The pictures
were so beautiful ....
They reminded me of your
fantastic cooking. Enjoy!! XX

THE GREAT ITALIAN COOKBOOK

THE GREAT ITALIAN COOKBOOK

The Italian Academy
of Cookery

International Culinary Society
New York

Picture Sources

Studio ADNA, Milan: 36, 44–5, 46, 62, 68–9, 92–3, 98, 102, 106–7, 110, 111, 114–15, 134–5, 190–1, 199, 205, 210–11, 216–17, 218–19, 234–5, 244, 245, 248–9, 252–3, 257, 266, 274–5, 291, 303, 304–5, 342–3, 346, 347, 348–9, 352, 353, 354–5, 358–9, 360–1.

AME, Milan: 308, 314, 318, 324, 329, 330, 331, 334, 335, 339.

Stelvio Andreis and Elvio Lonardi, Verona: 1, 5, 6, 10–11, 12–13, 15, 24–5, 28–9, 30, 31, 32–3, 34–5, 38–9, 40–1, 42, 47, 48, 49, 50, 51, 52–3, 54–5, 56, 57, 58, 59, 60–1, 63, 64–5, 67, 70, 72–3, 74–5, 76–7, 78, 79, 80–1, 82, 83, 84, 84–5, 89, 90–1, 97, 100–1, 104–5, 116–17, 118–19, 120–1, 124–5, 126, 127, 128–9, 130–1, 136, 137, 138, 140–1, 142, 147, 148, 152–3, 154–5, 157, 158, 159, 160–1, 163, 164–5, 166–7, 170–1, 172, 173, 174–5, 176, 177, 178–9, 180–1, 182–3, 184–5, 186, 187, 188–9, 196–7, 198, 200, 201, 202–3, 204, 206–7, 208, 214–15, 224–5, 228–9, 230–1, 232–3, 236–7, 240–1, 242–3, 246–7, 250, 251, 254, 255, 256, 260–1, 262, 264, 267, 268–9, 271, 272, 273, 278, 280–1, 282–3, 299, 306–7, 310–311, 312–313, 316–17, 320–1, 326, 332–3, 338–9, 344–5.

Paolo Belloni/Marzia Malli, Milan: 298.

Riccardo Marcialis, Milan: cover, 26–7, 86–7, 88, 94, 96, 99, 108–9, 112, 113, 122–3, 132–3, 144–5, 150–1, 168–9, 192–3, 194–5, 212–13, 221, 222–3, 226–7, 238–9, 263, 276–7, 284–5, 288–9, 294–5, 296–7, 300, 301, 302, 350–1.

Angela Prati, Trento: 356, 357. PRIMA PRESS, Milan: 258–9. Lino Simeoni, Verona: 309. Luca Steffenoni, Verona: 16–17, 18–19, 20, 23, 286–7, 292–3, 314–15, 319.

Acknowledgments

The Publisher would like to thank Lorenzo Nicoletti, Giuseppe Calcinone and Ruggero Bauli & C. S.p.A., Verona, for their kind assistance in the production of this book.

Photographs on pp. 24–5, 90–1, 104–5, 120–1, 164–5, 166–7, 180–1, 214–5, 282–3 were taken at the "Il Desco" restaurant, Verona, who also provided those particular recipes.

Contributors

Ada Boni   Roberto Bosi
Vittorio Camilla   Giorgio Marcolungo
Anna Martini   Lamberto Paronetto
Mariella Pizzetti   Francesco Spagnolli

Edited by Anna Bennett, Elaine Hardy, Helen Parker

Translated from the Italian by
Caroline Beamish   Juliet Haydock
Anna Bennett   Helen Parker
Ardèle Dejey   Elizabeth Stevenson
Nicoletta Flessati   Daphne Tagg
Elaine Hardy   Susan Wheeler
Sara Harris

This 1987 edition published by
International Culinary Society,
distributed by Crown Publishers, Inc.,
225 Park Avenue South,
New York, New York 10003.

ISBN 0-517-63553-4

h g f e d c b a

Contents

NOTE

All recipes serve four unless otherwise stated.

An asterisk after the title of a recipe indicates that the dish is illustrated.

*F*ood has never been as fashionable as it is today. Walk into any expensive but not necessarily top-quality restaurant in Manhattan, Mayfair or the rue Saint-Honoré and you will invariably be served an artistically presented concoction. In their pursuit of fashion, these illustrious establishments are contributing to the decline of "real" cuisine.

It is a modern-day paradox that never before has so much been spoken, written and published about food, while in actual fact we are not only eating less and less, but also, sadly, less and less well.

The eating habits of the twentieth century have replaced the dedicated glutton of yesteryear with the anxious pill-popper, who is terrorized by faddish diets, hounded by food technology's fiendish new weapon, deep-frozen convenience meals, and confused by a surfeit of culinary sophistication. The art of convivial conversation, that most agreeable of accompaniments that fed the minds of glorious past epochs and graced our once civilized dinner tables has also, sadly, fallen victim to this tragic modernity, swinging monotonously between two sole topics: high-fat versus low-fat, both of which subjects jar at table and offer no scope for scintillating after-dinner speeches. Fashionable diners today sit silently before a desultory one-course meal which is, typically, a plain little salad denied the uplift of any dressing.

Showered on to this unappetizing scene is a deluge of glossy culinary publications which nourish the eye rather than the stomach. Such works of exhibitionism are destined to adorn coffee tables, unconsulted reference works which will be ignored by the honest cooks they are supposedly aimed at. Common sense finally had to react against such absurd and trivial modishness, revolting against the trends created by an era characterized by gastronomic confusion and disquiet. This call to order was the principal inspiration behind the birth of the Accademia Italiana della Cucina (Italian Academy of Cookery), a body of professional experts whose aim is to revive the real Italian cuisine and rescue it from irrelevant and transient fashions. Our cultural heritage of regional and familial traditions has been dispersed by a wind of change, in an atmosphere of haste and vulgarity. The foremost cause of this devastation is the sacrificial worship of the slender Western mortal at the altar of slimming diets.

Over 30 years of dedicated work by good, honorable people have shown that we will associate with neither posturing gourmets nor blasé nostalgia mongerers. It is in a spirit of respect for both the institution of the family and our national culture, that we have to set out to defend the true riches Italy was in danger of squandering away, bewildered and confused as she was by so-called "modern living."

Just as monuments, museums, and age-old crumbling ruins are seen to be decaying against the neglected skyline of a betrayed Italy, yet another component of our cultural heritage – our gastronomic tradition – has of late also seemed to be vanishing. Swept along by the current wave of an anonymous, pseudo-international fast-food syndrome, our national cuisine has been lost in a morass of hamburgers, frozen pizzas that bear more relation to the Wild West than to Italy, and improbably fizzy drinks.

The many concerned Italians who are committed to the preservation of genuine Italian cuisine may be accused of fighting a rearguard action in a spirit of hopeless romanticism. Not so; we are the valiant champions of a worthy cause. Our belief is that God, having punished the sinner with hunger, then rewarded human endeavor with appetite. At the divine invention of water to quench thirst, man's ingenuity responded in turn with the invention of wine (and plenty of good wine is produced in Italy to this day to bear this out). As a reward for this inspired invention, God – in admiration – bestowed on man alone among all creatures on Earth the gift to enjoy drinking without being thirsty. Enslaved by hunger and forced to nourish himself for the survival of the species, man found a way to transform hunger into a chosen pleasure, elevating it to appetite. On this foundation civilization built up the science of gastronomy.

Let us not forget Mme de Sévigné's reminder to her daughter: "Yes, indeed, my dear, like the animals we too eat and make love: mais quand même, un peu mieux." And Descartes' comment to the Duc de Duras, who had arrogantly accused him of being a gluttonous intellectual: "Do you suppose that God created good things for fools alone?"

The Italian Academy of Cookery is proud to put its name to this book, in a tribute to Italy's national gastronomic tradition, founded on large family meals, where laughter and spirited conversation are felicitiously married with a noble and unashamed pleasure in good food.

This volume seeks to re-introduce the true Italian cuisine, which has in recent years fallen a little out of favor, or been

Foreword

distorted by passing culinary fashions into something different. Cuisine is a rich and continually evolving creative expression, drawing on contemporary life for its inspiration, interpreting all its vital elements against the backdrop of a constantly changing political and economic scene. This book sets the record straight as it were, returning us to a more sensible school of thought and dismissing much of the gratuitous modishness that has surreptitiously crept into the culinary field in recent years bearing labels such as "nouvelle cuisine," in a vulgar betrayal of original accepted culinary standards.

"Fruges consumere nati," as Horace so truly said. The ancients developed a kind of cookery upon which St Thomas pronounced: "This art is major; it nourishes mortals." Italy, perhaps more than any other country, has developed a cuisine which blends an incomparable wealth of tastes and aromas, and is closely linked to the infinite variety of natural produce available. This is a cuisine which bears the tradition of a great past enriched by many foreign influences through wars, invasions, trade and the like. A centuries-old historical tradition which harmonizes happily with the best of the current trends and also looks to the future, all the while retaining its inherent spontaneity. Ours is an unaffected and uncomplicated cuisine – echoing our entire national style – and it has thus unwittingly succeeded in meeting the approval of state-of-the-art dietetic science: many Italians, old-school gourmets and picky up-to-date health freaks alike eat good, healthy food without being aware of a Mediterranean diet as such. Let us also not forget that the spontaneous geniality of the Italian people has known throughout history how to overcome poverty, by turning it into an instrument of true culinary invention and elevating it to an art. The true Italian cookery which has its origins in a distant Golden Age has nothing to fear from the cumbersome trappings of commercial rhetoric or mundane frivolity; let us not lose our way along cuisines that are "haute" or "bourgeoise," "classique" or "nouvelle," "gourmande" or "minceur." To anyone who accuses Italian food of wallowing in an excessive and unadventurous simplicity we can only suggest in reply that they look at the undimmed popularity of wholesome home cooking. With all due respect to the culinary tradition of France, a reflection of the highest culture and of sophisticated manners, I think we can safely say that the subjugation of Italian cuisine has come to an end and an auspicious renaissance is in sight, particularly through promising young newcomers to the field, heirs to the natural talent of their forebears, who are back on familiar ground once again, pursuing culinary excellence along the well-trodden path to success with humility and a passion for experimentation.

Much hope is vested in these young descendants of traditional rural cooks who remain steadfastly faithful to the past in their concern for a revival which repudiates all that is intolerably baroque and heavy. They blend ancient traditions and future trends in their rediscovery of old country itineraries where food is still the most pleasurable way to restore both body and spirit, and the source of spectacular surprises. Such meals are invariably washed down by unpretentious bottles of wine. The comforting conviviality this creates recalls Dante's image of the warmth of the sun turning to wine mixed with the good humor dripping from the vine. The Italian saying is appropriately quotable here: "I have brought food before you, now feed yourself."

We are self-confessed and confirmed followers of a cuisine which is plain and good without recourse to any other adjectives. Italy still has the potential to remain the purest interpreter of such a cuisine.

At table man celebrates all his rituals in one—daily family interaction, social, diplomatic and even religious observances. Throughout history man has celebrated his triumphs with the sharing of food, from the primitive repasts cooked over fires in caves to the grandeur of Homeric banquets, from the exotic feasts of Oriental satraps to the orgies of ancient Rome, from the colorful tables of the Italian Renaissance to the splendors of the dining rooms at Versailles, and the jubilant "grande cuisine" meals of the Belle Epoque.

But even before the superfluous addition of a sumptuous style and a highly embellished culture, we Italians knew how to remain loyal to the wholesome cuisine for which we have always been naturally gifted. It is with irrefutable modesty that we combine the riches of our cuisine with the simplicity of style which is part and parcel of our national character. Just as a solitary but voluptuous layer of polenta can be as smooth and beautiful as the marmorially divine Paolina Borghese sculpted by Canova, so a humble popular dish can in its immaculate simplicity be elevated to princely heights. We Italians have no hesitation in proclaiming ourselves provincial, irredeemably and delightfully so. After all, our provinces are nothing less than the sovereign states of an incomparably glorious past, supreme rulers in each and every art over a country that is richly varied, always top of the class in history and geography and – why not – as far as we Italians are concerned – in the culinary sciences as well.

GIOVANNI NUVOLETTI PERDOMINI

President, Accademia Italiana della Cucina
(Italian Academy of Cookery)

The Recipes

Antipasti and Cured Meats

*A*lthough antipasti or hors d'oeuvres have never played a major role in the Italian gastronomic repertoire, the fact remains that when Italians sit down to a substantial meal of typical regional dishes they will be disappointed if the menu does not include antipasti. This must be due in part to the excellence of Italian cured meats which have become justly famed throughout the world. Who could refuse a few slices of flavorsome prosciutto or finocchiona, capocollo, or a coarse, country-style salami while waiting for a plate of steaming hot pasta to arrive?

Some people maintain that serving an antipasto before the pasta course makes for a very heavy meal. Often the best solution is to serve just a couple of chicken liver crostini, for example, or half a dozen mussels or a couple of slices of Parma ham to stimulate the appetite rather than blunt it, in anticipation of the courses to follow.

BRUSCHETTA *
(Garlic toast)

8 slices coarse white bread
2 cloves garlic, minced but still
   whole
olive oil
salt
freshly ground pepper

Crusty homemade bread is best for this recipe, but if unavailable use French sticks. Cut the loaf in half lengthwise. Heat in the oven at 325°F for a few minutes until both sides are golden brown and crisp. Peel the garlic, mince, and rub it all over the surface of the bread. Sprinkle with olive oil and plenty of salt and pepper, and serve very hot.

CAPE SANTE
(Sautéed scallops)

12 scallops
½ cup olive oil
small bunch parsley, chopped
1 clove garlic, minced
fine fresh breadcrumbs
1 clove garlic, peeled and finely
   chopped
scant ¼ cup butter
¼ cup dry white wine
2 tbsp lemon juice

Scrub the outside of the scallop shells under cold running water then heat in a large saucepan or skillet with a little of the oil, the parsley and the minced clove of garlic. When the shells have opened remove the scallops and roll in breadcrumbs. Peel the garlic and sauté with the rest of the parsley in the remaining oil and butter in a small saucepan; add the scallops and when they are lightly browned all over, moisten with the wine and lemon juice. Serve very hot, on the half shell.

COZZE AL RISO *
(Mussels with rice)

1½ lb mussels
1 clove garlic
3 tbsp olive oil
2 cups canned tomatoes
salt

freshly ground pepper
1½ cups Arborio (risotto) rice

Discard any mussels that do not close when tapped sharply. Scrub thoroughly, scraping off barnacles, and removing any beards. Rinse and place in a saucepan. Heat without adding water for about 5 min, shaking the saucepan frequently, until fully opened. Discard any that remain closed. Remove the mussels from their shells, strain their liquor and reserve. Peel the garlic clove and sauté in the oil in a large saucepan; remove and discard when golden brown. Add the sieved tomatoes and the strained mussel liquor to the flavored oil. Season with salt and pepper and simmer. Cook the rice according to the manufacturer's instructions; when half cooked, drain if necessary and add to the tomatoes. Continue cooking until the rice is done, adding the mussels a few minutes before serving.

COZZE AL FORNO
(Baked mussels)

4 dozen mussels (allow only 10 per
   person if very large)
1 tbsp vinegar
olive oil
juice of 2 lemons
small bunch parsley
salt
freshly ground pepper
2 cloves garlic
fine fresh breadcrumbs

Rinse the mussels thoroughly under cold running water. Scrub vigorously with a stiff brush to remove beards and barnacles. Discard any that are open. With a short, sharp knife open and discard one half of each shell. (Reserve any liquor or juice produced during preparation and pass through a fine sieve; mix it in a small bowl with the vinegar, 6 tbsp olive oil, the lemon juice and finely chopped parsley, season with salt and pepper and set aside.) Place the mussels on the half shell in a single layer in one or more large, shallow ovenproof dishes. Sprinkle with the prepared mixture, followed by more oil mixed with the peeled and minced garlic. Cover each shell

with a generous sprinkling of breadcrumbs. Bake in the oven at 400–450°F for about ¼ hr. Serve very hot straight from the dish.

CRESCENTINE
(Fritters)

2¾ cups all-purpose flour
1½ tbsp butter or shortening
¼ cup light stock
½ tsp active dry yeast
oil and shortening for deep frying
salt

Sift the flour on to a pastry board and make a well in the middle. Heat

the stock and melt the butter in it. Allow to cool a little and pour nearly all of it into the well when tepid; add the yeast. Gradually work in the flour from the sides of the well. The dough should be soft and pliable. Use a rolling pin to roll out into a thick square; fold in half and then in half again to give four thicknesses; roll out. Repeat the rolling and folding process 5 or 6 times, ending with a sheet of dough just under ¼ in thick. Cut this sheet into strips about 1½ in wide with a fluted pastry wheel or knife; cut into rectangles 3 in long. Heat plenty of oil and shortening in a deep fryer until boiling hot; lower a few fritters into the fat at a time.

They should puff up immediately, with little bubbles forming over the surface. Remove carefully with a slotted spoon so the bubbles do not break and fill with oil; drain on kitchen paper. Sprinkle with a little salt (or with confectioner's sugar for children); serve without delay on a hot platter.

CROSTINI DI FEGATINI
(Chicken liver crostini)

1 tbsp olive oil
2-3 slices fat bacon
½ onion
2-3 sage leaves
1 cup chicken livers
salt
freshly ground pepper
1 tbsp butter
½ lemon
8 slices bread, cut from a French
*   stick (1 day old)*
grated Parmesan cheese

Heat the oil in a saucepan. Coarsely chop the bacon, onion and sage leaves and cook for 5 min. Remove the thin skin surrounding the chicken livers, rinse them, chop coarsely and add to the saucepan once the onion has become transparent. Heat gently, adding 2–3 tbsp water, until tender. Sprinkle with salt and a little pepper. Discard the sage leaves, then sieve the livers (or liquidize in a blender). Place the mixture in a bowl, stir in the butter and a few drops of lemon juice and stir until smooth. Spread each slice of bread generously with the chicken liver pâté, sprinkle with a little grated Parmesan cheese and place in a hot oven (425°F) for a few minutes before serving.

CROSTINI ALLA NAPOLETANA
(Cheese and tomato crostini)

8 thick slices bread
8 canned anchovy fillets
4 large ripe tomatoes
2 Mozzarella cheeses
generous ¼ cup unsalted butter
salt
freshly ground pepper
oregano
olive oil

Trim a thick-cut large sandwich loaf if necessary, leaving plenty of room for the cheese to melt and spread without running over the edges. Cut each anchovy fillet lengthwise in half. Wash and dry the tomatoes and slice. Cut the Mozzarella cheeses into eight slices of even thickness. Spread each slice of bread sparingly with butter and place a slice of cheese on top. Place two strips of anchovy on top of each slice of cheese and top with a slice of tomato. Season with a little salt, pepper and dried oregano. Place the crostini on a lightly oiled cookie sheet and heat in a moderate oven (about 350°F) for up to 10 min. Serve immediately as an appetizer or snack.

CROSTINI GUSTOSI ALLA ROMANA
(Savory crostini Roman style)

8 canned anchovy fillets
¼ cup unsalted butter
8 slices crusty white bread
Mozzarella cheese

Chop the anchovies. Heat the butter in a small saucepan and when it begins to melt, remove from the heat. Add the anchovies, working them with a fork to a smooth cream. Spread evenly on the slices of bread and place a slice of Mozzarella on top of each piece (leave plenty of room around the cheese as it will spread out as it melts). Transfer to the oven preheated to 325°F for a few minutes and serve as soon as the cheese has started to melt.

GRANSEOLA
(Dressed crab Venetian style)

4 medium live crabs
olive oil
juice of 1 lemon
salt
freshly ground pepper
1 heaping tbsp chopped parsley

Leave the crabs in a sink or bowl full of cold water for at least 2 hr before plunging them into gently boiling water. Cook for 10–15 min depending on size, until the shells turn red. When cold break off the legs and pull the underside away from the top section. Discard the stomach sac and "dead men's fingers" (the grayish feathery gills). Take all the meat and soft parts from the shell, claws and legs. Place in a bowl. Flake the meat, picking out any shell fragments. Wash and dry the top section of each shell. Sprinkle the crab meat generously with olive oil, lemon juice, salt, pepper and parsley and fill the prepared shells with it. Chill slightly before serving.

INSALATA DI SEPPIE
(Cuttlefish salad)

1¼ lb cuttlefish
3 tbsp vinegar
scant ½ cup olive oil
juice of 1 lemon
salt
freshly ground pepper
1 clove garlic
1–2 tbsp chopped parsley
black olives
strips of yellow and red peppers
lemon wedges

Rub off the thin outer skin of the cuttlefish under cold running water. Use sharp scissors to cut away the eyes, the hard mouth parts, ink sac and to free the bone. The latter should be discarded. Rinse away every trace of sand. Beat with a meatbat or rolling pin. Bring a saucepan of water to a boil, add the salt and vinegar followed by the cuttlefish. Cover and simmer for about 1 hr. Test with a sharp knife or fork and remove from the heat when tender. Drain and allow to cool before cutting into strips. Mix with a dressing of olive oil, lemon juice, salt, pepper, minced garlic and chopped parsley. Serve in scallop shells if possible, decorating with black olives, strips of yellow and red peppers and lemon wedges.

LUMACHE ALLA BOBBIESE
(Snails Bobbio style)

2¼ lb large snails
1 cup olive oil
¼ cup butter
1 onion
5 tbsp tomato paste
salt
freshly ground pepper
2 large carrots
1 lb celery
1 lb leeks

Snails from the vicinity of Bobbio (Piacenza) are highly sought after, especially those found in December, during their hibernation period. Eaten locally as a Christmas Eve treat, they are also exported far and wide and can be sampled in international cities such as Milan and New York. If fresh snails are unavailable, canned or frozen snails may be substituted. Preparation of fresh snails takes time, so start several days before you plan to serve them. Live snails must be starved for a period, to eliminate any poisonous substances they may have ingested: place the snails in a loose weave sack with plenty of bran. After 6 days discard any dead snails and extract the live ones from their shells. Rub them with salt or maize flour and rinse repeatedly to get rid of the slime; pull off the black visceral spiral and discard. (If you are using canned or frozen snails, drain them and continue from this point.) Sweat the finely chopped onion in the butter and oil in a

flameproof casserole until almost translucent (do not allow to color), add the snails and the tomato paste mixed with 1 cup hot water. Bring to a boil and then turn down the heat; season lightly with salt and pepper, cover and simmer for 2 hr, stirring frequently and adding more hot water if necessary. Turn off the heat and leave to stand until the following day. Trim, slice and wash the carrots, celery and leeks. Turn on the heat again, add 1 cup water and the vegetables. Cover and cook slowly for another 2 hr, adding water when necessary and a little more salt if wished. The sauce should be smooth and creamy. Serve very hot, with polenta, a green salad or spinach sautéed in a little butter.

LUMACHE ALLA MILANESE
(Snails Milanese style)

24 large snails
1 cup vinegar
3 tbsp coarse salt
1 clove garlic
½ cup olive oil
¼ cup butter
8 anchovy fillets, chopped
4 fennel seeds
3 tbsp finely chopped parsley
½ onion, finely chopped
1½ tsp all-purpose flour
1¼ cups dry white wine
salt
freshly ground pepper
pinch of nutmeg

Prepare the snails as directed in the previous recipe, to eliminate any poisonous substances.
Scrub the snails' shells well under cold running water and leave to soak for an hour at a time in three changes of just enough cold water, vinegar and coarse salt to cover them. Place in a saucepan, in just enough fresh water, vinegar and salt to cover, and cook for 10 min. Extract the snails from their shells and remove the black tract (see previous recipe). Peel the garlic, crush it with the flat of a knife blade and sauté briefly in the oil and butter to flavor; discard the garlic clove and add the chopped anchovies, fennel seeds, parsley and onion. Sauté. Stir in the flour and add the snails, followed by the

wine, a little salt, pepper and nutmeg. Cook over moderate heat for about 1 hr, stirring occasionally. Return the snails to their shells, sprinkle with their cooking juices and serve very hot.

BOVOLONI
(Snails with garlic and wine)

1¾ lb large snails
corn meal
½ cup olive oil
5 cloves garlic
2–3 tbsp chopped parsley
1 cup dry white wine
salt
freshly ground pepper

Detoxify the snails as described in the "Lumache alla Bobbiese" recipe (see left), wash well and add them, still in their shells, to a large saucepan of boiling water; cook for 10–15 min. Drain; extract each snail with a fork. Remove the dark intestinal tract formerly at the top of the shell. Sprinkle the snails with plenty of corn meal and rub this over them with your fingers to remove as much slime as possible. Rinse very thoroughly afterward under cold running water. Spread out to dry on clean cloths. Place the snails in a flameproof casserole containing the oil, whole peeled garlic cloves and the coarsely chopped parsley, cover and heat from cold. Cook for 4 hr over very low heat, moistening with the wine and, when this has all evaporated, with a little water when necessary. Halfway through cooking, season to taste with salt and pepper.

MOZZARELLA
ALL'ORIGANO
(Cheese and tomato fans)

2 very large ripe tomatoes
2 Mozzarella cheeses
5 tbsp olive oil
salt
freshly ground pepper
oregano
a few basil leaves

Mozzarella combines perfectly with sun-ripened flavorsome tom-

atoes for a light summer appetizer. Wash and dry the tomatoes and place stalk end downward; slice vertically, leaving the slices attached at the base, into a fan shape. Place a slice of Mozzarella inside each opening in the tomato fan. Dress with oil, salt, pepper, oregano and decorate with basil leaves.

OSTRICHE ALLA
TARANTINA
(Oysters Taranto style)

24 very fresh oysters
salt
3 tbsp chopped parsley
3 tbsp fine breadcrumbs
freshly ground pepper
olive oil
1–2 lemons

Make sure you use absolutely fresh, sound oysters. Open them with an oyster knife; rinse the half shells containing the oysters in cold salted water, drain and then cover the bottom of a large ovenproof pan (or two) with a single layer of them. Sprinkle plenty of parsley, breadcrumbs and freshly ground pepper on to each oyster on its half shell. Drizzle a little olive oil over them and cook in a preheated oven, at 325°F, for ¼ hr. Serve hot, with lemon wedges.

OLIVE AL FORNO
(Baked olives)

24 very large green olives
24 thin slices smoked pancetta
olive oil

Pancetta is an Italian bacon, usually sliced very thinly. Allowing a few extra for mistakes, pit 24 extremely large, perfect olives, keeping them neat. Wrap each olive in a slice of pancetta. Thread on to cocktail sticks, in pairs, and place on a lightly oiled cookie sheet. Heat in a moderate oven until the pancetta fat starts to melt. Place briefly on kitchen paper to absorb excess fat and serve on a hot plate. Remove the cocktail sticks if wished.

OLIVE FARCITE *
(Stuffed olives)

2 tbsp butter
scant 1 cup finely ground meats
  (use a mixture of veal, pork,
  mortadella, prosciutto)
salt
freshly ground pepper
pinch of nutmeg
½ cup dry white wine
2 eggs
3 tbsp grated Parmesan cheese
40 green olives preserved in brine
flour
oil for frying

Melt the butter in a heavy sauce-pan; add the meat and cook briskly for 5 min, stirring and turning it frequently. Add a little salt and pepper and a tiny pinch of freshly grated nutmeg; pour in the wine, turn up the heat and continue cooking until the wine has evaporated. Beat 1 whole egg with the Parmesan cheese. Turn the heat as low as possible and stir in the egg and cheese mixture. Use this filling to stuff the olives. Beat the remaining egg and dip each stuffed olive in this. Roll the olives in flour and then deep fry briefly in very hot oil.

OLIVE NERE ALL'ACCIUGA
(Black olives in anchovy dressing)

14 oz firm black olives
scant 1 cup olive oil
½ onion, finely chopped
1 clove garlic, peeled and finely chopped
4 anchovy fillets
oregano

Pit the olives with the appropriate utensil, keeping them as neat as possible. Sauté the onion, garlic, anchovy fillets and oregano in the olive oil for 5 min over moderate heat, then pour the flavored oil through a sieve on to the pitted olives.

CUSCINETTI DI PANDORATO
(Deep-fried sandwiches)

approx. 14 oz sandwich loaf
¾ lb Mozzarella cheese
¼ lb thinly sliced prosciutto (or a few anchovy fillets)
flour
1 cup milk
2 eggs
salt
oil for deep frying

Cut the loaf into very thick slices; remove the crusts, then cut each slice horizontally in half, stopping short of the edge so the two slices are attached. Place a few thin slices of Mozzarella and prosciutto (or anchovies) inside; coat both sides of the sandwiches in flour, dip briefly in the milk and then place in a single layer in a deep dish and pour the lightly salted beaten eggs all over them. Leave to stand and soak up the egg for up to 1 hr. Lower carefully into very hot oil and deep fry briefly until golden. Drain on kitchen paper and serve at once.

POLENTA LODIGIANA
(Polenta Lodi style)

1 pint milk
scant 1 cup polenta (corn meal)
salt
½ lb thinly sliced Gruyère cheese
1 egg, beaten

flour
fine breadcrumbs
scant ½ cup butter

Bring the milk to a boil in a double boiler; pour in the corn meal gradually, stirring all the time. Add a pinch of salt and continue to cook while stirring until the mixture is very thick. Rinse a large chopping board about ¼ in thick in cold water. When the polenta is cooked, spread it out on the rinsed board and leave until cold. Cut out circles with a 1¼-in circular pastry cutter and sandwich a slice of Gruyère between pairs of these disks. Flour the sandwiches before dipping them in beaten egg and then coat with breadcrumbs. Heat the butter in a skillet and fry a few at a time.

POLIPI VERACI ALL'AGLIO
(Octopus with garlic)

2 large octopus
½ cup olive oil
4 cloves garlic
1 bay leaf
½ tsp cumin seeds
salt
1 chili pepper
rosemary
parsley

Neapolitans call the common octopus (octopus vulgaris) "verace"(true) because it alone has the true savor of the sea. Cut out the eyes and "beak" and discard the internal organs, including the ink sac. Slit the skin to facilitate its removal. Beat the skinned octopus, tentacles and body, energetically on a chopping board with a meatbat or rolling pin to tenderize. Wash well under cold running water until white; do not dry. Place in a heavy saucepan with the oil, the peeled and minced garlic cloves, bay leaf and cumin. Tie a covering of wax paper tightly over the saucepan with string, place the lid on top and cook over gentle heat for 1–2 hr depending on the size and age of the octopus. When tender, take up the octopus, remove the suckers and serve with a dressing of olive oil, salt, crumbled chili pepper, rosemary and parsley.

PROSCIUTTO E MELONE
(Parma ham with melon)

8 slices ripe melon
12 slices prosciutto (Parma ham)

Slice a melon lengthwise in half; discard the seeds and filaments; cut into wedges and remove the rind. Spread most of the paper-thin slices of prosciutto out on a large platter and arrange the melon slices round the outer edge, wrapping the occasional slice in a piece of the remaining prosciutto.

SPECK AL CREN
(Speck with horseradish)

12 thin slices Speck
2 bunches radishes
½ cup heavy cream
3 tbsp horseradish sauce (see p. 128)

Arrange the sliced Speck on a platter and garnish with small bunches of washed and dried radishes. To prepare the sauce, peel a horseradish root (sunglasses will help prevent your eyes watering) and grate finely into a bowl. Choose a small root or half a root if you do not like very strong horseradish. Add a pinch each of salt and sugar. Beat ½ cup heavy cream (more, if you prefer a milder tasting sauce) until fairly thick, but not stiff; fold, a spoonful at a time, into the horseradish. Hand the sauce round separately.

TARTINE DI CARNE CRUDA
(Veal tartare)

14 oz veal leg rump roast
1 clove garlic
2 anchovy fillets
salt
6 tbsp olive oil
3 lemons
1 fresh white truffle (optional)

Grind the meat finely and then pound in a mortar with the peeled garlic clove and anchovy fillets until smooth. Transfer to a bowl and use a wooden spoon to stir in a little salt (if needed) followed by the

Capocollo calabrese

olive oil and lemon juice, adding these a little at a time. Shape into hamburgers and finish each serving with a few slices of truffle (if available) or raw button mushrooms.

SALAM D'LA DÜJA

A traditional pure pork sausage, also known as "salame dell'olla" (*olle* is a dialect word for small earthenware pots but glass pots are also used), preserved in pork fat. Tender and flavorsome, it is soft enough to cut with a fork.

SALAME DI TACCHINO
(Turkey sausage)

1 neck of turkey (with the skin)
6 oz raw turkey breast
2 chicken livers
¼ lb prosciutto
1 egg
salt
freshly ground pepper
nutmeg
1 small carrot
1 onion
1 stick celery

Starting at one end, peel the skin off the entire turkey neck just as you would remove a glove: it will come away very easily. Reserve the neck. Rinse the skin then sew up one end tightly and neatly with kitchen thread (use a trussing or darning needle) to form a bag. Prepare the stuffing: chop the turkey breast, chicken livers and prosciutto together finely and mix well in a bowl with the egg, salt, pepper and a small pinch of grated nutmeg. Carry on blending, using your hands. Pack into the skin "bag;" sew up the other end. Pierce the skin with a needle in several places, then wrap in a clean cloth, tying the latter tightly at both ends and sewing where necessary to keep in place. Take an oval or rectangular casserole (or a fish kettle), add 2 quarts cold water, the turkey neck, any trimmings, the peeled carrot, onion and the celery and a little salt. Heat until near boiling point, add the prepared sausage and simmer gently for 1½ hr. Place on a plate with a small weight on top and leave until cold.

SARDINE IN SAÓR
(Marinated sardines)

1 lb fresh sardines
all-purpose flour
olive oil
salt
2 large onions
1⅛ cups white wine vinegar

A famous Venetian dish traditionally served on the feast of Corpus Christi. Gut the sardines, snip off their fins and rinse well, then flour them. Heat plenty of olive oil in a large skillet and fry the sardines until golden brown on both sides. Take out and drain on kitchen paper. Sprinkle with salt. Slice the onions into thin rings. Pour off the oil; clean the skillet and heat ½ cup fresh olive oil in which to sweat the onions. When tender, pour in the vinegar and reduce considerably over low heat for the marinade. Place a layer of sardines in a high-sided dish, pour half the marinade and onions over them, cover with the remaining sardines and finish with the rest of the onions and marinade which must completely cover the fish. Cover and leave to stand in a cool place for at least 48 hr.

Cured Meats

Bresaola

Parts of Lombardy (such as the Valtellina district) and Switzerland (Canton of Grisons) have the ideal cold, dry climate for curing and keeping this traditional specialty; these conditions are vital for the treatment of highly perishable beef.

In Italy bresaola is much sought after as an antipasto, sliced very thinly and dressed with oil, lemon, and perhaps freshly ground pepper. Once sliced it must be used as quickly as possible as its taste, aroma and in particular its color deteriorate once exposed to the air, turning an unattractive brownish hue through oxidization. It can also be cooked: sautéed in butter and salt pork with onions, garlic, pepper, herbs and sometimes other vegetables to add to the flavor.

Capocollo calabrese

Capocollo (or capicollo) means "top of the neck," the part of the pig's carcass which provides the raw material for this salted, cured meat which originates in central and southern Italy (Umbria, Abruzzo, Campania, Apulia, Calabria, etc.). Methods vary from region to region giving each variety its own distinctive flavor.

Calabria's version of capocollo starts off with the selected cuts being immersed in a brine bath. After a few days the meat is removed from the brine, given a protracted and thorough soaking in red wine and then sprinkled with finely crushed peppercorns before being packed into casings of pig's intestines ready for maturing and keeping. Strips of reeds are then tightly wrapped around these sausages, providing the perfect packaging for curing the meat and giving it a dry appearance on the outer surface. The capocollo is hung up to dry in a well ventilated place where it is smoked. Once the reed casings are removed the capocollo, like most other Italian cured meats, is bound with string.

Capocollo pugliese

In Apulia, capocollo is prepared in two ways. It is most often flavored with peppercorns but there is a more highly spiced version which involves the addition of chili pepper, much favored in the cooking of Apulia and throughout southern Italy.

Preparation is along the same lines as in Calabria but the appearance and taste are different. The Apulian version is much smaller and has a far smokier flavor, due to the meat being cold-smoked during the early stages of maturation, using the smoke from green oak wood funneled toward the suspended capocollo. Curing lasts 5–6 months, during which time the meat dries out just the required

amount. In summer it is kept in earthenware jars filled with olive oil to prevent excessive dehydration.

Capocollo umbro

Umbria produces capocollo of a particularly high quality, with a delicious yet delicate taste. Only prime lean pork is used, from pigs which have been fed the best possible foodstuffs.

The flank is trimmed and rolled into a cylindrical shape and then given several "washings" by being immersed in dry white wine; it is then enveloped in wax paper left unsealed at each end. After about ten days the wax paper is replaced by vegetable parchment, in which the capocollo is tightly wrapped and sealed; it is then tied with

Coppa

Mortadella di Bologna

string and hung up to cure in a cool, well ventilated spot. At least three months should then elapse if the capocollo is to measure up to the high quality of mature Umbrian capocollo.

Coppa

Neck and loin of pork are used for one of Italy's most popular and widely used cured meats; several regions lay claim to the best variety.

Selected cuts are salted and then carefully matured for a comparatively short time under stringently controlled conditions to ensure that the end product is moist and tender. The high proportion of lean meat in coppa means that it becomes hard and stringy if kept for

too long in a hot dry environment. One way of avoiding this is to wrap the meat in a cloth soaked in white wine. A cool, moist cellar is the ideal environment but this technique can protect capocollo in a very dry climate and can also revive coppa when it is has already started to dry out. The wine penetrates the meat very gradually, restoring the moisture content and dispersing the excess salt produced by undesirably rapid dehydration.

Cotechino

A mixture of tender and gristly parts from the pig's gullet and snout is chopped medium fine and blended with lean, sinewy meat and skin (*cotenna*) from which the

cotechino derives its name.

It is then seasoned with salt and a sprinkling of peppercorns and stuffed into pig's intestines before undergoing a brief drying process in wood-fired stoves; the same stuffing mixture goes into natural casings shaped into spherical bondiola sausages and into pigs' trotters for sale as zamponi.

As cotechino does not keep very well, it must be cooked and eaten within a short time. It needs gentle boiling but care needs to be taken to preserve its special flavor and aroma. Even with very slow simmering, which should last at least 2–3 hours, the stuffing swells and the skins sometimes burst, turning the contents into an unappetizing sludge; to prevent this the skin

should be pricked all over with a needle, or the string ties loosened slightly at each end and the sausage wrapped and secured in muslin.

Finocchiona

One of Tuscany's outstanding products, the greatest quantities being consumed by the inhabitants of that region. Pork and beef (half fat cuts, half lean) are very finely chopped together to form a smooth paste. The addition of fennel (*finocchio*) seeds which gives the product its name, imparts a unique flavor.

Luganega

This sausage originated in Lucania (*lucanica* meaning "from Lucania") but its name was changed by Venetian dialect since the region of the Marches and Treviso adopted the product as its own.

Packed into long lengths of small intestines and knotted into small links, the stuffing comes from the pig's neck and jowl or cheek. Luganega's distinctive savor is partly due to the omnipresent peppercorns but also to a varying selection of flavorings, for which no set recipe exists. In recent times producers have tended to place more emphasis on the quality of the meat used rather than on spiciness.

Mortadella di Bologna

One of the most popular and commercially successful of all Italian sausages, combining a universally pleasing taste with practicality when eaten sandwiched in fresh crusty rolls for an inexpensive snack. Mortadella is made with the less prized cuts of pork, ground very finely and sometimes mixed with beef. It varies in price and quality depending on the proportion of fat cuts used.

The prepared mixture is mixed with ¼–½-in dice of pork fat which give the slices their unmistakable mosaic marbled pattern. The all-important flavor is added in the shape of natural ingredients such as peppercorns (long ago these were unavailable in Europe and myrtle berries were used instead, the original Latin name for this sausage being *myrtatella*). The producers then subject their mortadella to long, slow cooking in

Cotechino

Prosciutto toscano

special ovens at about 195°F. The sausages are almost always wrapped in manmade skins.

Pancetta arrotolata

The Italian cured meat and sausage industry processes the layer of adipose tissue of the pig's belly in varying ways depending on whether the carcass has a lot of fat on it or not. In the case of very fat animals, pancetta looks much like pure pork fat except for being less hard and dense and having thin streaks of red meat running through it. This type will be salted unskinned and kept flat. It is used as flavoring or diced and added to other meats in cooking and sometimes as a garnish when thinly sliced.

In Italy pancetta has traditionally served as a substitute for finer, more expensive meats, providing a high-fat, high energy content food when used as a filling for rolls and sandwiches. Careful maturing enhances pancetta's delicate flavor and tenderness and cuts from prime carcasses with a high proportion of red meat to fat are flavored with various spices, rolled and tied, then matured for several months, often in smokehouses like their inferior, more fatty counterparts.

Prosciutto di Parma

Each cured meat has its aficionados but gourmets all over the world agree that prosciutto or Parma ham is one of the finest.

Only the best pigs' carcasses are selected for the legs which are then cured, with no artificial preserving process except for refrigeration. The hams are matured for varying lengths of time, depending on their weight and prevailing conditions but once salting has taken place those weighing 15–19 lb will be cured for at least 10 months and larger hams for at least a year. Parma ham is distinguished by a stamp on the outer, rounded side showing its authenticity. Laws have been passed to delineate those areas which may use this famous name, situated in central Italy and stretching from Emilia-Romagna to Piedmont. Regulations even stipulate the breed of pig to be used and how it is to be reared and fed to provide the raw material

for these exquisite hams. Parma ham is sold either on or off the bone. The latter may take various shapes but the former has the distal (trotter) removed and looks almost like a giant chicken drumstick, due to the excess fat having been pulled away from the inner, flatter side and the partial removal of the skin and underlying layer of fat, while the muscular section near the top of the femur has been trimmed away to within ¾ in.

Whether on or off the bone, the color, flavor and aroma are identical, the first varying from rose to red when sliced, with delicate streaks of fat. The taste is mild and delicate, not too salty with a fragrance which improves as the ham matures. Parma ham is never smoked.

Boned hams weigh at least 11¾ lb and those on the bone usually 17–19 lb.

Prosciutto di San Daniele

San Daniele prosciutto is one of the glories of the Italian cured meat industry and its reputation is jealously guarded by law.

Fresh hams weighing no less than 20 lb are selected from only the best pigs which are butchered and completely bled under rigorously controlled conditions. The hams are then pressed between spruce or pine boards, giving them their characteristic violin shape; the trotter is left attached. A finished San Daniele ham owes much of its appearance to a complicated and skillful technique of partially boning the hindquarters of the freshly killed pig, the expert butchers making the incisions between the muscles and along the natural lines of separation of the meat with virtually surgical skill.

Salting is then carried out and the method is crucial to success; it must take place during the period between October 1 and March 31. After this the hams are hung up to cure for not less than 9 months, certain atmospheric conditions being vital to produce the distinctive flavor. In San Daniele (in the province of Friuli) the prevailing moisture-laden winds provide the ideal conditions in which the salt can penetrate through to the bone. No artificial process (except refrigeration) is used to hasten the

curing process and San Daniele hams benefit from this natural treatment, being world famous for their tenderness when sliced or tested with a needle probe; their low proportion of absolutely pure white fat contrasts with the lean rosy red delicately marbled meat. The taste is delicate and sweet, with a superbly fragrant aroma.

Prosciutto toscano

Tuscany is renowned for its cured meats based on pork and boar. The method of curing is essentially artisanal, with the hams being generously salted prior to the curing process. This imbues them with a unique and very distinctive flavor, setting them apart from the hams of other regions.

Salama da sugo

One of Ferrara's traditional products: a sausage made of finely chopped pork and pigs' tongue mixed with spices and red wine, the recipe for which is said to have originated from none other than Lucrezia Borgia in the days when the cuisine at the ducal Este court was at its most elaborate.

The stuffing is packed into gut skins or into pig's bladders and dried off rapidly in a warm place (it was once the custom to bury the salami in the ashes of the hearth); they are then hung up to cure for 6 months or longer in a cool, well ventilated place. The end product's Italian name which means "sauce sausage" is descriptive of the delicious juices which are produced as it cooks and which must not be wasted. When hot, these sausages go well with mashed potatoes and when cold, with melon.

Salame di Milano

There are sufficient differences between the salami which come from Milan and the myriad other, related salami produced elsewere to warrant a separate name and classification.

Milano salami has a very dense, well blended texture, consisting of predominantly lean meats from pork leg and from the neck and shoulder of the pig's carcass; these are processed at length to give a very even mixture of lean and fat. Once this stage has been completed (the change to large scale

mechanized production from the original artisanal methods has not noticeably affected the product's quality), the mixture is packed into large skins and then cured under controlled conditions for 3–4 months.

Salame Varzi

Lean pork, pancetta (pork bacon piece), pepper, saltpeter, cooking salt, white wine and garlic make up this type of salami.

The resulting mixture (in the proportions of seven parts lean meat to three parts fat bacon piece) is finely chopped, moistened with white wine mixed with minced garlic and blended once more with the other ingredients until smooth and homogenous. This is then packed into a long pig's intestine which has been thoroughly cleaned and dried beforehand; the sausage is knotted into links every 12 in and tied tightly.

Methods have changed considerably since production switched from a cottage industry to industrial manufacture but still consist of two phases: the salami is usually matured for about 2 months in cool, damp surroundings once it has been heated for a few hours to rid it of excess moisture.

Salamini or salsicce di cinghiale

These "little salami" or boar's meat sausages mainly comprise the lean parts of the animal and the home of this traditional specialty is the once marshy and wild region of the Maremma in Tuscany.

They are often preserved in oil and sold in jars, which keeps the salamini moist and their full, gamey flavor intact. There is always the risk that this very lean sausage may become too dry and hard as it matures, given the climate of this region. As with other, similar products special curing conditions and techniques are vital.

Salsiccia della Basilicata

The generic word "salsiccia" covers a variety of sausages for which pork, beef, donkey and horse meat, etc. may be used and which are sold fresh, cured, smoked, cooked, raw, etc.

Lucania sausage was enormously popular in Roman times and

countless classical Latin writers refer to it. It is made mainly of pork along almost identical lines to the recipe for *lucanica*: a high proportion of lean meat is ground and flavored, black pepper and chili pepper or sweet red pepper predominating. Served in all sorts of ways with each area having its own preferred process of maturing.

Salsiccia siciliana

Preparation and use of this sausage is much the same as for other sausages of this general type but in Sicily lean pork and pork fat in a proportion of 4:1 are finely chopped together and then mixed with a variety of seasonings: salt, pepper, parsley, fennel seeds, small pieces of mature Caciocavallo cheese and slices of tomato.

This highly flavored and appetizing sausage is sometimes used as a stuffing in certain meat dishes but frying or broiling is traditional and more popular.

Sopressata calabrese

Nearly three-quarters lean pork and just over a quarter fat cuts (pork fat and bacon piece) make up the basic mixture for this product. In contrast with nearly all the other types of Italian sausage, the meat is rather unevenly chopped with a knife and then mixed with salt, pepper, chili pepper and red wine. Sometimes pig's blood is added, or paprika to color the mixture a vivid red.

There are two steps in treating the sausage: it is first hung up inside the fireplace to dry rapidly and acquire a faintly smoky aroma. Afterward it is pressed to get rid of any air pockets and then cured for 2–3 months in a cool, well ventilated spot before being ready for consumption.

Sopressata della Basilicata

As famous as the renowned Basilicata sausages, sopressata is suspended within the wide hearths of the farmhouses of that region until perfectly matured and permeated by a unique aroma. The sausage mixture consists of 80% lean pork and 20% pork fat, flavored with salt and peppercorns. It is then packed into natural gut skins and pressed (hence *sopressata*) in order to produce a dense texture but also, more importantly, to eliminate any air bubbles which could jeopardize its keeping qualities. As with other Italian sausages, sopressata needs to be briefly cured in a cool, well ventilated place and is occasionally smoked.

Sopressa veneta

A remarkably fragrant and tender sausage from the Veneto region, it is packed into very large skins, conserving moisture and flavor most successfully. Selection of ingredients plays an important part, as do the surroundings where the sausages are matured.

Lean cuts are used for two-thirds of the mixture and come from the pig's shoulder, neck and leg, while the fatter sections of the underside of the neck and of the belly account for the remainder. The meat is first coarsely chopped, flavored with salt, pepper and, more often than not, minced garlic and a little wine. In the days of artisanal production, grappa was often used instead of wine to slow down the normal fermentation process which tends to make the stuffing harden.

The chopped mixture is then processed thoroughly until completely blended, and the skins are then stuffed with it (the pig's large intestine is used, known in Italy as *maniche grosse*, "wide sleeves"). It then undergoes several pressings (hence *sopressa*) to make sure that no air pockets remain to jeopardize its keeping qualities.

Once the sausage has been cured it can be sliced and eaten cold or broiled and eaten with toasted polenta cake: a meal which was once a humble peasant staple is still a popular mouthwatering snack.

Speck

The inhabitants of the Alto Adige region in northern Italy are famous for their cured meats; the climate is perfect for this purpose.

One of their greatest gastronomic achievements is Speck, for which either the belly or the leg is used, the former resulting in a product which is effectively a type of smoked pancetta or fat bacon while the latter is a smoked version of prosciutto.

The all-important smoking process which gives Speck its own distinctive flavor and aroma is still carried out according to the time-honored methods handed down from generation to generation. Once the selected cuts of pork have spent a few weeks being salted in brine and being marinated in various substances and spices they are ready to undergo the crucial smoking process. Nothing is left to chance in the choice of surroundings, duration and, above all, the type of wood for the smoking fire. A mixture of spruce and pine is used, with juniper berries to add extra aroma to the smoke which will penetrate the meat and give it a very distinctive flavor.

The finished Speck keeps well in a dry, preferably dark, well ventilated place and the slight mold which sometimes forms on the inner, flatter side of the leg is harmless and can be gently scraped off.

Lean Speck is usually sliced and served as an appetizer with other cured meats; the fat version is widely used in cooking.

Zampone

A traditional specialty of the Reggio Emilia region, production centering on Modena. The pig's skin is chopped up together with other cuts from the shoulder, jowl and hock, then mixed with salt, pepper and other seasonings, after which it is used as a stuffing for the pig's trotters.

These are then dried in special stoves for longer than is the case with their first cousin cotechino, and slightly cooked in the process which improves their keeping qualities. Eventually, when the skin has turned a reddish brown, the zampone has been successfully cured. When it comes to cooking zamponi, they must first be soaked in plenty of cold water for about 12 hours, then punctured by pushing a large needle right through the skin in several places to prevent the filling swelling and bursting the encasing trotter while they are gently boiled for 3 hours or more. Zampone is also available in cans and jars, ready cooked and only needing reheating.

Zampone should be served piping hot, cut into thick, round slices, ideally accompanied by mashed potatoes and, traditionally, boiled lentils.

Speck

BUDINO DI FORMAGGIO CON FONDUTA AL PROFUMO DI FUNGHI
(Hot cheese molds with mushroom-flavored sauce)

for the mold:
3½ oz piece Parmesan cheese
3½ oz Taleggio cheese
scant ½ cup milk
3 whole eggs
salt

for the sauce:
2 oz dried porcini (cèpes) soaked
   overnight in ¼ cup milk
3½ oz Fontina cheese, diced

Melt the Parmesan and Taleggio cheeses in the hot milk in the top of a double boiler. Beat the eggs and stir gently into the melted cheese and milk mixture, adding salt to taste. Pour into small heatproof molds and place these in a roasting pan half filled with water. Bake in the oven at 300°F for 1 hr.

Remove the mushrooms from the milk (they can be used for other dishes), place the milk in a double boiler and melt the Fontina in it. Turn the cooked molds out on to hot plates, pour the sauce over them and serve while still very hot.

CALAMARI CALDI ALLO SCALOGNO *
(Calamari with beetroot)

12 calamari (approx. 1¼ lb)
salt
½ carrot
1 onion
½ stick celery
½–1 tbsp butter
1 shallot
1 cup dry white wine
1 cup heavy cream
1 cooked beetroot

Clean, skin and prepare the calamari (for method see recipe for cuttlefish on p. 13, removing the quill instead of the cuttlefish bone). Boil in salted water with the carrot, onion and celery for about ½ hr. Heat the butter in a skillet and sauté the very thinly sliced shallot; add the white wine, followed by the cream and 1 cup of the cooking stock. Reduce until fairly thick. Place slices of beetroot on hot plates, place the calamari in the center and cover with the sauce.

INSALATA TIEPIDA DI PORCINI CON LATTUGA ALL'ACETO *
(Warm lettuce and mushroom salad with raspberry vinegar dressing)

scant 1 tbsp butter
1 lb porcini (cèpes)
1 lettuce
1–1½ tbsp raspberry vinegar
salt
freshly ground pepper

Shred the lettuce into an ovenproof bowl, sprinkle with the raspberry vinegar, salt and pepper and stir. Slice the mushrooms thinly. Heat the butter and sauté the mushrooms briskly for 2 minutes, stirring and turning continuously. Place the lettuce in a hot oven for 30 sec. Transfer to hot plates and place the mushrooms on top. Serve immediately.

FONDI DI CARCIOFO AL FEGATO GRASSO
(Artichoke bottoms with foie gras)

4 artichokes
vinaigrette dressing
4 large lettuce leaves
4 slices foie gras (smaller diameter than the artichoke bottoms)
4 slices white truffle

Boil the artichokes in salted water until the leaves pull off easily. Once these are removed, trim the bottoms and dip in the well beaten vinaigrette before placing on the lettuce leaves. Put a small round slice of foie gras on each artichoke base and top with a slice of truffle.

25

Pasta

*I*talian cuisine is renowned for its pasta dishes, which are many and varied. Until quite recently, the serving of the pasta course, which in Italy precedes the main course, was nothing short of a ritual, with the family gathered round the table waiting in silent anticipation for the appearance of a steaming tureen. This ritualistic element still survives, although it has been subdued by an increased awareness of weight-reducing diets.

Some Italian athletes, to the surprise of some non Italians, have been known to dine off pasta meals on the eve of a momentous sporting event, but, as the Italians maintain, if you are healthy and active, eating pasta regularly will do you no harm.

Pasta is unique in its versatility, the many ways of serving it being governed by traditional regional recipes, or by whatever the cook's imagination may conjure up. Sauces can be as simple or sophisticated as you like, sometimes consisting of nothing more than melted butter and a generous sprinkling of Parmesan cheese, or leftovers imaginatively converted into a delicious accompaniment. Creative new recipes have greatly enriched the repertoire of Italian pasta dishes, adding new flavors and seasonings.

As well as experimenting with sauces, it is very rewarding to make your own fresh pasta. The best flour to use is durum wheat, known in Italian as "tipo 00" and available from Italian delicatessens, but perfectly good results can be obtained by using all-purpose flour.

TAGLIATELLE COL PROSCIUTTO
(Tagliatelle with Parma ham)

2½ cups all-purpose flour
3 eggs
salt
¼ cup butter
4 oz prosciutto
¼ cup grated Parmesan cheese
freshly ground pepper

Make a dough by mixing together with a fork the flour, eggs and a pinch of salt. Knead well for about 10 min until smooth and elastic. Roll out into a thin sheet using a floured rolling pin and leave to dry for ½ hr. Roll up and cut into strips ⅓ in wide. Cook the tagliatelle for 3 min in plenty of boiling salted water. Meanwhile, heat the butter in a wide skillet together with the prosciutto cut into narrow strips. When the tagliatelle are *al dente*, drain and pour into the skillet with the butter and prosciutto. Mix for a few minutes over low heat and sprinkle with freshly ground pepper; remove from the heat and add the Parmesan cheese. Stir quickly and serve immediately.

TAGLIATELLE ALLA ROMAGNOLA
(Tagliatelle with tomato and parsley sauce)

1 sprig parsley
1 clove garlic
1 lb tomatoes (not too ripe)
4 tbsp olive oil
salt
freshly ground pepper
1 lb fresh egg tagliatelle (see p.30)

Chop the parsley and garlic. Cut the tomatoes into pieces and discard the seeds. Put the chopped ingredients, oil and tomatoes in a heavy saucepan with salt and freshly ground pepper to taste. Cook over moderate heat for about ½ hr or until the sauce is thick. Remove from the heat and sieve. Cook the tagliatelle in plenty of boiling salted water for 3 min until *al dente*. Drain and transfer to a warm serving dish. Cover with the sauce, mix and serve.

TAGLIATELLE SMALZADE
(Tagliatelle with onion and cream sauce)

2½ cups all-purpose flour
3 eggs
salt
1 lb veal stew meat, cubed
¼ cup butter
1 medium onion
½ cup white wine
a little stock
⅔ cup light cream
freshly ground pepper
grated Parmesan cheese

This dish is typical of the Trento region. Make a dough by mixing together the flour (reserving 1 tbsp), eggs and a pinch of salt. Knead for about 10 min until smooth and elastic, adding a few tablespoons of warm water if too dry. Roll out evenly into a thin sheet. Leave to dry for ½ hr then cut into strips ⅓ in wide. Coat the veal pieces with the remaining flour. Heat the butter in a saucepan until it begins to brown, then add the meat and the onion cut into pieces. When the meat has browned, add the wine and leave to evaporate with the saucepan uncovered. Add a little stock or diluted meat extract. When the veal is tender, season with salt and freshly ground pepper and then pour in the cream. Remove the pieces of veal and keep hot. Cook the tagliatelle for 3 min in plenty of boiling salted water; drain and then toss in the meat sauce. Sprinkle with Parmesan cheese. The meat may be served separately, as a main course with a side salad or with the tagliatelle.

TAGLIATELLI AL SUGO
(Tagliatelli with tomato and ham sauce)

grated Parmesan cheese
2½ cups all-purpose flour
2 eggs
2 egg yolks
1 ⅓-in thick slice cooked ham
1 stick celery
1 small carrot
¼ cup butter
1 lb ripe or canned tomatoes
salt
freshly ground pepper

This is a typical Piedmont dish. Add 2 tbsp Parmesan cheese to the flour and knead together with the eggs and egg yolks until you have a firm, elastic dough. Roll out very thinly then leave to stand for ½ hr. Cut into strips 1½ in wide. Pile these strips on top of one another and cut into ribbons ⅓ in wide. Dice the ham and chop the celery and carrot finely. Heat half the butter in a skillet with the ham and chopped vegetables. When they begin to soften, add the sieved tomatoes. Season with a little salt and cook over low heat for about ½ hr until the sauce thickens. Cook the tagliatelli for 3 min in plenty of boiling salted water; drain and transfer to a warm serving dish. Dot the remaining butter over the pasta and pour over the hot sauce. Serve the Parmesan cheese separately.

TAGLIATELLINE CON LA FONDUTA
(Thin tagliatelle with melted cheese)

8 oz Fontina cheese, thinly sliced
½ cup milk, warmed
2 tbsp butter
3 egg yolks
salt
freshly ground pepper
10 oz thin tagliatelle
1 white truffle

This dish is typical of the Val d'Aosta. Put the slices of Fontina cheese in a bowl, and cover with the warmed milk. Leave for at least 2 hr. Melt the butter in a stainless steel saucepan, then over low heat add the Fontina cheese and 2 tbsp of the milk used to soak the cheese. Whisk until the cheese has melted completely. Turn up the heat and add the egg yolks one by one, beating hard to obtain an even, creamy consistency. Season with salt and pepper. Cook the tagliatelline for 3 min in plenty of boiling salted water; drain and transfer to a serving dish. Mix with the melted cheese. Garnish with thin flakes of white truffle.

TAGLIATELLE COL POLLO *
(Tagliatelle with chicken)

2½ cups all-purpose flour
3 eggs
salt
12 oz boned chicken
1 small onion
4 tbsp olive oil
¼ cup butter
½ cup dry red wine
1⅛ cups milk
1 tsp meat extract
freshly ground pepper
1 tsp tomato paste
¼ cup grated Parmesan cheese

Make a dough by mixing together the flour, eggs and a pinch of salt. Knead well for about 10 min until smooth and elastic. Roll out into a thin sheet using a floured rolling pin and leave to dry for ½ hr. Roll up and cut into strips ⅓ in wide. Cut the chicken into pieces. Chop the onion finely. Heat the oil and butter in a skillet. When they start to bubble, add the onion and stir until it begins to brown. Add the chicken pieces and brown evenly. Raise the heat and pour in the wine; leave to evaporate and then add the milk containing the dissolved meat extract. Season with salt and freshly ground pepper. Lower the heat and leave to simmer for about ¼ hr. Mix the tomato paste with a little warm water and pour into the skillet. Leave to cook slowly until the meat is tender, gradually adding enough warm water to give a thick coating sauce for the tagliatelle. Cook the tagliatelle for 3 min in plenty of boiling salted water until *al dente*. Drain and transfer to a warm serving dish. Cover with the chicken sauce and serve with grated Parmesan cheese. (The chicken pieces can be served separately as a main course with new potatoes and a crisp green salad.)

TAGLIATELLE VERDI ALLA MARINARA
(Spinach tagliatelle with mussels)

1¾ lb mussels
4 tbsp olive oil
¼ onion
1 clove garlic
4 large ripe tomatoes
salt
freshly ground pepper
1 tbsp chopped parsley
1 lb fresh spinach tagliatelle

Leave the mussels in a bowl under cold running water for ½ hr. Discard any that do not close when tapped sharply. Scrub well and trim the beards. Place in a skillet with 1 tbsp oil over high heat for 5 min until the shells open. Discard any that remain closed. Reserve a few of the mussels in their shells. Remove the rest and set aside. Pour the remaining liquor through a fine sieve and set aside. Heat the remaining oil in a saucepan and brown the sliced onion and minced garlic for a few minutes. Add the seeded and chopped tomatoes and season with salt and pepper; add the chopped parsley and cook over high heat until the sauce is well-flavored and thick. Add the mussels and a few tablespoons of the reserved liquor. Cover and leave to simmer. Meanwhile cook the spinach tagliatelle for 3 min in plenty of boiling salted water. Drain and transfer to a warm serving dish and cover with the mussel sauce. Garnish with a few mussels still in their shells. Sprinkle with black pepper before serving.

TAGLIATELLE ALL'UOVO IN SALSA DI FEGATINI (Tagliatelle with chicken liver sauce)

8 oz chicken livers
2 tbsp olive oil
2 tbsp butter
1 slice onion
8 oz ripe or canned tomatoes
salt
freshly ground pepper
1 lb fresh egg tagliatelle (see p.30)
¼ cup grated Parmesan cheese

Rinse the chicken livers and cut into pieces. Fry in a skillet in the oil and butter, together with the onion, which should be removed as soon as it begins to soften. Cook over high heat at first, then cover and turn down the heat. Peel, drain and seed the tomatoes before chopping and adding to the chicken livers. Season with salt and freshly ground pepper and continue to cook slowly. Meanwhile, cook the tagliatelle for 3 min in plenty of boiling salted water until *al dente*. Drain and transfer to a warm serving dish. Cover with the chicken liver sauce, extra butter and grated Parmesan cheese.

TAGLIATELLE IN SALSA DI FUNGHI (Tagliatelle in mushroom sauce)

8 oz ripe or canned tomatoes
3 tbsp olive oil

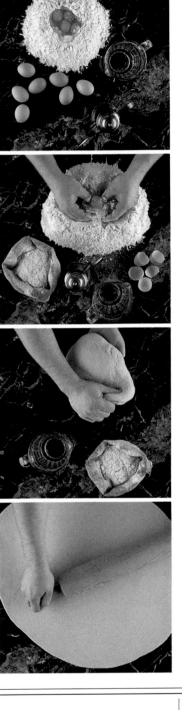

Basic pasta dough for fresh tagliatelle, fettuccine, etc.

To make four portions (about 1 lb) of egg pasta you will need 2½–3 cups all-purpose flour, 3 eggs and a pinch of salt. In some regions a little oil or milk is added to the eggs; in others the flour is mixed with water alone.

Sift the flour into a mound and break the eggs into the center. Add a pinch of salt and mix the ingredients together slowly with a fork or your fingertips.

Knead well for about 10 min until the dough is smooth and elastic (you should see air bubbles when you cut the dough). Leave to stand for ¼ hr wrapped in a floured cloth.

Roll out into a fairly thin sheet, working from the center outward, making sure that the pasta is of even thickness. Leave to dry for up to ½ hr.

Roll up the sheet of pasta and cut into ribbons with a sharp knife.

¼ onion
1 clove garlic
8 oz fresh porcini (cèpes) or 1 oz dried
salt
1 lb fresh egg tagliatelle (see p.30)
freshly ground pepper
2 tbsp butter
¼ cup grated Parmesan cheese

Peel the tomatoes if fresh. Remove the seeds, drain and fry in a skillet with the oil, chopped onion and a clove of garlic. Clean the mushrooms: Scrape away any soil with a knife, wipe with a cloth and slice. Add to the skillet and season with salt and pepper. Cook the sauce over high heat at first, then

cover, turn down the heat and simmer until the mushrooms are tender. Cook the tagliatelle for 3 min in plenty of boiling salted water until *al dente*. Drain and transfer to a warm serving dish. Sprinkle with melted butter and cover with the tomato and mushroom sauce. Serve hot with grated Parmesan cheese.

TAJARIN ALL'ALBESE CON FEGATINI (Tagliatelle with chicken livers)

2½ cups all-purpose flour
3 eggs
¼ cup butter
4 oz chicken livers
1 tsp meat extract
salt
nutmeg
freshly ground pepper
¼ cup grated Parmesan cheese
1 white truffle

This dish is typical of Piedmont. Make a dough by mixing together the flour and eggs. Knead for about 10 min until smooth and elastic. Roll out into a very thin sheet and cut into "tajarin" (tagliatelle ⅙–¼ in wide). Heat the butter in a small skillet and when it starts to bubble, add the rinsed and finely sliced chicken livers. Sauté for 2–3 min. Add the meat extract dissolved in a ladle of warm water; season with salt and a pinch of grated nutmeg. Cook over moderate heat until the sauce is quite thick. Cook the pasta for 2–3 min in plenty of boiling salted water. Drain when *al dente* and transfer to a warm serving dish. Sprinkle with black pepper and grated Parmesan, and pour over the sauce. Mix well and garnish with thin flakes of white truffle.

TAGLIATELLE CON FUNGHI E SALSICCIA (Tagliatelle with mushrooms and spicy sausage)

8 oz fresh porcini (cèpes) or 1 oz dried
4 oz spicy sausage
3 tbsp olive oil
1 clove garlic

¼ onion
salt
freshly ground pepper
1 lb fresh egg tagliatelle (see p.30)
¼ cup grated Parmesan cheese
¼ cup butter
2 tbsp chopped parsley

Do not spoil the flavor of the mushrooms by washing, but clean off the soil with a knife, scraping the cap and stalk delicately. Wipe with a cloth and slice. Prick the sausage with a fork, immerse briefly in boiling water, remove the skin and cut into rounds. Heat the oil in a saucepan with the garlic and onion which should be discarded as soon as they begin to brown. Add the pieces of sausage, sliced mushrooms, salt and pepper. Cook over high heat for a few minutes, then lower the heat. Add a little stock if necessary and cook until the mushrooms are tender. Cook the tagliatelle for 3 min in boiling salted water until *al dente*. Drain, transfer to a warm serving dish and add melted butter and cheese. Toss with two forks and cover with the mushroom sauce. Garnish with chopped parsley and serve with grated Parmesan cheese.

TAGLIOLINI ALLA MARINARA
(Tagliolini in fish sauce)

2½ cups all-purpose flour
3 eggs
1 tsp grated lemon peel
1 scorpionfish
2 small hake (or cod)
2 medium sole
1 monkfish tail
4 tsp olive oil
1 clove garlic
1 sprig parsley
1 tbsp tomato paste
salt
freshly ground pepper

Make a fairly firm dough by mixing together the flour, eggs and 1 tsp grated lemon peel. Roll out into a very thin sheet and leave to stand for ½ hr. Roll up and cut into "tagliolini" (very thin tagliatelle). Prepare a fish stock: Clean and gut the fish in the usual way but leave the heads attached. Place in a large saucepan, add a little salt, cover with 2 pints water and boil for about ¼ hr. Put the olive oil, garlic and half the parsley, finely chopped, in a separate saucepan and add the tomato paste and the strained fish stock. Remove the heads from the fish and squeeze out any remaining stock. Season with salt and freshly ground pepper and cook slowly for 15–20 min to thicken. The sauce should be fairly liquid. Meanwhile cook the tagliolini for 2 min in plenty of boiling salted water. Drain and pour into the fish sauce. Stir for 1 min until the tagliolini are *al dente*. Sprinkle with the remaining freshly chopped parsley and serve piping hot.

Do not serve cheese with this dish. Fillet and skin the fish to serve as a main course; dress with olive oil, salt, freshly ground pepper and lemon slices and serve with boiled potatoes.

TAGLIOLINI AI CARCIOFI
(Tagliolini with artichokes)

4 artichokes
juice of 1 lemon
3 tbsp olive oil
¼ cup butter
¼ onion
salt
freshly ground pepper
1 lb fresh egg tagliolini (see p.30)
2 eggs
¼ cup grated Parmesan cheese

Pull away the tough outer leaves from the artichokes and slice the inner leaves, cutting off any sharp tips. Trim and thinly slice the stalks, then immerse in water acidulated with lemon juice. Heat the oil and butter in a skillet and gently fry the onion in one piece for 5 min. Discard the onion, then add the drained artichokes. Cover and cook over low heat, adding water when necessary. To prevent discoloration do not add salt until the artichokes are tender. Add a little freshly ground pepper at the same time. Cook the tagliolini for 3 min in plenty of boiling salted water. Beat the eggs with a little Parmesan. Drain the tagliolini and transfer to a warm dish. Add the beaten eggs, the artichokes in their sauce and the remaining cheese. Mix carefully, transfer to a warmed serving dish and serve with more grated Parmesan cheese.

TAGLIOLINI ALLA FRANCESCANA
(Tagliolini with tomato and thyme sauce)

1 medium onion
1 small carrot
1 stick celery
¼ cup butter
14 oz very ripe or canned tomatoes
1 sprig parsley
1 sprig thyme
10 oz fresh egg tagliolini (see p.30)
salt
¼ cup grated Parmesan cheese

Chop the onion, carrot and celery finely. Fry in the butter in a wide skillet over very low heat for 5 min. Add the sieved tomatoes, chopped parsley and sprig of thyme. Raise the heat, cover the skillet and let the sauce thicken for about ¼ hr. Cook the tagliolini for 3 min in plenty of boiling salted water. Drain and mix with the sauce in a warm serving dish so that the pasta is completely coated. Sprinkle over half the Parmesan cheese and mix again. Serve with the remaining Parmesan.

LINGUINE AGLIO E OLIO
(Linguine noodles with garlic and oil)

½ cup olive oil
4 cloves garlic
2 tbsp chopped parsley
10 oz linguine noodles
salt
freshly ground pepper

Heat the oil in a skillet and fry the garlic cloves. When the garlic starts to brown, remove the skillet from the heat and add the parsley. Cook the linguine in plenty of boiling salted water for 5 min. Drain when *al dente*. Pour into the skillet with the flavored oil and sprinkle with pepper. Mix well and serve without grated cheese.

TRENETTE AL PESTO ✳
(Trenette noodles with pesto sauce)

pesto (see p. 130)
1 medium potato
salt
10 oz trenette noodles

Prepare the pesto sauce in advance. Peel and dice the potato and cook for 5 min in a large saucepan of salted water. Add the trenette. (Trenette are long and flattened noodles; the Genoese variety are darker and take longer to cook.) Drain the pasta when *al dente*, reserving a little of the cooking water. Transfer to a warm serving dish and mix with the pesto sauce diluted in a little of the reserved cooking water. Serve hot.

BAVETTINE AL POMODORO
(Bavettine with tomatoes)

14 oz fresh tomatoes
salt
freshly ground pepper
1 sprig parsley
4 basil leaves
4 tbsp olive oil
1 clove garlic
10 oz bavettine (thin noodles)
¼ cup grated Parmesan cheese

Peel the tomatoes and scoop out the seeds. Slice the tomatoes and place in a colander, sprinkled with salt, pepper, parsley leaves and chopped basil to drain for ¼ hr. Heat the oil in a saucepan and add the garlic clove. Remove as soon as it begins to brown and add the tomatoes with the chopped basil and parsley. Cook for a few minutes only, making sure they do not break up. Cook the bavettine for 8–10 min in plenty of boiling salted water until *al dente*. Drain and transfer to a warm serving dish; cover with the tomato sauce and serve with grated Parmesan.

PAPPARDELLE ALL'ARETINA
(Pappardelle with duckling)

1 duckling, with liver
1 lb pappardelle
2 oz prosciutto
1 medium onion
1 stick celery
1 small carrot
2 tbsp butter
salt
freshly ground pepper
stock or meat extract
1 tbsp tomato paste

Ask the butcher to clean the duckling for you, reserving the liver. To prepare the pappardelle, mix together 3 cups all-purpose flour, 3 eggs, 1 egg yolk and a pinch of salt and knead for about 10 min until the dough is smooth and elastic. Roll out not too thinly and cut into 1¼-in strips. Use a serrated cutting wheel if preferred. Rinse and dry the duckling. Chop up the prosciutto, onion, celery and carrot. Melt the butter in a large saucepan and brown the duckling evenly with the liver. Add the chopped ingredients and season with salt and pepper. Cook the duckling over moderate heat for about 1 hr or until tender, gradually adding stock mixed with the tomato paste. If you have no stock, use 1 level tsp meat extract dissolved in boiling water. When the duckling is tender, remove from the saucepan, cut the meat into strips, and keep warm.

Reduce the stock by boiling fast. Mash the liver with a fork and stir into the reduced stock. Cook the pappardelle for 4 min in plenty of boiling salted water. Drain and cover with the reduced stock and strips of duckling meat. Alternatively, serve the meat as a main course with a side salad.

PAPPARDELLE AL CINGHIALE
(Pappardelle with wild boar sauce)

4 oz porcini (cèpes)
1 onion
1 carrot
8 oz ham from wild boar (or other strong-flavored ham)
2 oz salt pork
½ cup olive oil
¼ cup butter
salt
freshly ground pepper
1⅛ cups red wine
1 liqueur glass grappa
14 oz fresh pappardelle (see previous recipe)
⅓ cup grated Parmesan cheese

Do not wash the mushrooms or they will lose their fragrance. Brush off the soil and scrape cap and stalk with a knife before wiping with a cloth and slicing. Mince the onion, carrot, ham and salt pork in a food processor. Transfer this mixture to a skillet and brown in the oil and 1 tbsp butter. Add the sliced mushrooms and season with salt and pepper. Cook over high heat for a few minutes, then add the wine and grappa. When the liquid has evaporated, cover the skillet, turn down the heat and simmer gently for about ½ hr. Prepare the pappardelle as directed in the previous recipe, and cut into 1¼-in wide strips. Cook for 4 min in plenty of boiling salted water. Add a ladle of cold water before draining to prevent the strips of pasta sticking together. Transfer to a serving dish, cover with melted butter and cheese and pour over the wild boar sauce. Serve with grated Parmesan cheese.

PAPPARDELLE SULLA LEPRE
(Pappardelle with hare)

3 cups all-purpose flour
3 eggs
1 egg yolk
salt
1 oz pancetta
½ onion
½ stick celery
½ carrot
2 sprigs parsley
¼ cup butter
4 hare legs
1 tbsp tomato paste
freshly ground pepper
1 cup red wine
2–3 cups stock

Mix together the flour (reserving 1 tbsp), the eggs, egg yolk and a pinch of salt and knead for about 10 min until the dough is smooth and elastic. Roll out, not too thinly, and cut into pappardelle about ¾ in wide. Chop the pancetta, onion, celery, carrot and parsley. Melt the butter in a saucepan and brown the chopped ingredients for 5 min. Strip the meat from the hare legs, add to the saucepan and brown for a few minutes. Sprinkle in 1 tbsp flour, stir for 2–3 min, then add the tomato paste dissolved in a little stock. Season with salt and pepper. When this has thickened, pour in the wine and allow to reduce a little before adding 2 cups hot stock. Cover and cook over moderate heat for at least 1 hr. The sauce should be rich and quite thick. Cook the pappardelle for 4 min in plenty of boiling salted water; drain well, transfer to a warm serving dish and cover with the sauce. Mix carefully before serving.

PAPARÈLE E FEGATINI
(Paparèle and chicken livers)

4 oz chicken livers
2½ cups all-purpose flour
3 eggs
salt
1 tbsp butter
freshly ground pepper
3 cups meat stock
¼ cup grated Parmesan cheese

This dish is typical of the Veneto region. Clean the chicken livers, removing all the membranes. Rinse thoroughly and cut into pieces. Mix together the flour, eggs and a pinch of salt. Knead well for 10 min until the dough is smooth and elastic. Roll out thinly, leave to stand for a few minutes then roll up and cut into ¼-in wide ribbons known as "paparèle." Heat the butter in a saucepan. When it begins to bubble, add the chicken livers, season with salt and pepper and brown evenly for 2–3 min. Bring the meat stock to a boil in a large saucepan and add the chicken livers, followed by the paparèle. Cook for about 4 min, by which time nearly all the stock will have been absorbed. Serve the Parmesan cheese separately.

LINGUE DI PASSERO AL TONNO
(Ribbon noodles with tuna)

3 tbsp butter
1 tbsp all-purpose flour
1¼ cups dry white wine
¼ cup grated Parmesan cheese
1 can tuna in oil
freshly ground pepper
10 oz ribbon noodles
salt
2 tbsp oil

Melt the butter over low heat in a saucepan. Add the flour and stir for 2–3 min. Gradually pour in the white wine, stirring constantly. Once the sauce thickens, remove from the heat and add the Parmesan cheese, the tuna – drained and mashed with a fork – and freshly ground pepper. Cook the noodles in plenty of boiling salted water until al dente. Drain and transfer to a warm serving dish; sprinkle with the oil and pour over the tuna sauce.

BÌGOLI IN SALSA
(Wholewheat noodles with anchovy sauce)

4 salted anchovies
1 medium onion
¼ cup olive oil
1 tbsp chopped parsley

freshly ground pepper
1 lb bìgoli (fresh wholewheat
    noodles)
salt

Rinse the anchovies to remove the salt, bone and chop together with the onion. Heat the oil and chopped ingredients in a skillet. Add a little water, cover and simmer gently for ¼ hr. A few minutes before removing from the heat, add the chopped parsley and freshly ground pepper. The sauce should have an even, creamy consistency. Cook the bìgoli in plenty of lightly salted water until *al dente*. Drain and cover with the hot sauce. This dish is not served with grated cheese.

BÌGOLI CON REGAGLIE DI POLLO
(Wholewheat noodles with chicken giblets)

4 oz chicken giblets
4 oz chicken livers
salt
¼ cup butter
3 sage leaves
stock (or bouillon cube)
1 lb bìgoli (fresh wholewheat
    noodles)
¼ cup grated Parmesan cheese

This dish is typical of the Veneto region. Clean and rinse the chicken giblets and livers and cut them into small pieces. Heat the butter and sage leaves in a heavy saucepan until browned. Add the giblets and cook for about ½ hr, adding a ladle of stock if necessary. Add the livers for the last 5 min only so that they stay soft. Meanwhile cook the bìgoli in plenty of lightly salted boiling water until *al dente*. Drain, cover with the sauce, and serve piping hot with Parmesan cheese.

BÌGOLI CON LE SARDELLE
(Wholewheat noodles with sardines)

3 salted sardines
salt

1 lb bìgoli (fresh wholewheat
    noodles)
¼ cup oil

This dish is typical of the Veneto region. Rinse the sardines well to remove the excess salt; bone and chop. (The salt may also be removed from the sardines by frying them with a slice of lemon.) Bring a saucepan of lightly salted water to a boil, add the bìgoli and cook until *al dente*. Meanwhile, heat the oil and sardines in a skillet over low heat. Mash with a fork to produce a smooth sauce. Drain the bìgoli when *al dente* and cover with the sardine sauce. Do not serve Parmesan cheese with this dish.

PASTA ALL'AGLIO E OLIO DEL DUCA
(Spaghetti with garlic sauce)

6 cloves garlic
2 tbsp butter
2 tbsp all-purpose flour
1 cup milk
salt
freshly ground white pepper
10 oz spaghetti
5 tbsp olive oil

Put the garlic cloves in a saucepan, add 2½ cups water and simmer gently for about 2 hr. Prepare a white sauce by heating the butter in a saucepan. When it starts to color, add the flour and cook for 1–2 min, stirring constantly. Gradually pour in the milk. Season with salt and freshly ground white pepper and simmer for 10–15 min. Remove from the heat and set aside, stirring occasionally. Cook the spaghetti for 10–12 min in plenty of boiling salted water until *al dente*. Meanwhile push the garlic cloves through a sieve together with their cooking water and return to their saucepan. Pour in the oil and return the saucepan to the heat to reheat the puréed garlic. Drain the spaghetti and transfer to a serving dish. Cover first with the white sauce, then with the garlic sauce. Toss the spaghetti well, using two forks so that the sauces are well blended and the spaghetti evenly coated. Contrary to expectations, this dish does not have the disadvantages of most garlic-

flavored dishes: You may enjoy it without fear that it will linger heavily on the breath.

BÌGOLI CO' L'ANARA ✳
(Wholewheat noodles with duck sauce)

1 duckling
1 onion
1 stick celery
1 small carrot
salt
¼ cup butter
3 sage leaves
stock (or bouillon cube)
freshly ground pepper
1 lb bìgoli (fresh wholewheat
    noodles)
¼ cup grated Parmesan cheese

Thoroughly clean and rinse the duckling, reserving the liver and giblets. Place the duckling in a large saucepan of lightly salted water with the onion, celery and carrot. Bring to a boil, cover and cook over moderate heat for about 1½ hr. Heat the butter in a small saucepan and fry the sage leaves for 2–3 min before adding the liver and giblets cut into very small pieces. Add a ladle of stock, season with salt and pepper and simmer for ¼ hr. When the duckling is tender, lift out, reserving the stock, and place in a warm oven. Cook the bìgoli in the reserved stock. Drain when *al dente* and transfer to a serving dish; cover with the sage and giblet sauce and sprinkle with Parmesan cheese. Mix carefully and serve hot. Serve the duckling as a main course accompanied by one of the many sauces suitable for braised meats (see chapter on sauces, p. 122).

PASTA CON LA CARNE "CAPULIATA"
(Pasta with ground beef)

1 onion
1 clove garlic
1 sprig parsley
2 basil leaves
¼ cup butter
1 cup lean ground beef
½ cup dry red wine
4 very ripe tomatoes
salt

freshly ground pepper
10 oz spaghetti (or macaroni)
¼ cup grated Parmesan cheese
4 oz Caciocavallo or strong
  Provolone cheese

This dish is typical of Sicily. Chop the onion, garlic, parsley and basil finely together. Heat the butter in a skillet (reserving ½ tbsp) and add the chopped vegetables and herbs when it starts to bubble. Fry for a couple of minutes, then add the meat. Mix well and brown, uncovered, for a further 3–4 min. Raise the heat, pour in the wine and when this has evaporated, add the peeled, seeded and chopped tomatoes. Season with salt and freshly ground pepper; cover and cook over moderate heat for about ½ hr, stirring occasionally and adding a little hot water if necessary. Cook the pasta in plenty of boiling salted water for 10–12 min or until *al dente*. Drain and transfer to a warm dish. Cover with the sauce and grated Parmesan. Grease an ovenproof dish with the remaining butter and spread a layer of pasta in the bottom; lay slices of Caciocavallo cheese on top, and then cover with pasta. Finish with a layer of cheese. Place in a moderate oven (350°F) for about 20 min. Remove from the oven and serve immediately. If you prefer a more pronounced flavor use Pecorino cheese instead of Parmesan.

FETTUCCINE AL PESTO
(Fettuccine with pesto sauce)

pesto (see p. 130)
1 lb fresh egg fettuccine (see p. 30)
salt

Prepare the pesto sauce in advance. Cook the pasta for 3–4 min in plenty of boiling salted water. (Add 1 tbsp oil to stop the pasta sticking together.) Drain and toss in the pesto sauce. Serve immediately.

FETTUCCINE ALLA ROMANA
(Fettuccine Roman style)

1 oz dried mushrooms
1 onion

¼ cup salt pork
1 clove garlic
8 oz ripe tomatoes
¼ cup + 2 tbsp butter
salt
8 oz chicken giblets
⅛ cup dry white wine
freshly ground pepper
stock
1 cup clove gravy (see p. 129)
10 oz dried fettuccine
grated Parmesan cheese

Soak the mushrooms in warm water for ½ hr. Chop the onion and fry in a saucepan with the salt pork and minced garlic clove. Discard the garlic as soon as it begins to brown and add the peeled, seeded

and chopped tomatoes together with the mushrooms, squeezed dry. Add salt and cook over high heat for about 20 min. Meanwhile brown the finely chopped giblets in 1 tbsp butter, sprinkle with salt and add the wine. When the wine has evaporated, add pepper and pour in a few tablespoons of hot stock. Add the cooked giblets and the clove gravy to the tomato sauce and simmer gently for 10–15 min. Cook the fettuccine for 5–6 min in plenty of boiling salted water and stir immediately to prevent sticking. Drain and cover with the hot sauce, melted butter and a good sprinkling of grated Parmesan. Serve steaming hot.

PASTA CON LE ZUCCHINE ✳
(Pasta with zucchini)

10 oz pasta (spaghetti, penne,
    tagliatelle, etc.)
salt
3 zucchini
olive oil
freshly ground pepper

Cook the pasta in plenty of boiling salted water for 10–12 min or until *al dente*. Rinse, dry and thinly slice the zucchini, then fry on both sides in the hot oil until tender. Season with salt and freshly ground pepper, stirring frequently to prevent them sticking. Drain the pasta and transfer to a serving dish. Add

the zucchini with their cooking oil, mix well and serve.

FETTUCCINE ALLA TRASTEVERINA
(Fettuccine with shrimp and clams)

3 cups all-purpose flour
3 eggs
3 tbsp olive oil
salt
½ onion
1 clove garlic
¼ cup butter
14 oz ripe or canned tomatoes
2 lb clams

⅓ cup shrimp
freshly ground pepper
1 tbsp chopped parsley

Mix together the flour, eggs, 1 tsp olive oil and a pinch of salt. Knead for about 10 min to obtain a smooth, elastic dough. Roll out into a fairly thin sheet, then roll up and cut into ribbons ½ in wide. Chop the onion and garlic and heat in a skillet with the remaining oil and butter. When soft, add the peeled, seeded tomatoes cut into strips (if you use canned tomatoes, sieve them). Meanwhile place the clams in a skillet with ½ cup water over high heat for 5–10 min or until the shells open. Remove the clams from their shells and reserve the cooking liquor. Rinse the shrimp and cut into pieces. Add the shrimp to the tomatoes and cook over moderate heat. Pour the reserved clam liquor through a very fine strainer (or muslin cloth) into the skillet with the shrimp and tomatoes. Turn up the heat, season with salt and freshly ground pepper and let the sauce thicken slightly. Add the clams 2–3 min before removing from the heat. Cook the fettuccine for 3–4 min in plenty of salted water. Drain and transfer to a warm serving bowl and cover with sauce. Sprinkle with finely chopped parsley, mix well and serve.

FETTUCCINE AL TRIPLO BURRO MAESTOSE (ALL'ALFREDO)
(Fettuccine Alfredo with "triple" butter)

2½ cups all-purpose flour
3 eggs
salt
½ cup grated Parmesan cheese
½ cup butter

Mix together the flour, eggs and a pinch of salt. Knead for about 10 min until the dough is smooth and elastic (you should see air bubbles when you cut through the dough). Cover with a cloth and leave to stand for ¼ hr. Roll out into a fairly thin sheet, leave to dry slightly then cut into ½-in ribbons. Cook the fettuccine for 3–4 min in plenty of boiling salted water until

al dente. Drain, but not too thoroughly otherwise the fettuccine may stick together. Transfer to a warm serving dish and cover with Parmesan cheese. Mix quickly to insure the pasta does not become cold. Flake the butter into the fettuccine a little at a time (the fettuccine will be "double" or "triple" butter, as the Italians say, depending on the amount of butter used – the quantity must always be generous). Serve in warm dishes. As in all similar pasta dishes served with butter, the grated cheese should always be sprinkled on before adding the butter.

FETTUCCINE ALLA PAPALINA
(Fettuccine with prosciutto, cream and eggs)

2½ cups all-purpose flour
5 eggs
1 tbsp olive oil
salt
3 oz prosciutto
½ onion
¼ cup butter
¼ cup grated Parmesan cheese
½ cup light cream
freshly ground pepper

Mix together the flour, 3 eggs, 1 tbsp oil and a pinch of salt. Knead well for 10 min until the dough is smooth and elastic (you should see air bubbles when you cut through the dough). Roll out into a fairly thin sheet and cut into ½-in ribbons. Cook the fettuccine for 3–4 min in plenty of boiling salted water. Meanwhile cut the prosciutto into narrow strips, finely chop the onion and brown both gently in a small skillet in 2 tbsp butter. When the pasta is almost ready, heat the remaining butter in a large skillet. Beat the remaining two eggs with 2 tbsp grated Parmesan cheese and the cream and add to the skillet when the butter begins to bubble. Stir the mixture. Drain the pasta and add to the skillet together with the chopped prosciutto and onion. Sprinkle with freshly ground pepper. Mix quickly and remove from the heat. Serve in warm dishes and sprinkle with grated Parmesan. Serve this delicately flavored dish very hot.

FETTUCCINE CON PROSCIUTTO E PANNA
(Fettuccine with prosciutto and cream)

2½ cups all-purpose flour
3 eggs
salt
1 egg yolk
1 cup light cream
2 oz prosciutto
¼ cup grated Parmesan cheese
freshly ground white pepper

Mix together the flour, 3 eggs and a pinch of salt and knead well for 10 min until the dough is smooth and elastic. Roll out into a fairly thin sheet and cut into ½-in ribbons. Pour the cream into a bowl, add the prosciutto cut into narrow strips, together with half the grated Parmesan cheese, the egg yolk, salt to taste and freshly ground white pepper. Stir with a wooden spoon until the ingredients are well blended. Cook the fettuccine for 3–4 min in plenty of boiling salted water. Drain while still al dente and transfer immediately to the bowl. Mix carefully until the pasta is well coated with the sauce. Serve the remaining grated Parmesan cheese separately.

TESTAROLI AL PESTO
(Testaroli with pesto sauce)

2½ cups all-purpose flour
salt
4 tbsp olive oil
pesto (see p. 130)
⅓ cup grated Parmesan cheese

At one time testaroli were cooked in terracotta dishes known as testi, from which the dish takes its name. Hot cinders were piled on the lid of the dish and the testaroli would cook within 4–5 min. Nowadays they are made in a 10–12-in cast-iron skillet or crêpe pan and the same procedure is followed as for cooking crêpes. Prepare a fairly liquid batter by mixing together the flour, approx. 3¾ cups water and a little salt. Beat the batter until smooth. Heat a little oil in the skillet and pour in sufficient batter to cover the bottom in a thin layer. Cook for 1–2 min over medium heat, then invert and cook the

other side for 30 sec. For convenience the testaroli may be cooked in advance. To reheat simply immerse in a saucepan of boiling salted water. Turn off the heat and leave for 4–5 min. Drain the testaroli, cut into strips and cover with the pesto sauce. Serve in warm dishes with grated Parmesan cheese.

STRANGOZZI DI SPOLETO
(Fettuccine Spoleto style)

3 cups all-purpose flour
water
1 clove garlic
½ cup olive oil
1¾ lb ripe tomatoes, peeled and chopped
1 sprig parsley
1 sprig basil
salt
freshly ground pepper

The fettuccine prepared without eggs in Spoleto are given the name of "strangozzi." Mix the flour with sufficient cold water to obtain an elastic dough. Knead until smooth and full of air bubbles. Roll out thinly. Leave to dry out for ¼ hr and then cut into ribbons ¼ in thick. Spread out the ribbons and leave to dry for about ½ hr. Meanwhile, fry the minced garlic with the oil in a saucepan. Discard as soon as it begins to brown, then add the tomatoes, chopped parsley and basil, and a pinch of salt and pepper. Stir and cook briskly over high heat for about 20 min. Put the strangozzi in plenty of boiling salted water and drain as soon as the water returns to a boil (if made the same day, leave them to boil for a minute longer if dry). Cover with the tomato sauce and serve immediately. Do not serve Parmesan cheese with this dish.

SPAGHETTI ALLE VONGOLE
(Spaghetti with clams)

1¼ lb clams (or 1 can shelled clams)
4 large ripe tomatoes (or 14 oz canned tomatoes)
2 cloves garlic
1 sprig parsley
3 tbsp olive oil

salt
freshly ground pepper
12 oz spaghetti

Rinse the clams thoroughly, place in a skillet with ½ in water and boil over high heat until the shells open. Remove the clams from their shells when cool enough to handle. Reserve the cooking water and leave to stand to allow any sand to settle. Pour through a strainer lined with a piece of muslin.

Rinse the tomatoes and push through a sieve using a wooden spoon. Finely chop the garlic cloves and half the parsley and place in a skillet with the oil and reserved cooking water from the clams. Season with salt and reduce by boiling rapidly until only a few tablespoons remain. Add the sieved tomatoes and reduce over high heat. Season with freshly ground pepper and add the clams. These should not be allowed to boil as they need only be heated through (the same applies if canned clams are used). Cook the spaghetti for 10–12 min in plenty of boiling salted water. Drain and transfer to a warm serving bowl. Cover with the clam sauce and the remaining parsley, finely chopped (parsley should be chopped at the very last minute so that it does not lose its flavor). Cheese should not be served with this dish.

PASTA CON LE MELANZANE
(Pasta with eggplant)

2 eggplant
salt
olive oil
¼-in piece red chili pepper
1 clove garlic
12 oz pasta (spaghetti, vermicelli, etc.)
1 tbsp chopped parsley

This is a typically Sicilian dish. Peel the eggplant if the skin is tough and cut into cubes. Sprinkle with salt and leave to drain for 2 hr to draw out the bitter juices. Heat plenty of olive oil in a skillet with the chili pepper and minced garlic clove. Discard the garlic when it browns and add the eggplant cubes. Fry until they are tender and golden brown, adding more oil if necessary. Remove and drain on kitchen paper. Meanwhile cook the pasta for 10–12 min in plenty of boiling salted water. Drain when al dente and transfer to a warm serving dish; trickle over a little oil, sprinkle with finely chopped parsley, mix well and garnish with the eggplant cubes. Do not serve cheese with this dish.

SPAGHETTI AL TONNO
(Spaghetti with tuna)

1 clove garlic, minced
½ cup olive oil
14 oz ripe tomatoes
salt
freshly ground pepper
4 oz tuna in oil
1 tsp oregano
10 oz spaghetti
grated Pecorino cheese (optional)

Fry the garlic in the oil in a small saucepan. Remove the garlic as soon as it begins to brown and add the peeled, chopped and seeded tomatoes. Season lightly with salt and pepper and cook over high heat for about 20 min. Flake the tuna with a fork and add to the saucepan. Sprinkle in the oregano. Stir and cook gently for a further 5 min. Cook the spaghetti for 10–12 min in plenty of boiling salted water. Drain when al dente and cover immediately with the hot sauce. Serve without cheese or, if desired, with grated Pecorino cheese.

SPAGHETTI ALLA
SANGIOVANNIELLO
(Spaghetti with anchovies)

1 lb very ripe fresh (or canned) tomatoes
3 salted anchovies
6 tbsp olive oil
1 clove garlic
2–3 basil leaves
¼-in piece red chili pepper
salt
12 oz spaghetti
1 tbsp chopped parsley

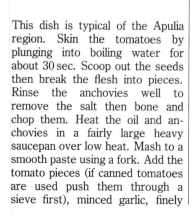

SPAGHETTI COI BROCCOLI * (Spaghetti with broccoli)

4 salted anchovies
1 ¼ lb broccoli
salt
12 oz spaghetti
4 tbsp olive oil
1 clove garlic

This dish is typical of the Apulia region. Rinse, bone and chop the anchovies. Rinse and trim the broccoli into florets. Cook for 10 min in plenty of boiling salted water. Drain, reserving the cooking water. Cook the spaghetti for 10–12 min in the reserved water. While the pasta is cooking, heat the olive oil with the finely chopped garlic and anchovies in a small saucepan. Mash the anchovies to a paste. When the spaghetti is *al dente*, drain, transfer to a warm bowl, cover with the anchovy sauce and add the broccoli florets. Mix gently and serve without cheese. Add a pinch of finely chopped red chili pepper to the anchovies for a hotter dish if preferred.

SPAGHETTI CON LE SEPPIE (Spaghetti with cuttlefish)

14 oz cuttlefish
1 small onion
1 stick celery
1 clove garlic
1 piece carrot
4 tbsp olive oil
½ cup dry white wine
salt
freshly ground pepper
2 cups stock (or 1 tsp meat extract dissolved in water)
1 sprig parsley
12 oz spaghetti

Rinse and clean the cuttlefish: Pull away the head and hard central bone from inside the cuttlefish. Reserve the body sacs and tentacles and discard the rest. Cut the tentacles into pieces. Rub off the purplish outer skin and cut the body sacs into narrow strips. Finely chop the onion, celery, garlic and carrot. Heat the olive oil in a saucepan and gently fry the chopped vegetables until the onion becomes transparent and the other ingredients begin to soften. Add the pieces of cuttlefish and cook for 5 min before adding the wine. Cook, uncovered, for a further 5 min until the wine evaporates. Season with salt and freshly ground pepper, then cook over moderate heat for ¼ hr adding a ladle of hot stock from time to time (or 1 tsp meat extract dissolved in boiling water). Add the chopped parsley just before removing from the heat. Cook the spaghetti for 10–12 min in plenty of boiling salted water until *al dente*. Drain, transfer to a warm serving dish and cover with the cuttlefish sauce.

SPAGHETTINI AROMATICI (Spaghetti with mint, olives and anchovies)

12 oz spaghettini
½ cup olive oil
1 clove garlic
2–3 anchovy fillets
4 mint leaves
1–2 tbsp chopped parsley
8 black olives, pitted and chopped
1 tsp capers

Bring a large saucepan of salted water to a boil and add the spaghettini. Stir with a fork to separate. Cook for 10–12 min over high heat until *al dente*. Meanwhile, heat the oil in a small skillet. Fry the minced garlic clove and discard as soon as it begins to brown. Then add the chopped anchovy fillets and fry gently until they break up. Remove from the heat and add the chopped mint and parsley to the anchovy paste. Drain the spaghettini, transfer immediately to a warm serving dish and cover with the anchovy sauce. Add the chopped olives and the capers. Mix thoroughly and serve without grated cheese.

SPAGHETTI ALLA CAPRESE (Spaghetti with tomatoes and Mozzarella cheese)

12 oz ripe tomatoes
olive oil
salt

chopped basil and chili pepper. Cook over moderate heat until the sauce reduces but is not too thick. Taste the sauce and remove the chili pepper when the dish is sufficiently hot. Cook the spaghetti for 6 min in plenty of boiling salted water. Drain, reserving a little of the cooking water, and add the spaghetti to the sauce. Raise the heat and cook for 5 min or until the spaghetti is *al dente*, stirring continually. Add a few tablespoons of the reserved cooking water if necessary. Add the chopped parsley just before the pasta is ready. Serve piping hot without cheese.

This dish is typical of the Apulia region. Skin the tomatoes by plunging into boiling water for about 30 sec. Scoop out the seeds then break the flesh into pieces. Rinse the anchovies well to remove the salt then bone and chop them. Heat the oil and anchovies in a fairly large heavy saucepan over low heat. Mash to a smooth paste using a fork. Add the tomato pieces (if canned tomatoes are used push them through a sieve first), minced garlic, finely

2 oz anchovy fillets
3 oz tuna in oil
⅓ cup black olives, pitted
14 oz spaghetti
4 oz Mozzarella cheese
freshly ground pepper

Scald the tomatoes for 1 min in boiling water before skinning, chopping and discarding the seeds. Heat 3 tbsp oil in a skillet, add the tomatoes, salt lightly and cook over high heat for about ¼ hr. Rinse the anchovies, dry on kitchen paper and pound well in a mortar with the tuna and olives. Sieve the mixture and dilute the resulting paste with a few tablespoons of olive oil. Then heat gently over low heat. Cook the spaghetti in plenty of boiling salted water for 10–12 min until *al dente*. Drain and cover immediately with the hot tomato sauce, diced Mozzarella and warm anchovy paste. Sprinkle with black pepper, mix well and serve immediately.

SPAGHETTI ALLA VIAREGGINA
(Spaghetti with clams and chili pepper)

2 lb clams
1 clove garlic
1 cup olive oil
1 small onion
½ cup dry white wine
12 oz tomatoes
1 piece chili pepper
salt
10 oz spaghetti
2 tbsp finely chopped parsley
freshly ground pepper

Soak the clams in water to remove the sand; rinse and place in a large skillet with the garlic and a few tablespoons of oil. Cover with a tightly fitting lid and leave over moderate heat until the shells open. Remove the clams and reserve the cooking liquor. Slice the onion and fry in the oil until it begins to brown. Pour in the wine and leave to evaporate before adding the chopped tomatoes and the reserved liquor from the clams. Add the chopped chili pepper and a pinch of salt and cook over high heat for about 20 min. Meanwhile cook the spaghetti for 10–12 min in plenty of boiling salted water. Add the clams, parsley and plenty of pepper to the tomato sauce and simmer gently for 1 min. Drain the spaghetti, cover with the piping hot sauce and serve immediately.

SPAGHETTI AL FORMAGGIO
(Spaghetti with cheese)

1–2 cloves garlic
1 tbsp chopped parsley
1 tbsp chopped basil
½ cup oil
12 oz ripe tomatoes
salt
freshly ground pepper
10 oz spaghetti
3 oz Pecorino cheese

Fry the chopped garlic, parsley and basil in the oil over very low heat. Add the peeled, chopped and seeded tomatoes. Season with salt and pepper and leave to cook over high heat for about ¼ hr. Cook the spaghetti for 10–12 min in plenty of boiling salted water until *al dente*. Drain and cover immediately with the tomato sauce. Mix well and transfer to an ovenproof casserole. Cover with the grated Sardinian Pecorino cheese and place in a preheated oven at 350°F for a few minutes until the cheese has melted. Serve immediately.

SPAGHETTI CON SALSA DI POMODORO
(Spaghetti with tomato sauce)

1 lb plum tomatoes
½ cup olive oil
10 oz spaghetti
salt
¼ cup grated Parmesan cheese
freshly ground pepper
few basil leaves

Choose four of the firmest tomatoes, immerse in boiling water for 1 min then peel off the skin. It is important to scald tomatoes for as short a time as possible so that their consistency remains unchanged. Cut the tomatoes into quarters, scoop out the seeds and discard the stalks. Cut each quarter in half lengthways so that you are left with eight slices for each tomato. Set aside. Scald, peel and seed the remaining tomatoes. Cook over medium heat for about ¼ hr until smooth and reduced. Add ¼ cup olive oil and heat for a further 5 min. Meanwhile cook the spaghetti for 10–12 min in plenty of boiling salted water. Drain and cover with the tomato sauce to which the reserved tomato slices should be added at the last minute. Adjust the quantity of oil according to the thickness of the sauce; the sauce should coat the pasta without running off on to the dish. Add a little Parmesan cheese and, if desired, a little freshly ground pepper. For a more flavorsome sauce, leave a few basil leaves to soak overnight in the olive oil. Discard the leaves before use.

SPAGHETTI ALLA NORMA
(Spaghetti with eggplant and matured ricotta cheese)

3 eggplant
salt
14 oz ripe (or canned) tomatoes
olive oil
small bunch fresh basil
2 cloves garlic
freshly ground pepper
12 oz spaghetti
3 oz matured, hard ricotta cheese (or Parmesan) for grating

Thinly slice the eggplant, sprinkle with salt and drain in a plastic colander for 1 hr to draw out the bitter juices. Scald the tomatoes in boiling water for 1 min then peel off the skin. Scoop out the seeds and chop the flesh. If canned tomatoes are used push through a sieve. Heat 3 tbsp olive oil in a skillet together with the tomatoes, chopped basil and garlic, salt and freshly ground pepper. Cook the sauce over moderate heat until reduced and thickened. Heat ½ cup oil in a skillet until very hot: dry the eggplant slices and fry a few at a time until golden brown on both sides, adding more oil as necessary. Remove with a fork, drain on kitchen paper and sprinkle with salt and pepper. Cook the spaghetti for 10–12 min in plenty of boiling salted water until *al dente*. Drain and transfer to a warm serving dish. Cover with the eggplant slices and tomato sauce and sprinkle with the grated ricotta or Parmesan cheese. This tasty dish from Catania is dedicated to Vincenzo Bellini, one of the city's most celebrated sons, who composed the famous opera *Norma*.

SPAGHETTI ALLA TARANTINA *
(Spaghetti Taranto style)

10 oz clams
8 oz mussels
6 oz shrimp
6 tbsp olive oil
1 clove garlic
4 sea dates
4 oz eel
salt
freshly ground pepper
9 oz ripe or canned tomatoes
1 tbsp parsley
12 oz spaghetti

Scrub the clams and mussels thoroughly with a stiff brush. Discard any mussels that do not close when tapped sharply. Rinse and place in a skillet with ½ cup water over high heat until the shells open. Remove as the shells open and discard any that remain closed. Take out the meat, then rinse in cold water to remove all traces of sand. Reserve the cooking liquor in the skillet. Leave to stand before straining through a muslin cloth or fine sieve into a bowl. Rinse and shell the shrimp. Heat the olive oil in a skillet and gently brown the chopped garlic. Scrub and rinse the sea dates. Lower the heat and add the clams and mussels, shrimp, the sea dates in their shells and the chopped eel. Season with salt and freshly ground pepper, then add the peeled, seeded tomatoes cut into slices (sieve canned tomatoes, if used). Cook for 5 min over moderate heat, adding the reserved cooking liquor. Add the chopped parsley a few minutes before taking off the heat. Meanwhile cook the spaghetti for 10–12 min in plenty of boiling salted water until *al dente*. Drain, transfer to a warm serving dish and cover with the sauce. Serve onto individual plates, making sure each is garnished with a sea date.

SPAGHETTI ALLA SIRACUSANA
(Spaghetti with pepper and Pecorino cheese)

1 tbsp salted capers
1 salted anchovy
5 tbsp olive oil
1 clove garlic
1 lb very ripe tomatoes
1 yellow pepper
salt
freshly ground pepper
12 oz spaghetti
¼ cup grated Pecorino cheese

Rinse the capers and anchovy to remove excess salt. Bone and chop the anchovy. Heat the oil in a saucepan with the chopped garlic and peeled, seeded and coarsely chopped tomatoes. Simmer uncovered for about 10 min, then add the chopped anchovy, capers and pepper cut into thin strips. Season with salt and freshly ground pepper and cook over moderate heat until the sauce is fairly thick. Meanwhile cook the spaghetti for 10–12 min in plenty of boiling salted water until *al dente*. Drain, transfer to a warm serving dish and cover with the sauce. Sprinkle with Pecorino cheese, mix well and serve immediately.

SPAGHETTI ALLA CARRETTIERA
(Spaghetti with bacon, tuna and mushrooms)

*8 oz fresh porcini (cèpes) or ½ cup
    dried mushrooms*
4 tbsp olive oil
1 clove garlic
2 oz bacon
salt
freshly ground pepper
½ tsp meat extract
2 oz tuna in oil
12 oz spaghetti
¼ cup grated Parmesan cheese

Clean the mushrooms thoroughly by wiping with kitchen paper. If you are using dried mushrooms, soak in warm water for 1 hr. Drain and cut into pieces. Put the olive oil in a skillet with the chopped garlic and bacon cut into thin strips. Heat until the bacon fat is transparent; add the sliced mushrooms, season with a little salt and freshly ground pepper. Simmer for about 10 min, adding the meat extract dissolved in a few tablespoons of boiling water. Now add the flaked tuna and stir over low heat for 2 min until well blended. Cook the spaghetti for 10–12 min in plenty of boiling salted water until *al dente*. Drain, transfer to a warm serving dish and cover with the sauce. Mix and serve. Serve the Parmesan cheese separately.

SPAGHETTI CON LE COZZE
(Spaghetti with mussels)

1¾ lb mussels
12 oz spaghetti
4 tbsp olive oil
2 cloves garlic
2 tbsp chopped parsley
salt
freshly ground pepper
1 tsp grated lemon peel

Scrub the mussel shells thoroughly with a stiff brush, removing beards and barnacles. Discard any that do not close when tapped sharply. Rinse and place in a skillet with ½ cup water over high heat for about 5 min or until the shells open. Discard any that do not. Remove the mussels from their shells and rinse

off all traces of sand with warm water. Reserve the cooking liquor and leave to stand before straining through a fine muslin cloth. Cook the spaghetti for 10–12 min in plenty of boiling salted water. Meanwhile heat the oil in a skillet with the finely chopped garlic, 1 tbsp parsley and the reserved cooking liquor. Pour this carefully into the skillet leaving any sediment behind. Boil over high heat to reduce slightly, then add the mussels for 1 min. Just before removing from the heat, season with salt, freshly ground pepper and the grated lemon peel. Drain the spaghetti when *al dente* and transfer to a warm serving dish. Cover with the mussel sauce and sprinkle on the remaining parsley. Mix well and serve. Do not serve cheese with this dish.

SPAGHETTI ALLA MARINARA
(Spaghetti with olives and capers)

4 tbsp olive oil
20 black olives
1 tbsp capers
1 clove garlic
1 lb ripe or canned tomatoes
a few basil leaves
12 oz spaghetti
salt

This sauce is best if prepared a little in advance and is traditionally cooked in an enamel or flameproof earthenware saucepan. Put the oil in the saucepan with the pitted black olives cut into pieces, the finely chopped capers and garlic, the peeled, seeded and chopped tomatoes (sieved if you are using canned) and the basil leaves. Leave to stand for ½ hr so that the flavors mingle, then cook over moderate heat for 15–20 min or until the sauce is smooth, thick and quite dark. Meanwhile cook the spaghetti for 10–12 min in plenty of boiling salted water until *al dente*. Drain and transfer to a warm serving dish. Remove the basil leaves and pour the sauce over the spaghetti. Cheese should not be served with this dish.

For a sharper flavor a red chili

pepper can be added to the sauce ingredients. Leave whole so that it can be removed easily when the sauce is sufficiently hot for your taste.

SPAGHETTI AL POMODORO E BASILICO
(Spaghetti with tomato and basil)

1¼ lb firm ripe tomatoes
4 tbsp olive oil
1 sprig basil
salt
freshly ground pepper
12 oz spaghetti
¼ cup grated Pecorino or Parmesan cheese

Immerse the tomatoes for 1 min in boiling water then peel off the skin. Scoop out the seeds then cut the tomatoes into strips and drain. If using canned tomatoes, drain off the liquid and then sieve. Heat the oil in a skillet and when hot, add the tomatoes and basil; season with salt and pepper and cook over moderate heat for about ½ hr. Stir gently from time to time to prevent the sauce from sticking. Remove the basil when the sauce is ready. Meanwhile cook the spaghetti for 10–12 min in plenty of boiling salted water until *al dente*. Drain and cover with the sauce. Serve the Pecorino cheese separately.

SPAGHETTI ALLA CARBONARA
(Spaghetti with bacon, cream and eggs)

4 oz pancetta or bacon
1 tbsp olive oil or butter
12 oz spaghetti
salt
4 egg yolks
2 tbsp light cream
¼ cup grated Parmesan cheese
freshly ground pepper

This dish is typical of Latium. Cut the pancetta (or bacon) into strips. Heat the oil and pancetta in a fairly wide skillet and fry over moderate heat until the pancetta fat melts. Remove from the heat and keep

warm. Cook the spaghetti for 10–12 min in plenty of boiling salted water. Meanwhile beat the egg yolks in a bowl, then add the cream, half the Parmesan and a generous sprinkling of freshly ground pepper. The mixture should be neither too thick nor too liquid. Return the skillet with the pancetta to the heat and add the drained spaghetti. Stir for a few moments, remove from the heat immediately and pour over the egg mixture, stirring quickly to prevent the egg from setting. Add a little more cream at this point if necessary. Serve in individual, warm dishes with the remaining Parmesan cheese.

SPAGHETTI CACIO E PEPE ✳
(Spaghetti with cheese and pepper)

12 oz spaghetti
salt
freshly ground pepper
⅓ cup grated Pecorino cheese

This dish is typical of the mountainous region of Abruzzo. Cook the spaghetti for 10–12 min in plenty of boiling salted water. Drain when *al dente*, reserving a few tablespoons of the cooking water, and transfer to a warm serving dish. Season with plenty of coarsely ground pepper, sprinkle with grated Pecorino cheese and add a few tablespoons of cooking water. Mix and serve immediately.

BUCATINI ALL'AMATRICIANA
(Bucatini with bacon and chili pepper)

3 large firm tomatoes
1 tbsp olive oil
4 oz bacon, diced
1 tbsp finely chopped onion
½ red chili pepper
salt
12 oz bucatini
¼ cup grated Pecorino cheese

This dish comes from the Amatrice area, on the borders of Abruzzo

and Latium. Immerse the tomatoes in boiling water for 1 min to loosen the skin, scoop out the seeds and slice the flesh. Heat the oil in a skillet and brown the bacon over low heat. When the fat is transparent, remove the bacon from the pan and set aside and keep warm. Add the onion and chopped chili pepper. When the onion is golden brown, add the well drained tomatoes. Season with a little salt, stir and leave to cook for about 10 min. Remove from the heat and add the bacon to the sauce. Cook the bucatini in plenty of boiling salted water until *al dente*. Drain and transfer to a warm serving dish. Cover with the sauce and sprinkle with Pecorino cheese. Mix well and serve piping hot. An essential feature of this dish is that the pasta should not be covered in a tomato sauce but barely colored by the tomato. The bacon should be crisp as if just removed from the pan.

SPAGHETTI CON CAPPERI E OLIVE NERE
(Spaghetti with capers and black olives)

10 oz spaghetti
salt
1 tbsp pickled capers
20 large black olives, pitted
4 tbsp olive oil
1 red chili pepper
1 tbsp tomato paste

Cook the spaghetti for 10–12 min in plenty of boiling salted water. Squeeze the capers to remove excess vinegar, and chop finely. Place in a bowl with the quartered olives, the oil and the seeded, whole chili pepper. Add the tomato paste and mix with a spoon to produce a fairly smooth sauce. Drain the spaghetti when *al dente* and cover with the caper and olive sauce, stirring continually. Before serving remove the chili pepper which will have flavored the hot spaghetti. Do not serve cheese with this dish.

This sauce may be made a few days in advance and kept in the refrigerator. Leave in a bowl and pour a thin layer of olive oil over the top of the sauce.

SPAGHETTI CON POLPI E TOTANI
(Spaghetti with octopus and squid)

10 oz baby octopus
8 oz baby squid
2 cloves garlic
1 medium onion
5 tbsp olive oil
14 oz canned tomatoes
salt
12 oz spaghetti
freshly ground pepper

This dish is typical of the Tyrrhenian coast of Calabria. Rinse and clean the octopus and squid; cut the squid into rings and the octopus into pieces. Chop the garlic and onion together and put into a skillet together with the oil, octopus and squid. Brown over low heat for 5 min then add the sieved tomatoes. Season with salt to taste and cook over moderate heat for ½ hr until the sauce has reduced and thickened, adding a little hot water if necessary. Meanwhile cook the spaghetti for 10–12 min in plenty of boiling salted water until *al dente*. Drain, and transfer to a warm serving dish. Cover with the sauce and a sprinkling of freshly ground pepper. Do not serve cheese with this dish.

SPAGHETTI ALLA GIARDINIERA
(Spaghetti with mixed vegetables)

1 yellow pepper
2 small artichokes
1 lemon
4 oz mushrooms
1 onion
1 clove garlic
¼ cup butter
½ cup olive oil
1 cup shelled peas
½ cup shelled beans
salt
freshly ground pepper
1 cup dry red wine
12 oz canned tomatoes
10 oz spaghetti
grated Parmesan cheese

Place the pepper under a broiler until the skin blisters, then rub off the skin; cut open and remove the seeds. Rinse the pepper and cut into strips. Remove the hard outer leaves from the artichokes and trim any sharp tips with scissors. Cut the artichokes into four, removing the central hairy choke, and slice each quarter. Rinse in water acidulated with lemon juice. Rinse the mushrooms and dry on kitchen paper before slicing. Heat the butter and oil in a skillet and add the chopped onion and minced garlic. When the onion and garlic begin to brown, add the sliced pepper, artichokes and mushrooms, the shelled peas and beans, salt to taste, and freshly ground pepper. Stir and fry gently. Pour in the red wine, allow to evaporate then add the tomatoes. Cover and cook over medium heat for ½ hr or until all the vegetables are tender. Add a little water if the sauce becomes too dry. Cook the spaghetti for 10–12 min in plenty of boiling salted water. Remove from the heat when *al dente*; drain and transfer to a warm serving dish. Cover with the mixed vegetable sauce. Serve grated Parmesan cheese separately.

SPAGHETTI AL GORGONZOLA
(Spaghetti with Gorgonzola cheese)

12 oz spaghetti (or bucatini, etc.)
salt
2 tbsp butter
¾ cup light cream
2 oz Gorgonzola cheese
2 sage leaves
freshly ground white pepper

Cook the spaghetti for 10–12 min in plenty of boiling salted water. Meanwhile heat the butter, cream, Gorgonzola and sage leaves in a bain marie or double boiler, stirring constantly and without allowing to boil. When smooth and well blended, remove from the heat and keep warm. Drain the pasta when *al dente* and transfer to a warm serving dish. Cover immediately with the cheese sauce (remove the sage leaves) and sprinkle generously with freshly ground white pepper. Mix well so that the sauce coats the spaghetti evenly and then serve immediately on warm plates.

SPAGHETTI AGLIO E OLIO
(Spaghetti with garlic and oil)

12 oz spaghetti
salt
4 tbsp extra virgin olive oil
4 cloves garlic
1 sprig parsley
freshly ground pepper

This dish is typical of southern Italy. While the spaghetti is cooking in plenty of boiling salted water, put the oil in a skillet, mince the garlic and fry until golden brown then discard. Keep the oil warm. Chop the parsley very finely. Drain the pasta when *al dente*, season with freshly ground pepper, and cover with the garlic-flavored hot oil and chopped parsley. Mix well and serve hot.

For a stronger taste, fry 1 red chili pepper together with the garlic, removing at the same time as the garlic.

SPAGHETTI AI FRUTTI DI MARE ✳
(Spaghetti with seafood)

9 oz shrimp
salt
2 lb assorted molluscs (mussels, clams, etc.)
½ cup olive oil
1 clove garlic
2 ripe tomatoes
freshly ground pepper
12 oz spaghetti

Rinse the shrimp and remove the shells. Scrub the mussels well with a brush in several changes of cold water, removing beards and barnacles. Discard any that do not close when tapped sharply. Scrub the clams. Heat the mussels and clams in a skillet with 2 tbsp olive oil to open, shaking the skillet from time to time. After about 5 min, remove from the heat and lift out the molluscs with a spoon. Keep to one side. Never try to open any shells that remain closed; they are not fresh and should be discarded. Chop the garlic clove and fry in ½ cup olive oil, add the peeled, chopped, seeded tomatoes; season with salt and pepper and cook for about 10 min over high heat. Meanwhile cook the spaghetti in plenty of boiling salted water. Heat the molluscs and shrimp in the sauce for just a few minutes; do not overcook or they will become tough. Drain the spaghetti when *al dente* and cover immediately with the prepared sauce.

SPAGHETTI COL TARTUFO NERO
(Spaghetti with black truffle)

1 large black truffle
2 salted anchovies
4 tbsp olive oil
12 oz spaghetti
salt
1 sprig parsley

This dish is typical of Umbria. Clean the truffle (it should be scrubbed hard but never washed) and cut into wafer-thin slices. Rinse the anchovies well to remove excess salt, bone and chop. Put the anchovies into a bowl

SPAGHETTI DELL'ADRIATICO
(Spaghetti with baby octopus)

1¾ lb baby octopuses
½ cup oil
1 sprig rosemary
1 bay leaf
pinch oregano
pinch cumin seeds
1 tbsp chopped parsley
6 oz tomato slices
salt
freshly ground pepper
12 oz spaghetti

Rinse the baby octopuses, dry with kitchen paper and cut away the mouth part. Heat the oil in a skillet with the rosemary, bay leaf, oregano, cumin and parsley. Add the tomato slices and lay the octopuses on top, seasoned with salt and pepper. Cover the skillet with a tightly fitting lid and simmer for about ¾ hr. Meanwhile cook the spaghetti for 10–12 min in plenty of boiling salted water until *al dente*. Drain, transfer to a warm serving dish and cover with the sauce. Serve piping hot.

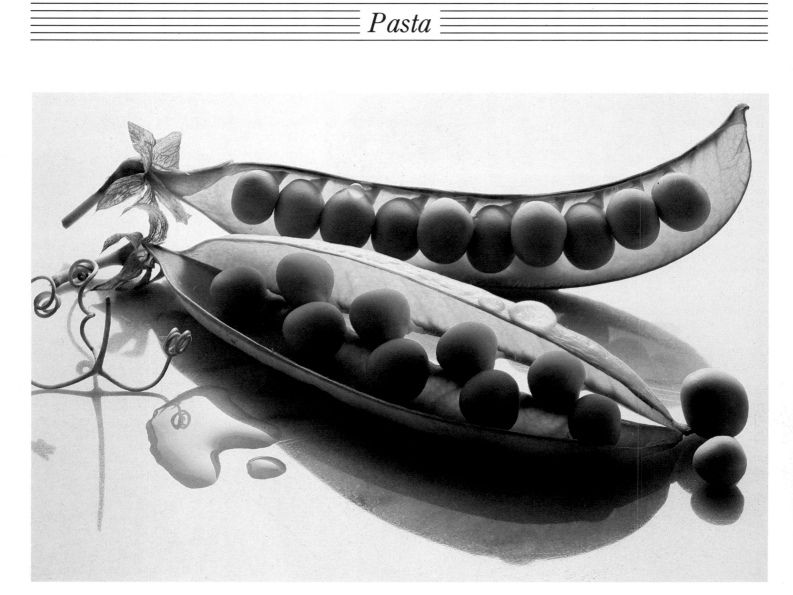

and add the oil drop by drop, stirring continually. Mash the anchovies up with a fork. Put to one side. Cook the spaghetti in plenty of boiling salted water until *al dente*, drain and transfer to a serving bowl. Add the truffle slices and the chopped parsley to the anchovy mixture and pour the sauce over the spaghetti. Serve immediately.

SPAGHETTINI AL BASILICO TRITATO
(Spaghettini with chopped basil)

14 oz fresh or canned tomatoes
12 oz spaghettini
¼ cup butter
1 tbsp chopped onion
salt
freshly ground pepper
2–3 tbsp chopped basil
¼ cup grated Parmesan cheese

This dish is typical of the Ligurian coast.

Chop the tomatoes and put into a saucepan (if you are using canned tomatoes, pour in the entire contents), boil for about ½ hr, then sieve. While the spaghettini are cooking in plenty of boiling salted water, melt half the butter in a saucepan. When it begins to bubble, add the onion and cook until soft. Then add the tomato sauce, season with salt and pepper and leave to cook over moderate heat for about 10 min.

When the spaghettini are cooked *al dente*, drain and transfer to a warmed serving dish. Cut the remaining butter into flakes, and add them to the pasta, together with the chopped basil and half the Parmesan cheese. Mix thoroughly, then pour over the tomato sauce. Mix thoroughly again and serve the remaining Parmesan cheese separately.

VERMICELLI CON PROSCIUTTO E PISELLI
(Vermicelli with ham and peas)

1 cup fresh shelled peas
¼ cup butter
2 oz cooked ham
1 small onion
freshly ground pepper
salt
meat stock
½ cup dry white wine
12 oz vermicelli
½ cup grated Parmesan cheese

Choose very fresh peas for this recipe; shell, and cook briefly in order to preserve their attractive green color. Place the butter, the diced fat from the ham and the chopped onion in a saucepan. Fry over very low heat without letting the onion brown. Then add the peas, a little pepper and a little meat stock. Turn up the heat and cook quickly, stirring continually. When almost done, add salt, the wine and the chopped ham. Allow the wine to evaporate, take the saucepan off the heat and keep warm. Cook the vermicelli in plenty of well salted boiling water. Drain when *al dente*, transfer to a serving dish and cover with peas and sliced ham. Sprinkle with Parmesan cheese and serve.

TIMPANO DI VERMICELLI GRANITO
(Vermicelli and fish timbale)

1 oz dried mushrooms
5 tbsp olive oil
8 oz white fish fillets
salt
freshly ground pepper
2 tbsp chopped parsley
10 oz vermicelli
3 salted anchovies

1 tbsp butter
4 tbsp breadcrumbs
1 small can peas
2 tbsp capers
10 pitted green olives

Soften the mushrooms in a little warm water for about 20 min. Flake the fish fillets into a bowl, add 1 tbsp oil, and season with salt and pepper. Heat a little oil in a saucepan, add the flaked fish, salt, chopped parsley together with the mushrooms and a little of their strained water. Take off the heat when the sauce is thick. Cook the vermicelli in plenty of salted water until *al dente*, then sauté in a wide saucepan with the rest of the oil and the rinsed, boned and chopped anchovies. Take off the heat and leave to cool. Grease an ovenproof pan with half the butter, sprinkle with breadcrumbs and spread at least half the vermicelli over the sides and bottom of the dish. Cover with the fish and mushroom sauce, and spread the fish, peas, capers and olives over the top. Lay the rest of the vermicelli on top and add a few flakes of butter and a handful of breadcrumbs to complete the dish. Put in a moderate oven (350°F) for about 20 min until golden brown.

VERMICELLI CON CIPOLLINE E PISELLI
(Vermicelli with onions and peas)

8 pickling onions
¼ cup butter
1 slice pancetta
1 cup shelled peas
freshly ground pepper
1 tbsp tomato paste
salt
2–3 tbsp meat stock
10 oz vermicelli
¼ cup grated Parmesan cheese
chopped parsley

Skin the onions and put into cold water. Chop and fry in a saucepan with a little butter and the pancetta cut into squares. Cover and steam briefly. Add a little water if necessary. Add the peas, pepper and tomato paste diluted in 2–3 tbsp hot meat stock. Turn up the heat and cook for a further 20 min.

Season with salt when the peas are cooked; this will help them stay more tender and green. Cook the vermicelli in plenty of salted water until *al dente*. Drain, transfer to a bowl, and cover with melted butter, cheese and part of the sauce. Mix well, arrange on a serving dish and pour over the remaining sauce. Sprinkle with chopped parsley. Serve extra Parmesan cheese separately.

VERMICELLI ALLA TURIDDU
(Vermicelli with olives and chili pepper)

5 tbsp olive oil
12 oz peeled tomatoes
10–12 pitted black olives
½ red chili pepper
salt
10 oz vermicelli
¼ cup grated Parmesan cheese
pinch of oregano

Heat the oil in a saucepan and when it is hot, add the peeled, seeded, drained tomatoes, whole pitted black olives and half a chopped chili pepper. Season with salt and cook until the sauce is thick. Cook the vermicelli until *al dente* in plenty of salted water. Drain and add a trickle of oil, the cheese and a pinch of oregano. Arrange on a serving dish and pour over the piping hot Turiddu sauce.

VERMICELLI ARROSTO CON SPINACI
(Baked vermicelli with spinach)

2 lb spinach
2 salted anchovies
1 clove garlic
1 sprig parsley
4 tbsp olive oil
1 oz finely chopped pine nuts
salt
10 oz vermicelli

Clean the spinach and cook in the water left on the leaves, adding a little salt. Rinse the anchovies well to remove excess salt and chop with the garlic clove, parsley and spinach. Heat the oil in a saucepan

and brown the chopped mixture for a few minutes. Add the pine nuts and cook for a few more minutes. Half cook the vermicelli in plenty of boiling salted water, then drain. Arrange the vermicelli in a fairly wide buttered ovenproof pan and cover evenly with the sauce. Cook in a hot oven (400°F) for about 10–15 min. Serve without Parmesan cheese.

VERMICELLI ALLE ALICI SALSE
(Vermicelli with anchovies)

4 salted anchovies
12 oz vermicelli
4 tbsp olive oil
1 clove garlic, minced
salt
freshly ground pepper

This dish is a specialty of the Gulfs of Naples and Salerno. Clean, bone and chop the anchovies. Cook the vermicelli in plenty of boiling salted water until *al dente*. Heat the oil in a wide skillet and add the minced garlic. As soon as it browns, discard. Mash the anchovies to a smooth paste and add to the garlic-flavored oil. Drain the pasta and pour it into the skillet, mixing well. Stir over moderate heat for 1–2 min so the pasta absorbs the anchovy flavor. Season to taste with salt and freshly ground pepper. Serve without cheese.

VERMICELLI ALLA SICILIANA
(Vermicelli with sardines Sicilian style)

4 ripe tomatoes
1 tbsp butter
salt
freshly ground pepper
4 fresh sardines
5 tbsp olive oil
10 oz vermicelli

Sieve the tomatoes and make a fairly thick sauce: Melt the butter in a saucepan, add the tomatoes, a little salt and a sprinkling of freshly ground pepper. Keep warm. Clean, bone and fillet the sardines. Fry half of these in 2 tbsp oil until golden brown and drain on kitchen paper. Sprinkle with a pinch of salt and set aside. Chop the remaining fish fillets and fry until soft in the rest of the oil in a wide skillet. Season with salt and pepper and mash to obtain a paste (add 1 tbsp milk if necessary to dilute). Cook the vermicelli in plenty of boiling salted water until *al dente*, drain and transfer to the skillet containing the sardine paste. Add the reserved sardine fillets, the tomato sauce and stir until the sardine fillets are heated through. Add one of the sardine fillets to each serving.

ORECCHIETTE CON LE CIME DI RAPA STRASCICATE
(Orecchiette with turnip tops)

12 oz orecchiette (see right)
14 oz turnip tops
salt
4 tbsp olive oil
¼-in piece red chili pepper
1 clove garlic

Make the orecchiette according to the instructions given on the right or buy ready-made. Rinse the turnip tops and cook for 5 min in plenty of boiling salted water. Take off the heat while still firm. Drain and reserve the cooking water. Put the oil in a skillet with the red chili pepper and the finely chopped garlic clove. Add the turnip tops and salt to taste. Cook for 1–2 min and remove the chili pepper when

the vegetables are as hot as required. Boil the orecchiette for 5 min in the reserved cooking water. Drain and pour into the skillet. Mix carefully with the turnip tops and serve piping hot. Cheese is not served with this dish.

How to make orecchiette

Mix together 1½ cups fine semolina, 1 cup all-purpose flour and sufficient warm, lightly salted water to produce a fairly firm dough, similar in consistency to bread dough, but not too soft.

Knead well for 10 min. Break the dough into two or more pieces then roll each one into sausages about 1 in in diameter and 12–16 in long.

Cut into disks about ⅛ in thick. Indent each disk by pressing in the middle with your thumb to produce the characteristic "little ear" shape.

When the orecchiette are all ready, spread out on a clean cloth and leave to dry for at least a day.

VERMICELLI ALL'OLIO E POMODORI CRUDI
(Vermicelli with oil and raw tomatoes)

3–4 basil leaves
½ cup olive oil
1 clove garlic

1¼ lb ripe tomatoes
1 sprig chopped parsley
juice of ½ lemon
salt
freshly ground pepper
14 oz vermicelli

Soak the basil leaves in the olive oil overnight. Mince 1 garlic clove and rub the inside of a bowl with it, then discard. Slice and remove the seeds from the tomatoes and put into the bowl. Add the chopped parsley, the basil-flavored olive oil, the juice of half a lemon and a little salt and pepper. Cover and leave for about ½ hr.
Bring plenty of salted water to a boil in a saucepan, cook the vermicelli until *al dente* and drain. Transfer to a serving bowl, pour on the sauce, mix well, and serve.

ORECCHIETTE AL SUGO D'AGNELLO ✱
(Orecchiette with lamb sauce)

1½ cups fine semolina
1 cup all-purpose flour
salt
2 lb boned lamb
½ cup butter
2 tbsp olive oil
1 sprig rosemary
freshly ground pepper
¼ cup grated Parmesan cheese

Mix together the semolina, flour and warm, lightly salted water to produce a fairly firm dough. Knead well for 10 min until smooth and elastic. Roll into sausages (see left) and then cut into slices about ⅛ in thick. Press in the middle of each small disk with the thumb to form the characteristic hollowed shape. Spread the orecchiette out on a clean cloth and leave to dry for at least a day. Rinse and dry the lamb. Cut into very small cubes and place in a heavy saucepan together with butter, oil and rosemary. Cover the saucepan and place over low heat. Stir the meat occasionally until evenly browned. Season with salt and freshly ground pepper and cook over moderate heat for about 20 min, adding a few tablespoons of water from time to time if necessary. Remove the rosemary when the lamb is cooked. Boil the orecchiette in plenty of salted water for 5 min until *al dente*. Drain and transfer to a warm serving dish, then cover with the lamb sauce which should be dark and thick. Mix well and serve with grated Parmesan cheese. Orecchiette, literally "little ears," are also known as "strascinati" in some parts of Italy.

MACCHERONI ALLE ERBE AROMATICHE (Macaroni with creamy veal sauce)

1–1½ lb lean veal
2 oz pork fat or bacon
1 clove garlic
1 medium onion
1 small carrot
2 sticks celery
1 sprig parsley
2–3 basil leaves
2 tbsp butter
3 tbsp olive oil
½ cup dry red wine
1 tsp meat extract
2 tbsp tomato paste
salt
freshly ground pepper
1 red chili pepper
10 oz macaroni
¼ cup grated Parmesan cheese

Wrap the pork fat or bacon around the veal and tie with kitchen string. Finely chop the garlic, onion, carrot, celery, parsley and basil. Put the butter and oil in a heavy saucepan with the veal and brown the meat on all sides over moderate heat. Pour in the wine, turn up the heat and allow to evaporate. Add the chopped vegetables and herbs and cook for 5 min, stirring occasionally. Add a ladle of hot water containing the dissolved meat extract and tomato paste; season with salt and pepper and add the halved and seeded red chili pepper. Cover and simmer over low heat for ¾–1 hr until the meat is tender and the sauce thick and creamy. Stir occasionally to prevent sticking and add a little hot water as necessary. Discard the chili pepper when the sauce is hot enough for your taste. Remove the meat, discard the string and set aside in a warm place. Cook the macaroni for 10–12 min in plenty of boiling salted water until *al dente*. Drain, transfer to a warm serving dish and cover with part of the meat sauce. Sprinkle with Parmesan cheese and serve immediately. Slice the meat, cover with the remaining sauce and serve as the main course with a green salad.

49

MACCHERONI ALLA PESARESE
(Baked filled macaroni with meat and cream sauce)

1 small onion
4 oz lean veal
½ cup butter
1⅛ cups stock

salt
freshly ground pepper
4 oz chicken livers
1 black truffle
6 oz cooked ham, chopped
1½ cups light cream
10 oz large macaroni for filling
½ cup grated Parmesan cheese

Chop the onion and the veal finely. Melt ¼ cup butter in a skillet and fry the chopped mixture over moderate heat for a couple of minutes, stirring continually; pour in the stock (or 1 tsp meat extract dissolved in water). Season with salt and pepper and cook, uncovered, for about ½ hr over low heat, stirring occasionally. Skin, rinse and then sieve the chicken livers into a bowl. Scrub and finely chop the truffle and add to the chicken livers together with the cooked ham. Mix the ingredients well with a spatula or wooden spoon; season with salt and pepper and gradually stir in about two-thirds of the cream. The filling should be smooth but not too soft. Cook the macaroni for 5 min in salted boiling water, then drain and hold in a colander under cold water. Spread out on a cloth to dry. Generously butter a wide ovenproof dish. Fill the macaroni using a decorating bag with a wide tube and arrange them in a single layer in the dish. Spoon a few tablespoons of the meat sauce over the top and sprinkle with a little grated Parmesan cheese. Repeat the operation, making a second layer of stuffed macaroni and pouring over the remaining meat sauce. Sprinkle with grated Parmesan cheese, pour over the remaining cream and dot with butter. Cook in a preheated oven at 400°F for 15–20 min or until the top is golden brown. Serve very hot.

This dish is different from the baked macaroni of Reggio Emilia which contains tomato and white sauce. The filling in this version is more evenly distributed since it is inserted by hand and the resulting flavor is perhaps more delicate, thanks to the truffle.

MACCHERONCELLI ALLA CAMPOFILONE
(Fine macaroni with veal, pork and chicken liver)

2½ cups all-purpose flour
3 eggs
½ cup butter
4 oz lean veal
6 oz pork loin
1 lb peeled tomatoes
salt
freshly ground pepper
4 oz chicken livers
grated Pecorino cheese

This dish is typical of the Marches. Mix together the flour and eggs and knead well to produce a smooth, elastic dough. Roll out into a very thin sheet, then roll up and leave to dry for ½ hr. Using a sharp knife, cut into very fine "maccheroncelli," almost like fine vermicelli. Heat the butter in a saucepan, cut the veal and pork into cubes and brown slowly all over. Sieve the peeled tomatoes, add to the saucepan and season with salt and freshly ground pepper. Cook over low heat for about 1½ hr. Add a little hot stock (or water) if necessary during cooking. Shortly before taking the saucepan off the heat, add the well rinsed, cleaned and chopped chicken livers. Cook the fine macaroni in plenty of boiling salted water (this will take little more than 1 min).

Transfer to a warm serving dish, cover with the meat sauce, and sprinkle with a little grated Pecorino cheese (use Parmesan cheese for a milder flavor).

MACCHERONI ARROSTO
(Baked macaroni)

2 cloves garlic
1 sprig rosemary
¼ cup butter
¾ cup ground beef or veal meat
1 tbsp all-purpose flour
½ cup dry white wine
4 ripe fresh or canned tomatoes
salt
freshly ground pepper
¾ cup stock (or 1 tsp meat extract dissolved in hot water)
12 oz macaroni
¼ cup grated Parmesan cheese

Chop the garlic and rosemary very finely. Heat the butter in a saucepan and add the ground meat, flour, chopped garlic and rosemary. Brown for a few minutes, stirring well over moderate heat. Turn up the heat and pour in the wine; allow to evaporate, stirring continually. Skin the tomatoes, scoop out the seeds and slice the flesh (or sieve canned tomatoes). Pour into the saucepan and season with salt and freshly ground pepper. Stir in the stock, cover and simmer gently for about ½ hr or until the sauce thickens. Cook the macaroni for 10–12 min in plenty of boiling salted water. Drain when *al dente* and arrange in layers with the meat sauce and a sprinkling of Parmesan cheese in a buttered ovenproof dish. Cover the final layer with a few pieces of butter and bake in a moderate oven (375–400°F) for about 20 min. Remove from the oven when the top is golden brown and serve immediately from the baking dish.

MACCHERONI ALLA CHITARRA *
(Macaroni made with a "guitar")

2½ cups very fine semolina
4 eggs
salt
¼ cup butter

2 oz pancetta
4 large ripe tomatoes
¼ cup grated Pecorino cheese
freshly ground pepper

This characteristic pasta dish from Abruzzo is made from very fine semolina and requires a special piece of equipment known as a "guitar" (see illustration, right). This is a rectangular frame on which are strung fine steel wires, equally spaced, about 1⁄16 in apart, over which the pasta is pressed and then cut into fine macaroni. If you do not have a "guitar," use a pasta-making machine (the sheets of pasta should be quite thick) and then cut with the attachment for making tagliatelle. Mix together the semolina, eggs and a pinch of salt. Knead well for about 20 min until the dough is very elastic and malleable (softer than a normal tagliatelle dough). The secret of this dish lies in the thorough kneading of the dough. Leave to stand for ¼ hr. Meanwhile prepare the sauce: Cut the pancetta into narrow strips and fry in the butter for a few minutes. Peel and seed the tomatoes, add to the pancetta and cook over moderate heat until the sauce thickens a little. Roll out the pasta dough into a fairly thick sheet (as thick as the gaps between the wires on the "guitar"). Cut the pasta into rectangles the same length and width as the frame and lay one sheet at a time over the "guitar." Roll the rolling pin over the top so that the pasta is cut into strips of "square" spaghetti. Cook in plenty of boiling salted water for a few minutes only until *al dente.* Drain very well and cover with the sauce. Serve with Pecorino cheese and a little freshly ground pepper.

MACCHERONI ALLA NAPOLETANA DI ARTUSI
(Macaroni with tomato sauce)

1 small onion
1 sprig basil
¼ cup butter
14 oz ripe or canned tomatoes
salt
freshly ground pepper
10 oz macaroni
¼ cup grated Parmesan or Pecorino cheese

How to prepare macaroni with a "guitar"

You will need a special piece of equipment known as a "guitar" to make this pasta. This utensil is used in Abruzzo and is so called because of its similarity to the musical instrument. It consists of a wooden frame strung with closely spaced steel wires.

Put the very fine semolina on a floured surface or in a mixing bowl; break the eggs into the middle, add a pinch of salt, mix with a fork, then knead the dough well for about 20 min. Leave the dough to stand for ¼ hr.

Roll out into a fairly thick sheet. The thickness of the sheet should be equal to the distance between the steel wires of the "guitar" so that the pasta, when cut, will be square in cross section.

Cut the sheet of pasta into rectangles the same size as the "guitar."

Place one piece of pasta at a time over the "guitar" and press down with a rolling pin so that the pasta is cut into strips of square spaghetti. Use a teaspoon to loosen the strips from the "guitar" and sprinkle lightly with flour so they do not stick together. Repeat the process until all the pasta has been used.

Finely chop the onion and basil. Melt 2 tbsp butter in a skillet, add the chopped mixture and fry over moderate heat for a few minutes. Peel, seed and chop the tomatoes (or sieve if canned). Season with salt and freshly ground pepper and simmer, uncovered, for about ½ hr or until the sauce has thickened. Cook the macaroni in plenty of boiling salted water for 10–12 min until *al dente*. Drain and transfer to a warm serving dish and add the remaining butter in flakes. Cover with the tomato sauce, sprinkle with grated Parmesan cheese (use Pecorino cheese for a stronger taste), mix well and serve piping hot.

MACCHERONI ALLA BOLOGNESE *
(Macaroni with Bolognese sauce)

4 oz lean veal
1 small onion
1 stick celery
1 piece carrot
4 oz pancetta
¼ cup butter
1 tsp all-purpose flour
1 cup stock
salt
freshly ground pepper
pinch of nutmeg (or 1 clove)
½ cup light cream
1 chicken liver
12 oz ridged macaroni (or quills)
¼ cup grated Parmesan cheese

Grind or finely dice the veal. (According to Emilian tradition, the meat should not be ground but chopped very finely on a board with a knife to avoid losing the meat juices.) Finely chop the onion, celery, carrot and pancetta. Put the mixture in a heavy saucepan with the butter and ground meat and brown slowly, stirring frequently so that the meat does not stick to the bottom. Sprinkle in the flour and add the stock (or 1 tsp meat extract dissolved in boiling water if you have no stock). Add a little salt (the pancetta is already salted), pepper and, if desired, a pinch of nutmeg or a clove. Simmer the sauce for about ½ hr over low heat, stirring from time to time. A few minutes before removing the

saucepan from the heat, add the cream and finely chopped chicken liver. Cook the macaroni in plenty of boiling salted water for 10–12 min until *al dente*. Drain and transfer to a warm serving dish. Cover with the sauce which should be smooth and creamy. Mix well and serve immediately with grated Parmesan cheese.

MACCHERONI COL RAGÙ
(Macaroni with meat sauce)

8 oz lean beef
1 clove garlic
4 tbsp olive oil
14 oz ripe fresh or canned tomatoes
1 tsp meat extract
1 sprig basil
salt
freshly ground pepper
12 oz macaroni
¼ cup grated Parmesan or Pecorino cheese

Dice the meat finely. Mince the garlic clove and fry in a saucepan with the olive oil. Remove the garlic when it begins to brown and add the pieces of meat. Brown well all over. Scald the tomatoes for about 1 min, remove the skin and seeds and squeeze lightly to remove excess water. Add the tomatoes to the saucepan. Simmer for a while. Dissolve the meat extract in a little boiling water and add to the saucepan. Add the basil, season with salt and freshly ground pepper, cover the saucepan and continue cooking for about ½ hr over moderate heat. Cook the macaroni in plenty of boiling salted water until *al dente* (about 10–12 min), drain, transfer to a serving dish and cover with the meat sauce. Serve with Parmesan or Pecorino cheese.

MACCHERONI AI QUATTRO FORMAGGI
(Macaroni with four cheeses)

2 oz Mozzarella cheese
2 oz Gruyère cheese
2 oz Fontina cheese
2 oz mild Provolone cheese
¼ cup butter
½ tsp all-purpose flour

1⅛ cups milk
10 oz macaroni
salt
freshly ground pepper
¼ cup grated Parmesan cheese

Cut the cheeses into narrow strips. Heat half the butter in a skillet and add the flour as soon as it begins to bubble. Mix for 1 min then gradually stir the milk. Simmer for about 5 min, stirring constantly, until the sauce has thickened. Remove from the heat, add the cheese strips, stir well and set aside. Cook the macaroni in plenty of boiling salted water for 10–12 min until *al dente*. Drain and transfer to a warm serving dish. Sprinkle with freshly ground pepper and the remaining melted butter. Stir well. Return the cheese sauce to a high heat and stir quickly for a few moments. Pour the cheese sauce over the macaroni, mix once more and serve immediately. Serve the Parmesan cheese separately.

The types of cheese used to prepare this dish may be varied according to taste and availability. One cheese in particular which is essential to the successful outcome, however, is Fontina.

MACCHERONI ALLA NAPOLETANA
(Macaroni with tomato and cheese sauce Neapolitan style)

1 medium onion
1 clove garlic
generous 1 lb ripe or canned
   tomatoes
¼ cup + 2 tbsp butter
salt
freshly ground pepper
12 oz macaroni
8 oz fresh Scamorza or Mozzarella
   cheese

Peel and finely chop the onion and garlic, sieve the tomatoes and heat with ¼ cup butter in a saucepan. Season with salt and freshly ground pepper, then cook the sauce until fairly thick over moderate heat. Half cook the macaroni in plenty of salted water, then drain. Arrange alternate layers of the macaroni, diced Scamorza or Mozzarella cheese and tomato sauce in an ovenproof dish. Distribute even dots of the remaining butter over the surface of the final layer (of tomato sauce). Cook in a preheated oven at 350°F for about ½ hr. Serve piping hot.

MACCHERONI ALLA CALABRESE
(Spicy macaroni Calabrian style)

1 garlic clove
1 red chili pepper
½ cup oil
1 onion
4 oz prosciutto
generous 1 lb ripe tomatoes
salt
freshly ground pepper
12 oz macaroni (or pasta tubes)
4 oz grated Caciocavallo cheese

Mince the garlic clove and chop the chili pepper and onion. Fry the garlic and chili pepper in a saucepan with the oil. Remove the garlic as soon as it starts to brown, add the onion and cook over very low heat until transparent. Chop the prosciutto and add. Heat through for 1–2 min. Skin, seed and chop the tomatoes and add to the saucepan. Season with salt and pepper and leave to cook over high heat for about ½ hr. Cook the macaroni in plenty of boiling salted water, until *al dente* (about 10–12 min), drain and cover with a little of the prepared sauce. Put a layer of macaroni on a warmed serving dish, sprinkle with plenty of grated Caciocavallo cheese and add 2 tbsp sauce. Continue to build up layers in this way until the ingredients are used up, then serve piping hot.

MACCHERONI ALLE ALICI FRESCHE
(Macaroni with fresh anchovies)

4 oz fresh anchovies
6 large ripe tomatoes
1 cup olive oil
2 cloves garlic
salt
freshly ground pepper
4 oz tuna in oil

1 tbsp chopped parsley
2 tbsp chopped fresh basil
12 oz macaroni or pasta tubes

Cut the anchovies, remove their backbones, rinse thoroughly and dry with kitchen paper. Scald 6 large, ripe tomatoes in boiling water; skin, cut into slices and remove the seeds. Heat the oil in a saucepan with the garlic cloves until the garlic begins to brown, then add the anchovies and tomatoes. Add a little water, season with salt and pepper and cook for about ½ hr. Flake the tuna and add to the sauce. Boil for a little longer and complete the preparation by adding the chopped parsley and basil. Cook the macaroni in boiling salted water for 10–12 min and drain. Put half the pasta in a large round dish and cover with half the tomato and anchovy sauce. Cover with the remaining pasta and pour over the remaining sauce. Leave to stand for a few minutes and serve immediately.

MACCHERONI ALLA PASTORA
(Macaroni with ricotta cheese and spicy sausage)

12 oz macaroni
salt
scant 1 cup ricotta cheese
freshly ground pepper
4 oz spicy sausage
oil
¼ cup grated Pecorino cheese

Bring a large saucepan of salted water to a boil. Meanwhile beat the ricotta with a little salt and pepper in a bowl. Crumble the sausage and fry in a little oil. As soon as the water boils, cook the macaroni until *al dente* (about 10–12 min) and drain, reserving some of the cooking water. Soften the ricotta with a little of the cooking water, and add the crumbled sausage, the Pecorino and a little pepper. Mix well and serve immediately.

MACCHERONI CON LA RICOTTA
(Macaroni with ricotta cheese and cinnamon)

14 oz macaroni
salt
generous 1 cup ricotta cheese
6 tbsp warm milk
2 tbsp sugar
pinch of powdered cinnamon

This macaroni dish is very popular with children. Put the macaroni in a large saucepan of boiling salted water, stir and cook for about 10 min until soft. Meanwhile, beat the ricotta, milk, sugar and cinnamon well in a bowl to form a smooth paste. Drain the macaroni and transfer to a warmed serving bowl. Add the ricotta mixture, stir well and serve immediately.

TORTIGLIONI CON FONDUTA
(Tortiglioni with melted cheese sauce)

4 oz Fontina cheese
2 cups milk
2 egg yolks
freshly ground white pepper
salt
12 oz tortiglioni
¼ cup butter
¼ cup grated Parmesan cheese
1 white truffle

Slice the Fontina thinly, place in the bottom of a deep bowl, cover with 1 cup milk and leave to infuse for a few hours. Pour the cheese into a flameproof bowl over a saucepan of gently simmering water (alternatively use a double boiler) and heat, whisking continuously, until the mixture thickens. Mix the egg yolks with 1 cup warm milk and blend well. Gradually add the egg and milk mixture to the cheese sauce. Complete the preparation with a sprinkling of white pepper. Cook the tortiglioni in plenty of boiling salted water until *al dente*. Melt the butter in a saucepan. Drain the pasta and transfer to a warm serving bowl. Cover with the melted butter and grated Parmesan and coat with the fondue sauce. Slice the white truffle on top and serve immediately.

TORTIGLIONI ALL'ITALIANA
(Tortiglioni with Mozzarella and olives)

8 black olives
1 Mozzarella cheese
4 tomatoes
2 tbsp oil
basil leaves
12 oz tortiglioni
salt
¼ cup butter
grated Parmesan cheese
1 tsp oregano
2 cloves garlic

Pit and chop the olives. Dice the Mozzarella. Skin and seed the tomatoes and cook gently in a saucepan with olive oil, 1 clove garlic and a few basil leaves. Set aside and keep warm. Cook the tortiglioni in plenty of boiling salted water until *al dente*. Melt the butter in a saucepan. Drain the pasta and transfer to a round serving bowl. Cover with the melted butter and Parmesan cheese, the diced Mozzarella and chopped olives. Flavor with oregano and the minced garlic clove and pour over the tomato mixture. Serve immediately.

PASTA E BROCCOLI
(Pasta with broccoli)

1 head of broccoli
2 salted anchovies
2 oz prosciutto
1 small onion
1 clove garlic
2 tbsp chopped parsley
3 tbsp olive oil
1 red chili pepper
½ cup dry white wine
10 oz tomatoes
salt
meat stock
10 oz pasta (e.g. quills, macaroni, etc.)
grated Parmesan cheese

Cut the broccoli into florets. Rinse, bone and chop the anchovies. Chop the prosciutto, onion and garlic. Skin the tomatoes and sieve. Heat the olive oil in a saucepan and add the chopped mixture, together with the red chili pepper, parsley and chopped anchovies. Fry gently for a few minutes then add the wine, the sieved tomatoes and a little salt. Simmer for about ¼ hr. Add the broccoli florets and cook for 5 min, pour on 1–2 ladlefuls boiling meat stock and add the pasta. Cook until *al dente* (about 10 min), adding more boiling stock if necessary. Transfer to a bowl and serve with grated Parmesan cheese.

For a simple but flavorsome variation to this dish mix in a few thin strips of prosciutto before serving.

PASTA CON LE SARDE
(Pasta with sardines)

½ cup seedless white raisins
8 oz wild fennel
salt
12 oz sardines
1 onion
2 cups olive oil
4 boned anchovies
freshly ground pepper
1 cup pine nuts
14 oz small macaroni

This dish is typical of Sicily. Soak the seedless white raisins in a little water to soften. Clean the fennel, discarding the tough outer parts, rinse and put in a saucepan with 8 cups salted cold water. Bring to a boil and cook for about 10 min, then drain, reserving the cooking water, squeeze well and chop. Gut the sardines, remove the head and the backbone. Wash in plenty of salted water and dry with kitchen paper. Fry the onion over low heat in a little olive oil in a saucepan. As soon as it begins to soften, add half the sardines and mash well with a wooden spoon to form a paste.

Rinse, drain and mash the anchovies with a little olive oil in a small skillet over low heat. Add to the onion and sardine mixture. Season with a little salt and a generous sprinkling of pepper. Drain the seedless white raisins, and squeeze out excess moisture. Add to the saucepan together with the pine nuts and the fennel. Cover and leave to cook for a few minutes. If the sauce is too thick, add a little of the fennel cooking water. Keep the sauce warm. Cook the other half of the sardines over low heat in a skillet with a little hot olive oil. Turn over with a wooden spoon, taking care not to break the fish, season with a little salt and remove from the heat after about 10 min. Add plenty of salted water to the fennel cooking water and bring to a boil. Add the macaroni, cook until *al dente* (about 10–12 min) and drain. Cover immediately with half the prepared sauce. Spread a layer of cooked pasta over the base of an ovenproof pan, cover with a few whole sardines and a few tablespoons of sauce. Continue in this way until all the ingredients are used up. Finish with macaroni covered with sauce. Cover the pan and transfer to an oven preheated to 325°F. Cook for about 20 min.

This dish is equally good served hot or cold.

How to prepare garganelli

Mix together the flour, eggs, Parmesan cheese and a pinch of salt. Knead well to produce a smooth and elastic dough.

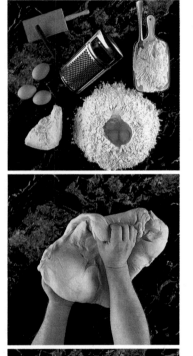

Roll out to a thin sheet.

Cut the sheet into squares with sides measuring 2½ in.

Starting at one corner of the squares, wrap the pasta pieces round a stick or tube about the same size as a little finger, running a fork over them at the same time to form a ridged pattern (in Italy a special ribbed board is used for the purpose). Remove the stick or tube to obtain large, transversely fluted quills (see illustration opposite).

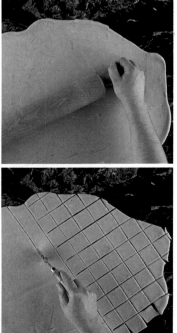

GARGANELLI ✻
(Garganelli with meat sauce)

2½ cups all-purpose flour
3 eggs
¼ cup grated Parmesan cheese
1 medium onion
1 small carrot
1 stick celery
2 oz pancetta
¼ cup butter
8 oz ground meat (beef or veal)
½ cup dry white wine
10 oz tomatoes
salt
freshly ground pepper
2 chicken livers

Mix together the flour, egg and half the Parmesan cheese. Knead to produce a smooth, elastic dough. Roll out quite thinly, then cut into squares with sides measuring about 2½ in. Starting with one corner of the square, roll the pasta pieces around a stick or tube about the size of a little finger, running a fork over them at the same time to create a ridged pattern – a special ribbed board is used in Italy (see left). Remove the stick or tube to produce the shape illustrated on p. 57. Finely chop the onion, carrot, celery and pancetta. Melt 1 tbsp butter in a saucepan and add the chopped mixture and ground meat. Fry for 4–5 min to brown the meat, then pour on the wine and leave to evaporate for 4–5 min over high heat. Skin and sieve the tomatoes, season with salt and pepper and add to the saucepan. Cook slowly, uncovered, until the sauce is smooth and thick. Clean and chop the chicken livers and add to the sauce a few minutes before taking the saucepan off the heat. Cook the garganelli in plenty of salted boiling water until *al dente*, drain and dot with the remaining butter. Cover with the sauce and the other half of the Parmesan cheese.

PASTA INCACIATA
(Pasta with eggplant and cheese)

2 eggplant
salt
olive oil
1 egg
1 clove garlic
1 sprig basil
2 oz Mozzarella
14 oz ripe or canned tomatoes
2 oz ground veal
½ cup fresh shelled peas
freshly ground pepper
2 chicken livers
10 oz macaroni
¼ cup grated Pecorino or Parmesan cheese

Dish typical of Sicily. Slice the eggplant thinly. Sprinkle with salt and leave in a colander for at least ½ hr to draw out the bitter juices. Rinse and pat dry with kitchen paper. Fry the eggplant in hot olive oil, drain on kitchen paper and keep warm. Hard-boil the egg and cut into rings. Chop the garlic and basil and slice the Mozzarella. Peel the tomatoes. Put 4 tbsp olive oil in a saucepan together with the basil, garlic, tomatoes, ground veal and shelled peas. Season with salt and freshly ground pepper. Bring to a boil, cover and simmer for about ½ hr. Clean and chop the chicken livers and add to the sauce just before it is ready. Cook the pasta in plenty of boiling salted water until *al dente* (about 10–12 min) and drain. Oil an ovenproof pan, line the bottom and sides with eggplant slices. Then pour in half the pasta and cover with half of the Mozzarella slices, the egg slices and one third of the sauce. Add the remaining pasta, cover with another one third of the sauce followed by the rest of the Mozzarella slices. Lastly, add a sprinkling of Pecorino cheese. Press

down the pasta a little to form a more compact pie, then cook in a preheated oven at 400°F for about 20 min. Take out of the oven and unmold on to a serving dish. Pour on the remaining hot sauce and sprinkle with a little Pecorino cheese. Serve immediately.

MACCHERONI AL SUGO DI PESCE
(Macaroni with fish sauce)

14 oz ripe or canned tomatoes
2 medium hake (about 8 oz each)
1 onion
4 tbsp oil
4–5 basil leaves
salt
freshly ground pepper
3 tbsp chopped parsley
12 oz macaroni

Dish typical of Sicily. Blanch the tomatoes for 1–2 min, remove the skin, cut in half and remove the seeds (if using canned tomatoes, put them through a sieve). Clean, gut, and fillet the hake. Rinse thoroughly. Slice the onion thinly, then heat in a saucepan with the oil. As soon as it is transparent, add the fish fillets. Fry for a few minutes, then add the tomatoes and basil. Season with salt and freshly ground pepper, cover and simmer over low heat until the sauce thickens, stirring from time to time to prevent the sauce sticking. Add the parsley a few minutes before removing from the heat. Cook the macaroni in plenty of boiling salted water until *al dente* (about 10–12 min) then transfer to a warm serving dish and cover with the fish sauce.

PASTA ALLA CACCIATORA
(Pasta with teal)

1 teal (about 10 oz)
1 stick celery
1 small carrot
1 sprig parsley
salt
10 oz pasta (e.g. penne, macaroni, etc.)
¼ cup butter
¼ cup grated Parmesan cheese

This highly digestible and delicately flavored dish made with teal, a small wild duck, is typical of Tuscany. Ask your butcher to pluck and draw the teal. Singe the skin, then put the bird in a flameproof casserole with the carrot, celery and parsley. Cover with cold water and add a little salt. Bring to a boil and cover. Simmer for 1–1½ hr or until done. When the teal is cooked, lift it out, reserving the cooking liquid, then cut the meat away from the carcass and chop. Keep warm. Bring the teal stock to a boil and cook the pasta in it until *al dente* (about 10–12 min). Melt the butter in a saucepan. Drain the pasta and cover with the melted butter, chopped meat and plenty of grated Parmesan cheese. Mix well and serve piping hot.

PAGLIA E FIENO
(Yellow and green ribbon noodles)

4 oz spinach
3½ cups all-purpose flour
2 eggs
salt
2 tbsp butter
1 slice cooked ham (about 2 oz)
½ cup light cream
grated Parmesan cheese

This famous dish of mixed plain and spinach noodles is known as "paglia e fieno," straw and hay.

Rinse the spinach thoroughly then cook in the water left on the leaves, adding a pinch of salt. Drain, squeeze out excess moisture and purée. Make a fairly firm dough with the flour, eggs and a pinch of salt. When the dough is well kneaded and elastic, divide it into two unequal parts, one large and one small. Put the smaller portion to one side and roll the other out not too thinly. Leave to dry for a while, then cut into ribbons about ¼ in thick. Knead the remaining pasta together with the spinach purée, adding a little flour, then proceed as for the first piece of dough. While the *paglia e fieno* are cooking in plenty of boiling salted water, dice the ham. Melt the butter in a wide skillet, and add the ham. Cook until the ham fat becomes transparent, then pour on the cream; season to taste with salt and simmer for 1–2 min. Drain the pasta when *al dente* and transfer to the skillet. Stir to finish cooking the pasta then serve with grated Parmesan cheese.

PENNE AL MASCARPONE *
(Pasta quills with cream cheese)

12 oz ridged penne (quills)
salt
2-oz slice lean cooked ham
2 tbsp butter
¼ cup grated Parmesan cheese
2 oz mascarpone (cream cheese)

While the pasta is cooking in plenty of boiling salted water, chop the ham finely, discarding any fat. When the pasta is cooked *al dente*, (about 10–12 min) add a ladleful of cold water to the saucepan to stop the cooking and prevent the pasta sticking together. Drain and transfer to a serving dish. Keep warm. Melt the butter in a saucepan, add to the pasta with the Parmesan cheese and mix. Dot the mascarpone cheese over the surface, spread evenly with the chopped ham and serve.

PASTA ALLA ZINGARA
(Pasta in spicy tomato and olive sauce)

10 oz pasta (e.g. quills, macaroni, etc.)
salt
4 ripe tomatoes
8 black olives
1 clove garlic
1 red chili pepper
3 tbsp olive oil
oregano
grated Parmesan cheese

Skin the tomatoes, remove the seeds, and chop. Pit the black olives and chop. Fry the garlic clove and chopped chili pepper in the oil, add the tomatoes, olives and oregano and salt to taste. Cook until the sauce thickens. Cook the pasta in plenty of boiling salted water for about 10–12 min. Drain and cover with the sauce. Serve with grated Parmesan cheese.

PENNE ALL'ARRABBIATA *
(Spicy pasta quills)

1 medium onion
1 clove garlic
4 oz bacon or pancetta
generous 1 lb ripe tomatoes (or 14 oz canned)
12 oz ridged penne (quills)
1 tbsp butter
1 red chili pepper
¼ cup grated Pecorino cheese

Dish originating in northern Latium. Finely chop the onion and garlic and cut the bacon into thin strips. Scald the tomatoes for 1 min in boiling water, then skin and remove the seeds. Chop or slice. (If you are using canned tomatoes, put them through a sieve.) Melt the butter in a wide skillet and cook the chopped onion, garlic and bacon over low heat until golden brown. Add the tomatoes and the red chili pepper. Simmer over moderate heat, and discard the chili pepper when the sauce is sufficiently spicy to suit your taste. Half cook the pasta and drain after about 5 min, reserving a little of the cooking water. Transfer to the saucepan, add 1–2 tbsp grated Pecorino cheese and stir gently for about 5 min until the pasta is cooked. Dilute the sauce with some of the pasta cooking water if it is too thick. Serve with the rest of the grated Pecorino cheese.

PENNE ALLA VESUVIANA
(Pasta quills with capers, olives and Mozzarella)

12 oz ridged penne (quills)
salt
4 large ripe tomatoes (or 1 lb canned)
12 black olives
1 Mozzarella cheese
1 clove garlic
basil leaves
4 tbsp olive oil
freshly ground pepper
2 tbsp capers
pinch of oregano

While the pasta is cooking in plenty of boiling salted water, sieve the tomatoes, pit and halve the olives, dice the Mozzarella and mince the garlic clove. Put the sieved tomatoes in a saucepan with the garlic and a few basil leaves, season with salt and cook the sauce over high heat until thick. Remove the garlic, take the saucepan off the heat and keep warm. Drain the pasta when *al dente* (about 10–12 min), transfer to a serving dish, cover with the olive oil and a little freshly ground pepper and mix well. Add the capers, olives and Mozzarella, pour on the tomato sauce, and sprinkle with oregano. Garnish the dish with a few basil leaves to add a contrasting note of color and serve immediately. Cheese should not be served with this dish.

INSALATA DI PENNE
(Pasta salad with tuna and olives)

12 oz penne (quills)
salt
2 hard-boiled eggs
1 large tomato
1 small can tuna
12 black olives
8 stuffed olives
½ yellow pepper
½ red pepper
4 tbsp olive oil

This dish is the perfect choice for a summer meal. While the pasta is cooking in plenty of boiling salted water, slice the eggs and tomato, flake the tuna, pit the black olives and cut the stuffed olives in half. Dice the peppers. Drain the pasta when *al dente* (about 10–12 min) add the olive oil and all the prepared ingredients except the eggs and tomato. Mix well, then decorate with the tomato and egg slices arranged alternately. Cheese should not be served with this dish.

PENNE CON I CARCIOFI
(Pasta quills with artichokes)

4 tender globe artichokes
juice of 1 lemon
4 tbsp olive oil
1 clove garlic
salt
freshly ground pepper
3 tbsp chopped parsley
2 tbsp butter
¼ cup grated Parmesan cheese

Remove the outer leaves from the artichokes and trim off the sharp points to leave only the succulent, tender hearts. Slice thinly, and place the slices in a bowl of unsalted water containing lemon juice. Transfer to a saucepan with the oil and ½ cup water, and add the finely minced garlic. Season with salt and freshly ground pepper, cover and simmer over low heat until the artichokes are well done. A few minutes before removing from the heat, add the parsley. Cook the pasta in plenty of boiling salted water until *al dente* (about 10–12 min), then transfer to a serving dish and dot with butter. Add the prepared sauce, mix well, and serve with grated Parmesan cheese.

FUSILLI ALLA NAPOLETANA ✳
(Pasta spirals with Mozzarella)

1 medium onion
1 stick celery
1 small carrot
1 clove garlic
2 oz pancetta
4 oz Mozzarella cheese
3 tbsp olive oil
½ cup dry white wine
4 ripe or canned tomatoes
1 tbsp tomato paste
salt
freshly ground pepper
12 oz fusilli (pasta spirals)
¼ cup grated Pecorino cheese
pinch of oregano

Finely chop the onion, celery, carrot and garlic. Cut the pancetta into narrow strips and dice the Mozzarella. Put the mixture in a wide skillet together with the pancetta and the oil. Fry until the vegetables and pancetta are soft, then pour on the white wine and evaporate over high heat. Skin and seed the tomatoes (if you are using canned tomatoes, put them through a sieve) and add to the skillet together with the tomato paste. Season with salt and pepper, lower the heat and cook until the sauce has thickened, stirring from time to time. Cook the fusilli in plenty of boiling salted water until *al dente* (about 10 min),

drain and transfer to the skillet. Add 1 tbsp grated Pecorino cheese and mix well. If the sauce is too thick, dilute with a few tablespoons of water. Transfer to a serving dish, cover with an even layer of Mozzarella cubes, sprinkle with oregano and serve immediately. Serve the remaining Pecorino cheese separately.

ROLLATO DI SPINACI
(Spinach roll)

1 lb spinach
1 tbsp butter
3 tbsp olive oil
½ onion
4 oz smoked ham
salt
freshly ground pepper
pinch of nutmeg
1 cup all-purpose flour
melted butter to serve
¼ cup grated Parmesan cheese

Rinse the spinach in several changes of water and cook, using only the water left on the leaves. When cooked, drain, squeeze well to remove excess moisture, and chop. Put 1 tbsp butter and 1 tbsp olive oil in a saucepan and cook the spinach with the chopped onion and part of the ham cut into cubes.

Season with salt and pepper to taste, then add a pinch of nutmeg and leave to cool. Mix the flour, 2 tbsp olive oil, a little salt and sufficient water to form a dough. On a floured surface knead well until soft and elastic. Using a floured rolling pin roll out thinly in an oblong shape. Spread the spinach mixture and the remaining ham out on the dough and roll up, tucking both ends under to seal. Wrap the roll tightly in a cloth, tie up securely at both ends and cook in salted, boiling water for about ½ hr. Remove the cloth wrapping from the roll and cut into slices. Serve with melted butter and grated Parmesan cheese.

RAVIOLI AI FILETTI DI SOGLIOLA ALLA MARCHIGIANA
(Ravioli with sole and ricotta cheese)

3 cups all-purpose flour
4 eggs
6 oz ricotta cheese
4 oz grated Parmesan cheese
nutmeg
salt
2 medium sole (approx. 8 oz each)
1 small carrot
1 stick celery
2 cloves garlic
5 tbsp olive oil
½ cup dry white wine
14 oz fresh or canned tomatoes
freshly ground pepper
1 sprig parsley

Prepare the ravioli in advance (see p. 63). To make the filling: In a bowl blend the ricotta, 1 egg, a handful of grated Parmesan, a pinch of nutmeg and salt to taste. Clean, gut, bone and fillet the fish. Chop the carrot, celery and 2 cloves garlic. Heat the oil in a skillet with the chopped vegetables and fry briefly. Peel the tomatoes (if using canned tomatoes, drain them of their juice) and put through a sieve. Add the fillets of sole to the skillet and cook on both sides. Raise the heat and pour on ½ cup white wine. When this has evaporated, lower the heat and add the sieved tomatoes. Season with salt and freshly ground pepper. Cover the skillet and simmer until the

tomatoes are cooked. Add the finely chopped parsley a few minutes before taking off the heat. Cook the ravioli in plenty of boiling salted water for 5 min, drain, serve in individual dishes and pour on the prepared sauce. Place two fillets of sole on each plate, and serve the remaining grated Parmesan separately.

RAVIOLI RIPIENI DI PESCE E SPINACI
(Ravioli filled with fish and spinach)

1 medium hake (about 10 oz)
14 oz spinach
3 tbsp olive oil
2 salted anchovies
salt
freshly ground pepper
¼ cup butter
2½ cups all-purpose flour
3 eggs

Clean the hake then gut, bone, fillet and chop. Wash the spinach and place in a saucepan. Lightly salt and cook over low heat, using only the water left on the leaves. Run under the cold faucet, squeeze out excess moisture, and chop finely. Rinse the anchovies to remove excess salt. Chop and mash with a fork until broken down. Heat the oil in a saucepan, add the anchovies and the spinach and cook for 1–2 min. Add the hake, season with salt and freshly ground pepper and stir over moderate heat for 5–6 min. Take off the heat and pass the mixture through a sieve in order to obtain a smooth paste. Use this to fill the ravioli (see p. 63).

Boil the ravioli in plenty of boiling salted water for 5 min. Drain, transfer to a serving dish, cover with melted butter and serve piping hot.

RAVIOLI RIPIENI DI RAGÚ DI PESCE
(Ravioli filled with fish sauce)

1 oz dried mushrooms
1 hake (approx. 10 oz)
3 tbsp olive oil
2 salted anchovies

1 medium onion
1 small cårrot
1 celery stalk
1 clove garlic
1 sprig parsley
2 tbsp tomato paste
salt
freshly ground pepper
3 cups all-purpose flour
3 eggs
salt
¼ cup butter
¼ cup grated Parmesan cheese

Soak the mushrooms in warm water. Rinse and clean the hake well before boning, filleting and chopping finely. Rinse, bone and chop the anchovies, and mash with a fork to break up. Finely chop the onion, carrot, celery, garlic and parsley. Drain the mushrooms, squeeze out excess moisture and chop. Heat the olive oil in a skillet and add the anchovies and chopped vegetables. Cook over moderate heat for a couple of minutes. Dissolve the tomato paste in a little warm water and transfer to the skillet. Season with salt and freshly ground pepper. Simmer until the sauce has thickened. Add the prepared hake a few minutes before removing from the heat, add salt to taste and stir well. Make the pasta dough with the flour, eggs and a pinch of salt. Follow the basic recipe on p. 63 to make the ravioli and fill with the prepared mixture. Cook the ravioli in plenty of boiling salted water for 5 min, then drain and transfer to a serving dish. Serve with melted butter and grated Parmesan cheese.

RAVIOLI CON LA ZUCCA
(Ravioli with pumpkin)

1¼ lb pumpkin
4 oz calf sweetbreads
2 oz prosciutto
¼ cup + 2 tbsp butter
4 oz lean veal
salt
freshly ground pepper
4 eggs
⅓ cup ricotta cheese
2½ cups all-purpose flour
¼ cup grated Parmesan cheese

Cook the pumpkin in salted water, drain well, remove the hard green

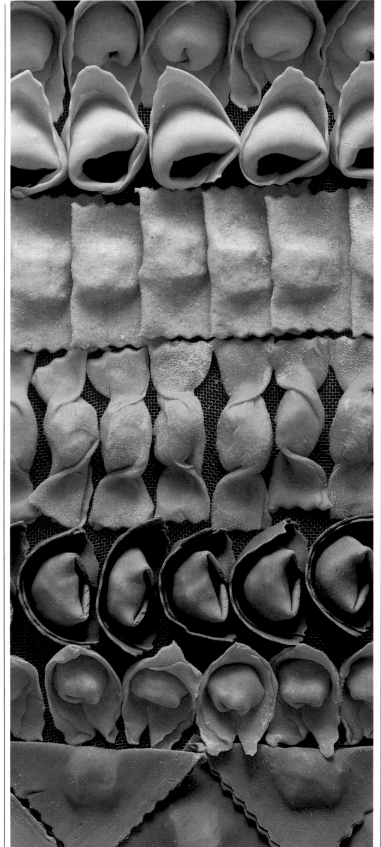

parts and chop the flesh very finely. Soak the sweetbreads in cold water for 1–2 hr to remove all the blood then drain. Put in a saucepan with fresh water and bring to a boil. Drain, fill the saucepan with fresh water and bring to a boil once again. Drain, rinse under cold water and remove the veins and membranes. Chop the sweetbreads. Heat 2 tbsp butter in a saucepan, add the veal and brown all over. Season with salt and freshly ground pepper and cook, adding a few tablespoons of water if necessary. Grind the meats. Break 1 egg into a bowl, beat well and then add the ground sweetbreads and veal together with the veal cooking juices, the mashed ricotta, prosciutto and chopped pumpkin. Season with salt to taste and blend well with a wooden spoon to form a smooth, firm paste. Mix the flour, 3 eggs and a pinch of salt, then knead well on a board until smooth and elastic. Roll out quite thinly into two sheets and then distribute evenly spaced portions of the pumpkin filling over one sheet. Brush the spaces between the portions of filling with water. Lay the other sheet of pasta over the first, pressing the pasta down between the portions of filling so the sheets stick together, then cut into small squares, using a pastry wheel, to produce the ravioli. Cook the ravioli in plenty of boiling salted water until *al dente* and drain. Cover with melted butter and serve immediately with Parmesan cheese.

RAVIOLI AI FUNGHI
(Ravioli with mushrooms)

4 oz spinach
¼ cup butter
6 eggs
salt
8 oz ricotta cheese
4 oz ham
¼ cup grated Parmesan cheese

for the sauce:
7 oz porcini (cèpes) or 1 oz dried
    mushrooms
2½ cups all-purpose flour
2 tbsp butter
1 onion
1 clove garlic

This dish is a typical Ligurian specialty. Heat the oven to 425°F and once it has reached this temperature turn it off. Wash the spinach, steam, squeeze out excess water and put through a food mill or processor. Collect the resulting paste in an ovenproof bowl and dry it in the hot oven (do not turn on). Make a dough with 4 eggs, a little salt and the spinach purée. Knead well and roll out thinly. Cut into 2½-in squares. Blend the ricotta with 2 eggs, the chopped ham, grated Parmesan cheese and salt into a paste. Place 1 tsp of this paste on to half the pasta squares. Place another square on top of each, pressing the edges together with your fingers to seal. To make the mushroom sauce, slice the mushrooms; melt the butter in a saucepan, add the onion and garlic and cook until softened. Do not brown. Add the mushrooms and cook briefly. Season to taste with salt and pepper. Cook the ravioli in plenty of boiling salted water for 5 min then drain well. Coat with melted butter and Parmesan cheese and serve with the mushroom sauce. Serve extra grated Parmesan cheese separately.

RAVIOLI ALLA GENOVESE
(Ravioli Genoese style)

(serves 6)
for the filling:
8 oz chicory
4 oz borage
2 tbsp butter
3 oz lean veal
3 oz lean pork
3 oz brains
1 sweetbread
3 eggs
soft inside of 1 bread roll
2 tbsp grated Parmesan cheese
salt
freshly ground pepper
marjoram

for the pasta:
3½ cups all-purpose flour
3 eggs
pinch salt

for the sauce:
1 cup meat sauce (see p. 129)
¼ cup grated Parmesan cheese

How to prepare filled pasta

Make a smooth, firm dough with flour, eggs, a pinch of salt and, if wished, a little oil as when making tagliatelle (see instructions on p. 30). Roll out to form two fairly thin sheets. Dot one sheet with evenly spaced amounts of filling rolled into little balls (the filling may

consist of meat, ricotta cheese or vegetables). Brush the spaces between the portions of filling with egg beaten with water, then cover with the second sheet and press lightly with the finger tips around each mound of filling. Cut the pasta into squares, each containing a portion of filling, with a pastry wheel to produce the ravioli (see above).

Another way of making the pasta is by spacing the portions of filling further apart, then cutting out rounds containing the filling with a special cutter (or upturned glass), brushing the edges with beaten egg or milk and – after folding the pasta over on itself – pressing the edges of the pasta together to obtain filled semicircles. Pinch the two corners of the semicircle together to form cappelletti, tortellini etc. (see above right).

The left-hand column shows how square ravioli are obtained using a ravioli cutter.

Soak and prepare the sweetbread as directed in the previous recipe. Soak the brains in cold salted water to remove traces of blood. Remove bone particles and fibers. Bring to a boil in fresh water and simmer for 20 min. Drain. Wash the chicory and borage and cook in a very small amount of boiling water for 5 min. Drain, squeeze out excess moisture and chop finely. Melt the butter in a saucepan, and brown the pork and veal then chop finely with the brains and sweetbread. Add the chopped greens, eggs, the soft inside of 1 bread roll soaked in the butter left in the saucepan after cooking the meat, 2 tbsp grated Parmesan, salt, pepper and a pinch of marjoram. Mix well with a wooden spoon. Mix the flour with the eggs, salt and sufficient water to produce a dough. Roll out two thin sheets.

Dot small portions of filling over one sheet, cover with the other sheet and cut into ravioli using a pastry wheel. Let the ravioli stand for 1–2 hr before cooking a few at a time in boiling water for 3–4 min. Drain and arrange in a serving dish, cover with meat sauce and serve with grated Parmesan cheese.

RAVIOLI ALL'ABRUZZESE *
(Ravioli filled with ricotta cheese Abruzzi style)

5 eggs
2 tsp sugar
pinch of cinnamon
8 oz ricotta cheese
3 cups all-purpose flour
salt
¼ cup butter
generous ½ cup ground meat
1 small onion
1 clove garlic
1 clove
salt
freshly ground pepper
4 tbsp dry white wine
4 tbsp tomato paste
¼ cup grated Parmesan or Pecorino
   cheese

Beat 1 egg, add the sugar, a pinch of cinnamon and the ricotta. Mix gently to produce a fairly soft paste that will be used to fill the ravioli. Mix the flour on a board with 3 eggs, add a pinch of salt and knead well to produce a smooth, even dough. Roll out thinly. Beat the remaining egg and brush over the sheet of pasta. Dot small amounts of filling over half the sheet. Cover with the other half of the pasta sheet and press together between the filling, then cut into small squares using a pastry cutter. Leave the ravioli to stand on the board. Peel and finely chop the onion and garlic. Melt the butter in a saucepan. When it starts to color, add the ground meat, onion, garlic and clove. Season with salt and freshly ground pepper. Fry, stirring constantly, for a few minutes. Pour in the white wine and boil over high heat until evaporated. Remove the clove. Dilute the tomato paste in a little warm water and add. Cover the saucepan and cook the sauce over low heat until thick. Cook the ravioli in plenty of boiling salted water for 5 min, drain and place on individual warmed plates. Cover with sauce and serve immediately. Serve the Parmesan separately. Use Pecorino cheese instead of Parmesan if you prefer a stronger taste.

RAVIOLI AGLI ORTAGGI *
(Ravioli with vegetables)

4 oz zucchini
1 stick celery
4 oz French beans
½ cup peas
½ cup Navy beans
4 oz pancetta
½ tsp meat extract
salt
freshly ground pepper
14 oz ravioli
¼ cup grated Parmesan cheese

Wash the vegetables. Cut the zucchini into thickish slices, dice the celery and chop the French beans. Boil the vegetables briefly to soften. Cut the pancetta into strips, place in a saucepan and melt its fat over low heat. Remove the pancetta pieces and keep warm. Add the vegetables to the fat left in the saucepan and cook for a few minutes, stirring occasionally. Dissolve the meat extract in 2–3 tbsp water and add to the saucepan. Season with a little salt and freshly

ground pepper. Add a few ladlefuls of water and boil over high heat, stirring continuously. Return the pancetta pieces to the saucepan shortly before removing from the heat. Cook the ravioli in plenty of boiling salted water for 5 min, drain and transfer to a serving dish. Cover with the contents of the saucepan and serve with Parmesan cheese.

RAVIOLI DI MAGRO ALLA PANNA
(Spinach-filled ravioli with cream)

4 oz spinach
salt
¼ cup butter
freshly ground pepper
scant 1 cup ricotta cheese
2½ cups all-purpose flour
3 eggs
¾ cup light cream
¼ cup grated Parmesan cheese

Clean the spinach well, and cook in the water left on the leaves. Drain, squeeze out excess moisture and chop. Melt 2 tbsp butter in a saucepan, add the spinach, season with salt and freshly ground pepper and cook for 3–4 min. Put the spinach and ricotta in a bowl and blend to a smooth paste with a wooden spoon. Season with salt to taste. Prepare the pasta using the flour, eggs and a pinch of salt. Fill the ravioli with the prepared paste following the basic recipe on p. 63. Boil the pasta in plenty of boiling salted water until *al dente* (about 5 min) then drain. Bring the butter and cream to a boil in a large skillet. Transfer the ravioli to the skillet and coat in the mixture. Add grated Parmesan cheese, mix again and serve accompanied by more Parmesan cheese.

RAVIOLINI ALLA MILANESE
(Small ravioli with beef and ham Milanese style)

½ cup butter
8 oz lean beef
1 sprig rosemary
salt
freshly ground pepper
1 thick slice ham

¼ cup grated Parmesan cheese
pinch of cinnamon (optional)
3 cups all-purpose flour
4 eggs

Melt ¼ cup butter in a saucepan, add the beef and rosemary and brown well on all sides over fairly high heat. Lower the heat, season with salt and freshly ground pepper, cover the saucepan and finish cooking, adding a little water from time to time. Reserve the cooking juices and keep warm.

Chop the ham and the cooked beef finely. Transfer to a bowl, add 1 egg, 1 tbsp grated Parmesan, a little of the juices left over from cooking the meat and, if desired, a pinch of cinnamon. Mix all the ingredients well and use this mixture to fill the raviolini as described in the basic recipe on p.63 using 3 cups all-purpose flour, 3 eggs and a pinch of salt to make the pasta dough.

Cook the raviolini in plenty of boiling salted water for 5 min and drain. Melt the remaining butter in the cooking juices over moderate heat. Serve the pasta with the resulting sauce poured over and a generous sprinkling of grated Parmesan.

CULINGIONES
(Sardinian ravioli with spinach and Pecorino)

8 oz spinach
¼ cup butter
salt
5 eggs
1 cup fresh Pecorino or ricotta cheese
pinch of nutmeg
freshly ground pepper
1 tbsp all-purpose flour
2½ cups all-purpose flour
14 oz fresh or canned tomatoes
¼ cup grated Pecorino cheese

Culingiones are a Sardinian type of ravioli. Clean the spinach and cook in the water left on the leaves. Drain, squeeze out excess moisture and chop finely. Melt 1 tbsp butter in a saucepan, add the chopped spinach and a pinch of salt and cook for 1–2 min. Transfer to a bowl, add 2 eggs, the fresh Pecorino, a pinch of grated nutmeg, a little freshly ground pepper, salt to taste and 1 tbsp all-purpose flour. Mix well with a wooden spoon to obtain a smooth, firm paste. Make the culingiones with the flour, 3 eggs and a pinch of salt following the basic recipe on p. 63. Make a tomato sauce by sieving the tomatoes and cooking them in the remaining butter with a pinch of salt over moderate heat until thick. Cook the pasta in plenty of boiling salted water, until *al dente*, drain, transfer to a serving dish and cover with the tomato sauce. Serve with grated Pecorino cheese.

CASONSÈI DI BERGAMO
(Ravioli Bergamo style)

8 oz spinach
¼ cup butter
½ onion
1 clove garlic
salt
freshly ground pepper
1 tbsp chopped parsley
10 oz potatoes
2 tbsp dry breadcrumbs
½ cup grated Parmesan cheese
4 eggs
4 oz spicy sausage
3 cups all-purpose flour

The filling for casonsèi, a specialty of Bergamo, should be prepared up to 24 hr in advance. Clean the spinach and cook in the water left on the leaves. Drain, squeeze out excess moisture and chop. Peel and finely chop the onion and garlic, and fry with 1 tbsp butter in a saucepan. Add the chopped spinach. Season with salt and freshly ground pepper, cook briefly, then remove from the heat and add the chopped parsley. Peel the potatoes, then boil and mash. Transfer to a bowl, add the breadcrumbs, ¼ cup grated Parmesan, the spinach mixture, 1 egg and the finely chopped sausage. Season with salt and pepper to taste, mix thoroughly so that the ingredients are well blended, then cover the bowl and leave in a cool place. Meanwhile, prepare the pasta dough in usual way, as for tagliatelle, using the all-purpose flour, 3 eggs and a pinch of salt. Knead well until the dough is soft and elastic

and roll out thinly. Using a special cutter (or the edge of an upturned glass), cut rounds from the dough. Place ½ tbsp filling in the center of each round and make the casonsèi: Fold a flap of dough over the filling and then fold over first the flap on the left, and then that on the right to obtain a tightly sealed package. Boil the casonsèi for about 5 min in plenty of salted water, drain and serve with the remaining butter, melted, and Parmesan sprinkled on top.

AGNOLOTTI ALLA PIEMONTESE
(Agnolotti with beef and spinach Piedmont style)

for the filling:
¼ cup butter
1 tbsp olive oil
1 small chopped onion
1 clove garlic
1 sprig rosemary
8 oz lean beef
1 heaping tbsp all-purpose flour
meat stock
2 ripe tomatoes
salt
generous ½ cup boiled, chopped spinach
¼ cup grated Parmesan cheese
2 eggs
freshly ground pepper

for the pasta:
3 cups all-purpose flour
3 eggs
salt

Peel and chop the onion and garlic and fry with the rosemary in a saucepan with ½ the butter and 1 tbsp olive oil. Add the meat and brown well all over, seasoning with salt and pepper. When the meat is well browned, sprinkle with 1 tbsp flour and then add about 2 ladlefuls of stock, and the peeled, strained tomatoes. Season to taste with salt, cover and leave to cook slowly for about 1–2 hr, to produce a thick sauce with which to cover the agnolotti. When the meat has cooked, grind it and make into a paste with the spinach, ½ the grated Parmesan and the eggs. Season to taste with salt and pepper and blend the mixture well. Prepare a pasta dough with the

flour, eggs and a good pinch of salt. Knead well until soft and elastic, then roll out as thinly as possible into two sheets. Dot small, well spaced amounts of the filling over one sheet. Cover with the other sheet and press together the spaces between the filling. Cut out the agnolotti with a pastry wheel. Cook in plenty of salted water, for 3–5 min, drain, then cover with the prepared sauce and the rest of the butter. Serve with grated Parmesan.

PANSOÒTI CON SALSA DI NOCI ALLA LIGURE *
(Ligurian ravioli with walnut sauce)

10 oz fresh greens and borage
salt
1 clove garlic
1 egg
4 oz ricotta
¼ cup grated Parmesan cheese
freshly ground pepper
3 cups all-purpose flour
½ cup dry white wine
⅔ cup whole shelled walnuts
1 large slice bread, crusts removed
4 tbsp olive oil
4 tbsp sour milk or buttermilk

Wash the greens, reserving the borage, then blanch in a few table-spoons of salted water. Drain, squeeze out excess moisture and put through a sieve. Chop the garlic clove and put into a bowl with the sieved greens, borage, egg, ricotta and 2 tbsp grated Parmesan. Season to taste with salt and freshly ground pepper. Mix well until all the ingredients are blended. For the pansoòti, make a fairly firm dough with the all-purpose flour, wine, a pinch of salt and water. Knead well, then roll out into quite a thick sheet. Cut into small squares. Put a small amount of filling on each piece of pasta, brush the edges with water, then fold in two to form a triangle shape and press to seal the dough. Blanch the walnuts for 1–2 min to make them easier to peel, then put into a mortar with the soaked, squeezed bread. Season with salt and pound well to produce a homogenous paste. Sieve and transfer to a bowl.

Mix with the olive oil and sour milk (or buttermilk). Cook the pansoòti in plenty of salted water. Drain and cover with the walnut sauce. Serve hot with the rest of the grated Parmesan cheese.

AGNOLOTTI TOSCANI
(Agnolotti with veal Tuscan style)

2 oz stale bread
2–3 tbsp milk
4 oz calf brains
¼ cup + 2 tbsp butter
6 oz ground veal
salt
freshly ground pepper
4 eggs
5 heaping tbsp Parmesan cheese
2½ cups all-purpose flour

Soak the bread in the milk. Soak the brains in cold salted water to remove all blood. Cut away any bone particles and fibers. Drain and bring to a boil in fresh water. Simmer for 20 min, drain and cool. Chop. Cook the ground veal slowly with 2 tbsp butter in a covered saucepan, seasoning with salt and freshly ground pepper. Add a few tablespoons of water if necessary. Squeeze out excess moisture from the bread. In a bowl put 1 egg, the squeezed bread, chopped brains, ground veal and 2 tbsp Parmesan. Season to taste with salt and freshly ground pepper. Blend all the ingredients well with a wooden spoon. Prepare the agnolotti according to the basic recipe on p. 63, using this filling. Cook the agnolotti in plenty of boiling salted water for 3 min, then drain, transfer to a serving bowl and cover with melted butter. Sprinkle on grated Parmesan cheese and serve immediately.

AGNOLOTTI ALLA MARCHIGIANA
(Agnolotti with beef and mortadella Marches style)

3 cups all-purpose flour
3 eggs
salt
½ cup butter
scant 1 cup ground meat

8 oz spinach
1 slice mortadella
freshly ground pepper
generous 1 lb fresh or canned
    tomatoes
¼ cup grated Parmesan cheese

Prepare the agnolotti according to the basic recipe on p.63, with the following filling: brown the ground meat in a saucepan with 2 tbsp butter and a pinch of salt. Transfer to a bowl. Wash the spinach and cook in the water left on the leaves for a few minutes. Drain, squeeze out excess moisture and chop finely. Transfer to a small skillet with 2 tbsp butter and a pinch of salt. Cook for a few minutes, then add to the meat. Finely chop the mortadella and add this to the meat as well. Season to taste with salt and freshly ground pepper and blend all the ingredients well to complete the filling. Put the tomatoes through a sieve. Melt the remaining butter in a saucepan, add the tomatoes and a pinch of salt and simmer gently to produce a thick sauce. Boil the agnolotti in plenty of salted water for 3 min, drain, transfer to a serving dish and cover with the tomato sauce and grated Parmesan.

RAVIOLI DI ROMAGNA
(Ravioli Romagna style)

6 oz ricotta cheese
2 eggs
¼ cup + 2 tbsp grated Parmesan
    cheese
1 ¼ cups all-purpose flour
salt
½ cup + 2 tbsp butter

These ravioli, typical of the Romagna region and known locally as "orecchioni" or "tortelloni," are not made of a pasta envelope with a filling but in the following way: put the ricotta, eggs, ¼ cup grated Parmesan cheese, almost all the flour, and salt to taste, in a bowl. Blend well with a wooden spoon, then transfer the mixture to a floured board and shape into a roll approx. 1½ in diameter. Cut this into slices about ¼ in thick, and lay out on the floured board so that they do not stick together. Cook these "ravioli" in plenty of water without salt, remove with a slotted spoon when they float to the surface and, taking care they do not break, transfer on to individual dishes and cover with melted butter and grated Parmesan cheese.

CAPPELLETTI ASCIUTTI ALL'USO DI ROMAGNA
(Cappelletti with chicken and ricotta cheese Romagna style)

2 chicken breasts
½ cup butter
⅔ cup ricotta cheese
pinch of nutmeg
4 eggs
salt
freshly ground pepper
3 cups all-purpose flour
¼ cup grated Parmesan cheese

Brown the chicken breasts in a saucepan with 2 tbsp butter. Season with salt and freshly ground pepper and cook, adding a few tablespoons of hot water from time to time. When the meat is cooked, chop very finely and blend with the ricotta, nutmeg, 1 egg and salt to taste, in a bowl.

To make the cappelletti, mix the flour, 3 eggs and a pinch of salt to form a soft, elastic dough. Roll out to a thin sheet, then cut rounds with a special cutter or with an upturned glass. Place a little filling at the center of each round and then fold in half to form a semicircle. Press the edges together and then join the two points of the semicircle, pinching together so that they stick properly (wetting slightly will help). Cook in plenty of boiling salted water until *al dente*, drain, cover with the remaining melted butter and sprinkle with grated Parmesan.

TORTELLINI ALLA PANNA CON TARTUFI
(Tortellini with cream and truffles)

4 oz lean veal
4 oz lean pork
2 oz ham
1 tbsp olive oil
1 clove garlic

1 sprig rosemary
freshly ground pepper
salt
1 cup dry white wine
6 eggs
grated Parmesan cheese
nutmeg
3 cups all-purpose flour
¼ cup butter
2 cups light cream
3 oz white truffle

This dish is a specialty of Bologna and the surrounding area. To prepare the tortellini filling, finely chop the veal and pork and brown in a pan with the oil, garlic clove, rosemary, a little freshly ground pepper and salt. When browned, add the white wine, and allow to evaporate. Cover and cook gently. Discard the rosemary and garlic and grind all the veal, pork and the ham together. Bind the mixture with 1 egg, plenty of Parmesan cheese and a pinch of nutmeg. Make a dough with the flour, 3 eggs and a pinch of salt. Roll out to a thin sheet and cut into 2-in squares. Place a portion of filling at the center of each square and fold over, drawing the points together (see illustration on p. 63). Cook the tortellini in plenty of boiling water with the salt and a piece of butter. Melt the remaining butter in a skillet and heat the cream. When cooked *al dente*, transfer the pasta to the skillet. Coat the tortellini in the cream, then take off the heat and mix in the egg yolks and Parmesan. Transfer to a warmed ovenproof dish and grate on the truffle. Cover with melted butter and grated Parmesan cheese. Put the dish briefly in a hot oven before serving.

TORTELLINI AL SUGO DI CARNE
(Tortellini with meat sauce)

1 onion
1 carrot
1 stick celery
½ cup olive oil
¼ cup butter
2 oz lean pork
2 oz lean beef
salt
freshly ground pepper
½ cup dry red wine
1 tbsp tomato paste
6¼ cups stock or water
2 oz prosciutto
2 oz mortadella
14 oz meat-filled tortellini

Chop the vegetables, then dice the pork and beef. Fry all the chopped vegetables in the oil and half the butter until browned. Add the diced pork and beef. Brown, mix and season with salt and pepper. Pour the wine into the saucepan, allow to evaporate; then add the tomato paste diluted in a little stock or water. Cover and cook over moderate heat for approx. ½ hr. Before removing the saucepan from the heat, mix the chopped prosciutto and mortadella into the sauce. Boil the prepared tortellini in the stock until *al dente*. Drain and transfer to a serving dish. Melt a piece of butter over the meat sauce, and pour this over the tortellini. Serve piping hot.

ANOLINI ALLA PARMIGIANA ("Anolini" Parma style)

1 carrot
1 stick celery
1 clove garlic
1 medium onion
½ cup butter
1 tbsp olive oil
10 oz lean beef
salt
freshly ground pepper
½ cup dry white wine
1 tbsp tomato paste
5 tbsp dry breadcrumbs
½ cup grated Parmesan cheese
4 eggs
3 cups all-purpose flour

Chop the carrot, celery, garlic and onion finely. Heat ¼ cup butter and the oil in a flameproof casserole and fry the vegetables gently. Then add the meat and brown over high heat. Pour over the wine. When this has evaporated, lower the heat, season with salt and pepper, dilute the tomato paste in a little hot water and pour over. Cover the saucepan and simmer until the meat is cooked, by which time the sauce should be fairly thick. Lift out the meat and reserve.

Put the breadcrumbs and ¼ cup grated Parmesan cheese in a bowl, then add ⅔ of the meat sauce and 1 egg, blending all the ingredients well to form a firm filling (add a pinch of grated nutmeg or cinnamon at this point if you wish to make the mixture more spicy). Prepare the pasta dough according to the basic recipe for making filled pasta on p. 63, using the flour, 3 eggs and a pinch of salt; cut out rounds and fold in two over ½ tbsp of filling. Press the edges together to seal the anolini while cooking. Cook the anolini in plenty of salted water, drain and serve with the remaining butter, the sauce and the remaining grated Parmesan. Slice the meat and use for the main course.

TIMBALLO DI LASAGNE ALLA MODENESE (Spinach lasagne Modena style)

meat sauce
3 cups all-purpose flour
2 eggs
½ cup cooked chopped spinach
salt
2 cups white sauce
grated Parmesan cheese
2 tbsp butter

Prepare the meat sauce in advance (see p. 129). To make the lasagne, heap the flour on to a board and add the eggs, cooked spinach and a pinch of salt. Knead and roll out to a fairly thick sheet. Cut out 4-in squares – use up the offcuts. Bring a saucepan of lightly salted water to a boil (add ½ tbsp oil to prevent the pasta from sticking) and cook the lasagne squares a few at a time. Remove while still very firm, drain and lay out on damp cloths to cool. In the meantime make the white sauce (see p. 127). Butter a deep baking pan and arrange a layer of lasagne in the bottom. Cover with meat sauce and plenty of Parmesan cheese. Continue to add layers of lasagna covered with

69

meat sauce and Parmesan cheese. Cover the final layer of lasagne with the white sauce, spreading the surface evenly with a palette knife. Sprinkle over Parmesan cheese and dot with butter. Cook in a moderate heated oven for ½ hr. Serve immediately.

TIMBALLO DI FETTUCCINE *
(Fettuccine mold with mushroom sauce)

1 oz dried porcini (cèpes)
1 clove garlic
3 tbsp olive oil
1 ladle meat stock
1 lb fresh egg fettuccine
3 egg yolks
8 tbsp white sauce
5 oz cooked ham
¼ cup grated Parmesan cheese

Soak the dried mushrooms in warm water. Drain, squeeze out excess moisture, and slice. Peel and mince the clove of garlic. Heat the oil in a saucepan and brown the minced garlic. Add the mushroom slices. When they have absorbed the garlic flavor, cover the saucepan and cook slowly in a little stock. Boil the fettuccine in plenty of salted water for 3–4 min. Before draining, add a ladleful of cold water so that the pasta is lighter and does not stick together. Transfer to a bowl containing the beaten egg yolks, white sauce (see p. 127) and diced ham. Coat well in this sauce. Butter a baking pan and sprinkle with grated Parmesan. Transfer the fettuccine to the baking pan. Put in a hot oven (425°F) for 10 min. Place a serving dish over the mold and turn upside down. Wait for a few minutes before unmolding then pour over the mushroom sauce and serve.

TIMBALLO DI TORTELLINI
(Tortellini mold)

1 small onion
1 sprig parsley
1 stick celery
1 small carrot
½ cup butter
½ cup ground veal
½ cup white wine
14 oz peeled tomatoes
salt
freshly ground pepper
2 oz chicken livers
2-oz slice prosciutto
1¼ cups all-purpose flour
¼ cup sugar
12 oz fresh tortellini
¼ cup grated Parmesan cheese

Chop the onion, parsley, celery and carrot. Heat 2 tbsp butter in a saucepan. As soon as the butter begins to brown, add the chopped vegetables and veal. Fry for a few minutes, then pour on the white wine and evaporate over high heat. Lower the heat and add the sieved tomatoes, season with salt and freshly ground pepper, cover the saucepan and simmer until the sauce is thick, stirring from time to time. Shortly before removing from the heat, add the chopped chicken livers and diced prosciutto. Make a smooth dough with the flour (keeping a small amount back with which to dust the base of the dish), 2 oz melted butter, the sugar and a pinch of salt. Wrap in a cloth and leave to stand for ½ hr. Then roll out two sheets; one large enough to line the base and sides of an ovenproof pan and the other to act as a lid. Cook the tortellini in plenty of boiling salted water for 4 min and remove while still very firm. Drain and put to one side. Butter an ovenproof dish, dust with flour and line with the larger piece of dough. Trim the edges. Arrange a layer of tortellini in the dish, cover with a few tablespoons of meat sauce and sprinkle on a little Parmesan cheese. Then add a second layer of tortellini and continue in this way until all the ingredients have been used up. Dot the dish with butter and lay over the second sheet of pastry, sealing the edges. Cook in a preheated oven at 350°F for approx. 20 min.

SAGNE CHINE
(Lasagne with meatballs)

for the meatballs:
8 oz fresh porcini (cèpes) (or 1 oz dried)
4 oz lean pork
2 tbsp Pecorino cheese
1 egg
salt
freshly ground pepper
oil for frying
½ chopped onion
1 chopped carrot
1 stick chopped celery
½ cup oil
2 globe artichokes
lemon
oil for frying

for the pasta:
2½ cups all purpose flour
salt
water
1 cup meat gravy
3 hard-boiled eggs
5 oz diced soft Provola or Mozzarella cheese
¼ cup grated Pecorino cheese

This is a dish typical of Calabria and Lucania. Thoroughly clean the mushrooms and slice (if you are using dried porcini, soften them first in warm water, then rinse well, and squeeze out excess moisture). Put the pork loin through the grinder twice. Brown the ground meat in the hot oil, then remove from the heat and mix with the Pecorino cheese, 1 egg, a pinch of salt and a generous sprinkling of black pepper. Form walnut-sized meatballs and fry in plenty of hot oil until golden brown. Drain on kitchen paper to remove excess oil. Fry the chopped onion, carrot and celery in oil. As soon as the vegetables are soft, add the chopped mushrooms. Season lightly with salt and cook over low heat for about 10 min. Remove the toughest leaves from the artichokes, rinse in water acidulated with lemon juice and chop. Fry in hot oil

with a pinch of salt over low heat for approx. 20 min, adding a few tablespoons of hot water (or stock). Make a fairly firm dough with the flour, a pinch of salt and water. Knead for about ½ hr until the dough is smooth and elastic and contains air bubbles. Roll out a very thin sheet, cut squares with sides measuring 3 in and cook these lasagne a few at a time in plenty of boiling salted water until they float to the surface. Drain and lay out on a cloth that has been soaked in water and well wrung out (if the pasta has been standing for a long time, it will take a few more minutes to cook). Take a high-sided ovenproof dish approx. 12 in in diameter and wet the bottom with 2 tbsp very hot meat gravy. Arrange a layer of lasagne in the bottom and cover with 1 tbsp gravy, a few meatballs, a few cooked porcini and chopped artichokes, some slices of hard-boiled egg, a few pieces of Provola or Mozzarella cheese and a good sprinkling of Pecorino cheese. Repeat this procedure until all the ingredients are used up. Finish up with a layer of pasta, a few tablespoons of gravy and a good sprinkling of grated Pecorino. Cook in a preheated oven at 325°F for approx. ½ hr. Serve piping hot from the baking pan.

PASTICCIO DI MACCHERONI ALL'USO DI ROMAGNA
(Baked macaroni Romagna style)

2 cups white sauce (see p. 127)
1 oz dried mushrooms
4 oz sweetbreads
salt
freshly ground pepper
4 oz prosciutto
12 oz macaroni
1 small black truffle
nutmeg (optional)
¼ cup butter
½ cup grated Parmesan cheese

Make the white sauce (see p. 127). Soak the dried mushrooms in warm water. Soak the sweetbreads in cold water for 1–2 hr to remove all blood. Drain and place in a saucepan filled with fresh water. Bring to a boil and drain. Rinse in cold water

then bring to a boil once again in fresh water, drain and remove the membranes. Cut the sweetbreads and the prosciutto into narrow strips. Half cook the macaroni in plenty of boiling salted water, then drain and spread out on a cloth. Heat the butter in a saucepan and as soon as it starts to brown, add the sweetbreads. Season with salt and a little freshly ground pepper, cover with half of the white sauce and cook. Now add the prosciutto, mushrooms, flaked truffle and a pinch of nutmeg (optional). Arrange a layer of macaroni in a buttered ovenproof pan, dot with a few pieces of butter and pour over a little white sauce. Repeat until the ingredients are all used up. Sprinkle plenty of grated Parmesan cheese over the final layer and dot with butter. Cook in a preheated oven at 350°F for approx. 20 min. Serve hot from the baking pan.

VINCISGRASSI
(Baked lasagne in the style of the Marches)

for the sauce:
4 oz brains
1 oz dried mushrooms
2 oz prosciutto fat or salt pork
¼ cup butter
1 small onion cut in half
1 carrot cut in half
8 oz chicken giblets and lamb offal
⅛ cup dry white wine
1 generous tbsp tomato paste
½ cup meat stock
salt
freshly ground pepper
½ cup milk
cinnamon

for the pasta:
4 cups all-purpose flour
¼ cup butter
3 eggs
salt
⅛ cup sweet white wine or Marsala

for the white sauce:
¼ cup butter
¼ cup all-purpose flour
1 cup milk
salt
nutmeg
¼ cup + 2 tbsp grated Parmesan cheese
1 truffle (optional)

71

Vincisgrassi is a stuffed lasagne dish said to have been created by the chef of the Prince of Windisch-Graetz, an Austrian general who came to the Marches during the Napoleonic wars ("vincisgrassi" is a corruption of his name).

Soak the brains in cold salted water for 1–2 hr to remove all blood. Cut away any bone particles and fibers. Drain and bring to a boil in fresh water. Simmer for 20 min, drain and cool. Chop. Soak the mushrooms in water. Chop the onion and carrot and fry with the prosciutto fat (or salt pork) in the butter. When they are well browned, remove the vegetables and add the chopped chicken giblets and lamb offal (reserve the liver and chop). Stir, pour over the dry white wine, and cook until evaporated. Now pour on the tomato paste dissolved in the hot stock, season with salt and pepper, put a tightly fitting cover on the saucepan and cook over low heat for approx. 2 hr. Half an hour before cooking is completed, add the chopped liver and brains, the mushrooms and approx. ½ cup milk. Finally, sprinkle on a little cinnamon.

Mix the flour, butter, eggs, a pinch of salt and the sweet white wine or Marsala on a board. Knead the dough well for about 20 min until smooth and elastic. Roll out into a thin sheet and cut into strips 4 in wide and as long as the baking pan. Leave to stand on the board. Prepare a fairly liquid white sauce (see p. 127). As soon as it is ready, boil plenty of salted water in a shallow, wide saucepan. Cook the pasta a few strips at a time and drain as soon as they float to the surface. Butter a baking pan well and line with a layer of pasta. Then add a few tablespoons of white sauce and a few of meat sauce. Sprinkle with a little Parmesan cheese and put a few flakes of truffle here and there (optional). Repeat this procedure until all the ingredients are used up. Finish up with a layer of pasta, topped with white sauce, grated Parmesan and a few pieces of butter.

Leave the dish to stand in a cool place for about 6 hr (or overnight) before baking. Cook in a preheated oven at 400°F for approx. ½ hr, until the top becomes slightly crisp. Pour over a little melted butter and serve piping hot.

LASAGNE ALLA FERRARESE
(Lasagne with beef Ferrara style)

1 small onion
½ carrot
1 stick celery
4 oz prosciutto
¼ cup butter
scant 1 cup ground beef
½ cup dry white wine
generous 1 lb peeled tomatoes
salt
freshly ground pepper
10 oz dried lasagne
2 cups white sauce
½ cup grated Parmesan cheese

Finely chop the onion, carrot, celery and prosciutto. Fry in 2 tbsp butter in a flameproof casserole for a few minutes. Then add the ground meat and brown. Turn up the heat, add the white wine and allow to evaporate. Add the strained peeled tomatoes and, after lowering the heat, season with salt and freshly ground pepper. Cover the casserole and cook for approx. 1 hr, adding a few tablespoons of stock or water if necessary. Cook the lasagne in plenty of salted water and remove when still very firm. Run under the cold faucet, drain and lay out on a cloth. Butter an ovenproof pan, arrange an even layer of lasagne in the bottom, spread with some of the meat sauce, cover with few tablespoons of white sauce (see p. 127) and sprinkle on a little grated Parmesan cheese. Continue to build up layers in this way until all the ingredients have been used up. Dot pieces of butter over the final layer. Cook in a preheated oven at 400°F for at least ½ hr. Serve hot.

LASAGNE VERDI ALLA RICOTTA *
(Spinach lasagne with ricotta cheese)

1 cup meat sauce
4 oz lean beef
4 oz lean pork
1 slice mortadella
1 slice cooked ham
1 stick celery
1 small carrot
1 medium-sized onion
salt
freshly ground pepper
oil
¼ cup butter
½ cup red wine
1 cup tomato sauce
generous 1 cup ricotta cheese
nutmeg
1 tbsp milk
1 lb fresh spinach lasagne
Parmesan cheese

Chop the lean beef, pork, mortadella and cooked ham together with the celery, carrot and onion. Fry all the ingredients in a saucepan with butter and oil. Season with salt and pepper and when browned, pour on ½ cup red wine. Allow the wine to evaporate and add the tomato sauce (p. 127) or the equivalent quantity of fresh tomatoes, sieved. Simmer until the meats are cooked and the sauce thick. Beat the ricotta cheese in a bowl, season with salt, pepper and nutmeg and add milk. Cook the lasagne a few at a time in plenty of boiling salted water, and as they come to the surface, remove with a slotted spoon and lay on a cloth. When all the pasta strips are cooked, arrange in layers in an ovenproof pan with the ricotta and meats. Pour melted butter over the final layer and then bake in a hot oven (425°F) for 10 min. Serve the lasagne immediately, with grated Parmesan cheese served separately.

LASAGNA IMBOTTITA
(Stuffed lasagne)

3 cups all-purpose flour
salt
generous 1 lb pork loin
1 oz dried mushrooms
¼ cup grated Pecorino cheese
3 eggs
freshly ground pepper
olive oil
4 oz Mozzarella cheese
1 stick celery
1 small onion
1 small carrot
½ cup fresh shelled peas

This is a main course dish from Calabria. Mix the flour, a pinch of salt and warm water. Roll out to a fairly thick sheet on a board and then cut into very broad strips. Cut four slices from the pork loin and keep to one side. Grind the rest of the meat. Soak the mushrooms in water, drain, squeeze out excess moisture and chop. Put 2 tbsp grated Pecorino cheese into a bowl with 1 egg, the ground meat, salt and freshly ground pepper. Blend these ingredients well with a spoon, then form walnut-sized balls and fry in boiling oil. Hard-boil 2 eggs, then shell and slice. Dice the Mozzarella cheese. Fry the pork slices in the hot oil as well. Chop the onion, celery and carrot very finely. Heat 2 tbsp olive oil with the chopped vegetables and mushrooms. Brown for a few min-

utes, then add the peas and a little water. Cover and simmer while you cook the pasta. Boil the lasagne in plenty of salted water, remove carefully when still very firm and lay out to dry on a cloth. Arrange layers of lasagne in an oiled ovenproof pan, covering each layer with a few hard-boiled egg slices, Mozzarella cubes, meatballs and, on one layer, the pork slices. Cover each layer with a few tablespoons of sauce and grated Pecorino cheese. Finish with a layer of pasta covered only with sauce and Pecorino. Bake for approx. ½ hr in a moderate oven (375°F). Serve very hot.

LASAGNA ALL'ABRUZZESE (Lasagne with veal, eggs and Mozzarella)

6 eggs
1 Mozzarella cheese
10 oz lean veal
¼ cup + 2 tbsp butter
4 tbsp dry white wine
14 oz peeled tomatoes
1 tbsp tomato paste
½ cup grated Parmesan cheese
2¾ cups all-purpose flour
salt
freshly ground pepper

Hard-boil and chop 2 eggs. Chop the Mozzarella. Grind the veal finely. Heat ¼ cup butter in a saucepan; when it begins to bubble, add the ground veal and brown for a couple of minutes. Then pour on the white wine and allow to evaporate. Skin and sieve the tomatoes and add them to the saucepan with 1 tbsp tomato paste. Bring to a boil. Put 3 tbsp grated Parmesan cheese in a bowl with 1 egg. Season with salt and freshly ground pepper. Blend all the ingredients well, then spoon the mixture into the saucepan. Thicken the sauce over low heat. Mix 3 eggs, the flour and a pinch of salt on a board. Knead to produce a smooth, elastic dough, then roll out to a thin sheet and cut into strips large enough to fit the bottom of a narrow ovenproof pan. Cut one longer, broader strip that is large enough to cover also the sides of the dish. Half-cook the pasta in plenty of boiling salted water, then

73

drain and gently transfer to a cloth. Butter the ovenproof pan well and line the dish with the largest piece of pasta. Cover with a few tablespoons of sauce, sprinkle evenly with chopped Mozzarella and hard-boiled egg, then sprinkle on the grated Parmesan. Cover with another layer of pasta, add more meat sauce and continue in this way until all the ingredients have been used up. The final layer should be pasta covered only with a little melted butter. Cook in a preheated oven at 400°F for approx. ¼ hr. Serve immediately.

LASAGNE AL SANGUE ✳
("Black" lasagne)

4 oz pig sweetbreads
salt
½ onion
2 tbsp chopped parsley
2 tbsp olive oil
2 tbsp butter
scant 1 cup fresh sausage meat
10 oz fresh lasagne
1¼ cups pig's blood
½ cup milk
¼ cup grated Parmesan cheese

This dish is typical of the Piedmont region. Soak the sweetbreads in cold water for 1–2 hr to remove all blood. Drain. Put in a saucepan, cover with fresh water and bring to a boil. Drain, fill the saucepan with fresh water and bring the sweetbreads to a boil once again. Drain, rinse under cold water and remove the veins and membranes. Chop. Peel and chop the onion. Heat the oil and butter in a saucepan, then add the onion, parsley, sausage meat and the chopped sweetbreads. Cover and cook over slow heat for approx. ½ hr. Meanwhile, cook the lasagne in plenty of boiling salted water and drain when half done. Pour the pig's blood and milk into a wide saucepan. When the mixture is hot, add the lasagne and stir gently over moderate heat until the blood is brown and creamy (do not allow to thicken). Add the contents of the saucepan and, after removing from the heat, the grated Parmesan. Mix well and serve piping hot.

LASAGNE BOLOGNESI
(Lasagne with Bolognese sauce)

for the pasta:
2 eggs
2¼ cups all-purpose flour

for the white sauce:
¼ cup butter
4 tbsp all-purpose flour
1 tsp salt
4 cups milk

for the sauce:
10 oz meat sauce
2 oz dried mushrooms soaked in warm water
1 clove garlic
1 cup milk
2 tbsp chopped parsley
2 tbsp butter
½ cup Parmesan cheese
¼ cup butter

Prepare the pasta according to the basic recipe (see p. 30), the meat sauce (using little tomato) and the white sauce (see p. 127). Simmer the latter for about 20 min. Soak the mushrooms in water. Drain, squeeze out excess moisture and slice. Peel 1 clove garlic and leave whole. Fry in a small skillet. When it has browned, discard and add the mushrooms, salt, milk and parsley. Cook slowly for approx. ¼ hr. Butter a round pan about 9 in in diameter. Arrange a layer of pasta over the base followed by a layer of white sauce and one of meat sauce, replacing the meat sauce with the mushrooms on 2 or 3 layers (this permits the flavor of the mushrooms to be appreciated). Sprinkle with grated Parmesan. Repeat until all the ingredients have been used up. Finish with a layer of pasta, a few tablespoons of meat sauce, a few pieces of butter and a sprinkling of Parmesan. Cook in a hot oven (about 350°F) for approx. 1 hr until the top is slightly crispy.

LASAGNETTE AGLI SPINACI
(Lasagne with spinach)

generous 1 lb spinach
salt
1 clove garlic
2 tbsp olive oil
2 oz butter
freshly ground pepper
½ cup grated Parmesan cheese
9 oz dried narrow lasagne strips ("lasagnette")

Rinse the spinach and blanch briefly in the minimum of water, adding a little salt to preserve the bright green color. After a few minutes, remove from the cooking water, squeeze out excess moisture and chop. Peel and mince the garlic clove. Heat the oil and butter in a saucepan with the minced garlic. When this begins to brown, discard and add the spinach, season with salt to taste and freshly ground pepper. Shortly before removing from the heat, add half the grated Parmesan and mix well.

Cook the lasagne in plenty of salted, boiling water until *al dente*. Drain and transfer to a serving dish. Cover with an even layer of spinach. Serve the remaining Parmesan cheese separately.

LASAGNETTE AL MASCARPONE
(Lasagne with cream cheese)

2½ cups all-purpose flour
3 eggs
salt
2 egg yolks
3 tbsp olive oil
4 oz fresh mascarpone (cream cheese)
freshly ground pepper
¼ cup grated Parmesan cheese

Mix the flour with the eggs and pinch of salt to obtain a smooth, firm dough. Roll out a sheet, roll up and cut pasta strips about ½ in wide. Leave to dry on the board or on a cloth. Bring a large pan of salted water to a boil and add the "lasagnette." While this is cooking, put the egg yolks in a bowl and add the olive oil drop by drop, stirring gently all the time. Then gradually add the mascarpone and season with salt and freshly ground pepper. Drain the lasagne when cooked but still firm. Transfer to a serving dish and cover with the sauce. Mix well, sprinkle generously with grated Parmesan cheese and serve.

Bought, dried lasagne may be used instead of homemade.

LASAGNE AL BASILICO
(Lasagne with basil)

3 oz Pecorino or Parmesan cheese
1 large bunch basil
10 whole, shelled walnuts
2 tbsp olive oil
10 oz dried lasagne
salt

This easy to prepare, strongly flavored dish, is typical of Tuscan cuisine. Pound the cheese well with the basil and walnuts in a mortar. Gradually add the oil. Cook the lasagne in plenty of salted water until *al dente*, drain, cover with the cold basil sauce, mix and serve immediately.

LASAGNE AL SUGO DI FUNGHI
(Lasagne with mushroom sauce)

4 large fresh tomatoes
7 oz fresh porcini (cèpes) or 1 oz dried
½ onion
1 sprig parsley
1 clove garlic
2 tbsp oil
salt
freshly ground pepper
10 oz dried lasagne
¼ cup butter
¼ cup grated Parmesan cheese

This dish is a specialty of Liguria. Blanch the tomatoes briefly and remove their skins, then seed and slice. Clean the mushrooms thoroughly (if using dried mushrooms, soak in water, drain, and squeeze out excess moisture). Slice. Finely chop the onion, parsley and the garlic clove. Heat the oil in a saucepan. As soon as this is hot, add the chopped ingredients and the sliced tomatoes (if you have no fresh tomatoes, use 2 tbsp tomato paste diluted in 1 cup boiling water or meat stock). Add the mushrooms. Season with salt and pepper to taste, cover the saucepan and cook slowly for approx. ½ hr, or until the sauce is smooth. Cook the lasagne in plenty of boiling salted water until *al dente*, drain, transfer to a serving dish and cover with pieces of butter, the sauce and grated Parmesan cheese. For a lighter dish, add olive oil instead of butter.

LASAGNE AL SUGO
(Lasagne with meat sauce)

2½ cups all-purpose flour
3 eggs
salt
1 onion
1 stick celery
1 small carrot
1 sprig parsley
¼ cup butter
12 oz lean veal or beef chopped into very small pieces
½ cup dry white wine
4 ripe fresh or canned tomatoes
freshly ground pepper
¾ cup stock (or 1 tsp meat extract)
¼ cup grated Parmesan cheese

Mix the flour (reserve 1 tbsp), eggs and a pinch of salt to form a smooth dough. Roll out into a thin sheet and cut into squares with 2½-in sides. Finely chop the onion, celery, carrot and parsley. Place in a saucepan with the butter and meat and fry gently over moderate heat for 5–6 min. Pour on the wine and turn up the heat to evaporate, stirring all the time. Plunge the tomatoes in boiling water for 2–3 min, skin, remove the seeds, chop and add to the meat. Season with salt and freshly ground pepper, cover the saucepan and simmer for approx. ¼ hr. Toast the remaining flour in a steel or aluminum saucepan, stirring continuously, until it is biscuit-colored. Wet the flour with the hot stock (or with the same amount of boiling water containing the dissolved meat extract) and then pour into the saucepan containing the meat and vegetables. Cover and cook until the resulting sauce is fairly thick. Cook the pasta in plenty of boiling salted water until *al dente* and drain. Place a layer on a serving dish, cover with part of the sauce and Parmesan cheese. Cover with a second layer and so on. Serve the lasagne hot.

LASAGNE COI FAGIOLI
(Lasagne with beans)

2½ cups all-purpose flour
salt
generous 1 lb French beans
2 cloves garlic
2 oz salt pork
freshly ground pepper
1 sprig parsley

This dish is typical of the Lucania region. Heap the flour on a board, add salt and sufficient water to make a firmish dough. Knead for at least ½ hr. Roll out to a thin sheet, then cut into broad strips. Boil the beans in plenty of lightly salted water. Drain, and keep warm. Peel and mince the garlic cloves. Chop the salt pork finely and put in a saucepan with the minced garlic. When the garlic is browned, remove from the saucepan and discard. Meanwhile, cook the pasta in plenty of boiling salted water until *al dente*. Transfer to a bowl and cover with the hot salt pork and beans. Sprinkle with plenty of freshly ground pepper and finely chopped parsley. Mix well and serve immediately without grated Parmesan.

PICCAGGE AL SUGO
(Broad lasagne with meat sauce)

2½ cups all-purpose flour
3 eggs
salt

1 oz dried mushrooms
¼ cup butter
1 onion
10 oz lean veal
4 ripe fresh or canned tomatoes
salt
freshly ground pepper
¼ cup grated Parmesan cheese

Dish typical of Liguria. Reserve 1 level tbsp flour and blend the rest with the eggs and a pinch of salt to produce a firmish dough. Knead well until smooth and elastic. Roll out to a fairly thin sheet, leave to stand for a while and cut into broad lasagne strips (called "piccagge" in Genoese dialect). Lay out on the board, taking care they do not stick to one another. Soak the mushrooms in a little warm water. Heat the butter, chopped onion and meat in a saucepan over low heat and brown the meat well all over, stirring continuously. When the veal is well browned, skin, seed and chop the tomatoes (if you are using canned tomatoes it will be sufficient to sieve them). Add the tomatoes and chopped mushrooms to the saucepan, season with salt and pepper, cover and simmer for approx. ¼ hr. Meanwhile, toast the remaining 1 tbsp flour in a small saucepan, stirring continuously, until well browned. Transfer the flour to the saucepan containing the meat, add hot stock if necessary and finish cooking the meat with the saucepan covered. Cook the piccagge in plenty of boiling salted water until *al dente*, transfer to a serving dish and cover with the sauce and a generous sprinkling of grated Parmesan cheese. If you slice the meat thinly and cover with a little of the remaining sauce, it will make an excellent main course accompanied by a green salad. Alternatively, distribute the meat among the individual dishes of pasta after adding the cheese.

PIZZOCCHERI DELLA VALTELLINA *
(Buckwheat pasta with potatoes, sage and cabbage)

scant 1 cup fine ground buckwheat
    flour
1 cup all-purpose flour
1 egg

1 cup milk
salt
3 medium potatoes
few Savoy cabbage leaves
3–4 sage leaves
4 oz Taleggio cheese
¼ cup butter
freshly ground pepper

Blend the two types of flour and mix with the egg, milk and warm water, if necessary, to form a fairly firm dough. Roll out to form a thickish sheet and then cut into strips ½ in long and ½ in wide. Peel and chop the potatoes, shred the Savoy cabbage leaves and cook in plenty of salted boiling water. When the vegetables are almost cooked, add the pizzoccheri and boil over high heat. Melt the butter in a small saucepan and add the sage leaves to flavor it. Drain all the ingredients when the pasta is cooked *al dente*. Alternate layers of the pasta and vegetables on a serving dish with thin slices of Taleggio cheese. Pour on the sage-flavored melted butter and season with freshly ground pepper.

STRASCINATI
(Ridged lasagne)

for the pasta:
3½ cups all-purpose flour
1 tbsp lard
salt
water
¼ cup + 2 tbsp grated Pecorino
    cheese

for the sauce:
1 chopped onion
1 tbsp oil
1 tbsp lard
7 oz pork or veal
½ cup red wine
12 oz ripe tomatoes
salt
freshly ground pepper
1 minced clove garlic
½ chopped chili pepper
2 tbsp olive oil

Dish typical of Lucania and Calabria. Pile the flour on a board with the lard and a pinch of salt. Work the lard into the flour using your fingertips. Add enough warm water to produce a firm dough. Knead the dough for about ½ hr until smooth and elastic. Roll out to a sheet about ¼ in thick and cut into strips about 2½ in wide and of the same length. Rest the strips on a board. Stretch out the pasta and make a ridged pattern across the surface with a fork. In Italy a special ridged board known as a *cavarola* is used for this purpose. Leave to stand for 1–2 hr. Grind the meat twice. Fry the onion over low heat with the oil and lard in a saucepan. As soon as it starts to color, add the ground meat. Brown for a couple of minutes, stirring well. Add the wine and allow to evaporate. Add the sieved tomatoes, season with salt and freshly ground pepper, cover the saucepan and leave to cook slowly for about 2 hr. Fry the garlic and chili pepper separately in oil in a small skillet. Remove the garlic as soon as it begins to brown and keep the oil warm. Cook the fresh lasagne in plenty of boiling salted water for about 5 min until *al dente*. Drain and immediately cover with some of the hot sauce. Put a little sauce on a warmed serving dish, add a little pasta, sprinkle with plenty of grated Pecorino cheese and continue to build up layers in this way. Pour on the hot oil with the chili pepper and serve immediately.

CANNELLONI ALLA NAPOLETANA
(Cannelloni with tomatoes, Mozzarella and anchovies)

1¾ cups all-purpose flour
2 eggs
salt
2 lb ripe tomatoes
½ cup oil
1 sprig basil
7 oz diced Mozzarella cheese
3 anchovies
¼ cup grated Parmesan cheese

Prepare a dough with the flour and eggs. Roll out to form a thin sheet and leave to stand on the board. Cut into squares with sides measuring approx. 2½ in. Bring a shallow, wide pan of slightly salted water to a boil. Lower the pasta squares into the water a few at a time; they will float almost immediately to the surface. Leave to cook for only a few minutes so they are still firm, drain and lay out on a damp, well wrung cloth at some distance from one another. Scald the tomatoes in boiling water to remove the skin, chop and remove the seeds. Heat the oil in a saucepan and add the tomatoes, season with salt and cook over high heat for approx. 20 min. Sieve about half the tomatoes. Flavor the sauce obtained with a sprig of basil and keep to one side. Fill each pasta square with a little Mozzarella, a few pieces of tomato, a few pieces of anchovy and a sprinkling of Parmesan cheese. Roll up the pasta pieces into tubes. Butter a wide ovenproof pan and arrange the cannelloni in a single layer. Pour on the tomato sauce and a good sprinkling of Parmesan cheese. Cook in a preheated oven at 350°F for about 20 min. Serve hot, straight from the oven.

CANNELLONI AL GRATIN *
(Cannelloni au gratin)

2½ cups all-purpose flour
4 eggs
7 oz lean veal
4 oz calf sweetbreads
1 small onion
4 tbsp olive oil
1 sprig rosemary
salt
freshly ground pepper
½ cup dry white wine
2 tbsp tomato paste
4 oz spicy sausage
¼ cup grated Parmesan cheese
1 tbsp breadcrumbs

Soak the sweetbreads for 1–2 hr to remove all blood. Drain. Put in a saucepan, cover with fresh water and bring to a boil. Drain, fill the saucepan with fresh water and bring the sweetbreads to a boil once again. Drain, rinse under cold water and remove the veins and membranes. Make a dough with the flour and 3 eggs and roll out to a fairly thick sheet. Cut into rectangles measuring about 4 × 6 in. Chop the veal and sweetbreads separately and finely chop the onion. Fry the sprig of rosemary in the oil for 2–3 min, then discard the herb. Add the onion and the pieces of veal, and brown the meat all over. Season with salt and pepper, then pour on the wine and leave to evaporate. Add the sweetbreads and immediately take the saucepan off the heat. Grind all the ingredients. Add 2 tbsp tomato paste diluted in 2 tbsp warm water to the cooking juices left in the saucepan and keep on one side. Mix the ground ingredients with the egg, sausage and half the Parmesan cheese (add a pinch of nutmeg if desired). Cook the pasta rectangles a few at a time in plenty of boiling water. Remove with a slotted spoon when half cooked and plunge into cold water. Then lay out on a damp cloth. Put a portion of filling in the center of each piece of pasta, roll up and pinch the ends to seal. Generously butter an ovenproof dish and lay the cannelloni in a single layer on the bottom. Cover evenly with the reserved sauce. Mix the remaining Parmesan cheese with 1 tbsp breadcrumbs and sprinkle over the top. Cook in an oven preheated to 350°F for 30–40 min until the top is golden brown.

STRANGULAPRIÈVETE
(Gnocchi Neapolitan style)

generous 1 lb potatoes
2¼ cups all-purpose flour
salt
14 oz canned tomatoes (or 4 large ripe tomatoes)
2 tbsp olive oil
freshly ground pepper
few basil leaves
¼ cup grated Parmesan cheese

"Strangulaprièvete" are gnocchi prepared in the Neapolitan style. Boil the potatoes, peel and mash while still very hot. Transfer to a board and gradually blend in the flour and 1 level tsp salt (add a little more flour if the mixture is too soft). Knead well to obtain a soft, elastic dough that does not stick to the hands. Form into rolls as thick as your finger and then cut into pieces. Press each piece against the board with your thumb to produce the characteristic gnocchi shape (see illustration, right). Spread out the strangulaprièvete on a lightly floured cloth and leave to stand for about ¼ hr. Make the sauce: Sieve the tomatoes and put in a saucepan with the oil. Season with salt and freshly ground pepper. Add a few basil leaves. Cook over low heat until thick. While the sauce is cooking, boil the strangulaprièvete in plenty of salted water, remove with a slotted spoon as they come to the surface and transfer to individual warmed plates. Pour over a few tablespoons of sauce and serve with Parmesan cheese.

GNOCCHI ALLA VENETA
(Gnocchi Veneto style)

1¾ lb potatoes
1¼ cups all-purpose flour
2 eggs
salt
generous 1 lb ripe or canned
   tomatoes
¼ cup butter
grated Parmesan cheese

Boil the potatoes, peel and mash. Transfer to a bowl containing the flour. Add the 2 eggs and season with a good pinch of salt. First knead in the bowl, then on a board until you have obtained a soft, elastic, smooth dough. Form the dough into rolls which you will then cut into segments about ¾ in long. Press against a grater or the back of a fork with the thumb to form the characteristic gnocchi shape. Spread out so they do not stick to one another. Sieve the tomatoes and put into a saucepan with the butter; season to taste with salt. Simmer uncovered until the sauce is thick and smooth. Cook the

gnocchi in plenty of salted water, remove from the water with a slotted spoon as soon as they are ready and transfer to individual dishes. Cover each portion with 1–2 tbsp tomato sauce. Sprinkle with grated Parmesan cheese and serve immediately.

GNOCCHI ALLA BAVA
(Gnocchi with Fontina cheese)

1¾ lb potatoes
1¾ cups all-purpose flour
salt
¼ cup butter
5 oz Fontina cheese

Boil the potatoes, peel and mash immediately (never allow the potatoes to cool before mashing if you wish to obtain a smooth result without lumps). Transfer to a board. When they have cooled slightly, add the flour and 1 tsp salt. Knead well to obtain a soft, smooth dough. Form the dough into finger-thick rolls, cut into ¾-in long segments and then form into the characteristic gnocchi shape against the back of a fork or a grater. Cook the gnocchi in plenty of boiling salted water for about 10 min, remove a few at a time with a slotted spoon, drain well and arrange in the bottom of a buttered ovenproof pan. Build up layers with the sliced Fontina cheese and cover with melted butter. Put the gnocchi in a very hot oven for about 10 min, until the dish starts to brown, then serve immediately.

GNOCCHI AL SUGO DI PAPERA
(Gnocchi with duck sauce)

1¾ lb potatoes
2 eggs
1¼ cups all-purpose flour
1 medium onion
1 sprig parsley
4 tbsp olive oil
1 duck, jointed
½ cup dry white wine
10 oz peeled tomatoes
salt
freshly ground pepper
¼ cup grated Parmesan cheese

Prepare the gnocchi dough with

How to prepare potato gnocchi

Boil the potatoes, peel and mash while still hot. (A potato ricer may be used for this purpose.) Transfer to a board together with the flour. Add a pinch of salt and knead the ingredients well to obtain a smooth, soft dough. Since eggs are not used in this recipe, you will need to compensate by adding more flour to bind the potatoes.

Divide the dough into portions and form rolls of finger thickness.

Cut the rolls into segments about 1¼ in long and press against a grater to give them their characteristic gnocchi shape (see illustration, top right). Spread out well on a cloth to dry, taking care they do not stick together.

the boiled, mashed potatoes, the eggs, a pinch of salt and the flour. Knead first in the bowl and then on a board until the dough is soft and elastic. Form into rolls, cut into segments about 1 in long and press into the characteristic shape with the thumb against a grater. Chop

the onion and parsley and put into a saucepan with the olive oil. Fry until the onion is transparent. Flour the duck portions (which should be fairly small), put into the saucepan and brown all over. Raise the heat and, over high heat, pour on the wine and allow to evaporate. Peel the tomatoes and sieve them into the saucepan. Season with salt and freshly ground pepper and turn the heat down when the sauce begins to boil. Simmer uncovered over low heat, stirring frequently so that it does not stick, for about ½ hr or until tender. Cook the gnocchi in plenty of boiling salted water, drain and serve on to individual plates. Cover each portion with 2–3 tbsp duck sauce, add a few pieces of meat cut away from the bone and serve immediately with grated Parmesan cheese. Any remaining meat can be served as a main course.

GNOCCHI ALLA VERONESE *
(Buttered gnocchi with cinnamon Verona style)

1¾ lb potatoes
1¾ cups all-purpose flour
salt
¼ cup + 2 tbsp butter
1 tsp sugar
1 tsp cinnamon
¼ cup grated Parmesan cheese

Boil the potatoes, peel and mash while still hot. Transfer to a board together with the flour. Add a pinch of salt and knead well until the dough is soft and smooth. (Since this recipe does not use eggs, more flour is necessary then usual to insure the potatoes bind properly.) Form the dough into finger-thick rolls, cut into segments ¾ in long and form into the characteristic gnocchi shape with the aid of a fork. Cook in plenty of salted water for about 3 min, remove with slotted spoon, leave to drain and transfer to individual plates. Melt the butter and when it is well browned, pour 2–3 tbsp over each portion. Add a pinch of sugar and the same amount of cinnamon. Sprinkle with plenty of Parmesan cheese and serve.

GNOCCHI DI POLENTA
(Corn meal gnocchi)

3 cups corn meal
4 cups water
salt

2 oz dried mushrooms
2 tbsp oil
½ cup butter
2 oz prosciutto fat
1 carrot
1 stick celery
2 oz pork sausage
7 oz tomato sauce (see p. 127)
freshly ground pepper
½ cup grated Parmesan cheese

Cook the polenta: Bring 4 cups salted water to a boil. Pour in the corn meal. Stir the mixture until thick, then simmer gently, stirring frequently, for about ¾ hr. Season to taste with salt. Wet a board with water and when the polenta is done, spread out evenly to ½ in thick and leave to cool.

Meanwhile, prepare the sauce. Soak the mushrooms in warm water for ½ hr. Squeeze out excess moisture, dry and chop finely. Heat the oil and butter and fry the prosciutto fat and chopped carrot and celery until soft. Add the crumbled sausage and brown for a few minutes. Dilute the tomato sauce in a little water and add. Cover and cook over low heat. Add the mushrooms after about ¼ hr, season with salt and pepper, then continue cooking for a further ¼ hr.

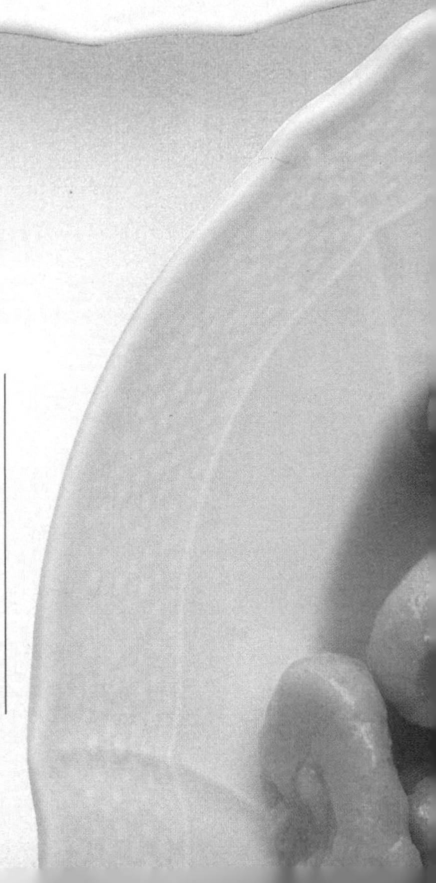

Cut the polenta into rounds and arrange a layer on the bottom of a buttered dish. Cover this layer with a few tablespoons of sauce, grated Parmesan cheese and a few pieces of butter. Continue to form layers in this way until all the ingredients are used up. Transfer the dish to an oven preheated to 400°F for about ¼ hr until the gnocchi have developed a crisp surface.

GNOCCHI DI ZUCCA MANTOVANI ✳ (Pumpkin gnocchi)

generous 1 lb pumpkin
salt
1¼ cups all-purpose flour
¼ cup + 2 tbsp butter
¼ cup + 2 tbsp grated Parmesan
    cheese

Remove the pumpkin rind and the underlying green part before cutting into large pieces and cooking in lightly salted water. When cooked, strain and transfer to a board. Add the flour a little at a time, and a pinch of salt, adding more flour if the dough is too soft; everything depends on the flouriness of the pumpkin itself. Knead all the ingredients well to obtain a fairly soft and elastic dough. Form the dough into finger-thick rolls, then cut into ¾ in segments. Form the gnocchi into their characteristic hollowed shape against the back of a fork or, better still, a grater. Boil the gnocchi in plenty of salted water a few at a time so that they do not stick together. Remove with a slotted spoon as they float to the surface. Transfer to individual plates, cover with plenty of melted butter and sprinkle with the grated Parmesan. Serve piping hot.

GNOCCHI DI CASTAGNE (Chestnut gnocchi)

3 cups chestnut flour
2½ cups all-purpose flour
½ cup whole shelled walnuts
⅓ cup pine nuts
1 cup oil
1 sprig parsley
2 cloves garlic
¾ cup grated Parmesan cheese

Mix the chestnut flour and the all-purpose flour on a board. Add sufficient water to produce a soft, smooth dough. Divide the dough into pieces as large as an orange, then form finger-thick rolls on the board. Cut these into segments about ¾ in long and press against the back of a fork or a grater to produce the characteristic gnocchi shape. Keep separated so they do not stick together. Blanch the walnuts in boiling water for 3–4 min to help remove their skins and toast the pine nuts in the oven. Put all the nuts in a mortar and pound well. Peel and finely chop the garlic cloves. Fry with the parsley and 4 tbsp oil in a saucepan. Add the nuts, stir and continue frying for a couple of minutes. Remove from the heat and then add the remaining oil mixed with a little boiling water (the water is necessary to obtain a smooth paste). Boil the gnocchi in plenty of salted water for about 7–8 min. Remove carefully with a slotted spoon, then transfer to individual plates. Cover each portion with some of the sauce and grated Parmesan cheese. Serve immediately.

GNOCCHI ALLA PIEMONTESE (Gnocchi with butter and sage)

1¾ lb potatoes
1¾ cups all-purpose flour
salt
¼ cup butter
few sage leaves
¼ cup grated Parmesan cheese

Peel the potatoes and boil in a covered saucepan with a little water so they are almost steamed. When cooked, drain and leave the potatoes on the heat for 15 sec. with the lid off so they dry out. Mash immediately and pile on to a board. Gradually incorporate the flour and 1 tsp salt and knead the dough well until it is smooth and elastic. Form into finger-thick rolls and cut into 1¼-in segments. Press into the characteristic gnocchi shape against the back of a fork or a grater. Remember that the inside should be very hollow like a shell if the gnocchi are to cook properly.

Boil the gnocchi in plenty of salted water for a few minutes over high heat. Melt the butter in a saucepan and add the sage leaves. Drain the gnocchi with a slotted spoon and transfer to individual plates. Cover with 1–2 tbsp of the sage butter. Finish up with a sprinkling of grated Parmesan cheese.

GNOCCHI ALLA ROMANA ✻ (Semolina gnocchi Roman style)

2¼ cups milk
generous 1 cup semolina
2 eggs yolks
½ cup butter
¾ cup grated Parmesan cheese

How to prepare gnocchi alla Romana

Bring the milk to a boil with a pinch of salt and gradually add the semolina, stirring continuously to prevent the formation of lumps. Leave to cook for 15–20 min.

When the semolina is thick, take off the heat and add half the butter, the egg yolks and a handful of grated Parmesan cheese. Continue to stir vigorously so that the hot semolina does not cause the egg to set.

Transfer the semolina to a wetted serving dish and smooth the surface with a wet knife blade.

When the semolina is cool and properly set, cut out small rounds using a cutter or upturned glass.

Oil an ovenproof pan and lay out the disks carefully in a single layer as shown in the photograph at the top.

Put the milk in a saucepan and bring to a boil. Slowly add the semolina, stirring continuously with a wooden spoon, taking care that the semolina does not stick to the bottom. Stop adding the semolina from time to time and stir harder. The paste should be fairly liquid at the beginning of the cooking process; leave to cook for 15–20 min and remove from the heat. In the meantime put the 2 egg yolks in a bowl and add a few tablespoons of milk to dilute. Add half the butter to the semolina after removing from the heat and while still hot. Stir well to dissolve. Then add the contents of the bowl and stir hard to prevent the egg from setting. Spread the contents of the saucepan on a wetted serving dish to form a ½-in thick layer. Leave to cool for at least 1–2 hr. Upturn the contents of the plate on to a board and cut disks using a round cutter or upturned glass. Oil an ovenproof pan and carefully set out the gnocchi in a single layer. Melt the butter and pour it over the gnocchi. Place in an oven preheated to 350°F and remove when the gnocchi begin to brown. Sprinkle with grated Parmesan cheese. Serve.

GNOCCHI ALLA PASTISSADA (Gnocchi with meat)

1¾ lb potatoes
1¼ cups all-purpose flour
salt
14 oz lean beef
¼ cup butter
1 tbsp olive oil
1 cup red wine
1 onion
generous 1 lb ripe tomatoes or 14 oz canned tomatoes
grated Parmesan cheese
freshly ground pepper
pinch of cinnamon

Dish typical of the Veneto region. Boil the potatoes, peel and mash while still hot (to avoid leaving lumps.) Transfer to a board together with the flour. Add a pinch of salt and knead well to obtain a soft, smooth dough. Use the minimum flour so that the potato binds properly. Form the dough into finger-thickness rolls, cut into

segments ¾ in long and press into the characteristic gnocchi shape against the back of a fork or a grater. Spread out on a cloth so they do not stick together. Now prepare the meat sauce ("pastissada"). Chop the meat very finely. Heat the butter and oil in a saucepan and brown the meat over high heat for a few minutes. Add the wine and allow to evaporate. Thinly slice the onion. Skin the tomatoes, remove the seeds and add to the saucepan together with the onion. Cover and leave to cook for 2–3 hr, or until the meat is tender enough to cut with a fork. Cook the gnocchi in boiling salted water and remove with a slotted spoon as soon as they come to the surface. Arrange on the individual plates, then cover with the meat sauce. Add grated Parmesan, freshly ground pepper and a pinch of cinnamon to taste.

MALLOREDDUS (Gnocchi with saffron Sardinian style)

2½ cups all-purpose flour
salt
pinch saffron
1 onion
1 clove garlic
3–4 basil leaves
4 tbsp olive oil
generous 1 lb ripe or canned tomatoes
salt
freshly ground pepper
1 tsp meat extract
¼ cup grated Pecorino cheese

"Malloreddus," traditional small gnocchi from Sardinia, should be prepared the day before you intend to serve them. Prepare the pasta dough as usual on a board with the flour, a pinch of salt and a little warm water in which the saffron has been dissolved. Knead well to obtain a fairly firm, smooth dough. Form rolls about the diameter of a pencil and then cut into segments no more than ½ in long. Flour each piece well to prevent sticking and form into a curled gnocchi shape by pressing with a thumb against the back of a grater or fork. Spread out on a cloth to dry and leave until the next day. Peel and chop the onion and garlic clove and roughly chop the few basil leaves. Heat the oil in a saucepan and cook the chopped ingredients for a few minutes. (The dish may be enriched by adding sausage meat or ground meat to the sauce at this point.) Sieve the tomatoes into the saucepan, and season with salt and freshly ground pepper, then add the meat extract dissolved in 1 tbsp hot water. Simmer uncovered over low heat until the sauce is thick. Boil the malloreddus in plenty of boiling salted water, and remove with a slotted spoon as they float to the surface. Transfer to individual plates and pour on a few table-spoons of the prepared sauce. Serve the grated Pecorino cheese separately.

TROFIE AL PESTO ✳
(Pasta twists with pesto sauce)

3 cups all-purpose flour
salt
4 tbsp olive oil
3 bunches basil leaves
1 clove garlic
1 tbsp toasted pine nuts
2 tbsp grated Pecorino cheese
2 tbsp grated Parmesan cheese
freshly ground pepper
pesto (see p.130)

Mix the flour, a pinch of salt and sufficient water to make a firm dough. Knead well, then detach small pieces (about the size of a cherry) and roll these out on a board to form short sticks with pointed ends. Coil each stick round a large knitting needle, then remove the needle to leave a pasta twist. Cook these "trofie" for a few minutes (if fresh) in plenty of boiling salted water. Drain and cover with pesto sauce.

MALFATTI
(Spinach and ricotta gnocchi)

generous 1 lb spinach
salt
½ cup butter
½ onion
4 oz ricotta
¼ cup + 2 tbsp grated Parmesan
  cheese

83

nutmeg
freshly ground pepper
2 eggs and 1 yolk

This recipe for gnocchi is from the Lombardy region. Rinse the spinach and cook in the water left on the leaves, adding salt. Coarsely chop the onion and fry in 2 tbsp butter. As soon as it begins to brown, add the chopped spinach. Cook for a few minutes, then take the saucepan off the heat and leave to cool. Beat the ricotta with a wooden spoon, and blend with half the Parmesan cheese, a pinch of nutmeg, salt and pepper to taste, the 2 whole eggs and the yolk, and lastly, the flour (reserving 1 tbsp). Mix the ingredients well. Form small gnocchi of about the size of a walnut and boil for a few minutes in plenty of salted water. Melt the remaining butter in a saucepan. When the gnocchi float to the surface, drain and transfer to a bowl. Pour on the melted butter, sprinkle with Parmesan cheese and cook in a hot oven (400°F) for 5 min. Serve immediately.

How to prepare canèderli

Beat the eggs with a little milk and a pinch of salt. Cut the bread into small cubes and put to soak in a bowl with the egg and milk mixture. Leave to stand for about 20 min, stirring from time to time so that the liquid is all absorbed.

Brown the finely diced pancetta or Speck and salami for a few minutes together with the chopped onion and parsley. Transfer to the bowl and carefully blend in a little flour until the mixture is soft and of uniform consistency.

There are two ways to form the paste into the characteristic "canèderlo" shape. The first method involves forming 1 heaping tbsp of mixture into an apricot-sized ball with wetted hands: in the second method (see bottom photograph), you put 1 tbsp mixture into a ladle and roll with a teaspoon to produce an egg-shaped dumpling.

CANÈDERLI *
(Bread dumplings with pancetta and salami)

4 eggs
¾ cup milk
salt
9 oz stale bread
2 oz pancetta or Speck
2 slices salami (approx. 2 oz)
1 medium onion
1 sprig parsley
3 tbsp all-purpose flour
freshly ground pepper
¼ cup butter
grated Parmesan cheese

Beat the eggs in a bowl with the milk and a little salt. Cut the bread into cubes and soak in the bowl for about 20 min, stirring frequently and gently with a wooden spoon to insure the bread absorbs all the liquid. Dice the pancetta and salami, peel and chop the onion and finely chop the parsley. Cook for a few minutes over moderate heat in a saucepan. Pour the contents of the saucepan into the bowl containing the bread and add all the flour while stirring slowly. Season with salt to taste and add a pinch of freshly ground pepper. There are two ways of making these dumplings ("canèderli"): Either wet your hands, take a heaping tbsp of the mixture and roll into a ball the size of an apricot or, alternatively, put 1 tbsp of the mixture into a ladle and turn with a teaspoon until you have obtained an egg-shaped dumpling. Canèderli should be cooked in boiling salted water a few at a time. (It is advisable to try cooking one canèderlo at first to test the consistency of the mixture. If the dumpling tends to come apart in the boiling water, add a further 1–2 tbsp flour to the mixture). Melt the butter in a saucepan. Once the canèderli are cooked, drain them, then cover with the melted butter and grated Parmesan cheese. Canèderli may also be served in a well flavored stock.

POLENTA CONDITA
(Polenta with sausage and cheese)

2½ cups coarse corn meal
salt
½ cup oil
½ onion
1 sprig parsley
few basil leaves
4 ripe tomatoes
8 oz spicy sausage
1 tbsp butter
4 oz Sardinian cheese (e.g. Pecorino)

Prepare the polenta in advance. Bring about 6¼ cups salted water to a boil. Pour in the corn meal. Stir the mixture until thick, then simmer gently, stirring frequently, for about ¾ hr. Season to taste with salt. Turn out, leave to cool then slice. Heat the oil in a saucepan with the onion, parsley and chopped basil. When the ingredients are soft, sieve the tomatoes and cut the skinned sausages into rounds. Add these to the saucepan. Thicken the sauce over moderate heat. Put a layer of polenta slices in the bottom of a wide, buttered ovenproof pan, cover with grated cheese and a good helping of the prepared sauce. Build up layers in this way, ending up with a layer of polenta covered with cheese. Dot the surface with butter and transfer to a preheated moderate oven (325°F) removing when the top is golden brown.

POLENTA PASTISSADA
(Polenta with veal sauce)

3½ cups corn meal
11 cups water
salt
1 oz dried mushrooms
½ cup + 2 tbsp butter
14 oz chicken giblets
freshly ground pepper
2 tbsp oil
½ onion
1 stick celery
1 carrot
2 oz pancetta
8 oz peeled tomatoes
8 oz veal stew meat
½ cup dry white wine
grated Parmesan cheese

Dish typical of Venetian cuisine. Make the polenta: Put the water on to boil in a large saucepan, add salt and pour in the corn meal a little at a time so lumps are not formed. Cook for about ¾ hr, stirring continuously. Turn out on to a board and leave to cool, then cut into ¾-in slices. Soak the mushrooms in a little warm water for about 20 min, then rinse, squeeze out excess moisture and chop. Put one third of the butter into a saucepan with the mushrooms. Cook for 1–2 min. Finely chop the chicken giblets, and add to the saucepan, seasoning with a little salt and pepper to taste. Cook for 5 min over low heat, stirring the ingredients. Take off the heat and put to one side. Heat the oil and 1 tbsp butter in another small saucepan and fry the chopped onion, celery, carrot and pancetta. Brown for a while, stirring continuously, then add the veal stew meat, stir and pour on the wine. When the wine has evaporated, sieve the tomatoes into the saucepan, season with salt and freshly ground pepper; cover the saucepan, lower the heat and cook for about 1 hr. Take off the heat when the meat is tender and the sauce thick. Butter an ovenproof pan and arrange a layer of polenta slices in the bottom, cover with a few table-spoons of sauce and meat, a second layer of polenta covered with mushroom and chicken sauce and a sprinkling of grated Parmesan cheese. Repeat from the first layer of polenta and end up with a sprinkling of grated Parmesan cheese and a few pieces of butter. Put the dish in a moderate oven (about 350°F) for about ½ hr, then serve immediately.

POLENTA E FONTINA IN TORTA
(Baked polenta and Fontina cheese)

6¼ cups water
scant 2 cups corn meal
salt
6 oz Fontina cheese
freshly ground white pepper
2 tbsp butter

This dish is a specialty of the Val d'Aosta region in Piedmont. Boil the salted water in a large saucepan and pour in the corn meal, stirring continuously with a long wooden spoon. Cook the polenta, stirring frequently, for about ¾ hr until it comes away from the sides of the saucepan.

Rinse a deep dish in cold water, pour the polenta into it, and leave to cool. Cut into ¼-in slices. In a buttered ovenproof pan alternate layers of polenta with layers of Fontina cheese, sprinkling a little white pepper on each layer of cheese. Dot butter over the final layer of polenta and cook in a hot oven (475°F) to brown.

POLENTA TARAGNA
(Buckwheat polenta with cheese)

2½ cups buckwheat flour
½ cup corn meal
6¼ cups water
salt
½ cup + 2 tbsp butter
8 oz Taleggio cheese

This dish is typical of the Valtellina area in Lombardy. Mix the buckwheat flour with the corn meal. Bring the water to a boil, add a pinch of salt and pour in the buckwheat flour and corn meal. Cook for at least 1 hr, stirring all the time. Cut the butter into pieces and the cheese into strips and add to the saucepan. Mix and cook for a further 10 min. Turn the polenta out on to a serving dish or a wooden board from which everyone can serve themselves.

POLENTA SMALZADA TRENTINA
(Polenta with anchovies)

6¼ cups water
salt
2¼ cups corn meal (or buckwheat flour)
¼ cup butter
10 anchovy fillets
¼ cup grated Parmesan cheese

Put the water into a large saucepan, add salt, bring to a boil, then slowly add the corn meal or buckwheat flour. Stir continuously for about ¾ hr. When the polenta is done, transfer to a buttered ovenproof pan. Melt the butter in a saucepan. Smooth the surface of the polenta, spread with anchovy fillets, sprinkle with grated Parmesan cheese and pour on the melted butter. Cook in a very hot oven preheated to 400–425°F for 5–10 min, then serve immediately.

POLENTA DI PATATE
(Potato polenta)

2 lb potatoes
½ cup oil
4 oz salt pork
4 oz smoked bacon
1 onion
2 tbsp all-purpose flour
2 large slices salami
salt
freshly ground pepper

Dish typical of the Trento region. Boil the potatoes, peel and mash immediately. Put the oil in a skillet with the salt pork, diced bacon and finely chopped onion. Fry, stirring continuously, until the ingredients are well browned. Add the flour and stir in thoroughly. Put the potatoes into a saucepan or skillet and add the prepared mixture plus the salami cut into strips or cubes. Season with salt and pepper to taste. Cook the polenta over fairly high heat, stirring continuously. When the mixture comes away from the sides of the saucepan, turn out on to a board and serve immediately with pickles, cucumber salad or any green salad.

This polenta is also excellent the following day, reheated in a moderate oven (350°F) for 15–20 min.

How to prepare couscous

Mix the two types of semolina well in a wide bowl, then add 1 cup water in which the saffron has been dissolved.

Rub the semolina across the bottom and sides of the bowl (known as a "mafaradda") to form small granules about the size of peppercorns.

As the granules start to form transfer to a sieve and shake to separate from the semolina which has not been absorbed. Then spread out on a cloth and leave to dry. Continue in this way until all the semolina is used up.

CUSCUSU *
(Couscous)

scant 1 cup fine semolina
scant 1 cup coarse semolina
pinch saffron threads
1 nutmeg
salt
freshly ground pepper

for the fish sauce:
olive oil
1 clove garlic
1 sprig parsley
1 onion
1 tomato
2 lb assorted fish (try to include 1 scorpionfish and 1 small sea bream; some shellfish may also be added)
salt
freshly ground pepper

Couscous is a dish which is traditional fare throughout the Mediterranean. The base is always prepared in the same way although the type of sauce used to accompany it varies from region to region; this may be made from various types of meat or, as in the case of Sicilian couscous, from fish. The dish is laborious to prepare and usually requires special equipment. Mix the two types of semolina in a wide-bottomed bowl. (This is called a "mafaradda" in Sicilian dialect.) Soak the saffron threads in 1 glass warm water. Add this to the bowl. Rub your hand over the bottom of the bowl to form small lumps of semolina. The amount of water added is crucial in insuring these lumps are of equal size and about as large as peppercorns. If too much water is added, the lumps become too big and more semolina will be needed. If not enough water is added, the grains will not form at all. As the grains are formed, remove them from the bowl and sieve through a colander which will retain the small grains and allow the rest of the semolina to fall through. Spread the grains of semolina out to dry on a cloth for a while once the operation is complete. Using a special couscous steamer or a steaming saucepan (a colander lined with muslin will also do) prepare the fish. Clean, gut and chop. Pour ½ cup oil into the saucepan; add the garlic, parsley and onion; cook for a while then add the tomato. Before the ingredients start to brown, add the fish.

Pour in about 6¼ cups water and season with salt and pepper. Cook the fish until done. (The time will vary according to the type of fish.) Strain the soup to separate out the larger pieces. Reserve about 2¼ cups of the fish stock and make the remaining liquid up to 6¼ cups with water. Return this fish stock to the saucepan used to cook the fish and place the couscous steamer on top. Carefully transfer the semolina grains to the steaming saucepan and pour on ½ cup oil, mixing thoroughly to insure the oil does not drop through to the pan underneath. The saucepan is put on to the heat. Take care that the steam does not escape since the success of this dish depends on impregnating the semolina with the flavor of the fish stock during a slow cooking process that lasts about 1½ hr. For best results, keep the holes in the steaming pan unblocked by piercing with a knitting needle or similar implement.

When the couscous is cooked, transfer to another saucepan and separate the grains gently with a fork, taking care not to break them. Occasionally pour on a little of the stock (originally put to one side) until it is all used up. The couscous should slowly absorb this extra liquid.

Keep the saucepan tightly covered and warm during this process which should take no longer than 1 hr. Transfer to a serving dish and cover with boned pieces of fish. Add a little pepper and nutmeg (if wished). Serve hot.

RAVIOLI DI MELANZANE AL BURRO FUSO *
(Eggplant ravioli with butter)

1 lb eggplant
salt
¼ cup butter
olive oil
2 cloves garlic
1 small onion
8 oz ripe tomatoes
few basil leaves
¼ cup grated Parmesan cheese
1 cup all-purpose flour
2 eggs
parsley

Peel and slice the eggplant, sprinkle with salt and place in a colander. Leave for 1 hr to draw out the bitter juices. Rinse and dry. Chop finely. Heat 1 tsp butter and 1 tsp oil in a saucepan. Peel and finely chop the garlic and onion. Fry for a few minutes. Plunge the tomatoes into boiling water for 1 min; peel and chop. Add to the saucepan, together with the basil. Cook for about ¼ hr. Add the eggplant and cook until the mixture reaches the consistency of a thick paste. Add the Parmesan cheese. Prepare the pasta dough with the flour and eggs, roll out to a thin sheet and make ravioli (see p. 63), filling them with the eggplant mixture. Cook the ravioli in plenty of boiling salted water for 5 min. Melt the remaining butter in a saucepan. Drain the pasta and transfer to a serving dish. Pour on the melted butter, and garnish with parsley.

SPAGHETTI ALL'ARAGOSTA *
(Spaghetti with lobster)

2 lb ripe tomatoes
1 cooked lobster weighing approx.
  2 lb
¼ cup butter
2 tbsp oil
1 small onion
1 small clove garlic
2 tbsp chopped parsley
salt
freshly ground pepper
2–3 tbsp brandy
1⅛ cups dry white wine
12 oz spaghetti
basil leaves

Skin and seed the tomatoes, then chop and set aside. Crack the claws and legs off the lobster, leaving the tail intact and extract the meat. Remove the dark vein and discard. Cut the head away from the tail and pick out all the meat from the head. Remove and discard the stomach sac and gills. Sauté the lobster meat and the whole tail in half the butter and the oil, together with the chopped onion, garlic and parsley. Season with salt and pepper, cover with the brandy and wine and set alight. When the flames have died down, add the tomatoes. Cover and cook for 20 min. Remove from the heat and put the tail to one side. Purée the lobster sauce in a blender or food processor. Cook the spaghetti in plenty of boiling salted water until *al dente*. Drain and toss in the lobster sauce, adding the remaining butter. Serve the pasta decorated with slices of lobster tail and basil leaves.

Soups

*E*arliest versions of soup were
probably obtained simply by
boiling a few basic foods in water. What is
known in Italy today as "minestra in brodo"
(literally, "soup in broth") is therefore the
gastronomic evolution of a method of cooking
intended to make the most of humble
ingredients that were easy to find, especially
in the countryside. In the Middle Ages, by
which time meats were available for
consumption at least once or twice a week,
soups developed into sustaining broths
containing pieces of chicken or mutton or
beef. Then new vegetables, particularly the
bean, were introduced into Europe from the
New World and were added to vegetable
soups.

In Italian cuisine a good "minestra" can
contain not only vegetables but various kinds
of pasta as well. When food was short
peasants would break an egg or two into
broth thus creating the now famous
"stracciatella" soup; but in the more
prosperous regions women delighted in
concocting varieties of stuffed pasta which
would swell up in a rich, steaming broth that
was delicious to eat and almost a meal in
itself.

The basis of a good soup is a good stock,
although if time is short, bouillon cubes and
water may be substituted. For meat (beef,
veal or chicken) stock, place the bones in a
large saucepan or stockpot together with 1
onion, 1 carrot, 1 celery stick, 1 leek, some
fresh herbs or a bouquet garni, salt and a few
peppercorns. Add cold water, bring to a boil,
then lower the heat and simmer for 3 hr. (For
vegetable stock, omit the bones, double the
vegetable quantities, and follow the same
recipe.) Strain the liquid, and skim off any
fat. This is best done by leaving the stock to
cool and allowing the fat to rise to the
surface.

ACQUACOTTA
(Tuscan mushroom soup)

14 oz fresh porcini (cèpes)
8 slices stale bread
7 oz ripe or canned tomatoes
2 cloves garlic
6 tbsp olive oil
1 bouillon cube
salt
freshly ground pepper
3 eggs
¼ cup grated Parmesan cheese

Rinse the mushrooms, dry thoroughly and slice into medium-sized pieces. Trim the slices of bread, toast them lightly in the oven and place 2 slices in each soup plate. Peel and finely chop the garlic and fry gently with the oil and the mushrooms in a covered saucepan for about 10 min. Plunge the tomatoes into boiling hot water for a few seconds to split the skins. Peel, remove the seeds and chop coarsely. If canned tomatoes are used you need only put them through a sieve. Add the tomato and bouillon cube to the saucepan with a little salt and pepper. Pour in 4½ cups boiling water, stir well and simmer for 30–40 min. Break the eggs into a soup tureen, add the grated cheese and blend thoroughly with a fork. Add the boiling tomato liquid, 1 ladleful at a time, stirring constantly. Pour on to the bread slices in each soup plate and serve.

CIPOLLATA
(Onion and tomato soup)

2¼ lb large white onions
¼ cup salt pork
6 tbsp olive oil
4–5 basil leaves
salt
freshly ground pepper
generous 1 lb ripe or canned
  tomatoes
2 eggs
generous ¼ cup grated Parmesan
  cheese
toasted rounds of crusty bread

Cut the onions into thin slices and leave overnight in a deep bowl filled with cold water. The next day pound the salt pork and fry with the oil for a few minutes in a large

saucepan. Drain the onions thoroughly and place in the saucepan together with the roughly chopped basil leaves, and a little salt and pepper. Cover and gently sweat the onions until they are transparent. Do not allow them to brown. Put the tomatoes through a sieve and add the juice to the onions together with 5 cups cold water. Stir well, cover and simmer gently for 1 hr or until the liquid has reduced to a thick consistency. When the soup is almost ready beat the eggs and grated cheese in a bowl or tureen until smoothly blended. Remove the saucepan from the heat and pour it into the egg and cheese mixture, stirring quickly. Serve with rounds of lightly toasted crusty bread.

CREMA VELLUTATA DI VERDURE
(Cream of vegetable soup)

¾ lb mixed vegetables (e.g. asparagus, marrow, cauliflower)
9 cups water
3 tbsp cornstarch
2 egg yolks
salt
freshly ground pepper
¼ cup butter
grated Parmesan cheese

Chop the vegetables and boil in water until the liquid has acquired a good aromatic flavor. Mix the cornstarch with 1 ladleful of the hot liquid and stir it into the rest. Simmer until thickened to a creamy consistency then remove from the heat. Put the egg yolks in a tureen, pour in the soup and blend thoroughly. Season with salt and pepper and add 1 tbsp butter and 1 tbsp grated Parmesan to each serving.

FAVATA
(Pork and fava bean soup)

generous 1 cup dried fava beans
7 oz small pork loin chops
7 oz pork sausage
½ cup oil
½ white cabbage
2–3 bulbs fennel

2 onions
2 ripe tomatoes
3 oz pancetta
salt
freshly ground pepper
slices of toasted bread
grated Parmesan cheese

Soak the fava beans in a bowl of tepid water for 12 hr. Heat the oil in a deep saucepan and gently fry the chops and the pricked sausages until well browned. Drain the fava beans, add to the saucepan and pour in enough water to cover the meat and beans. Cover and simmer for 1 hr. Chop the cabbage, fennel and onions, then peel and chop the tomatoes and add to the saucepan with the pancetta. Season lightly with salt and pepper and continue simmering very slowly for 2 hr, adding more water if necessary. The meat should by now be tender and the liquid should have the consistency of a thin gravy. Remove the pancetta and the chops, cut into small pieces, discarding any bones from the chops, and return to the saucepan. Serve piping hot with grated Parmesan and toasted bread.

MINESTRA DI FARRO
(Ham and barley soup)

1 ham bone
1 small carrot
1 stick celery
½ onion
3 ripe tomatoes or 1 cup canned tomatoes
salt
1 cup pearl barley
generous ¼ cup equal portions of grated Parmesan and Pecorino cheese

Boil the ham bone in water for ¼ hr to reduce the saltiness. Drain and refill the pan with 6¼ cups fresh water. Chop the carrot, celery and onion, peel the tomatoes, remove the seeds and chop (canned tomatoes should be pressed through a sieve). Add to the saucepan and boil for 1 hr. Remove the bone, strain the liquid and reheat. Test for seasoning and when the liquid begins to boil pour in the barley, stirring with a wooden spoon. Simmer for ½ hr.

Just before removing from the heat, add any meat from the ham bone, cut into small pieces, and the two types of grated cheese. Stir well and serve immediately.

MINESTRA DI CICORIA
(Endive soup)

generous 1 lb Belgian endive
salt
2 eggs
½ cup grated Parmesan cheese
6½ cups meat stock
croûtons

Rinse the endive and simmer for 5 min in lightly salted water. Drain well and chop. Mix the eggs with 3 tbsp grated Parmesan and a generous pinch of salt. Heat the stock in a saucepan. Just before it comes to a boil remove from the heat, add the egg and cheese mixture together with the endive and stir briskly with a fork. Serve immediately accompanied by croûtons and sprinkle the remaining grated cheese on top.

MINESTRA DI PISELLI FRESCHI E CARCIOFI
(Pea and artichoke soup)

14 oz unshelled peas
2 young artichokes
1 lemon
1 clove garlic
3 tbsp olive oil
3 tbsp chopped parsley
pinch of baking soda
salt
1 tsp meat extract (optional)
grated Parmesan or Pecorino cheese
toasted bread

Shell the peas. Discard the outer leaves of the artichokes, cut the rest into very small wedges and steep in water acidulated with the juice of 1 lemon. Peel and chop the garlic; gently fry in oil; when it begins to color remove it from the pan and discard. Put in the peas, the artichokes and the chopped parsley. Sauté lightly. Add the baking soda, a little salt and the meat extract (if used) to 6¼ cups water and pour this into the saucepan. Cover and cook over medium heat for 30–45 min. Serve the pea and artichoke soup piping hot with grated cheese and toasted bread.

MINESTRA D'ERBE MARITATA
(Neapolitan vegetable soup)

3 oz pork rind
1 chicken
¾ lb beef flank steak
4 oz salami in one piece
4 oz lean bacon
4 oz prosciutto
salt
1 onion
1 carrot
1 stick celery
1 small white cabbage
¾ lb Belgian endive
7 oz chicory
1 clove garlic
¼ cup salt pork

This delicious and filling soup is traditionally eaten in Naples on Easter Day. Cook the pieces of pork rind and drain off fat. Place them in a large casserole together with the chicken, steak, salami, bacon and prosciutto. Cover with water and simmer. Season with salt and add the onion, carrot and celery to flavor the broth. Remove the meats as they become tender and keep warm in a separate dish with a little of the hot liquid. When all the meat is cooked, strain the broth and set it aside. Separate the cabbage leaves and halve each leaf, discarding the central rib. Clean the Belgian endive and the chicory, cut the endive into quarters and tear the chicory into small pieces. Rinse well, place in boiling water and cook for 4–5 min. Cool in fresh cold water then gently squeeze out the moisture and arrange a bed of vegetables at the bottom of the casserole.

Finely chop the salt pork and the garlic, mix together and spread over the vegetables. Slice the salami, the bacon and the prosciutto, chop up the pork rind and add to the casserole with the sliced chicken and beef. Cover with the hot broth and simmer very slowly for at least 2 hr.

Turn off the heat and leave for several minutes before serving.

MINESTRA DI TRIPPA E VERDURE *
(Tripe and vegetable soup)

1½ lb tripe
2 small onions
2–3 cloves
1 carrot
1 stick celery
salt
3 black peppercorns
½ cup salt pork
1 small cabbage
3 potatoes
1 leek
salt
freshly ground pepper

Buy tripe ready-washed and boiled by the butcher. Cut into strips; place in a large pan together with 1 onion stuck with cloves, the carrot, ½ stick celery, a little salt and the peppercorns. Cover all the ingredients with plenty of water and simmer for 1 hr. Remove the tripe, strain the liquid and set aside. Finely chop the remaining onion and celery, shred the cabbage, cut the leek into pieces and dice the potatoes. Pound the salt pork and fry until soft. Sauté the onion and celery lightly, then add the tripe, stock, cabbage, leek and potatoes. Adjust the seasoning and simmer for 1 hr.

MINESTRA DEL PARADISO
(Paradise soup)

6½ cups meat stock
4 eggs
½ cup grated Parmesan cheese
6 tbsp fresh breadcrumbs
salt
freshly ground pepper
pinch of nutmeg

Heat the stock in a saucepan. Break the eggs into a bowl and mix with generous ¼ cup of the grated Parmesan and the breadcrumbs (some recipes recommend frying the breadcrumbs in butter to a golden brown first). Season with salt, pepper and nutmeg. Beat the mixture with a fork and add to the saucepan as the stock begins to boil. After a moment or two stir and continue cooking for another minute. Pour the soup into a tureen and sprinkle on the rest of the grated cheese before serving.

MINESTRA DI PASSATELLI ✳
(Pasta and cheese soup)

1 ¼ cups fresh breadcrumbs
pinch of salt
pinch of nutmeg
½ lemon
3 eggs
⅓ cup grated Parmesan cheese
2 tbsp butter, softened
scant 4 ½ cups meat stock

First make the passatelli: place the breadcrumbs in a bowl with a pinch of salt, a pinch of nutmeg, the grated peel of ½ lemon and the eggs. Beat with a fork. Add the grated Parmesan and the softened butter. Still using a fork, blend all the ingredients into a doughy paste, cover and set aside (see step-by-step illustrations below right). Bring the stock to a boil. Force the paste through a potato ricer or similar mincing implement, squeezing the handles firmly together. Drop the short lengths of paste that will emerge straight into the boiling stock, simmer for a few minutes and serve hot. There is no need for a cheese garnish because the "passatelli" in the soup are already flavored with Parmesan.

MINESTRONE ABRUZZESE
(Abruzzo vegetable broth)

1 pig's head weighing 1 lb
1 onion
½ stick celery
2 carrots
1 tbsp olive oil
generous 1 tbsp salt pork
½ clove garlic
1–2 sprigs parsley
3 medium potatoes
1 turnip
½ leek
½ cabbage
salt
⅓ cup cooked lentils or large white
 beans
½ cup pasta
grated Pecorino cheese

Cook the pig's head in boiling water for 5 min then drain. Clean and rinse it thoroughly. Place it in fresh water, bring again to a boil and remove any scum that forms. Add half the onion, the celery and 1 carrot and simmer for 3 hr. Remove the pig's head, bone it and cut the meat into large cubes. Place the meat in a separate saucepan, cover with a little of the broth and keep warm. Reserve the remaining broth.

Put 1 tbsp oil into a deep saucepan together with the chopped salt pork, the garlic, the remaining ½ onion and the parsley. Sauté lightly for a minute or two. Strain the reserved broth and add to the saucepan. Clean and peel the remaining uncooked vegetables, chop the carrot and potatoes, dice the turnip and thinly slice the leek. Discard the stem of the cabbage and the central ribs of the leaves, and cut into ribbons. Gently boil these vegetables for 5 min. Add them to the broth, cover the saucepan and lightly boil until all the ingredients are tender. Add the salt, the cooked lentils or large white beans and the pasta. When the pasta is cooked, add a generous sprinkling of grated Pecorino cheese and stir well. Leave off the heat for a moment or two before serving in individual soup bowls with some pieces of the meat in each bowl.

MINESTRONE D'ORZO
(Pearl barley soup)

¾ cup dried large white or Navy
 beans
1 cup pearl barley
¼ cup smoked pancetta or bacon
1 clove garlic
1 sprig parsley
salt
freshly ground pepper
1 small smoked sausage
2 potatoes

Soak the beans in water for 12 hr. It also helps the cooking if the pearl barley is left overnight in water. The next day strain the beans and the barley and place in a large saucepan. Finely chop the pancetta, the garlic and the parsley, pound together to a smooth paste and add to the saucepan. Pour in 9 cups water, season with salt and pepper then bring to a boil. Cover and simmer over low heat for 2 hr.

Grind the sausage, dice the potatoes and add to the saucepan just before the beans are fully tender. When the potatoes are cooked set the pan aside, keep covered and allow the soup to cool. Serve when just warm.

MINESTRONE TOSCANO
(Tuscan vegetable soup)

1 ½ cups large white beans
salt
½ cup oil
1 clove garlic
½ onion
1 stick celery
1 carrot
2 sprigs rosemary
¼ cup pancetta or bacon (optional)
1 heaping tbsp tomato paste
½ cabbage

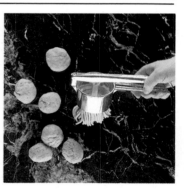

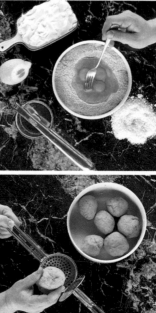

2 leeks
2 zucchini
1 sprig basil
1 clove
½ cup long-grain rice or pasta
 (optional)
rounds of toasted bread

Boil the beans in a pan with 9 cups salted water for about 2 hr. Remove half the beans from the pan and pass through a sieve, letting the pulp fall back into the water. Cover and set aside. Peel and finely chop the garlic, then chop the onion, celery, carrot, rosemary and pancetta (if used). Heat 4 tbsp oil in a deep saucepan and gently fry the chopped onion. Thin the tomato paste in a little warm water and add it to the saucepan when the onion begins to color. Chop the remaining vegetables, add them to the saucepan

How to prepare "passatelli"

Place in a bowl the breadcrumbs, a pinch of salt, a pinch of nutmeg, the grated lemon peel and the eggs. Beat with a fork then add the grated Parmesan and 1 tbsp butter. Blend all the ingredients thoroughly into a paste which is slightly more solid in consistency than mashed potatoes. Cover the bowl and set aside.

Heat the soup; after ¼ hr, press the paste through a potato ricer, squeezing the handles tightly together. Let the short round filaments of paste that emerge drop straight into the boiling soup.

together with the chopped basil, the clove and the beans (including their liquid). Pour in a little more water, adjust the seasoning and simmer for ½ hr. Add the rice or pasta if desired, otherwise garnish the soup with rounds of toasted bread and 1 tbsp olive oil but no cheese.

MINESTRONE COL PESTO
(Vegetable soup with pesto)

1 cup dried borlotti beans
2 potatoes
2 ripe tomatoes
2 carrots
2 zucchini
1 onion

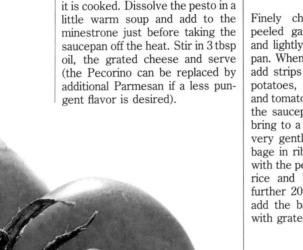

1 sprig borage
1 leek
3 sticks celery
salt
6 tbsp olive oil
5 oz short cut pasta suitable for minestrone
3 tbsp grated Parmesan cheese
1 tbsp grated Pecorino cheese
1 tbsp pesto (see p. 130)

Soak the beans in water overnight. Clean and peel the vegetables and cut into thick slices. Pour 9 cups water into a saucepan, add some salt and bring to a boil. Add the vegetables, the chopped borage and 3 tbsp oil. Cover and simmer for approximately 2 hr or until the soup is thick and the beans are tender (do not overcook). Add the pasta and continue simmering until it is cooked. Dissolve the pesto in a little warm soup and add to the minestrone just before taking the saucepan off the heat. Stir in 3 tbsp oil, the grated cheese and serve (the Pecorino can be replaced by additional Parmesan if a less pungent flavor is desired).

MINESTRONE ALLA MILANESE
(Milanese vegetable soup)

⅓ cup pancetta
1 clove garlic
1 sprig parsley
1 onion
¾ cup pork rind
2 potatoes
2 carrots
2 sticks celery
2 zucchini
1 ripe peeled tomato
1 cup cooked large white beans or Navy beans
salt
1 white cabbage
generous ½ cup shelled peas
¾ cup long-grain rice
1 tbsp chopped basil
grated Parmesan cheese

Finely chop the pancetta, the peeled garlic, parsley and onion and lightly sauté in a deep saucepan. When the onion is transparent add strips of pork rind. Chop the potatoes, carrots, celery, zuchini and tomato. Pour 9 cups water into the saucepan, add a little salt and bring to a boil. Cover and simmer very gently for 4 hr. Cut the cabbage in ribbons and add, together with the peas. After 20 min add the rice and beans, and cook for a further 20 min. At the last minute add the basil and stir. Serve hot with grated Parmesan.

PANCOTTO
(Bread and tomato soup with egg)

1 cup fresh or canned tomatoes
½ cup olive oil
1 clove garlic
1 sprig parsley
2 bay leaves
1 stick celery
salt
freshly ground pepper
generous 1 lb stale bread
4 eggs
grated Pecorino cheese

Chop the tomatoes and place in a saucepan with the oil. Finely chop the garlic, parsley, bay leaves, and celery. Add these to the saucepan, together with 5 cups water, add

seasoning and simmer for ½ hr. Meanwhile toast rounds of bread in the oven. Strain the tomato broth and pour the strained liquid into a clean saucepan. Add the toasted bread and let it absorb the liquid for a moment or two. Remove the rounds of bread and distribute them into soup plates. Bring the liquid to a boil and carefully break in 1 whole egg. As soon as it sets, remove it and lay it on top of the bread. Repeat with each egg. Top generously with grated Pecorino and serve hot.

PASTA E CECI
(Pasta and chick pea soup)

1 cup dried chick peas
1 clove garlic
1 tbsp olive oil
1 sprig rosemary
1 tsp tomato paste
salt
freshly ground pepper
8 oz short cut pasta (about 1 in in length)

Soak the chick peas in water overnight. The next day drain and simmer them in a covered saucepan with 6 cups slightly salted water until tender. Peel and chop the garlic. Gently fry in the olive oil with the sprig of rosemary. When the garlic has turned a light gold, dilute the tomato paste in ½ cup hot water and add to the saucepan. Remove half of the chick peas from the saucepan and put them through a sieve. Return the chick peas to the saucepan, stir in the prepared tomato sauce, season to taste and add the pasta. Cook until the pasta is tender and the consistency of the soup is very thick. Discard the sprig of rosemary before serving.

PAPPA COL POMODORO
(Thick tomato soup)

9 oz stale coarse bread
1½ lb ripe or canned tomatoes
4 cloves garlic
1 sprig parsley
2 basil leaves
scant 4½ cups stock (or 1 bouillon cube and ½ tsp meat extract

dissolved in the same amount of
water)
1 tbsp olive oil
salt
freshly ground pepper

Cut the bread into even rounds and toast lightly in the oven. Rinse the tomatoes, cut them in half and scoop out the seeds. Peel the garlic cloves and leave whole. Place with the tomatoes, parsley and basil leaves in a saucepan. Sauté lightly for a few minutes then put the contents through a sieve and return to the saucepan. Add the stock, the toasted bread, the oil, salt to taste and plenty of pepper. Simmer slowly until the soup is thick. Serve hot or chilled.

PASTINA CON VERDURA
(Rice pasta soup with vegetables)

2 zucchini
2 potatoes
1 small can tomatoes
2 tbsp butter
scant 4½ cups meat stock
generous 1 cup pastina (very small
    rice-like pasta for soups)
salt
grated Parmesan cheese

Wash, peel and dice the zucchini and the potatoes. Put the tomatoes through a sieve. Melt the butter in a saucepan and fry all the vegetables gently. Let the flavors draw a little then add generous 1 ladleful of the hot stock and simmer the vegetables for 4–5 min. Add the rest of the stock, bring to a boil and pour in the pastina. After 5 min, test the seasoning and pour the soup into individual bowls. Serve piping hot with grated cheese.

PASTA E FAGIOLI
(Pasta and bean soup)

2 cups dried large white or Navy
    beans
1 onion
1 cup olive oil
6¼ cups meat stock (or 1 bouillon
    cube and 1 tsp meat extract
    dissolved in the same amount of
    water)

1 cup canned tomatoes or tomato
    paste
salt
freshly ground pepper
8 oz tagliatelle
¼ cup grated Parmesan cheese

Soak the beans overnight in water. Finely chop the onion. Heat the oil in a large saucepan and sauté the onion for a few minutes. Drain the beans and add to the saucepan together with the boiling stock. Cover and simmer very slowly for 1 hr. Put the tomatoes through a sieve (if using tomato paste, you need only dilute it in a little water), add to the saucepan and continue simmering, covered, for 2 hr. Lift out about one-third of the beans with a skimming spoon and press them through a sieve, letting the pulp drop back into the pan. This gives the soup a deliciously smooth and creamy texture. Check at this stage whether there is enough soup for 4 servings and if necessary top up with a little boiling water. Add salt and pepper to taste and the tagliatelle. Continue cooking and when the tagliatelle are *al dente* (done but still with some bite to them), remove from the heat and add the grated cheese before serving.

QUADRUCCI E PISELLI
(Pea, prosciutto and pasta soup)

¼ cup salt pork
1 clove garlic
1 stick celery
1 sprig parsley
1 onion
generous ¼ cup prosciutto
¼ cup butter
1 cup shelled peas
scant 4½ cups meat stock
1 tbsp tomato paste
salt
9 oz fresh quadrucci (pasta squares)
    or 7 oz dried
grated Parmesan or Pecorino cheese

Finely chop the salt pork, the peeled garlic clove, celery and parsley. Slice the onion and dice the prosciutto. Melt the butter in a saucepan and fry the vegetables, together with the peas. Heat the stock and dilute the tomato paste in some of it. Add the tomato paste to the vegetables in the saucepan. Season with salt and simmer slowly for ¼ hr. In a separate saucepan bring the remaining stock to a boil, add the pasta, stir and cook until *al dente* (done but with a bite to it). Add the contents of the other saucepan and stir well. Serve piping hot with grated cheese.

RAVIOLI DI MAGRO IN BRODO
(Fish ravioli in clear stock)

to make the ravioli:
2¼ cups flour
1 egg

pinch of salt
milk

to make the filling:
10 oz boiled fish
scant ½ cup grated Parmesan
    cheese
2 eggs
salt
pinch of nutmeg
scant 4½ cups clear skimmed stock

Place the flour on a pastry board, make a hollow in the center and put in the egg and a pinch of salt. Fold the egg into the flour with your hands or a fork then add enough milk to make a stiff dough (see p. 63). Knead well for about 10 min until the dough is no longer sticky. Finely chop the fish and mix with the grated cheese and the eggs, a little salt and the nutmeg. Roll out the dough thinly and cut into 1½ in disks. Place a little of the filling in the center of each disk, then press the edges together to seal in the filling. Leave to dry on a cloth for 2 hr. Bring the stock to a boil, add the ravioli and cook for 3–4 min. Serve the ravioli in the stock with grated cheese.

SCRIPPELLE 'MBUSSE
(Cheese crêpes soup)

3 eggs
1 cup flour
scant ½ cup grated Parmesan
    cheese
salt
nutmeg
1⅛ cups milk
pork fat or olive oil
¼ cup grated Pecorino cheese
chicken giblets ready-cooked in
    butter (optional)
scant 4½ cups chicken or turkey
    stock

This most satisfying and unusual soup comes from the Abruzzi mountains of central Italy. Beat together the eggs, the flour, 1 tbsp grated cheese, a little salt and a pinch of nutmeg. Gradually stir in the milk until a fairly runny batter is made. Thoroughly grease a 6-in skillet with fat or oil, and heat. Drop in 2 tbsp batter and fry on each side for 1 min. Keep warm, and repeat until all the batter is used up. Dust the crêpes lightly with Parmesan and Pecorino cheese. Place the cooked giblets (if used) in the middle of each crêpe, fold and seal the edges. Lay the crêpes in the serving bowls and pour over the boiling stock.

STRACCIATELLA ALLA ROMANA
(Egg and cheese soup Roman style)

3 eggs
¼ cup grated Parmesan cheese
pinch of nutmeg (optional)
salt
scant 4½ cups meat stock

Break the eggs into a bowl, add the grated cheese, a pinch of nutmeg, season lightly and blend thoroughly with a fork. Bring the stock to a boil in a saucepan, pour in the egg mixture and beat with a whisk. The action will make the egg separate into small uneven strands (stracciatelle) giving the soup its name. Simmer for 3 min and serve.

TORTELLINI IN BRODO
(Tortellini in stock)

3 oz lean pork
2 oz turkey or capon breast
2 oz beef bone marrow
scant ¼ cup butter
2 oz mortadella
generous 1 oz prosciutto
scant ½ cup grated Parmesan
    cheese
1 egg
salt
freshly ground pepper
nutmeg
scant 4½ cups meat stock
pasta dough (see p. 63) made with
    2¼ cups flour and 2 eggs

Melt the butter in a saucepan and brown the pork, the turkey or capon breast and the bone marrow. Put the meats through a food processor or finely chop together with the mortadella and the prosciutto then blend to a smooth mixture with the grated cheese and the egg. Season to taste with salt, pepper and a pinch of nutmeg. Spoon ½ tsp of the mixture on to the center of each disk of pasta, fold and press the edges together then curl the ends to form a ring shape. Set the tortellini on a cloth, allow at least 1 hr to dry out then simmer them in boiling stock for 4 min. Serve about 20 tortellini in stock per portion.

ZUPPA SANTÉ
(Meat ball soup)

generous 1 cup ground veal
1 egg
3 tbsp grated Pecorino or Parmesan
    cheese
salt
freshly ground pepper
flour
¼ cup butter
8 slices stale bread
5½ cups chicken stock
generous ¼ cup chicken giblets
⅓ cup Caciocavallo cheese

Place the ground veal in a bowl with the egg and the grated Pecorino (substitute with Parmesan if a less pungent flavor is desired). Add a little salt and pepper and mix thoroughly with a spoon. Flour the palms of your hands and roll the mixture into small olive-sized balls. In a skillet, heat the butter to a light gold color and fry the meat balls, turning them gently so they brown all over. Toast the slices of bread in the oven. Skim the stock and heat in a saucepan. Chop the giblets, add to the saucepan and simmer until cooked. Place 2 slices of toast and some of the finely diced Caciocavallo cheese in each of 4 soup bowls. Distribute 4 portions of the meat balls, the stock and the giblets and serve immediately while the toast is crisp.

ZUPPA DI FAGIOLI ✳
(Bean soup)

1 cup dried cannellini beans
salt
1 onion
1 clove garlic
1 sprig parsley
1 stick celery
3–4 bay leaves
6 tbsp olive oil
2 dark leaves and 2 light leaves of a
  Savoy cabbage
freshly ground pepper
4 tbsp tomato paste
8 slices stale coarse brown bread
grated Parmesan cheese (optional)

Soak the beans in water overnight. Drain, place in a saucepan with 11 cups lightly salted water and boil for 2–3 hr. Finely chop the onion, the peeled garlic, the parsley, celery and basil leaves and fry lightly in a deep saucepan with the oil. When the vegetables are tender and are about to turn brown, add 2 ladlefuls of the bean broth together with the coarsely chopped cabbage leaves. Season to taste with salt and plenty of pepper. Dilute the tomato paste in 1 ladleful of the bean broth and add to the vegetables. Cover and cook over moderate heat for at least 1 hr taking care not to let the liquid run dry, then remove the saucepan from the heat. Take half the beans out of the saucepan, press them through a sieve and add the pulp to the saucepan with the vegetables. Transfer the rest of the beans to the saucepan using a slotted spoon. Pour over just enough of the broth

to make the consistency liquid but still thick then set aside and keep warm. Toast the bread in the oven for a few minutes then place the slices in a tureen and pour on the vegetable soup. Add a sprinkling of grated cheese if desired.

ZUPPA DI CIPOLLE
(Onion soup)

14 oz onions
generous ¼ cup butter
2 tsp flour
salt
white pepper
6¼ cups beef stock
1 stick bread
½ cup grated Emmental cheese
¼ cup grated Parmesan cheese

Slice the onions finely and gently fry in a saucepan with two-thirds of the butter. When the onions are transparent, stir in the flour and season with salt and pepper. Pour in the stock and simmer for ¾ hr. Meanwhile slice the bread and lightly toast in the oven. In an ovenproof pan arrange layers of toasted bread dotted with the remaining butter, with a generous covering of the two cheeses between each layer. Pour the onion broth over the layers, cover and place in a preheated oven at 275°F for 10 min before serving.

ZUPPA DI MANZO CON PAPRICA
(Beef soup with paprika)

1 onion
1 clove garlic
3 tbsp salt pork
1¼ lb flank steak
salt
1 tsp paprika
2 red peppers
3 potatoes
2 tomatoes
2 pork sausages, cooked
brown bread

Slice the onion, peel and finely chop the garlic and gently fry in a saucepan with the salt pork. Cube the meat and brown in the saucepan. Season with salt and 1 tsp paprika, mix well and cover so that the flavors absorbed by the meat become more concentrated. Simmer gently for ¼ hr. Cut the peppers into strips and dice the potatoes. Peel the tomatoes, remove the seeds and chop. Add to the saucepan, together with the peppers and potatoes. Pour in 9 cups boiling water and simmer for 1 hr. Finely dice the sausage and add at the last minute. Check the seasoning and the tenderness of the meat before serving the soup accompanied by slices of brown bread.

ZUPPA DI FUNGHI
(Mushroom soup)

3 oz dried mushrooms (porcini)
1 onion
½ cup olive oil
2 tbsp cornstarch
4 potatoes
salt
freshly ground pepper
4½ cups chicken stock
½ cup light cream
1 tbsp butter
2–3 tbsp chopped parsley
grated Parmesan cheese

Rinse the mushrooms well and soak in warm water for ½ hr. When they have plumped up, drain and squeeze excess water out with your hands; chop coarsely. Chop the onion and brown in the oil, then add the mushrooms. Mix the cornstarch with a little cold water and add to the saucepan. Peel and rinse the potatoes and leave whole. Add to the saucepan, season with salt and pepper, then add the stock. Simmer for 1 hr. Remove the potatoes and put through a ricer; return to the saucepan. Stir in the cream and butter, adjust the seasoning and cook for a few minutes longer. Sprinkle with freshly chopped parsley and serve piping hot with freshly grated Parmesan.

ZUPPA DI PORRI
(Leek soup)

2¼ lb leeks
2 tbsp olive oil

2 tbsp butter
3 tbsp rice flour
3 small potatoes
6¼ cups stock
salt
grated Parmesan cheese

Cut away the root and the green end of the leeks leaving only the tender white part. Rinse well and plunge into boiling water to reduce the acidity. Cut in half lengthwise then across into ¼-in slices and fry gently in a deep saucepan with the oil and the butter. Peel the potatoes, rinse thoroughly and leave whole. Mix the rice flour with a little water and add to the saucepan together with the potatoes. Pour in the stock, add salt to taste and simmer for 2 hr. Remove the potatoes, squeeze them through a ricer and return to the pan to thicken the soup. Leave on the heat for a minute or two before transferring to a soup tureen. Serve with grated Parmesan.

ZUPPA DI CECI
(Chick pea soup)

1¼ cups dried chick peas
salt
pig's head weighing 1 lb
2 small onions
2 sticks celery
1 clove
1 bay leaf
3 tbsp butter
1 cup dry white wine
3 tbsp salt pork
1 carrot
1 sprig sage
1 tbsp tomato paste
chopped parsley

Soak the chick peas overnight: drain and simmer in a deep pot with 9 cups lightly salted water for 3 hr. Clean and rinse the pig's head, place in a saucepan with 1 sliced onion, 1 finely chopped stick celery, the clove, the bay leaf, the butter and let it brown. Pour in the wine, let it reduce then add a little salt and cover the ingredients with warm water. Simmer, covered, for 1½ hr, skimming from time to time.
Finely chop the salt pork, the carrot, and the remaining celery and onion; place in a skillet with the

sage and sauté lightly before adding to the chick peas together with the tomato paste, diluted in ½ cup water. Stew for 20 min then bone the meat, cut it into small slices and put it into the chick pea soup. Serve with a sprinkling of chopped parsley.

ZUPPA ALLA PAVESE
(Poached egg broth)

scant 4½ cups fat-free meat stock
1 tbsp butter
4 slices stale French bread
4 eggs
freshly ground white pepper
grated Parmesan cheese

Preheat the oven to 350°F. Have a good clear meat stock standing by on a slow simmer. Fry the bread in butter until a light gold on both sides, turning carefully so that the slices do not crumble. Place 1 slice each in 4 ovenproof bowls. Break 1 egg on to each slice and put the bowls quickly into the preheated oven so that the white sets. Just before serving pour 1 ladleful boiling stock into each bowl and sprinkle the top with ground pepper and grated cheese.

ZUPPA DI FAGIOLI ALLA TOSCANA
"LA RIBOLLITA"
(Tuscan bean soup)

1½ cups Navy beans
1 clove garlic
1 onion
1 carrot
1 stick celery
1 leek
1 sprig rosemary
1 chili pepper
3 tbsp oil
1 ham bone
salt
freshly ground pepper

for the garnish:
1 clove garlic
pinch of thyme
1 cup olive oil
8 slices coarse toasted bread
generous ¼ cup grated Parmesan cheese
1 onion

Soak the beans in water overnight and drain. Finely chop the garlic, onion, carrot, celery, leek, rosemary and the chili pepper. Place in a deep saucepan with the oil and gently fry until the vegetables begin to color. Put in the beans and the ham bone, cover with water, add seasoning and cook slowly for 2 hr. Remove the ham bone. Put half of the beans through a sieve, and add the pulp into the soup. Set aside and keep warm.
Gently fry the minced garlic and the thyme with the oil. After 2–3 min stir half the flavored oil into the bean soup. Toast the bread in the oven, place in an ovenproof serving dish and cover with half the grated cheese. Pour in the bean soup, cover with fine slices of onion and the remaining oil and cheese. Place in a preheated oven at 350°F for ½ hr or until the onions are a deep golden brown.

ZUPPA DI CAVOLO NERO
(Cabbage soup)

2 sticks celery
1 carrot
½ onion
1 clove garlic
1 cup olive oil
3–4 basil leaves
1 sprig sage
pinch of thyme
6 leaves black cabbage or 6 dark leaves of a Savoy cabbage
1 cup cooked beans
1 tbsp tomato paste
salt
3–4 slices brown bread
freshly ground pepper
¼ cup grated Parmesan cheese

Chop the celery, the carrot and onion. Peel and chop the garlic; place in a deep saucepan and fry gently with the oil. When the vegetables begin to color, put in the chopped basil, sage and thyme; cut the cabbage leaves into ribbons, add to the saucepan together with the beans. Add the tomato paste, diluted in a little warm water. Season to taste, cover with 9 cups water and simmer very slowly. When the cabbage is tender lay slices of brown bread in a tureen and pour the soup over. Add plenty

of pepper and grated cheese, stir and serve hot.

CREMA DI ZUCCA CON AMARETTO
(Creamed marrow soup with macaroons)

1 onion
1 tbsp butter
1 lb marrow
salt
4½ cups milk
1 tsp sugar
3½ oz macaroons (amaretti)

Finely chop the onion and gently fry in a saucepan with the butter. Add the chopped marrow and stir for a few minutes. Season to taste, add the milk, the sugar and half of the amaretti. Simmer slowly for ½ hr. Put the contents of the saucepan through a blender, pour into soup plates, crumble the remaining amaretti on top and serve.

ZUPPA DI LENTICCHIE
(Lentil soup)

1 cup red lentils
3 bay leaves
salt
3 tbsp olive oil
¼ cup salt pork
15 roasted chestnuts
2–3 basil leaves and 1 pinch each of marjoram, rosemary and thyme
1 tbsp tomato paste
freshly ground pepper
8 slices coarse bread

Lightly boil the lentils with the bay leaves in 6¼ cups salted water until tender (about ¼ hr). Meanwhile, in a skillet over low heat, mix the oil with the finely chopped salt pork, chestnuts, basil, marjoram, rosemary and thyme. When the fat begins to color, dilute the tomato paste in a little warm water and add. Season with salt and pepper. Take the bay leaves out of the cooking liquid; add the contents of the skillet, stir well and simmer for a further ½ hr (but do not let the liquid reduce below 4½ cups). Place 2 slices of bread in each soup plate, cover with hot lentil soup and serve.

ZUPPA DI CARCIOFI
(Artichoke soup)

2 onions
4 tbsp olive oil
1 tbsp butter
10 small artichokes
salt
scant 4½ cups vegetable stock
¼ cup grated Parmesan cheese

Use small young artichokes for this recipe and if necessary remove the tough outer layer. Chop roughly. Heat the oil and butter in a saucepan, chop the onions and fry until transparent. Season with salt, and add the stock. Bring to a boil and simmer for 20 min. Purée in a blender, then strain the soup through a sieve and serve with the grated cheese.

ZUPPA DI ASPARAGI
(Asparagus soup)

1 bunch asparagus
3 onions
1 tbsp butter
4 tbsp olive oil
salt
9 cups vegetable stock
1 sprig parsley
½ cup Parmesan cheese
oven-toasted croûtons

Clean the asparagus and discard ¾ in from the bottom; cut off the tips and reserve. Gently fry the onion in a saucepan with the butter and the oil. When the onion is soft add the asparagus stalks and cook for 4–5 min. Season lightly with salt, add the stock and simmer for 2 hr. Put the contents of the saucepan through a sieve or blender and return the creamed soup to the saucepan. Add the asparagus tips, cook very slowly for 5 min and serve in soup plates with finely chopped parsley, fine slivers of Parmesan cheese and hot oven-toasted croûtons.

ZUPPA DI FINOCCHI *
(Fennel soup)

2 onions
4 tbsp olive oil
1 tbsp butter
6 heads fennel
salt
scant 4½ cups vegetable stock
¼ cup grated Parmesan cheese

Heat the oil and butter in a saucepan and fry the chopped onions until transparent. Clean and finely slice the fennel, add to the saucepan and stir for 2–3 min. Add salt and the stock, bring to a boil and simmer for 20 min. Put through a blender, garnish with chopped fennel leaves and serve in a tureen with Parmesan cheese.

Rice

*R*ice was unknown in Italy until it was introduced from Spain during the Renaissance. Yet in the short space of 500 years, it has become a staple and often irreplaceable food in Italian cuisine. This is borne out by the numerous rice dishes to be found in almost every region, from the fish, shellfish and crustacean varieties of the coast to the mushroom, game and truffle risottos of the interior. A subtle distinction once existed between "riso" and "risotto." The plain vegetable "riso" was rice that had been boiled in water and garnished with oil whereas the more elaborate first course "risotto" was made by first frying the rice briefly in fat and then boiling it in stock. The difference in the taste is, however, so small that the distinction has largely disappeared and we now often come across "riso" served as a first course or as an attractive salad dotted with colorful vegetables.

Italian rice dishes are made mainly with short-grain rice and tend to be very moist. The rice should be fried in butter or oil first and the liquid added gradually, allowing each addition to be absorbed before pouring in more. Stir continuously as the rice cooks. Like pasta, risotto rice should be cooked until al dente *(done, but still retaining some bite)*.

SFORMATO DI RISO BIANCO
(Savory rice mold)

generous ½ cup sweetbreads and
  brains
6¼ cups chicken stock
1¼ cups Arborio (risotto) rice
¼ cup butter
scant ½ cup flour
2 cups chicken stock
salt
pepper
1 tbsp butter
1¼ cups chicken livers
¼ cup butter
mushrooms, chopped
scant ¼ cup peas (fresh or frozen)
3 tbsp fresh breadcrumbs
grated Parmesan cheese

Soak the sweetbreads and brains in
cold water for 1–2 hr, to remove
all traces of blood. Drain, and place
in a saucepan with cold water.
Bring to a boil and drain again.
Cover with cold water once again,
bring to a boil and simmer for ¼
hr. Drain and set aside. Bring 6¼
cups stock to a boil, add the rice
and lightly boil for 15–20 min.
Meanwhile, make the sauce: Melt
the butter in a saucepan. When it
foams, add the flour and stir for 2
min. Add 2 cups hot stock slowly,
stirring until the sauce thickens.
Add the seasoning and butter.
  Sauté the chicken livers lightly in
butter. Add the mushrooms,
sweetbreads and brains. Blend
well. Add the peas, two-thirds of
the sauce and simmer very gently
for 10–15 min. Line a well buttered
ovenproof bowl with breadcrumbs.
Fill it with alternate layers of rice
and sauce dotted with grated
Parmesan. Place the bowl in a slow
oven preheated to 300°F just long
enough to warm through. Unmold
the rice on to a serving plate and
spoon round the chicken livers,
brains and sweetbreads. Pour any
remaining sauce over the rice.

MINESTRA DI RISO CON FAVE
(Rice soup with fava beans)

2¼ lb unshelled fava beans
1 onion
generous ¼ cup salt pork
3 very ripe tomatoes (or 3 tbsp
  tomato paste)
salt
freshly ground pepper
scant 1 cup Arborio (risotto) rice

Shell the beans and finely chop the
onion. Pound the salt pork and melt
in a saucepan. Add the onion and
fry gently for 3 min. Add the beans
and the juice from the sieved tomatoes (or 3 tbsp tomato paste diluted in 2 ladlefuls of boiling water).
Simmer for ¼ hr. Pour in scant 4½
cups water, season with salt and
pepper and bring to a boil. Add the
rice and boil until it is *al dente*.

SUPPLÌ
(Rice balls)

makes 20
1½ oz dried mushrooms
3 oz sweetbreads
1¾ cups Arborio (risotto) rice
1 generous cup tomato sauce (see
  p. 127)
⅓ cup butter
scant ½ cup grated Parmesan
  cheese
2 eggs
¼ onion
3 tbsp butter
1½ oz prosciutto
2 chicken livers
3 oz ground meat
1 tbsp tomato paste
salt
4 oz Mozzarella cheese
breadcrumbs
oil or lard for frying .

Leave the dried mushrooms to
swell in warm water for 2 hr. Soak
the sweetbreads in cold water for
1–2 hr, to remove all traces of
blood. Drain, place in a saucepan,
and cover with cold water. Bring to
a boil and drain. Cover with fresh
cold water, and bring to a boil a
second time. Drain. Place the rice
in a saucepan with the tomato
sauce and scant 4½ cups boiling
water. Cook, stirring from time to
time, until the rice is *al dente* (10-
15 min). Remove from the heat.
Add salt to taste, butter, grated
Parmesan and eggs. Amalgamate
well and set aside. Lightly sauté
the onion in butter until transparent. Chop the prosciutto, chick-
en livers, and sweetbreads and
stir. Add to the saucepan with the
ground meat. Drain the mushrooms, squeeze out the water by
hand, chop and add to the saucepan
with the tomato paste diluted in a
little warm water. Add salt and
simmer for about 20 min. When the
liquid has reduced and the filling is
ready, spread a handful of rice on
the palm of the hand, place a little
of the filling in the middle and dot
with Mozzarella. Enfold the filling
in the rice and form a large ball
about the size of a small orange.
Repeat until the ingredients are
used up. Roll each rice ball carefully in breadcrumbs. Fry the
supplì in hot oil, turning each one
until a crisp golden brown. Drain
on kitchen paper. Serve piping hot.

RISI E BISI *
(Rice with peas Venice style)

2 slices pancetta
1 sprig parsley
scant ¼ cup butter
1¾ cups tender new peas or petit
    pois
sugar
1 tsp meat extract
1 bouillon cube
generous 1 cup Arborio (risotto) rice
salt
freshly ground pepper
¼ cup grated Parmesan cheese

Chop the pancetta, parsley and onion and gently fry in a saucepan with half of the butter. Add the peas, 1 cup water and a pinch of sugar. Cook with the lid on for 5 min (or ¼ hr if large peas are used). Dissolve the meat extract and bouillon cube in scant 4½ cups hot water. Bring this liquid to a boil, add the rice and seasoning. When the rice is *al dente*, add the remaining butter and grated cheese. Blend thoroughly and serve. For a true "risi e bisi" the liquid should have reduced enough to provide a thick, almost glutinous consistency.

POLPETTINE DI RISO
(Rice rissoles with vegetables)

1¾ cups Arborio (risotto) rice
generous 1 cup grated Fontina
    cheese
¼ cup butter
¼ cup grated Parmesan cheese
2 egg yolks
3 tbsp flour
6 tbsp olive oil
1 carrot
1 turnip
1 celeriac
3–4 lettuce leaves
6¼ cups meat stock

Boil the rice in plenty of salted water until *al dente*. Dice the Fontina cheese and place in a large shallow dish. Drain the rice and lay it on top of the Fontina. Allow a minute or so for the cheese to melt, then mix with the rice. Add butter, grated Parmesan and the beaten egg yolks. Blend thoroughly. Make small nut-sized balls with the rice mixture. Roll the rice balls lightly on a floured board and fry in a skillet in hot oil until a light golden brown. Drain on kitchen paper. Clean and rinse the vegetables, finely slice the carrot, turnip and celeriac and shred the lettuce. Place the vegetables in a saucepan, cover with stock and bring to a boil. After 10 min, lower the heat and add the rissoles, giving them a few moments to warm through. Serve with grated Parmesan separately.

SARTÙ DI RISO ALLA NAPOLETANA
(Neapolitan rice timbale)

½ cup ground meat
3–4 tbsp fine breadcrumbs
6 tbsp grated Parmesan cheese
2 eggs
1 clove garlic
1 sprig parsley
salt
freshly ground pepper
olive oil
4 oz fresh mushrooms (or ¾ oz dried
    mushrooms)
2 small spicy sausages (combined
    weight 4 oz)
butter
4 oz chicken giblets
2 oz prosciutto
scant 1 cup peas
4 very ripe tomatoes
4 oz Mozzarella cheese
generous 1 cup Arborio (risotto) rice

Place the meat, 1 tbsp breadcrumbs, 3 tbsp grated Parmesan and 1 egg in a bowl with finely chopped garlic and parsley. Season with salt and pepper. Stir thoroughly with a wooden spoon. Form the mixture into olive-sized rissoles. Roll lightly in breadcrumbs, and fry in hot oil until golden brown. Remove with a slotted spoon.
Wash the mushrooms and dry thoroughly (if dried mushrooms are used, soak in warm water for 15 min and squeeze dry). Using the same oil, sauté the mushrooms. When they are well coated with oil, add a little salt and lower the heat. Cook for 10 min. Set aside.
Cut the sausage into thin rounds, sauté in a skillet for a few minutes and remove. Melt a piece of butter in the same pan, add the chopped giblets, a little salt and cook for 10 min. Set aside.
Cut the prosciutto into small strips, melt a little butter in a small casserole and sauté. Add the peas, a little water and salt and pepper. Simmer gently until the peas are done and the liquid has reduced (5 min). Remove from the heat. Put the sieved tomato in a saucepan with a little salt and 1 tbsp butter. Cook, uncovered, over moderate heat until the juice has thickened. Last of all, cut the Mozzarella in thin slices. Now all the ingredients are ready for the filling of this elaborate and delicious timbale.
Boil the rice in salted water until it is *al dente* (about 10 min). Drain and place in a shallow bowl. Using a wooden spoon, carefully stir in the tomato gravy, the remaining egg and the grated Parmesan. Line a soufflé dish with butter, sprinkle the sides and bottom lightly with breadcrumbs, saving a few for later. When the rice is almost cold, put a little aside and pile the rest into the soufflé dish. Distribute the rice evenly against the sides leaving a hollow in the middle. Fill the hollow with the rissoles, mushroom, sausage, giblets, peas and Mozzarella slices. Cover with the remaining rice, sprinkle with breadcrumbs and dot with butter. Bake in a preheated oven at 350°F until a golden brown crust has formed (about ¾ hr). Remove and leave to stand for 10 min. Insert a spatula around the edge of the timbale and turn out on to a serving platter.

RISOTTO ALLA ROSSINI
(Rice with mushrooms and tomatoes)

4 mushroom caps (use porcini)
6 tbsp butter
4 ripe tomatoes
salt
¼ cup beef bone marrow
1½ cups Arborio (risotto) rice
6¼ cups meat stock
2 egg yolks
scant ½ cup grated Parmesan
    cheese

Clean and chop the mushrooms. Place in a skillet with half the butter. Add the peeled and quartered tomatoes, season with salt, cover and cook slowly for 20 min. Chop the bone marrow and fry gently with the rest of the butter in a saucepan. Add the rice and stir until the fat is absorbed. Pour in 2 ladlefuls of boiling stock. As the liquid is absorbed, add more stock in small amounts, stirring the rice continually with a wooden spoon.

and immediately stir in the remaining butter, ¼ cup grated Parmesan (or mixed Parmesan and Pecorino if a sharper flavor is desired) and 1 egg to bind the mixture. Shape the rice into large croquettes, the size of a small orange. Make a hole in each croquette with your finger and fill it with a little of the meat and pea stuffing. Close the hole and restore the shape. Beat the remaining egg on a plate. Dip each croquette in the egg, then roll it in breadcrumbs. Heat plenty of oil or lard in a skillet until bubbling and brown the croquettes until nut-colored. Drain on kitchen paper and serve hot. Serve with tomato sauce (p. 127) if desired.

RISOTTO DI GAMBERI
(Rice with saltwater crayfish)

14 oz saltwater crayfish
1 clove garlic
½ onion
½ cup olive oil
1½ cups Arborio (risotto) rice
½ cup dry white wine
salt
freshly ground pepper
2–3 sprigs parsley
1 tbsp butter

Wash the saltwater crayfish and boil in water for 5 min to make them easy to shell. Peel and finely chop the garlic and onion and place in a large saucepan. Lightly fry in oil for a few minutes, stirring with a wooden spoon. Add the rice, stir and turn in the oil until the grains are soaked. Raise the heat, pour in the wine and let it evaporate. Add the shelled crayfish, season with salt and pepper to taste. Add small amounts of water as the rice absorbs the liquid and keep stirring until the rice is *al dente*. Add finely chopped parsley and butter, remove from the heat, stir well and serve.

POMODORI RIPIENI DI RISO
(Stuffed tomatoes)

4 large tomatoes
scant ½ cup Arborio (risotto) rice
6 tbsp olive oil
freshly ground pepper

After 10 min add the mushrooms, tomatoes and remaining stock. After 5 min remove from the heat. The rice should be *al dente* and have a thick, moist consistency. Fold in the egg yolks and grated Parmesan with quick movements to prevent the yolks hardening. Cover, leave for 2 min then serve, with additional grated Parmesan if desired.

INSALATA DI RISO E FRUTTI DI MARE
(Rice and shellfish salad)

1 carrot
1 stick celery
1 clove garlic
1 sprig parsley
½ onion
salt
scant 1 cup shrimp
4 razor clams
1¼ cups Arborio (risotto) rice
1 lemon
salt
½ cup oil
freshly ground pepper

Coarsely chop the carrot, celery, garlic, parsley and onion. Place in a saucepan with plenty of salted water and bring to a boil. Rinse the shrimp and razor clams under running water. When the water is boiling, add the shrimp and razor clams and simmer for ¼ hr. Drain and save the cooking water. Shell and finely chop the shrimp. Leave the razor clams whole and set aside with the shrimp. Bring the cooking water back to a boil, add the rice and boil until it is *al dente*. Drain and cool. Place the rice in a shallow bowl with the juice of ½ a lemon, salt, oil, plenty of pepper and the shrimp. Mix thoroughly. Make 4 servings, each garnished at the center with 1 slice of lemon and 1 razor clam.

ARANCINI DI RISO
(Rice croquettes)

scant ¼ cup butter
3 tbsp oil
½ small onion

---

scant ½ cup ground meat (veal, pork, beef or a mixture)
scant 1 cup tender new peas or petit pois
salt
freshly ground pepper
2 ripe tomatoes
scant 1 cup Arborio (risotto) rice
stock
grated Parmesan or Pecorino cheese
2 eggs
fine fresh breadcrumbs
oil or lard for frying

Sieve the tomatoes and reserve the pulp. Melt half the butter with the oil in a saucepan. When the fat begins to foam, add the finely chopped onion and fry gently until transparent. Add the meat, peas, salt and pepper to taste and the tomato pulp. Cover and cook over low heat, stirring often, until a thick, moist consistency is obtained. Put the rice in a separate saucepan with about 2 ladlefuls of boiling stock. Boil lightly, adding more stock if necessary, until the rice is *al dente*. Remove from the heat

3 tbsp grated Parmesan cheese
1 clove garlic
6 anchovy fillets
generous 1 tbsp capers
1 sprig parsley
3–4 basil leaves
salt

Slice the top off each tomato to form a lid and scoop out the seeds. Put the seeds through a sieve and save the juice. Boil the rice in plenty of salted water for about 10 min and drain. Add the tomato juice, 3 tbsp olive oil, pepper, grated Parmesan and the finely chopped garlic, anchovy, capers, parsley and basil. Mix well. Brush the inside of the tomatoes with salt, fill with the rice mixture and replace the tops. Space the tomatoes well apart in a baking pan with the remaining oil and 1 cup water. Bake in a slow preheated oven at 280°F for ½ hr.

PANISSA DI VERCELLI
(Rice with sausage and beans Vercelli style)

generous ½ cup borlotti beans
3½ oz pork rind
3 tbsp olive oil
1 tbsp butter
1 cup pork sausage meat
¼ cup salt pork or lard
1 onion
1¼ cups Arborio (risotto) rice
freshly ground pepper
salt
grated Parmesan cheese

Soak the beans in water overnight. Drain, and boil the beans with the pork rind in 4½ cups water for about 1 hr until tender. Reserve the water. Finely chop the onion and place in a large saucepan with the oil, butter, sausage meat and salt pork or lard. Fry gently, stirring with a wooden spoon, until the onion is transparent. Add the rice, and stir to coat the grains with the fat. Pour 1 ladleful of the hot bean water over the rice. Add a little more bean water when it is absorbed and repeat until the rice is nearly done. Mix in the beans and pepper. Add salt if necessary. When the rice is al dente, remove from the heat, add the grated cheese, stir well and serve immediately.

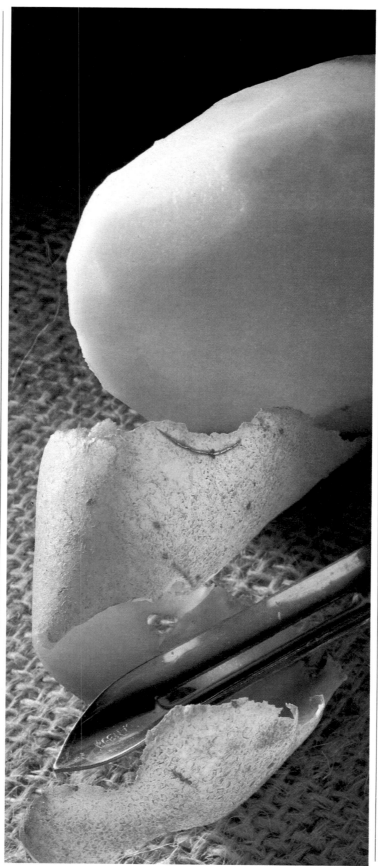

RISOTTO COI CARCIOFI
(Artichoke risotto)

6 young artichokes
1 lemon
4½ cups meat stock
2 oz prosciutto
¼ cup butter
1¼ cups Arborio (risotto) rice
salt
freshly ground pepper
1 sprig parsley
6 tbsp grated Parmesan cheese

Discard the outer leaves of the artichokes and cut off the hard tips. Slice the hearts in half vertically and plunge in water acidulated with the juice of 1 lemon to preserve their color. Heat the stock. Chop the prosciutto and fry gently with the butter in a saucepan. After 2–3 min add the drained artichokes with 1 ladleful of the hot stock. Simmer uncovered for about 10 min or until the liquid has almost all evaporated. Add the rice, stir and coat the grains in the artichoke juice with a wooden spoon. Add hot stock in small amounts as the rice absorbs it. Season with salt and pepper to taste. When the rice is al dente, add the finely chopped parsley and grated cheese. Remove from the heat, stir well and serve at once.

RISO E PATATE
(Rice with potatoes)

6¼ cups meat stock
3 tbsp olive oil
1 onion
4 oz ham
14 oz potatoes
salt
1 cup Arborio (risotto) rice
1 sprig parsley
grated Parmesan cheese

Heat the stock and keep hot. Chop the onion and the fat part of the ham. Place in a saucepan with the oil and sauté lightly until the onion is a pale brown. Dice the potatoes, cut the remaining ham in strips, add to the pan and stir. Add half of the hot stock and boil, covered, until the potatoes are cooked. Pour in the remaining stock and adjust the seasoning. Bring to a boil, add the rice and cook until it is al dente.

Add finely chopped parsley and mix well. Remove from the heat and serve piping hot with grated cheese.

RISO IN BRODO CON FEGATINI
(Rice with chicken livers)

6¼ cups chicken stock
generous 1 cup Arborio (risotto) rice
salt
6 chicken livers
¼ cup butter

Bring the stock to a boil in a saucepan. Add the rice, and boil briskly so that the grains do not stick. Do not cover. Season to taste. Clean the chicken livers, remove any yellowish traces and rinse thoroughly. Drain and chop the livers, sauté in butter for a few minutes and add to the saucepan just before the rice is cooked. Mix thoroughly, remove from the heat and serve piping hot.

RISO E FAGIOLI ALLA FIORENTINA
(Florentine rice and beans)

1½ lb unshelled Navy beans
salt
¼ cup salt pork or lard
½ cup oil
1 sprig parsley
1 medium onion
1 small carrot
1 stick celery
2 cloves garlic
1 small piece red chili pepper
14 oz ripe tomatoes
1 cup Arborio (risotto) rice

Shell and rinse the beans. Boil in a saucepan with 9 cups water for 2 hr. Add salt only when the beans are almost cooked (otherwise the skins become tough). Peel and finely chop the onion and garlic; chop the parsley, carrot and celery and the chili pepper. Peel and seed the tomatoes. Pound the fat or cut it with a hot knife, then place in a separate pan with the oil and gently fry the parsley, onion, carrot, celery, garlic, the chili pepper and tomatoes. Stir well, cover and simmer over low heat for 15–20 min. Sieve the vegetables if a smooth texture is desired or add them as they are to the cooked beans; stir well, adjust the seasoning and simmer for another 4–5 min. Add the rice to the saucepan with the beans and lightly boil until al dente. Remove from the heat, stir well and serve. If preferred the rice can be omitted and the beans eaten as a soup, garnished with croûtons crisped in the oven.

RISO ALLA PARMIGIANA
(Rice Parma style)

¼ cup butter
½ onion
1¼ cups Arborio (risotto) rice
scant 4½ cups meat stock (lightly salted)
⅓ cup grated Parmesan cheese
salt

Finely chop the onion. Put two-thirds of the butter in a saucepan and gently fry the onion until transparent. Add the rice, turn and stir in the fat for a few minutes, using a wooden spoon. Add 2 ladlefuls of boiling stock, simmer and continue stirring until the liquid has been absorbed. Replenish with more stock, stirring all the time, until the rice is done. Add the grated cheese and remaining butter, adjust the seasoning and blend thoroughly. Remove from the heat and serve immediately.

RISOTTO COI TARTUFI
(Rice with truffles)

1 small onion
¼ cup butter
1¼ cups Arborio (risotto) rice
scant 4½ cups meat stock
1 white (or black) truffle
scant ¼ cup grated Parmesan cheese

The success of this dish depends on the perfect balance of cheese and truffle flavors. Take care that the Parmesan does not overpower the more subtle taste of the truffle.

Finely chop the onion and gently fry in a saucepan with half of the butter until transparent. Add the rice and stir until the grains are coated with the butter. Pour in a little hot stock and add a little more each time the liquid is absorbed, stirring the rice all the time. When the rice is al dente, add the remaining butter, blend well and remove from the heat. Arrange the rice on a hot platter and sprinkle with thinly cut flakes of truffle and a handful of grated cheese.

RISOTTO CON LA ZUCCA *
(Pumpkin risotto)

1 pumpkin weighing approx. 1 lb
½ onion
6 tbsp olive oil
1¼ cups Arborio (risotto) rice
1 tsp meat extract
salt
freshly ground pepper
grated Parmesan cheese

Clean the pumpkin, remove the skin, seeds and membrane and cut the flesh into small cubes. In a large saucepan, cook the pumpkin and the finely chopped onion with the oil over low heat for 5 min, stirring with a wooden spoon. Have 6¼ cups boiling water ready. Add the water to the pumpkin 1 ladleful at a time as the liquid reduces. When the pumpkin is half cooked, add the rice and the meat extract. Season with a little salt. Keep adding boiling water, stirring continuously, until the rice is al dente. Season with a little pepper if desired, remove from the heat and add the grated cheese, blending thoroughly. This risotto should have a rather creamy texture. Serve immediately.

RISO CON LE RANE
(Rice with frogs' legs)

8 oz frogs' legs
½ onion
1 stick celery
1 tbsp butter
1 tbsp oil
scant 4½ cups meat stock
generous 1 cup Arborio (risotto) rice
salt
1 sprig parsley

Wash the frogs' legs. Finely chop the onion and celery and gently fry in a large saucepan with butter and oil until transparent. Add the frogs' legs and cook gently for a few minutes. Pour in the hot stock, bring to a boil and add the rice. Simmer, stirring often, for 10 min or until the rice is *al dente*. Remove from the heat, check the seasoning and sprinkle with chopped parsley.

RISO ALLA PILOTA
(Rice with sausage Mantua style)

scant 4½ cups water
salt
1¼ cups Arborio (risotto) rice
4 oz spicy sausage
¼ cup butter
pinch of nutmeg
pinch of cinnamon
generous ¼ cup grated Parmesan
* cheese*

Fill a large saucepan with 4½ cups salted water and bring to a boil. Pour in the rice through a spout or a folded piece of paper so that it makes a hill in the center. The tips of the rice grains should be just above the water level. If not, take out some of the water with a ladle. Boil, uncovered, for 5 min. Remove from the heat. Shake the saucepan to settle the rice, cover with a teacloth folded in four, then put the lid on; on top of that place a heavy cloth or folded towel, so that the rice goes on cooking in its own heat, away from a direct flame, for 25 min (alternatively, if you are using an ovenproof casserole,

place with the lid on in a preheated oven at the lowest temperature for 18–20 min). When it is cooked, the rice should be barely moist. While the rice is cooking, remove the sausage skin, grind or cut the sausage into small pieces and fry in butter for a few minutes. Add a pinch of nutmeg and cinnamon and a little salt if necessary. Combine the sausage and the butter it has cooked in with the rice, add the grated cheese, mix well and serve.

RISOTTO CON L'ANGUILLA
(Rice with eel)

1 medium eel
generous 1 tbsp butter
6 tbsp olive oil
1 onion
1¼ cups Arborio (risotto) rice
1 bouillon cube
½ tsp meat extract
salt
freshly gound pepper
1 sprig parsley

This dish is a specialty of the Veneto region. Clean and wash the eel thoroughly, leaving the skin on. Cut into thickish slices and place in a saucepan with the butter and oil. Finely chop the onion and add to the saucepan. Brown for a few minutes. Cover the pan and cook over low heat for 1 hr, adding small amounts of boiling water to thin the sauce as it reduces. Remove the eel slices and set aside. Strain the eel sauce and pour it into a sauce-

pan with the rice. Cover the rice with a little stock prepared from the bouillon cube and meat extract diluted in approx. 5 cups boiling water. As the liquid reduces add small amounts of hot stock, stirring, until the rice is *al dente*. Season with salt and pepper to taste. Skin the eel, remove the vertebrae and add the flesh to the rice. Stir well and serve with finely chopped parsley.

RISOTTO NERO ALLE SEPPIE *
(Rice and cuttlefish)

1¾ lb cuttlefish
½ onion
1 clove garlic
1 sprig parsley
oil
½ cup dry white wine
scant 4½ cups fish stock or water
1¼ cups Arborio (risotto) rice
salt
freshly ground pepper

Rinse the cuttlefish, and remove the tentacles and head; remove the ink sacs from the head and reserve. Discard the head tentacles and all internal organs. Remove the cuttlebone from the tail and discard. Wash again, and cut into thin strips. Finely chop the onion, garlic and parsley, place in a large saucepan and lightly sauté in hot oil. Add the cuttlefish and cook in the saucepan juices for a few minutes. Add the wine and the ink from some of the ink sacs. Cook over low heat, adding a little stock if necessary. After about 20 min, pour in the rice and as it absorbs the liquid, keep it fluid with small amounts of fish stock or water until it is *al dente*. Add more salt if required and add plenty of pepper. Remove from the heat, mix thoroughly and serve at once. The rice should be moist enough to slide to the edge of the plate.

RISOTTO ALLA MILANESE
(Saffron rice Milan style)

1 onion
¼ cup butter
1 small piece beef bone marrow

½ cup dry white wine (or red wine)
1¼ cups Arborio (risotto) rice
4½ cups meat stock
1 sachet saffron
scant ¼ cup grated Parmesan cheese

Finely chop the onion and place with half of the butter and the bone marrow in a large saucepan. Fry gently until the onion is transparent. Pour in the wine and simmer briskly. When the wine has evaporated, add the rice and stir until the grains are coated with the pan juices. Add two ladlefuls of boiling stock. Add two more when the liquid has been absorbed. Keep stirring the rice and moistening it with stock. After about 10 min, dissolve the saffron in a little stock and pour over the rice, mixing thoroughly. When the rice is *al dente*, add the remaining butter and the grated cheese. Remove from the heat, mix well and leave to stand with the lid on for 2–3 min before serving.

RISOTTO CON GLI ASPARAGI
(Asparagus risotto)

2¼ lb asparagus
salt
1 onion
scant ¼ cup butter
1¼ cups Arborio (risotto) rice
½ cup dry white wine
1 bouillon cube
½ tsp meat extract
freshly ground pepper
grated Parmesan cheese
1 tbsp butter

Soak and rinse the asparagus. Cut off the tips and put aside. Boil the stalks in lightly salted water. When tender, press the stalks through a sieve and return the pulp to the cooking water. Keep hot. Finely chop the onion. Melt the butter in a saucepan and gently fry the onion and the asparagus tips for a few minutes. Add the rice, mixing and turning with a wooden spoon until the grains are coated in the fat. Pour the wine over the rice, raise the heat and boil briskly until the wine has evaporated. Dilute the bouillon cube and the meat extract in the hot asparagus water. Add a

little of the liquid to the rice, lower the heat, stir and add more liquid as it reduces, until the rice is *al dente*. Adjust the seasoning if necessary, glaze the rice with 1 tbsp butter and add the grated cheese. Stir well and serve immediately.

RISOTTO ALLA CERTOSINA
(Rice with shrimp and wine)

1 lb shrimp

1 onion
½ cup oil
1 clove garlic
1 carrot
1 stick celery
1 sprig parsley
2 cups ripe or canned tomatoes
salt
freshly ground pepper
¼ cup butter
½ cup dry white wine
2 cups Arborio (risotto) rice

Wash the shrimp thoroughly. Peel and finely chop the garlic and half of

RISOTTO AI FUNGHI
(Mushroom risotto)

1 small onion
¼ cup butter
9 oz porcini (cèpes)
scant 1 cup dry white wine
1¼ cups Arborio (risotto) rice
scant 4½ cups meat stock
salt
freshly ground pepper
scant ¼ cup grated Parmesan
  cheese

Chop and gently fry the onion in a saucepan with half of the butter until transparent. Clean and chop the mushrooms, add to the pan and stir. Pour in the wine, let it evaporate a little then add the rice, mixing and turning the grains until coated in the juices. Add 2 ladlefuls of hot stock and as it reduces add more, a little at a time, to keep the rice moist. When the rice is *al dente* (10–15 min), remove from the heat, season with salt and pepper, add the remaining butter and the grated cheese and mix thoroughly. Cover and let stand for 3 min. Serve accompanied by more grated Parmesan if desired.

RISOTTO ALLA
VALTELLINESE
(Cabbage and bean risotto)

generous 1 cup dried borlotti beans
salt
8 oz cabbage
1¾ cups Arborio (risotto) rice
2–3 sage leaves
generous ¼ cup butter
¼ cup grated Parmesan cheese

Wash the beans and soak overnight in water. Drain. Cook the beans in boiling water for 1 hr or until tender, adding salt to taste and more water if necessary. Drain and keep hot. Rinse the cabbage and remove the stalks and the central rib of the leaves. Plunge the leaves into boiling water for a few minutes, drain and shred. Bring 9 cups salted water to a boil, pour in the rice and simmer briskly for 5 min. Add the cabbage, continue simmering for another ¼ hr, then add the beans and stir. Drain and arrange the risotto on a serving dish. In a small saucepan sauté the sage leaves in butter until they are a nut color. Discard the leaves, pour the flavored butter over the rice and serve with grated Parmesan cheese.

RISOTTO CON LE ZUCCHINE
(Rice with zucchini)

¾ lb zucchini
¼ cup butter
2 oz pancetta
1 clove garlic
1 small onion
2–3 sprigs parsley
salt
1½ cups Arborio (risotto) rice
scant 4½ cups stock
freshly ground pepper
grated Parmesan cheese

Clean the zucchini and slice finely. Melt the butter in a saucepan. Chop pancetta, garlic and onion and sauté in the butter until the onion is a light gold color. Remove the garlic and add the zucchini and the chopped parsley. Cook over low heat until the zucchini are tender. Add a little salt and then the rice, stirring the grains thoroughly to coat in the fat. Add 2 ladlefuls of boiling stock and keep stirring and adding stock in small amounts as the rice absorbs it, until the rice is *al dente* (10–15 min). Remove from the heat, adjust the salt to taste, add the pepper and the grated cheese, mix well and allow to stand, covered, for 2–3 min before serving.

RISO E VONGOLE ALLA
VENETA
(Rice with clams Veneto style)

2¼ lb clams
1 clove garlic
½ cup olive oil
¾ lb ripe tomatoes
4 anchovy fillets
salt
freshly ground pepper
1¾ cups Arborio (risotto) rice
basil leaves
parsley

Rinse the clams and if it is necessary to remove sand from them, place a bowl upside down in a deep

the onion, the carrot, celery and parsley. Place in a large saucepan and sauté lightly in the oil. Add the shrimp and mix well. Peel and sieve the tomatoes and add to the saucepan with salt and pepper. Pour in approx. 4½ cups hot water and bring to a boil. After 10 min, remove, drain and shell the shrimp, reserving the stock. Set aside half of the shelled shrimp. Mash the remaining shrimp in a mortar, press through a sieve and return the pulp to the stock. Cut the remaining half onion into fine slices and gently fry in a large saucepan with half of the butter.

Pour in the wine and allow to evaporate. Add the rice and coat the grains in butter. Pour in two ladlefuls of the reheated stock. Simmer, stirring the rice and adding more stock as the rice absorbs the liquid. After 8–10 min, when the rice is half cooked, put in the whole shrimp and stir. Remove from the heat when the rice is *al dente*, stir in the remaining butter and leave to stand, covered, for 3 min before serving.

saucepan. Put the clams on top of the bowl and cover with water. Leave to soak so that the sand will be freed from the clams and sink to the bottom of the saucepan. After about 2 hr, pick out the clams with care, disturbing the water as little as possible. Steam the clams in a covered saucepan (no water is needed as they will cook in their own moisture). As soon as the shells are open, remove from the heat. Remove the clams from their shells and set aside. Sieve the liquid left in the saucepan and reserve it for the sauce.

Fry the finely chopped garlic in a

saucepan with the oil. Peel, seed and chop the tomatoes. Add to the saucepan together with the anchovy fillets. Season with a little salt and plenty of pepper. When the tomato starts to boil, add the clam juice previously set aside. Simmer briskly for 20 min or until the sauce has thickened. Add the clams, remove from the heat and keep warm. Boil the rice in 9 cups salted water until it is *al dente*. Drain, place in a tureen and pour on the hot clam and tomato sauce. Serve garnished with finely chopped basil and parsley.

RISOTTO ALLA BOLOGNESE
(Rice with Bolognese sauce)

2 oz pancetta
2 oz ham
¼ cup butter
1¼ cups Arborio (risotto) rice
1 cup dry white wine
4½ cups stock
6 tbsp meat sauce (p. 129) or tomato sauce (p. 127)
salt
freshly ground pepper
¾ cup grated Parmesan cheese
1 medium truffle

Cut the pancetta and the ham into small pieces; place in a saucepan with just over half of the butter and gently fry until softened. Add the rice and cook for 5 min, mixing and turning it so that the grains are coated in the fat. Pour in the wine, allow it to evaporate for a minute or two, then add 1 ladleful stock. Stir the rice continuously, over low heat, and when the stock has been absorbed add more, a little at a time as it reduces, until the rice is *al dente*. Add the meat or tomato sauce and blend with the rice before removing from the heat. Adjust the seasoning, stir in the rest of the butter and the grated cheese and sprinkle the top with fine slices of truffle before serving.

CRESPELLE DI RISO ALLA BENEDETTINA
(Sweet fried rice balls)

3 cups milk
salt
1 cup pudding rice
grated peel of 1 small orange or
    lemon
½ tsp baking powder
plain flour
oil
1 tbsp confectioners' sugar
pinch of cinnamon

Put the milk in a saucepan with 2 cups water and a little salt. Bring to a boil, add the rice and cook until all the liquid has been absorbed and the rice is very tender. Cool, then add the grated peel and the baking powder and let stand for ½ hr. Form the mixture into small balls the size of walnuts. Heat plenty of oil in a skillet. Roll the rice balls in flour and fry in the hot oil until a golden brown. Remove with a slotted spoon and dry on kitchen paper. Arrange the rice balls on a serving plate, dust with confectioners' sugar mixed with a little cinnamon and serve at once.

RISOTTO ALLA SARDA *
(Sardinian rice)

4 oz pork
4 oz veal
¼ cup salt pork or ½ cup oil
½ onion
½ cup red wine
8 oz very ripe tomatoes
½ tsp saffron
salt
freshly ground pepper
1 tbsp butter
1¼ cups Arborio (risotto) rice
scant 4½ cups meat stock or 1
    bouillon cube diluted in the same
    amount of water
¼ cup grated Pecorino cheese

Cut the pork and veal into very small dice; pound the salt pork, slice the onion into thin rings and gently fry in a shallow saucepan. Add the meat and fry until it has browned, then pour in the wine and allow to evaporate uncovered. Plunge the tomatoes for just a few seconds into boiled water to split the skins; peel and remove the seeds. Chop the tomatoes coarsely, add to the meat together with the saffron, a little salt and plenty of pepper. Mix thoroughly, cover and simmer until the sauce thickens. Melt the butter in a large saucepan. When it begins to foam, add the rice and mix the grains in the butter with a wooden spoon for 3–4 min. Pour in the thickened meat sauce and simmer briskly, stirring often and adding small amounts of boiling stock to keep the rice moist. When the rice is *al dente*, turn off the heat, add the grated Pecorino (use Parmesan if a less pungent flavor is preferred) and more pepper. Stir well and serve.

RISOTTO AL SALTO
(Rice cake)

This is an ideal way to use up rice leftovers. Butter a skillet and heat over moderate heat. When the butter is hot, add the cooked rice and pat it into the shape of a cake. Let it fry, shaking the pan now and again to prevent the rice from sticking, until a light golden crust has formed on the underside. Turn the rice and similarly crisp the other side. The same result can be obtained by putting the rice in a lightly buttered nonstick oven pan, baking in a preheated oven at 400°F for 5–10 min, until the top has a golden crust. Cut like cake and serve each portion with a topping of grated Parmesan cheese.

PEPERONI FARCITI ALLA TORINESE
(Stuffed peppers Turin style)

4 large peppers (green or yellow)
⅔ cup Arborio (risotto) rice
salt
8 anchovy fillets
1 tbsp butter
6 tbsp olive oil
1 clove garlic
1 sprig parsley

Cut the peppers in half and cut off a small piece from the bottom to leave a flat base. Remove the seeds and pith. Plunge in boiling hot water for 2–3 min. This will split the skins and make them easy to peel. Cook the rice in boiling salted water for approximately 10 min. Meanwhile cut the anchovy fillets in small pieces and finely chop the garlic. Place in a skillet with the butter, 1 tbsp olive oil and cook over low heat, prodding now and then with a fork to make the anchovies break up. When it is *al dente*, drain the rice and stir in 2 tbsp oil and a sprinkling of chopped parsley. Spoon the rice into the peppers, put them in an oiled ovenproof pan and sprinkle them with the anchovy sauce. Bake in a preheated oven at 350°F for ½ hr. These stuffed peppers may be eaten hot or cold.

RISOTTO CON I FINOCCHI
(Fennel risotto)

¾ lb small tender fennel
generous ¼ cup butter
1 onion
1¼ cups Arborio (risotto) rice
scant 4½ cups stock
grated Parmesan cheese

Clean the fennel, discard the fibrous outer leaves, rinse and cut into fine slices. Finely chop the onion and fry slowly in a saucepan with two-thirds of the butter. Add the fennel, raise the heat and sauté until a golden brown. Pour in the rice, cook in small amounts of boiling stock, stirring continually and adding the liquid as it reduces. When the rice is *al dente*, add plenty of grated Parmesan and the remaining butter. Cover, keep over low heat for 2–3 min and serve.

RISOTTO ALLA TOSCANA
(Tuscan-style risotto)

½ onion
1 small carrot
1 stick celery
3 tbsp olive oil
generous ¼ cup butter
4 oz ground lean beef
3 oz chopped veal or sheep's kidneys
3 oz chopped calf's liver
1 chicken liver
½ cup red wine
1 tbsp tomato paste
salt
freshly ground pepper
pinch of nutmeg
1½ cups Arborio (risotto) rice
scant 4½ cups meat stock
1 tbsp butter
generous ¼ cup grated Parmesan cheese

Fry the chopped onion, carrot and celery in oil and butter until a light color. In the same saucepan brown the beef thoroughly and then the kidneys and liver. Pour in the wine, let it reduce, then add tomato paste diluted in a little hot stock. Season with salt, plenty of pepper and a pinch of nutmeg. Cover and simmer for ½ hr. Add the rice, coat it in the fat, then add the stock little by little, stirring continually.

When the rice is *al dente* and the consistency slightly runny, remove from heat, add the butter and the grated cheese. Cover, let stand for 2 min and serve.

RISOTTO ALLA CHIOGGIOTTA
(Fish risotto)

½ onion
1 clove garlic
3 tbsp olive oil
generous 2 tbsp butter
generous 1 lb sprats or whitebait
salt
1¼ cups Arborio (risotto) rice
½ cup dry white wine
freshly ground pepper
1 sprig parsley

Fry the chopped onion and garlic in a saucepan with the oil and half of the butter. Wash and drain the fish, add to the saucepan, season and cover. After ¼ hr, put everything through a sieve and dilute the pulp with a little boiling salted water. Fry the rice in the remaining butter, constantly stirring and turning the grains. Add the fish broth a little at a time and cook for about ¼ hr. When the rice is *al dente*, add the wine, plenty of pepper and sprinkle with parsley.

RISOTTO DI GAMBERETTI
(Rice with shrimp)

4 oz small shrimp
4 oz jumbo shrimp
¼ onion
1 clove garlic
6 tbsp olive oil
salt
freshly ground pepper
2 cups dry white wine
¼ cup butter
1¼ cups Arborio (risotto) rice
scant 4½ cups fish stock (see p. 131)

Wash the shrimp, remove the heads and leave the tails intact. Lightly brown the chopped onion and garlic in a saucepan with ¼ cup oil. Add the shrimp tails, season with salt and pepper and fry gently for 1–2 min. Pour in the wine; simmer for 10 min. Set aside and keep warm. Melt the butter in a

separate saucepan; add the rice, mixing and turning so that the grains absorb the butter. Pour in a little boiling fish stock. Keep stirring the rice and adding small amounts of fish stock alternated with the shrimp broth, until the rice is *al dente*. Stir in 1 tbsp oil, which will glaze the rice and give it a smooth texture. Pile on to a warmed serving dish and garnish with the shrimp.

RISOTTO ALL'UOVO
(Rice with creamed egg)

scant 4½ cups meat stock
generous ¼ cup butter
1¼ cups Arborio (risotto) rice
4 egg yolks
1 cup light cream
¼ cup grated Parmesan cheese
pinch of nutmeg

Have hot meat stock ready. Melt the butter in a saucepan. Add the rice and stir well while it absorbs the fat. Adding the hot stock a little at a time, boil the rice, keeping it moist and stirring constantly, until it is *al dente*. Lower the heat and glaze the rice with the remaining butter. Mix the yolks, the cream, the grated cheese and the nutmeg in a blender. Carefully fold the egg mixture into the rice, holding the saucepan off the heat. Let stand for 2 min and serve in soup plates with more grated Parmesan cheese on top.

RISO CON RICOTTA
(Rice with ricotta cheese)

generous 1 lb peeled tomatoes
1 onion
1 stick celery
1 carrot
3–4 basil leaves
salt
1 tbsp oil
scant ½ cup ground lean veal
1¼ cups Arborio (risotto) rice
4 oz ricotta cheese
2 eggs
1 Mozzarella cheese
pinch of nutmeg
¼ cup grated Parmesan cheese
¼ cup butter

Simmer the tomatoes in a saucepan with the finely chopped onion, celery, carrot and basil. When the vegetables are soft, put the mixture through a vegetable mill or blender and return to the saucepan. Add a little salt and oil and reduce the heat. While the sauce is thickening, form the ground veal into small balls. Add the meat balls to the saucepan to cook in the sauce. Boil the rice in plenty of salted water until it is *al dente*. Drain, turn the rice with a wooden fork and when it has cooled, add the ricotta, the beaten eggs, the diced Mozzarella, the nutmeg, a little tomato sauce and the grated Parmesan. Put the rice in a well buttered ovenproof bowl. Place in an oven preheated to 350°F. After 5 min, turn out on to a serving plate and arrange the meat balls and the remaining tomato sauce around the base.

RISO ALLA PUGLIESE *
(Rice Apulia style)

10 oz fresh mussels
3 tbsp olive oil
1 clove garlic
7 oz fresh sardines
2 onions
1 potato
3 tbsp peeled tomatoes
½ tsp saffron
salt
1¼ cups Arborio (risotto) rice
4½ cups fish stock (see p. 131)
1 egg yolk
¼ cup tomato sauce (see p. 127)
1 green pepper
black olives
1 sprig parsley

Wash and scrub the mussels under running cold water until free of grit. Remove beards and barnacles and discard any that do not close when tapped sharply. Dry the shells, rub them with oil and garlic and cook in a skillet until they open. Discard any that are closed. Remove the molluscs from the shells, filter the mussel juice through a muslin cloth and set aside. Scale, wash and fillet the sardines and chop. Slice the onions and potato. Heat 1 tbsp olive oil in a flameproof casserole; add the sliced onions and brown; add the sliced potato, chopped sardines and the tomatoes. Let them soak in the onion and fat. Mix the saffron in the mussel juice; add to the casserole with a little salt. Gently simmer until the broth has reduced a little. Add the mussels and the rice. Cover with the hot fish stock and place in a preheated oven (350°F) for 15–18 min or until the rice is tender and moist. Remove from the oven, mix with a drop of olive oil and the beaten egg yolk. Place the rice in a serving dish, and and garnish with a ring of tomato sauce interspersed with small pieces of pepper, olive and parsley.

RISOTTO CON RADICCHIO ROSSO
(Rice with radicchio)

1 onion
scant ½ cup butter
3¼ oz smoked pancetta
1¼ lb radicchio
1 sprig parsley
salt
freshly ground pepper
1¼ cups Arborio (risotto) rice
1 cup red wine
scant 4½ cups stock
grated Parmesan cheese

Heat half of the butter in a saucepan and gently fry the chopped onion. Dice the pancetta and add to the saucepan. Wash and drain the radicchio; shred the leaves, add to the saucepan with chopped parsley, salt and pepper to taste and cook over low heat for 20 min. Melt the remaining butter in a large saucepan. Add the rice and mix it with the butter for 1–2 min. Pour in the wine and let it reduce. Add the stock, a little at a time, until the rice is *al dente*. Mix the radicchio leaves and the grated cheese into the rice and serve.

RISOTTO AL FONDO BRUNO *
(Rice with thickened meat stock)

1 onion
generous ¼ cup butter
scant 2 cups Arborio (risotto) rice
6¼ cups meat stock
salt
scant ½ cup grated Parmesan cheese
¼ cup fondo bruno (see p. 131)

Gently fry the chopped onion with half the butter. Add the rice, mix it in the butter for 2–3 min. Pour in the stock, season to taste and simmer for 20 min. Remove from the heat, stir in the remaining butter and the grated cheese. Serve with 1½ tbsp of the *fondo bruno* on each helping of rice.

RISOTTO CON FEGATINI E PISELLI *
(Rice with chicken livers and peas)

1 small onion
½ cup butter
10½ oz chicken livers
salt
6¼ cups meat stock
2 oz prosciutto
1¼ cups Arborio (risotto) rice
2 cups shelled peas
generous ¼ cup grated Parmesan
    cheese
1 sprig parsley

Chop half of the onion and lightly sauté in a small saucepan with one third of the butter. Add the livers, a little salt and ½ cup stock. Simmer for 10 min. Chop the remaining half onion and the prosciutto. Fry the onion in a separate saucepan with half of the remaining butter. Add the prosciutto; after 2 min add the peas, ½ cup stock and slowly simmer for 15–20 min. Melt the remaining butter in a saucepan. Add the rice, stir well, pour in the hot remaining stock and boil for 20 min. Remove from the heat, add the grated Parmesan, chopped parsley, peas and livers, mix well and serve.

Sauces

*I*n some national cuisines – the French and Chinese for example – sauces have always been considered the most important ingredient for many dishes, to the extent that the original flavor of the food is sometimes drowned entirely by the accompanying sauce. In Italian cooking, sauces – and dressings in general – do not mask the other flavors but complement them. Indeed, there is such a great variety of sauces (we need only consider the example of pasta dishes) that almost every region with a culinary reputation can boast its own specialties.

Tomatoes, basil, anchovies, eggplant, clams, turnip tops, mussels, liver, sardines, mushrooms, truffles, cream, garlic and olive oil are just some of the many ingredients that are used in sauces to accompany every type of bought or homemade pasta. Oregano, rosemary and basil are just a few of the herbs cooked with meat, while such ingredients as parsley and onions add fragrance and distinctive flavor to fish dishes of all kinds.

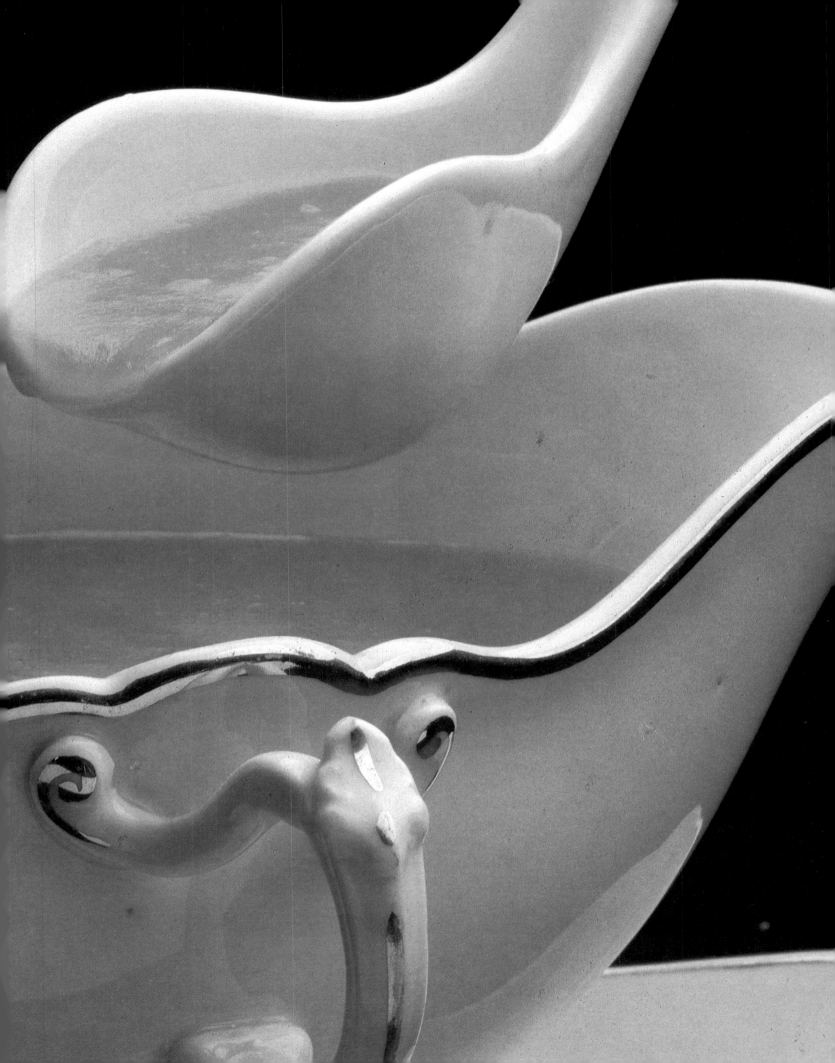

POMODORO IN BOTTIGLIA
(Preserved tomatoes[1])

This is the simplest way to preserve tomatoes all winter so that you can cook them as in their fresh state when needed. Use as many plum tomatoes as you require (depending on the number of canning jars or bottles you have available); remove the stalk, wash thoroughly and leave to drain well. Do not remove the skins. Chop into small pieces in a bowl to catch the juice, fill the bottles up to their necks with the pieces (leaving a gap of 3–4 in) and divide the juice in the bowl between the bottles. (More convenient, hermetically-sealed canning jars are also sold for the purposes of sterilization; follow the manufacturer's instructions.) Seal the bottles with crown caps using a crown capping machine and stand them in a large saucepan or cauldron, wrapped in cloths and up to their necks in cold water. Bring the water to a boil and sterilize by simmering gently for about 1 hr. Leave to cool, remove the bottles from the water once they are cold and store in a cool place.

POMODORI PELATI IN BOTTIGLIA
(Preserved tomatoes[2])

Proceed exactly as for the tomatoes in the above recipe but first scald with boiling water for 1–2 min so that the skins can be easily removed. Cut in half and remove the seeds. Put the pieces (halves or quarters depending on the size of the tomatoes and that of the bottle neck) into the bottes, seal well and sterilize for 1 hr. Hermetically-sealed canning jars can also be used in this case; follow the manufacturer's instructions.

SALSA DI POMODORO *
(Bottled tomato sauce)

It is useful to have a supply of tomato sauce in the refrigerator for use in various recipes. Plum tomatoes are best for this purpose.

For a tomato mixture to form the basis of a sauce or indeed for use in any recipe requiring the use of tomatoes, place the tomatoes in boiling water for 5 min, then drain well. Sieve, taking care to collect not only the juice that falls into the bowl but also the denser liquid attached to the underside of the strainer. Place in a saucepan, bring to a boil and simmer for about ½ hr, stirring occasionally with a wooden spoon. If the tomatoes are a little watery they may need a few more minutes' cooking. If you are not going to use the tomato mixture immediately, and wish to preserve it, proceed as follows: Warm the bottles well so that they do not crack when the hot sauce is poured in. Pour the mixture into the bottles or canning jars slowly and carefully, a little at a time, using a funnel. Seal the bottles or jars immediately and cool gradually, taking care not to move them or subject them to drafts. Tomatoes prepared in this way should be used within 1 week. Once opened, keep refrigerated and use within 1–2 days.

To make a tomato sauce that will keep for longer use the following method: Once the tomatoes have been washed, drained and chopped, cook with salt and other ingredients as required (chopped onion, celery, basil, pepper, carrot) as if you were preparing a basic tomato sauce for pasta (see p. 127). Cook for about ½ hr then sieve or put through a blender. Leave to cool. Fill bottles to the base of their necks and seal. Wrap the bottles in cloths and stand in cold water in a large saucepan. Bring to a boil and simmer for 1 hr. Allow to cool, remove the bottles and store in a cool place. This tomato sauce should keep for up to 6 months. Once opened, keep refrigerated and use within 1–2 days.

POMODORI PELATI COTTI
(Bottled tomato and basil sauce)

Scald the tomatoes for 1 min in boiling water then peel. Chop into halves or quarters, discarding the seeds if preferred. Heat a few tablespoons of olive oil in a saucepan and fry a little very finely chopped onion and celery until soft

but not brown. Add the tomatoes and cook the sauce for about ½ hr, adding a few basil leaves just before it is ready. If you wish to bottle the sauce, leave it to cool, mix well (otherwise the oil tends to float on top) and put into bottles. Cool, fill bottles to the base of their necks and seal. Wrap the bottles in cloths and stand in cold water in a large saucepan. Bring to a boil and simmer for 1 hr. Allow to cool, remove the bottles and store in a cool place. Hermetically-sealed canning jars are recommended for this method; follow the manufacturer's instructions. Once sealed, the tomato and basil sauce should keep for up to 6 months. Once opened, keep refrigerated and use within 1-2 days.

SALSA AL DRAGONCELLO
(Tarragon sauce)

the soft inside of 1 fresh bread roll
½ cup red wine vinegar
1 sprig tarragon
2 cloves garlic
oil
salt

Crumble the bread and add to the vinegar in a bowl. Trim and wash the tarragon, then chop together with the garlic. Remove the bread from the bowl, squeeze gently to eliminate excess vinegar and sieve into a bowl together with the chopped tarragon and garlic. Mix in the oil gradually with a wooden spoon, add salt as required and continue to beat until a thick sauce is obtained.

This sauce can be served with boiled or braised meat. It will keep for a few days in the refrigerator.

SALSA TARTUFATA
(Truffle sauce)

1 small onion
1 clove garlic
1 sprig parsley
1½ tbsp butter
½ cup white wine or dry Marsala
1 tsp all-purpose flour
salt
freshly ground pepper
½ cup light meat stock
1 white truffle

Chop the onion, garlic and parsley very finely and sauté in a small saucepan in the melted butter. Mix the wine (or Marsala) and flour in a bowl, then pour into the saucepan, stirring constantly with a wooden spoon. Season with salt and pepper and when the sauce begins to thicken, add the stock (or the same quantity of boiling water with ½ tsp of meat extract dissolved in it) and cook for a few minutes longer. Shortly before removing from the heat, add the truffle cut into wafer-thin slices. Serve the sauce hot with cutlets, steak or roasted meats.

SALSA DI NOCI
(Walnut sauce)

½ cup pine nuts
1 cup shelled walnuts
½ clove garlic
1 sprig parsley
salt
1 cup ricotta cheese
½ cup olive oil

Toast the pine nuts in a hot oven for a few minutes. Soak the walnuts for a couple of minutes in boiling water and remove their outer skins. Using a mortar and pestle pound together the garlic, parsley and a pinch of salt to make a paste. Place in a bowl and stir in the ricotta, diluted with 2–3 tbsp of water, and the oil.

This sauce is a Genoese specialty typically served with *pansoòti* (see p. 66).

SALSA PIEMONTESE
(Piedmontese anchovy and truffle sauce)

1⅛ cups water
1 tbsp meat extract
4 anchovy fillets
1 small white truffle, grated
1 small shallot, chopped
1 clove garlic
1 sprig parsley
1 hard-boiled egg yolk
1 tsp cornstarch
olive oil
lemon juice
pinch freshly ground white pepper

SALSA ALLA TARTARA
(Tartare sauce)

mayonnaise, using 2 egg yolks and
   1 cup olive oil
½ onion
1 clove garlic
½ green pepper
1 tbsp capers
2 tbsp chopped parsley

Unlike the mayonnaise recipe (see below left), one egg yolk must be raw and one hard-boiled for tartare sauce. The procedure is then the same. Mix one raw and one hard-boiled egg yolk in a bowl with a wooden spoon until they form a smooth paste. Pour the oil into this paste a drop at a time. Add vinegar and lemon juice to dilute, then season with salt. Now add the following ingredients finely chopped: onion, garlic, pepper, capers and parsley. Mix carefully and serve with fish or meat dishes.

SALSA AL PEPERONCINO *
(Chili pepper mayonnaise)

2 egg yolks
scant 1 cup sunflower seed oil
lemon juice
salt
1 tbsp chili powder

Put the egg yolks in a bowl and mix with a wooden spoon or small whisk. Begin by beating slowly and regularly. Add half the oil a drop at a time, pour in a little lemon juice and a pinch of salt. Continue to whisk and pour in the remaining oil. Finish by adding the chili powder to this mayonnaise.

Put the water in a saucepan, bring to a boil and mix in the meat extract. Using a pestle and mortar or blender, pound the anchovies, truffle, shallot, garlic, parsley and hard-boiled egg yolk. Push the mixture through a sieve and add to the boiling liquid. Add the cornstarch, diluted in a little water, a few drops of oil, a few drops of lemon juice and the pepper. Stir and serve this sauce piping hot.

Stop the thickening by adding drops of lemon juice. Season with salt and pepper and gently stir in the remaining oil. Lastly, beat in 1 tbsp hot vinegar so that the mayonnaise holds its consistency and is lighter.

SALSA MAIONESE *
(Mayonnaise)

2 egg yolks at room temperature
juice of 1 lemon
1⅛ cups oil (half olive oil, half
   sunflower oil)
salt
freshly ground white pepper
1 tbsp vinegar

Mix the egg yolks and a little lemon juice evenly and continuously in a deep bowl using a wooden spoon or a small whisk. Add half the oil, drop by drop at first and then pouring as the mayonnaise begins to thicken.

SALSA VERDE *
(Green sauce)

3½ cups parsley
3 salted anchovies
juice of ½ lemon
1 green pepper
¼ onion
1 clove garlic
3 tbsp capers
1⅛ cups olive oil
salt

Choose fresh parsley and rinse thoroughly. Scrape the salt off the anchovies, rinse with lemon juice and bone. Broil the pepper until the skin blisters and can be rubbed off. Slice open, discard the seeds and rinse. Put the parsley, anchovy, pepper slices, onion, garlic and capers into a blender or food processor. Blend until smooth, then dilute with olive oil and lemon juice. Adjust the seasoning as required. Serve with main courses and vegetables.

SALSA DI POMODORO *
(Tomato sauce)

2 cups ripe or canned plum
    tomatoes, chopped
1 small carrot
1 small onion
1 stick celery
2 basil leaves (optional)
½ clove garlic
1⅛ cups olive oil
salt
freshly ground pepper

Choose ripe, plump and juicy summer tomatoes for this sauce. Rinse thoroughly, chop, salt lightly and leave to sweat in a colander placed over a bowl. Sauté the chopped vegetables, basil and garlic in a heavy skillet in a few tablespoons of oil. Add the tomatoes immediately, bring to a boil and cook over moderate heat for about ½ hr. When the tomatoes are no longer watery, strain in a vegetable mill or blend in a food processor. If the sauce is too thin, reduce by cooking briefly over high heat. Check the seasoning and add some more oil and a little sugar if desired. Pour into a sauceboat when hot. This sauce goes well with pasta.

SALSA BESCIAMELLA
(White sauce)

(makes 4½ cups)
½ cup butter
4 tbsp flour
½ tsp salt
4½ cups milk

Cut the butter into small pieces and melt in a heavy saucepan. Stir in the flour with a wooden spoon, add the salt and mix over medium heat until smooth. Gradually add the milk, stirring constantly until the sauce has thickened. If a richer sauce is required, remove from the heat and stir in 1 egg yolk or a little grated Parmesan cheese.

SALSA AL CREN
(Horseradish sauce)

with vinegar
1 horseradish root (4 oz)
¾ cup fresh breadcrumbs soaked in
  milk and squeezed to remove
  excess moisture
pinch of salt
pinch of sugar
½ cup white wine vinegar

Scrape the horseradish root thoroughly before rinsing and grating. Place the pulp in a sauceboat. Add the breadcrumbs which have been soaked in milk and then squeezed to remove the excess moisture, a pinch each of salt and sugar. Mix well and stir in the white wine vinegar.

with cream
1 horseradish root (4 oz)
pinch of salt
pinch of sugar
½ cup light cream

Scrape, rinse and grate the horseradish root. Add a little sugar to the pulp in a sauceboat and mix gently while adding the lightly whipped cream. Serve the two horseradish sauces in sauceboats. The first goes well with boiled meats while the second is served with antipasti, cold meat or cold fish.

SALSINA PER ARROSTI E CACCIAGIONE
(Sauce for roasted meats and game)

2 oz Parma ham (fat and lean meat)
2 chicken livers
2 cloves garlic
2¼ cups dry white wine
3 sage leaves
1 sprig rosemary
few juniper berries
½ lemon
½ cup olive oil
1⅛ cups red wine vinegar
salt
freshly ground pepper

Finely chop the ham together with the chicken livers and the garlic, then place in a saucepan (not aluminum) with the white wine, sage, rosemary, juniper berries, ½ lemon, peeled and chopped, oil and

vinegar. Add salt and pepper as required. Simmer over low heat, stirring frequently, until the sauce is thick (it should reduce by about half). This sauce is particularly suitable for roasted meats and game.

SALSA AI CAPPERI E ACCIUGA
(Caper and anchovy sauce)

4 tbsp capers
3 tbsp anchovy fillets
1 tbsp chopped onion
½ cup butter
a little vinegar
2 tbsp creamed butter

Scrape the salt off the anchovies, and chop together with the capers. Sauté the finely chopped onion in butter in a small saucepan. Brown gently then remove from the heat before adding the chopped capers and anchovies. Stir in a little vinegar and the creamed butter.

SALSA ALLE OLIVE
(Olive sauce)

1 cup black olives
½ onion
1⅛ cups olive oil
2 tbsp peeled, seeded and sieved
   tomatoes
salt
freshly ground pepper

Pit the black olives and chop finely. Slice the onion and brown in the oil in a small saucepan. Add the chopped olives and sieved tomatoes. Cook over low heat for 10 min, seasoning with salt and pepper. Pour into a sauceboat when ready.

SALSA AI PEPERONI
(Pickled sweet pepper sauce)

1 cup pickled sweet peppers (see p. 304)
½ cup grated Parmesan cheese
½ tsp mustard
½ cup olive oil
salt

Remove the seeds from the pickled peppers and chop finely. Gently

mix the pulp with the coarsely grated Parmesan. Add the mustard, season with salt and stir in the olive oil. Pour into a shallow dish and garnish with gherkins, whole pickled peppers and pickled onions. This sauce goes well with boiled meats.

SALSA PER IL PESCE
(Sauce for fish)

2 hard-boiled egg yolks
3–4 anchovy fillets
½ cup olive oil
few drops lemon juice

Chop the egg yolks and the anchovy fillets separately, then pound them together using a pestle and mortar until a soft, well blended paste is produced. Add the oil and lemon juice drop by drop until the sauce is creamy in consistency, like mayonnaise. This flavorsome sauce goes well with broiled fish.

SUGO DI CARNE
(Meat sauce)

⅓ cup suet
¼ cup butter
1 generous cup ground beef
½ onion, chopped
½ stick celery, chopped
½ carrot, chopped
½ clove garlic
1 sprig rosemary
2 large ripe tomatoes
1⅛ cups red wine
salt
freshly ground pepper
1⅛ cups meat stock

Melt the suet and the butter in a saucepan and add the ground beef. When the meat is browned, add the chopped onion, celery, carrot, garlic and rosemary. Season with salt and pepper and leave to cook for 5–10 min, stirring occasionally. Meanwhile, peel the tomatoes, remove the seeds and chop coarsely. Pour in the red wine and when it has evaporated, add the tomatoes. Continue to cook over moderate heat for at least 2 hr, occasionally adding a ladle of stock, until the meat is cooked and the sauce thick.

Sieve the meat together with its juice or purée in a blender.

SALSA "PEARÀ" *
(Peppered sauce)

3 tbsp butter
¼ cup ox marrow
1½ cups fresh white breadcrumbs
3 tbsp grated Parmesan cheese
2½ cups light stock
salt
freshly ground pepper

This peppered sauce, called *pearà* in Veronese dialect, is a thick, tasty sauce served with braised or boiled meats. It is traditionally cooked in a terracotta pot. Melt the butter and ox marrow, add the breadcrumbs and mix with a wooden spoon until they have absorbed the fat. Ladle in the boiling stock and stir until a smooth sauce is obtained. Simmer very gently for 30–40 min, stirring occasionally. Before serving, add the grated Parmesan, salt if required, and plenty of freshly ground black pepper. Serve piping hot.

"GAROFOLATO"
(Beef casserole with clove gravy)

1¾ lb lean beef rump
4 oz slice fat bacon
2 cloves
½ clove garlic, chopped
few marjoram leaves, chopped
salt
freshly ground pepper

for the sauce:
¼ cup butter (or olive oil)
1 oz bacon, chopped
½ clove garlic, minced
salt
freshly ground pepper
½ cup red wine
2 cloves
1 onion, chopped
1 stick celery, chopped
1 carrot, chopped
1 sprig parsley, chopped
1 tbsp tomato sauce (or strained
   tomatoes)

A sauce from the countryside around Rome which takes its name from the Roman word for cloves, *garofolo*. Pound the meat well with a meatbat, then lard as follows: make small incisions with a sharp knife and insert the cloves and the fat bacon cut into pieces and rolled in chopped garlic, marjoram, salt and pepper. Roll up the meat and tie with string, then brown slowly in the butter with the chopped bacon and minced garlic. When the garlic is browned, remove and turn the meat until it is browned all over. Season with salt and pepper and pour over the wine. Cook until the wine has evaporated; remove the meat and set aside; add the cloves, chopped onion, celery, carrot and parsley to the remaining gravy. Simmer the vegetables over low heat for 5 min then return the meat to the saucepan. Cook for a further 10 min over low heat. Add the tomato sauce dissolved in a little warm water and pour over enough warm water to cover the meat. Cover and cook very slowly for about 2 hr.

The gravy from this dish is often served as a sauce for fettuccine, risotto, etc., or with tripe; the meat is served in slices as a main course.

RAGÙ ALLA BOLOGNESE
(Bolognese sauce)

2 oz pancetta
1 medium onion
1 small carrot
1 stick celery
¼ cup butter
¾ cup ground mixed meats (pork, veal, beef)
½ cup dry red wine
2 tbsp tomato sauce
1 tsp meat extract
salt
freshly ground pepper
1 cup milk

Chop the pancetta very finely with the onion, carrot and celery. Melt the butter in a heavy saucepan; when it is bubbling, add the chopped vegetables and the ground meats. Brown for a few minutes, turn up the heat and pour in the red wine. When this has completely evaporated, add the tomato sauce, diluted in a little hot water, and the dissolved meat extract. Season

with salt and pepper as required. Cover and leave to simmer over low heat for 30–40 min until the sauce is quite thick. Pour in the milk, stir well, cover and simmer over very low heat until the milk is absorbed.

This is the original recipe for Bolognese sauce. Other variations have been developed which in no way detract from the traditional recipe – indeed they make the sauce richer. In addition to the traditional ingredients listed above, other recipes for Bolognese sauce may include chicken livers, or a few dried mushrooms previously softened in warm water and then chopped together with the vegetables and the pancetta, or the fat and lean parts of Parma ham slices, or even – and this produces the very best results – all three of these ingredients. Prepare the sauce the previous day and keep in a cool place in a covered casserole.

Bolognese sauce is an excellent accompaniment to ravioli, tortellini, spaghetti and many other types of pasta. It also makes a tasty filling for baked green lasagne.

RAGÙ D'AGNELLO E PEPERONI
(Lamb and pepper sauce)

½ lb lean lamb
salt
freshly ground pepper
1 clove garlic, minced
2–3 bay leaves
½ cup oil
½ cup dry white wine
3 peeled ripe tomatoes
2 sweet peppers, cut into strips
meat stock (optional)

Cut the lamb into small chunks, season with salt and pepper, then leave to stand for about 1 hr. Fry the minced garlic and bay leaves in the oil and remove when they start to brown.

Add the meat to the saucepan and brown evenly. Pour in the wine and allow to evaporate. Add the chopped tomatoes and the peppers, and season with salt if required; cover and leave to cook slowly for about 1½ hr, stirring occasionally and adding a little stock if the sauce becomes too dry.

Serve the lamb and pepper sauce with fresh fettuccine and macaroni.

PESTO ALLA GENOVESE *
(Basil sauce)

handful of pine nuts
bunch of basil (about 30 leaves)
2 cloves garlic
pinch salt
1 tbsp grated Parmesan cheese
1 tbsp grated Pecorino cheese
½ cup olive oil

Toast the pine nuts in a hot oven. Using a pestle and mortar (preferably marble) pound the basil leaves (not washed but wiped with a cloth) with the toasted pine nuts, garlic and salt. Do not mash the ingredients but try to crush them against the sides of the mortar. Gradually add the two cheeses then transfer the paste to a bowl. Blend in the oil a little at a time with a wooden spoon. The resulting mixture should be bright green and not too thick.

Pesto is most commonly served with pasta dishes, but can also be added to soups, particularly minestrone.

AGLIATA
(Garlic sauce)

the soft inside of 1 bread roll
1 tbsp white wine vinegar
2 cloves garlic, minced
2 sprigs parsley, chopped
handful of basil leaves, chopped
1⅛ cups olive oil
salt
freshly ground pepper

This sauce is typical of Ligurian cuisine. *Agliata* is similar to a Provençale sauce, *aïoli*, containing garlic, egg yolks and olive oil. Several versions of this sauce may be found throughout Latin countries and the Balkans. This sauce makes an excellent accompaniment to a variety of dishes including fried *baccalà* (salt cod), veal liver or lamb liver cooked in a casserole with oil.

Soak the bread in vinegar, squeeze well and pound in a mortar

with the finely minced garlic, parsley and basil. Transfer to a sauceboat and stir in the oil, salt and pepper before serving.

BAGNA CAUDA
(Garlic and anchovy dip)

6 salted anchovies
scant ½ cup butter
¼ cup olive oil
4 large cloves garlic
1 white truffle (optional)

Wash the anchovies thoroughly to remove the salt; bone and chop. Put the butter, oil and garlic into a saucepan, preferably terracotta,

and fry gently until the garlic is soft but not browned. Remove from the heat, add the anchovies and mix to a paste using a fork. Clean the truffle thoroughly and cut into wafer-thin slices. Return the saucepan to the heat and add the truffle. Stir the ingredients over low heat until they are well mixed and then serve immediately. *Bagna cauda* must be eaten very hot. It is traditionally kept hot over a spirit stove (a fondue pot will do) and used as a dip for tender raw vegetables cut into small pieces or matchstick strips. Serve with a selection of celery, carrots, red and green peppers, broccoli, mushrooms, etc.

PEVERADA
(Savory Venetian sauce)

generous ½ cup chicken livers
2 slices sopressa veneta *or other sausage (about 4 oz)*
2 anchovy fillets
1 clove garlic
1 sprig parsley
grated peel and juice of 1 lemon
8 tbsp olive oil
½ cup dry wine (or 4 tbsp vinegar)
salt
freshly ground pepper

Chop the chicken livers, sausage, anchovy fillets, garlic, parsley and grated lemon peel very finely. Heat the oil in a saucepan. When hot, add the chopped mixture and season with salt and a little pepper. Fry gently, adding the lemon juice and white wine (or vinegar), and simmer until the sauce is smooth and thick. *Peverada* is very good as an accompaniment to chicken or roast guinea fowl.

FONDO BRUNO

Into a large stock pot put 13 lb of veal and beef bones broken into pieces. Add 3 lb of lean meat, 1 lb onions, 1 lb carrots, 1 lb celery, all chopped up, a bouquet garni consisting of parsley, 1 bay leaf, 2 sprigs of thyme and 1 clove minced garlic. Put the stock pot over heat and stir frequently until all the ingredients are well browned. Remove the fat as it is produced. Pour in 2 cups dry white wine and leave to evaporate. Add 7½ cups peeled tomatoes and continue to stir until the mixture is almost completely dry. At this point, add about 2 gallons water, 10 peppercorns and salt to taste. Simmer for 2 hr, continuing to skim off the fat and any other scum that comes to the surface. Pass through a fine sieve and continue to cook over high heat until reduced by one third. *Fondo bruno* will keep in the refrigerator for about 3 weeks. It is used to add flavor to meat dishes.

FONDO BRUNO DI SELVAGGINA
(Game fondo bruno)

Follow the same method as for basic *fondo bruno* (see previous recipe), replacing the beef and veal bones with game bones and carcasses. Use to add flavor to game dishes.

FONDO DI PESCE
(Fish stock)

Into a large stockpot put 6½ lb fish trimmings and bones, 1 cup onion, 1 cup celery, a bouquet garni consisting of parsley, ½ bay leaf and some slices of carrot, 1 cup dry white wine, juice of ½ lemon, a few peppercorns and salt to taste. Add about 1 gallon water. Bring to a boil and simmer for 4 hr. Sieve. Use as a base for a variety of fish sauces.

Meat

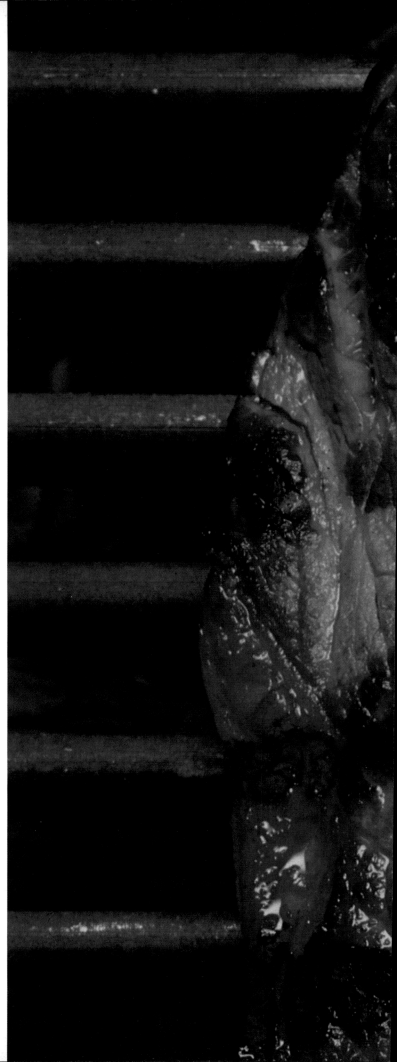

*T*his section includes all meat except poultry and game.

In Italy the culinary tradition varies widely from region to region. In central Italy, for example, dishes based on mutton, lamb and kid tend to predominate. These traditional dishes are eaten more often during religious festivals, such as Easter. The extensive grasslands of the Po Valley region naturally give rise to more beef and pork dishes (pork reigns supreme on tables from Bologna along the Via Emilia to the Po); while in Tuscany, birthplace of the renowned steak Florentine, it is said that the true steak, which can only be termed an authentic steak Florentine if it comes from a certain breed of swampland cattle, is now as hard to find as snow in summer. Throughout southern Italy and the islands mutton, lamb and kid are also popular – and pork is also used (in Sardinia and Calabria for example) to prepare delicious rustic dishes, such as pórchetta (roast suckling pig).

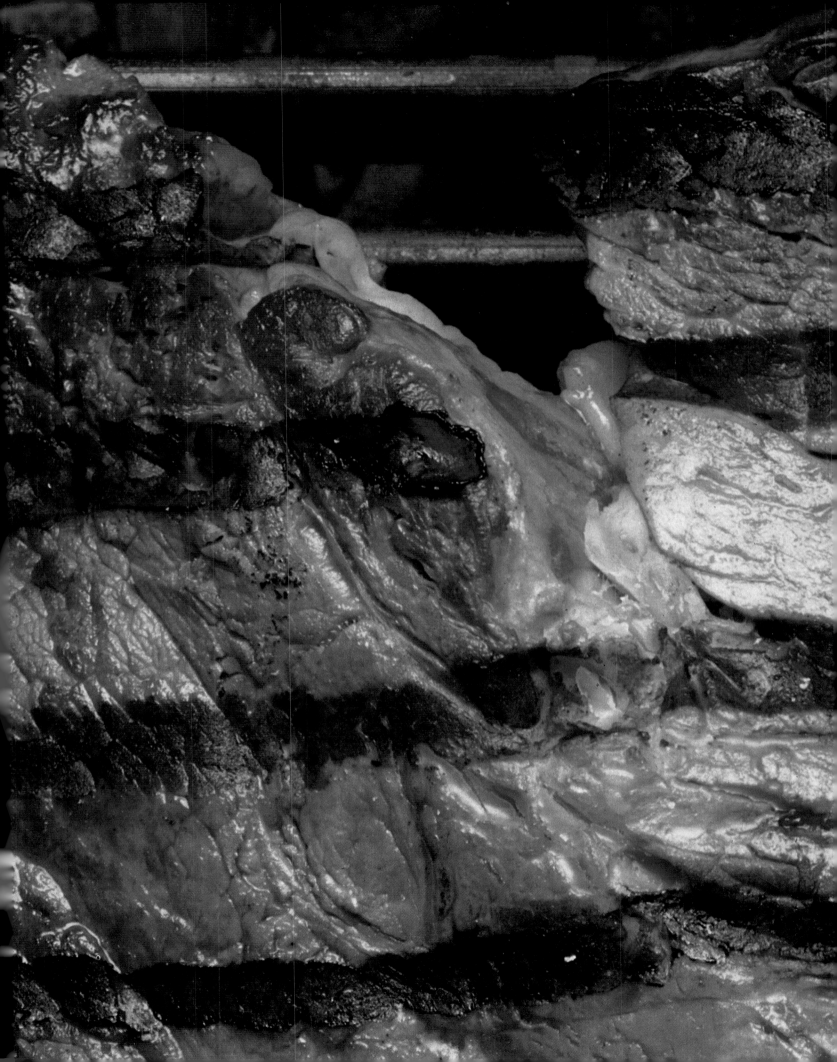

Beef

STRACOTTO
(Braised beef)

2 cloves garlic
2 lb beef, cut from the rump
¼ cup butter
½ onion
1 stick celery
1 small carrot
¼ cup salt pork
1 tsp meat extract
2 tbsp tomato paste
salt
freshly ground pepper

Cut the garlic into slivers and place inside small cuts made in the meat. Put the butter and the chopped vegetables into a large heavy saucepan together with the salt pork and fry for a few minutes. Add the meat and brown well, stirring frequently. Add a few ladles of hot water in which the meat extract and tomato paste have been dissolved. Cover the saucepan and bring to a boil over low heat. Turn the meat occasionally and add more hot water when necessary. Simmer gently for 3 hr, then add salt and pepper to taste. For perfect braised beef, the meat should be cooked over very low heat for at least 4 hr. The result will be very tasty, tender meat in a smooth, creamy gravy. Cut into thick slices to serve and cover with a little of the strained gravy. Accompany with fresh green vegetables.

POLPETTINE ALLA SALVIA *
(Meat balls with sage)

2 cups lean ground beef
8 sage leaves
¼ cup butter
2 tbsp grated Parmesan cheese
¼ tsp salt
all-purpose flour
4 tbsp Marsala

Mix together the meat, the finely chopped sage leaves, half the butter, the grated Parmesan cheese and the salt. Mix until well blended and shape into small balls with floured hands. Melt the remaining butter in a skillet and then fry the balls in the hot butter for 5–7 min until golden brown. Pour in the Marsala, leave to evaporate, then serve the meat balls piping hot with their cooking juices.

CODA ALLA VACCINARA
(Oxtail ragoût)

2½ lb oxtail
1 onion
1 clove garlic
1 carrot
1 sprig parsley
¼ cup salt pork
1 tbsp butter, or oil or lard
salt
freshly ground pepper
1⅛ cups dry white wine
2 tbsp tomato paste
1 stick celery

This is a typical Roman dish. Rinse the oxtail well and leave to soak in cold water for a few hours before cutting into small sections along the vertebral joints. Chop the onion, garlic, carrot and parsley very finely. Pound the salt pork well and put into a saucepan together with the butter and chopped ingredients. Fry for a few minutes until the vegetables begin to soften, then add the oxtail and stir over moderate heat until the meat is golden brown. Add salt and pepper and pour in the white wine. When the wine has evaporated, add 3 cups water with the tomato paste dissolved in it. Stir well, cover, and simmer over low heat for 3–4 hr, adding more water if necessary. Add the sliced celery and cook for a further ½ hr. Transfer the oxtail to a warm serving dish and cover with the gravy.

CODE DI BUE ALLA CAVOUR
(Oxtail stew)

2½ lb oxtail
½ cup olive oil
2 oz pork rind
2 onions
4 carrots
1 large stick celery
1 sprig parsley
salt
freshly ground pepper
1⅛ cups red wine
1 tsp meat extract
1 tsp cornstarch
2 tbsp butter
2 oz dried mushrooms

Rinse and dry the oxtail and cut into sections. Pour the oil into a saucepan, then add the pork rind, cut into strips, the coarsely chopped onions, carrots, celery, parsley and, lastly, the pieces of oxtail. Season with salt and pepper before pouring in the wine. Cook over moderate heat until the wine has evaporated and the vegetables have softened. Add enough hot water to cover the oxtail, then stir in the meat extract. Cook for at least 3 hr, adding more hot water if necessary. Soak the mushrooms in cold water for ½ hr in a little oil; drain, dry, then sauté briefly. Transfer the oxtail to a large heavy skillet and thicken the gravy with the cornstarch mixed with the butter. Add the mushrooms and simmer gently over low heat for a further 10 min.

FARSUMAGRU
(falso magro)
(Meat roll)

2 cups lean ground beef
1 egg
1 egg yolk
2 tbsp grated Caciocavallo cheese
salt
freshly ground pepper
nutmeg
1 sprig parsley, chopped
marjoram (optional)
thyme (optional)
1 clove garlic, chopped (optional)
1 thinly cut, lean beef steak (about 10 oz)
1 hard-boiled egg
3 oz Caciocavallo cheese
1 slice prosciutto (about 3 oz)
1 slice salt pork (about 4 oz)
¼ cup lard
1 onion
½ cup red wine
1 cup freshly made tomato sauce (see p.127), (optional)

Put the ground beef in a bowl and mix with the egg and egg yolk,

grated Caciocavallo cheese, a pinch of salt, plenty of freshly ground pepper, grated nutmeg, parsley, and, if desired, the marjoram, thyme and garlic. Mix the ingredients to a smooth paste and set aside. Pound the steak into a rectangle with a meatbat and make small incisions around the edge to prevent it from rolling up during cooking. Slice the hard-boiled egg and cut the Caciocavallo cheese, the prosciutto and salt pork into strips. Place the steak on a board and spread with the prepared meat paste, taking care to leave about ½ in around the edges uncovered. Place the egg slices, the Caciocavallo cheese, the prosciutto and salt pork on top of the meat filling. Roll up carefully from the shortest side and tie securely. Melt the lard in a heavy saucepan; add the chopped onion and the meat roll and fry very gently, turning occasionally. As soon as the onion and the meat start to brown, pour in the wine and cook until it evaporates. Add salt and pepper, cover and leave to cook over moderate heat for about 1½ hr, adding a little hot water if necessary. The meat roll can be served hot or cold, cut into slices. Serve with hot tomato sauce if desired.

ROLLÈ DI FILETTO
(Fillet roll)

1 lb beef fillet
salt
freshly ground pepper
2 tbsp olive oil
1 sprig rosemary
2 bay leaves
½ lemon
3 tbsp butter
1 tsp all-purpose flour
1 cup dry white wine (or 2 tbsp wine vinegar)

Season the fillet generously with salt and pepper and place in a heavy saucepan with the oil, rosemary, bay leaves and sliced lemon. Cover and cook over moderate heat for about ½ hr, turning frequently. Remove the lemon, rosemary and bay leaves, then add the butter and the flour mixed with a few tablespoons of cold water. Pour the white wine (or vinegar)

over the meat and bring to a boil, stirring constantly. Remove the meat and keep in a warm place. Reduce the sauce by stirring over high heat for a few minutes. Cut the fillet into thick slices and serve in its own gravy.

MANZO STUFATO
(Barolo braised beef)

1½ lb beef rump roast
2 oz pancetta, cut into strips
2 cloves garlic
2 tbsp butter
2 tbsp olive oil
1 onion, chopped
1 stick celery, chopped
1⅛ cups red wine (Barbera or Barolo)
salt
freshly ground pepper
1 tbsp tomato paste
meat stock

Lard the meat with a few pieces of pancetta and then rub with a cut garlic clove. Heat the oil and butter in a large saucepan and add the meat, tied with kitchen string. Then add the second garlic clove and the chopped vegetables. Brown and add the wine. When the wine has evaporated, add salt and pepper and pour in the tomato paste mixed with a little hot meat stock. Cover and simmer gently for about 4 hr, adding more hot stock as necessary. Strain the sauce (it should be quite thick) and serve piping hot with the sliced meat. This dish is best reheated and served the following day. It is traditionally eaten with polenta.

MANZO BRASATO ALLA MODA DI TRENTO
(Braised beef Trento style)

1½ lb beef rump roast (or veal)
2 oz salt pork, cut into strips
¼ cup butter
½ onion
1 sprig rosemary
1⅛ cups vinegar
1⅛ cups milk
1 tbsp light cream
salt
freshly ground pepper
meat stock or meat extract
1 tsp cornstarch

Lard the meat with salt pork and tie securely to form a firm roll. Put the butter and the finely chopped onion into a large heavy saucepan and fry until soft. Then add the meat and the rosemary. Brown the meat for 5–10 min over moderate heat, stirring frequently. Pour in the vinegar and cook until evaporated, turning up the heat slightly. Add the milk and cream, and season with salt and pepper; cover and cook for about 1 hr, adding a little hot meat stock as necessary (or hot water containing 1 tsp meat extract). Just before serving, strain the gravy and thicken with 1 tsp cornstarch mixed with 2 tbsp cold water. Slice the meat, cover with the gravy and serve with hot polenta.

STUFATINO
(Beef stew)

1½ lb round steak
salt
¼ cup lard
1 onion, chopped
¼ cup ham fat, chopped
1 stick celery
1 clove garlic
pinch of marjoram
1⅛ cups red wine
2 tbsp tomato paste
meat stock
1½ lb cooked celeriac or cardoons

Salt the meat and cut into pieces.

Heat the lard in a heavy saucepan and fry the onions until soft. Add the ham fat, chopped celery and garlic, and fry for a few minutes. Then add the meat and a pinch of marjoram; brown over gentle heat, pour in the wine and cook slowly until it evaporates. Dilute the tomato paste in a cup of hot stock and add to the saucepan. Cover and cook slowly for about 2 hr, adding more stock as necessary.

Cut the cooked celeriac or cardoons into pieces and add to the saucepan at the last moment. Cook for a few more minutes. This dish is typically eaten with vegetables from the celery family, especially cardoons.

CULATTA DI MANZO ALLA TRIESTINA
(Beef rump Trieste style)

1¾ lb beef round steak or rump roast
2 oz prosciutto
4 tbsp olive oil
2 tbsp butter
½ onion
1 stick celery
1 carrot
a few cloves
salt
freshly ground pepper
1⅛ cups dry white wine
3 cups boiling water containing 1 bouillon cube and ½ tsp meat extract
1 tsp cornstarch (optional)

Lard the meat with strips of prosciutto, then place in a heavy saucepan with the oil and butter. Brown the meat evenly over low heat until golden brown. Then add the finely chopped onion, the celery and carrot cut into pieces, and the cloves. Add salt and pepper, then pour in the wine. Cover and cook for about 1½ hr, adding a little stock when necessary. When the meat is tender, remove from the saucepan, leave to cool slightly, then slice thinly. Strain the meat juices in the saucepan and reduce over high heat until thick and smooth. If preferred, thicken with 1 tsp cornstarch mixed with 2 tbsp cold water. Reheat and pour over the meat.

Serve with mashed potatoes.

GULASCH ALLA TRIESTINA
(Goulash Trieste style)

2 oz salt pork
¼ cup lard
1½ lb onions
1½ lb beef stew meat
salt
paprika
1 sprig rosemary
2 bay leaves
1 cup freshly made tomato sauce (see p. 127)

Put the pounded salt pork, lard and thinly sliced onions into a saucepan. Fry the onions over low heat until soft. Then add the beef, cut into 1-in cubes; raise the heat and brown all over, stirring frequently. Add salt and paprika to taste. Tie the herbs together in a piece of muslin and tie with string. Mix the tomato sauce with 2 ladles of hot water and pour over the meat. Cover and simmer gently for about 1½ hr until the meat is very tender, adding a little hot water from time to time during cooking if necessary. When the goulash is ready, take out the herbs and serve immediately.

This dish may be served with freshly prepared polenta, ribbon noodles or boiled potatoes.

GAROFOLATO DI MANZO ✻
(Beef with clove gravy)

1½ lb beef round steak or sirloin
2 cloves garlic
2 oz salt pork
cloves
¼ cup olive oil
1 tsp butter
1⅛ cups dry red wine
4 ripe tomatoes
salt
freshly ground pepper

Using the point of a sharp knife, make incisions in the meat, then insert the garlic, salt pork pieces and a few cloves. Heat the oil and butter in a heavy saucepan. As soon as they begin to bubble, add the meat and brown, turning frequently. When the meat is browned pour in the wine (leaving to evaporate over high heat) and then add the sieved tomatoes. Add salt and pepper, cover and leave to

cook slowly for about 1 hr, stirring and adding water occasionally. When the meat is tender, remove from the heat, slice thickly and serve immediately. The gravy from this dish goes well with pasta dishes.

INVOLTINI ALLA BARESE
(Roulades Bari style)

4 6-oz beef steaks
salt
freshly ground pepper
3 oz salt pork
3 oz Pecorino cheese
1 sprig parsley
4 cloves garlic (or less if desired)
4 tbsp oil
1 lb ripe tomatoes

Pound the steaks with a meatbat to flatten before seasoning with salt and pepper. Cut the salt pork and the Pecorino cheese into narrow strips. Chop the parsley and the garlic coarsely. Divide the chopped mixture and the salt pork and cheese strips into four and spread on top of the steaks. Carefully roll up each steak to enclose the filling, then tie each roulade with thread. Heat the oil in a skillet, add the roulades and brown for a few minutes, turning frequently. Add the skinned, seeded and chopped tomatoes. Season with salt, cover and leave the sauce to thicken over moderate heat for about ½ hr.

When the meat is tender, remove the roulades, untie the thread and transfer to a serving dish. Heat the sauce and pour over the roulades. Serve hot.

BISTECCHINE ALLA MODA DI NAPOLI
(Steaks Neapolitan style)

4 oz mushrooms
4 oz prosciutto
1 sprig parsley
olive oil
salt
freshly ground pepper
8 small sirloin steaks
½ lemon

Rinse and thinly slice the mushrooms; chop the prosciutto and the parsley. Grease a baking pan large enough to accommodate all the steaks without overlapping and lay the prosciutto on the bottom. Add a layer of mushrooms, season with salt (only a little because the prosciutto is already salty) and pepper, then sprinkle with chopped parsley. Pour a little oil over all the ingredients. Place the steaks on top and cook in a hot, preheated oven (about 400°F) for ¼ hr. Then, using a spatula, turn the steaks and sprinkle with the juice of ½ lemon and a little salt. Cook for a further 5 min and then serve immediately from the baking pan. Use a large serving spoon in order to pick up some of the sauce under each steak at the same time.

MANZO ALLA PIZZAIOLA
(Beef with tomatoes, garlic and oregano)

1 ½ lb tender, lean beef
½ cup olive oil
2 cloves garlic
1 lb ripe tomatoes
salt
freshly ground pepper
oregano
½ cup dry white wine

Cut the meat into very thin slices. Heat the oil and chopped garlic in a large skillet. When the garlic starts to brown, fry the slices of meat for a few minutes, then remove from the skillet and keep warm. Skin, seed and chop the tomatoes, then add them to the meat juices in the skillet. Season with salt and pepper, sprinkle generously with oregano and pour in the wine. Reduce rapidly by cooking, uncovered, over high heat, stirring carefully so that the tomatoes do not break up. Return the meat to the skillet, cover with the sauce and heat for no more than a couple of minutes. This tasty dish owes its distinctive flavor to the oregano and is a great favorite in the Naples area.

POLPETTINE AI CAPPERI
(Meatballs with capers)

3 tbsp fresh breadcrumbs
a little milk
scant 2 cups lean ground beef
1 tsp butter
salt
pinch of marjoram
1 ½ tbsp capers
1 tbsp all-purpose flour
½ cup olive oil
½ cup white wine

Soak the breadcrumbs in a little milk for 1 min and then squeeze out. Put the ground beef, breadcrumbs and butter into a bowl and season with salt and marjoram. Knead all the ingredients well and then shape into small balls. Press 2 or 3 capers into each and then roll in the flour. Heat the oil in a wide skillet and brown the meatballs in it in a single layer, turning frequently but gently. Pour in the wine and cook for 10 min. Remove the meatballs and arrange on a warm serving dish. Add a few tablespoons of water to the juices in the skillet, stir and heat. Pour over the meatballs and serve immediately.

BISTECCHE ALLA SICILIANA
(Sicilian steaks)

⅓ cup black olives
4 ripe tomatoes
2 tbsp pickled chili peppers
1 stick celery
½ cup olive oil
2 cloves garlic
4 steaks (beef tenderloin or sirloin)
¼ cup capers
salt
freshly ground pepper
oregano

Pit the olives and cut in half. Skin the tomatoes, remove the seeds and chop. Cut the chili peppers in half lengthwise and remove the seeds. Dice the celery. Heat the oil and the minced garlic in a large skillet. When the garlic starts to brown, discard and put the steaks in the skillet. Cook on both sides over high heat for a couple of minutes. Remove the steaks and set aside. Add the chopped celery, olives, chili peppers, capers and tomatoes to the meat juices in the skillet, season with salt and pepper, then sprinkle with oregano. Thicken the sauce over moderate heat, stirring gently, for a few minutes. Return the steaks to the skillet to absorb the flavors, turning a couple of times. Serve piping hot straight from the skillet.

FILETTO ALLA SARDA
(Beef Sardinian style)

1½ lb beef tenderloin
2 cups dry white wine
1 clove garlic
1 sprig parsley
salt
freshly ground pepper
½ cup olive oil
2 salted anchovies
1 lemon

Put the beef, wine, minced garlic, whole sprig of parsley, and a generous pinch of salt and pepper into a heavy saucepan. Leave to marinate for at least 2 hr, turning the meat frequently so that it absorbs the liquid evenly. Add the oil, cover the saucepan and cook over low heat until very tender, adding more hot water as necessary. When the meat is cooked, remove from the saucepan, allow to cool slightly, then slice thinly. Arrange the slices on a serving dish. Strain the cooking juices, return to the saucepan and add the rinsed, boned and finely chopped anchovies. Add the lemon juice and heat for 1 min, stirring thoroughly. Pour the sauce over the meat and serve immediately.

"PASTISSADA" ALLA VENETA *
(Marinated beef Venice style)

for the marinade:
2 cups vinegar
1 clove garlic
2 cloves
pinch of cinnamon
2 sticks celery
1 sprig rosemary
salt
4 peppercorns

1 onion, chopped
generous ¼ cup butter
2¼ lb beef rump roast or round steak
salt
freshly ground pepper
1 cup Marsala
1 cup white wine

Mix together the vinegar, garlic, cloves, cinnamon, celery, rosemary, salt and pepper, and marinate the meat for 12 hr, turning frequently. After this time, remove the meat, drain well and dry. Melt the butter in a heavy saucepan and fry the chopped onion together with the vegetables from the marinade. Add the meat and brown evenly. Season with salt and pepper and pour in the Marsala and the wine. Cover the saucepan with a sheet of buttered wax paper and a lid. Leave to cook slowly for 2½ hr. Cut into fairly thick slices; strain the gravy and pour over the meat. Serve with polenta.

MANZO BRASATO AL BAROLO
(Beef in red wine)

1 bottle Barolo wine
1 onion
1 stick celery
1 carrot
a few peppercorns
salt
1 bay leaf
2 lb beef rump roast or chuck pot roast
⅛ cup butter
⅛ cup ham fat, chopped
1 tsp cornstarch

Pour the wine into a bowl and add the chopped onion, celery and carrot, the peppercorns, a pinch of salt and the crumbled bay leaf. Put the beef into the liquid and marinate for at least 24 hr, turning occasionally. When ready to cook, dry thoroughly and tie securely. Place in a heavy saucepan and brown evenly in the melted butter and ham fat. Meanwhile, reduce the marinade over high heat in a separate saucepan. When it is fairly concentrated, strain and pour over the meat. Add salt to taste, cover the saucepan and cook over low heat for about 2 hr until the meat is

very tender. Remove from the saucepan and place on a warm serving dish. Mix the cornstarch with a little water and stir in to the gravy. Cook for a few minutes, stirring continuously. Serve the meat with the piping hot gravy.

MEDAGLIONI ALLA ROSSINI
(Beef medallions with Marsala sauce)

4 1-in thick round fillet mignon steaks
2 tbsp olive oil
¼ cup butter
1 tbsp all-purpose flour
½ cup Marsala
salt
freshly ground pepper
4 slices prosciutto
4 slices Gruyère cheese
½ cup thick white sauce (see p. 127)
4 slices fried bread
1 white truffle (optional)

Fry the steaks in the oil and butter over high heat. When the meat begins to brown, sprinkle with flour and then pour in the Marsala. Cook until the liquid evaporates. Season generously with salt and pepper on both sides. Leave the meat to cook until it has absorbed all the juices, then transfer to an ovenproof casserole. Lay slices of prosciutto and Gruyère cheese over the steaks, cover with the white sauce and place in a hot oven (400°F) for a few minutes until the cheese has melted. Serve the steaks on slices of bread fried to a golden brown in butter. Sprinkle with sliced truffle if available.

Veal

NOCE DI VITELLO FARCITO
(Stuffed veal)

(serves 6–8)
2¼ lb boneless veal rump roast (or knuckle)
salt
freshly ground pepper

chopped rosemary
few drops lemon juice
½ lb pork or turkey meat
nutmeg
2 tbsp Marsala
2 oz cooked ham
2 oz cooked tongue
2 oz mortadella
2 oz calf's liver
2 hard-boiled egg yolks
1 cooked carrot, diced
1 cup cooked peas
3 tbsp olive oil
milk (optional)

Pound the veal with a meatbat and flatten into a rectangle. Season with a little salt, pepper, chopped rosemary and a few drops of lemon juice. Leave to stand for ½ hr. Meanwhile, prepare the stuffing: Chop the pork or turkey meat and season with salt, nutmeg and Marsala. Add the ham, the tongue and the mortadella, all cut into cubes, the liver, cut into pieces, the hard-boiled egg yolks, the carrot and the peas. Mix all the ingredients together and spread the mixture over the meat, leaving the edges free. Roll up carefully and tie securely with kitchen string. Place the meat in an ovenproof dish. Sprinkle with olive oil and cook in a moderate oven (310°F) for about 1½ hr until the veal is tender. Add a little milk if necessary during cooking to moisten the meat. Serve hot or cold, cut into slices.

SALTIMBOCCA ALLA ROMANA
(Veal cutlets with prosciutto and sage)

8 veal cutlets
8 slices prosciutto
8 sage leaves
¼ cup butter
salt
freshly ground pepper
dry white wine

Pound the cutlets with a meatbat until very thin. Lay a slice of prosciutto and a sage leaf on each and secure with a toothpick. Heat the butter in a wide skillet and add the cutlets. Brown on both sides over high heat adding a pinch of salt, pepper and a few tablespoons of white wine. Let the wine evaporate quickly (the cutlets should be cooked for no longer than 5 min) and then transfer the cutlets to a warm serving dish. Pour over the juices from the skillet and serve immediately. If there is insufficient liquid in the skillet, add a few tablespoons of water after the cutlets have been removed and stir over high heat for 1 min. Pour the meat juices over the cutlets and serve at once.

TOURNEDOS CON FINANZIERA
(Tournedos à la financière)

¾ lb calf sweetbreads
salt
1 tbsp vinegar
½ onion
1 carrot
1 stick celery
freshly ground pepper
½ cup butter
¾ cup Madeira (or dry Marsala)
½ cup diced pickled mushrooms
¼ cup diced pickled gherkins
4 1-in thick slices boneless veal roast
1 tbsp all-purpose flour

Soak the sweetbreads in cold water for 1 hr. Drain, place in a saucepan with cold water, bring to a boil and drain again. Put the sweetbreads in a saucepan of lightly salted water. Add the vinegar, onion, carrot, celery, a little salt and pepper, and boil for about 10 min. Drain, skin and dice the sweetbreads. Melt ¼ cup butter in a small skillet, add the sweetbreads and sauté briefly. Season with salt and pepper and pour in ¼ cup Madeira. Allow to evaporate, then add the mushrooms and gherkins. Mix well, cover and keep warm. To prepare the tournedos, tie up the slices of veal with kitchen string so that they keep their shape, then coat with flour. Melt the remaining butter in a skillet, add the tournedos and fry gently on both sides. Pour in ½ cup Madeira and cook very slowly until the liquid evaporates. Untie the tournedos, place them on a warm serving dish and pour a little of the sauce over each.

SOUFFLÉ CON FINANZIERA
(Soufflé à la financière)

(serves 6)
4 oz calf sweetbreads
½ cup dried mushrooms
3 tbsp olive oil
salt
6 chicken livers
1 tbsp butter
¼ cup dry white wine

for the soufflé:
generous ¼ cup butter
¾ cup all-purpose flour
2 ¼ cups milk
salt
freshly ground white pepper
pinch of nutmeg
¼ cup grated Parmesan cheese
2 oz prosciutto, cut into strips
4 eggs, separated
1 white truffle

Soak the sweetbreads in cold water for 1 hr. Drain, and place in a saucepan with cold water. Bring to a boil and drain again. Cover with cold water, bring to a boil and simmer for ¼ hr. Drain and set aside. Soak the mushrooms in warm water for ½ hr; drain, squeeze out excess water and cook in the oil with a pinch of salt. Dice the livers, sprinkle with salt and fry over high heat in the butter for a few minutes. Cut the sweetbreads into pieces and add to the liver. Stir in the wine and allow to evaporate. Remove from the heat and keep warm. To prepare the soufflé: Preheat the oven to 350°F. Melt the butter in a large saucepan over low heat, add the flour and when it has absorbed the butter stir in the hot milk a little at a time. Season with salt, a pinch of white pepper and nutmeg and cook for about ¼ hr, stirring constantly. Remove from the heat and stir in the grated Parmesan cheese and the prosciutto. Beat in the egg yolks one at a time, then gently fold in the stiffly beaten egg whites. Pour the mixture into a buttered 2-quart soufflé dish and transfer immediately to the hot oven. Cook for 40–50 min or until well risen and golden brown. Serve immediately with the reheated sweetbread and chicken liver mixture and the mushrooms. Finally, sprinkle with finely grated truffle.

COSTOLETTE ALLA VALDOSTANA *
(Veal chops Val D'Aosta)

4 large veal rib chops
4 oz Fontina cheese
4 slices prosciutto
salt
freshly ground pepper
1 tbsp all-purpose flour
1 egg, beaten
fine dry breadcrumbs
¼ cup butter

Make a horizontal slit in each chop to form a pocket for the filling. Cut the cheese into thin strips, divide into four portions, then divide equally between the slices of prosciutto. Roll up, flatten slightly and insert one into each of the pockets made in the chops. Then pound the edges of the pockets with a meat-bat to close. Season each chop on both sides with salt and pepper; dip first into the flour, then into the beaten egg and then into the breadcrumbs. Melt the butter in a wide skillet and cook the chops for about 20 min until golden brown on both sides. Serve hot with a fresh seasonal salad.

VITELLO ALLA MARENGO
(Veal Marengo)

1¾ lb boneless veal rump roast (or knuckle)
½ cup olive oil
1 onion, finely chopped
salt
freshly ground pepper
1 tbsp all-purpose flour
1 cup dry white wine
2¼ cups stock
4 ripe tomatoes, skinned and chopped into slices
1 clove garlic, minced
½ bay leaf
pinch of thyme
8 shallots
¼ cup butter
8 button mushrooms
4 slices bread fried in oil
2 tbsp chopped parsley

Cut the veal into large chunks and place in a skillet with the hot oil. Brown evenly, add the onion, a little salt and a pinch of pepper and cook for 5 min. Sprinkle in the flour and stir until the meat is well browned. Pour in the wine and stock. Stir to prevent the mixture from sticking to the skillet. Bring to a boil and add the tomato slices, garlic, bay leaf and thyme. Cover, lower the heat and simmer for about ¾ hr. Meanwhile sauté the shallots briefly in the butter. Rinse and dry the mushrooms, add, together with the shallots, to the skillet with the meat and cook for a further ¼ hr. Leave to stand so that the fat comes to the surface; skim off with a spoon and reheat. Transfer the meat to a serving dish, with its gravy, and arrange the fried bread slices around it. Sprinkle with chopped parsley.

COSTOLETTE ALLA MILANESE
(Milanese chops)

4 veal loin chops
2 eggs, beaten
fine dry breadcrumbs
½ cup butter
salt
lemon slices

To prepare the meat, trim away from the bone slightly, pound the meat lightly with a meatbat and cut the fat around the edge to prevent curling during cooking. Pound lightly again, dip into the beaten egg and then into the breadcrumbs, making sure that they are evenly coated. Heat the butter in a large skillet until it starts to brown, then add the chops, which should fit easily into the skillet. Cook over high heat without turning until a golden crust has formed on one side. Turn over with a wooden spatula and cook until a crust has formed on the other side. Lower the heat and cook for a further 5 min (the chops should be soft and lightly browned). Sprinkle with salt. Place the chops on a warm serving dish and garnish with lemon slices. The chops are also excellent eaten cold.

VITELLO AL VINO ROSSO
(Veal with red wine)

1 onion
generous ¼ cup butter
1½ lb veal stew meat
salt
freshly ground pepper
2¼ cups red wine
1 tsp meat extract
3–4 sprigs parsley
1 clove garlic
1 bay leaf
1 sprig thyme
1 tbsp all-purpose flour

Put the finely chopped onion and ¼ cup butter into a skillet over moderate heat. When the onion starts to fry, add the pieces of veal and brown. Season with salt and pepper and pour in the red wine, together with 1 cup water in which the meat extract has been dissolved. Reduce the liquid over fairly high heat. Prepare the herbs by wrapping the parsley, the minced garlic, bay leaf and thyme in a piece of muslin. Tie with thread and place in the skillet with the meat. Cover, turn down the heat and simmer for about 2 hr, adding a little water if necessary. Discard the herbs, lift out the meat with a slotted spoon and transfer to a warm serving dish. Blend the remaining butter with 1 tbsp flour and add to the sauce a little at a time to thicken. Pour the sauce over the veal and serve.

VITELLO CON MELANZANE
(Veal with eggplant)

4 ¼-lb slices veal fillet
2 eggplant
salt
oil for frying
4 ripe tomatoes
2 tbsp olive oil
½ cup pitted green (or black) olives
2–4 chopped basil leaves
all-purpose flour
¼ cup butter

Peel the eggplant, cut them into rounds ¼ in thick, salt lightly and place in a colander for 1 hr to drain away the bitter juices. Dry well and then deep fry a few at a time in hot oil. As soon as they are cooked, drain on kitchen paper. Dip the tomatoes into boiling water for 1 min; peel off the skin, cut into pieces and remove seeds. Put the tomatoes into a large skillet with the olive oil and a good pinch of salt and cook over high heat for about 10 min. Add the olives, basil and fried eggplant and cook over low heat for a couple of minutes. Coat the veal slices with flour and fry in another skillet in the butter over high heat for about 6 min turning once. Season with a pinch of salt and when well browned, transfer to a warm serving dish. Cover with the sauce and serve at once.

TESTINA DI VITELLO ALLE OLIVE
(Calf's head with olives)

1 calf's head
1 onion
1 carrot
1 stick celery
1 sprig parsley
salt
1 cup green olives
1 onion
2 carrots
2 sticks celery

Scrape and rinse the head thoroughly then place in a large saucepan with the whole onion, carrot, celery, parsley and a little salt. Cover with plenty of water, bring to a boil, then cover and simmer for at least 1 hr until the meat comes away from the bone easily. Remove all the meat and slice thinly. Reserve the stock. Pit all the olives and pound half with a pestle in a mortar. Put the chopped onion, carrots and celery into a saucepan with a few tablespoons of the reserved stock. Cook over low heat until the vegetables soften, then add the chopped olives and sliced meat. Cook for a few minutes, add another ladle of hot stock and then add the remaining pitted olives. Add salt if required, and simmer over low heat for about 10 min, shaking the saucepan from time to time to prevent the sauce from sticking. Serve piping hot.

INVOLTINI CON FAGIOLONI BIANCHI
(Roulades with white beans)

8 small veal cutlets
2 oz ham fat
1 clove garlic, chopped
6 tbsp olive oil
3 tbsp chopped parsley
4 ripe tomatoes, peeled and
    chopped
2 cups cooked white beans
salt
1 clove garlic, minced
¼ lb mushrooms, sliced
2 tbsp stock
scant 1 cup ground pork loin
2 tbsp grated Parmesan cheese
1 egg
freshly ground pepper
¼ cup butter

Pound the veal cutlets until ⅛ in thick. Fry the ham fat and the chopped garlic in half the oil. Add 2 tbsp parsley and the tomatoes followed by the cooked white beans. Season with salt and simmer gently for ½ hr. Meanwhile, fry the minced garlic clove in a small skillet in the remaining oil. As soon as it begins to brown, remove and add the mushrooms. Add salt and stock and cook over moderate heat for about 20 min.

Drain and chop finely. Mix the ground pork in a bowl with the Parmesan cheese, egg, a pinch of salt and pepper, the remaining parsley and mushrooms. Put a little of the mixture in the center of each cutlet and roll up, securing with a toothpick. Cook the roulades in hot butter until they are evenly browned, then add the white beans with their sauce. Continue cooking over low heat for a further ¼ hr.

PICCATE DI VITELLO
(Veal in lemon sauce)

4 ¼-lb veal cutlets
salt
1 tbsp all-purpose flour
1 tbsp butter
juice of ½ lemon
1 sprig parsley

Pound the veal cutlets until they are all the same thickness; sprinkle with salt and coat with flour. Melt the butter in a skillet. When it starts to color, add the cutlets and brown on both sides. As soon as the meat is cooked (if the veal is tender it will only take a few minutes), pour in the lemon juice and sprinkle with finely chopped parsley. Serve piping hot.

VITELLO IN GELATINA ALLA MILANESE
(Milanese veal in aspic)

2 lb veal breast (in one piece)
2 carrots
2 sticks celery
salt
freshly ground pepper
2 thick slices lean prosciutto
¼ cup butter
1 oz salt pork, chopped
2 bay leaves
1 clove garlic
1 calf's foot
2 envelopes unflavored gelatin
1 egg white
1–2 tbsp Marsala
pickles to garnish

Lay out the piece of veal and beat out to a ½-in thick square. Dice 1 carrot and chop 1 stick celery, mix together and spread over half the meat. Fold the meat in half, season

with salt and pepper on both sides and place between the two slices of prosciutto. Tie up securely with string so that the prosciutto stays in place while the meat is cooking. Melt the butter in a large skillet and add the salt pork, the remaining chopped carrot, celery and the bay leaves. Add the veal and cook evenly over moderate heat. Add the garlic clove and the calf's foot split in two; cover with water. Cover, bring to a boil, lower the heat and leave to simmer for about 2 hr. Turn off the heat and leave the meat to cool in its stock before cutting into thick slices. Arrange the slices in a serving dish.

Prepare the aspic using the cooking stock. Pour the stock through a muslin-lined sieve twice to eliminate excess fat. Dissolve the gelatin in the hot stock (add a little hot water if necessary to make up to 4 cups of liquid). Add a little salt, a beaten egg white to clarify the stock and 1–2 tbsp Marsala to add flavor. Place in a saucepan over heat and beat the liquid with a whisk until it reaches boiling point. Cover the saucepan and leave to simmer very gently for 4–5 min. Strain through a muslin-lined sieve to remove any sediment, then pour over the slices of meat. Leave to cool and then place in the refrigerator until the aspic is set. This dish may be served garnished with pickles.

NERVETTI IN INSALATA
(Cold veal with scallions in vinaigrette)

2 calf's feet and 2 slices veal rump roast (or knuckle)
1 carrot
1 stick celery
3 scallions
olive oil
wine vinegar
salt
freshly ground pepper

Clean, singe and rinse the calf's feet; rinse the veal slices. Simmer in plenty of salted water together with the carrot and the celery for at least 2 hr. Remove from the stock, leave to cool then strip the meat from the calf's feet. Cut the slices of veal into strips, and transfer

both to a bowl. Add the finely sliced scallions and dress, while still warm, with oil, good wine vinegar, salt and pepper.

FRITTURA PICCATA
(Veal and prosciutto in lemon sauce)

8 small veal cutlets
all-purpose flour
½ lb prosciutto
¼ cup butter
juice of 1 lemon
2 sprigs parsley, finely chopped
2 tbsp hot stock

Pound the veal cutlets lightly until they are very thin and coat with flour. Cut the prosciutto into thin strips, heat two-thirds of the butter in a large skillet and fry the veal cutlets and prosciutto over high heat for a few minutes. Salt lightly. As soon as the meat is cooked, transfer to a warm serving dish. Put the remaining butter, lemon juice, chopped parsley and stock into the skillet. Stir well and pour over the meat as soon as the mixture starts to boil. Serve immediately.

OSSOBUCO ALLA MILANESE *
(Braised shin of veal)

¼ cup butter
4 1½-in thick pieces shin of veal
1 tbsp all-purpose flour
½ cup dry white wine
1 cup peeled tomatoes
1 sprig parsley
grated rind of ½ lemon
1 clove garlic
1 anchovy (optional)

Melt the butter in a large saucepan, coat the meat with flour and add to the pan. Brown well on both sides, then slowly pour in the wine. Once the wine has evaporated, add the sieved tomatoes, cover and leave to simmer over low heat for about 1½ hr, stirring frequently, until the meat comes away from the bone (add a little hot water or stock if necessary but remember that the sauce must be fairly thick).

Now prepare a *gremolada* by chopping the parsley, lemon rind and garlic (and the rinsed and boned anchovy if desired). Remove the lid from the saucepan and divide the *gremolada* equally between the pieces of meat. Leave to simmer over moderate heat without further stirring for another 5 min. Serve very hot (the marrow is best when hot) accompanied by Milanese risotto or plain boiled rice.

COTOLETTE ALLA BOLOGNESE
(Bolognese veal cutlets [1])

4 6-oz veal cutlets
salt
1 tbsp all-purpose flour
1 egg
fine dry breadcrumbs
¼ cup butter
4 slices prosciutto
4 slices fresh Parmesan cheese (or 4 processed cheese slices)
½ cup, freshly made tomato sauce (see p. 127)
2 tbsp dry white wine (or dry Marsala)
milk (optional)

Pound the cutlets until thin; sprinkle with salt and coat with flour. Dip the cutlets first into the beaten egg, then coat with breadcrumbs. Melt the butter in a skillet, add the cutlets and brown on both sides. Remove from the pan and arrange side by side in a wide ovenproof dish. Put a slice of prosciutto and a slice of Parmesan (or processed cheese) on each. Pour in the tomato sauce, wine and a little milk, then place in a hot oven (400°F) for ¼ hr until the meat has absorbed almost all the wine. If preferred, stuffed cutlets can be prepared in the following way: Place a slice of prosciutto and a slice of cheese on each cutlet (in this case they should be smaller than those used above), cover with a second cutlet and press together; dip in flour, beaten egg and breadcrumbs as before, cook as above and when golden, pour in a little milk and the tomato sauce. Season with salt and pepper, cover and simmer gently over low heat for about 20 min.

SCALOPPE DI VITELLO ALLA BOLOGNESE
(Bolognese veal cutlets [2])

8 small veal cutlets
2 tbsp all-purpose flour
¼ cup butter
salt
freshly ground pepper
½ cup dry white wine
8 slices prosciutto
8 slices Gruyère cheese

Lightly pound the cutlets with a meatbat and coat with flour. Melt the butter in a skillet and brown the cutlets well on both sides. Transfer to a large ovenproof dish and season with salt and pepper to taste. Return the skillet in which the meat was cooked to the heat and pour in the wine (or 4 tbsp dry Marsala if preferred). When hot, pour over the cutlets in the ovenproof dish. Place a slice of prosciutto and a slice of Gruyère cheese on each cutlet and transfer to a hot oven (about 400°F) for a few minutes until the cheese is melted. Serve hot with vegetables or a green salad.

UCCELLINI DI CAMPAGNA
(Veal kabobs)

¼ lb salt pork
thick slices of bread, cut into cubes
1 lb veal cutlets, cut into cubes
a few sage leaves
olive oil
salt
freshly ground pepper

Finely slice the salt pork and thread alternate pieces of bread, veal, sage leaves and salt pork on to metal skewers. Brush with olive oil and sprinkle with salt and pepper. Put the skewers into an ovenproof dish and place in a hot oven (375°F) for about ½ hr, adding a few tablespoons of water to the dish as the juices dry up. Serve when the veal is tender and the bread golden brown.

This dish has several variations to accommodate different tastes. Some prefer to add slices of sausage or small pieces of pancetta to the veal.

BISTECCA ALLA FIORENTINA
(Steak Florentine)

2 T-bone steaks
salt
freshly ground pepper
4 tbsp olive oil
1 lemon

The secret of good steak Florentine lies in the quality of the meat and the cooking. The meat must be tender, red, succulent, and each steak should be 1 in thick and weigh no more than 1½ lb. Take the steaks (not pounded) and, without any type of seasoning, barbecue over a charcoal fire or under an electric broiler. Once the steaks are browned on one side, turn and season the cooked side with salt and pepper. Turn a second time and remove when the steaks are well browned on the outside and rare inside. Place on a serving dish and, if desired, sprinkle with a little olive oil. Garnish with lemon slices. For the Tuscan gourmet, the only seasonings necessary for this dish are salt, pepper and lemon juice.

144

COTECHINO IN FAGOTTO
(Veal stuffed with sausage)

1 ¾-lb cotechino sausage
1 lb veal rump roast (in a single
     slice)
3 slices prosciutto
¼ cup butter
1 stick celery
1 small carrot
½ onion
1 cup dry red wine
1 tsp meat extract

Remove the string from the sausage. Place the sausage in a large saucepan of cold water, bring to a boil and then simmer for ½ hr. Take the sausage out of the saucepan, remove the skin and leave to cool. Flatten out the veal with a meatbat. Place on a board, lay the slices of prosciutto on top and then place the sausage in the center. Roll up carefully and tie with string like a salami. Place the butter with the coarsely chopped celery, carrot and onion in a saucepan and cook until soft. Then add the prepared meat roll and brown all over. When the meat is evenly browned pour in the wine and let it reduce over high heat. Add 1 cup hot water containing the dissolved meat extract; cover and simmer over very low heat for about 1 hr (adding more hot water if necessary). Take the roll out of the saucepan, remove the string and cut into fairly thick slices (½ in). Arrange on a serving dish and keep warm in the oven. Stir the sauce over high heat until slightly reduced and thickened. Pour the sauce over the slices and serve immediately. This dish can be served with a green salad or, as in Romagna, with parboiled carrots sautéed in butter and seasoned with a pinch of salt and freshly ground pepper.

ROGNONI ALLA FIORENTINA
(Kidneys Florence style)

2 calves' kidneys
¼ cup butter
salt
freshly ground pepper
2 tbsp parsley
fine dry breadcrumbs
1 lemon

Cut the kidneys in half lengthwise and remove the membrane and hard white fat. Rinse the four kidney halves under cold water and dry thoroughly. Heat the butter in a skillet and when it is bubbling, add the pieces of kidney and sauté gently for a few minutes. Remove the skillet from the heat, season with salt, freshly ground pepper and chopped parsley. Set aside for a couple of hours, turning from time to time so that the kidneys are coated with the seasoning. Coat the kidneys in breadcrumbs and return to the skillet (or broiler) for a few minutes, browning well on both sides. Serve with mixed vegetables or a green salad, and garnish with lemon slices.

ARROSTO FARCITO
(Pot-roast stuffed veal)

10 oz spinach
2 eggs
¼ cup grated Parmesan cheese
2 oz Bolognese mortadella
salt
¼ cup + 2 tbsp butter
3 tbsp oil
1 lb veal rump roast (in a single slice)

145

4 oz pancetta
1 cup milk
freshly ground pepper

Trim and wash the spinach thoroughly. Cook for about 5 min, using only the water remaining on the leaves; drain thoroughly and chop finely. Place in a bowl and add the eggs, grated cheese and diced mortadella. Stir well and add salt to taste. Heat 1 tbsp butter and 1 tbsp oil in a large skillet. When they bubble, pour in the mixture from the bowl and spread out to form a thin omelet. Cook on one side and then turn gently so that it is evenly cooked on both sides. Place the meat on a board and flatten out with a meatbat until thin enough to roll. Cover with pancetta slices, followed by the spinach omelet, taking care to leave a border around the edge so that the filling ingredients do not spill out. Roll up carefully and sew up with kitchen thread so that all the ingredients are securely enclosed. Tie up with string like a large salami. Heat the remaining butter and oil in a large saucepan, add the meat roll and cook over low heat, turning frequently, until golden brown all over. When the meat is browned, add the milk and the same quantity of water. Cover the saucepan and bring to a boil. Simmer gently for about 1 hr.

This dish can be served hot in its own gravy or cold. It should be cut into thick slices (about ¾ in) and accompanied by a salad of radicchio.

ROGNONE IN UMIDO
(Braised kidneys)

2 calves' kidneys
salt
2 tbsp all-purpose flour
2 tbsp butter
2 tbsp oil
freshly ground pepper
1 sprig parsley
2 cloves garlic

Cut the kidneys in half lengthwise and remove the membrane and hard white fat. Slice and sprinkle with 1 tsp fine salt. Rub the salt well into the kidneys with your hands. Put the kidneys in a strainer and rinse under cold water. Place on kitchen paper to dry a little, then coat with flour, making sure that the slices are all well-floured and not stuck together. Heat the butter in a saucepan and when it starts to bubble add the slices of kidney. Stir the pieces of kidney over low heat until the flour is crusty and brown in color. Add sufficient warm water to produce a relatively thin sauce, about the consistency of light cream. Pour in the oil, salt to taste and a sprinkling of pepper. Finely chop plenty of parsley and the garlic and add to the saucepan. Leave to cook over very low heat for a further 10–15 min, stirring occasionally. Take care not to overcook the kidneys or they will toughen. When cooked, the sauce should have the same consistency as a white sauce. Serve immediately with hot, freshly made polenta.

VITELLO TONNATO
(Cold veal with tuna sauce)

1 bottle dry white wine
1 tbsp vinegar
1 bay leaf
2 cloves
1 stick celery
½ onion
1¼ lb veal rump roast
salt
4 salted anchovies
7 oz tuna in oil
2 hard-boiled eggs
½ cup olive oil
1 tbsp pickled capers
1 lemon

Put the wine, vinegar, chopped bay leaf, cloves, celery and chopped onion into a bowl. Tie up the veal securely, place in the marinade and leave to stand for about 24 hr (turn from time to time to insure the meat is thoroughly marinated). Remove the veal from the marinade and place in a saucepan. Strain the marinade over the meat and add sufficient water to cover the meat completely. Add a little salt, cover and leave to cook for about ¾ hr or until the stock has reduced. Rinse and bone the anchovies, mash up the tuna and chop the boiled eggs. Put the mixture into a sieve and pour the meat stock over it. Rub through the sieve and gradually stir in the oil and 1 tbsp capers, after squeezing well to remove the vinegar. When the veal is cool, remove the string and, using a sharp knife, cut the meat into thin slices (about ¼ in). Place on a serving dish and pour over the sauce. Serve with a dish of capers for those who may prefer a stronger taste.

A variation on this recipe involves a much simpler sauce. Prepare a mayonnaise sauce using two egg yolks, 2 tbsp olive oil, salt and vinegar or lemon juice. Finely chop the tuna, a few capers and a washed, boned anchovy (a blender or food processor would produce a tuna sauce of more even consistency). Add the tuna sauce to the mayonnaise together with a few more capers. This last version can be made at the last moment if ready-made mayonnaise is used.

CIMA ALLA GENOVESE
(Genoese stuffed breast of veal)

1¼ lb breast of veal, boned
1 calf's sweetbread
3 oz calves' brain
2 oz bone marrow
2 oz lean veal
½ onion, chopped
1 clove garlic
¼ cup butter
1 cup peas
3 eggs
3 tbsp grated Parmesan cheese
marjoram
salt

for the stock:
2 quarts water
1 onion
1 carrot
1 stick celery
salt

Prepare the stock in advance: Dice the vegetables; place in a large saucepan with the water and a little salt; bring to a boil and simmer for ½ hr. Set aside until needed.

Ask the butcher to cut the veal belly into a pouch so that it is open along one side and can be filled. Soak the sweetbread and brains in cold water for 1 hr. Drain, cover with cold water, add the bone marrow and bring to a boil. Drain, cover with cold water again, bring to a boil then simmer for 10 min. Drain, then remove the skin from the brains and sweetbread. Brown together with the lean veal and chopped onion and garlic in the butter. Take the meats out of the saucepan, cut into small pieces and mix with the peas, the eggs beaten with Parmesan cheese, a pinch of marjoram and salt. Spoon the stuffing into the veal pouch and sew up with kitchen thread. Put the meat in the hot vegetable stock, bring gently to a boil then simmer, uncovered, for 1 hr. Cover and cook for a further 1 hr. Remove the meat from the saucepan, cover with a cloth and place a heavy weight on top to compress the meat and filling. Remove the thread and serve hot or cold, cut into slices. The stock left over will make excellent soup.

LOMBATINE ALLA PARMIGIANA
(Veal cutlets with Parmesan cheese)

4 veal cutlets
salt
2 tbsp butter
¼ cup chopped ham
2–3 sprigs parsley, chopped
3 tbsp grated Parmesan cheese
½ cup Marsala

Pound the cutlets gently to flatten them, sprinkle with salt and place in a large buttered skillet. Brown slowly on both sides until the cutlets are golden brown. Mix together the ham, parsley and Parmesan cheese. Spread this mixture over the cutlets and pour in the Marsala. Cover the skillet and cook until the steam from the Marsala has melted the cheese. Serve hot.

"ZAMPI DI VITELLO"
(Calf's feet)

4 calf's feet
1 carrot
2 onions
2 sticks celery

¼ cup butter
2 tbsp oil
1 sprig parsley, chopped
salt
freshly ground pepper
1 tbsp meat extract
½ cup tomato paste
2 tbsp grated Parmesan cheese
pinch of cinnamon

Scrape the calf's feet with a knife and singe. Rinse in several changes of water and bring to a boil in a large saucepan of salted water together with the carrot, one onion and the celery. Simmer the calf's feet for about 2 hr until the meat falls away from the bone. Then take the feet out of the stock, strip the meat from the bones and cut into pieces. Put the butter, oil, parsley and the remaining chopped onion into a saucepan. Cook over moderate heat for a few minutes, then add the meat together with a few tablespoons of the cooking stock. Season with salt and pepper. When the stock has reduced slightly, add 1 tbsp meat extract and the tomato paste mixed with 1 tbsp stock. Add a little more stock and continue cooking until the sauce is quite thick. Sprinkle with Parmesan cheese and cinnamon before placing on a warm serving dish.

STUFATO DI MUSCOLO
(Braised veal)

1 lb lean veal stew meat, cut into
    cubes
all-purpose flour
2 tbsp tomato paste
3 tbsp oil
¼ cup butter
2 cloves garlic, minced
½ cup dry white wine
salt
freshly ground pepper
2–3 tbsp chopped parsley

Coat the cubes of veal in flour. Dilute the tomato paste in a little warm water. Heat the oil and butter in a heavy saucepan and fry the garlic, which must be removed as soon as it browns. Add the veal and brown all over. Pour in the wine and leave the liquid to reduce over moderate heat. Add the diluted tomato paste, salt and

pepper. Turn down the heat, cover and continue to cook for about 1 hr until the meat is tender and the sauce quite thick. Garnish with parsley and serve with the traditional accompaniment of boiled peas, or mushrooms fried in butter.

Pork

SCALOPPE DI MAIALE AL MARSALA
(Pork escalopes with Marsala)

1 lb pork tenderloin
¼ cup lard
salt
freshly ground pepper
½ cup Marsala
1 tbsp flour
2 tbsp butter

Cut the fat off the tenderloin and slit halfway through the meat. Open up as though the tenderloin were a book and pound with a dampened meatbat to obtain a single large slice. Cut several small steaks about 4 in long and 1½ in wide, which must then be pounded until thin. Heat the lard in a skillet and cook the escalopes for a couple of minutes on each side over high heat. Season with a little salt and a generous sprinkling of pepper then arrange on a serving dish so that the escalopes overlap. Keep warm. Meanwhile, pour the Marsala into the skillet together with the meat juices. Add the flour and stir with a wooden spoon over low heat until the sauce thickens. Add the butter, cut into pieces, and pour the hot sauce over the meat.

COSTINE AL FINOCCHIO *
(Spareribs with fennel)

2 tbsp oil
2 tbsp butter
2 lb pork spareribs
salt
freshly ground pepper
4 tbsp Marsala
½ cup red wine
1 clove garlic, chopped

147

pinch of fennel seeds
1 tbsp tomato paste

Heat the oil and the butter in a skillet and cook the spareribs over moderate heat. Season with salt and pepper and brown on both sides. When the ribs are cooked through, place on a serving dish, cover and keep warm. Put the Marsala, red wine, garlic, fennel and tomato paste into the skillet. Stir and boil over high heat. When the sauce has reduced by about two-thirds and appears quite thick, pour over the spareribs and serve immediately.

RÔSTIDA
(Braised pork variety meats in tomato sauce)

1 lb pork variety meats (heart, liver, kidneys, tongue, lights, etc.)
½ lb pork loin
¼ cup butter
3 large ripe or canned tomatoes
salt
freshly ground pepper

This is a typical Piedmont dish.

Select preferred variety meats, and together with the pork loin, cut into pieces and fry in butter in a skillet for a few minutes. Add the sieved tomatoes and season with salt and pepper to taste. Cover and simmer until the meats are tender, stirring from time to time and adding water if necessary. The cooking time will vary according to the types of variety meats used. The sauce should be fairly thick and is excellent served with hot polenta.

INVOLTINI DI MAIALE AL FORNO
(Baked pork roulades)

¾–1 lb pork loin
4 oz pork liver
2 oz chopped salt pork
1 chopped clove garlic
1 chopped sprig parsley
the soft inside of half a bread roll
2 egg yolks (or one whole egg)
bread slices
½ cup oil
salt
freshly ground pepper

Cut the meat into about a dozen thin slices and pound with a meat-bat. Soak the bread in a little warm, salted water and squeeze well. In a bowl mix the chopped liver and the salt pork with the garlic and parsley and add the bread and egg yolks (or whole egg). Mix well. Divide the filling among the meat slices. Roll up to form roulades and sew up the ends with kitchen thread so the filling does not seep out during cooking. Thread the roulades on to skewers in pairs, sandwiching a small slice of bread in between. Arrange the roulades in a pan, sprinkle with oil, add salt and pepper and cook in a preheated oven at 325°F for about ½ hr until they are well-browned and the bread is crispy. Serve hot.

INVOLTINI ALLA MILANESE
(Milanese pork roulades)

¾–1 lb lean pork or veal slices
2 small Italian pork sausages
2 chopped chicken livers
1 chopped clove garlic
2 tbsp chopped parsley
2 tbsp grated Parmesan cheese
2 egg yolks
4 oz pancetta
sage leaves
all-purpose flour
¼ cup butter
salt
½ cup white wine
½ cup hot water or stock

Only very tender meat is suitable for this recipe. Pound the pork or veal slices gently until they are thin. Try to make them all the same size, about 2¾ × 4 in.

Remove the skin from the sausages and crumble the sausage meat with the chicken livers, garlic, parsley, Parmesan cheese and beaten egg yolks in a bowl to form a thick paste. Spread on the meat, roll up the slices and secure with a toothpick. Thread a slice of pancetta and a sage leaf on to each toothpick. Flour the roulades lightly and fry in the butter in a large skillet until brown all over. Season with salt, add the wine and simmer over moderate heat until all the wine has evaporated. Add the stock, cover the skillet and continue to cook over moderate heat for about 20 min until the roulades are tender. Serve with risotto or polenta.

MORSEDDU
(Pork variety meats in tomato sauce)

9 oz pork or veal liver
5 oz pork or veal lights
5 oz pork or veal heart
½ cup oil (or lard)
2 chopped cloves garlic
12 oz ripe tomatoes
salt
freshly ground pepper
1 piece chili pepper, chopped
slices of toast or a pita

The name *morseddu* derives from the fact that this dish is eaten in bites or *morsi*. Dip the tomatoes into boiling water for 1 min, peel, seed and chop. Thinly slice the liver and grind the lights and heart. Heat the oil (or lard) in a skillet and brown the meats, then add the garlic and the tomatoes. Season with salt and pepper and add the chili pepper. Cover and cook over low heat for about ½ hr. Spread the mixture over slices of toast or fill halved pitas. Cook in a preheated oven at 375°F for ½ hr.

LOMBATINE DI MAIALE ALLA NAPOLETANA *
(Neapolitan pork loin cutlets)

2 yellow or red peppers
1 cup mushrooms
olive oil
1 clove garlic
4 pork loin cutlets
salt
freshly ground pepper
1 tbsp tomato paste

Clean the peppers, remove the core, seeds and membrane and cut into rings; clean the mushrooms and slice. Put a little oil in a skillet and fry the garlic without browning. Remove the garlic and use the same oil to fry the cutlets until golden brown; season with salt and pepper. Remove from the heat and keep warm. Put the tomato paste diluted in a little water into the skillet and add the peppers, mushrooms and then the cutlets. Cover and cook for ½ hr. Serve hot.

"CAZZOEULA"
(Spareribs with cabbage)

1 pig's trotter and 1 pig's ear
5 oz pigskin
1 onion, thinly sliced
2 tbsp butter
1 tbsp oil
1 lb pork spareribs
½ cup dry white wine
2 chopped sticks celery
2 chopped carrots
1 ladle stock
4 Luganega sausages
2 lb tender white Savoy cabbage
 leaves
salt
freshly ground pepper

A dish typical of Lombardy.

Singe the pig's ear and trotter; cut the pigskin into large pieces and boil in water for about 1 hr. Reserve the stock. Fry the onion until soft in the oil and butter, add the spareribs and brown. Pour in the wine and when it has evaporated, add the celery, carrots, pig's trotter, ear and skin. Pour in the hot stock and cook for about ½ hr.

Now add the sausages and the thoroughly washed Savoy cabbage and cook for a further ½ hr. Skim off the fat from time to time, season with salt and pepper. The "cazzoeula" should not be too runny.

BRACIOLINE DI MAIALE AL VINO BIANCO
(Pork chops in white wine)

4 pork chops
1 chopped clove garlic
1 chopped sprig rosemary
salt
pinch of chili pepper
2 tbsp oil
½ cup dry white wine
1 ladle stock

Pound the pork chops gently. Cut away the surrounding fat, chop finely and mix it with the chopped garlic, rosemary, a good pinch of salt and a little red chili pepper. Rub this seasoning well into both sides of the chops. Pour the oil into a skillet, add the chops, brown on both sides, then pour in the wine. When the wine has evaporated, add the hot stock, cover and cook over low heat until the stock has evaporated. Serve very hot.

"LOMBELLO" ARROSTO
(Roast pork tenderloin)

1 lb pork tenderloin
homemade bread
thickly sliced ham
3 tbsp lard
salt
freshly ground pepper

In Rome the pork tenderloin used to prepare this delicious dish is called "lombello."

Clean the meat thoroughly and remove the fat. Cut the tenderloin into slices at least ¾ in thick. Cut the same number of bread chunks and double the number of ham chunks. Take one large skewer and thread on it a slice of bread, one each of ham and pork, another slice of ham and one of bread and so on until the skewer is full. Melt the lard and pour it over the meat and bread, season with salt and freshly ground pepper and barbecue, occasionally adding more fat. After about ½ hr, the meat will be cooked through and the bread will be golden brown and crisp.

COSTARELLE CON LE "PANUNTELLE"
(Pork chops with bread rolls)

4 pork chops
2 tbsp oil or 1 tbsp lard
salt
freshly ground pepper
4 bread rolls

A dish typical of Campania.

Coat the pork chops in oil or melted lard and season with salt and pepper. Cut the rolls in half and arrange them cut side upward in the base of a broiling pan. Lay the chops on the rack directly above the bread so that it catches the drippings. Broil under moderate heat until one side of the meat is brown and crisp. Turn the chops and brown them on the other side. Make sure the meat is thoroughly cooked. Serve the chops hot, one on each piece of bread, sprinkled with freshly ground pepper.

PORCEDDU
(Roast suckling pig)

(serves 10–12)
1 11–13 lb suckling pig
1 large piece salt pork
myrtle leaves
salt
freshly ground pepper

Suckling pig spit-roasted in the open air is a Sardinian specialty. It is traditionally cooked by shepherds on rudimentary spits driven into the ground and placed

149

about 18 in from a fire of aromatic woods, which impart a unique flavor to the meat. The spit itself consists of a single wooden pole with two crossed pieces of wood at the top so that it can be turned occasionally during cooking, and another two placed further down to hold the meat in position. Today suckling pigs are generally prepared for special occasions and spit-roasted on large, automatic rotisseries.

Remove all the entrails, wash and dry the pig, and cut it in half lengthwise. Impale on two spits. Turn the ribs of the pig toward the the fire and cook until golden brown; then turn from time to time. During the cooking, skewer a big piece of salt pork on the spit and occasionally rub this over the meat. Allow at least 3–4 hr cooking time to ensure that the meat is thoroughly and evenly roasted. The *porceddu* should be served hot on a bed of myrtle leaves and cut into slices. It may also be eaten cold, arranged on a plate with myrtle leaves. Every part of the animal can be eaten, including skin and ears.

RAMBASICCI
(Stuffed cabbage leaves)

scant 2 cups mixed ground meat
   (pork and beef)
1 clove garlic
1 sprig parsley
1 tbsp grated Parmesan cheese
1 tsp paprika
salt
8 small tender leaves Savoy
   cabbage
1 tbsp butter
3 tbsp oil
1 onion, sliced into rings
1 tsp meat extract (or 1 bouillon
   cube)
2 tbsp fine fresh breadcrumbs

A dish typical of the province of Trieste and Istria.

Mix the meat, garlic, finely chopped parsley, Parmesan cheese, paprika and a good pinch of salt in a bowl. Blanch the cabbage leaves in boiling salted water for 3– 4 min, then remove carefully one by one and spread on a cloth to dry. Place a little of the meat mixture on each leaf and roll up into little rectangular parcels. Tie up with thread or secure with toothpicks. Heat the butter and oil in a skillet and add the onion. Fry for a few minutes and then add the stuffed cabbage parcels, arranged side by side. Cover and cook, gradually adding hot water containing the dissolved meat extract. After ½ hr, remove the lid, sprinkle with breadcrumbs and simmer for a few minutes to allow the sauce to thicken. Serve immediately.

INVOLTINI ALLA CALABRESE
(Calabrian pork, ham and cheese roulades)

4 slices pork tenderloin
4 slices pancetta
1 very fresh Mozzarella cheese
4 slices hot, spicy salami
salt
freshly ground pepper
oil

Pound the slices of pork until they are thin and flat. On each one place a slice of pancetta, a little Mozzarella cut into strips and a chopped slice of salami. Season with a little salt and pepper to taste, then roll up and secure with a toothpick. Brush the roulades with a little oil and cook under a hot broiler, turning frequently. When the meat is cooked, sprinkle with salt and serve immediately.

MAIALE AL LATTE
(Pork braised in milk)

1 2-lb leg of pork
scant 4½ cups white wine
¼ cup butter
salt
freshly ground pepper
scant 4½ cups milk
sage leaves
1 sprig rosemary

Place the meat in a bowl, cover with white wine and leave in a cool place to marinate for 1 day turning frequently. Remove the meat, dry thoroughly and bind securely to maintain the shape. Brown in the butter in a flameproof casserole, adding salt and pepper to taste. Cover the pork with milk, add the sage and rosemary, then simmer over low heat for about 1 hr. Turn up the heat to reduce the milk. Cut the meat into slices and arrange on a heated serving dish. Pour over the strained sauce and serve with mashed potatoes.

MAIALE UBRIACO
(Pork chops braised in wine)

1 clove garlic
1 sprig parsley
pinch of fennel seeds
4 pork chops
salt
freshly ground pepper
oil
1 cup red wine

Chop the garlic, parsley and fennel seeds very finely together. Spread this mixture over the pork chops, adding salt and pepper to taste. Place the meat in a skillet containing a little oil and cook over moderate heat until the pork chops are golden brown. Pour in the red wine, cover and allow the sauce to reduce slightly. Arrange the pork chops on a serving dish, pour over the sauce and serve hot.

FETTINE DI MAIALE IN SALSINA
(Pork slices in wine and caper sauce)

1 lb lean, tender pork
3 tbsp oil
½ cup dry red wine
juice of ½ lemon
salt
freshly ground pepper
1 tbsp capers

A dish typical of Umbria.

Cut the pork into thin slices. Put the oil in a skillet and fry the meat over low heat. When the slices are browned on both sides, pour in the wine and lemon juice. Add a little salt and pepper to taste. Wash the capers thoroughly to rid them of excess salt and chop them slightly. Add to the skillet, cover and allow the sauce to reduce over low heat. Serve hot.

ARISTA ALLA FIORENTINA
(Florentine roast pork)

pinch of salt
freshly ground pepper
grated peel of 1 lemon
2 cloves garlic, minced
1 sprig fresh or 1 tbsp dried
    rosemary
2 lb pork loin center rib roast

Mix together a little salt, a good pinch of pepper, the lemon peel, and rosemary leaves in a bowl. Prick the pork here and there with the point of a knife and insert a little of the prepared mixture in the slits. Place the meat in a roasting pan fat side up and roast in a moderate oven (about 325°F) for 1½–2 hr. No oil is needed as the meat already contains sufficient fat. Baste the meat from time to time with the juices that drip down into the pan and turn occasionally. When the meat is well done, remove it from the pan and keep it hot.

The cooking juices can then be used to cook sliced potatoes or other vegetables such as carrots, red cabbage or turnips. Serve these as an accompaniment to the thickly sliced roast pork.

ZAMPONE CON LENTICCHIE *
(Stuffed pig's trotter with lentils)

1 1½-lb zampone (see p. 22)
1 cup soaked green lentils
salt
1 onion
1 stick celery
oil
¼ cup chopped ham fat
1 chopped onion
½ stick celery, chopped

Rinse the zampone, prick all over with a fork, wrap in a cloth and tie securely. Put the zampone in cold water in a pan in which it will lie flat. Bring the water slowly to a boil and simmer gently for 2 hr.

Meanwhile, boil the lentils in water, together with the salt, an onion and one stick of celery for about 1½ hr. Heat a little oil in a saucepan, add the ham fat and the chopped onion and celery and allow to brown. Add the well drained lentils and a few ladles of stock from the zampone and leave to simmer gently until the lentils have absorbed all the water. Slice the zampone and serve hot on a bed of lentils.

ARISTA AL FORNO
(Pork loin pot roast)

1 tbsp vinegar
1 sprig rosemary
2 cloves garlic
salt
freshly ground pepper
1½ lb pork loin center rib roast
½ cup oil
1 cup milk

Make a marinade in a bowl by mixing the vinegar, rosemary, minced garlic cloves, salt and a pinch of pepper. Tie the meat with string so that it does not lose its shape and place in the marinade. Leave to marinate for 1 day, turning frequently; remove and dry thoroughly. Strain the marinade and reserve. Heat the oil in a flameproof casserole and add the meat. Turn constantly until it browns evenly all over then cover with the strained marinade and the milk. Cover the casserole and cook in a moderate oven (375°F) for about 1½ hr. When the meat is ready the sauce should be fairly thick. Add a few ladles of hot water to the meat during cooking if the sauce appears to be drying out.

CRAUTI E LUCANICA TRENTINA
(Sauerkraut and sausages)

4 oz salt pork
1½ lb sauerkraut
1 tsp meat extract
salt
1 lb lucanica or similar mild sausage

Lucanica trentina is a lightly flavored sausage made of pork and beef.
    Place the pounded salt pork in a saucepan and fry. Add the sauerkraut and sufficient water to cover (rinse the sauerkraut if a less acidic dish is preferred). Add the meat extract dissolved in a little hot water. Salt to taste, then cover the saucepan and boil for 4 hr, stirring from time to time and adding more hot water as necessary. After about 3 hr add the sausages. As soon as these are well done, serve with freshly made polenta.

Rabbit

CONIGLIO AI CAPPERI
(Rabbit with capers and anchovies)

2 lb rabbit pieces
1 sliced onion
2 tbsp lard (or oil)
3 boned anchovies
2 tbsp olive oil
¼ cup salted capers
1 sprig chopped parsley
1 tbsp all-purpose flour

for the marinade:
1 cup vinegar
1 cup red wine
1 sliced onion
1 diced stick celery
1 diced carrot
salt
freshly ground pepper

Wash and dry the rabbit pieces and put to marinate in a bowl with the vinegar, wine, onion, celery, carrot and a pinch of salt and pepper. Cover and leave overnight in a cool place (but do not refrigerate). Remove the meat from the marinade and dry thoroughly. Strain the marinade to remove the vegetables and reserve. Heat the lard (or oil) in a large saucepan over very low heat and brown the meat and sliced onion. Pour in half the marinade then cover and cook over very low heat for about ½ hr. Meanwhile, heat the olive oil in a small saucepan and cook the washed, chopped anchovies, stirring them to a paste. Add the washed and drained capers and the parsley. Pour in the remaining marinade, add 1 tbsp flour mixed with a little warm water and simmer for about 20 min, stirring constantly to prevent lumps from forming. Pour the sauce into the saucepan with the rabbit and allow to cook for a further 10 min before serving.

CONIGLIO FARCITO
(Roast stuffed rabbit)

1 young rabbit
vinegar

2 oz salt pork
3 cups fresh breadcrumbs
salt
¼ cup grated Parmesan cheese
1 tbsp chopped parsley
2 cloves garlic
grated peel of ½ lemon
oil
pinch of cinnamon
freshly grated nutmeg
freshly ground pepper
2 eggs

Slit the underside of the rabbit from the hind legs to the center of the belly and carefully remove all the internal organs, reserving the liver and the heart. Rinse out the body cavity well. Cover the rabbit with equal parts of water and vinegar in a bowl and leave for 12 hr. Remove from the marinade, dry thoroughly and stuff as follows: Pound the salt pork and heat in a small saucepan. Add the finely chopped heart and liver and cook for a few minutes. Mix together the breadcrumbs, salt, Parmesan cheese, finely chopped garlic, parsley, the cooked liver and heart, lemon peel, 1 tbsp oil, cinnamon, nutmeg and a pinch of pepper and bind together with the eggs. Check the seasoning. Mix the ingredients well and stuff the rabbit with the mixture. Sew up the cavity and brush the rabbit with oil. Place on a wire rack in a baking pan and cook in a moderately hot oven (350°F) for about 1 hr. Turn several times and brush with the juices from the pan. Cut into quarters and serve very hot with some stuffing on top of each portion.

CONIGLIO IN PORCHETTA *
(Stuffed rabbit with bacon and rosemary)

1 3¼-lb rabbit
1 cup vinegar
salt
freshly ground pepper
2 slices bacon, cut into squares
2 finely chopped cloves garlic
fennel seeds
1 finely chopped sprig rosemary
1 cup olive oil
2 oz chopped salt pork
½ cup dry white wine
2 potatoes, peeled and diced

Clean the rabbit and wash in a mixture of water and vinegar; dry with a cloth and season the inside with salt and pepper. Finely chop the heart and liver and mix with half the bacon and half the chopped garlic, fennel and rosemary. Add a little salt and stuff the rabbit with the mixture. Sew it up with thread and bind the rabbit along its whole length so that it maintains its shape during cooking.

Heat the oil and the salt pork in a saucepan and gently brown the rabbit together with the remaining bacon, garlic and herbs, turning from time to time. When the meat is well browned, pour in the wine and cook until it evaporates. Add the diced potatoes, cover the saucepan and cook over moderate heat for 30–40 min until the rabbit is tender.

CONIGLIO ALLA MOLISANA
(Rabbit and sausage kabobs)

1 2-lb rabbit
salt
freshly ground pepper
1 tbsp chopped rosemary
1 tbsp chopped parsley
8 slices prosciutto
4 small sausages
8 sage leaves
½ cup oil

Clean and bone the rabbit carefully, keeping the pieces of meat as large as possible. Cut into eight pieces and season with salt, pepper, rosemary and parsley. Place a slice of prosciutto on each piece of rabbit and roll up. Prick the sausages. Take four skewers. On each thread a rabbit roulade, a sage leaf, a sausage, a roulade and another sage leaf. Barbecue or bake in an oven preheated to about 350°F for about 1 hr, turning frequently and brushing with oil from time to time.

CONIGLIO ALLA CACCIATORA
(Rabbit with capers and garlic)

1 2-lb rabbit
½ cup oil

1 sprig sage
2 cloves garlic
salt
freshly ground pepper
2 cups vinegar
¼ cup capers
1 boned anchovy
½ tbsp cornstarch

Clean and joint the rabbit. Wash and dry the pieces thoroughly. Put the meat into a large skillet with the oil, sage leaves and garlic; brown over high heat, then season with salt and pepper to taste. Pour in half the vinegar and the same amount of hot water and heat to boiling. Cover the skillet, reduce the heat to low and leave to cook for ¾ hr, adding a little more hot water and vinegar as necessary if the sauce appears to be reducing too much. Place the rabbit on a heated serving dish when it is fork-tender. To the sauce left in the skillet add the capers, chopped anchovy and cornstarch mixed with ½ cup of vinegar. Stirring frequently, bring the sauce back to a boil and allow it to thicken before pouring over the rabbit.

CONIGLIO CON LE OLIVE
(Rabbit with olives)

1 2-lb rabbit
1 clove garlic
3 peeled tomatoes
1 carrot
2 tbsp oil
2 tbsp butter
3 tbsp brandy
salt
freshly ground pepper
1 cup green and black olives

Clean and joint the rabbit, then wash and dry each piece thoroughly. Put the meat into a skillet together with the garlic, tomatoes, finely sliced carrot, oil and butter. Cook over moderate heat. Sprinkle the meat with brandy, allow it to evaporate then add ¼ cup hot water. Season with salt and pepper and continue to cook for about 1 hr. Add the olives cut into slices, reduce the heat and braise gently for a further ¾ hour until the rabbit is fork-tender.

CONIGLIO IN AGRODOLCE
(Sweet and sour rabbit)

3½ lb rabbit pieces
all-purpose flour
1 finely chopped onion
¼ cup butter
¼ cup lard
salt
freshly ground pepper
1 cup stock
2–3 tbsp sugar
½ cup vinegar
4 tbsp seedless white raisins
4 tbsp pine nuts

for the marinade:
2 cups red wine
1 small onion, sliced
2 cloves garlic
1 tbsp chopped parsley
1 bay leaf
pinch of thyme
4–5 black peppercorns
salt

Clean the rabbit pieces and wipe with a damp cloth. Put all the ingredients for the marinade in a saucepan and bring to a boil over moderate heat. Remove the saucepan from the heat and leave to cool. Put the pieces of rabbit in a bowl and pour the marinade over them. After a couple of hours, remove the pieces of meat from the marinade, dry them and dust with flour. Fry the onions in the oil until soft and then add the pieces of rabbit. Pour in the marinade and cook over moderate heat, uncovered, for about 20 min. When the wine has evaporated, season with salt and pepper, add 1 cup hot stock or water, cover and cook for a further 20 min until the meat is tender and the sauce fairly thick.

Dissolve the sugar in 1 tbsp water in a saucepan over low heat. As soon as it begins to brown, add the vinegar and seedless white raisins and simmer for a few minutes. Pour this sauce over the cooked rabbit and mix well. Add the pine nuts and serve.

SALMÌ DI CONIGLIO *
(Braised rabbit with anchovy butter)

1 2-lb rabbit
½ cup olive oil
½ cup vinegar
1 sliced onion
1 sliced lemon
1 clove
2 crumbled bay leaves
a little meat extract
salt
freshly ground pepper
2 anchovies
1 tbsp butter

Clean and joint the rabbit. Wash and dry the pieces with a cloth. Prepare a marinade by mixing the oil, vinegar, onion, lemon, clove and bay leaves in a bowl. Put the pieces of rabbit into the marinade and turn so that they are well soaked. Cover and leave for 1 day. Transfer the contents of the bowl to a saucepan, removing only the pieces of lemon. Brown the rabbit over moderate heat. Pour over ¼ cup water containing the dissolved meat extract, season with salt and pepper, cover the saucepan and cook, gradually adding more water so that the sauce does not become too thick. Meanwhile, bone the anchovies, pound in a mortar and mix with the butter. Blend the anchovy mixture into the sauce in the saucepan. Transfer the rabbit to a serving dish and pour over the sauce.

CONIGLIO IN UMIDO ALLA REGGIANA
(Braised rabbit Reggio Emilia style)

1 2-lb rabbit
1 stick celery
1 onion
1 clove garlic
2 oz pancetta
¼ cup butter
½ cup dry white wine
2 tbsp tomato paste
salt
freshly ground pepper
2 tbsp chopped parsley

Recipes for braised rabbit are to be found in most regions of Italy. The ingredients will however, often vary slightly in quantity and proportion to accentuate the different flavors of the dish. The recipe given here comes from Reggio Emilia. Clean and joint the rabbit. Soak the pieces in a bowl of cold water for ½ hr, drain and dry thoroughly. Finely chop the celery, onion, garlic and pancetta and gently fry in a large skillet with the butter. Stir for a few minutes then add the pieces of rabbit and cook until they are nicely browned. Increase the heat and pour in the white wine; stir and cook until evaporated. Dilute the tomato paste in 1 cup water and pour into the skillet. Add salt and pepper to taste. Cover and simmer over low heat for about 1 hr until the rabbit is very tender. Add a little hot water if necessary to prevent the sauce from boiling away. Before removing the rabbit from the heat add the chopped parsley. Serve each portion with a few tablespoons of the sauce.

Lamb and kid

ABBACCHIO ALLA ROMANA
(Roman spring lamb)

2 lb leg of spring lamb
¼ cup olive oil
3 cloves garlic
1 sprig rosemary
3 salted anchovies
4 tbsp white wine vinegar

Abbacchio is the Roman word for spring lamb, which is eaten mainly at Easter time.
Cut the lamb into 1½-in chunks. Heat the oil together with 2 cloves of garlic in a skillet. When the garlic begins to brown, remove and discard. Add the pieces of lamb and fry until they are golden brown all over then continue to cook over low heat. Meanwhile, crush the remaining garlic clove with the rosemary and the boned, washed anchovies in a mortar and cover with the vinegar. Mix well to obtain a fairly liquid sauce. When the meat is tender, add the prepared sauce to the skillet and mix with the meat juices over high heat. Transfer the pieces of lamb to a heated serving dish and cover with the sauce. Serve immediately.

"CORDULA"
(Skewered lamb intestines)

intestines of 3 young lambs
salt
freshly ground pepper
4 oz slice salt pork
pinch of marjoram
pinch of thyme
1 bay leaf
1 sprig sage

"Cordula" or "corda" is one of the oldest and most traditional of all Sardinian dishes, clearly of shepherd origin.
Clean and wash the lamb intestines thoroughly, braid them, cut them into four equal lengths and thread them on to four skewers. Season with salt and pepper. Heat the salt pork in a small skillet and pour the fat over the skewered intestines. Sprinkle with marjoram, thyme, crumbled bay leaf and chopped sage. Barbecue until well browned on both sides. Serve the "cordula" very hot. In a more modern version of this recipe the braided intestines are cooked in oil in a skillet and served with a sauce of fresh tomatoes and peas.

AGNELLINO AL FORNO
(Roast lamb)

1 2-lb leg of lamb
5 oz prosciutto
1 sprig rosemary
3 tbsp salt pork
salt
freshly ground pepper
3 tbsp grated Pecorino or Parmesan cheese
3 tbsp fresh breadcrumbs

Wipe the meat with a damp cloth and make several deep incisions in the leg with a sharp pointed knife. Insert a piece of prosciutto and a few rosemary leaves into each. Put the prepared meat in a roasting pan, add the chopped salt pork, season with salt and pepper to taste and sprinkle on the grated cheese mixed with the breadcrumbs. Roast in a moderate oven (325°F) for about 40 min. Make sure that the meat is tender and serve with the cooking juices.

GNIUMMERIEDDI
(Lamb or kid variety meat kabobs)

1 lb lamb or kid variety meats (heart, liver, lights)
8 oz lamb or kid intestines
1 sprig sage
½ cup oil
salt
freshly ground pepper
2 oz salt pork
juice of 1 lemon

This dish, also called "torcinelli," is typical of the promontory of Gargano. It would traditionally have been barbecued over olive wood. Cut the variety meats into walnut-sized pieces. Gently flatten the intestines without breaking them. Squeeze them between forefinger and thumb, rinse thoroughly in several changes of cold water and dry. Take 1 long skewer (or a few shorter skewers) and thread with a piece of liver, one of lights and one of heart, placing a fresh sage leaf between every two or three pieces. When all the variety meats have been skewered, take the intestines and secure one end to the end of the skewer with string. Wrap the intestine back and forth around the skewer in long spirals to form a kind of net around the meats. Continue working up and down until you reach the end of the intestines. Tie up the end with string.
Pour on the oil, season with salt and pepper and barbecue over moderate heat so that the meats cook through to the middle. When they are cooked, after about ¼ hr, put the piece of salt pork on the end of a carving fork and heat it over the barbecue. Let big drops of fat from the salt pork fall on to the skewers. Remove the meats from the skewer, arrange on a plate and squeeze on lemon juice. Serve hot.

SPIEDINI DI CAPRETTO
(Baked kid or lamb kabobs)

1¾ lb boned leg of kid or lamb
20 small squares of bread
32 small squares of ham
salt
freshly ground pepper
½ cup olive oil

Cut the meat into 16 cubes of approximately the same size as the pieces of bread and ham. Season with salt and pepper. Take four skewers and on each thread a piece of bread, one of ham, a cube of meat, a piece of ham and a piece of bread in that sequence until each skewer holds four pieces of meat, five pieces of bread and eight pieces of ham.

Place the skewers in an oiled pan and pour a little oil over them. Sprinkle with salt and pepper and bake in a hot oven (400°F) for about ½hr, turning two or three times until browned and crisp. Remove the pieces of meat and bread from the skewers and arrange them on a warmed serving dish.

COSTOLETTE DI AGNELLO AI PEPERONI
(Lamb chops with peppers)

4 green bell peppers
6 tbsp oil
salt
8 lamb rib chops
freshly ground pepper
3–4 anchovy fillets
½ chopped clove garlic
4 tbsp chopped parsley

Char the peppers under a hot broiler or place in a very hot oven until their skin blisters. Peel off the skin while warm, slice off the end, cut in half and scrape out the seeds and membrane. Put the halved peppers in a greased pan, sprinkle with salt and 2 tbsp oil, and cook in a moderate oven (375°F) for 10 min. Heat the remaining oil in a skillet over moderate heat and brown the chops. Season with salt and pepper. Arrange the pepper halves on a serving dish and pour their cooking juices over them. Place a chop on top of each pepper. Stir 2–3 tbsp water into the cooking juices from the meat in the skillet. Add the anchovies, garlic and parsley and simmer until the sauce has thickened slightly and the anchovies have broken up. Pour a little of this sauce over each chop and serve.

AGNELLO AL FORNO CON PATATE E POMODORI *
(Baked lamb with potatoes and tomatoes)

2 lb boned leg of lamb
1 onion, sliced
¼ cup butter
½ cup olive oil
2 sprigs rosemary
1 cup dry white wine
salt
12 oz ripe tomatoes
1 lb new potatoes
salt
freshly ground pepper

Cut the lamb into large chunks. Heat in a large flameproof casserole and fry the onion in the butter and oil over low heat until soft. As soon as the onion is transparent, add the lamb and chopped rosemary. Brown the meat evenly over moderate heat, then pour in the wine and cook until it evaporates. Season with salt and add the chopped tomatoes, peeled and seeded if preferred. Cook over high heat for about ½hr, uncovered. Scrape and dice the potatoes, sprinkle with salt and pepper to taste and add to the meat in the casserole. Transfer the casserole to a preheated oven (350°F) and bake for about 40 min. Turn the lamb from time to time to prevent it sticking to the bottom. Serve as soon as the potatoes are browned and well done.

CAPRETTO ALLA PAESANA
(Country-style casserole of kid)

1¾ lb boneless kid or lamb
¼ cup lard
2 large onions, sliced
1 lb new potatoes
14 oz ripe tomatoes
½ cup grated Pecorino cheese
salt
freshly ground pepper
oregano
1 cup olive oil

Cut the meat into large chunks. Melt the lard in a flameproof casserole and brown the meat, together with the onions. Scrape and dice the potatoes, peel, seed and chop the tomatoes and add to the meat. Sprinkle on the grated Pecorino cheese, a little salt, pepper and oregano. Pour in the oil. Put a tight-fitting lid on the casserole and cook in a preheated moderate oven (350°F) for 1 hr or until tender. Keep the lid on until you are ready to serve the dish.

AGNELLO ALLA PECORARA
(Lamb with onion)

2 lb spring lamb
salt
1 onion
¼ cup butter
slices of toasted bread

Use a flameproof casserole with two handles and a very tight-fitting lid for this dish. Wash the meat and cut into 1-in chunks. Sprinkle with salt and leave for 1 hr. Put the lamb in the casserole with the whole onion and the butter, cut into pieces. Cover and cook over low heat for about 1 hr or until done. Do not remove the lid while the lamb is cooking but shake the casserole from time to time to insure the meat does not stick. Serve in its own gravy on slices of toasted bread.

CAPRETTO E CARCIOFI
(Kid with artichokes)

1¾ lb boneless kid or lamb
1 cup olive oil
2 oz chopped ham
1 medium onion, chopped
3 tbsp chopped parsley
1 tbsp all-purpose flour
1 cup dry white wine
salt
freshly ground pepper
4 young artichokes (or 1 9-oz
    package frozen artichoke hearts)
2 egg yolks
2 lemons
marjoram

Cut the meat into serving pieces and put into a saucepan with the oil and the chopped ham, onion and 2 tbsp parsley. Fry very gently and sprinkle on the flour when the meat is golden brown. Cook for a further 10 min, pour in the wine and boil over high heat until evaporated. Season with salt and pepper, cover and cook over low heat for at least ½hr. Meanwhile, prepare the artichokes. It is important that young artichokes be used in the preparation of this dish since these are very tender, have no chokes and require less cooking. If these are not available substitute frozen artichoke hearts. Remove the tougher outer leaves from the bottom of the artichokes, cut off the leaf tips and cut into quarters. Wash in water containing the juice of ½ lemon, drain well and add to the kid. Season with salt and leave to cook for ½hr, stirring from time to time. If the sauce seems too thick, thin it with a little hot stock (or water) taking care not to make it too liquid. Beat the egg yolks in a bowl with a pinch of salt and pepper and the juice of 1½ lemons. Add the remaining parsley and a pinch of marjoram. Pour the egg mixture into the saucepan with the meat, stir well and remove from the heat at once so that the egg sauce becomes creamy but does not curdle. Serve immediately.

BRACIOLINE D'AGNELLO
(Lamb loin chops)

8 lamb loin chops
4 tbsp olive oil
few sage leaves
salt
freshly ground pepper
½ cup dry white wine
juice of ½ lemon

Cook the lamb chops in a large skillet with a little olive oil and a few sage leaves. Brown well on both sides, season with salt and pepper and pour on the white wine. Continue to cook until the chops are tender and the sauce has reduced and thickened. Serve immediately sprinkled with lemon juice.

AGNELLO CON SALSINA ALL'UOVO E LIMONE
(Lamb with egg and lemon sauce)

1¾ lb lamb for stews
½ cup oil
1 clove garlic

½ cup dry white wine
salt
freshly ground pepper
2 egg yolks
juice of 1 lemon

This dish from Abruzzo is traditionally prepared at Easter.

Cut the lamb into 1-in chunks. Heat the oil in a saucepan and add the garlic clove and the pieces of lamb. As soon as the garlic browns, remove and discard. Turn the lamb pieces constantly so that they brown all over. Pour the white wine over the meat. Cook over fairly high heat until the wine evaporates, then season with salt and pepper. Cover the saucepan, turn down the heat and allow to simmer for about 1 hr, adding a little water from time to time if necessary. When the meat is very tender, remove the pieces one by one and keep them warm on a serving dish. Beat the egg yolks with the lemon juice and pour the mixture into the sauce. Remove the saucepan from the heat as you do this so that the eggs do not curdle. Continue to stir over very low heat until you obtain a light sauce with a custard-like consistency. Pour over the lamb and serve immediately.

AGNELLO AI FUNGHI CARDONCELLI
(Lamb with oyster mushrooms)

1 lb oyster mushrooms
2 lb lamb (or kid)
2 cloves garlic
salt
freshly ground pepper (or tip of a red
    chili pepper)
½ cup oil

Clean, wash and drain the mushrooms. Cut the meat into large pieces and put in an ovenproof dish with the mushrooms, finely chopped garlic, a pinch of salt and plenty of pepper (or, if preferred, the finely chopped chili pepper). Pour on the oil and then transfer to a preheated moderate oven (325°F) for 1 hr, turning the meat from time to time and basting with the cooking juices. Serve hot straight from the cooking dish.

157

AGNELLO, CACIO E UOVA *
(Lamb, cheese and eggs)

2 lb lamb (preferably leg)
salt
freshly ground pepper
1 onion, sliced
½ cup oil
1 cup dry white wine
2 whole eggs (or 4 yolks)
¼ cup grated Pecorino cheese

Wash the meat and cut into chunks. Sprinkle with salt and pepper and leave for 1 hr. Fry the onion in the oil in a large flameproof casserole. As soon as it is soft, add the pieces of lamb and brown slowly. Pour over the wine and cook, uncovered, until it has evaporated. Cover the casserole and stir occasionally adding a little hot stock if necessary. Cook for about 1 hr or until the meat is tender. Beat the eggs with the Pecorino cheese and a pinch of salt and pepper in a bowl and pour the mixture into the casserole with the lamb just before serving. Stir well and remove from the heat after a couple of minutes. Serve immediately.

AGNELLO AL FORNO CON PATATE E CIPOLLE
(Roast lamb with potatoes and onions)

2 lb lamb (preferably leg)
½ cup oil
1 tbsp butter
1 clove garlic
1 sprig rosemary
1¾ lb small new potatoes (or ordinary potatoes cut into quarters)
salt
freshly ground pepper
6 shallots (or 2 large onions)

Wash and dry the meat. Heat the oil, butter, garlic and finely chopped rosemary in a flameproof casserole. When the mixture begins to bubble, add the lamb and fry until it begins to brown. Scrape or peel the potatoes, sprinkle with salt and pepper and add to the dish together with the shallots. Transfer the dish to a very hot oven (400–425°F) and cook for about 1 hr, stirring frequently and adding a little oil if necessary. Remove the dish from the oven when the meat and potatoes are golden brown. Serve immediately on its own or with a green salad. This dish is excellent eaten very hot.

CALDARIELLO
(Lamb cooked in milk)

1 clove garlic
1 sprig parsley
wild fennel leaves
1 onion
½ cup oil
2 cups creamy milk
1¾ lb lamb, cut into 1-in chunks
salt
freshly ground pepper
8 slices crusty bread

This dish, a specialty of the inland areas of Apulia, takes its name from the small, rounded cauldron in which it would traditionally have been cooked.

Chop the garlic, parsley and wild fennel leaves and finely slice the onion into rings. Put these, along with the oil and milk into a large, flameproof casserole and add the pieces of lamb. Season with salt and pepper to taste. Cover the casserole and simmer over very low heat for 2–2½ hr or until the meat is fork-tender. Stir occasionally so that the meat does not stick. Serve hot with slices of bread.

COSTOLETTE D'AGNELLO ALLA COSENTINA
(Cosenza lamb rib chops)

1 cup oil
8 lamb rib chops
14 oz very ripe tomatoes
2 large, green bell peppers
2 tbsp green olives
1 onion
2 cloves garlic
1 sprig parsley
salt
freshly ground pepper
red chili pepper

Heat 4 tbsp oil in a large skillet, add the lamb chops and cook until browned on both sides. Remove the meat and keep warm. Peel, seed and chop tomatoes, cut the peppers into strips, halve and pit the olives and chop the onion, garlic and parsley. Put these into the skillet with the remaining oil and season with salt and pepper to taste and a little finely chopped red chili pepper if desired. Cook over moderate heat for ¼ hr. Add the chops to the sauce and cook for a further ¼ hr, turning several times. Serve immediately.

"SGUAZETO" D'AGNELLO ALLA FRIULANA
(Friuli braised lamb)

1¾ lb lamb leg meat
3 oz salt pork, chopped
1 onion, chopped
1 clove garlic
¼ cup butter
2–3 tbsp oil
salt
freshly ground pepper
pinch of cinnamon
1 tbsp tomato paste
⅓ cup stock

Cut the meat into cubes. Fry the salt pork, onion and garlic in the oil and butter. When these begin to brown, remove the garlic and add the meat. Season with salt, pepper and cinnamon. When the meat is evenly browned, add the tomato paste dissolved in the hot stock. Cover and cook over low heat, adding more water if necessary, for 1½–2 hr or until the meat is tender and the sauce thick.

COSCIOTTO DI AGNELLO ARROSTO
(Lamb braised in white wine)

1 2-lb leg of lamb
3 oz prosciutto, cut into thin strips
3 tbsp chopped parsley
2 chopped cloves garlic
1 chopped sprig marjoram
2 chopped sprigs rosemary
salt
freshly ground pepper
¼ cup lard
1 cup dry white wine

Wash and thoroughly dry the leg of lamb. Trim off some of the fat and make about a dozen incisions with a sharp knife point all over the surface. Lightly brown the prosciutto in a skillet with the chopped parsley, garlic, marjoram and rosemary. Season with a little salt and pepper and, using a spoon, insert a little of the mixture into each incision. Rub a little salt and pepper and any remaining mixture into the surface of the meat. Put into a flameproof casserole with the lard and cook over moderate heat, turning from time to time until the meat is browned on all sides. Pour in the wine, cover and cook slowly for a further 40 min, or until the meat is fork-tender adding a little more wine if necessary. Some cooks prefer to cook the meat on a rotisserie, basting with the melted lard, but the meat is more succulent if cooked in a saucepan with wine.

ABBACCHIO O CAPRETTO BRODETTATO
(Lamb or kid brodettato)

2 lb spring lamb or kid
1½ lemons
2–3 tbsp olive oil
2 tbsp butter
2 slices of ham, shredded
1 finely chopped onion
salt
freshly ground pepper
1 tbsp all-purpose flour
1 cup dry white wine
hot water or stock
2 egg yolks
½ cup finely chopped parsley
few leaves marjoram, finely chopped

Cut the meat into pieces, dry with a cloth and rub with ½ lemon (reserve the peel). Heat the oil and butter in a large saucepan, add the meat, prosciutto and onion and fry gently, stirring from time to time. Season with salt and pepper. When the meat begins to brown, coat all the pieces thoroughly in flour. Add the wine, cover and cook over low heat for ½ hr or until the meat is tender. Add a few ladles of hot stock if necessary so that the sauce is neither too thick nor too liquid.

Beat the egg yolks together with the grated peel of the ½ lemon and the juice of 1 whole lemon, the chopped parsley and marjoram and a pinch of salt. Lower the heat when the meat is cooked and pour the egg mixture into the saucepan. Simmer for 2 min, stirring constantly to prevent the egg from curdling. Serve immediately.

CACCIATORA DI CAPRETTO
(Braised kid)

2 lb kid or lamb
1 clove garlic
2 tbsp oil
¼ cup butter
½ onion, chopped
2 oz chopped bacon
1 cup red wine
6 oz tomatoes
salt
freshly ground pepper
3 tbsp chopped parsley

Cut the meat into evenly-sized pieces. Dip the tomatoes into boiling water for 1 min, peel and chop. Fry the whole garlic clove in the oil and butter. Remove when browned and add the onion and bacon. Add the pieces of kid and when they are well browned, pour in the wine and cook until it evaporates. Add the chopped tomatoes and parsley and season with salt and pepper. Cover and cook for about 1 hr or until the meat is fork-tender.

Variety meat

ANIMELLE DI VITELLO
(Calf sweetbreads)

1¼ lb calf or lamb sweetbreads
2 oz chopped bacon
¼ cup lard (or oil and butter)
½ onion, chopped
salt
freshly ground pepper
stock
2 tbsp butter
2 cups petits pois
¼ cup melted butter
1 oz chopped ham

Soak the sweetbreads in cold water for 1–2 hr to remove the blood. Drain and cover with cold water in a saucepan. Bring to a boil, drain immediately and pour on cold salted water. Bring to a boil again over low heat, rinse in cold running water, drain and remove the twin outer membrane, veins and connective tissue. Cut into pieces. Fry the bacon with the lard and onion in a skillet. As soon as the onion is soft, add the sweetbreads. Season with salt and pepper, add a little stock, cover and cook slowly for 20 min, stirring from time to time. Remove the sweetbreads from the saucepan and keep warm. Continue to cook the sauce until it thickens slightly, add a little butter and pour the hot sauce over the sweetbreads. Meanwhile, cook the petits pois in the melted butter with the ham. Season with salt and pepper and serve as a side dish with the sweetbreads (or mix with the sweetbreads and leave to cook for a couple of minutes over very low heat).

CERVELLA ALLA NAPOLETANA *
(Brains with capers and olives)

¾ lb lamb or calf brains
salt
oil
freshly ground pepper
1 tbsp salted capers
⅓ cup black olives
¼ cup fresh breadcrumbs
olive oil

Soak the brains for 1 hr in cold water, rinse and remove as much of the outer membrane as possible. Put the brains in a saucepan with a little cold water and some salt, bring to a boil and simmer for a couple of minutes. Then remove carefully with a skimmer or wide slotted spoon and immerse in a bowl of cold water. Lightly oil a shallow ovenproof dish and lay out the brains in a single layer without breaking them. Season with salt and freshly ground pepper, then add the rinsed capers and halved, pitted olives. Sprinkle on the breadcrumbs, followed by a trickle of olive oil. Cook in a preheated oven at 350°F for about 20 min. Serve in the ovenproof dish.

CERVELLA IN CARROZZA
(Brains on bread)

1 set calf brains
salt
2 eggs
4 tbsp milk
1 tbsp all-purpose flour
8 slices of bread
breadcrumbs
oil for frying

A dish typical of the province of Trento.
Soak the brains in cold water for 1 hr. Rinse to remove bone fragments and peel off the transparent outer membrane. Bring to the boil in a little salted water and simmer for ¼ hr. Drain, put into a bowl and mash with a fork. Beat the eggs with the milk and add the salt and flour, taking care that lumps do not form. A fairly liquid batter should result. Spread one side of each bread slice with an even layer of mashed brains. Dip the slices into the batter and coat with breadcrumbs. Heat plenty of oil in a skillet. When it is very hot, add the bread slices and fry on both sides. They are ready when the crust is golden brown. Serve immediately.

FEGATELLI ALLA TOSCANA
(Tuscan liver)

7 oz pig's caul
1¾ lb pork liver cut into large chunks
pinch of fennel seeds
salt
freshly ground pepper
breadcrumbs
bread chunks
bay leaves

Soak the caul in warm water to soften it, cut into squares and drain. Put the liver on a plate and sprinkle the pieces with the fennel seeds, salt, pepper and bread-crumbs. Individually wrap the prepared liver pieces in the squares of caul. Thread the liver pieces on to four skewers and intersperse with bread and bay leaves. Barbecue over a wood fire or fry in a skillet with a little oil over moderate heat for 10 min. Serve hot.

SGUAZZETTO "A LA BECHERA"
(Calf variety meats in vegetable sauce)

1½ lb calf variety meats (heart, liver, lights and spleen)
1 onion
1 clove garlic
1 stick celery
2 carrots
¼ cup butter
2 tbsp oil
½ cup dry white wine
salt
freshly ground pepper
1 sprig thyme
1 tbsp tomato paste
⅓ cup stock

Blanch the variety meats for 5 min in salted boiling water, drain and cut into chunks. Finely chop the onion, celery and carrot. Heat the butter and oil in a flameproof casserole and gently sauté the chopped vegetables and the garlic clove. When they begin to soften, remove the garlic clove, add the meats and pour on the wine. When this has evaporated, season with salt and pepper and add the thyme. Add the tomato paste mixed with the stock, cover and cook slowly for ½ hr until the sauce thickens. Serve hot.

FEGATO ALLA VENEZIANA
(Liver Venice style)

1 lb calves' liver
2 large onions
1 sprig parsley
3 tbsp oil
¼ cup butter
salt

Remove the membrane from the liver, then slice thinly. Thinly slice the onions and chop the parsley. Heat the oil and butter in a skillet and as soon as they start to bubble, add the onions and parsley. Cover and cook over low heat so that the onions do not brown too much. Remove the skillet from the heat and leave to cool for a few minutes before adding the slices of liver (this is done to prevent the meat from becoming too tough). Return the skillet to the stove, turn up the heat and cook the liver until it is browned on both sides; this will only take a few minutes. Remove from the heat and add salt to taste. If the liver is prepared in this way it will remain tender. Serve hot.

FEGATO ALL'ACETO
(Liver with vinegar)

1 lb calves' liver
¼ cup butter
salt
freshly ground pepper
2 tbsp vinegar
2–3 sprigs parsley, finely chopped

Trim any membrane from the liver and slice very finely. Heat the butter in a skillet and fry the slices of liver for 3 min over high heat until they are brown all over. Season with salt and pepper and add the vinegar. Stir well. Transfer the liver to a warmed serving plate. Sprinkle with chopped parsley and serve hot.

FEGATO AL POMODORO
(Liver with tomato sauce)

1 lb calves' liver
all-purpose flour
4 tbsp olive oil
1 clove garlic, chopped
5–6 sage leaves

salt
freshly ground pepper
1 cup freshly made tomato sauce
   (see p. 127)

Cut the liver into very thin slices and coat lightly with flour. Heat the oil in a skillet and add the chopped garlic clove and sage. When the oil is hot, lay the liver slices in the skillet and cook for about 4 min until brown on both sides (be careful not to overcook them or they will become tough). Season with salt and pepper, then add the tomato sauce. Lower the heat, simmer for a few minutes, arrange on a dish and serve.

FEGATO "GARBO E DOLCE"
(Breaded liver with lemon glaze)

1 egg
salt
¾–1 lb calves' liver
all-purpose flour
fine dried breadcrumbs
⅓ cup butter
juice of 1 lemon
1 tsp sugar

Trim any membrane from the liver, slice very finely and coat in flour. Beat the egg with a pinch of salt. Dip the lightly floured liver slices in the egg mixture and coat in breadcrumbs. Heat the butter in a skillet and fry the battered liver slices on both sides until brown. Transfer to a serving dish and keep warm. Slowly heat the lemon juice with the sugar, stirring until the sugar dissolves. Pour this mixture over the liver and serve hot.

BIANCO E NERO (fegato alla genovese)
(Liver Genoa style)

½ lb calf brains
salt
½–¾ lb calves' liver
all-purpose flour
1 lightly beaten egg
fine dried breadcrumbs
oil for frying

Soak the brains in cold water for 1 hr. Rinse to remove any bone

161

fragments and peel off the transparent outer membrane. Bring to a boil in a saucepan of lightly salted water and simmer for 20 min. Cut into walnut-sized pieces. Remove the membrane from the liver and slice finely. Coat the brain and liver pieces in flour, dip in egg and then in breadcrumbs and fry in a skillet a few pieces at a time in plenty of hot oil.

BÜSÊCA
(Lombardy tripe)

1 lb fresh tripe
1 onion
1 stick celery
4 sage leaves
1 carrot
½ cup oil
¼ cup butter
2 oz salt pork
salt
freshly ground pepper
nutmeg (optional)
clove, crushed (optional)
4 large ripe or canned tomatoes
½ cup grated Parmesan cheese

A dish typical of Lombardy.

Fresh tripe is sold blanched and partly cooked and additional cooking time can vary. Always check with the butcher how much longer the tripe should be cooked. Cut the tripe into strips about ¼ in wide. Chop the onion, celery, sage and carrot and pound the salt pork in a mortar. Put the oil, butter and salt pork in a saucepan together with the chopped vegetables. Fry, stirring constantly. Add the tripe and fry for about another 10 min. Season with salt and pepper to taste and a pinch of grated nutmeg and crushed clove if desired. Sieve the tomatoes, add to the saucepan and cook until the sauce has reduced and thickened. Pour in about 1 cup hot water, cover the saucepan tightly and cook over gentle heat for about 2 hr or until the tripe is tender. Add more hot water during cooking as necessary if the sauce becomes too dry. The sauce should not be too liquid. Serve this dish hot, sprinkled with the grated Parmesan cheese. The Milanese recommend that this dish be eaten with a slice of bread fried in butter.

TRIPPA ALLA ROMANA
(Tripe Roman style)

1 lb fresh tripe
salt
1 onion, chopped
2 sticks celery, chopped
1 carrot, chopped
meat sauce (see p. 129) or tomato sauce (see p. 127)
grated Parmesan or Pecorino cheese
4–5 mint leaves, chopped

This famous Roman dish may be prepared with a meat or tomato sauce. In both cases the same basic preparation is used.

The tripe you buy will be blanched and partly cooked. Check with your butcher how much longer the tripe should be cooked as this will vary. You should generally allow about 2 hr. Cut the tripe into fairly large pieces and place in a saucepan containing plenty of cold salted water together with the onion, celery and carrot. Bring to a boil, cover and simmer over low heat for about 2 hr, skimming the surface from time to time. When the tripe is tender, cut it into strips about ½ in wide and boil for about 3 min in the tomato or meat sauce. Salt to taste and sprinkle with grated cheese mixed with chopped mint leaves. The cheese may be either Parmesan or Pecorino, or a mixture of both. Serve the dish with plenty of grated cheese and mint.

TRIPPA E ZAMPA ALLA FIORENTINA
(Tripe and calf's foot Florence style)

1 lb fresh tripe
salt
1 onion
2 sticks celery
2 small carrots
1 sprig parsley
1 calf's foot
1 clove garlic
2–3 basil leaves
1 sprig rosemary
½ cup oil
¼ cup butter
7 oz ripe tomatoes
freshly ground pepper
3 tbsp grated Parmesan cheese

The tripe you buy will be blanched and partly cooked. Check with your butcher how much longer it should be cooked. Cut the tripe into pieces the size of the palm of your hand and put in a saucepan containing plenty of salted water. Coarsely chop half the onion, a stick of celery, a carrot and a few parsley leaves and add these to the saucepan. Put the well rinsed calf's foot in a second saucepan with plenty of salted water. Cover both saucepans, bring to a boil and simmer for 2 hr or until the tripe is tender and the meat of the calf's foot comes away from the bone. Remove the pieces of tripe from the saucepan and cut into narrow strips on a cutting board. Strain the stock and reserve. Remove the calf's foot and cut the meat into chunks. Finely chop the remaining vegetables and herbs – the onion, carrot, garlic clove, basil leaves, stick of celery and a few rosemary leaves. Heat the butter and oil in an ovenproof casserole and add this chopped mixture. Fry over low heat for a few minutes. Dip the tomatoes into boiling water for 1 min, peel, quarter and seed and add to the casserole together with the tripe strips and meat chunks. Season with salt and pepper to taste. Cover the casserole and cook over low heat for about 2 hr, gradually adding the strained stock from the tripe if the sauce becomes too thick. Remove from the heat, add the grated Parmesan cheese, stir gently and serve.

TRIPPA DORATA ALLA BOLOGNESE ✳
("Golden" tripe Bologna style)

1¾ lb fresh tripe
salt
2–3 tbsp olive oil
7 oz smoked pancetta, chopped
1 thinly sliced onion
1 chopped garlic clove
¼ cup chopped parsley
freshly ground pepper
3 eggs
1 tsp meat extract
4 tbsp grated Parmesan cheese

Buy the tripe ready blanched and boil in salted water for about 1½ hr or until tender. Drain and cut into 1½-in chunks. Heat a few tbsp of oil and the pancetta in a skillet. When the fat is hot, add the onion, garlic and parsley. Leave to soften slightly, then add the tripe, season with salt and pepper and cook for about 20 min, stirring frequently.

Just before serving, beat the eggs in a bowl and add 2 tbsp water mixed with the meat extract. Remove the tripe from the heat and pour in the egg mixture. Add the Parmesan cheese and, stirring lightly, return to the heat for 2 min. Serve immediately.

TRIPPA ALLA TREVISANA
(Tripe Treviso style)

1 lb fresh tripe
¼ cup chopped salt pork
1 sliced onion
¼ cup butter
1 sprig rosemary
3 cups beef stock
8 small slices toasted bread
grated Parmesan cheese

Buy the tripe ready blanched and cook it in boiling water in a covered saucepan for 1½ hr or until tender. Drain well and cut into thin strips. Heat the butter in a saucepan and fry the salt pork and the onion. Add the tripe and a sprig of rosemary and cook gently for a few minutes. Pour on the stock and simmer for ½ hr. Put two slices of toasted bread into each bowl, add the tripe and ladle some of the stock over the top. Sprinkle with Parmesan cheese and serve immediately.

SPIEDINI MISTI SPOLETINI
(Spoleto mixed kabobs)

4 cubes pork loin
4 small lamb chops
4 small pieces boned chicken
4 slices pork liver
8 slices pancetta
few sage leaves
2 tbsp chopped rosemary
freshly ground pepper
3–4 juniper berries
½ cup olive oil

On to four skewers thread the pork, chicken, liver and lamb chops, interspersing them with the slices of pancetta and sage leaves.

Put the skewers in a shallow dish and sprinkle with a little rosemary and plenty of pepper and add the juniper berries. Pour the olive oil over them and leave to marinate for 5–6 hr. Barbecue or cook in a saucepan over high heat for ¼ hr or until all the meats are tender.

UCCELLINI SCAPPATI
(Kabobs of calves' variety meats)

7 oz calves' or pork liver
7 oz calf kidneys
4 oz calf sweetbreads
5 oz pancetta
few sage leaves
¼ cup butter
salt
freshly ground pepper

Soak, peel and precook the sweetbreads as described in the recipe for calf sweetbreads on p. 160. Remove membranes and any fatty parts from the kidneys and liver. Cut the variety meats into cubes and slice the pancetta. Thread skewers in the following order: Pancetta, sage, sweetbreads, kidney, liver, sage and pancetta. Melt the butter in a large skillet and put in the skewers. Season with salt and pepper and brown for 5–10 min.

SELLA DI CONIGLIO ALL'ARANCIA
(Saddle of rabbit with orange)

2 saddles of rabbit

1 tbsp butter
salt
½ cup game fondo bruno (see p. 131)
1 cup white wine
juice of 1 orange
3 tbsp chopped parsley

Cut four fillets from the two saddles of rabbit. Brown in the butter in a flameproof casserole. Add salt and pour in the white wine, add the game fondo bruno and put in an oven preheated to 475°F for 10 min. Remove the meat from the oven, slice lengthwise and fan out on a serving dish. Add the orange juice to the sauce, reduce over high heat, add the chopped parsley and pour over the rabbit slices.

Serve at once with a selection of cooked vegetables.

CERVELLA AL BURRO NERO E CAPPERI
(Brains with black butter and capers)

2 calf brains
1 bouquet garni
¼ cup + 2 tbsp butter
parsley leaves
2 tbsp herb vinegar
¼ cup capers

Soak the brains in cold water for 1 hr, drain, and remove the outer membrane. Boil in salted water with the bouquet garni for ¼ hr and arrange on serving plates. Heat the butter in a saucepan until it browns, take off the heat and add the parsley leaves, herb vinegar and capers. Stir well. Pour over the brains and serve.

163

AGNELLO COTTO A VAPORE IN FOGLIE DI LATTUGA AI TRE PURÈ *
(Lamb steamed in spinach leaves with chestnut, apple and carrot purées)

for the chestnut purée:
1 medium potato, peeled and diced
4 oz canned, unsweetened chestnut
   purée
1 tbsp butter
salt
freshly ground pepper
freshly grated nutmeg

for the apple purée:
2 medium potatoes, peeled and
   diced
1 onion, chopped
1 tbsp butter
1 medium cooking apple, peeled
   and diced
salt

for the carrot purée:
⅛ cup chopped onion
1 tbsp butter
2 medium carrots, chopped
salt
freshly ground pepper
8 large spinach leaves
1 8-rib lamb rib roast
salt

First prepare the three purées.
   For the chestnut purée: Boil the potatoes in salted water until soft. Mash and add to the chestnut purée and butter in a small saucepan. Heat gently, stirring constantly. Season with salt and pepper and a sprinkling of nutmeg. Keep warm.
   For the apple purée: Boil the potatoes in salted water until soft. Fry the onion in the butter, add the apples and cook for about 10 min until the apple is soft; add the potatoes and continue cooking for another 10 min. Salt and mash the mixture. Keep warm.
   For the carrot purée: In a small saucepan fry the onion in the butter, add the carrots, cover and cook for 10 min over low heat. Add a little stock if necessary. When the ingredients are soft season with salt and pepper and blend. Keep warm.
   Dip the spinach leaves in boiling water for 2 min to blanch them. Divide the rib roast into eight, cutting carefully between each rib.

Salt and wrap one spinach leaf around each piece of meat. Steam for ½ hr or until the meat is tender. Test by inserting a fork on the underside of the lamb so as not to break the spinach leaf. Serve immediately with a little of each purée, as illustrated.

164

FILETTO DI MANZO ALL'AMARONE *
(Beef loin tenderloin in red wine)

1 lb red onions
2 cups Amarone or any full-bodied, dry wine
2 cups meat stock
2 tbsp butter
4 beef loin tenderloin steaks

Coarsely chop the onions and cook in the wine, allowing the liquid to reduce by half. Add the stock and continue to cook until the liquid is reduced to a quarter of its original volume. Remove the onions and boil the stock down still further. Add 1 tbsp butter and stir well. Melt the butter in a skillet over medium-high heat and cook the steaks for about 4 min until the underside is browned. Turn and cook the other side according to taste: 5 min for rare, 7 min for medium and 10 min for well done. Arrange on serving plates, pour over the sauce and serve immediately.

ANIMELLE AI FUNGHI PORCINI *
(Sweetbreads with cèpes)

2 lb calf sweetbreads
¼ cup butter
1 cup meat stock
salt
freshly ground pepper
7 oz fresh porcini (cèpes)
1 sprig parsley

Soak the sweetbreads in cold water for 1–2 hr. Drain, cover with fresh water and bring to a boil. Drain, cover with salted water and bring to a boil again. Rinse in cold water, drain and cut into small pieces. Heat 2 tbsp butter in a skillet, add the sweetbreads and cook over low heat for ¼ hr, adding a little stock from time to time. Season with salt and pepper to taste. Meanwhile, thinly slice the porcini and fry them in a little butter for a few minutes. Add to the sweetbreads and cook for 3 min. Add a little chopped parsley and serve.

166

ROGNONE ALLA VERZA E ACETO DI LAMPONI *
(Kidney with Savoy cabbage and raspberry vinegar)

12 ½-in thick slices calves' kidney
    with their own fat
2 tbsp butter
salt
½ cup white wine
20 green peppercorns
3 tbsp raspberry vinegar
1 tsp fondo bruno (see p. 131)
1 sprig parsley
8 boiled Savoy cabbage leaves

Brown the kidney slices in the butter over high heat for 5 min, add salt, pour on the white wine and then remove the kidneys from the pan. To the sauce left in the pan add the peppercorns, vinegar, fondo bruno and chopped parsley. Reduce the sauce to thicken. Arrange two cabbage leaves on each serving plate, put the kidney slices on top and pour over the sauce.

FEGATO DI VITELLO ALL'UVA
(Calves' liver with grapes)

1¾ lb calves' liver
¼ cup butter
salt
½ cup sweet white wine
20 green grapes, peeled and
    seeded
¼ cup chopped parsley
2 tbsp fondo bruno (see p. 131)

Cut off any membrane from the liver, slice thinly and sauté for 1 min over high heat in 2 tbsp butter. Add salt, pour in the wine and take the liver off the heat immediately. To the sauce in the skillet add the grapes, chopped parsley, fondo bruno and remaining butter. Pour the sauce over the liver and serve.

Poultry

*T*urkey, duck, goose, guinea fowl and the humble and often denigrated chicken are an extremely versatile main-course choice, lending themselves to a variety of sauces and cooking methods as well as forming the basis of a cheap and nutritious meal. Birds may be simply braised, or roasted with garlic, butter and herbs to enhance their flavor. Married with interesting and unusual ingredients such as pomegranates, truffles, eggplant, olives, prunes and chestnuts, Marsala or green peppercorns, they can assume a sophistication worthy of the most formal meal. Try port, lemon juice or a touch of chili as an interesting and flavorsome alternative to white wine when cooking succulent poultry dishes, or a combination of anchovies, gherkins and capers.

Italian cuisine abounds with classic poultry dishes, each region contributing its own traditional touches to this already vast repertoire. In recent years adventurous and innovative new recipes have shown us how to elevate the most ordinary of birds to dishes of the highest culinary excellence. Whichever way you choose to cook poultry, you will always be sure to serve a pleasing and welcome dish.

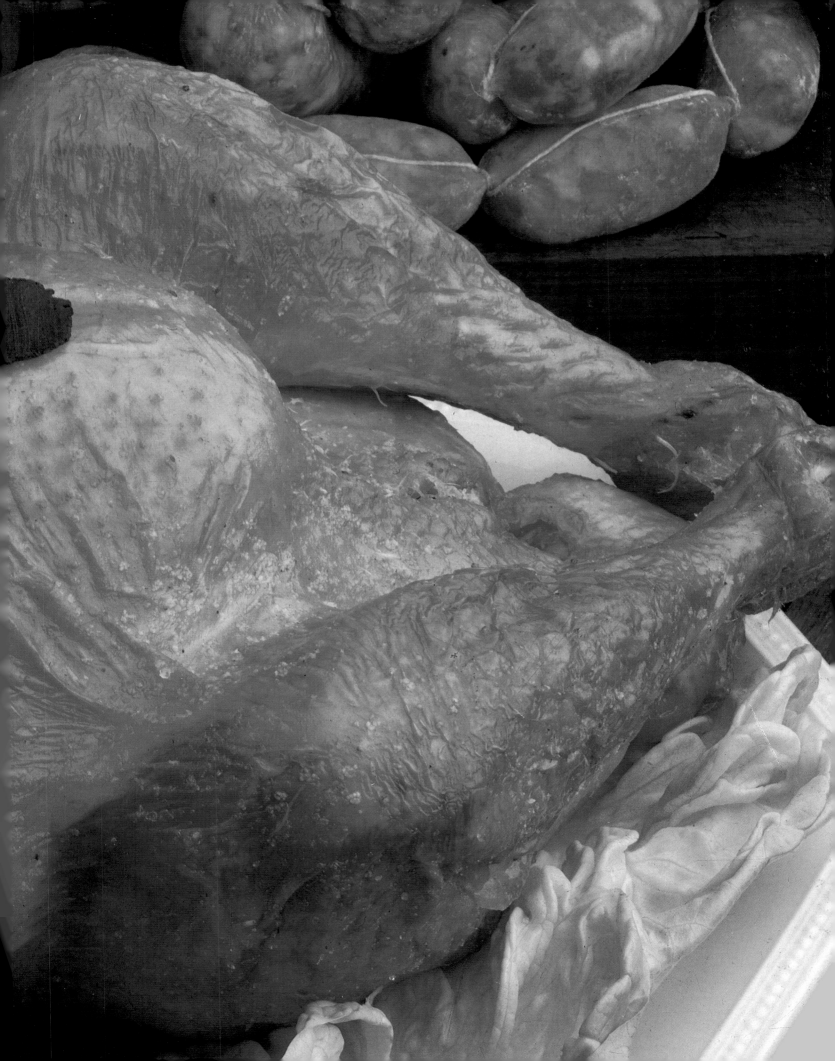

POLLO ALLA CACCIATORA
(Hunter's chicken)

1 2¼ lb oven-ready chicken
1 tbsp olive oil
¼ cup pancetta, diced
1 clove garlic
2–3 tbsp dry white wine
3–4 ripe tomatoes
1 cup stock
salt
freshly ground pepper
chopped parsley

Joint the chicken. Heat the oil in a skillet over moderate heat and add the diced pancetta and the clove of garlic. When the pancetta begins to fry, add the chicken pieces and brown carefully. As the chicken begins to brown, sprinkle it with the dry white wine and, when this has evaporated, add the seeded, chopped tomatoes. Pour in a little stock or hot water. Season with salt and pepper. Lower the heat and simmer gently for ¾ hr–1 hr. The sauce should remain fairly liquid and the chicken take on a nice rosy color. If you like, you can add some chopped parsley just before serving.

POLLO ARROSTO
(Chicken pot roast)

¼ cup butter
1 medium oven-ready chicken
3 tbsp oil
salt
freshly ground pepper

Place a piece of butter inside the chicken. Truss the bird with string if necessary and rub more butter all over it and especially into the creases where the legs and wings join the body. Heat 3 tbsp of very good quality oil in a saucepan and, when it begins to sizzle, put in the chicken. Season sparingly with salt. Cover and cook over low heat for about 1 hr. It is advisable to turn the chicken several times during cooking so that it cooks evenly. Uncover the saucepan for the last 7–8 min of cooking so the bird can brown. (For a more browned effect place the chicken in a preheated oven at 325–350°F for the last 10 min.) When the bird is browned check it is done by prick-ing it with a fork at the fattest part of the thigh. If the juices run clear, the chicken is ready.

POLLO AL LIMONE
(Lemon chicken)

1 2¼ lb oven-ready chicken
2–3 lemons
salt
freshly ground pepper
½ cup dry white wine

Remove any string from the chicken and spread the bird out without actually cutting it apart. Pour over the juice of 2–3 lemons, making sure that the juice moistens every part of the chicken. Season with salt and pepper and leave overnight to marinate in the juices. Next day, put the chicken in an ovenproof pan with the remaining juices. Do not add any butter or oil. Preheat the oven to 325–350°F and place the bird in the oven. Roast for about 1 hr, basting two or three times during the cooking with spoonfuls of the dry white wine.

POLLO IN PORCHETTA
(Chicken Florentine)

1 1¾ lb young oven-ready chicken
½ cup prosciutto, coarsely chopped
3 cloves garlic
whole peppercorns
wild fennel leaves
1 tbsp butter
sprigs rosemary
freshly ground pepper
3 oz Pecorino cheese
herbs of your choice
1 lemon

Fill the inside of the chicken with the prosciutto, the whole garlic cloves, a few peppercorns and some fennel leaves. Grease an ovenproof pan generously with butter and place the chicken in it. Sprinkle over some rosemary, pepper and little flakes of Pecorino cheese. Add other herbs to taste. Preheat the oven to 325°F and cook the chicken for about ¾ hr. Serve garnished with slices of lemon.

POLLO AL TEGAME *
(Braised chicken)

1 2¼ lb young oven-ready chicken
1 onion, sliced
1 carrot, chopped
1 stick celery, chopped
¼ cup butter
1 tbsp oil
½ cup dry white wine
salt
1 clove
pinch cinnamon
freshly ground pepper
7 oz tomatoes
12 oz fresh mushrooms

Joint the chicken, rinse and dry. In a saucepan, soften the onion, carrot and celery in the butter and oil. Add the chicken pieces and sprinkle with the wine. Salt, add the clove, a pinch of cinnamon and pepper and, when the chicken has browned all over, the peeled, seeded and chopped tomatoes. Cook for at least 1 hr. Wash and slice the mushrooms and, ¼ hr before the end of the cooking time, add them to the saucepan. Check the seasoning, adding more salt if necessary.

SPEZZATINO DI POLLO
(Chicken with tomato and white wine sauce)

1 1¾ lb chicken
¼ cup butter
2 tbsp oil
salt
white pepper
½ cup white wine
14 oz tomatoes

Joint the chicken. Heat the butter and oil in a large saucepan or skillet and brown the chicken pieces over high heat. Season with salt and white pepper, lower the heat and continue to cook until the meat begins to get tender (about 25 min). Remove the chicken pieces from the saucepan and keep them warm. Deglaze the pan with the white wine and allow it to evaporate. Meanwhile rinse, blanch and sieve the tomatoes. Add them to the saucepan. Cook the sauce for 10 min and, when it has reduced a little, return the chicken pieces to the saucepan and let them absorb the flavors for a few minutes. Transfer the chicken to a warmed serving dish and accompany with the tomato sauce.

BUDINO DI POLLO
(Chicken mold)

1 2¼ lb boiling fowl
salt
freshly ground pepper
1 egg, beaten
grated lemon peel
½ cup light cream
1 black truffle, diced (optional)
butter for the mold

Skin the chicken and cut all the meat away from the carcass; put the meat twice through a mincer or food processor. Season with salt and pepper and add the beaten egg, a little grated lemon peel, the cream and, if you like, the diced truffle. Butter an ovenproof bowl or mold and spoon in the chicken mixture. When the mold is full, tap it on the work surface to settle the contents and eliminate air bubbles. Then cover with a piece of wax paper and place in a pan half-filled with hot water. Preheat the oven to 325°F and cook the mold for about 1 hr. Remove from the oven and leave to rest for a few minutes before turning out on to a flat serving dish.

POLLO ALLA MARENGO
(Chicken Marengo)

1 2¼ lb young oven-ready chicken
8 tbsp oil
4–5 tomatoes
1 cup white wine
2 cloves garlic
salt
freshly ground pepper
½ tsp meat extract
croûtons fried in butter
4 shrimp poached in white wine (optional)
4 eggs fried in butter
2 tbsp chopped parsley

Joint the chicken into pieces, wash and dry. Heat the oil in a skillet and brown the chicken over high heat. As soon as the breasts have cooked, remove them from the skillet and continue to cook the other pieces.

When the rest of the chicken is almost cooked, drain off the oil and add the peeled, seeded and chopped tomatoes, the white wine and

171

the garlic, and season with salt and pepper. Cook the sauce to reduce it and add the meat extract. Add the breast meat and cook for several more minutes. Arrange the chicken on a serving plate and garnish with the croûtons of fried bread, the poached shrimp and fried eggs. Sprinkle over the chopped parsley and serve.

POLLO RIPIENO
(Boned stuffed chicken)

1 2¼ lb oven-ready chicken
5 oz veal
2 oz prosciutto or sausage
crumbs of 1 dry bread roll
few tbsp milk
salt
freshly ground pepper

grated nutmeg
2 egg yolks
1 tbsp butter

Bone the chicken without cutting into pieces, turning back the neck and wings once the bones have been taken out and removing membranes, tendons and veins. Grind the veal meat, cut the prosciutto into slivers and soak the breadcrumbs in a little milk. Put the veal, prosciutto and breadcrumbs into a

bowl, season lightly and add a pinch of nutmeg. Add the egg yolks and mix well. Spread the stuffing on the inside of the chicken, roll and then sew it up. Wrap the roll in a piece of muslin, tie up with care and poach in simmering water for about 2 hr. Unwrap the muslin from the chicken. Heat a little butter in a pan and brown the roll of chicken over low heat. Remove the strings used to sew up the bird and serve the chicken, cut into slices, with a seasonal green salad.

POLLO ALLA LUCANA
(Chicken Lucania style)

1 2¼ lb young oven-ready chicken
2 oz lard, firm salt pork or streaky
   bacon

172

4 chicken livers
salt
freshly ground pepper
2 eggs
1 sprig rosemary (optional)
2 tbsp grated Pecorino cheese

Mash the lard (to make it easier to spread, heat the knife blade over the flame). Put 1 tsp of the lard in a little saucepan and, when it is sizzling, add the chicken livers. Season with salt and pepper and let the livers cook for a few minutes, turning them several times. Chop them finely. In a bowl, beat the eggs for a minute or two with the Pecorino cheese, then add the livers and mix thoroughly. Sprinkle the inside of the chicken with a little salt and pepper, then fill it with the prepared mixture and sew up the opening with string. Rub the bird with a little salt and pepper, smear with the remaining lard and place in a roasting pan together with the sprig of rosemary, if used. Preheat the oven to 325°F and roast the bird for about 1 hr. Baste frequently with the cooking juices, and turn the chicken several times so that it cooks evenly. When it is ready, place on a warmed serving platter and spoon over some of the cooking juices. Serve very hot accompanied by a mixed salad.

POLLO ALLA DIAVOLA
(Spatchcocked chicken)

1 2¼ lb young oven-ready chicken
1 cup dry white wine
1 sprig sage
a little oil
salt
freshly ground pepper

Rinse the bird inside and out. Cut in half vertically. Flatten the two pieces of chicken with a meatbat until they are almost level. Pour the wine into a wide deep dish, add the chopped sage and immerse the two chicken pieces in this marinade. Leave for several hours, making sure to turn the pieces several times. Take the chicken pieces out of the marinade, dry them and spread oil all over them. Place the pieces on the barbecue or under the broiler and cook slowly; when the meat is almost

cooked, season it generously. If necessary, baste the chicken with more oil ·while it cooks to stop it drying out too much. If you cannot broil the chicken, cook it over moderate heat in a wide pan where it can be spread out, and moisten it every now and then with some of the marinade. A young chicken should only take about 20 min to cook.

POLLO IN POTACCHIO *
(Braised chili chicken)

1 2¼ lb young oven-ready chicken
½ cup oil
2 tbsp butter
1 medium onion, sliced
2 cloves garlic, minced
salt
½ cup dry white wine

for the sauce:
½ cup oil
1 onion, finely chopped
1 sprig rosemary, chopped
14 oz ripe tomatoes
salt
1 piece red chili pepper, finely chopped
1 tbsp butter

This is a typical dish from the Marches region. Cut the chicken into small pieces, rinse and dry them. Heat the oil and butter in a skillet and brown the chicken, the onion and the garlic. Add a little salt. Once the garlic has browned, remove it from the skillet and, when the chicken has begun to cook through, pour over the wine. Meanwhile, prepare the sauce in a small saucepan. Heat the oil and fry the onion and rosemary; as soon as the onion has softened, add the peeled, seeded and chopped tomatoes. Salt sparingly and sprinkle with the chopped chili pepper. Let the sauce cook gently for about 20 min, then add the chicken and a few flakes of butter. Finish cooking for about 20 min in an oven preheated to 400°F.

POLLO ALLA BOLOGNESE
(Chicken Bologna style)

1 2¼ lb young oven-ready chicken
2 tbsp oil
¼ cup butter
1 slice prosciutto
2 cloves garlic
1 sprig rosemary
2 large ripe tomatoes (or 3 tbsp tomato paste)
salt
freshly ground pepper
generous 1 lb potatoes

Cut the chicken into pieces and bone carefully. Heat the oil and butter in a saucepan large enough to hold all the chicken pieces. Fry the prosciutto, the finely chopped garlic and the rosemary for a few minutes. Then add the chicken pieces and brown, turning them frequently. Peel and seed the tomatoes, chop coarsely and add to the saucepan (if fresh tomatoes are not used, mix 2–3 tbsp tomato paste with a little water, or use 1 cup

sieved, canned tomatoes). Season with salt and pepper, cover and simmer over very moderate heat, adding a little water if the sauce becomes too thick. When the chicken is tender, remove from the saucepan and keep warm. Add a little more water to the sauce, then add the potatoes, cut into small pieces. Cook over moderate heat and, just before the potatoes are ready, return the chicken pieces to the saucepan and heat thoroughly before serving.

POLLO IN PADELLA (ALLA ROMANA)
(Chicken Roman style)

1 2¼ lb oven-ready chicken
1 generous tbsp lard
2 slices prosciutto, diced
salt
freshly ground pepper
1 clove garlic, finely chopped
pinch marjoram
1 cup dry white wine
4–5 ripe tomatoes
stock or water

Joint the chicken. Melt the lard in a saucepan and add the diced prosciutto. When the lard begins to sizzle, add the chicken pieces, season with salt and pepper and brown well. Then add the garlic and marjoram and gradually add the wine, letting it evaporate between additions. When all the wine has been added, put in the peeled, seeded and chopped tomatoes; if the chicken seems to be getting too dry, add some stock or water. Cook over high heat; the chicken should be done in about 20 min or so if it is a tender one. The sauce should be thick, dark and not very plentiful as this is characteristic of authentic Roman-style chicken.

POLLO SPEZZATO E MELANZANE
(Chicken with eggplant)

1 2¼ lb oven-ready chicken
3 medium eggplant
salt
1 cup olive oil
1 clove garlic
freshly ground pepper
1 cup dry white wine
10 oz ripe tomatoes
½ cup prosciutto, chopped
stock or water
2–3 sprigs parsley, chopped

Rinse the eggplant and cut into cubes but do not peel. Sprinkle the cubes with salt and place them in a colander for ½ hr to drain away the bitter juices. Joint the chicken. Heat a few tablespoons of oil in a large skillet and brown the garlic. Remove the garlic and brown the chicken pieces. Season with salt and pepper and pour over the white wine. As soon as this has evaporated, add the peeled, seeded and chopped tomatoes and the chopped prosciutto. Add a little hot stock if necessary. Meanwhile, heat the remaining oil in a large saucepan and cook the drained eggplant for 10 min over high heat. Season with salt and pepper and sprinkle with chopped parsley. A few minutes before the chicken portions are cooked, transfer to the saucepan containing the eggplant, pour over the sauce and cover. Heat gently for a few minutes, then serve straight from the saucepan.

POLLO IN SALSA PICCANTE *
(Chicken in piquant sauce)

1 2¼ lb oven-ready chicken
6 tbsp olive oil
1 onion, chopped
1 tbsp all-purpose flour
½ cup dry white wine
1 tbsp concentrated tomato paste
salt
freshly ground pepper
6 tbsp wine vinegar
1 anchovy, filleted and chopped
3 gherkins, chopped
1 tbsp capers, chopped
2 sprigs parsley, chopped
1 small clove garlic, chopped

Joint the chicken. Heat the oil in a saucepan, add the onion and the chicken pieces and brown them gently. As soon as they are golden, sprinkle the pieces of chicken with the flour and moisten with the wine. After the wine has evaporated, add the tomato paste diluted with a little hot water. Season generously with salt and pepper.

Cook the tomato for a few minutes, then cover the chicken with boiling water and, over moderate heat, continue cooking until the sauce is well reduced. In a separate small saucepan, boil the vinegar until it has reduced by nearly two-thirds. Add the anchovy, gherkins, capers, parsley and garlic. Stir the mixture and pour into the chicken saucepan 5 min before removing it from the heat. Stir well, letting the chicken pieces absorb the flavors for a minute or two, before serving with the thick sauce.

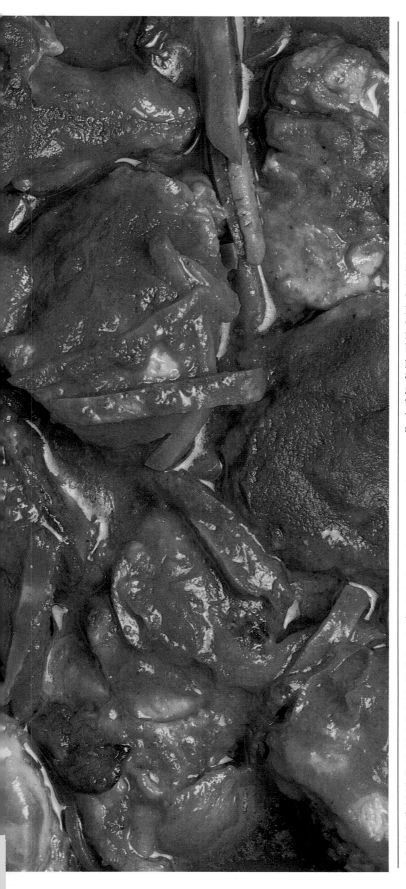

POLLO FRITTO
(Fried chicken)

1 2¼ lb very young oven-ready
   chicken
about ½ cup oil
juice of 1 lemon
1 sprig parsley, chopped
salt
freshly ground pepper
all-purpose flour
2 eggs, beaten
oil for deep frying

Cut the chicken into small pieces: Make two pieces out of each leg and thigh, two out of each wing, four pieces from the breast and about four pieces from the back. Put the pieces to marinate in the oil, lemon juice, parsley, salt and pepper for at least 1 hr. Drain the chicken pieces from the marinade, flour them and dip them in the beaten egg. Deep fry the pieces in plenty of very hot oil, over moderate heat for about 20 min until golden brown on both sides. Drain them on kitchen paper and serve very hot, accompanied by a fresh seasonal salad.

POLLO ALLA MACERATESE
(Blanquette of chicken)

1 2¼ lb oven-ready chicken, giblets
   reserved
salt
¼ cup butter
5 tbsp oil
2¼ cups beef stock
2 egg yolks
juice of 1 lemon

Wash the chicken, dry it and salt it generously inside and out, then truss it with string so that it keeps its shape. Wash and trim the chicken giblets, then chop them finely. Heat the butter and oil together in a saucepan large enough to hold the chicken, then add the giblets. Let them cook for a minute or two, turning them over, then add the chicken. When it begins to cook, pour in the boiling stock. Place a piece of wax paper under the lid, cover tightly and cook slowly for about 1 hr. Then reduce the remaining stock over high heat, uncovered. Joint the chicken, arrange the pieces on a serving dish, and keep warm. Beat the egg yolks, and mix a little of the hot liquid from the saucepan into them. Add this mixture to the saucepan together with the lemon juice and a pinch of salt. Cook over very low heat for 1 min or so, stirring all the time so the egg thickens the sauce (without curdling). Do not allow to boil. Pour the sauce over the chicken and serve at once.

POLLO ALL'ARRABBIATA
(Chicken in spicy sauce)

1 2¼ lb young oven-ready chicken
6–8 tbsp olive oil
2 tbsp butter
salt
1 cup dry white wine
3 large ripe tomatoes
pinch chili powder

Joint the chicken into medium-sized pieces then wash and dry carefully. Heat the oil and butter in a saucepan and let the chicken pieces brown and the meat begin to cook through. Sprinkle with salt, moisten with the dry white wine and cook until it evaporates. Meanwhile, peel and seed the tomatoes, then chop coarsely. Add to the chicken, lower the heat and add a generous pinch of chili powder. Cover the saucepan and leave to cook over moderate heat until the chicken is tender – about 40 min. Serve hot, covered with the sauce.

STECCHI ALLA GENOVESE
(Deep-fried Genoese kabobs)

4 oz calf sweetbreads
¼ cup butter
4 oz chicken livers
8 oz fresh mushrooms
stock
salt
all-purpose flour
1 egg yolk, lightly beaten
breadcumbs
oil for deep frying

for the sauce:
1 cup white sauce (see p. 127)
3 tbsp grated Parmesan cheese
1 egg yolk
2 oz prosciutto

1 sprig parsley, chopped
1 small truffle, sliced

Soak the sweetbreads in cold water for 1–2 hr to remove all traces of blood. Drain and put in a saucepan filled with cold salted water. Bring to a boil and drain. Cover once again with cold salted water and bring to a boil a second time. Drain and rinse. Heat a little butter in a small saucepan and cook, separately, the livers, sweetbreads and mushrooms, adding if necessary a little stock or water. Cut into small pieces and salt lightly. On skewers measuring about 4 in in length, thread the various cooked ingredients alternately. Prepare the white sauce so that it is quite thick and add a generous amount of grated Parmesan cheese, the egg yolk, the chopped prosciutto and parsley and, when the sauce is ready, the truffle slices. Dip the kabobs into the sauce so that they are well covered and line them up on the work surface. When the coating sauce is cold and has thickened, carefully pick up the kababs one by one, roll them in the flour, then in the beaten egg, then in the breadcrumbs and deep fry them in plenty of very hot oil until they are golden brown.

FARAONA AL CARTOCCIO ✳ (Roast guinea fowl)

1 2¾ lb guinea fowl, cleaned, giblets reserved
1 tbsp butter
1 sprig sage
1 clove garlic
salt
freshly ground pepper
3½ oz pancetta slices or bacon
1 tbsp oil

Wash the guinea fowl well inside and out and dry it. Melt the butter in a small saucepan, add the giblets, some sage leaves and the minced garlic clove. Fry for a few minutes, stirring, and season well. Take the saucepan off the heat and finely chop the giblets (discard the garlic and sage). Put the giblets back in the saucepan, stir to allow them to absorb the cooking juices, then stuff the guinea fowl with the mixture. Sprinkle the bird with salt, then lay the pancetta or bacon over it. Wrap it in a piece of foil, lightly greased with oil on the inside and pricked with a few holes here and there. Place in a preheated oven at 325–350°F and roast for about 1–1½ hr. Bring the bird to table still enclosed in the foil so it stays very hot, and accompany it with fresh seasonal salad and roast potatoes.

TACCHINELLA ALLA MELAGRANA
(Turkey with pomegranates)

(serves 6–8)
1 4½ lb young oven-ready turkey, giblets reserved
7 oz sliced pancetta or bacon
3 pomegranates
½ cup oil
salt
freshly ground pepper

Bard the turkey with the pancetta or bacon so that every part is well covered, place in a roasting pan and cook in a preheated oven at 375°F for about 1½ hr. Turn the bird several times during roasting so that it cooks evenly and is well basted with its own juices. Halfway through the cooking, baste the bird with the juice squeezed from two of the pomegranates. Meanwhile, in a small saucepan, prepare the sauce. Heat the oil and add the very finely chopped turkey giblets – the liver, lungs and heart. Add salt and moisten with the juice of the remaining pomegranate. Allow the sauce to thicken over low heat. When the turkey is well done, joint it into serving pieces, arrange on a heated serving dish, pour over the sauce and bring to the table at once.

FARAONA ALLA CAMPAGNOLA
(Country-style guinea fowl)

1 2¼ lb oven-ready guinea fowl, giblets reserved
salt
freshly ground pepper

2 tbsp oil
1 carrot
1 stick celery
1 small bunch parsley
1 sprig rosemary
¼ cup butter
1 cup dry white wine
1 white truffle (optional)

Season the guinea fowl inside and out, place it in a roasting pan and oil it all over. Roast it in a preheated oven at 325°F for 1–1½ hr, turning it now and again. Finely chop the vegetables and herbs (use only tender leaves of rosemary) together with the bird's liver and heart. Melt the butter in a small saucepan and cook the chopped ingredients gently. When they are softened, add the white wine and, if necessary, some water. Allow to thicken a little, then sieve the sauce. If the sauce is too liquid, put it back on the heat for a few minutes, stirring all the time. When the guinea fowl is done, remove it from the saucepan and joint it into four. Remove as many bones as possible. Arrange the portions of guinea fowl on a serving dish and moisten with the sauce. Sprinkle with very thin slices of white truffle.

FILETTI DI TACCHINO AL MARSALA *
(Turkey breasts with Marsala)

2 turkey breast fillets
all-purpose flour
¼ cup butter
salt
white pepper
1 cup Marsala
1 truffle

Trim the breast fillets, pound lightly with a meatbat and cut each one in two. Flour the pieces of turkey. Heat most of the butter in a saucepan and brown the breasts over high heat, seasoning them with salt and pepper. Reduce the heat and cook the meat for about 20–25 min or until tender. Remove from the saucepan and keep warm.

Deglaze the pan with the Marsala and when it has partly evaporated melt the remaining butter into the Marsala sauce. Arrange the turkey pieces on a warmed serving dish and pour over the sauce. Sprinkle with the grated truffle.

SPEZZATINO DI TACCHINO
(Braised turkey with olives)

½ cup olive oil
1 clove garlic
1¾ lb turkey meat, cubed
½ cup dry white wine
1¼ cups sweet black olives, pitted
salt
freshly ground pepper

This is a typical recipe from Umbria. In a large skillet heat the oil and fry the whole clove of garlic. When the oil is hot, remove the garlic and replace with the turkey meat. Brown the turkey pieces over high heat, moisten them with the wine and, when the wine has evaporated, add the pitted olives, salt, a pinch of pepper and a generous ladleful of hot water. Cover the saucepan and leave to cook on very low heat for at least 2½ hr until the water has reduced and become a delicious sauce.

PETTO DI TACCHINO ALLA NAPOLETANA
(Turkey breast Neapolitan style)

¾ lb turkey breast
¼ cup butter
4 oz Mozzarella cheese
3 ripe tomatoes
salt
freshly ground pepper
2 bunches parsley

Poach the turkey breast in simmering water until tender; allow to cool and cut into thin slices. Butter a small ovenproof pan and arrange the slices over the bottom, spread over them a layer of sliced Mozzarella cheese and on top of them the sliced tomatoes. Season with salt and pepper and dot pieces of butter over the surface. Put the pan in a preheated oven at 350°F and cook for 20 min. When the cheese has melted, garnish with the chopped parsley and serve.

TACCHINO ALLA TRIESTINA
(Turkey with chestnuts and prunes Trieste style)

1 4½ lb young oven-ready turkey
6 chestnuts, peeled
8 prunes
2 celery hearts
salt
4 oz sliced pancetta or bacon
freshly ground pepper

Stuff the turkey with the chestnuts, prunes, the chopped celery and a good pinch of salt. Bard it well with the slices of pancetta or bacon, truss it with a piece of string and put it on to the rotisserie skewer. Roast it slowly on the rotisserie or in a preheated oven at 375°F for about 1½ hr, basting occasionally with the fat that collects from the cooking. Adjust the seasoning. When it is done, divide the turkey into pieces and arrange on a serving plate with the stuffing. Accompany with fried potatoes.

ANATRA ARROSTO
(Roast duck)

1 4–5 lb oven-ready duck
salt
freshly ground pepper
1 clove garlic
sprigs rosemary
pieces of butter or 2 tbsp oil

Truss the duck with string and season inside and out with a generous pinch of salt and pepper, 1 minced garlic clove and the rosemary. Heat the butter or oil in a roasting pan. When it is hot, place the duck in the pan. It is not necessary to grease the meat of the duck itself as it contains plenty of fat. Place in a preheated oven at 350°F. Do not worry that the roasting pan will dry out since the cooking liquid will be replenished with juices from the duck. Turn the bird several times during cooking and baste the meat with spoonfuls of dripping from the base of the pan. Allow a roasting time of 20 min per 1 lb, or less if you have a preference for slightly pink meat. It is a good idea to test with a fork several times to be sure.

ANATRA RIPIENA *
(Roast duck with stuffing)

(serves 6–8)
1 4½ lb oven-ready duck
½ cup ground veal
¼ cup pounded salt pork
¼ cup salami, finely chopped
1 egg, beaten
2 tbsp grated Parmesan cheese
1 clove garlic, finely chopped
1 sprig parsley, chopped
* the crumbs of 1 bread roll soaked*
* in milk and squeezed out*
salt
freshly ground pepper
4 oz sliced pancetta or bacon
1 cup oil
¼ cup butter
2 sprigs rosemary

In a bowl mix together the veal, salt pork, salami, egg, Parmesan cheese, garlic, parsley, breadcrumbs and salt and pepper to taste. Stuff the duck with this mixture and sew up the opening with thread. Bard the bird with the slices of pancetta or bacon and tie with string. Put the duck in a roasting pan with the oil, butter and rosemary. Salt and roast evenly in a preheated oven at 350°F allowing 20 min per 1 lb. Reserve the cooking juices and serve as gravy with the duck.

ANATRA IN SALSA
PICCANTE
(Duck in piquant sauce)

(serves 6–8)
1 4½ lb oven-ready duck
¼ cup + 2 tbsp butter
1 sprig rosemary, finely chopped
4–5 sage leaves, finely chopped
¼ cup pancetta or bacon, finely
* chopped*
1 lemon, halved
salt
freshly ground pepper
8 oz pork sausage meat
1 clove garlic, finely chopped
6 oz anchovies, finely chopped
½ cup wine vinegar

Melt the butter in a large ovenproof pan and add the rosemary, sage and pancetta or bacon. Fry for a few minutes, remove from heat and place the duck in the pan together with the lemon. Season with salt and pepper and put in an oven preheated to 400°F. Roast the duck, uncovered, for 20 min per pound. After ½ hr remove from the oven, pour away the excess fat and prick the bird's skin over the breast and thighs. Replace in the oven and continue cooking, basting frequently with the cooking juices, until done. While the duck is cooking, combine the chopped sausages with the garlic and anchovies. Fry in a saucepan, season with salt and pepper and, when the mixture is well browned, add the wine vinegar. Put the duck into this piquant sauce and let it absorb the flavors for about ½ hr before bringing it to the table.

OCA ARROSTO RIPIENA
(Roast stuffed goose)

(serves 8)
1 6½ lb oven-ready goose, giblets
* reserved*
8 oz pork sausage meat
1 cup green olives, pitted
1 truffle (optional)
⅔ cup oil
salt
freshly ground pepper

Put the finely chopped sausage meat into a bowl with the coarsely chopped olives, the cleaned, diced truffle and cleaned, chopped goose giblets. Mix together and stuff the goose with the mixture. Sew up the opening with string and truss the bird to maintain its shape. Place the goose in a roasting pan, grease generously and season with salt and a sprinkling of pepper. Roast in a preheated oven at 375°F for about 3 hr, moistening from time to time with a little water.

PETTO D'ANITRA AL PEPE VERDE E PEPERONE *
(Duck breast with green peppercorns and sweet pepper)

2 tbsp goose fat
2 duck breasts
salt
2 tbsp brandy
1 cup white wine
1 cup fondo bruno (see p. 131)
1 tbsp green peppercorns
1 tbsp finely chopped sweet red
    pepper

Heat the goose fat and brown the duck breasts over high heat for 5 min; while they are still pink salt them and sprinkle them with brandy. Ignite the brandy and, when the flames have gone out, remove the meat from the saucepan and keep warm. Pour the wine into the saucepan with the cooking juices and add the *fondo bruno*, the peppercorns and sweet pepper; reduce for a few minutes. Cut the duck breasts into slices, arrange them on a plate and pour over the sauce. Serve with diced carrots and zucchini.

ROTOLO DI FARAONA ALLE SPUGNOLE *
(Guinea fowl roulades with morel mushrooms)

1 2¼ lb guinea fowl
rosemary
3 oz prosciutto
¼ cup butter
salt
freshly ground pepper
6 tbsp white wine
7 oz morel mushrooms
⅔ cup port
6 tbsp light cream
1 cup game fondo bruno (see recipe
    p. 131)

Clean the bird carefully. Remove the two breast fillets and the thighs and bone the thighs. Prepare four rolls of meat by enclosing inside each breast fillet and boned thigh some rosemary and diced prosciutto. Place the roulades in a roasting pan with some butter and roast in a preheated oven (350°F) for 20 min. Season with salt and pepper and sprinkle with the white wine. At the end of the cooking time, remove the roulades from the pan and arrange them on serving plates. Put the halved mushrooms into the pan with the remainder of the roasting juices; adjust the seasoning if necessary, add the port, cream and *fondo bruno* and cook until the sauce is quite thick. Pour over the roulades and serve at once.

181

Game

There are many delicious recipes for furred and feathered game to be found throughout Italy, dating from the days when people fed off such fare from necessity. Nowadays, hunger has been replaced by sport; indeed, many would argue that shooting is a sport man would do well to practice less frequently if at all.

There are many varieties of game in Italy, including venison from the Val d'Aosta, Tuscan wild boar, hare, pigeon, wild duck, partridge and quail. Woodcock are best found on the edge of the Umbrian forest, tired by their flight over the Adriatic, and thus easy prey.

Game is strongly flavored in itself and responds equally well to simple cooking or a more elaborate and well seasoned sauce.

BECCACCE ARROSTO
(Roast woodcock canapés)

(serves 2)
2 woodcock
2 oz firm pork fat or salt pork
1 tbsp butter
sage leaves
juniper berries
slices of fried bread
liver pâté

Hang the woodcock, heads down, unplucked, for two or three days in a cool, well ventilated place, but do not leave them to become too high. Pluck and clean them, rinse and singe off remaining feathers over a flame. Reserve the birds' livers. Either wrap the birds in the pork fat and roast them on a rotisserie over moderate heat, or roast them in the oven. To do this, melt 1 tbsp butter in a roasting pan with some sage leaves, juniper berries and little pieces of pork fat. Cook the birds for 20–30 min at 375°F. Serve the woodcock as canapés on slices of bread fried in butter, spread with liver pâté, and finally with the livers of the woodcock themselves, fried in butter and flavored with the juices reserved from the cooked birds.

BECCACCE IN SALMÌ
(Braised woodcock)

(serves 2)
2 woodcock, already hung
salt
4 slices prosciutto
½ cup oil
½ cup dry white wine
½ cup dry Marsala
1 tsp salted capers
2 salted anchovies
8 slices dry bread

Clean the woodcock, reserving the liver, stomach, heart and lungs. Salt the inside of the birds and then wrap each one in two slices of prosciutto. Tie with kitchen string so the slices do not slip off. Pour half the oil into a flameproof casserole and when it is hot, put in the birds and brown over low heat. Sprinkle with 2 tbsp white wine and 2 tbsp Marsala. Cover and cook in the oven at 325°F for about 1 hr, moistening if necessary with water. Meanwhile, rinse the salt from the capers and anchovies, filleting the latter, and chop with the reserved giblets. Pour the rest of the oil into a small skillet and fry the chopped mixture, salting it and moistening it with the remaining wine and Marsala. Stir frequently and continue to cook for another 10 min. Pound the mixture to a paste. Toast the slices of bread in the oven and spread them with the giblet paste. Serve the woodcock with the hot toast.

BISTECCHINE DI CINGHIALE *
(Wild boar steaks with prunes and chocolate)

¼ cup lard
3 tbsp oil
1¼ lb wild boar or venison steaks, cut from the rib
salt
2 tbsp sugar
4 bay leaves
1½ cups wine vinegar
⅓ cup seedless white raisins, soaked in warm water
⅓ cup prunes, soaked in warmed water
2 oz cooking chocolate, grated
pinch cinnamon or nutmeg
1 tbsp all-purpose flour

This is a typical Sardinian dish. Since wild boar is not readily available, venison may be substituted.

Melt the lard with the oil in a saucepan over low heat. Add the meat and brown on both sides; season with a good pinch of salt and cook for 10 min. Put the sugar, bay leaves and 1 cup vinegar in another saucepan and, when the sugar has dissolved but the syrup is still white and transparent, add the drained seedless white raisins and the drained, pitted prunes. Add the chocolate and the cinnamon or, if you prefer, the nutmeg. Stir well and simmer gently for about 10 min until the sauce has thickened.

Blend the flour with the remaining vinegar and add this light paste to the meat; stir, and cook for a few more minutes. Add the sweet-and-sour sauce to the meat and cook for another 10 min. Transfer to a warmed serving dish and serve immediately.

FAGIANO CON FUNGHI
(Pheasant with mushrooms)

(serves 2)
1 pheasant, already hung
1 onion
2 sticks celery
1 bunch parsley
4 sage leaves
pinch thyme
¼ cup butter
4 tbsp oil
2 tbsp brandy
salt
freshly ground pepper
1 ladleful stock
10 oz fresh porcini (cèpes)
lemon juice
1 white truffle

Clean the pheasant, singe it over a flame, rinse and joint it into serving pieces. Pat dry and arrange in a flameproof casserole. Add the finely chopped onion, celery, parsley, sage and thyme, the butter and 2 tbsp of the oil and brown very gently. When the vegetables are completely soft and the pheasant meat has turned a nice brown color, sprinkle with the brandy, season with salt and pepper and moisten with a ladleful of hot stock. Cover and cook gently for about 1 hr or until done. Peel the mushrooms, slice and rinse in water acidulated with a few drops of lemon juice. Drain well and cook in a little oil, with salt and a few tablespoons of water. Add the mushrooms to the casserole containing the meat and simmer for a little longer. Transfer to a serving dish and garnish with the very thinly sliced truffle.

FAGIANO TARTUFATO
(Truffled pheasant)

(serves 2)
1 young pheasant
2 small white truffles
¼ cup softened pork fat
3 slices firm pork fat or bacon
3 tbsp oil
salt

The day before you are going to cook the pheasant, clean it carefully, singe it over a flame, wash and dry. Scrape, wash and dry the truffles, cut them into very thin slices and place the slices inside the pheasant, together with the softened pork fat. Put the pheasant in a dish with a close-fitting lid and leave in a cool place until the next day. When it is time to cook the bird, bard the breast with the slices of pork fat or bacon and secure them with kitchen string. Place in a roasting pan, pour the oil over the bird and sprinkle with salt. Roast in a preheated oven at 375°F for about ¾ hr or until done. Joint the pheasant into serving pieces and arrange on a serving dish.

FOLAGA ALLA PUCCINI
(Mallard Puccini)

1 mallard, cleaned
2 anchovies
1 cup wine vinegar
1 carrot
1 onion
1 stick celery
1 bunch parsley
4–5 small basil leaves
1 bay leaf
½ cup oil
1 tbsp butter
salt
freshly ground pepper
6 tbsp dry white wine
3 tbsp tomato paste

This recipe was traditionally made with coot (folaga), which used to be found in abundance in the Maremma region of Tuscany. Mallard is equally successful. Rinse the anchovies well to get rid of excess salt; fillet and chop them. Joint the bird into four pieces and marinate in the wine vinegar for a couple of hours. Take out the pieces, rinse well under running water and dry them. Finely chop the carrot, onion, celery, parsley, basil, bay leaf and anchovies. Heat the oil and butter in a saucepan and gently fry the chopped vegetables and herbs for a few minutes. Add the mallard pieces, season with salt and pepper, and brown. Moisten with wine and cook until it evaporates. Then add the tomato paste diluted with a couple of tablespoons of hot water; stir. Cover and cook over low heat for about ½ hr or until fork-tender. Take out the mallard pieces and pass the sauce through a sieve. Serve at once.

185

LEPRE IN SALMÌ *
(Hare in red wine)

(serves 4–6)
1 medium hare, already hung
all-purpose flour
¼ cup butter
2 tbsp oil
1 onion, finely chopped

for the marinade:
1 carrot, finely chopped
1 onion, sliced
1 stick celery, chopped
1 clove garlic, minced
1 sprig thyme
1 sprig marjoram
1 sprig sage
2 bay leaves
2 juniper berries
4 peppercorns
salt
scant 4½ cups red wine

Skin and clean the hare, reserving the heart, lungs and liver. Wash the hare well and joint it into pieces. Mix together all the ingredients for the marinade and put the pieces of meat into it. Cover and keep in a cool place for at least 48 hr. Take the hare pieces out of the marinade, reserving the latter, dry them and coat with flour. In a large saucepan or flameproof casserole, melt the butter and oil and fry the onion. Add the hare meat and, when it has begun to cook, add the chopped heart, lungs and liver. Pour in the marinade with all the flavorings and season. Cover and cook gently for 2–3 hr depending on the age and tenderness of the hare. Arrange the meat on a serving plate and keep warm. Pass the cooking liquid through a sieve and reheat the sauce. Serve accompanied by polenta.

LEPRE ALLA MARENGO
(Hare Marengo)

1 hare, skinned and cleaned
5 tbsp oil
1 onion, finely chopped
1 carrot, finely chopped
1 stick celery, chopped
1 clove
2 sage leaves
1 bay leaf
1 sprig rosemary
2 cloves garlic, chopped
1¼ cups red wine
3 tbsp wine vinegar
½ cup dried mushrooms
1 tbsp butter
salt
2 tbsp tomato paste
⅔ cup dry white wine
2–3 tbsp chopped parsley

Joint the hare. Wash the pieces, dry them and put them in a marinade prepared in the following way: Heat 2 tbsp oil in a saucepan and add the finely chopped onion, carrot and celery. Cook gently for about ¼ hr without letting the vegetables brown. Then add the clove, sage leaves, 1 bay leaf, the rosemary and 1 chopped garlic clove. Cook for another couple of minutes and then add the red wine and about 3 tbsp vinegar. Stir, bring to a boil, then remove from the heat and transfer the marinade to an earthenware bowl. Leave to cool.

Put the pieces of hare in a deep dish and when the marinade is cold, pour it over the hare. Leave for about 18 hr. Heat the remaining 3 tbsp oil in a large saucepan or flameproof casserole. Drain the pieces of hare, reserving the marinade, dry them and brown in the hot oil over moderate heat. Pour the marinade over them, cover and cook over low heat for 2–3 hr or until fork-tender.

Meanwhile soak the dried mushrooms in warm water and when they have softened, rinse them. Cook them in a small saucepan with 1 tbsp butter, a couple of spoonfuls of water and a pinch of salt. When the mushrooms are cooked, stir in the tomato paste and the other chopped clove of garlic. About 20 min before the hare pieces are done, pour the sauce into the saucepan containing the meat, and add the white wine. Serve sprinkled with the chopped parsley.

PERNICI IN SALSA D'ACETO
(Cold poached partridges in caper vinaigrette)

2 partridges, plucked and cleaned
salt
1 onion
2 sticks celery
2 carrots

for the sauce:
1 cup olive oil
2 tbsp wine vinegar
salt
1 tbsp chopped parsley
1 tbsp chopped capers

Put the partridges in a saucepan of lightly salted water with the onion, celery and carrots and poach, covered, over moderate heat for about 1 hr or until fork-tender. Remove the partridges from the saucepan, divide each one in two and arrange on a serving plate. Meanwhile, prepare the sauce by mixing together the oil, vinegar, a little salt, the parsley and capers. Season the partridge halves with this sauce and leave to cool thoroughly before bringing to the table.

PERNICI ALLE OLIVE
(Partridges with olives)

4 partridges
salt
freshly ground pepper
several sage leaves
8 slices prosciutto
½ cup olive oil
1¼ cups dry white wine
1¼ cups olives, pitted
1 cup stock

This is a typical Sicilian dish. Clean the partridges, reserving the livers, then wipe the birds with a damp cloth. Sprinkle the inside of each partridge with salt and pepper and put a couple of sage leaves inside each one. Lightly rub the birds with salt as well, then wrap each one in two slices of prosciutto and secure with kitchen string.

Heat the oil in a large saucepan or flameproof casserole and brown the partridges on all sides, then moisten with the wine and cook until it evaporates. Add the finely chopped livers, the pitted olives and the hot stock. Cover and cook for about 1–1¼ hr. Remove the string and arrange the partridges on a serving plate. Pour over the cooking liquid and serve.

PICCIONI IN SALMÌ
(Pigeon salmi)

4 pigeons, plucked and cleaned, giblets reserved
4 sage leaves
2 bunches parsley
4 anchovy fillets
4 cloves garlic
1 generous tbsp capers
2 cups oil
grated peel of 1 lemon
6 tbsp wine vinegar (or ⅔ cup red wine)
salt
freshly ground pepper

Bone the pigeons, taking care to keep the breasts intact. Cut the rest of the meat into pieces. Mix the giblets (liver, heart and cleaned gizzard) with the sage, parsley, anchovies, garlic and capers and finely chop the mixture. Heat the oil in a saucepan, put in the pigeon breast meat and the grated lemon peel and stir over moderate heat until the meat is golden brown. Sprinkle over the vinegar and leave to evaporate, then add the other pieces of meat together with the chopped giblet mixture. Season with salt and pepper, place a piece of wax paper or foil over the saucepan, then place the lid on top to prevent any liquid escaping, and continue to cook for 1 hr.

PICCIONI ALLA DIAVOLA
(Deviled pigeons)

4 young oven-ready pigeons
8 tbsp olive oil
salt
cayenne pepper
grilled or baked tomatoes
2 lemons cut in wedges

Divide the pigeons in half lengthwise, and beat the carcasses lightly to flatten them. Marinate the birds for about 1 hr in oil seasoned with salt and a generous amount of cayenne pepper, turning them from time to time. Drain the pigeons, reserving the marinade. Broil, or cook on a charcoal barbecue for about 20 min, basting frequently with the marinade. Serve with the tomatoes and lemon wedges.

PICCIONI ALLA CAVOUR
(Pigeons Cavour)

4 oven-ready pigeons
4 oz butter
salt
1 tbsp all-purpose flour
2 tbsp Marsala
2 chicken livers
1 white truffle

Heat the butter in a saucepan and brown the birds gently. Sprinkle them with salt and with the flour, then add the Marsala; cook until the liquid evaporates a little and then add a ladleful of warm water. Cook very gently for about ½ hr or until fork-tender. Halfway through the cooking time, add the diced chicken livers and the thinly sliced truffle.

PICCIONI ALLO SPIEDO
(Rotisseried pigeon)

2 pigeons, plucked and cleaned,
    giblets reserved
3 tbsp oil
salt
⅔ cup dry red wine
1 tbsp herb-flavored wine vinegar
1 tbsp black olives
4–5 small leaves sage
1 lemon
toasted bread slices

Put the pigeons on to a rotisserie skewer (leave the heart, liver and cleaned gizzard inside the birds) and roast gently over low heat, basting them with oil and seasoning them with a little salt. Catch the drippings in a pan placed underneath the birds. Pour the wine and vinegar into the pan with the drippings, then add the black olives, the sage, and the peeled, sliced lemon. Baste the pigeons with this mixture frequently as they cook. While the birds are cooking, the

juices that drip into the pan will mix with the other ingredients and will simmer. When the pigeons are well cooked take out the giblets. Chop them finely and, stirring with a wooden spoon, mix them into the sauce in the drippings pan. Cut the pigeons in half, arrange them on a warmed serving plate, moisten them with sauce and leave in a warm place for a couple of minutes so the pigeons absorb the full flavor of the sauce. Serve accompanied by slices of bread toasted in the oven.

"POLENTA E OSEI"
(Polenta and small birds)

8 quail, cleaned
4 oz pancetta or bacon
1 bunch sage leaves
salt
8 slices polenta (see pp. 84–9)

This is a typical dish from the Veneto region where small birds may be shot as game. They are, traditionally, rotisseried whole on skewers. Quail may be used as a substitute. Thread the quail on to skewers, alternating them with slices of pancetta or bacon and sage leaves. Salt lightly and cook on the rotisserie, placing a pan underneath in which to catch the cooking juices. Fry the slices of polenta in this fat and serve with the golden brown birds.

QUAGLIE AI TARTUFI *
(Truffled quail)

(serves 2)
4 quail, cleaned
4 slices bacon
¼ cup + 2 tbsp butter
salt
1¾ cup rice
2 tbsp grated Parmesan cheese
1 white truffle

Wrap each quail in a piece of bacon and secure with a piece of string. Arrange the birds side by side in a roasting pan. Melt half the butter, pour it over the quail and season the birds with salt. Put them into a preheated oven at 400°F and roast them for 30–40 min, turning them

from time to time. Five minutes before the end of cooking, remove the strings and bacon so that the birds can brown. Meanwhile, cook the rice until al dente in plenty of boiling salted water. Melt the remaining butter and mix it into the rice together with the grated cheese. Serve the quail on a bed of rice and garnish with the grated truffle.

QUAGLIE ALLA VIGNAIOLA
(Quail with grapes)

8 quail, cleaned
knob of butter
1 cup grape juice
½ lb grapes
salt
freshly ground pepper

Arrange the quail in a flameproof casserole. Brown them in a little butter. As soon as the quail have begun to cook through, add the grape juice and the grapes. Season with salt and pepper. Put the dish in a preheated oven (375°F) and cook the quail slowly for about ½ hr.

QUAGLIE IN TEGLIA
(Quail with peas and prosciutto)

8 quail, cleaned
12 oz peas (fresh or frozen)
2 tbsp butter
4 oz prosciutto, diced
salt
freshly ground pepper
6 tbsp dry white wine
10 oz very ripe tomatoes

Rinse and dry the quail. Cook the peas, butter and a third of the diced prosciutto in a saucepan with sufficient water to cover. Drain, and season with salt and pepper. Put the rest of the chopped prosciutto into a large flameproof casserole. Soften the prosciutto for a few minutes over moderate heat, then add the quail and, turning frequently, brown well. Pour the wine into the casserole, let it evaporate over high heat, then add the peeled, seeded and chopped tomatoes. Cover and, stirring from time to time so nothing sticks to the

bottom, cook over moderate heat for about ½ hr. When the quail are done and the sauce is thick, add the cooked peas to the casserole, raise the heat a little and, stirring carefully, coat the peas with the sauce. Arrange the quail in a circle on a serving dish and pour the peas and sauce into the center. Serve immediately.

UCCELLINI DELL'UMBRIA
(Umbrian quail with herbs)

8 quail
½ cup oil
¼ cup butter
1 clove garlic, minced
1 sprig sage
2 bay leaves
12 pitted green olives, halved
3 slices lemon
6 tbsp dry white wine
salt
freshly ground pepper
juice of ½ lemon

Rinse and dry the quail. Heat the oil and butter in a skillet and add the garlic clove; when it has browned a little, remove it and add the quails, sage, bay leaves, the halved olives and the slices of lemon. Brown everything over high heat, and add the wine. Season and cook, covered, for 20–30 min over moderate heat. Discard the sage and bay leaves and the lemon slices, leaving only the olives. Sprinkle the lemon juice over the birds and serve very hot.

Fish and Shellfish

*T*hanks to the geography of the Italian peninsula, nearly all the regions of Italy border the sea on one side. When you remember that this entire coastline was the cradle of ancient civilizations it is easy to understand why fish dishes in Italy are among the noblest in her culinary repertoire. It is consequently extremely difficult to chose a representative selection of recipes, and virtually impossible to say that the fish soup or stew, the cacciucco or buridda from any particular region is the best. Local variations on a single dish may stimulate the interest of the gastronomically inclined visitor, but undoubtedly the most interesting of all is the extraordinary variety of fish to be found off the coast of Italy: From the eels of Comacchio or the tiny elvers caught at the mouth of the Arno to the gianchetti of Liguria; from the soft shell crabs of Trieste to the mussels of Taranto; from the mullet of the Tremiti islands to the grouper fish of Ustica; from Sicilian sardines to Calabrian swordfish; from the spider crabs of the Venetian lagoon to the gray mullet of the Lago di Lesina; from the lobsters of Sardinia to the tuna of the Gulf of Naples. Such a wide variety of fish obviously gives rise to a corresponding variety of recipes. And fish is not only served as a main course in Italy – it is also used for soups and stews, sauces, appetizers and marinades.

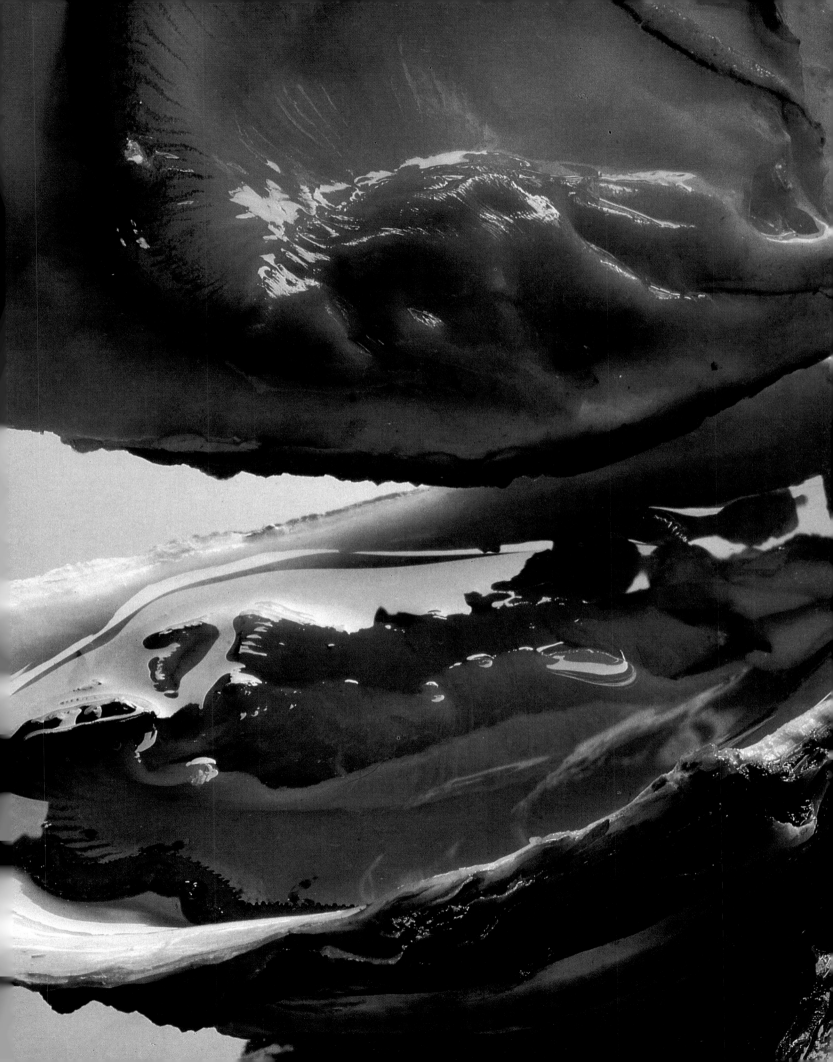

ACCIUGHE RIPIENE
(Stuffed anchovies)

1½ lb fresh large anchovies
4 oz mild cheese
anchovy fillets in oil
all-purpose flour
2 eggs, beaten
fine dried breadcrumbs
oil for frying
salt
2 lemons

Clean the anchovies and cut off the heads. Slit along the belly of each fish and carefully remove the backbone, taking care not to cut into fillets. Rinse the fish under cold water and pat dry. Cut the cheese into thin strips, then stuff each fish with a strip of cheese and an anchovy fillet. Close the anchovies and dip them first in flour, then in the beaten egg and finally in breadcrumbs. Heat a generous amount of oil in a deep skillet. When it is very hot fry the stuffed anchovies, a few at a time, until golden. Drain on kitchen paper, sprinkle with salt (remembering that the anchovy fillets in the stuffing are already salted), and arrange on a serving dish. Garnish with wedges of lemon and serve immediately.

TORTIERA DI ALICI
(Anchovy pie)

1¾ lb fresh anchovies
2 cups fresh breadcrumbs
2 tbsp grated Pecorino cheese
1 tbsp capers
1 sprig parsley
1 clove garlic
salt
oregano
olive oil
2 ripe but firm tomatoes

Clean the anchovies: Slit open, without separating the two sides of the fish, and remove the backbone. Rinse and pat dry. Reserving 1 tbsp, put the breadcrumbs into a bowl with the grated cheese. Add the chopped capers, parsley and garlic and sprinkle with a pinch of salt and oregano. Moisten this mixture with ½ cup oil and stir well. Generously grease a gratin dish and coat with breadcrumbs. Arrange a layer of anchovies in the dish, sprinkle with salt and spread part of the breadcrumb mixture over the top. Repeat with another layer of anchovies and so on until the ingredients are used up. Cover the pie with thin slices of peeled and seeded tomatoes; sprinkle the top with oil and cook in a preheated oven at 350°F for about ½ hr. Serve hot or cold.

ANGUILLA STUFATA
(Stewed eel)

2 1-lb eels
all-purpose flour
2 tbsp olive oil
1 finely chopped onion
1 cup dry white wine
12 oz tomatoes
salt
freshly ground pepper
1 clove garlic, minced
2 sprigs parsley, chopped
1 bay leaf

Prepare the eels: Cut off their heads, rinse well and chop into 4-in pieces. Plunge the pieces of eel into boiling water for a few minutes, then rinse in cold water; dry them and coat with flour. Heat the oil in a flameproof casserole and fry the chopped onion very gently. Add the floured pieces of eel and fry them over low heat, turning them from time to time. Pour in the wine and allow to evaporate. Peel, seed and chop the tomatoes and add them to the casserole with the eel. Season with salt and freshly ground pepper, then add the minced garlic, parsley and bay leaf. Cover and simmer for a further ½ hr or until the eel is tender. Serve hot from the same casserole.

ANGUILLA DORATA
(Fried eel)

2 1½-lb eels
2 eggs
salt
freshly ground pepper
2 tbsp grated Parmesan cheese
2 tbsp fresh breadcrumbs
oil for frying

few sage leaves
sprig rosemary
tomatoes
2 lemons

Make a circular cut just below the head of the eel. Hold the head firmly and pull off the skin from head to tail. Cut into 2-in long pieces, discarding the head, then rinse and pat dry. Beat the eggs in a basin with salt and pepper, dip the pieces of eel into the egg, then into the grated cheese and breadcrumbs mixed together. Heat the oil in a large skillet and as soon as it is hot fry the pieces of eel. When they are cooked through and golden, remove them with a slotted spoon, drain on kitchen paper and sprinkle with salt while still very hot. Transfer to a warm serving dish and garnish with sage leaves and rosemary, lemon wedges and tomatoes.

ANGUILLA IN GRATELLA
(Broiled eel)

1 2-lb eel (or 2 or 3 smaller ones)
squares of toast
few sage or bay leaves
salt
freshly ground pepper
1–2 lemons

A large eel must be skinned (see previous recipe) but it is not necessary to skin smaller ones. Cut the eel into pieces about 1½ in long and thread on to a skewer, alternating the pieces of eel with squares of toast. In the middle of each skewer put a sage or bay leaf. Sprinkle the eel with salt and pepper and broil or barbecue. Turn the skewers from time to time until the eel is cooked through. Serve at once with wedges of lemon.

ANGUILLA COI PISELLI
(Eel with peas)

1 1½-lb eel
½ cup olive oil
1 small onion, chopped
1 clove garlic, minced
½ glass dry white wine
1 large fresh or canned tomato
2¼ lb fresh peas (or ¾ lb frozen)
salt
freshly ground pepper
1 sprig parsley

Make a circular cut just below the head of the eel. Hold the head firmly and pull off the skin. Cut into 1½-in long pieces, discarding the head. Heat the oil in a saucepan and fry the onion and garlic; when the garlic begins to brown remove it and add the pieces of eel. Sauté the eel for a few minutes, turning the pieces gently and taking care not to break them, then raise the heat and add the wine. When the wine has evaporated add the juice of the sieved tomato and the peas; season with salt and a generous sprinkling of freshly ground pepper. Cover the saucepan and bring to a boil over low heat. Simmer for ½ hr, stirring gently from time to time and adding a ladleful of hot water if necessary. Garnish with parsley.

ANGUILLA MARINATA *
(Marinated eel)

2 1-lb eels
bay leaves
salt
freshly ground pepper

for the marinade:
6 cups wine vinegar
1 sprig fresh sage
2 cloves garlic
peel of 2 oranges (or 1 lemon)
1 tbsp pine nuts (optional)
1 tbsp seedless white raisins
1 tbsp chopped candied fruit
5–6 peppercorns

Rinse the eels and cut off the head, but do not skin them. Cut into 2-in pieces. Thread the eel on to skewers alternating each piece with a bay leaf. Season with salt and pepper and cook under the broiler. Meanwhile, pour the vinegar into a non metallic saucepan with the sage, garlic, orange peel and, if used, pine nuts and seedless white raisins. Bring to a boil, then simmer for ½ hr. Add the candied fruit and peppercorns, place the eels in a flameproof casserole and pour over the marinade. Bring to a boil and transfer to a preserving jar or deep dish. The eels must be covered by the liquid and should be kept for two days before serving. Serve cold.

Alternatively, skin the eels; leaving them whole, cover with water, and simmer gently for ½ hr or until cooked. Drain, then follow instructions for the marinade as above. Shape in to roulades and serve cold.

ANGUILLA IN UMIDO
(Eel stew)

1 2-lb eel
2 cloves garlic
1 onion
½ cup olive oil
½ glass dry white wine
8 oz ripe tomatoes (or canned)
1 sprig parsley
salt
freshly ground pepper

To skin the eel in one piece, make a circular cut just below the head. Then, holding the head firmly in one hand, pull the skin carefully downward. Discard the head, then cut into 2-in pieces. Sauté the finely chopped onion and garlic in the oil in a large skillet over medium heat until the onion begins to soften. Add the pieces of eel to the skillet, turn up the heat and brown the eel. Add the wine and when it has evaporated, add the sieved tomatoes and the chopped parsley. Season with salt and pepper, cover and cook for 20–30 min over low heat, stirring frequently to prevent sticking. Add a little water if necessary. The sauce should be thick, and the pieces of eel intact.

BRODETTO ALLA VASTESE
(Fish soup Vasto style)

2½ lb assorted fish (cod, red mullet, sole, dogfish, cuttlefish, squid, shrimp, clams, mussels, etc.)
½ cup olive oil
2 cloves garlic, finely chopped
8 long, thin sweet red peppers
1 glass red wine vinegar
salt
freshly ground pepper
1 sprig parsley, chopped
slices of crusty white bread

Clean and gut the fish and cut the larger ones into pieces. Put the oil, chopped garlic and whole peppers

BRODETTO DI RIMINI ✳
(Rimini fish soup)

2½ lb assorted fish (sole, shrimp,
　　turbot, dogfish, mullet, sardines,
　　squid, cuttlefish, mussels, clams,
　　etc.)
1 cup olive oil
2 onions, chopped
2 cups canned tomatoes
1 tbsp vinegar
salt
freshly ground pepper
1 sprig parsley, chopped
slices of bread, toasted

for the fish stock:
2 tbsp oil
1 onion, chopped
2 ripe tomatoes
1 sprig parsley, chopped
1 lb fish trimmings (heads, bones,
　　etc.)
salt
freshly ground pepper
5 cups water
1 tbsp vinegar

Choose a wide variety of fish,
bearing in mind that the greater the
variety the richer the flavor of the
soup. Clean and gut the fish, reserving the heads for the stock.
Wash the fish in salted water and
drain well. Prepare the stock: In a
deep saucepan fry the chopped
onion in the oil until soft, then add
the chopped and seeded tomatoes.
Cook over high heat for ¼ hr, then
add the parsley and the fish trimmings; season with a little salt and
pepper, then add the water and
vinegar. Cover and simmer gently
for about 40 min, then strain.

　Prepare the soup: Pour the oil in
to a shallow fireproof dish, large
enough to hold the fish in a single
layer. Fry the onions over low heat
and when they begin to soften add
the canned tomatoes and cook over
moderate heat for about 20 min.
Add the fish, putting in the firmer
fleshed varieties first and arranging
them in a single layer. Season with
a little salt and pepper. Cook until
the liquid begins to boil, then
sprinkle the vinegar over the fish
and allow it to evaporate. Cover
and cook very gently for ½ hr; the
fish must remain firm. Add the
chopped parsley and finally the hot
strained stock to the fish soup.
Serve hot, with the slices of
toasted bread.

into a wide skillet and fry over
moderate heat for about 10 min;
remove the peppers and crush in a
mortar. Gradually stir in the vinegar. Return the crushed peppers
to the skillet, add the fish, the
larger pieces first, and lower the
heat. Season with salt and pepper;
add just enough water to cover,
and sprinkle with the parsley.
Cover and simmer over low heat
for about 20 min or until the fish is
tender but still firm. Serve very
hot, with slices of crusty bread.

CAPITONE MARINATO
(Marinated eel)

1 2½-lb eel
2 cloves garlic, sliced
salt
freshly ground pepper
3–4 bay leaves
1 cup olive oil
2¼ cups wine vinegar

Rinse the eel thoroughly under
cold water and pat dry. Leaving the
head attached, coil the eel round
and place in a non-metallic saucepan that fits it exactly. Add the
garlic, a little salt and plenty of
pepper, the bay leaves, oil and
vinegar. Cover the saucepan and
bring to a boil. Simmer gently over
low heat for about 1 hr. When the
eel is cooked and the liquid reduced
carefully transfer to an earthenware dish, pour over the cooking
liquid and allow to cool. Leave to
stand for two days before serving.

ASTICI LESSATI
(Boiled lobster)

4 small lobsters
1 stick celery
1 onion
1 carrot
2 sprigs parsley
slices of lemon
1 bay leaf
mayonnaise (see p. 126)

Put the celery, coarsely chopped
onion, carrot, parsley, 1 slice of
lemon and the bay leaf into a large
saucepan of cold water and bring to
a boil. Simmer for ½ hr. Tie the
lobsters securely, add to the
saucepan and simmer for ¼ hr or
until cooked. Drain, leave to cool,
and then split in half lengthwise.
Carefully remove the black intestinal vein; the red coral can be
eaten. Garnish with slices of lemon
and serve with mayonnaise.

BRODETTO ALLA PORTO
RECANATI
(Porto Recanati fish soup)

2½ lb assorted fish (scorpionfish,
　　monkfish, turbot, sole, scampi,
　　squid, mussels, etc.)

1 onion
2 cloves garlic
1 cup olive oil
1 sprig parsley
1 envelope saffron
5 cups fish stock (see p. 131)
salt
freshly ground pepper
slices of bread, toasted

Clean and gut the fish and rinse
thoroughly. Chop the onion and
garlic very finely and cut the larger
fish into pieces. Fry the chopped
garlic and onion in the oil for a few
minutes, stirring constantly, then
add the fish, starting with those
requiring the longest cooking (the
monkfish and squid). Add the hot
stock. Shellfish, which are spoiled
by overcooking, should be added
last. Halfway through cooking
(after about ¼ hr), add salt and
pepper to taste, and stir in the
saffron, mixing it first in a spoonful
of stock; last of all add the chopped
parsley. When the fish is cooked
(after about ½ hr) the soup should
be quite thick and full of flavor.
Bring it to the table still boiling and
serve with thick slices of toasted
bread.

ARAGOSTA ARROSTO
(Baked lobster)

1 2½-lb cooked lobster
½ tbsp mustard powder
freshly ground pepper
2 tbsp chopped parsley
1 tsp marjoram
salt
1 cup olive oil
3 tbsp butter
2 tbsp fresh breadcrumbs
2 lemons

Cut the lobster in half lengthwise
and carefully remove the black intestine that runs from the end of
the tail to the main part of the
body. Place both halves in a baking
pan, flesh uppermost. In a small
skillet mix the mustard with a
generous amount of pepper, the
parsley, marjoram and a little salt.
Dilute this mixture with about ½
cup oil and a small piece of butter,
then warm it very gently over low
heat. Pour the sauce over the
lobster and sprinkle with breadcrumbs, pressing the crumbs down

with the blade of a knife so that they stick well. Sprinkle the remaining oil over the breadcrumbs and bake in a preheated oven (400°F) for about 25 min. Arrange the lobster on a serving dish, sprinkle with lemon juice and serve very hot with lemon wedges.

FILETTI DI BACCALÀ FRITTI
(Deep-fried salt cod)

1½ lb salt cod
oil for frying
1 lemon

for the batter:
3 tbsp all-purpose flour
1 cup water
2 tbsp oil
pinch of salt
1 egg white, whisked

Soak the salt cod for two days in cold water, changing the water frequently. Cover with boiling water and leave for 5 min; drain well, skin and bone the fish and cut into strips. To make the batter, place the flour in a bowl and whisk in the cold water; then add the oil, beating constantly, and a little salt. Leave the batter to stand for 1 hr. When ready to fry the fish fold in the whisked egg white. Dip the pieces of salt cod into the batter and fry until golden, a few at a time, in plenty of hot oil. Drain on kitchen paper and serve very hot with lemon wedges.

BACCALÀ ALLA BOLOGNESE
(Bolognese salt cod)

1½ lb salt cod, presoaked (see previous recipe)
½ cup olive oil
1 sprig parsley
2 cloves garlic
salt
freshly ground pepper
¼ cup butter
juice of 1 lemon

Cut the salt cod into large pieces and place them side by side in a generously greased skillet. Chop the parsley and garlic together and

scatter evenly over the salt cod; season lightly with salt and pepper and then pour the remaining oil over the fish. Dot with butter. Cook over high heat, turning the pieces carefully. (As the fish is not coated with egg and breadcrumbs or flour it is very easily broken.) When the fish is cooked pour the lemon juice over it and serve at once from the skillet.

BACCALÀ ALLA LIVORNESE
(Leghorn salt cod)

2 lb salt cod, presoaked (see "Deep-fried salt cod," left)
all-purpose flour
2 cloves garlic, chopped
1 cup olive oil
1 cup freshly made tomato sauce (see p. 127)
1 sprig parsley, chopped

Skin the salt cod, bone it and cut into regular pieces. Dry the pieces well and flour them. Fry the garlic in the oil, then add the pieces of salt cod and fry until evenly browned. Add the tomato sauce and simmer gently for 1 hr, stirring from time to time. Sprinkle with parsley and adjust seasoning.

BACCALÀ ALLA NAPOLETANA
(Neapolitan salt cod)

2 lb salt cod
all-purpose flour
olive oil
2 cloves garlic
8 oz ripe tomatoes
salt
freshly ground pepper
1 tbsp capers
2 oz black olives

Buy the salt cod already soaked, or soak it at home; let it stand in running water for at least 2 days (or change the water as often as possible). When it has softened, skin and bone it, and cut into 1½ in squares. Dry the pieces with a cloth, then flour them and fry them in plenty of hot oil. Drain them on kitchen paper. Put a little oil in another skillet and fry the garlic,

removing it as soon as it begins to brown. Add the peeled, seeded and chopped tomatoes to the garlic-flavored oil and season with salt and pepper. Cook over moderate heat for ¼ hr. Place the pieces of salt cod in a single layer in an ovenproof dish, and pour over the tomato sauce, capers and black olives. Transfer to a moderate oven (375°F) for about ¼ hr before serving.

BACCALÀ CON LE OLIVE VERDI
(Salt cod with green olives)

2 lb salt cod, presoaked (see "Deep-fried salt cod," far left)
all-purpose flour
olive oil
1 small jar tomato paste
½ onion, chopped
2 small gherkins
1 tbsp capers
4 oz pitted green olives
salt
freshly ground pepper
1 tbsp chopped parsley

Skin and bone the salt cod, then cut into 2½-in squares. Wash and dry the fish, and coat with flour. Heat a little oil in a flameproof casserole and place the salt cod inside in a single layer. Fry the slices until lightly browned, turn them carefully and fry on the other side. Drain off most of the oil. Make a tomato sauce by frying the onion in oil and adding a small jar of tomato paste; to this add the sliced gherkins, capers, olives and a pinch of salt and pepper. Heat for a few minutes until the sauce thickens slightly. Pour the sauce over the fish and cook for a few minutes. Using a spoon, baste the fish with sauce from the bottom of the casserole. Transfer to a moderate oven for 10 min before serving. Sprinkle with chopped parsley.

BACCALÀ ALLA VICENTINA *
(Dried cod Vicenza style)

2 lb dried cod
all-purpose flour
2 tbsp grated Parmesan cheese

2 large onions
1 clove garlic
1½ cups olive oil
2 salted anchovies
1 sprig parsley
2 cups milk

This dish is made with sun-dried cod that has not been salted. Beat the dried cod with a meatbat and put in a basin of water for 2–3 days, changing the water daily. Once it has softened, open it out lengthwise, pat dry and coat with flour. Sprinkle with grated Parmesan cheese. Sauté the chopped onions and garlic in a skillet in half the oil; discard the garlic as soon as it begins to brown. Meanwhile, rinse and bone the anchovies and chop them with the parsley. Add to the skillet with the onions and oil and stir well with a wooden spoon. Spread half the sauce over one side of the fish, then fold over carefully and cut into strips about 2 in wide. Place these stuffed strips side by side in a flameproof casserole, and pour over the remaining sauce, the milk and the remaining oil; the fish should be covered by the liquid. Cover the dish and simmer gently over very low heat for about 3 hr.

ZUPPA DI BACCALÀ
(Salt cod soup)

2 lb salt cod, presoaked (see "Deep-fried salt cod," p.196)
olive oil
2 onions, sliced
2 cloves garlic, chopped
1 stick celery, chopped
½ bay leaf
1 sprig thyme
3 sprigs parsley
1 tsp tomato paste or 2–3 chopped tomatoes
1 cup dry white wine
3 potatoes
2 sprigs parsley, chopped
salt
freshly ground pepper
slices of bread, toasted

Skin the salt cod and cut it into 2½-in squares; remove the bones. Heat ½ cup oil in a large saucepan and add the onions, very finely sliced, and the chopped garlic. Cook these together very gently without allowing the onion to brown, then add the chopped celery, and the bay leaf, thyme and parsley tied together. When the herbs have cooked for a moment add 1 tsp tomato paste diluted in a little water, or the peeled and chopped tomatoes. Cook the tomatoes for a moment, then add the white wine. Next, add the peeled potatoes, cut into pieces, and 5 cups water. When the potatoes are almost cooked, remove the herbs and add the salt cod and 2–3 tbsp olive oil. Lower the heat, cover the saucepan and simmer very gently for about 1 hr. Add a little water if the sauce becomes too thick. Garnish with freshly chopped parsley, and add salt and a sprinkling of pepper. Place slices of toasted bread in warmed serving dishes; pour the salt cod and broth over the bread and allow to stand for a moment before serving.

BRANZINO BOLLITO
(Poached sea bass)

1 2½-lb sea bass
4½ cups water
2 cups dry white wine
2 tbsp wine vinegar
1 lemon
1 carrot
1 onion
½ celeriac
1 bay leaf
few peppercorns
salt
parsley
mayonnaise (see p. 126)
vinaigrette

Prepare a court-bouillon: In a fish kettle or large saucepan combine the water, wine, vinegar, half the lemon, the chopped carrot, onion and celeriac, the bay leaf, crushed peppercorns and a little salt. Bring to a boil and simmer gently for ½ hr, skimming off any scum. Allow to cool. Scrape the scales off the fish, remove the gills and fins; gut and rinse thoroughly. Dry the fish and rub with the lemon to prevent the skin coming off during cooking. Place the fish carefully in the cooled court-bouillon and bring to a boil. Lower the heat and simmer gently for about 10 min or until tender. Remove from the heat and leave to stand for 5 min before taking out the fish. Drain the fish, then transfer to a long serving dish; garnish with slices of lemon and curls of lemon peel, rings of carrot and sprigs of parsley. Serve with mayonnaise and vinaigrette made with oil, pepper and lemon juice lightly whisked together.

CALAMARETTI ALLA NAPOLETANA
(Baby cuttlefish Neapolitan style)

2½ lb baby cuttlefish (or squid)
2 onions, sliced
1 clove garlic, minced
4 tbsp olive oil
½ cup dry white wine
12 oz ripe tomatoes
2 oz seedless white raisins
2 oz pine nuts
salt
freshly ground pepper
1 dozen pitted olives
1 sprig parsley, chopped
slices of bread, toasted

Rinse the baby cuttlefish and leave them whole. Fry the onion and garlic in oil in a saucepan. When they begin to soften remove the garlic and pour in the wine. While the wine is cooking cover moderate heat, dip the tomatoes into boiling water, then peel them; chop and remove the seeds. Soften the seedless white raisins in warm water and squeeze dry. Add the tomatoes and cook over high heat for about 10 min; add the cuttlefish, the seedless white raisins, the pine nuts and, if the sauce has reduced too much, a little warm water. Season with salt and pepper, cover the saucepan and simmer gently for about ½ hr. Finally, add the halved olives and plenty of chopped parsley. As soon as the cuttlefish are tender and the sauce is reduced, serve, with slices of toasted bread.

CALAMARI RIPIENI
(Stuffed cuttlefish)

8 medium cuttlefish (or squid)
1 sprig parsley
2 cloves garlic
1 sprig rosemary
salt
freshly ground pepper
4 tbsp olive oil
1 cup dry white wine
1 lemon
2 tomatoes

Take hold of each cuttlefish and pull away and discard the hard central bone and ink sac. Rinse in cold running water and rub off the purplish outer skin. Detach the tentacles from the body sac and chop the tentacles finely with the parsley, garlic and rosemary. Season this mixture with salt and pepper, and stir in 2 tbsp oil. Mix well and use it to stuff the cuttlefish. Stitch up the opening to prevent the stuffing from falling out. Place the cuttlefish in a large skillet with the hot oil, and brown gently, turning occasionally. Add the wine, allow to evaporate a little, then cover and simmer for about ½ hr. When the cuttlefish are tender and the sauce has reduced, remove from the heat and arrange on a warm serving dish. Garnish with wedges of lemon and fresh tomatoes. Serve immediately.

CACCIUCCO ALLA LIVORNESE
(Leghorn fish soup)

(serves 6)
3lb assorted fish (dogfish, gurnard,
    baby octopus, red mullet, squid,
    mussels, hake, eel, monkfish,
    sole, shrimp)
1 onion
4 cloves garlic
1 stick celery
1 carrot
few sprigs parsley
1 cup olive oil
1 lb ripe tomatoes (or canned)
1 cup dry white wine
pinch of cayenne pepper
6 thick slices white bread
salt

Use at least five of the varieties of
fish listed above, some large, some
small (the inhabitants of Leghorn
insist that at least as many varieties as there are "c's" in Cacciucco be used) and rinse thoroughly.
Leave the small fish whole; gut the
larger varieties and cut into pieces,
reserving the heads. Fillet the
sole, reserving the bones and skin.
Put the heads, bones and skin in a
saucepan with half the onion, 1
clove garlic, the celery, carrot and
6 cups lightly salted water. Boil for
about ½ hr, then sieve and reserve
the stock. Chop the other half
onion, 2 cloves garlic and a few
sprigs parsley and sauté in half the
oil. As soon as the onion begins to
soften add the sieved tomatoes.
Season with a little salt. When the
tomatoes have thickened slightly,
pour in the wine and cook, uncovered, over high heat to reduce
slightly. Sieve this sauce and pour
it back into the saucepan. Add the
fish, taking care to add the firmest
first (including the octopus and
squid, cleaned and cut into rings),
and the fillets later. Cover and
cook over low heat for about
20 min, adding the reserved fish
stock as necessary.

The soup should be stirred as
little as possible in order not to
break up the pieces of fish. When
the soup is quite thick and nearly
ready to serve, add the mussels
(these must be rinsed and scrubbed thoroughly, then heated in a
skillet until the shells open). Heat
for a few minutes more, then
remove from the heat and add

2 tbsp finely chopped parsley. Bake
the slices of bread in the oven until
golden and then rub with a clove of
garlic. Place a slice of bread in the
bottom of each serving dish and
cover with pieces of fish, and a
couple of ladles of broth.

CARPA ALLA GIUDEA
(Carp with juniper berries)

1 2-lb carp
salt
1 cup olive oil
2 onions
4 shallots
1 tbsp all-purpose flour
2 tbsp chopped parsley
3 juniper berries
freshly ground pepper

Clean, rise and dry the carp, then
cut in to slices at right angles to the
backbone. Sprinkle the slices with
salt and leave to stand for several
hours. Heat the oil in a large
skillet; when it begins to smoke
add the coarsely chopped onions;
after a few minutes add the finely
chopped shallots and flour, stirring
until the flour begins to brown.
Place the pieces of fish on top of
the onions and cover with warm
water. Bring to a boil, then add the
chopped parsley, juniper berries
and a sprinkling of freshly ground
pepper. Cook uncovered over
moderate heat for 30–35 min. Carp
cooked in this way can be eaten hot
or cold; if it is to be served cold it
may be cooked a day in advance.

CARPIONE AL VINO
(Carp in white wine)

1 2½-lb carp
1 onion
2 tbsp oil
3 tbsp butter
1 tbsp all-purpose flour
1 sprig parsley
1 glass dry white wine
salt
freshly ground pepper
1 tbsp vinegar
1 lemon

Clean, rinse and dry the carp, then
cut in to large pieces. Fry the finely
chopped onion in oil in a skillet.
Work the butter together with the

flour to make a *beurre manié* and
add to the skillet with the parsley
and wine. Add the pieces of carp,
season with salt and pepper, then
add the vinegar and 1 cup water.
Cover and simmer for ½ hr, stirring gently from time to time.
Serve hot with its cooking juices,
garnished with lemon wedges.

CARPIONE AI FERRI
(Broiled carp)

2 1½-lb carp
lemons
salt
freshly ground pepper
3 tbsp olive oil

Clean the carp carefully and scrape
off the scales; gut and rinse well,
then dry with a cloth. Rub the skin
with slices of lemon, season the
inside with salt and pepper, then
place on a rack under a preheated
very hot broiler. Turn the heat
down immediately; when one side
is browned turn the fish over and
brown the other side. When the
fish is cooked remove from the
heat and dress with olive oil and
lemon juice. Serve at once on a
dish garnished with green salad,
sliced tomatoes and lemon
wedges. Carp can also be prepared
in this way in the oven: Cook on a
rack in a preheated oven (320–
350°F) for 35–40 min.

FRITTO DI PESCE ALLA MODA DI NAPOLI *
(Neapolitan fried fish)

8 small red mullet
1 lb baby cuttlefish
½ lb shrimp
all-purpose flour
oil for frying
salt
2 lemons

Scrape the scales off the fish with a knife and gut them. Wash in salted water, drain them, then dry on kitchen paper. Leave the baby cuttlefish whole. (If they are large pull out and discard the hard central bone, separate the tentacles from the body and slice the body into rings.) Take the heads off the shrimp but do not peel. (If you wish to peel them, dip them in flour and beaten egg seasoned with a pinch of salt.) Dip the red mullet and cuttlefish in flour; do not flour the shrimp in their shells. Plunge the red mullet into a pan of hot oil, then lower the heat to allow the fish to cook right through. When cooked and golden, drain on kitchen paper, sprinkle with salt and keep hot in the oven. In the same oil fry the shrimp, a few at a time, and the cuttlefish. Drain as soon as they are cooked and sprinkle with salt. Serve very hot with wedges of lemon.

CODA DI ROSPO AL VINO BIANCO
(Monkfish in white wine)

4 ¾-lb monkfish tails
1 cup olive oil
1 onion
2 cloves garlic
chopped parsley
rosemary
1 stick celery
3 tbsp all-purpose flour
salt
freshly ground pepper
2 cups dry white wine

Wash the monkfish in salted or acidulated water and pat dry with a cloth. Heat some oil in a casserole and add the finely chopped onion, garlic, celery, parsley and rosemary; fry gently over low heat. Add the floured monkfish, brown on both sides and season with salt and pepper. Add the wine and transfer the casserole to a moderate oven (375°F) for ½ hr, basting the fish with the cooking liquid from time to time. Serve the fish with its sauce, garnished with sprigs of rosemary and radicchio.

CERNIA RIPIENA
(Stuffed sea bass)

1 2½-lb sea bass
1 tbsp butter
6 shallots
½ cup dried mushrooms
½ cup white wine

for the stuffing:
¾ cup fresh white breadcrumbs, soaked in milk and squeezed
6 shrimp
½ cup dried mushrooms
1 tbsp butter
2 tbsp grated Parmesan cheese
2 eggs, beaten
pinch of nutmeg
salt
freshly ground pepper

Slit the fish along the belly and carefully remove the entrails and backbone, without breaking the fillets. Rinse and dry. Mix together the soaked breadcrumbs, the shrimp (shelled and pounded in a mortar), the dried mushrooms (soaked in hot water for ½ hr, then drained), the butter, Parmesan cheese, eggs, nutmeg, salt and pepper. Fill the fish with this stuffing and stitch the two sides together. Melt the butter in a large flameproof casserole and add the shallots and the remaining soaked and drained mushrooms. Place the fish in the casserole and pour over the wine. Cook in a moderate oven for about 1 hr (350°F).

FRITTATA DI GAMBERETTI
(Shrimp omelet)

½ lb shrimp
salt
1 tbsp butter
5 eggs
freshly ground pepper
3 tbsp oil
1 sprig parsley

Boil the shrimp in a small quantity of salted water for 10 min; drain and remove their shells. Melt the butter in a saucepan, add the shrimp and a pinch of salt and stir for a few minutes. Beat the eggs lightly, seasoning with salt and pepper to taste. Heat the oil in a skillet; when very hot pour in a quarter of the beaten egg and allow to set. Scatter a quarter of the shrimp over the top, then fold the omelet neatly; transfer to a plate, garnish with parsley and serve. Make three more omelets in the same way.

FRITTATA DI MITILI
(Mussel omelet)

¾ lb mussels
½ onion, chopped
1 sprig parsley, chopped
2 tbsp oil
4 eggs
2 tbsp Parmesan cheese
salt
freshly ground pepper

Scrub the mussels and rinse well. Discard any that do not close when tapped. Place in a skillet. Cover and heat for about 5 min until the shells open. Discard any that remain closed. Remove from their shells and set aside. Fry the onion and parsley in a little oil for a few minutes, then add the mussels. Beat the eggs lightly; add the Parmesan cheese, salt and pepper and pour into the skillet. Cook until set.

FRITTATA DI GIANCHETTI
(Sardine and anchovy omelet)

10 oz salted sardines and anchovies
4 eggs
salt
freshly ground pepper
1 clove garlic
1 sprig parsley
2 tbsp oil

Wipe the salt off the fish, but do not rinse. Beat the eggs thoroughly; season with salt and pepper. Add the coarsely chopped fish and the finely chopped garlic and parsley; mix well. Heat the oil in a skillet and pour in the mixture. Lower the heat and brown the omelet lightly underneath. Turn and cook over low heat until set.

INSALATA DI FRUTTI DI MARE
(Seafood salad)

2 lb mussels
¾ lb clams
2 tbsp oil
¾ lb baby octopus
¾ lb shrimp
oil
1 tsp mustard
juice of 2 lemons
1 sprig parsley
salt
freshly ground pepper

Scrape the mussels and wash thoroughly with the clams in salted water. Discard any that do not close when tapped. Put the mussels and clams together in a wide skillet with 2 tbsp oil and a little water and heat for about 10 min or until the shells open, shaking the skillet from time to time. Discard any that remain closed. Remove the mussels and clams from the shells and sieve the cooking liquor. Clean the octopus (if they are big, clean as directed in *Octopus Luciana* on p. 203), and cook in the liquor from the mussels and clams over low heat for 20 min. Add the shrimp, with their shells, and remove from the heat after 10 min. Cut the octopus into small pieces, shell the shrimp, then add to the mussels and clams. Dress with plenty of oil, mixed with the mustard, lemon juice, parsley, a little salt and freshly ground pepper. Mix well and leave to stand for a couple of hours before serving.

GAMBERONI AGLIO E OLIO
(Deep-fried crayfish with garlic and oil)

16 saltwater crayfish
oil for frying
2 cloves garlic
2 tbsp all-purpose flour
salt

Shell the crayfish, rinse thoroughly in cold water and dry with a clean cloth. Heat the oil in a large skillet. As soon as it is hot, add the garlic and fry for a few minutes; discard the garlic and put in the floured crayfish. Fry briskly until they become red and shiny, then remove them with a slotted spoon. Sprinkle with salt and serve at once.

GAMBERONI ALLA GRIGLIA
(Crayfish kabobs)

16 saltwater crayfish
½ cup olive oil
salt
freshly ground pepper
1 clove garlic, chopped
chopped parsley
lemon wedges

Shell the crayfish, rinse thoroughly in cold water and pat dry with a cloth. Marinate them for 1 hr in the oil, seasoned with salt and pepper. Preheat the broiler. Drain the crayfish, put them on to skewers and place under the broiler, lowering the heat immediately. Cook both sides evenly for about 20 min altogether. When the crayfish are cooked transfer to a serving dish and dress with the olive oil, garlic and chopped parsley mixed together. Garnish with lemon wedges.

GRANCHIO DI MARE IN ZUPPIERA
(Crab with garlic and lemon juice)

2 2-lb crabs
salt
bouquet garni
1 cup olive oil
1 clove garlic, chopped
1–2 tbsp chopped parsley
1 lemon
freshly ground pepper

Bring to a boil a large saucepan of water to which has been added salt and a bouquet garni. Put in the rinsed crabs and boil for 10 min. Drain them and allow to cool. Break off the legs and open them at the lower end to extract the meat. Crack the claws and put all the meat, including that from the shell, into a dish. Season with salt and pepper, oil, garlic, chopped parsley and a few drops of lemon juice. Leave to stand for at least 1 hr before serving to allow the flavors to mingle. Transfer to a serving dish and garnish with lemon wedges. Accompany with a variety of salads.

GRIGLIATA MISTA
(Mixed fish grill)

1½ lb sole
1 ¾-lb slice monkfish
1½ lb sea bass

8 crayfish tails
salt
freshly ground pepper
½ cup olive oil
2 tbsp chopped parsley
juice of 1 lemon

Clean, gut and skin the sole. Clean and gut the sea bass, and scrape off the scales. Clean and shell the crayfish tails. Rinse all the fish in plenty of salted or acidulated water. Dry carefully and season with salt and pepper. Heat the broiler and first broil the monkfish (which needs the longest cooking); next add the sea bass, then the sole and finally the crayfish tails, threaded on a skewer. Lower the heat as the fish begin to brown; turn when the first side is browned. Cook for 15–25 min. Arrange the fish on a serving dish and dress with salt, olive oil, chopped parsley and lemon juice.

LAMPREDA AL VINO BIANCO
(Lamprey in white wine)

4–5 shallots
few leaves of thyme, chopped
½ cup olive oil
1 lamprey to serve 4
all-purpose flour
½ cup stock
salt
freshly ground pepper
1 cup dry white wine

Fry the finely chopped shallots and the thyme in the olive oil in a flame-proof casserole with a tightly fitting lid. Clean and skin the lamprey and cut into pieces; coat the pieces with flour and place in the casserole with the shallots and thyme. Add the stock (or hot water) and salt and pepper. Replace the lid tightly and cook for 10 min, then add the wine. Cook for a further 5 min, by which time the lamprey will be cooked. Serve in the same dish.

LUCCIO ALLA MARINARA
(Pike sailor style)

1 2½-lb pike
2 tbsp olive oil

1 finely sliced onion
1 clove garlic, minced
1 small carrot, diced
2 sprigs parsley
salt
freshly ground pepper
4½ cups red wine
¼ cup butter
2 tbsp all-purpose flour
croûtons

Clean and gut the fish; cut into pieces and arrange in a dish with the oil, onion, garlic, carrot, chopped parsley, salt and pepper. Pour over the red wine and leave the fish to marinate for about 1 hr. Transfer the contents of the dish to a flameproof casserole, bring to a boil and simmer gently over low heat for about ¼ hr. As soon as the fish is cooked, lift out and set aside. Strain the cooking liquid and reduce over moderate heat. Work the butter and flour together and add to the reduced liquid. Stir well until the sauce thickens and begins to look velvety. Return the pieces of fish to the casserole and reheat without boiling. Transfer to a serving dish and surround with the croûtons fried in butter.

FILETTI DI MERLUZZO
(Cod fillets with anchovy)

1 onion
1 clove garlic
1 sprig parsley
4 tbsp oil
1 lb cod fillets
salt
1 tbsp capers
2 salted anchovies
1 tsp all-purpose flour
small piece chili pepper
juice of 1 lemon

Finely chop the onion, garlic and parsley together and fry them in oil in a skillet, stirring frequently. After a few minutes add the cod fillets, sprinkle with salt and cook over low heat, turning once to cook each side. Remove the fillets and arrange on a serving dish. Into the same skillet put the roughly chopped capers, the rinsed, boned and chopped anchovies, the flour mixed with ½ cup cold water and the chili pepper. Stir over heat for 5 min, then remove the chili; add the

lemon juice and pour the sauce over the cod fillets. Serve at once.

MUGGINE ALLA MELAGRANA
(Broiled red mullet with pomegranate)

8–10 small red mullet
½ cup olive oil
salt
freshly ground pepper
2 pomegranates

Rinse the fish thoroughly; do not gut them or remove the heads. Dry and place under a preheated broiler. While they are cooking brush them with olive oil seasoned with salt and pepper. Once the fish are browned on both sides and cooked through place them in a warm serving dish. Cover and leave to stand for a few minutes. Before serving sprinkle generously with the juice squeezed from the two pomegranates.

PESCE PERSICO ALLA SALVIA
(Fillets of perch with sage butter)

8 perch fillets
all-purpose flour
1 egg
pinch of salt
fine dried breadcrumbs
¼ cup butter
2 tbsp oil
6 sage leaves

for the marinade:
½ cup oil
juice of 1 lemon
1 spring onion, finely chopped
salt
freshly ground pepper

Mix the marinade ingredients together and pour over the fish fillets in a shallow dish. Leave to stand for 2 hr, turning the fillets from time to time. Remove from the marinade and dry with a cloth. Dip in flour, then in the lightly salted beaten egg and lastly in the breadcrumbs. Heat half the butter with the oil in a large skillet. Place the fillets in the melted butter and oil

and brown on both sides. Transfer to a heated serving dish. Put the remaining butter in the skillet, add the sage leaves and heat gently for a few minutes. Pour over the fillets and serve at once.

ORATA ALLA PUGLIESE ✳
(Sea bream Apulia style)

1 2-lb sea bream
2 cloves garlic
1 sprig parsley
1 cup olive oil
4 medium potatoes
1 tbsp butter
salt
freshly ground pepper
2 tbsp grated Pecorino cheese

Scrape the scales off the fish, cut off the fins and the tail, and gut. Rinse very thoroughly and dry. Chop the garlic and parsley together and mix with the oil in a basin. Peel the potatoes, wash and cut into thin slices. Butter an oven-proof dish large enough to hold the fish when laid flat; sprinkle half the garlic and parsley in the dish, cover with a layer of sliced potatoes (about half), sprinkle with a pinch of salt, pepper, and 1 tbsp Pecorino cheese; lay the fish on top and sprinkle with the remaining cheese. Cover with the rest of the potatoes, sprinkle with salt and then the remaining parsley and garlic mixture. Cook in a preheated oven (350°F) for ¾ hr. Serve at once.

PALOMBO COI PISELLI
(Dogfish with peas)

4 dogfish steaks
salt
½ onion, sliced
2 tbsp olive oil
14 oz shelled peas
1 sprig parsley, chopped
1 tbsp tomato paste
freshly ground pepper

Wash the fish steaks in cold salted water and leave to drain. Fry the onion in oil in a large skillet over very low heat. Add the peas, the parsley and the tomato paste dissolved in 1 cup warm water. After about ¼ hr add the fish steaks.

Sprinkle with salt and pepper and simmer gently for 5 min on each side. Serve very hot.

POLIPETTI ARRABBIATI
(Baby octopus with chili)

2 lb baby octopus
½ cup olive oil
3 salted anchovies
1 clove garlic
1–2 tbsp capers
small piece chili pepper
4 large ripe tomatoes
salt
freshly ground pepper
1 sprig parsley

Clean the baby octopus, removing the skin and eyes. Rinse under cold water and drain. Put into a flame-proof casserole with no extra liquid, cover and cook gently for 10 min. Then add the oil, the rinsed, boned and chopped anchovies, the chopped garlic, the capers, chili pepper and the peeled, seeded and chopped tomatoes. Season with salt and pepper and stir well. Cover and cook for at least ½ hr, stirring occasionally. If the sauce becomes too dry add a little hot water as required. Before removing from the heat sprinkle with chopped parsley. Serve hot.

POLPO ALLA LUCIANA
(Octopus Luciana)

2½ lb octopus
2 cloves garlic, chopped
dried chili pepper
fresh parsley
few ripe tomatoes
½ cup olive oil
juice of 1 lemon
salt
freshly ground pepper

Clean the octopus by turning the body sac inside out and emptying it. Remove and discard the eyes and the hard central bone. Rinse well and beat vigorously to tenderize. Put the octopus into a large saucepan (the octopus should fill two-thirds of the saucepan) and cover with salted water (preferably seawater). Add a clove of garlic, a piece of dried chili, a sprig of parsley and a few ripe tomatoes, roughly chopped. Cover with a tightly fitting lid and cook over very low heat for 2 hr. The lid should not be removed from the saucepan during cooking. Drain the octopus, cut into pieces and dress while still hot with the minced garlic and parsley, oil, lemon juice and salt and pepper to taste. Serve while still warm, or leave a while to allow the flavors to be absorbed.

RANE IN GUAZZETTO
(Frogs' legs in white wine)

1 lb frogs' legs, skinned and cleaned
1 cup dry white wine
⅓ cup butter
1 tsp all-purpose flour
salt
2–3 tbsp chopped parsley
juice of 1 lemon

Rinse and dry the frogs' legs and put them in a skillet with the white wine and half the butter; bring to a boil and cook until the wine has reduced by half. Thicken the sauce with 1 tsp flour mixed with 1–2 tbsp cold water; season with salt and add the chopped parsley. Cover the skillet and simmer over low heat for at least ¼ hr. Before serving, stir the remaining butter into the sauce and sprinkle with lemon juice.

RANE FRITTE *
(Deep-fried frogs' legs)

1 lb frogs' legs
1 cup dry white wine
2 eggs
few tbsp milk
salt
all-purpose flour
oil for frying
1 lemon

Rinse and dry the frogs' legs. Place them in a shallow dish with the wine and leave to marinate for several hours. Beat together the eggs, milk, salt and enough flour to make quite a thick batter. Leave the batter to stand while the frogs' legs are in the marinade. Remove the frogs' legs from the wine, drain them and dip in batter. Heat plenty of oil in a deep skillet; when very hot fry the coated frogs' legs until crisp and golden. Remove with tongs and drain on kitchen paper. Serve hot with wedges of lemon.

SALMONE IN BELLAVISTA
(Cold poached salmon)

9 cups water
1 cup dry white wine
2 tbsp vinegar
peppercorns
1 bay leaf
1 onion
1 stick celery
1 carrot
salt
1 3-lb salmon
2¼ cups mayonnaise (see p. 126)
4 tomatoes
6 tbsp cooked peas
lettuce leaves

Prepare the court-bouillon: In a fish kettle or deep saucepan put the water, wine, vinegar, crushed peppercorns, bay leaf, onion, celery, sliced carrot and salt. Bring to a boil, removing any scum that may form on top, and simmer for ½ hr. Leave to cool. Clean, de-scale and rinse the salmon carefully and place in the cold court-bouillon. Bring to a boil and simmer very gently for about ½ hr, then remove from the heat and allow to stand for another ½ hr. Drain the salmon and remove the skin, taking care not to break the flesh. Arrange the fish on a serving dish and, using a pastry bag, decorate with mayonnaise. Fill the halved tomatoes with peas and place on lettuce leaves around the fish. Serve the remaining mayonnaise separately.

FILETTI DI SAN PIETRO
(John Dory fillets)

4 John Dory fillets
lemons
2 tbsp all-purpose flour
2 eggs
salt
fine dried breadcrumbs
¼ cup butter
2 tbsp olive oil
parsley
red and green peppers

Remove any bones from the fillets and rinse in water acidulated with lemon juice. Dry and then dip first in the flour, then in the eggs beaten with a pinch of salt and a few drops of lemon juice. Remove from the egg mixture and coat both sides with breadcrumbs. Heat the butter and oil in a wide skillet and when hot fry the fillets over high heat to brown them, then lower the heat to cook them through. Turn carefully with a fish slice so that they are evenly browned. When they are cooked through and golden arrange the fillets on a warm serving dish and garnish with lemon halves, sprigs of parsley, and slices of red and green pepper.

SARDE RIPIENE
(Stuffed sardines)

1 lb fresh sardines
salt
8 oz beet leaves (or spinach)
2 slices fresh white bread, crusts
*   removed, soaked in milk*
2 tbsp grated Parmesan cheese
1 clove garlic, chopped
2 tbsp chopped parsley
4 leaves marjoram (or basil),
*   chopped*
1 egg, beaten
1 cup olive oil
1 tbsp pine nuts
1 lemon

Clean the sardines and cut off their heads. Open them without separating the two fillets and remove the backbone. Salt the insides lightly and leave the fish to drain. Wash the beet leaves in several changes of salted water, then chop finely and mix with the soaked bread, the Parmesan cheese, garlic, parsley, marjoram, egg, a pinch of salt and

2 tbsp oil. Stuff the sardines with this mixture, place in an ovenproof dish with ½ cup oil and sprinkle with pine nuts. Bake in a preheated oven (350°F) for ¼ hr. Serve hot with wedges of lemon.

SARDE ALLA NAPOLETANA
(Neapolitan sardines)

1¾ lb fresh sardines
2 tbsp extra-virgin olive oil
salt
freshly ground pepper
1 sprig parsley
1 clove garlic
pinch fresh marjoram
4 large tomatoes

Cut the heads off the fish, gut them and remove the backbone; taking care not to separate the fillets. (Leave the tails attached as they help to hold the two fillets together.) Rinse and dry carefully. Choose an ovenproof dish large enough to hold all the sardines in not more than two layers. Pour a light film of oil over the fish, sprinkle with salt and freshly ground pepper, plenty of finely chopped parsley, finely chopped garlic and a pinch of marjoram. Cover the fish with the peeled, seeded and coarsely chopped tomatoes. Cook in a hot oven (400°F) for about 20 min.

SARDE AL VINO BIANCO
(Sardines in white wine)

1¾ lb fresh sardines
½ cup butter
2 salted anchovies
salt
freshly ground pepper
1 cup white wine

Cut the heads off the sardines, slit them open and, without separating the fillets, remove the backbone. Cut off the tail. Rinse the fish and dry with a cloth. Place half the butter in a mortar with the rinsed and boned anchovies, and pound together; spread the resulting anchovy butter inside the sardines. Press the fillets of each sardine together again and arrange them in a buttered ovenproof dish. Dot the

remaining butter over them, season with salt and pepper and sprinkle with white wine. Cover with foil and cook in a preheated moderate oven (350°F) for about 10 min. Serve hot.

SARDE IN TORTIERA
(Baked sardines)

1¾ lb fresh sardines
1½ cups fresh breadcrumbs
salt
freshly ground pepper
2 sprigs parsley, chopped
½–¾ cup olive oil
1 clove garlic, chopped
juice of 1–2 lemons

Clean the sardines and cut off their heads. Slit them open and, without separating the fillets, remove the backbone. Rinse the fish and press the two fillets together again. In a bowl, mix together the breadcrumbs, salt, pepper, parsley, oil and garlic; stir until well blended. Brush an ovenproof dish with oil and place a layer of sardines in the bottom. Spread a layer of the breadcrumb mixture over the sardines, then another layer of sardines followed by another layer of breadcrumbs. Continue in this way until the ingredients are used up, finishing with a layer of breadcrumbs. Pour a little oil over the top and transfer to a moderate oven (350°F) for 20–30 min or until the top is golden brown. Remove from the oven and sprinkle with lemon juice.

SEPPIE RIPIENE
(Stuffed squid)

4 medium squid
2 cloves garlic
1 sprig parsley
2 tbsp fresh breadcrumbs
salt
freshly ground pepper
olive oil
1 cup dry white wine

Clean the squid well, rubbing off the outer skin. Pull away and discard the hard, central bone and ink sac, then cut off the tentacles. Rinse well under cold water. Chop the tentacles finely with the garlic and parsley; put this mixture into a bowl and add the breadcrumbs, salt and pepper to taste and 2 tbsp oil. Mix well and fill the squid with this stuffing. Stitch up the opening with kitchen thread to prevent the stuffing from coming out during cooking. Heat 4 tbsp oil in a skillet large enough to hold all the squid side by side. When the oil is hot lay the squid in the skillet and brown lightly, turning frequently. Sprinkle with salt and pepper, add a little more oil then add the wine. Cover and cook very gently for about 20 min or until the flesh of the squid feels very tender when pierced with a fork. Serve at once.

SCAMPI GIGANTI AI FERRI
(Broiled saltwater crayfish)

12 saltwater crayish, heads attached
salt
freshly ground pepper
½ cup olive oil
juice of 1 lemon
chopped parsley

Choose large saltwater crayfish and rinse well. Remove the shell by cutting along the back with a sharp knife, leaving the head intact. Open them out in half and season with salt, pepper and oil. Heat the broiler until very hot and place the crayfish on the rack. Lower the heat immediately. Turn several times to prevent burning and to insure that they brown evenly. As soon as the crayfish are cooked, transfer to a serving dish and dress with a few drops of olive oil, lemon juice and chopped parsley.

SPIEDINI ALLA GRIGLIA
(Seafood kabobs)

8 saltwater crayfish tails
8 shrimp
8 medium cuttlefish
½ cup olive oil
salt
freshly ground pepper
chopped parsley
1 clove garlic
fresh breadcrumbs
lemon wedges

Clean and prepare the seafood: Shell, rinse and dry the crayfish and shrimp. Remove the hard, central bone and the ink sacs from the cuttlefish and rinse thoroughly under cold water until the flesh is white. Thread the seafood on to skewers. Mix together the oil, salt, pepper, chopped parsley, chopped garlic and breadcrumbs in a dish. Dip and turn the skewers in this mixture and then place under a very hot broiler. Reduce the heat at once and cook until evenly browned. Transfer the kabobs to a serving dish and season with a pinch of salt and pepper and a few drops of olive oil. Garnish with lemon wedges and serve with salad.

SCAPECE ALLA VASTESE
(Marinated fish Vasto style)

1¾ lb fish steaks (skate or dogfish)
all-purpose flour
oil for frying
salt
4½ cups vinegar
small pinch of saffron

Rinse the steaks and dry on kitchen paper. Coat lightly with flour and fry in plenty of hot oil. Drain on kitchen paper and sprinkle with salt. Heat the vinegar in a non metallic saucepan; mix the saffron with a little vinegar and add to the saucepan. Remove from the heat as soon as it boils. Lay half the fish in a dish and pour over some of the saffron vinegar; cover with the rest of the fish and pour over the remaining liquid. Cover and keep in a cool place for 24 hr. Drain the fish well before serving.

SEPPIE ALLA VENEZIANA
(Squid Venice style)

8 small squid
1 clove garlic
½ onion
8 tbsp olive oil
1 tbsp chopped parsley
1 cup dry white wine
freshly ground pepper
½ lemon
salt

Clean the squid, pulling away (and discarding) the hard, central bone. Reserve the ink sacs. Rinse the squid well and cut into strips. Fry the whole clove of garlic and the chopped onion in 6 tbsp oil; when they begin to soften remove the garlic and add the squid, including the tentacles, and the chopped parsley. Add the wine and raise the heat. Allow to reduce, then add a little of the reserved ink to taste. Sprinkle with pepper, cover and cook slowly for about ½ hr. If the squid become too dry add a few spoonfuls of boiling stock (or ½ tsp meat extract mixed with a little water). When the squid are cooked, add 2 tbsp oil and the juice of ½ lemon; taste and add salt if necessary. This dish is usually served with slices of toasted polenta.

SEPPIE IN UMIDO CON PISELLI ✳
(Stewed squid with peas)

2 lb squid, cleaned (see recipe above)

for the marinade:
1 cup wine vinegar
1 small onion, sliced
salt
freshly ground pepper

for the sauce:
4 tbsp olive oil
1 clove garlic, minced
1 small onion, finely chopped
2–3 sprigs parsley, chopped
2 tbsp tomato paste
8 oz shelled peas
salt
freshly ground pepper

Cut the squid into thin strips. Mix the marinade ingredients in a large dish, stir in the strips of squid and leave to stand for several hours. Heat the oil in a wide skillet and fry the garlic. When it begins to brown remove it, then brown the chopped onion in the flavored oil. Drain the squid well, reserving the marinade, and add to the skillet with the parsley, 1 tbsp of the marinade and the tomato paste mixed with a cupful of water. Cook over low heat for ¼ hr. Add the peas, season with salt and pepper and cook until the squid are tender. The cooking time depends on the size of the squid.

SARDINE AL FINOCCHIO
(Sardines with fennel)

1 large onion, sliced
½ cup olive oil
½ cup dry white wine
12 oz ripe tomatoes (or canned)
salt
freshly ground pepper
1¾ lb sardines
fine dried breadcrumbs
1 tbsp fennel seeds, minced in a
    mortar

In a small saucepan fry the onion in oil over low heat. When it is lightly browned add the wine and reduce. Add the peeled, chopped and seeded tomatoes. Season with salt and pepper and cook over moderate heat for ¼ hr. Clean the sardines: Remove their heads, rinse thoroughly in salted water and drain well. Season the fish with salt and pepper, dip in the breadcrumbs and sprinkle with fennel seeds. Pour the tomato sauce into an ovenproof dish, arrange the sardines in the sauce, and pour over a little oil. Cook in a preheated oven (325°F) for ½ hr until the breadcrumbs are golden brown. Serve very hot.

SOGLIOLA ALLA MUGNAIA
(Sole meunière)

2 large or 4 medium sole
all-purpose flour
¼ cup + 2 tbsp butter
2 tbsp chopped parsley

Skin, gut and rinse the fish. Dry on kitchen paper, then coat lightly in flour. Melt 2–3 tbsp butter in a skillet; when it begins to sizzle put in the sole and brown evenly on both sides over very low heat for about ¼ hr. When the sole are cooked transfer to a warm serving dish and sprinkle with chopped parsley. Melt the rest of the butter and pour over the fish.

FILETTI DI SOGLIOLA ALLA PUGLIESE
(Sole fillets Apulia style)

4 medium sole
1 sprig parsley
2 oz black olives
pinch of oregano
olive oil
salt
freshly ground pepper

Using a pair of kitchen scissors, trim away all the fins around the outside of the fish. Beginning with the dark side, cut into the skin at the tail with the point of a knife. Working from the tail toward the head, pull the skin firmly back to detach it. Repeat on the other side of the fish to remove the white skin. Using the point of a knife, make a cut under the first fillet, beginning at the head; cut around the outer edge of the fillet, then along the backbone. Cut off the head and detach the fillets. Rinse and dry the fillets and lay them neatly on a piece of foil, sprinkling them with the parsley and olives chopped together with a pinch of oregano. Sprinkle with olive oil, season with salt and pepper. Wrap the foil loosely around the fillets and fold over the edges to seal. Cook in a preheated oven (400°F)

TRANCI DI PESCE SPADA LESSATI
(Poached swordfish steaks)

4 4-oz swordfish steaks
salt
½ onion
1 stick celery
1 sprig parsley
1 carrot
oil
1 clove garlic, chopped
paprika
pickled vegetables

SOGLIOLA AL VINO BIANCO
(Sole in white wine)

4 8-oz sole
lemon juice or vinegar
all-purpose flour
¼ cup + 2 tbsp butter
salt
freshly ground pepper
4 sage leaves, chopped
½ glass dry white wine
2 tbsp dry Marsala
juice of 1 lemon
1 tsp mustard

BRACIOLE DI PESCE SPADA *
(Stuffed swordfish roulades)

1 lb swordfish
2 oz Mozzarella cheese
1 onion
3 tbsp olive oil
salt
freshly ground pepper
2–3 tbsp brandy
3 tbsp fresh breadcrumbs
1 sprig basil
thyme
1 lemon

for 15–20 min. Transfer the fillets to a lightly greased dish. Pour the juices from the foil into the dish and cook in a hot oven (475°F) for 5 min.

Remove the skin from the swordfish steaks; place in a saucepan and cover with cold water. Add salt and flavorings (onion, celery, parsley and carrot). Bring slowly to boil and simmer gently for 5 min. Drain the fish steaks and place in a dish. Dress with plenty of oil and season with chopped garlic and a generous sprinkling of paprika. Garnish with chopped parsley and chopped pickled vegetables.

Clean the sole; gut, skin and rinse them in water acidulated with lemon juice or vinegar. Dry, then dip in flour. Melt the butter in a wide skillet; season the sole with salt, pepper and the sage leaves. Place the sole in the skillet and turn the fish carefully to brown both sides. Add the wine, Marsala, lemon juice and mustard. Reduce the sauce over high heat and check the seasoning before removing from the heat. When the sole are cooked transfer to a serving dish and garnish with lemon wedges.

Cut the Mozzarella and the swordfish into eight thin slices. Chop any leftover fish with the onion. Heat the oil in a large skillet and add the chopped onion, and a pinch of salt and pepper. Brown the onion lightly and pour in the brandy. When the sauce has thickened remove from the heat and stir in the breadcrumbs. Place a slice of Mozzarella on each slice of fish, then some of the sauce and a couple of leaves of basil and a pinch of thyme. Roll up the slices and tie securely with kitchen thread, and cook gently under a hot broiler until browned on all sides. Serve at once garnished with lemon wedges.

208

PESCE SPADA AL FORNO
(Baked swordfish)

1 1¾-lb swordfish steak
3 tbsp all-purpose flour
1 cup olive oil
salt
freshly ground pepper
½ onion
2 cloves garlic
½ cup dry white wine
2 lemons
parsley

Scrape the scales off the fish and rinse; coat with flour and place in an ovenproof casserole the exact size of the fish. Season with oil, salt and pepper, the finely chopped onion and garlic, pour over the wine and the juice of one lemon. Place a piece of foil over the casserole, then cover with a tightly fitting lid. Cook in a hot oven (425°F) for ½ hr. The fish will cook in the steam from the other ingredients. As soon as it is cooked cut into serving pieces and garnish with parsley and slices of lemon.

FRITTURA DI PESCE SPADA
(Deep-fried swordfish)

1¾ lb swordfish
3 tbsp olive oil
salt
freshly ground pepper
juice of 1 lemon
all-purpose flour
2 eggs
fine dried breadcrumbs
oil for frying
1–2 lemons
2 tbsp chopped parsley

Skin the swordfish and cut into slices, rinse and pat dry. Transfer to a shallow dish and season with the olive oil, salt, pepper and lemon juice. Leave to marinate for 1–2 hr. Remove the slices from the marinade, dry them on kitchen paper, then dip first in flour, then in lightly salted beaten egg and finally in breadcrumbs. Put the fish at once into hot oil; lower the heat immediately and brown on both sides over moderate heat until cooked through. Remove from the skillet and drain off the excess oil on kitchen paper. Arrange the fish

on a serving dish and garnish with lemon wedges.

SPIGOLA AL FORNO
(Baked sea bass)

1 1¾–2 lb sea bass
rosemary
thyme
marjoram
sprigs of parsley
1 clove garlic, chopped
salt
1 tbsp fresh breadcrumbs
1 cup olive oil
juice of 1 lemon

Using the blunt edge of a knife, scrape the scales off the sea bass. Gut and rinse well. Into the belly cavity put the sprigs of rosemary, thyme, marjoram, parsley and the chopped garlic. Place the fish in a greased ovenproof dish. Salt lightly, sprinkle with breadcrumbs and pour over 1 cup oil with the juice of 1 lemon beaten into it. Cook for 40 min in a hot (425°F) oven.

TRIGLIE ALLA LIGURE
(Red mullet Ligurian style)

1½ lb red mullet
½ cup olive oil
1 clove garlic, chopped
2–3 sprigs parsley, chopped
2 anchovy fillets, chopped
½ cup white wine
4 tomatoes, peeled and chopped
salt
freshly ground pepper
1 tbsp capers
12 black olives, pitted and halved
2 lemons

Gut the fish, and rinse well. Heat the oil in a large skillet and fry the chopped garlic, parsley and anchovies until they just begin to brown. Add the wine and cook over fairly high heat for a moment, then add the tomatoes. Cook over moderate heat for ¼ hr, stirring occasionally. Add the fish, season with salt and pepper and continue to cook for a further 15–20 min or until done. Before serving add the capers, the pitted olives and a generous sprinkling of lemon juice. Garnish with lemon wedges.

TRANCI DI TONNO AI FERRI
(Broiled tuna steaks)

2 ¾-lb fresh tuna steaks
olive oil for dressing
2 cloves garlic, chopped
chopped parsley
1 tbsp chopped capers

for the marinade:
4 tbsp olive oil
salt
freshly ground pepper
1 bay leaf
few slices onion

Marinate the tuna steaks for 1 hr in the olive oil, mixed with salt and pepper, a bay leaf and a few slices of onion. Remove from the marinade and when the broiler is red hot place the steaks on the rack; brown on both sides, then lower the heat and continue cooking, basting from time to time with the rest of the oil from the marinade. Serve with a dressing of oil, garlic, parsley and chopped capers.

TRIGLIE DI SCOGLIO STUFATE
(Spicy red mullet)

4 8-oz red mullet
1 clove garlic, chopped
1 sprig parsley, chopped
4 tbsp olive oil
2 tbsp tomato paste
salt
pinch of chili pepper
all-purpose flour
2 tbsp dry white wine

Gut, rinse and dry the fish. Peel a clove of garlic and chop it with the sprig of parsley. Put the garlic and parsley in a skillet with 2 tbsp oil and fry gently until softened. Add the tomato paste mixed with a ladleful of water; season with salt and a pinch of chili pepper. Cook the sauce gently over low heat until it is reduced. Flour the mullet and place in a flameproof casserole in which the remaining oil has been heated. Fry the mullet for about 10 min, turning them carefully. Sprinkle with salt, add the white wine and when it has evaporated cover the fish with the tomato sauce mixed with a little more hot

water. Transfer to a hot oven (425°F) for 10 min, then serve the red mullet straight from the casserole.

TONNO FRESCO ALLA MARINARA
(Tuna steaks with tomatoes, olives and capers)

4 tuna steaks, 1¾ lb total weight
1 cup olive oil
1 sprig basil, chopped
3 oz pitted green or black olives
1 oz capers
14 oz ripe tomatoes
salt
freshly ground pepper
2 tbsp fresh breadcrumbs

Rinse the tuna steaks, skin them and drain. Pour about half the oil into an ovenproof dish, arrange the tuna steaks in a single layer, then sprinkle with basil, chopped olives, capers, the peeled, chopped and seeded tomatoes, a pinch of salt, a generous sprinkling of pepper and the breadcrumbs. Pour over the remaining oil and cook in a preheated oven (325°F) for ½ hr until the fish has cooked and the sauce reduced. Serve at once.

TONNO ALLA SICILIANA
(Tuna steaks Sicilian style)

1½ lb tuna
1 cup dry white wine
juice of 1 lemon
1 sprig rosemary
1 clove garlic
salt
freshly ground pepper
½ cup olive oil
3 salted anchovies
2 tbsp fresh breadcrumbs

The day before the fish is to be served, rinse the tuna in cold water, cut into four slices and place in the marinade, made by mixing together the wine, lemon juice, the sprig of rosemary, minced garlic and a pinch of salt and pepper. The next day drain the tuna, reserving the marinade, place them under the broiler and cook slowly, basting frequently with the marinade. When the steaks are nicely browned on both sides transfer to a serving dish and keep warm. Heat the oil in a saucepan and add the rinsed and filleted anchovies and the breadcrumbs; break up the anchovies with a fork, pour over the tuna and serve at once.

TINCHE MARINATE
(Marinated tench)

8 tench
all-purpose flour
oil for frying

for the marinade:
1 clove garlic, chopped
1 onion, chopped
½ cup olive oil
1 tbsp white wine vinegar
1 tbsp dry white wine
salt
3 black peppercorns
8 sage leaves

Clean the tench and rinse thoroughly to remove the muddy taste they usually have. Dry them on kitchen paper, coat lightly in flour and fry in hot oil. Arrange them in an earthenware dish. Fry the chopped garlic and onion in the olive oil in a small saucepan. Add the vinegar, wine, salt, peppercorns and the sage leaves. Bring the marinade to a boil and pour over the fish. Cover and leave for two days before serving.

TRIGLIE DI SCOGLIO ALLA GRATICOLA
(Barbecued mullet)

1½ lb red mullet
2 cloves garlic, chopped
2 sprigs parsley
salt
freshly ground pepper
½ cup olive oil
lemon juice

Gut the fish, taking care not to separate the fillets; rinse and dry them carefully. Chop together the garlic and parsley; add salt and pepper, and stuff the fish with this mixture. Taking care that the stuffing does not fall out, close the fish carefully by pressing with your fingers. Place the grill over the heat and when it is very hot arrange the fish on top. Move the fish a little away from the source of the heat as they are cooking; when you are sure that the first side is cooked, turn the fish carefully. When cooked on both sides, season with olive oil and lemon juice.

TRIGLIE ALLA LIVORNESE
(Leghorn red mullet)

8 small or 4 large red mullet
1 stick celery
3 cloves garlic
3 sprigs parsley
½ cup olive oil
1¼ lb ripe tomatoes (or canned)
salt
freshly ground pepper

Chop together the celery, garlic and parsley (reserving one sprig of parsley). Fry the chopped ingredients in the oil in a skillet and when they begin to brown add the peeled, chopped and seeded tomatoes. Season with salt and pepper and cook for about ¼ hr. Rub this sauce through a sieve and pour into a skillet or saucepan large enough to hold the fish in a single layer. Lay the fish in the sauce and bring to a boil over moderate heat. Simmer for about 20 min. If the mullet are small they will not need to be turned, but if they are larger they should be turned very carefully once. Just before removing from the heat sprinkle with the remaining parsley, finely chopped. The fish should be served at once from the same skillet.

TRIGLIE AL CARTOCCIO ✱
(Red mullet en papillote)

4 large red mullet
4 cloves garlic
1 bay leaf
olive oil
salt
½ tbsp fennel seeds

Clean the fish carefully, rinse and dry. If the mullet are fresh, gut them but leave the liver inside. This is less bitter than the liver of

other fish and is considered something of a specialty. Place each fish on a piece of wax paper or foil and season inside and out with chopped garlic, a piece of bay leaf, oil and salt. Sprinkle with fennel seeds. Fold over the edges of the paper or foil and bake in a preheated oven (425°F) for about 20 min or until the parcels look inflated and the fish inside are cooked through.

TRIGLIE ALLA CALABRESE
(Red mullet Calabrian Style)

2 lb red mullet
olive oil
salt
juice of 1 lemon
1 tbsp oregano

For this recipe each mullet should weigh about 4 oz. Allow two for each person. Clean and rinse the fish. Pour a thin film of oil in the bottom of an ovenproof dish and arrange the fish in a single layer on top. Season with salt, lemon juice and plenty of chopped oregano. Dribble oil over the fish until they are all well covered. Place the dish in a preheated oven (350–400°F) and cook for 10 min. The fish will not dry out but will cook in their own juices. Serve at once from the same dish.

TRIGLIE ALLA SICILIANA
(Red mullet Sicilian style)

4 8-oz red mullet
salt
freshly ground pepper
2 tbsp olive oil
peel of 2 oranges
2 tbsp meat juice or ½ tsp meat
    extract
½ cup dry white wine
½ cup butter
juice of 2 oranges and 1 lemon

Scrape the scales off the fish, taking care not to tear the skin. Rinse but do not gut the fish; season with salt and pepper, sprinkle with oil and leave to stand for about 10 min. Cook the red mullet on a barbecue or under the broiler for 5 min each side. Care-

fully peel the oranges, avoiding the pith; chop finely and blanch for 1 min in boiling water. Drain and place in a small saucepan with 2 tbsp meat juice (or ½ tsp meat extract mixed with a little water) and the wine. Boil for 1 min, remove from the heat and gradually stir in the butter and the juice from the oranges and one lemon. Arrange the fish on a warm serving dish and pour over the sauce.

TROTA ALLA PIEMONTESE
(Trout Piedmont style)

1 2-lb trout
⅛ cup seedless white raisins
1 small onion, chopped
1 clove garlic, chopped
1 stick celery, chopped
few sage leaves, chopped
1 sprig rosemary, chopped
2 tbsp olive oil
3 tbsp vinegar
grated peel of 1 lemon
1 cup light stock
salt
1 tbsp all-purpose flour

Clean the trout carefully and rinse well. Soak the seedless white raisins in warm water. Place the chopped onions, garlic, celery, sage and rosemary in a large skillet and fry them very gently in the oil. Add the fish, the vinegar, lemon peel, a little salt, the stock and the drained seedless white raisins. Cover and cook over low heat for about 15–20 min, depending on the size of the trout. Remove the fish, skin and fillet it and arrange on a serving dish; keep warm while you thicken the cooking liquid with the flour mixed with ½ cup water. Stir well, bring to a boil and simmer for 2 min. Pour over the fish and serve.

TROTE AFFOGATE
(Trout in white wine)

4 8-oz trout
2 tbsp all-purpose flour
1 cup olive oil
2 cloves garlic
1 large sprig parsley
salt
freshly ground pepper
1 cup dry white wine

Cut the tails and fins off the fish; gut, clean and rinse thoroughly, then dry on kitchen paper and dip in flour. In a skillet large enough to hold the fish in a single layer heat the oil and fry the chopped garlic and parsley very gently, stirring constantly with a wooden spoon. When the garlic begins to brown, add the fish and season with salt and pepper. Fry until light golden on both sides, then add the wine. Cook over low heat for about 20 min. Arrange the trout on a serving dish, pour over the cooking juices and serve at once.

TROTA AL FORNO
(Baked trout)

1 2-lb trout
butter for greasing
4 medium potatoes
salt
freshly ground pepper
olive oil
2 bay leaves
3 sprigs parsley, chopped
grated peel of 1 lemon

This dish can be prepared with a whole trout, or the fish can be cut into slices (the latter is preferable).

Clean the fish, rinse, dry and cut into thick slices. Place a layer of sliced potatoes in a buttered ovenproof dish and season with salt and pepper and a sprinkling of olive oil. Arrange the fish slices on the potatoes, add the bay leaves, and sprinkle with parsley, grated lemon peel, salt and pepper. Moisten with olive oil and cook in a moderate oven (350°F) for 45–50 min.

TROTE ALLA TRENTINA
(Trout Trento style)

4 small trout
1 tbsp all-purpose flour
1 cup olive oil
1 sprig rosemary
few sage leaves
½ onion
1 clove garlic
fresh parsley
2 lemons + peel of 1 lemon
1 cup white wine vinegar
salt
¼ cup seedless white raisins

Soften the seedless white raisins in warm water. Clean the trout, rinse, dry and dip in flour. Heat ½ cup oil in a large skillet with the rosemary and sage; when the oil begins to bubble remove the herbs and add the fish. Fry the fish for ¼ hr, turning frequently. In a non metallic saucepan heat 4 tbsp oil and gently fry the finely sliced onion over low heat. When the onion begins to soften add the garlic, one sprig finely chopped parsley, the grated lemon peel, vinegar, a little salt and finally the drained seedless white raisins. Boil this marinade for a few minutes. Arrange the trout side by side in a wide ovenproof dish and pour the marinade over them. Cover the dish and leave to stand for about 24 hr. To serve the trout take them from the marinade, place on a serving dish and garnish each fish with a wedge of lemon and a sprig of parsley.

ZUPPA DI ARSELLE
(Clam soup)

2¾ lb clams
2 tbsp olive oil
2 cloves garlic
2 cups dry white wine
salt
freshly ground pepper
1–2 tbsp finely chopped parsley
4 slices of bread fried in oil

Scrub the clams thoroughly with a stiff brush. Rinse in cold running water then leave to stand in salted water for 1 hr to remove all traces of sand. Place them in a large covered saucepan with 2 cups water. Heat gently for about 8 min until the shells open. Discard any that do not. Remove the clams and reserve the liquid. Heat the oil and fry a clove of minced garlic. As soon as it begins to brown remove it and add the wine and clams. Season with salt and pepper and add the reserved liquid from the clams. Cook over low heat for 5 min and sprinkle with chopped parsley just before serving. Mince the second clove of garlic, or cut it in half, and rub over the slices of fried bread; place one in each soup bowl before pouring in the clam soup.

CASSÓLA
(Sardinian fish soup)

3½ lb assorted fish (dogfish, sea bream, eel, John Dory, gray mullet, sea bass, scorpionfish, gurnard, squid, octopus, skate, crab, lobster)
½ cup olive oil
1 clove garlic
1 onion
1 sprig parsley
small piece chili pepper
4 ripe tomatoes
½ cup dry white wine
4 thick slices fried bread
salt

Clean all the fish thoroughly, wash them and cut into pieces, reserving the heads and other trimmings. Cut up the lobster tail and divide the body in two. Put the reserved heads and trimmings into 3 cups lightly salted water and boil for stock. Pour the oil into a large flameproof casserole (whence the name cassóla) and fry the chopped garlic, onion and parsley. When they begin to soften add the chili and the peeled, seeded and chopped tomatoes. Cook for a few minutes, then add the wine and allow to evaporate. Add 1 cup fish stock, then the squid and octopus, cut into pieces; season with salt and simmer for ¼ hr. Next add the fish needing the longest cooking, followed by the less firm varieties. Last of all add the lobster. Cover and simmer over low heat for a further ¼ hr, adding more fish stock as necessary. When the soup is ready (it should be fairly liquid) and the fish tender, serve in individual bowls with the slices of fried bread in the bottom.

BURIDDA
(Ligurian fish soup)

2½ lb monkfish, conger eel, presoaked salt cod, or other firm fish
1 whole clove garlic
1 onion, chopped
½ cup olive oil
1 anchovy fillet, chopped
1 sprig parsley, chopped
2 large ripe tomatoes, cut in pieces
4 walnuts, shelled and pounded
1 cup dry white wine
1 bay leaf
salt
thick slices of toasted bread

Clean the fish, cut into pieces and rinse well. In a large flameproof casserole fry the garlic and onion in oil. When the garlic begins to brown remove it and add the anchovy fillet, parsley and then the tomatoes. Mix together the pounded walnuts and the wine and add to the casserole. When the wine has reduced slightly add the fish, bay leaf and salt (add very little salt if you are using salt cod). Add 1 cup hot water and cook slowly for 20–30 min. Serve in the casserole with slices of toasted bread.

ZUPPA DI CAPE SANTE
(Scallop soup)

24 scallops
2 cups dry white wine
1 lb monkfish
1 carrot
1 onion
1 stick celery
salt
freshly ground pepper
9 cups water
1 cup olive oil
¼ cup + 3 tbsp all-purpose flour
4 anchovy fillets, chopped
3 tbsp chopped parsley
8 slices bread fried in oil

Remove the scallops from their shells and rinse them thoroughly under running water to get rid of any grit. Drain them, bring the wine to a boil and simmer the scallops in the wine for 5 min. Drain them again. Clean and rinse the monkfish, cut into pieces and put into a saucepan with all the vegetables and a little salt and pepper; cover with water, bring to a boil and simmer for ½ hr. Remove the fish (take out the bones) and vegetables with a slotted spoon and pass through a food mill. Reserve the stock. Heat the oil in a stockpot, add the flour and brown slightly. Add the chopped anchovy fillets, then gradually mix in some of the fish stock. Stir well to prevent lumps from forming. When well mixed pour in the remaining stock, together with the sieved fish and vegetables. Add the whole scallops and cook for a few minutes. Serve the soup in individual bowls, sprinkled with chopped parsley and accompanied by slices of bread fried in oil.

ZUPPA DI COZZE ALLA TARANTINA
(Mussel soup Taranto style)

2¾ lb mussels
2 tbsp olive oil
1 clove garlic, minced
small piece chili pepper
12 oz ripe tomatoes
salt
1 cup dry white wine
1 clove garlic, chopped
slices of fried or toasted bread

Scrub the mussels thoroughly with a stiff brush and rinse several times in cold running water. Scrape off the barnacles and trim the beards. Discard any that do not close when tapped sharply. Heat the oil in a large skillet and fry the garlic and chili. As soon as the garlic begins to brown remove it and the chili and add the peeled, seeded and chopped tomatoes. Cook over moderate heat for 10 min. Add the mussels and boil fast for about 5 min, shaking the skillet from time to time until all the shells open.

Discard any that do not. Pour in the wine and allow to evaporate over high heat. Sprinkle over the chopped garlic and serve the soup from the skillet, with slices of fried or toasted bread.

ZUPPA DI PESCE SIRACUSANA
(Fish soup Syracuse style)

2 lb assorted fish
1 onion, finely sliced
2–3 sprigs parsley, chopped
2 cloves garlic
2 sticks celery
1 bay leaf
8 oz ripe tomatoes
½ cup olive oil
1 cup dry white wine
salt
freshly ground pepper
thick slices of toasted bread

Any type of fish can be used, but the more varieties there are the richer the soup will be. Clean the fish and cut into evenly sized pieces (not too small); rinse in salted water. Put the pieces of fish in a casserole with the onion, chopped parsley, the whole garlic cloves, the chopped celery, the bay leaf and the peeled, seeded and chopped tomatoes. Pour ½ cup oil over this mixture, then add 1 cup white wine and enough water to reach the level of the fish but not to cover it. Season with salt and pepper, cover the casserole and cook in a preheated moderate oven (350°F) for about ½ hr or until the fish is tender. Remove the bay leaf and the cloves of garlic and serve the soup with thick slices of toasted bread.

ZUPPA DI PESCE DI POZZUOLI
(Fish soup Pozzuoli style)

2½ lb assorted fish (scorpionfish, gurnard, skate, eel, monkfish, swordfish, dogfish, octopus, baby squid)

¾ lb clams
¾ lb mussels
1 cup olive oil
2 cloves garlic
12 oz tomatoes
salt
3 sprigs parsley
small piece chili pepper
4 slices toasted bread

Clean the fish, leaving them whole if they are small. Otherwise cut them into pieces. Skin the dogfish and cut into slices. Clean the octopus and squid and cut into rings. Scrub the clams and mussels and open them by heating in a skillet for 5 min with a few tablespoons oil. When the shells have all opened keep the clams and mussels warm but do not remove from their shells. Put 2–3 cups water in a saucepan and add a few tablespoons oil, two whole cloves garlic, the peeled, seeded and chopped tomatoes, a generous pinch of salt, a sprig of parsley and the chili pepper. Bring to a boil and add the octopus and the squid. Bring to a boil again and simmer for 10 min before adding the other varieties of fish. Cook for a further 10 min, then add the mussels and clams to heat through. Place a slice of toasted bread in each soup dish; cover with fish broth, and garnish with chopped parsley.

BRANZINO AL FINOCCHIO
(Sea bass with fennel)

1 2½-lb sea bass
4 heads fennel
salt
freshly ground pepper
½ cup olive oil
1½ cups fish stock (see p.131)
1 sprig parsley

Clean the sea bass carefully and cut into four fillets. Only the hearts of the fennel are used; these should be finely sliced. Arrange the fish fillets in an ovenproof dish, add the sliced fennel, salt and pepper, olive oil and the fish stock and cook in a preheated oven (475°F) for 10 min. Remove from the oven and divide the fillets and fennel between the serving plates. Pour the sauce into a small saucepan and reduce over high heat. Add the chopped parsley, pour the sauce over the fish and serve.

CAPE SANTE AL PEPE ROSA *
(Scallops with pink peppercorns)

24 scallops
4 tbsp butter
salt
3 cups white wine
1–2 tbsp pink (or green)
   peppercorns
3 tbsp chopped parsley
1 tbsp sweet red pepper, finely
   chopped

Remove the scallops from their shells and rinse thoroughly in running water. Sauté in a large skillet for 1 min in 2 tbsp butter, sprinkle with salt and pour in the white wine. Bring to a boil and simmer for about 10 min. Remove the scallops and serve in individual dishes. Into the cooking liquid put the peppercorns, chopped parsley, finely chopped red pepper and the remaining butter; reduce slightly over high heat, then pour over the scallops and serve.

CODE DI GAMBERO CON ASPARAGI E RUCOLA *
(Jumbo shrimp with asparagus)

40 fresh jumbo shrimp
20 asparagus tips
4 oz corn salad
1 large cucumber, sliced
salt
freshly ground pepper
lemon juice
olive oil

Shell the shrimp, removing the black dorsal thread. Cut the hard part off the asparagus tips, tie them in a bundle, then steam upright in 1 in boiling salted water until tender. Arrange the corn salad and cucumber as illustrated on four serving plates; place the asparagus on top with the tips in the center, then add the shrimp which have been steamed for 2 min. Season with salt, pepper, lemon juice and plenty of olive oil.

SALMONE COTTO A VAPORE CON SALSA DI YOGURTH E ROSMARINO
(Steamed salmon with yogurt and rosemary sauce)

1 2½-lb salmon
¼ cup chopped onion
few sprigs fresh rosemary
1 tbsp butter
⅓ cup light cream
¾ cup natural yogurt
1 tbsp chopped parsley
salt

Clean and fillet the salmon and steam the fillets for about 4 min. Sauté the onion and rosemary in the butter, add the cream and yogurt and simmer over low heat for 20 min. Add the parsley and salt, simmer for 5 min more and then sieve. Arrange the salmon fillets on a serving dish and cover with the sauce.

215

Eggs

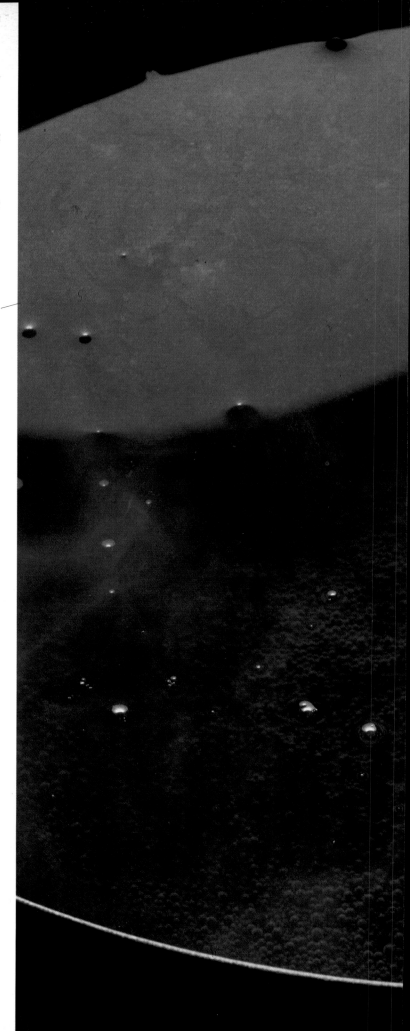

*H*ighly nutritious, relatively inexpensive and easy to store, the egg is above all immensely versatile, and one of the most fundamental and widely used ingredients in cookery. Its uses are manifold, from thickening soups and sauces to its vital place in dessert making and bakery.

Mixed with herbs, cheese, an assortment of vegetables, or fruit, they enable the cook to create an almost infinite repertoire of omelets, and crêpes both savory and sweet.

Eggs star in many celebrated classic recipes of Italian cuisine, from zabaglione to spaghetti alla carbonara. While they can be combined with other ingredients in a variety of delicious ways to make up elegant and imaginative appetizers or main-course dishes suited to formal entertaining, eggs are equally successful and satisfying as a meal in their own right, lightly boiled or poached with no other accompaniment than salt and pepper.

FRITTATA DI CIPOLLE
(Onion omelet)

4 large onions
salt
freshly ground pepper
4 eggs
oil
oregano

Slice the onions into rounds, place on a dish and sprinkle with salt and pepper. Put about 2 tbsp oil in a saucepan, add the onions and cook over low heat until they are very soft but not browned (stir frequently and, if necessary, add a few tablespoons of water from time to time). Meanwhile, beat the eggs with a pinch of salt, then stir into the cooked onions. Pour some oil into a nonstick omelet pan or skillet; when it starts to sizzle pour in the egg and onion mixture. Sprinkle with oregano and when the omelet is set, increase the heat slightly to cook the underside. Turn carefully and cook the other side.

FRITTATA ALLE ERBE
(Vegetable and herb omelet)

1½ lb mixed vegetables (e.g. spinach, leeks, onion)
2 sage leaves
4 basil leaves
4 tbsp oil
4 eggs
salt
freshly ground pepper

This dish is a typical Friulian specialty. Thoroughly clean the vegetables: Peel and slice the leeks and onion. Rinse the spinach well. Boil the vegetables (cook the spinach in a separate saucepan) in a small quantity of salted water until tender; drain well. Chop the spinach finely and coarsely chop the other vegetables. Rinse and chop the herbs. Put 4 tbsp oil in a saucepan, add the vegetables and herbs and simmer over low heat for a few minutes. Beat the eggs in a bowl with salt and pepper to taste, then add to the chopped vegetables and herbs; stir until well blended. Pour a little oil into a large nonstick omelet pan or skillet; when hot pour in the egg and vegetable mixture, gently level the surface

and cook until set; carefully turn the omelet over with a spatula and continue cooking until golden brown. The omelet should be soft in the center and slightly crispy on the outside.

FRITTATA ALLA MENTA
(Mint omelet)

1 tbsp all-purpose flour
½ cup milk
6 eggs
3 tbsp chopped mint
butter
salt

This dish is typical of Latium. Put the flour into a small bowl and gradually stir in the milk. Separate the eggs. Whisk the whites in a large bowl until they form peaks. Beat the yolks and fold into the whites. Add the flour and milk mixture and stir well. Finely chop the mint leaves and add them to the bowl. Melt the butter in a nonstick omelet pan or skillet and pour in one quarter of the egg mixture. As this omelet is cooked on one side only, it should be very thin and the skillet must be tilted during cooking to ensure that the eggs are evenly distributed over the bottom. Remove each omelet and set aside in a warm place until you have four omelets.

OMELETTE PIEMONTESE
(Truffle omelet Piedmont style)

2 white truffles
¼ cup butter
4 eggs
salt
freshly ground white pepper

Clean the truffles with a small hard brush. Cut one into fairly large dice, and the other into thin slices. Heat the diced truffle with the butter in a nonstick omelet pan or skillet; do not let it brown. Remove the pieces and drain on kitchen paper. Repeat the process with the slices of truffle leaving them in the butter for only an instant. Remove from the pan and keep warm.

Lightly beat the eggs, season with salt and white pepper, and pour into the skillet. Cook the omelet in the truffle-flavored butter, until it begins to set. Arrange the diced truffle along the center and fold the omelet over. Transfer to a hot plate, garnish with the truffle slices and serve immediately.

UOVA IN COCOTTE
(Baked eggs with cheese and ham)

3 tbsp butter
2 oz Fontina cheese
2 oz ham
4 eggs
pinch of salt

Preheat the oven to 325°F. Butter four ovenproof custard cups. Dice the ham and cheese and divide between them. Place in the oven for the cheese to melt. As soon as it has melted, take out of the oven and break an egg into each custard cup; season with a pinch of salt and top with a piece of butter. Place the custard cups in a shallow baking pan half filled with water and return to the oven for about 10 min or until set. Serve immediately.

CRÊPES PIEMONTESI
(Anchovy and truffle crêpes Piedmont style)

1 cup all-purpose flour
3 eggs
1 cup milk
pinch of salt
1 tbsp brandy
¼ cup + 2 tbsp butter
4 salted anchovies
1 white truffle

Heap the flour into a bowl; make a well in the center and break in the eggs. Add a pinch of salt, then gradually mix the eggs into the flour, pouring in the milk a little at a time. When the mixture is smooth and without lumps, melt one quarter of the butter and add it to the bowl together with the brandy. Leave to stand for ½ hr. Meanwhile bone, rinse and chop the anchovies. Dice the truffle. Sauté

the anchovies and truffle briefly in a small skillet in 2 tbsp butter; leave to cool.

Prepare the crêpes: Heat ½ tsp butter in a small skillet or crêpe pan about 8 in in diameter, tilting the pan so that it is evenly coated with melted butter. Pour about 2 tbsp crêpe batter into the skillet, tilting it again so that the batter covers the bottom in a thin film (the crêpes should be very thin). As soon as the batter has set, carefully invert the crêpe and cook the other side for 30 sec without browning too much. Lift the crêpe out of the skillet. Repeat the operation until all the crêpe batter is used up. When the crêpes are all cooked spread a little of the anchovy mixture in the center of each one and roll up. Arrange the crêpes side by side in a buttered ovenproof dish, dot with butter and place in a hot oven (325°F) for a few minutes to brown.

FRITTATA "IN ZOCCOLI"
(Smoked bacon omelet)

4 oz smoked bacon
6 tbsp olive oil
5 eggs
pinch of salt
freshly ground pepper
3 tbsp chopped parsley

This is a typically Tuscan dish. Dice the bacon and gently fry in a large skillet in 2–3 tbsp olive oil. As soon as the pieces start to brown but before they turn crisp, remove from the skillet and drain on kitchen paper. Heat the remaining oil in the same skillet; beat the eggs with a pinch of salt and some pepper and pour into the skillet. As soon as they begin to set, cover with the bacon and chopped parsley. Carefully fold the omelet over and slide on to a warmed serving plate. Serve immediately while still very hot.

UOVA ALLA FIORENTINA
(Eggs Florentine)

(serves 8)
for the pastry:
¼ cup butter
¾ cup all-purpose flour
pinch of salt
water

8 eggs
2 tbsp vinegar
1¾ cups cooked spinach
1 tbsp butter
2 tbsp milk
2 tbsp grated Parmesan cheese
salt

Melt 1 tbsp butter and mix with the flour, a pinch of salt and enough water to make a soft, malleable dough; knead well. Shape the pastry into a ball, cover with a clean teacloth and leave to rest for about ½ hr. Roll out the pastry thinly and use to line eight buttered custard cups. Put some dried beans into the bottom of each mold to prevent the pastry from rising, and place in an oven preheated to 375°F for about ¼ hr. Poach the eggs until lightly set in water acidulated with vinegar, then drain well. Discard the beans from the custard cups. Mix the well drained spinach with the butter, milk, a pinch of salt and the Parmesan cheese. Divide the spinach among the custard cups and place a poached egg in each one. Trim off any egg white overlapping the edges of the pastry and discard. Sprinkle with a little salt and some Parmesan cheese and return to the oven for a few minutes only to heat through. Remember that the eggs will continue to cook in the oven so do not allow to heat for too long.

FRITTATA CON LE ARSELLE
(Clam omelet)

14 oz clams
4 tbsp olive oil
4 eggs
pinch of salt
freshly ground pepper
3 tbsp chopped parsley

Wash the clams several times under cold running water. Place in a skillet with 2 tbsp oil; cover and cook over high heat until the shells open. Remove the clams from their shells and mix into the beaten eggs with a pinch of salt, a sprinkling of pepper and the chopped parsley. Heat 2 tbsp oil in a nonstick omelet pan or skillet, pour in the egg and clam mixture, cook the omelet on both sides and serve hot.

FRITTATA CON LE MELE
(Sweet apple omelet)

2 tbsp all-purpose flour
6 tbsp milk
pinch of salt
3 eggs
1 tbsp sugar
grated peel of 1 lemon
4 apples
⅛ cup butter
confectioners' sugar

Mix together the flour, milk and a pinch of salt. Beat the eggs and add to the mixture with the sugar and lemon peel. Peel and slice the apples and stir into the mixture. Whisk all the ingredients gently.

Melt the butter in a nonstick skillet about 8 in in diameter. Pour in the apple mixture, distributing the apple slices evenly over the pan. Cook over medium heat until the eggs begin to set and turn golden on the underside. Invert the omelet and cook on the other side, adding a little more butter if necessary. Transfer to a serving plate and sprinkle with confectioners' sugar.

OMELETTE AI TARTUFI
(Black truffle omelet)

2 small black truffles
3–4 tbsp oil
pinch of salt
2 tbsp chopped parsley
5 eggs
1 tbsp grated Parmesan cheese
¼ cup butter

Clean the truffles carefully with a small brush under running water. Pat dry and cut into slices. Heat the oil in a small saucepan, add the truffles, a pinch of salt and the parsley. Soften over low heat for 1–2 min. Beat the eggs in a bowl with a little salt and the grated Parmesan cheese. Heat the butter in a large skillet; pour the beaten eggs into it and when they begin to set, arrange the truffles in the center; fold over the omelet. Finish cooking over very low heat. This omelet is excellent served hot or cold.

UOVA IN TRIPPA ALLA ROMANA
(Omelet ribbons Roman style)

6 eggs
3 tbsp grated Parmesan cheese
salt
freshly ground pepper
2 tbsp oil
1 cup clove gravy (see p. 129)
2 tbsp grated Pecorino or Parmesan cheese
1 tbsp chopped mint

Beat the eggs in a bowl with 3 tbsp

grated Parmesan, a generous pinch of salt and a sprinkling of pepper. Coat a skillet with a little oil, and as soon as it is hot pour in one quarter of the mixture; lower the heat and brown the omelet on both sides. Set aside and keep warm. Cook three more omelets then cut them into strips and spread out a layer in an ovenproof pan. Heat the clove gravy. Cover the omelet "ribbons" with a little grated Pecorino or Parmesan cheese, pour over some of the hot sauce and sprinkle with a little chopped mint. Continue in this way until all the ingredients have been used up. Heat in the oven for about 10 min at 350°F.

FRITTATA CON LA RICOTTA
(Omelet with ricotta cheese)

for the sauce:
7 oz tomatoes
1 tbsp oil
1 small onion
salt
2 basil leaves

for the filling:
6 oz ricotta cheese
2 tbsp grated Parmesan cheese
salt
2 tbsp chopped parsley

for 4 omelets:
5 eggs
2 tbsp grated Parmesan cheese
salt
freshly ground pepper
2 tbsp lard or butter

Scald the tomatoes in boiling water for 30 sec then peel off their skins. Place the tomatoes in a small saucepan with the oil, the chopped onion, a pinch of salt and the basil, and cook over high heat for about ½ hr. In a bowl work together the ricotta with 1 tbsp Parmesan, a pinch of salt and the parsley to obtain a smooth, well blended mixture. In another bowl beat the eggs with the remaining Parmesan, a pinch of salt and some pepper. Melt one quarter of the lard (or butter) in a nonstick omelet pan or skillet. Pour one quarter of the egg mixture into the pan and when it begins to set and turn golden, place one quarter of the ricotta mixture on top; fold the omelet and cook for

just a few minutes more. Make three remaining omelets in the same way. Serve with the hot tomato sauce.

UOVA ALLA SARDA
(Sardinian-style eggs)

4 eggs
2 tbsp oil
2 tbsp vinegar
1 clove garlic
1 bunch parsley
1 tbsp fresh breadcrumbs
salt

Hard-boil the eggs. Run them under cold running water and shell. Cut in half lengthwise, then lay in a skillet in a single layer, yolks facing down. Sprinkle with a little salt, the oil and the vinegar. Cook over very low heat for a few minutes until the vinegar has evaporated. Lift the eggs from the pan with a spoon and arrange them on a serving dish, yolk side up. Return the skillet to the heat; add the garlic and the chopped parsley and let them soften. Finally, add the breadcrumbs and, stirring continuously, let them brown. Spread this mixture over the eggs and serve.

FRITTATA COI PISELLI
(Omelet with peas)

1 small onion
2 oz ham
1 small head fennel
¼ cup butter
2 cups fresh shelled peas
salt
freshly ground pepper
5 eggs
1 tbsp chopped parsley
2 tbsp oil

Finely chop the onion, dice the ham and slice the fennel. Melt the butter in a saucepan and lightly fry the onion, ham, fennel and peas for a few minutes. Season with salt and pepper, add a little boiling water (or meat stock) and simmer until the fennel is tender.
Lightly beat the eggs with a pinch of salt, then stir in the chopped parsley. Lift the vegetables and ham out of the saucepan, drain

and add to the beaten eggs; mix well.
Heat 2 tbsp oil in a large skillet. Pour in the egg mixture and cook until it begins to set and turn golden. Invert the omelet to cook the other side. Serve without folding over.

UOVA STRAPAZZATE AL POMODORO
(Scrambled eggs with tomatoes)

(serves 1)
2 tbsp butter
2 eggs
2 tbsp freshly made tomato sauce (see p. 127)
salt
freshly ground pepper
1 tbsp light cream

Melt 1 tbsp butter in a saucepan, and tilt the pan so that it is evenly coated. Do not let it brown. Break the eggs into a bowl, whisk with a fork and add the tomato sauce, salt and pepper. As soon as the butter is hot enough pour in the egg and tomato mixture; stir gently as the eggs thicken. Add 1 tbsp cream and 1 tbsp butter. When the mixture is setting but still soft and creamy, remove from the heat and serve.

UOVA AFFOGATE O IN CAMICIA
(Poached eggs)

(serves 1)
6 cups water
½ cup white wine vinegar
juice of 1 lemon
2 eggs

Bring the water to a boil with the vinegar and lemon juice in a large shallow saucepan. Break each egg in turn into a cup and, as the acidulated water starts gently simmering, lower the cup into the water, holding it by the handle, and gently slide the egg into the saucepan. Let the white set then lift the egg out very carefully with a slotted spoon. Drain on a teacloth and, using a small knife or a pastry cutter, trim the ragged edges.

Repeat the process with the other egg. Serve the poached eggs on a bed of lettuce.

UOVA SODE
(Hard-boiled eggs)

(serves 1)
2 eggs
olive oil
salt
freshly ground pepper

Carefully lower the eggs into a saucepan of boiling water using a spoon; the water must cover the eggs completely. Simmer gently for about 8 min. Remove the eggs and plunge them into cold water. This stops the cooking process, and makes them easier to shell. Slice the eggs and season with olive oil, salt and pepper.

UOVA AL BURRO
(Baked eggs)

(serves 1)
2 eggs
1 tbsp butter
salt
freshly ground pepper

Melt half the butter and pour into an ovenproof custard cup. Break the eggs into the custard cup, taking care not to break the yolks. Melt the remaining butter and pour over the eggs. Place the custard cup in the oven and bake at 350°F until set (about 5–8 min). Add salt and pepper, and serve at once.

UOVA CON CROSTINI E PATATE
(Scrambled eggs with croûtons and potatoes)

(serves 1)
1 slice white bread
1 large boiled potato
2 eggs
1 tbsp butter
salt
freshly ground pepper

Dice the slice of bread and the boiled potato and lightly fry in a skillet with a little butter. Beat the eggs in a bowl; add salt and pepper, and the diced fried bread and potato. Melt some butter in a skillet over low heat. Pour in the egg mixture and, stirring constantly, cook until the eggs are thick and creamy.

UOVA ALL'OSTRICA *
(Prairie oyster)

eggs
salt
freshly ground pepper
lemon juice

Separate one very fresh egg and place the yolk only into special porcelain or metal spoons, appropriately called the "prairie oyster" spoon. Season with a little salt, a generous sprinkling of pepper and a few drops of lemon juice. Set out the prairie oysters on a plate and garnish, if desired, with lemon slices and radicchio leaves. Prairie oyster is renowned in many countries as a cure for hangovers.

OMELETTE CON PEPERONI
(Omelet with sweet pepper)

(serves 1)
1 red or green sweet pepper
1 small onion
2 tbsp oil
2 eggs
salt
freshly ground pepper
1 tbsp butter

Scald the pepper in boiling water and remove the skin. Remove the seeds and cut into thin slices. Finely chop the onion. Put some oil into a saucepan and place over moderate heat; soften the onion without allowing it to brown. Add the sliced pepper, cover the saucepan and continue to cook slowly. Break the eggs into a bowl, season with salt and pepper and beat with a fork. Melt the butter in a nonstick omelet pan or skillet, tilting the pan so that it is evenly coated. Pour in the beaten eggs and turn up the heat. Shake the pan and when the eggs begin to set lower the heat.

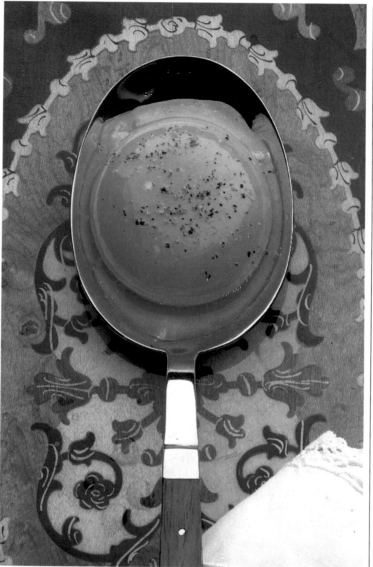

Using a spatula, lift the edges of the omelet from the sides of the pan; shake to detach the omelet from the base. Place two-thirds of the pepper and onion mixture over half the omelet and fold over. Slide on to a serving plate and decorate with the remaining pepper and onions.

UOVA FARCITE
(Stuffed eggs)

4 hard-boiled eggs
2 anchovy fillets
2 oz tuna in oil
½ tsp strong mustard
2 tbsp mayonnaise (see p. 126)
tomato slices
strips of red and green pepper

Hard-boil the eggs as directed on p. 220. Shell and cut in half lengthwise. Separate the yolks from the whites and rub the yolks through a sieve with the anchovy fillets and the tuna. (A blender or food processor will produce a smooth, even mixture.) Add the mustard and mayonnaise and mix well. Fill a pastry bag fitted with a star tube with the mixture and pipe a decorative rosette of the filling into each hollow egg white. Line a serving dish with lettuce leaves or other salad greens and grated carrot. Arrange the stuffed eggs in the center and garnish with tomato slices and pepper strips.

UOVA FRITTE ALLA FONTINA
(Fried eggs with Fontina cheese)

3 anchovy fillets
4 rounds white bread (about 2½ in in diameter)
¼ cup + 2 tbsp butter
4 slices Fontina cheese
4 eggs
¼ cup butter
salt
freshly ground pepper

This dish is typical of the Val d'Aosta. Mash the anchovy fillets. Fry the bread on one side only in 2 tbsp butter, then arrange the slices in an ovenproof pan. On each piece place a slice of Fontina cheese and some mashed anchovy (reserve some of the anchovy mixture); season with salt and pepper. Place in a moderate oven (350°F) until the cheese starts to melt. Meanwhile fry the eggs in ¼ cup butter, then lay them on the bread slices. Melt the rest of the butter with the remaining mashed anchovy and spoon over each egg. Serve immediately.

UOVA ALLA FONTINA
(Baked eggs with Fontina cheese)

1 tbsp butter
4 eggs
salt
freshly ground pepper
4 slices ham
4 slices Fontina cheese
2 tbsp dry white wine

Melt the butter in an ovenproof dish. Break the eggs on to a plate and slide very gently into the center of the dish. Season with salt and pepper; cover the yolks with a slice of ham and then with a slice of Fontina; baste with white wine. Bake in the oven at 400°F until the whites are firm, the cheese melted and the wine completely evaporated.

Vegetables and Salads

S uch is the profusion and diversity of vegetables produced in Italy, thanks to its geography and climate, that it deserves to be as famous for its vegetable dishes as for its pasta and pizza. Each region has its specialty: Tender zucchini and powerfully scented truffles from Piedmont; artichokes and broccoli from Latium; beans and turnips from Tuscany; eggplant and carrots from Apulia; wild fennel and saffron from Sicily; cabbage and potatoes from the Alto Adige; sun-drenched tomatoes from the Bay of Naples. Fresh local vegetables are married with the quintessentially Mediterranean flavor of fragant green olive oil.

ASPARAGI CON SALSA AL VINO BIANCO
(Asparagus in white wine sauce)

1¾ lb white or green asparagus
salt
4 egg yolks
8–10 tbsp dry white wine
butter

Wash and trim the asparagus and place in a small amount of cold, lightly salted water in a tall, narrow saucepan with a tightly fitting lid. Cook over high heat until the tips are tender; drain and keep warm. Place the egg yolks in a small heatproof bowl and beat together with the wine and salt. Heat gently over a saucepan of simmering water and continue to beat until the sauce is smooth. Add a piece of butter before removing from the heat. Place the hot asparagus on a heated serving dish and serve immediately, accompanied by the white wine sauce.

ASPARAGI ALLA LATTUGA
(Asparagus with lettuce sauce)

1¾ lb white asparagus
salt
butter
1 small onion, chopped
1 lettuce
scant ½ cup lean ham, diced
½ cup chicken stock
pepper
pinch of nutmeg
1½ cups light cream

Scrape the asparagus and trim the stalks to the same length. Wash well and tie into bundles. Place in a tall, narrow saucepan with cold, lightly salted water that comes two-thirds of the way up the stalks. Cover the saucepan and bring to a boil. Cook until the tips are tender, then untie the bundles and keep warm. Melt the butter in a saucepan and sauté the onion. Wash the lettuce and cut the leaves in half lengthwise. Add to the saucepan with the ham, pour over the stock and simmer for a few minutes. Season with salt, pepper and nutmeg. Remove from the heat and stir in the cream. Arrange the asparagus on a heated serving dish, pour over the hot sauce and serve immediately.

ASPARAGI IN TORTIERA
(Baked asparagus)

1¾ lb white asparagus
¾ lb green asparagus
salt
4 oz Fontina cheese
sliced white bread
4 oz prosciutto, chopped
freshly ground pepper
pinch of nutmeg
2 egg yolks
1 cup light cream
radicchio leaves

Clean the asparagus, trim the stalks to the same length and tie into bundles. Place in a small amount of salted water in a tall, narrow saucepan with a tightly fitting lid and steam until the tips are just tender. Slice half the Fontina and dice the rest. Butter a shallow baking pan, cover the bottom with a thin layer of bread and then a layer of sliced Fontina. Arrange the asparagus on top, alternating the white and green spears. Cover with the pieces of Fontina and prosciutto and season with salt, pepper and nutmeg. Beat the egg yolks in a bowl with the cream and pour over the asparagus. Place in a preheated oven (400°F) and bake for 20–30 min or until golden brown. Serve immediately, garnished with the radicchio.

ASPARAGI ALLA CREMA *
(Asparagus with cream sauce)

1¾ lb white asparagus
salt
2¼ cups light cream
freshly ground pepper
scant ½ cup grated Parmesan
    cheese
3 egg yolks
parsley

Wash the asparagus and peel the tough part of the stalks with a potato peeler. Tie into bundles and place upright in a tall saucepan with a small amount of salted water. Cook until the tips are tender; drain and keep warm. Bring the cream to a boil and remove from the heat. Season with salt and pepper, add the Parmesan and the egg yolks one by one, stirring in each one well. Place the hot asparagus on a heated serving dish, pour over the sauce and garnish with sprigs of parsley.

ASPARAGI ALLA PARMIGIANA
(Asparagus with Parmesan cheese)

1¾ lb white or green asparagus
salt
scant ½ cup butter
scant ½ cup grated Parmesan
    cheese
freshly ground pepper

Peel the tough part of the asparagus stalks with a potato peeler so that as much of the asparagus can be eaten as possible; wash well and tie into bundles. Place upright in a tall, narrow saucepan with a tightly fitting lid, with salted water to reach two-thirds of the way up the stalks. Cook over high heat until the tips are tender. Drain and arrange on a serving dish. Heat the butter in a saucepan until it browns. Sprinkle the asparagus with the Parmesan and pour over the melted butter. Season to taste with salt and pepper and serve immediately.

ASPARAGI ALL'OLIO E ACETO
(Asparagus with vinaigrette)

1¾ lb white or green asparagus
salt
½ cup olive oil
3 tbsp white wine vinegar
freshly ground pepper
sprigs of parsley

Wash the asparagus and peel the tough part of the stalks. Trim the stalks to the same length, tie into bundles and place in a tall, narrow saucepan with enough cold, salted water to come two-thirds of the way up the stalks. Cover the saucepan and cook over high heat until the tips are tender. Drain the

asparagus and allow to cool. Arrange on a serving dish and garnish with sprigs of parsley. Make the vinaigrette by mixing together the oil, vinegar, salt and pepper.

ASPARAGI IN SALSA TARTARA
(Asparagus with tartare sauce)

1¾ lb white or green asparagus
salt
1 egg yolk
3 hard-boiled egg yolks
1 tsp mustard
1 tbsp white wine vinegar
freshly ground pepper
generous 1 cup olive oil
1 tbsp capers, chopped
1 tbsp chopped parsley

Wash the asparagus and peel the stalks. Tie into bundles and stand upright in a tall, narrow saucepan with enough cold, salted water to reach two-thirds of the way up the stalks. Cover the saucepan but leave a gap for the steam to escape; the tips will thus be steamed while the tougher parts of the stalks will be boiled. Cook for 15–20 min, drain carefully and allow to cool. Meanwhile, prepare the sauce: Place all the egg yolks in a bowl and mix into a smooth paste. Stir in the mustard and vinegar and season with salt and a generous amount of pepper. Stirring continuously with a fork or a balloon whisk, pour in the oil drop by drop, as if making mayonnaise. When the sauce is the right consistency, stir in the capers and parsley; serve with the cold asparagus.

ASPARAGI CON LE UOVA
(Asparagus with fried eggs)

2¼ lb asparagus
salt
¼ cup grated Parmesan cheese
¼ cup butter
4 eggs

Choose only the tenderest asparagus. Wash them, then cook in a small amount of salted water for about 10 min, preferably in an asparagus steamer. Arrange around

225

the edge of a warm serving dish and sprinkle with the Parmesan. Melt the butter in a skillet and fry the eggs until the yolks just begin to set. Season with salt and place in the center of the serving dish.

BROCCOLI STRASCINATI
(Broccoli with anchovies)

2 lb broccoli
salt
2 salted anchovies
½ cup olive oil
freshly ground pepper

Rinse the broccoli, trim the stalks and divide into florets. Cook in boiling salted water until the stalks are barely tender. Rinse and dry the anchovies, then place in a large saucepan with the oil. Stir with a fork over gentle heat until they disintegrate. Drain the broccoli, add to the anchovies and toss well. Season with pepper. This dish is typical of Liguria, where it was traditionally served as a course in its own right. Nowadays it is usually served as an accompaniment to braised meat.

CAPONATA

1 tbsp seedless white raisins
1¼ lb eggplant
salt
olive oil
celery
1 onion
4 ripe tomatoes
2 tsp sugar
½ cup red wine vinegar
1 tbsp pine nuts
1 tbsp capers
2 cups pitted green olives

Soak the seedless white raisins in hot water for 20 min. Wash the eggplant. Without peeling, cut into cubes and place in a colander. Salt liberally and leave for about ½ hr to draw out the bitter juices. Rinse in cold water and pat dry on kitchen paper. Heat a generous amount of oil in a skillet, add the eggplant and stir-fry until golden brown. Remove with a slotted spoon and drain on kitchen paper. Using the whitest and most tender sticks of celery, cut into 1-in pieces, wash in

cold water, dry and fry in the oil used for the eggplant. When the celery is crisp and golden, remove and drain. Slice the onion. Skin the tomatoes, remove the seeds and chop. Pour off any excess oil, leaving 4–5 tbsp in the skillet, and add the onion and tomatoes. Cook for a few minutes, stirring frequently, and then stir in the sugar, vinegar, pine nuts, raisins, capers, olives, celery and eggplant. Cook over gentle heat for about ¼ hr. Transfer to a serving dish and leave to chill before serving. Red or green peppers, cooked in the same way as the celery, may also be added to this dish.

CARCIOFI AL TEGAME
(Stewed artichokes)

8 artichokes
1–2 cloves garlic, minced
few mint leaves, finely chopped
salt
freshly ground pepper
½ cup olive oil

Cut off the artichoke stalks, remove the tough, outer leaves and cut out and discard the central, hairy choke. Mix the garlic with the mint, season with salt and pepper and spoon a little into the center of each artichoke. Stand them in a flameproof casserole and pour over the oil and approximately twice the amount of water. Cover and cook over gentle heat for about 1 hr. Just before serving, increase the heat to reduce the cooking juices. This dish is excellent both hot and cold.

FRITTATA DI CARCIOFI
(Artichoke omelet)

4 large artichokes
juice of 1 lemon
½ cup olive oil
stock
5 eggs
salt
freshly ground pepper

This dish is typical of the countryside around Rome. Cut off the artichoke stalks and remove the tough, outer leaves. Cut in half

from top to bottom, discard the central, hairy choke, then cut into segments. Place in a bowl of water, adding the lemon juice to stop them turning black. Heat half the oil in a skillet and sauté the drained artichokes, adding a little stock if necessary. Break the eggs into a bowl, season with salt and pepper and beat with a fork. Remove the artichokes from the skillet with a slotted spoon and stir into the eggs. Heat the remaining oil in another skillet and cook the omelet over high heat. When the bottom is cooked but the top still soft, use a spatula to turn the omelet and cook the other side. It should be golden brown on both

sides. Serve immediately or leave until cold, if desired.

CARCIOFI IN FRICASSEA
(Artichoke fricassée)

6 young artichokes
juice of 1 lemon
¼ cup butter
1 tbsp chopped parsley
1 clove garlic, minced
salt
pepper
2 egg yolks
¼ cup grated Parmesan cheese

Rinse the artichokes, which must be very young and tender, cut off

CARCIOFI ALLA GIUDÍA
(Braised artichokes)

8 artichokes
juice of 1 lemon
generous 1 cup olive oil
salt
freshly ground pepper

The artichokes for this recipe must be very tender and young. Trim the stalks, leaving about 2 in, and scrape with a sharp knife. Starting at the bottom, cut off the inedible tip of each leaf. About a third from the top, cut straight across all the remaining leaves; the prepared artichokes will be lemon-shaped, with one blunt end and the stalk at the other. As soon as you have trimmed each artichoke place it in a bowl of water acidulated with the lemon juice to prevent it turning black. Heat the oil in a large flameproof casserole and put in the artichokes in a single layer, stalks downward. Season lightly, cover and cook over gentle heat for about 10 min. Turn the artichokes upside down, season with a little more salt and cook for 10 min more. When they are almost cooked, sprinkle with a few tablespoons of water, increase the heat and cook uncovered until the water has evaporated. Remove the artichokes from the saucepan with a slotted spoon and drain on kitchen paper. Serve while still hot.

FONDI DI CARCIOFO TRIFOLATI
(Artichoke hearts with garlic and parsley)

8 artichokes
juice of 1 lemon
½ cup olive oil
2 cloves garlic
2 tbsp all-purpose flour
salt
freshly ground pepper
2 tbsp chopped parsley

Prepare the artichokes by cutting off the stalk and discarding the tough, outer leaves; pull out the inner leaves and scrape away the hairy choke. Place the hearts in a bowl of water with the lemon juice until required. Heat the oil in a saucepan and fry the garlic. As

the stalks and remove any tough, outer leaves. Cut into segments and place in a bowl of water acidulated with the juice of half the lemon to stop them turning black. Melt the butter in a large saucepan and add the drained artichokes, together with the parsley and garlic. Pour over a ladleful of water and season to taste. Cover and cook over gentle heat until tender, adding more water as necessary. Beat the egg yolks with 1 tbsp water, the grated Parmesan, the remaining lemon juice and a pinch of salt. When the artichokes are tender, remove from the heat and pour over the egg mixture, stirring thoroughly. Serve at once.

CARCIOFI ALLA ROMANA
(Stuffed artichokes Roman style)

8 artichokes
lemon slices
fresh mint, chopped
1 glove garlic, minced
1 cup fresh breadcrumbs
generous 1 cup olive oil
salt
freshly ground pepper

Remove the outer leaves of the artichokes. Cut out the central, hairy choke and trim the hard, inedible tips of the remaining leaves. Using a sharp knife scrape and trim the stalks, leaving about 2 in. Rub all the cut surfaces of the artichokes with slices of lemon to stop them turning black. Mix together the mint, garlic and breadcrumbs, bind with a little olive oil and season. Stuff the center of the artichoke hearts with this mixture, closing the inner leaves over the stuffing. Place the artichokes side by side in an ovenproof casserole with the stalks uppermost, pour in a ladleful of water, cover with a sheet of oiled wax paper and then the lid. Cook in a hot oven (400°F) for about 1 hr. Serve hot as an accompanying vegetable, arranging the artichokes in a heated serving dish, or cold as an appetizer.

soon as the cloves begin to color, remove and discard. Coat the artichoke hearts in flour and sauté in the flavored oil; add a little water or stock, cover and braise gently until tender. Salt will make the artichoke hearts turn black, so season at the end of the cooking time. Transfer to a warm serving dish, pour over the cooking juices and sprinkle with the chopped parsley.

TORTINO DI CARCIOFI
(Baked creamy artichokes)

4 very young artichokes
juice of 1 lemon
½ cup oil
2 tbsp all-purpose flour
salt
4 eggs
2–3 tbsp milk
freshly ground pepper

Remove the tough leaves at the base of the artichokes, trim the tips of the remaining leaves and then slice the artichokes thinly; place in a bowl of water acidulated with the lemon juice to prevent them from turning black. Heat half the oil in a fairly large saucepan. Dry the artichokes on kitchen paper, coat in flour and fry in the hot oil, over very low heat, turning frequently. If they are in danger of sticking, pour in a ladleful of water. After about ¼ hr, remove from the heat, season with salt and transfer to a shallow ovenproof pan or casserole dish. Beat together the eggs and milk and season with salt and a generous amount of pepper. Pour the remaining oil over the artichokes, followed by the egg mixture and place in a preheated oven (350°F) for about 20 min. Serve hot from the dish.

CARDI ALLA PARMIGIANA
(Cardoons with Parmesan cheese)

1 small cardoon
juice of 1 lemon
½ cup butter, melted
scant ½ cup grated Parmesan
    cheese

Wash the cardoon thoroughly, discard the outer, prickly stems; remove the strings from the inner stalks and cut into pieces about 4 in long. Place the prepared cardoon pieces in a bowl of water, acidulated with the lemon juice, straight away to prevent discoloration. Cook in boiling salted water for about 30–40 min then drain. Butter an ovenproof pan and cover the bottom with a layer of cardoon pieces. Pour over a little melted butter and sprinkle with some Parmesan cheese. Continue to layer the cardoon pieces, butter and cheese until they have all been used up. Cook in a preheated oven (350°F) for 20–30 min until lightly browned. Serve hot sprinkled with extra Parmesan cheese if desired.

CAROTE ALL' ACCIUGA
(Carrot salad with anchovy dressing)

4 carrots
lettuce leaves
2 salted anchovies
1 onion slice
2 tbsp olive oil
1 tbsp white wine vinegar
freshly ground pepper

Scrape the carrots; rinse, dry and grate them into a salad bowl lined with lettuce leaves. Rinse and bone the anchovies. Chop finely with the onion slice and then sieve into a small bowl. Add the oil and vinegar, season with pepper, mix well and pour over the grated carrots just before serving.

CAROTE AL MARSALA ✳
(Carrots with Marsala)

14 oz carrots
¼ cup butter
6 tbsp dry Marsala
salt
freshly ground pepper

This is a typical Sicilian dish. Scrape the carrots, rinse, dry and cut into thin, even rounds. Melt the butter in a saucepan and when foaming add the carrots. Cook for a few minutes over high heat, then pour over the Marsala and season with salt; cover the pan and cook over gentle heat until the carrots are tender and most of the liquid has evaporated. Season with pepper just before serving.

CAVOLFIORE E FINOCCHI ALLA PANNA
(Cauliflower and fennel with cream)

1 cauliflower, weighing about 1¾ lb
2 heads fennel
1 onion
generous ¼ cup butter
generous 1 cup heavy cream
salt
freshly ground pepper
½ cup grated Parmesan cheese

Remove the leaves and stalk of the cauliflower and cut into florets. Wash and add to a saucepan of boiling salted water. Cook until barely tender, then drain. Remove the tough, outer leaves of the fennel, cut into segments and wash. Cook the fennel in a saucepan of boiling salted water until tender but still crisp, then drain. Finely chop the onion. In a large skillet fry the onion gently in the butter until golden, add the fennel and cauliflower and cook for a few minutes. Transfer the vegetables to an ovenproof pan and season with salt and pepper. Sprinkle with the Parmesan, dot with butter and pour over the cream. Bake in a preheated oven (350°F) for about ¼ hr until golden brown.

CIPOLLE AL FORNO
(Baked onions in oil and vinegar)

4 white onions
½ cup olive oil
2 tbsp vinegar
salt
freshly ground pepper

Peel the onions and parboil them whole for a few minutes to keep them white. Plunge in cold water, drain and then bake in a preheated oven (350°F) for about 1 hr. Leave until cold. Remove the outermost layer of skin and cut the onions into slices. Arrange in a serving dish, dress with the oil and vinegar, and season with salt and pepper. This vegetable dish is a good accompaniment to boiled meats.

CRAUTI AL VINO BIANCO
(Sauerkraut in white wine)

1¾ lb sauerkraut
1 onion
1 cooking apple
2 tbsp olive oil
salt
2¼ cups dry white wine
few juniper berries

Rinse the sauerkraut thoroughly in cold water, drain and squeeze dry. Chop the onion. Peel, core and thinly slice the apple. Heat the oil in a large saucepan, add the onion and apple and fry gently for a few minutes. Add the sauerkraut, season with salt and pour in the white wine. Bring to a boil, reduce the heat, cover the saucepan and cook for about 1 hr. Stir in the juniper berries and serve in a heated serving dish. In Italy this dish would be eaten with cotechino (a spicy pork sausage), zampone (stuffed pig's trotter) or roast pork.

FAGIOLI FRESCHI AL TONNO
(Beans with tuna)

1 cup dried cannellini beans
5–6 tbsp olive oil
1 clove garlic
4–5 large ripe tomatoes, skinned
    and chopped
salt
10 oz tinned tuna, drained and
    flaked
2–3 tbsp chopped basil
freshly ground pepper

Soak the beans overnight. Drain, and boil in plenty of water for about 1½ hr until tender. Drain. Heat the oil in a skillet and sauté the garlic. As soon as it begins to brown remove it and add the tomatoes. Season lightly with salt and cook over high heat for 10 min. Add the beans and the tuna, sprinkle over the chopped basil and season generously with pepper. Simmer for 10 min and serve hot.

FAGIOLI ALL'UCCELLETTO
(Beans in tomato sauce)

1 cup dried large white beans
few sage leaves
4 tbsp olive oil
salt
freshly ground pepper
2 tbsp tomato paste or 2 ripe,
    skinned tomatoes

Soak the beans overnight. Drain, and boil in plenty of water for about 1½ hr until tender. Drain. Wash and dry the sage and sauté the leaves in the oil for a few minutes. Add the beans and season with salt and pepper. Cook for a few minutes and then add the tomato paste diluted with a ladleful of hot water (alternatively add two sieved tomatoes). Simmer until the beans have absorbed some of the sauce. Serve the dish on its own or as an accompaniment to braised meat.

FAGIOLINI IN PADELLA
(French beans with tomatoes)

1 lb French beans
14 oz ripe tomatoes
1 tbsp butter
3 tbsp oil
1 onion, finely chopped
salt
freshly ground pepper
2 tbsp finely chopped parsley

Top and tail the beans, rinse well and keep in cold water until required. Skin the tomatoes, remove the seeds and chop coarsely. Heat the butter and the oil in a large saucepan. Fry the onion until golden, stir in the tomatoes and bring to a boil over gentle heat. Add the beans and season with salt and pepper; cover the saucepan and simmer for ½ hr or until the beans are tender and the sauce has reduced. Sprinkle with parsley and serve immediately.

FAGIOLI CON LE COTICHE *
(Beans with pork rind)

14 oz dried Navy beans
4 oz pork rind
2 oz pork fat
1 clove garlic
1 sprig parsley
1 tbsp lard
1 onion, thinly sliced
1–2 tbsp tomato paste
salt
freshly ground pepper

Wash the beans and soak overnight in cold water. Drain. Boil in plenty of unsalted water for 1½ hr and then keep warm in the cooking water. Scrape the pork rind and place in a saucepan of cold water. Bring to a boil, cook for a few minutes, drain and rinse in cold water. When the rind is quite clean cut into fairly large pieces and place in a saucepan with fresh cold water. Bring to a boil then simmer, covered, until cooked. Meanwhile, chop the pork fat, garlic and parsley and place in a large saucepan with the lard and onion. Sauté until the onion is transparent, then add the tomato paste diluted with a little water. Season with salt and pepper and cook for about ½ hr. Drain the beans and the pork rind and stir into the sauce. Simmer very gently for another ½ hr.

FUNGHI IMPANATI
(Fried mushrooms)

8 mushroom caps, preferably porcini (cèpes)
½ lemon
1 egg
salt
1–2 tbsp all-purpose flour
2 tbsp fine dried breadcrumbs
½ cup butter

Wipe the mushroom caps with a damp cloth and rub them with lemon. If they are very large slice in half horizontally. Beat the egg with a pinch of salt. Coat the mushrooms in the flour, dip in the egg and then in breadcrumbs. Heat the butter in a skillet, add the mushrooms when it is hot and fry for 10–15 min, turning them half-way through the cooking time.

FUNGHI TRIPPATI
(Sautéed mushrooms)

1 lb mushrooms
1 tbsp oil
3 tbsp butter
2 cloves garlic
salt
freshly ground pepper
2 tbsp grated Parmesan cheese

Clean the mushrooms, wash and dry them and slice thinly. Heat the oil and butter in a skillet. Peel and mince the garlic cloves and sauté until they begin to color. Remove from the skillet and add the mushrooms. Sauté for a few minutes, stirring with a wooden spoon; season with salt and pepper and add the Parmesan. Cook for a further 10–15 min.

FUNGHI TRIFOLATI
(Mushroms with garlic and parsley)

1 lb porcini (cèpes)
1 tbsp butter
2 tbsp olive oil
1 large clove garlic
1 tbsp chopped parsley
salt
freshly ground pepper

Clean the mushrooms and rub with a cloth; rinse them, dry in a tea-cloth and slice thinly. Heat the butter and the oil in a saucepan. Add the mushrooms, garlic and parsley and season to taste with salt and pepper. Cover and cook over low heat for 20–30 min, stirring occasionally. Before serving, remove the lid and reduce the cooking juices over high heat. This dish is an excellent accompaniment to steak, poultry and roasts.

FUNGHI PORCINI AL TEGAME
(Mushrooms with anchovies and mint)

1¼ lb porcini (cèpes)
2 anchovies
2–3 tbsp olive oil
4 ripe tomatoes
1 clove garlic
1–2 mint leaves

salt
freshly ground pepper
triangles of fried bread

Clean the mushrooms, cut into thick slices and rinse and dry them. Wash the anchovies and remove the bones. Heat the oil in a saucepan and cook the anchovies until they dissolve. Skin and chop the tomatoes and remove the seeds. Add to the saucepan with the mushrooms, garlic and mint. Season with salt and pepper, cover and cook over high heat, stirring occasionally, for ¼ hr. Discard the garlic clove, transfer the mushrooms to a serving dish and surround with triangles of fried bread.

FUNGHI ALL'OLIO E LIMONE
(Mushroom salad with olive oil and lemon)

1 lb mushrooms
juice of 1 lemon
4 tbsp olive oil
salt
freshly ground pepper
1 clove garlic, minced
¼ cup coarsely grated Parmesan
    cheese

Scrape the mushrooms, wipe with a cloth and sprinkle with lemon juice. Without removing the stalks, cut the mushrooms into very thin slices and place in a serving dish. Dress with the oil, season with salt, pepper and the minced garlic, and sprinkle with Parmesan cheese. This mushroom salad is excellent as an accompaniment to a variety of cold dishes.

CHAMPIGNONS CON ROGNONE
(Stuffed mushrooms)

8 large mushroom caps
½ veal kidney
vinegar
4 tbsp olive oil
1 clove garlic
1 bunch basil leaves
1 bunch parsley
salt
freshly ground pepper
¼ cup butter
1 cup dry white wine

Choose eight large flat mushrooms that are roughly the same size. Remove the stalks, clean them and set aside. Peel the caps. Remove the membrane and fat covering the kidney and cut away the central core. Cut into eight slices, rinse thoroughly under cold running water and then dip in water acidulated with vinegar. Pat dry. Heat the oil in a small skillet and sauté the kidney slices with the whole clove of garlic. Remove from the skillet and discard the garlic. Place a kidney slice in each mushroom cap. Finely chop the mushroom stalks, basil and parsley, and mix well, reserving 1 tbsp parsley. Season the mixture with salt and pepper and divide between the mushroom caps. Place in an oven-proof pan, dot with butter and cook in a preheated oven (400°F) for about ¼ hr. Pour over the wine, dot with a little more butter if necessary and continue cooking for ¼ hr. Serve sprinkled with the remaining parsley.

FUNGHI AL PREZZEMOLO
(Mushrooms with parsley and white wine)

14 oz mushrooms
1 lemon
2 tbsp chopped onion
1 clove garlic
4 tbsp olive oil
freshly ground pepper
1 cup dry white wine
salt
1 tbsp chopped parsley
1 tbsp grated Parmesan cheese

Scrape the mushrooms to remove the soil. Do not wash unless essential; wipe with a cloth and rub with a cut lemon. Heat the oil in a large skillet and fry the onion and garlic until they begin to brown. Roughly chop the mushrooms and add to the skillet. Cook over high heat until the moisture evaporates, then season with pepper. Pour over the wine. Cook until the wine has evaporated and then cover and simmer gently for 5–10 min. Add salt to taste, transfer to a warm serving dish and sprinkle with the chopped parsley and the Parmesan cheese.

231

FUNGHI PORCINI ALLA GRIGLIA *
(Broiled garlic mushrooms with parsley butter)

8 mushroom caps, preferably
   porcini (cèpes)
lemon slices
½ cup olive oil
1 clove garlic, minced
1 lemon
pinch of salt
freshly ground pepper
1 tbsp chopped parsley
1 tbsp butter, softened

Scrape the mushrooms, wipe with a cloth and rub with slices of lemon. Mix the oil, garlic and lemon, cut into wedges, season with salt and pepper and add the mushrooms. Marinate for ¼ hr. Stir the parsley into the softened butter and season with a pinch of salt. Drain the mushrooms. Turn the broiler on full. When it is hot, broil the mushrooms, until they have browned, then turn the heat down. As soon as they are done, transfer to a serving dish and pour over the marinade. Garnish with pieces of parsley butter.

PASTICCIO DI FUNGHI
(Mushroom pudding)

2¼ lb mushrooms
½ cup olive oil
scant ½ cup butter
1 clove garlic
freshly ground pepper
3 eggs
½ cup grated Parmesan cheese
1 tbsp chopped parsley
½ loaf sliced bread
2 ladlefuls chicken stock

Clean the mushrooms, preferably without washing them first as this can impair their very delicate flavor: Scrape and rub with a cloth. Slice and add to a saucepan with the oil, butter and garlic and sauté over high heat for 10 min. Season with pepper. Beat the eggs in a bowl with the Parmesan and parsley and add the cooked mushrooms. Line a round-bottom, oven-proof bowl with slices of buttered bread. Pour in half the egg mixture, cover with slices of bread and repeat with the remaining egg mixture and bread – the bowl should be two-thirds full. Carefully pour over the stock and leave to stand for ½ hr before cooking in a preheated oven (400°F) for ¼ hr. Leave to stand for a few minutes before unmolding on to a serving dish. Serve sprinkled with a little extra grated Parmesan cheese.

ped bacon and onion. Fry gently, stirring until the onion becomes transparent. Drain the lentils, add to the saucepan and sprinkle with salt. Add enough water to cover. Cover and simmer for about 1 hr, by which time the lentils should have absorbed all the water. If necessary add a little boiling water. This dish is excellent served with spicy pork sausages, stuffed pig's trotter, or freshly made polenta.

INSALATA DI SEDANI
(Celery and truffle salad)

1 large head celery
1 white truffle
1 cup mayonnaise (see p. 126)

Discard the tough, outer sticks of celery, wash the inner ones and cut into even-sized pieces or thin strips. Slice the truffle thinly, place in a salad bowl with the celery and fold in the mayonnaise. Chill before serving.

INSALATA CON TARTUFI
(Truffle salad)

1 head lettuce
1 large stick celery
olive oil
salt
freshly ground pepper
juice of ½ lemon
1 white truffle
½ cup light cream

Wash the lettuce, removing the outer leaves. Dry and shred the inner leaves. Remove the stringy filaments from the celery and cut into strips. Mix together the oil, salt, pepper and lemon juice and toss the lettuce and celery in the dressing. Slice the truffle thinly and add to the salad. Stir in the cream and serve.

INSALATA IN PINZIMONIO
(Crudités with vinaigrette dip)

2 heads celery
1 head fennel
1 yellow pepper
2 lettuce hearts
1 carrot

1 bunch radishes
10 tbsp olive oil
2 tbsp wine vinegar
salt
freshly ground pepper

Divide the celery into sticks. Remove the outer leaves of the fennel and cut into quarters. Remove the seeds and membrane inside the pepper and cut into strips. Cut off the base of the lettuce and separate the leaves. Scrape the carrot and cut into strips. Make a cross in the base of each radish and leave a few of the tenderest leaves attached. Wash all the prepared vegetables. Make the vinaigrette by mixing together the oil, vinegar, salt and pepper. Stir vigorously to emulsify. Guests help themselves to the vegetables and dip them into the dressing, so either serve the crudités on special individual plates that have a hollow for the vinaigrette, or arrange on large plates, with the vinaigrette in small bowls within reach of each guest.

INSALATA DI LATTUGHELLA
(Lamb's lettuce salad)

8 oz lamb's lettuce
1 clove garlic
1 anchovy
1 tbsp vinegar
juice of 1 lemon
freshly ground pepper
salt
3 tbsp olive oil

Discard any wilted or damaged leaves; wash the lamb's lettuce and dry in a teacloth. Chop the garlic and anchovy finely, stir in the vinegar and lemon juice and season with pepper and a little salt. Pour this dressing over the salad, sprinkle over the olive oil and toss gently.

INSALATA DI FONTINA
(Fontina, pepper and olive salad)

6 yellow peppers
10 oz Fontina cheese
2 oz green olives, pitted

Remove the outer leaves of the endives and rinse under running water. Without drying them, place in a large skillet together with the garlic, oil and herbs. Season with salt and pepper, cover and simmer gently until soft and tender. Remove the garlic and herbs before serving. This dish may be served as a separate course or as an accompaniment to a variety of roasted meats.

LENTICCHIE IN UMIDO
(Stewed lentils)

1½ cups continental lentils
5 tbsp olive oil
¼ cup bacon
1 small onion
salt

Soak the lentils in plenty of water overnight. Heat the oil in a heavy saucepan and add the finely chop-

INDIVIE INTERE "A CRUDO"
(Braised Belgian endives)

4 heads Belgian endive
1 clove garlic, minced
4–5 tbsp olive oil
few mint or basil leaves
salt
freshly ground pepper

4–5 tbsp olive oil
salt
freshly ground pepper
1 tsp mustard
2 tbsp light cream

This dish is typical of the Val d'Aosta. Broil the peppers until the skin is charred. Peel and rinse the peppers, remove the stalk and seeds, then cut into strips. Cut the Fontina into strips. Put the peppers, cheese and olives in a salad bowl. Mix together the oil, salt, pepper, mustard and cream and pour over the salad. Toss well and chill for 2 hr before serving.

INSALATA SICILIANA
(Sicilian salad)

8 large, firm tomatoes
½ cup mushrooms preserved in oil
½ cup pickled vegetables
10 olives, pitted
1 tbsp capers
½ cup peas, cooked
½ cup French beans, cooked
3 tbsp mayonnaise (see p.126)
salt
freshly ground pepper

Wash the tomatoes and slice off the tops. Remove the seeds with a teaspoon, salt the insides and leave upside down on a plate to drain. Mix the remaining ingredients together and fill the tomatoes with the mixture. Pile any remaining mixture in the center of a serving dish and surround with the stuffed tomatoes.

INSALATA MISTA *
(Mixed salad)

1 head lettuce
3 oz chicory
1 lb tomatoes
1 yellow pepper
½ cucumber
1 bunch radishes
1 onion
1 tbsp capers
1 anchovy fillet
1 clove garlic, minced
2 tbsp olive oil
few drops wine vinegar
salt
freshly ground pepper

Remove any brown or wilted leaves from the lettuce and chicory, cut off the base, wash the leaves in plenty of water and dry in a teacloth. Tear the large leaves into small pieces. Wash the tomatoes, pepper, cucumber and radishes. Cut the tomatoes into wedges. Discard the seeds and membrane inside the pepper and cut into strips. Finely slice the cucumber and radishes. Peel the onion and slice very thinly. Put all the ingredients in a salad bowl. Chop the capers and anchovy very finely and mix with the garlic. Add the oil, vinegar, salt and pepper and stir vigorously. Serve the dressing separately.

MELANZANE AL FORNO
(Baked eggplant stuffed with anchovies, olives and capers)

4 large, eggplant
salt
olive oil
4 salted anchovies
½ cup black olives
2 cloves garlic
1 sprig parsley
2 tbsp fresh white breadcrumbs
¼ cup capers
oregano
2 ripe tomatoes

Wash the eggplant, slice in half lengthwise and cut out the flesh, leaving about ¼ in inside the skin.

Salt the eggplant cases and leave upside down on a plate for 1hr to draw out the bitter juices. Meanwhile, heat plenty of oil in a skillet and sauté the diced eggplant flesh until crisp. Drain on kitchen paper and season with salt. Wash the anchovies to remove the salt, bone them and chop very finely. Pit the olives and chop with the garlic and parsley. Place in a small bowl with the anchovies, breadcrumbs, capers, and pinch of oregano and mix well. Rinse and dry the eggplant cases and place side by side in an ovenproof dish. Divide the filling between the cases. Slice the tomatoes and arrange on top of the stuffed eggplant, sprinkle with salt

skillet. Season with salt, pepper and sugar. Chop the parsley and basil. Rinse and dry the diced eggplant and add to the tomatoes with the herbs. Reduce over high heat for about ¼ hr then stir in the breadcrumbs. Rinse and dry the eggplant cases and fill with the tomato mixture. Stand the stuffed eggplant upright in a flameproof casserole and cover with the reserved tops. Skin and sieve the remaining tomatoes, dilute with a ladleful of water and pour over the eggplant. Season with salt and pepper, and pour over the remaining oil. Cover and simmer for about ¾ hr. Check occasionally that the eggplant are not sticking to the bottom of the casserole. Serve hot or cold.

MELANZANE ALLA CAMPAGNOLA
(Cold barbecued eggplant)

4 large eggplant
salt
2 cloves garlic
1 sprig parsley
few mint leaves
3–4 basil leaves
freshly ground pepper
½ cup olive oil

Wash the eggplant and cut lengthwise into ½-in slices. Sprinkle with salt and leave on a plate covered with a heavy lid for about 1 hr to draw out the bitter juices. Rinse well, dry and place the slices on the barbecue grid. Cook until golden brown, turning once, and arrange on a serving dish. Finely chop the garlic and herbs and sprinkle them over the eggplant. Season with a little salt and plenty of pepper and slowly pour over the oil. Leave to cool. To enjoy this dish at its best, leave for at least 7–8 hr before serving.

PARMIGIANA DI MELANZANE
(Eggplant bake)

2¼ lb eggplant
salt
olive oil
1¼ lb ripe tomatoes
3 tbsp oil

1 bunch basil
salt
freshly ground pepper
½ cup grated Parmesan cheese
6 oz Mozzarella cheese, sliced
1 egg, beaten or hard-boiled
  (optional)

Slice the eggplant lengthwise, sprinkle with salt and leave on a plate for about 1 hr to draw out the bitter juices. Rinse and dry thoroughly. Fry the slices a few at a time in plenty of hot oil. Drain on kitchen paper. Meanwhile, make the sauce. Skin the tomatoes and remove the seeds. Heat the oil in a saucepan, add the tomatoes and basil and season with salt and pepper. Cook over high heat for about 20 min until the sauce is reduced. Place a layer of eggplant slices in an ovenproof pan and sprinkle with Parmesan; cover with a few slices of Mozzarella, followed by a few spoonfuls of the tomato sauce and some beaten egg (or, if preferred, a few slices of hard-boiled egg). Continue layering in this way until all the ingredients are used up. Cook in a preheated oven (350°F) for 40 min. Serve hot or cold.

MELANZANE TRIFOLATE "A FUNGITELLI"
(Eggplant with tomatoes and capers)

1 lb eggplant
salt
½ cup olive oil
2 ripe tomatoes
1 tbsp capers
1 sprig parsley
1 clove garlic

Wash and dice the eggplant, sprinkle with salt and leave for about 1 hr to draw out the bitter juices. Put into a sieve, rinse and dry. Heat the oil in a large skillet and sauté the eggplant; salt to taste. Sieve the tomatoes and add to the skillet with the drained capers. Simmer, stirring, until the sauce begins to thicken (about 10 min). Chop the parsley and garlic very finely, add to the skillet and cook for a further 1–2 min. This dish is delicious served with steak or braised meat and is also excellent cold.

and then slowly pour over plenty of oil. Cook in a preheated oven (325°F) for 1 hr. This dish is delicious served hot or cold.

MELANZANE RIPIENE
(Eggplant stuffed with tomato and basil)

4 round eggplant
salt
½ cup olive oil
1 clove garlic
1 lb ripe tomatoes
freshly ground pepper
½ tsp sugar
1 sprig parsley

few basil leaves
2 tbsp breadcrumbs

This dish is typical of Apulia. Wash the eggplant, remove the stalk, cut off the tops about ¾ in thick, and set aside. Scoop out the flesh, leaving about ¼ in inside the skin. Sprinkle with salt inside, turn upside down on a plate and leave for 1 hr to draw out the bitter juices. Dice the scooped out flesh and put in a colander, sprinkle with salt and leave to drain. Heat half the oil in a large skillet. Add the garlic, then discard as soon as it begins to brown. Skin half the tomatoes and remove the seeds; chop the flesh and add to the

TIMBALLO DI MELANZANE *
(Baked eggplant with cheese and prosciutto)

3 long eggplant
salt
2 tbsp all-purpose flour
olive oil
8 oz Scamorza or Mozzarella cheese
4 oz prosciutto
¼ cup butter

Slice the eggplant, sprinkle with a little salt and leave in a colander for 1 hr to draw out the bitter juices. Dry the slices, dip in the flour and fry in plenty of oil. Drain and dry on kitchen paper. Slice the cheese and cut the prosciutto into strips. Put a layer of eggplant in a buttered ovenproof pan, with a few strips of prosciutto; dot with butter and cover with a layer of cheese. Continue layering, ending with a layer of eggplant. Melt the remaining butter, pour over the top and cook in a preheated oven (325°F) for about ½ hr, until the eggplant are golden brown.

PATATE FARCITE
(Stuffed potatoes)

8 large potatoes
½ cup butter
1 cup light cream
salt
freshly ground pepper
pinch of ground nutmeg
1 egg yolk, beaten

Scrub the potatoes. Steam in a large covered saucepan with a small amount of salted water until tender. Peel carefully, then trim the bottom of each potato to provide a firm base; cut off the top to form a lid. Gently scoop out two-thirds of the insides with a teaspoon. Place the potato shells in a buttered ovenproof pan. In a small bowl mash the scooped out potato with the cream, salt, pepper and nutmeg to make a smooth purée. Using a decorating bag with a large tube, fill the potato shells with the purée and brush with the egg. Place in a preheated hot oven (400°F) for ¼ hr or until the potatoes are crisp and golden brown. Serve hot with a roast.

PATATE AL SALE PROFUMATO
(Potatoes with sage and rosemary)

1½ lb potatoes
3–4 tbsp olive oil
¼ cup butter
5–6 fresh sage leaves
1 sprig fresh rosemary
1 sprig parsley
1 tsp salt
freshly ground pepper
1 clove garlic, minced

Peel, rinse and dice the potatoes. Dry in a teacloth and sauté in a flameproof casserole with the oil and butter. When they are golden brown, transfer to a moderate oven (350°F) for 20 min or until tender. Finely chop the sage, rosemary and parsley. Mix with the salt, pepper and minced garlic. Toss the hot potatoes in this mixture and serve as a vegetable accompaniment.

PATATE AL LATTE
(Potatoes cooked in milk)

1¾ lb potatoes
salt
¼ cup butter
2 cups milk
1 cup light cream
1 tsp cornstarch
freshly ground pepper
1 tbsp chopped parsley

Scrub but do not peel the potatoes. Place in a small amount of salted water; cover with a piece of wax paper and then the lid, and steam for ¼ hr or until barely tender. Peel them, leave until cold and then dice. Melt the butter over moderate heat and add the potatoes. When they begin to brown pour in the milk and cream. Simmer for 10 min. If necessary, thicken the sauce by adding the cornstarch blended with a little water and cook for a further 5 min. Season with salt and pepper, transfer to a serving dish and sprinkle with the parsley.

PATATE FRITTE
(Potato chips)

2½ lb potatoes
oil for deep frying
salt

Peel and rinse the potatoes. Cut some into strips approximately ½ in thick and then into wafer-thin slices using a mandoline cutter or food processor. Cut the remaining potatoes into julienne strips, dice, and other decorative shapes. Place in cold water until you are ready to fry them. Dry in a teacloth and

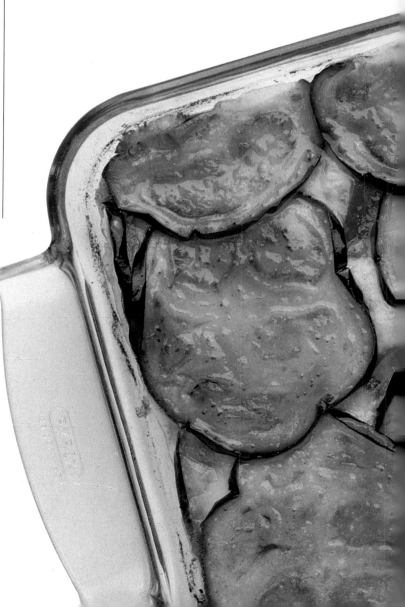

deep fry in small batches in the following way: Lower the basket into the hot oil for a minute or so, lift it out to drain the chips then turn up the heat so that the oil returns to a boil; plunge the basket in the oil for a few seconds, remove and drain the crisp, golden potato shapes on kitchen paper. Sprinkle with salt and serve with fried meat or fish.

PATATE AL POMODORO
(Potatoes in tomato sauce)

2½ lb potatoes
¼ cup butter
4 tbsp olive oil
1 medium onion
12 oz canned tomatoes
salt
freshly ground pepper
pinch of saffron threads

Peel and rinse the potatoes, cut into even-sized pieces and dry in a teacloth. Heat the butter and oil in a large skillet and sauté the chopped onion until transparent. Add the potatoes and fry until they begin to color, then add the tomatoes. Season with salt and pepper and stir in the saffron, soaked in a little water. Cover and simmer for ½ hr, or until the potatoes are tender, adding a little hot water if the sauce becomes too thick. Adjust the seasoning and transfer to a heated serving dish.

CROCCHETTE DI PATATE
(Deep-fried potato croquettes)

1¾ lb potatoes
salt
¼ cup butter or lard
3–4 tbsp grated Parmesan cheese
1 tbsp chopped parsley
pepper
3 eggs
all-purpose flour
fine dried breadcrumbs
oil for frying

Boil the potatoes in salted water until tender; peel and mash while still hot. Melt the butter or lard and stir into the potatoes with the Parmesan, parsley, salt and pepper, and one whole egg yolk. Beat two egg whites until stiff and mix with the remaining yolk. Shape the potato purée into croquettes; dip in flour, then in the egg mixture and finally in breadcrumbs. Fry a few at a time in plenty of very hot oil until the breadcrumbs form a crisp coating and turn golden brown. Drain on kitchen paper and serve hot.

CROCCHETTINI DI PATATE
(Potato, cheese and salami croquettes)

1¾ lb potatoes
salt
4 oz cup Scamorza or Mozzarella cheese, diced
5 eggs, beaten
3 oz salami, chopped
3–4 tbsp grated Parmesan cheese
1 tbsp chopped parsley
freshly ground pepper
fine dried breadcrumbs
oil for frying
lemon wedges

Boil the potatoes in salted water until tender; peel and mash while still hot. Stir in the Scamorza or Mozzarella, three beaten eggs, the salami, Parmesan and parsley. Season with salt and pepper and mix well. Shape the mixture into small croquettes and dip in the remaining beaten egg and then in the breadcrumbs. Heat plenty of oil in a skillet and deep fry the croquettes a few at a time. Once golden brown, remove with a slotted spoon; drain on kitchen paper. Arrange on a heated serving dish; serve at once, garnished with the lemon wedges.

TORTINO DI PATATE
(Gratin of potatoes)

1¾ lb potatoes
salt
1 packet sliced cheese
freshly ground pepper
¼ cup butter
1 cup milk

Boil the potatoes in salted water until barely tender. Peel them, allow to cool and then slice. Place a layer of potatoes in a buttered ovenproof pan, cover with cheese slices, a little pepper and dot with butter. Continue layering the ingredients in this way, finishing with a layer of potatoes. Pour over the milk, dot with butter and place in a preheated oven (375°F) for about ¼ hr.

PATATE TARTUFATE
(Potatoes with truffles)

1½ lb potatoes
salt
1 truffle
¼ cup grated Parmesan cheese
pepper
¼ cup butter
juice of ½ lemon

Place the potatoes in cold salted water, parboil and drain. Peel when cold and slice thinly. Butter a deep ovenproof pan and fill with layers of potato and wafer-thin slices of truffle. Sprinkle each layer with Parmesan, season with salt and pepper and pour over a little melted butter. Finish with a layer of potatoes, pour over the remaining butter and place in a preheated moderate oven (300–325°F) for about ¾ hr, or until the top is golden brown. A few minutes before removing from the oven pour over the lemon juice.

PATATE DUCHESSA
(Duchesse potatoes)

1¾ lb potatoes
salt
4 eggs
½ cup butter

This dish is typical of the Emilia-Romagna region. Wash and peel the potatoes, dice roughly, rinse and boil in a flameproof casserole in plenty of salted water. Drain thoroughly when cooked and place in the oven for a few minutes to dry out. Mash the potatoes. Beat the eggs and stir quickly into the potatoes. Return the casserole to the heat and stir in the butter. Fill a decorating bag fitted with a large tube with the mixture and pipe "nests" of the potato mixture on to an oiled baking sheet. Bake in a preheated hot oven (375°F) for about ½ hr, or until they begin to turn brown. Serve hot with roasted

meat. For a delicious finishing touch, fill the center of each "nest" with small pieces of cheese, such as Gorgonzola or Fontina.

PEPERONI ALLA BAGNA CAUDA
(Peppers with garlic and anchovy sauce)

4 large yellow peppers
3 ripe tomatoes
4 anchovy fillets
1 clove garlic, minced
bagna cauda (see p. 130)

Put the peppers in a hot oven for a few moments to char the skins. Peel, then rinse well; remove the stalk and seeds, cut into strips and place in a serving dish. Plunge the tomatoes in hot water for 1–2 min to loosen the skin. Remove the seeds, slice and add to the peppers. Chop the anchovies and add to the peppers with the garlic. Pour over the bagna cauda.

PEPERONATA *
(Braised peppers and tomatoes)

1½ lb yellow and red peppers
¾ lb ripe tomatoes
¾ lb onions
½ cup olive oil
salt
½ cup wine vinegar

Rinse the peppers, remove the stalk and seeds and cut into strips. Skin the tomatoes and remove the seeds. Chop the onion. Place the vegetables in a large saucepan with a tightly fitting lid, add the oil and season with salt. Cover and simmer for about 1 hr. Add the vinegar and cook for a few more minutes. Transfer to a serving dish and serve hot, warm or cold.

PEPERONI RIPIENI
(Stuffed peppers)

1 cup white breadcrumbs
milk
½ cup canned tuna
10 black olives
salt
freshly ground pepper
olive oil
4 large yellow or green peppers

Soak the breadcrumbs in a little milk. Drain and flake the tuna, finely chop the pitted olives and place in a bowl with the drained and squeezed breadcrumbs. Season with salt and pepper. Gradually add 4 tbsp oil, stirring well with a wooden spoon. Mix until the ingredients are well blended. Cut the peppers in half lengthwise, discard the seeds and fill with the tuna and olive mixture. Place the stuffed peppers on a lightly oiled baking sheet; brush lightly with oil and cook in a preheated oven (325°F) for 40 min. Serve hot or cold.

PEPERONI CON ARINGHE E CIPOLLA
(Peppers with herrings and onions)

2 yellow peppers
3 oz smoked herring fillets
½ onion
2 tbsp olive oil
juice of ½ lemon
freshly ground pepper
1 tbsp anchovy paste

Hold the peppers over a flame or place under a broiler until the skin blisters and can be rubbed off easily. Cut the peppers in half and remove the seeds and membrane, then dip in cold water. Drain and dry the peppers, then cut into strips. Finely chop the onion and smoked herring fillets. Place the ingredients together in a bowl and dress with a mixture of olive oil, lemon juice, pepper and anchovy paste.

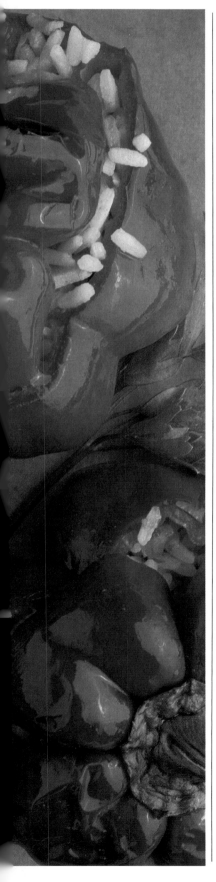

PEPERONI E CIPOLLE
(Peppers and onions in tomato sauce)

4–5 onions
3 tbsp olive oil
¾ lb tomatoes
salt
4 green, yellow or red peppers

Peel the onions and slice thinly. Rinse and pat dry and then fry gently in the oil until transparent. Peel the tomatoes, remove the seeds, chop roughly and add to the pan. Season with salt and simmer for about ¼ hr, or until the sauce thickens. Meanwhile, broil the peppers until the skin is charred, rinse well, remove the stalks and seeds and cut into strips. Add to the tomato sauce, adjust the seasoning, cover and simmer for at least ½ hr.

PEPERONI AL RISO *
(Rice-stuffed peppers)

4–6 peppers
1 onion
4 tbsp olive oil
1 cup rice
2 slices salami, chopped
3 oz ham, chopped
2¼ cups stock
1 Mozzarella cheese, diced
1 tbsp chopped parsley
1 clove garlic, minced
salt
freshly ground pepper

Char the peppers over a flame or under a broiler until the skin blisters and can be rubbed off. Slice off the tops to form lids and set aside. Remove the seeds with a teaspoon. Chop the onion and sauté gently in the oil for a few minutes. Add the rice, salami and ham and cook for a few minutes before adding the hot stock. Cook over high heat, without stirring, until the stock has been absorbed and the rice is just tender. Remove the saucepan from the heat and stir in the Mozzarella, parsley and garlic. Season with salt and pepper. Fill the peppers with the mixture, top with their lids and place upright in an oiled ovenproof pan. Bake in a preheated hot oven (375°F) for about ½ hr, or until the peppers are tender.

PISELLI AL PROSCIUTTO
(Peas with ham)

2¼ lb fresh, unshelled peas
1 onion, chopped
3 tbsp lard or butter
salt
freshly ground pepper
1 ladleful stock (or water)
2 oz ham, cut into strips
triangles of fried bread

This is a specialty of Rome. The countryside around Rome produces especially sweet, flavorsome peas, which make this dish a real delicacy. Shell the peas. Sauté the onion in the lard or butter and as soon as it begins to color, add the peas. Season with salt and pepper and pour in the stock or water. Cook over high heat for about 10 min if the peas are young and tender, or for slightly longer if they are less so, in which case a pinch of sugar should be added. A couple of minutes before the peas are cooked, stir in the ham. Serve hot, garnished with fried triangles of bread if desired.

PISELLI ALLA MAIONESE
(Peas in mayonnaise)

¾ lb shelled peas
4 tbsp mayonnaise (see p. 126)

Rinse the peas and boil rapidly for about ¼ hr, or until tender, in plenty of salted water. Drain and refresh in cold water so that they stay bright green. Fold into the mayonnaise and serve as part of a cold table.

PISELLI COL GUANCIALE
(Peas cooked with bacon)

2½ lb fresh, unshelled peas
2 onions
½ cup bacon
4 tbsp oil
salt
freshly ground pepper

Shell and rinse the peas. Chop the onions and bacon and sauté in the oil for a few minutes until the onion becomes transparent. Add the peas, season with salt and pepper and pour over 1–2 ladlefuls water. Cover and cook over moderate heat for ¼ hr or until the peas are tender, stirring occasionally and adding more water if necessary. Serve hot.

POMODORI GRATINATI
(Baked stuffed tomatoes)

4 large, ripe firm tomatoes
salt
1 clove garlic
1 sprig parsley
1 tsp capers
3 tbsp breadcrumbs
1 tsp oregano
oil

Wash and dry the tomatoes; cut them in half and scoop out the seeds with a teaspoon. Sprinkle with a little salt and turn upside down on a plate to drain away excess moisture. Finely chop the garlic, parsley and capers. Mix with 2 tbsp of the breadcrumbs, a pinch of salt and the oregano. Fill the tomato halves with this mixture; place in an oiled ovenproof pan, pour over a little oil and sprinkle with the remaining breadcrumbs. Place in a preheated oven (350°F) for about ½ hr. Serve piping hot.

POMODORI FARCITI
(Cold anchovy-stuffed tomatoes)

8 tomatoes
salt
½ onion, chopped
2–3 tbsp olive oil
2 tbsp breadcrumbs
2 salted anchovies
slices of lemon
2 hard-boiled eggs
2 oz ham, diced

Wash and dry the tomatoes, cut off the tops to form lids and scoop out the seeds with a teaspoon. Salt lightly and place upside down in a colander to drain. In a small saucepan sauté the onion in the oil and then add the breadcrumbs. Rub the anchovies with the lemon to remove the salt, bone them and chop finely. Sieve the hard-boiled eggs into a bowl and stir in the anchovies, the fried breadcrumbs and the ham. Fill the tomatoes with this mixture, cover each tomato with its lid and arrange on a serving dish. Garnish with lettuce leaves and chill. Serve as a summer appetizer, or as part of a cold table.

POMODORI ALLA SICILIANA *
(Sicilian stuffed tomatoes)

8 ripe tomatoes
1 onion, finely chopped
½ cup olive oil
2–3 anchovies
2 tbsp chopped parsley
1 tbsp capers
1 cup breadcrumbs
salt
freshly ground pepper
pinch of ground nutmeg

Wash the tomatoes, cut off the tops to form lids, scoop out the seeds, sprinkle with salt and turn upside down to drain. Gently fry the onion in 2 tbsp oil until it begins to turn brown. Wash, bone and chop the anchovies. Add to the onion off the heat, together with the parsley, capers and 2 tbsp breadcrumbs. Season with salt, pepper and nutmeg and stir well. Fill the tomatoes with this mixture, top with their lids and place in an oiled ovenproof pan. Heat the remaining oil in a small saucepan, fry the remaining breadcrumbs, stirring, until brown and sprinkle over the tomatoes. Place in a preheated hot oven (400°F) for about ½hr. Serve hot or cold.

RADICCHIO ALLA VICENTINA
(Radicchio salad)

12 oz radicchio
2 oz bacon fat
salt
freshly ground pepper
3 tbsp vinegar

Wash and dry the radicchio and place in a salad bowl. Pound the bacon fat and fry until brown. Season with salt and pepper, pour in the vinegar and boil over high heat until it evaporates. Toss the radicchio in this dressing and serve immediately before the fat cools.

RADICCHIO ROSSO FRITTO
(Fried radicchio)

12 oz radicchio
2 tbsp all-purpose flour
1 egg, beaten
fine dried breadcrumbs
oil for frying
salt

Remove the tough outer leaves from the radicchio, wash and dry and cut each head in half. Dip in the flour, then in the egg and finally in the breadcrumbs. Heat plenty of oil in a skillet until boiling. Fry the radicchio briefly, remove and drain on kitchen paper. Sprinkle with salt and serve hot.

RADICCHIO ROSSO AI FERRI
(Barbecued radicchio)

8 tight heads radicchio
2 tbsp olive oil
salt
freshly ground pepper

Wash the radicchio well and cut the heads in half lengthwise. Shake off the excess water and dry carefully in a teacloth. Mix the oil with salt and pepper and spoon over the radicchio. Cook on a hot barbecue, turning occasionally so that they brown evenly. Serve at once. This dish is particularly good with spit-roasted game.

CIME DI RAPA STUFATE
(Stewed turnip tops)

3 lb turnip tops
2 onions, sliced
salt
freshly ground pepper
½ cup oil

This is a specialty of Apulia. Discard the tough, stringy parts of the stalks and wash well. Place the turnip tops in a saucepan with the onions and 2 cups boiling water. Season with salt and pepper. Bring to a boil, cover and cook for about 10 min. Pour over the oil and cook over moderate heat for a further 10 min or until tender. Stirring constantly, turn up the heat to evaporate the cooking juices just before serving. This dish is good with braised, roasted or broiled meat.

SEDANO ALLA MAIONESE
(Celeriac salad)

2 celeriac
salt
juice of 1 lemon
4 tbsp mayonnaise (see p. 126)

Peel the celeriac, rinse and cut into julienne strips. Sprinkle with salt and pour over the lemon juice to prevent the celeriac turning brown. (The celeriac can be blanched briefly at this stage, if preferred.) Fold gently into the mayonnaise.

SPINACI DI MAGRO
(Spinach with garlic)

1 lb spinach
1 clove garlic
1 sprig parsley
4 tbsp olive oil
salt
freshly ground pepper
pinch of sugar

Wash the spinach thoroughly. Cook with just the water clinging to the leaves until tender but not soggy, and then press out as much moisture as possible. Chop the garlic and parsley very finely and sauté in the oil in a large saucepan. Add the spinach, season with salt, a little pepper and a pinch of sugar. Stir over gentle heat for 5–10 min. Serve as an accompaniment to meat or egg dishes. Traditionally, in Romagna, a few seedless white raisins, soaked in water, would be added to this dish.

TARTUFI ALLA
PIEMONTESE
(Gratin of truffles)

white truffles
Parmesan cheese
olive oil
salt
freshly ground pepper
lemon wedges

243

Clean the truffles by rubbing with a damp cloth and slice very thinly. Coarsely grate the Parmesan and fill a small ovenproof pan with layers of truffle and Parmesan, sprinkling each layer with a little oil, salt and pepper. Place in a preheated hot oven (375°F) for 10 min. Serve garnished with lemon wedges.

FRITTO DI FIORI DI ZUCCA
(Fried pumpkin flowers)

1lb pumpkin flowers
2 salted anchovies
2 tbsp fresh breadcrumbs
1 tbsp olive oil
1 tbsp chopped parsley
freshly ground pepper
2 eggs
1¼ cups all-purpose flour
1 cup milk
salt
oil for frying

The pumpkin flowers have to be very fresh for this recipe. Trim the stalks, remove any stringy parts and wash and dry the flowers carefully. Bone and chop the anchovies and mix with the breadcrumbs, oil and parsley. Season with pepper and stuff the flowers with a little of this mixture. Make a batter by beating the eggs and stirring in the flour, milk and a pinch of salt. Dip the flowers in the batter and deep fry a few at a time in plenty of boiling oil. As soon as they turn golden, remove, drain on kitchen paper and serve hot. For a simpler version of this recipe, put a small piece of anchovy or cheese inside each flower instead of the breadcrumb stuffing.

ZUCCHINE RIPIENE DI CARNE *
(Stuffed zucchini)

8 small zucchini
½ cup lean, ground beef
1 egg
2 tbsp grated Parmesan cheese
2 slices cooked ham, chopped
½ cup fresh white breadcrumbs
salt
freshly ground pepper
4 oz Fontina cheese

Wash the zucchini, slice in half lengthwise and scoop out the center with a potato peeler. Blanch in boiling salted water for 2 min. Make the stuffing by mixing together the beef, egg, Parmesan and ham. Soak the breadcrumbs in some water, squeeze well and stir into the stuffing. Season with salt and pepper and fill the zucchini with the stuffing mixture. Slice the Fontina into thin strips and decorate the zucchini with them. Place in a single layer in an oiled ovenproof pan and bake in a preheated moderate oven (350°F) for 20 min, or until the zucchini are tender.

ZUCCHINE IN AGRODOLCE
(Sweet-and-sour zucchini)

4 medium zucchini
1 clove garlic
2 tbsp olive oil
2 tbsp vinegar
2 salted anchovies
1 tbsp pine nuts
2 tbsp seedless white raisins

This dish is a Sicilian specialty. Top and tail the zucchini, cut into long pieces, remove the seeds and rinse well. Fry the garlic in the oil until it begins to brown and then discard. Add the zucchini and vinegar, cover and cook over moderate heat for 10 min, moistening with a few spoonfuls of water if necessary. Rinse and bone the anchovies and cut into strips. Add to the saucepan with the pine nuts and seedless white raisins. Season with salt, cook for a few more minutes and then transfer to a serving dish.

ZUCCHINE GRATINATE
(Zucchini baked with tomatoes and Mozzarella)

4 medium zucchini
salt
freshly ground pepper
1¾ lb ripe tomatoes
oil
2 tbsp all-purpose flour
8 oz Mozzarella cheese, thinly sliced

Wash the zucchini, top and tail them and slice lengthwise. Sprinkle with salt and pepper and leave for ½ hr. Meanwhile, plunge the tom-

atoes in boiling water; skin and chop them, remove the seeds and sieve. Heat 2–3 tbsp oil in a flameproof casserole, add the tomato pulp, season with salt and pepper and cook over high heat for about 20 min. Dry the zucchini, dip in the flour and fry a few at a time in plenty of hot oil. Drain on kitchen paper and then add to the tomato sauce. Simmer for 5 min, remove from the heat and cover with a layer of Mozzarella. Moisten with a little oil and bake in a preheated hot oven (375°F) for about 20 min.

TORTINO DI ZUCCHINE
(Gratin of zucchini)

1½ lb zucchini
3 tbsp oil
1 tbsp butter
1 tbsp chopped parsley
1 clove garlic, minced
salt
freshly ground pepper
white sauce (see p. 127)

Wash the zucchini, top and tail, and slice thinly. Heat the oil and butter in a saucepan, add the zucchini, parsley and garlic, and cook for 5 min, stirring constantly so that the zucchini do not brown. Season with salt and pepper, turn into an ovenproof pan and pour over the white sauce. Place in a preheated oven (400°F) for 5–10 min to brown the top.

ZUCCHINE E PEPERONI
(Zucchini baked with peppers and anchovies)

4 medium zucchini
1 yellow pepper
3–4 ripe tomatoes
1 tbsp oil
1 clove garlic, minced
salt
freshly ground pepper
few basil leaves
2 anchovies
8 slices Caciocavallo cheese

Top and tail the zucchini, cut in half lengthwise, scoop out the center and blanch in boiling salted water for 2 min. Drain and arrange in an oiled ovenproof pan. Char the pepper, then rub off the skin; rinse well, remove the stalk and seeds and cut into strips. Plunge the tomatoes in boiling water for 1 min, skin and chop them and remove the seeds. Place the tomatoes in a small saucepan with the oil and garlic. Season with salt and pepper and add the coarsely chopped basil. Cook over high heat for about 20 min. Cover each half zucchini with a spoonful of tomato sauce, a few strips of pepper, a slice of cheese and half an anchovy fillet. Moisten with a little oil and place in a preheated oven (325°F) for about ¼ hr, or until the cheese has melted and the zucchini are beginning to brown. Serve hot or cold.

PIATTO FREDDO DI ORTAGGI *
(Cold vegetable platter)

3–4 medium eggplant
2 yellow peppers
2 red peppers
1 medium onion
1 cup olive oil
1 clove garlic, minced
pinch of thyme
1 bay leaf
½ cup wine vinegar
salt
freshly ground pepper

Dice the eggplant without peeling. Char the skins of the peppers, rinse well, and cut into strips. Slice the onion. Place the vegetables in a flameproof casserole and pour over the oil and an equal amount of water. Add the garlic, thyme and bay leaf, and bring to a boil, stirring frequently. Cover, placing a piece of greased wax paper or foil under the lid. Place in a preheated moderate oven (325°F) for 1½ hr. When cooked, sprinkle with the vinegar, season with salt and pepper, transfer to a serving platter and chill.

Pizzas and Bread

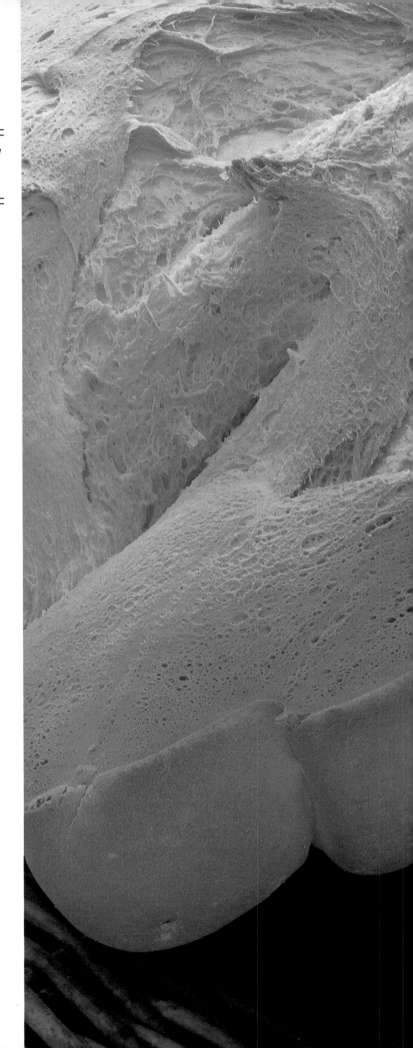

Wherever you travel, among nations of diverse culture and origin, you may be greeted by the universal sight of locals busily kneading various types of flour and water on a work top, a wooden board or a simple stone slab. This dough will be transformed into a pizza, a focaccia, a loaf of bread, a tortilla or some other creation produced by the skilled hand of the baker. Italy is no exception to this tradition: the Neapolitans – perhaps the country's most resourceful inventors – were indeed the creators of the pizza, a nourishing meal in itself which has found fortune worldwide. Today, pizza and Italy are synonymous – but beware! There are pizzas and pizzas, some of the modern variations often bearing little resemblance to the original idea. When the Neapolitans invented the pizza, they combined traditional methods with locally available ingredients to produce a simple yet substantial popular dish. So why the need for change? Although simple and unpretentious fare, the traditional pizza is immensely popular and versatile, in that a variety of toppings may be used.

This section also includes some recipes for savory breads, a useful addition to any cook's repertoire. As the basis of a filling snack, these can make an interesting and welcome change from more usual breads and, served at table, make novel accompaniments to a meal.

PIZZA ALLA NAPOLETANA *
(Neapolitan)

(makes 4 small or 1 large pizza)
basic bread dough:
4 cups all-purpose flour
1 tsp salt
1½ cakes (1 oz) compressed yeast
or
1 envelope active dry yeast
about 1 cup warm water
or
1 lb ready-made bread dough
2 tbsp oil

topping for 1 small pizza:
½ cup canned tomatoes, drained
    and chopped
2 oz Mozzarella cheese, diced
1 anchovy, chopped
salt
freshly ground pepper
1 tsp oregano
2 tbsp olive oil

Basic bread dough

Sift the flour and salt into a large bowl and make a well in the center. Blend the yeast and warm water, mixing until smooth. (If dried yeast is used, mix with the flour before adding the water or follow manufacturer's instructions.) Pour the blended yeast mixture into the flour and beat well with a wooden spoon. With floured hands, work the dough into a smooth ball. Turn the dough on to a floured surface and knead for about 10 min until smooth and elastic. Place in a large greased bowl, cover with a clean cloth and leave to rise in a warm place for about 2 hr or until doubled in size. Flatten the dough lightly with a rolling pin, then shape into a 12-in circle (or 4 small circles) pushing gently outward with the fingers and pinching up the edges to make a rim. Place on a well-oiled cookie sheet or in a special pizza pan.

If ready-made bread dough is used knead with 2 tbsp oil for about 10 min.

Pizzas are traditionally baked in very hot wood-burning brick ovens. To bake pizzas in a conventional oven, preheat to 450°F before use.

Topping

Spread the tomatoes evenly over the pizza base; sprinkle with the Mozzarella, anchovy pieces, salt and pepper, oregano and the oil. If cooked in a wood-burning oven the pizza will take only 4–5 min. With a conventional oven, place pizza near the top of the oven and allow ¼ hr for small pizzas, and 20–30 min for a large one.

PIZZA MARGHERITA
(With cheese, tomato and basil)

basic bread dough (see
    p. 250)
6 tbsp canned tomatoes, sieved
2 oz Mozzarella, sliced
3 fresh basil leaves (or pinch of
    oregano)
olive oil
salt

Arrange the ingredients on the pizza base in the above order. Pour over a little olive oil, sprinkle with salt and bake in a preheated oven at 450°F for 20–30 min or until the crust is golden.

PIZZA QUATTRO STAGIONI
(Four seasons)

basic bread dough (see
    p. 250)
2 large tomatoes, peeled and
    chopped
4 oz Mozzarella, sliced
⅔ cup button mushrooms, cooked
    for ¼ hr in a little butter
2 oz cooked ham
2–3 pickled baby artichokes
8 black olives
olive oil
salt

Cover the pizza base with the tomatoes and Mozzarella and arrange the remaining ingredients on top, each occupying a quarter. Bake in a preheated oven at 450°F for 20–30 min or until the crust is golden.

PIZZA AL PROSCIUTTO
(With ham)

basic bread dough (see
    p. 250)
2 oz cooked ham, cut into strips
⅓ cup canned tomatoes, sieved
2 oz Mozzarella, sliced
olive oil
salt

Arrange the ingredients on the pizza base in the above order. Pour over a little olive oil, sprinkle with salt and bake in a preheated oven at 450°F for 20–30 min or until the crust is golden.

PIZZA PUGLIESE
(With tomato and Pecorino cheese)

basic bread dough (see
    p. 250)
3 tbsp olive oil
1 onion
1 oz grated Pecorino cheese
3 tbsp canned tomatoes, sieved
salt

Work 1 tbsp oil into the pizza dough and roll out as usual. Cover with the finely chopped onion, grated Pecorino and sieved tomatoes. Sprinkle with the remaining oil and a little salt and bake in a preheated oven at 450°F for 20–30 min or until the crust is golden.

PIZZA ROMANA
(With anchovies)

basic bread dough (see
    p. 250)
⅓ cup canned tomatoes, sieved
2 oz Mozzarella, sliced
pinch of oregano
2 salted anchovies, rinsed and
    boned
olive oil
salt

Arrange the ingredients on the pizza base in the above order. Pour over a little olive oil, sprinkle with salt and bake in a preheated oven at 450°F for 20–30 min or until the crust is golden.

PIZZA AL FORMAGGIO
(With cheese)

3 oz Parmesan cheese
3 oz Gruyère cheese
3 oz Provolone cheese
1 oz Pecorino cheese (optional)

How to make pizza

Sift the flour and salt into a mound and make a well in the center. Blend the fresh yeast with a little warm water (follow manufacturer's instructions if using dried) and pour into the well.

Mix the ingredients together with a wooden spoon then knead well for about 10 min until the dough is smooth and elastic. If the dough is too wet or a little dry add more flour or water as necessary. Place in a greased bowl, cover with a clean cloth and leave to rise in a warm place for 2–3 hr. When the dough has doubled in size divide it into four and shape into balls.

Flatten the balls of dough lightly with a rolling pin then roll or push out with your fingers to make a pizza base ¼ in thick. Pinch up the edges to make a rim.

Add the topping of your choice and the pizzas are ready for the oven. Bake at the hottest possible setting, allowing 15–20 min for small pizzas and 30–40 min for large.

3 cups all-purpose flour
1 cake (1 oz) compressed yeast
salt
olive oil
2 eggs

Grate 2 oz Parmesan and 1 oz each Gruyère and Provolone. Cut the remaining cheese into small cubes.

Place a third of the flour on a work surface. Blend the yeast with a little warm water and then work into the flour, kneading until the dough is smooth and firm. Shape into a small loaf and place in a lightly floured bowl. Using a sharp knife make a cross on the top, cover with a cloth and leave to rise in a warm place until doubled in size. Meanwhile, pour the remaining flour on to the work surface, add a little salt and 1 tbsp oil. Gradually work in enough warm water to obtain a consistency similar to that for tagliatelle dough – firm but quite elastic. Beat the eggs in a bowl, stir in both the grated and cubed cheese and gradually work into the dough; finally, incorporate the smaller yeast "loaf," kneading well until the dough is smooth and soft. Place the dough in a high-sided baking pan, greased with a little oil; cover with a cloth and leave to rise in a warm place for at least 2–3 hr. The ideal temperature is about 86°F. To prevent the dough from drying out place an upturned colander on top and cover with a damp cloth. When the dough is well risen bake in a preheated oven at 450°F for 20–30 min or until the crust is golden. Remove from the oven, turn on to a serving dish and serve immediately.

PIZZETTE AL GORGONZOLA
(Gorgonzola mini pizzas)

¼ cup butter
4 oz Gorgonzola cheese, grated
1¾ cups all-purpose flour
2 eggs, separated
pinch of nutmeg
salt
freshly ground pepper

Mix together the softened butter and grated Gorgonzola. Work in the flour, together with 2 egg yolks, the nutmeg, salt and pepper. Shape into a ball and leave to stand in a covered dish in the refrigerator for ½ hr. Roll out into a thin sheet and cut out circles 3 in in diameter. Place on a buttered and floured cookie sheet and brush with beaten egg white. Bake in a preheated oven at 450°F for about ¼ hr or until the crusts are golden.

PIZZA AI FUNGHI
(With mushrooms)

basic bread dough (see p. 250)
1 lb mushrooms
2–4 cloves garlic
⅔ cup olive oil
2–3 sprigs parsley, chopped
salt
freshly ground pepper

Trim and rinse the mushrooms and slice thinly. Mince the garlic and fry in the oil. Remove as soon as it begins to brown; add the mushrooms, chopped parsley and a pinch of salt and pepper. Cook for about 10 min. Spread the mixture over the pizza base and cook in a very hot oven.

PIZZA ALLE VONGOLE
(With clams)

basic bread dough (see p. 250)
8 oz tomatoes, peeled, chopped
    and drained
salt
1 tsp oregano
⅓ cup olive oil
1 lb clams (or mussels), in their
    shells
1 clove garlic
1 sprig parsley
freshly ground pepper

Spread the tomatoes over the pizza base, salt lightly, sprinkle with oregano and 1 tbsp oil. Bake in a very hot oven for 20–30 min. Scrub the clams (or mussels) and heat for 5 min in a skillet with the remaining oil, the chopped garlic and parsley. When the shells have all opened, pick out the mussels and keep warm in the reserved cooking liquor. Pour over the cooked pizza and sprinkle with black pepper.

PIZZA CON UOVA E CIPOLLA
(With egg and onions)

basic bread dough (see p. 250)
4 onions
1–2 tbsp olive oil
salt
freshly ground pepper
2 eggs
2 tbsp chopped parsley

Finely slice the onions and heat gently in a skillet in a few tbsp oil. Make sure the heat is kept low and that the onions cook without browning. Add a few tbsp water if necessary and cook until the onions are soft and lightly colored. Season with salt and pepper.

Meanwhile, boil the eggs for 7 min. Place under cold running water, then leave to cool slightly. Peel and slice. Spread the onions over the pizza base and bake in a preheated oven at 450°F for 20–30 min or until the crust is golden. Remove from the oven and arrange the sliced eggs on top. Pour a trickle of olive oil over the pizza and garnish with parsley. Serve hot or cold.

PIZZA AI CICENIELLI
(With fish)

basic bread dough (see p. 250)
1 lb whitebait or sprats
2 cloves garlic
olive oil
salt
oregano (optional)

Whitebait are tiny fish which are eaten whole without being gutted, topped or tailed. Rinse thoroughly in cold water and pat dry with kitchen paper. Prepare the pizza base as usual and sprinkle the fish and chopped garlic on top. Pour over a little olive oil, salt and oregano and bake in a preheated oven at 450°F for 20–30 min or until the crust is golden.

PIZZA CALABRESE
(With tuna, olives and capers)

basic bread dough (see p. 250)
4 oz black olives
2 oz salted anchovies
4 oz canned tuna
1¼ lb firm ripe tomatoes
salt
⅓ cup olive oil
2 oz lard
freshly ground pepper
1–2 tbsp capers

Pit the olives and cut in half; rinse, bone and chop the anchovies; flake the tuna. Skin, seed and chop the tomatoes. Sprinkle the tomatoes with salt and place in a large saucepan with 5 tbsp oil over high heat for ¼ hr, stirring occasionally. Lightly grease a high-sided 10-in pizza pan with lard. Place the dough on a work surface, make a

well in the middle and put in the lard and a generous pinch of salt and pepper. Knead well until the lard is completely incorporated. Divide the dough in half and roll out two circles, one slightly larger than the other; use the larger circle to line the pizza pan. Spoon equal layers of tomatoes, anchovies, tuna, olives and capers over the bottom and cover with the smaller circle of dough. Fold the edges of the bottom layer over the top one and press gently to seal. Brush with the remaining oil and bake in a preheated oven at 350°F for 1 hr until golden brown. Serve hot or cold.

PIZZA LIEVITATA DI VERDURE
(With vegetables)

2¼ cups all-purpose flour
½ cake (½ oz) compressed yeast
salt
freshly ground pepper
1½ lb green leaf vegetables
⅓ cup olive oil
1 clove garlic
1 tbsp capers
8 black olives

Sift the flour in a mound on to a work surface. Crumble the yeast, dissolve in a little warm water and pour into the middle of the flour. Season with salt and pepper, then add another ladle of warm water. Knead well until the dough is soft and smooth. Place in a bowl covered with a damp cloth and leave to rise in a warm place until doubled in size. Trim and rinse the vegetables. Cut up and place in a saucepan with 6 tbsp oil, the whole garlic, salt and pepper. Cover and simmer until tender. Remove the garlic and leave the vegetables to cool. Divide the dough in two, roll out each half thinly, one larger than the other, and use the larger to line an oiled pizza pan. Place the vegetables on top, followed by the capers and olives. Cover with the second circle of dough. Press gently round the edges with your fingers to seal. Trickle a little olive oil over the top and place in a very hot oven (450°F) for about 20–30 min until golden brown. Serve hot or cold.

253

PIZZA ALL'ANDREA
(With anchovies and olives)

*basic bread dough (see
    p. 250)*
2 onions, sliced
½ cup olive oil
1¾ lb ripe tomatoes
3 oz salted anchovies
salt
2 basil leaves
12 black olives or 1 tbsp capers
1 clove garlic (optional)

This is a typical Ligurian dish. Fry the sliced onions in the oil in a large saucepan. As soon as they begin to brown add the skinned, seeded and chopped tomatoes. Cook over high heat for about ½ hr until all the liquid has evaporated. Meanwhile, knead the dough with 2 tbsp oil. Rinse, bone and chop the anchovies, then add to the tomato sauce. Adjust the seasoning and cook for a few minutes. Roll out the dough ½ in thick and place in a large oiled pizza pan. Spread the dough out with oiled fingers and pinch up the edges. Pour the cooled tomato sauce over the pizza base; add the basil, olives (or capers) and thinly sliced garlic and pour over a little olive oil. Bake in a preheated oven at 450°F for about ½ hr until crisp and golden.

PANZAROTTI ✲
(Fried cheese-filled crescents)

for the dough:
2¼ cups all-purpose flour
¼ cup + 3 tbsp butter
salt
1 egg yolk

for the filling:
4 oz Mozzarella
3 oz cooked ham
2 eggs
½ cup grated Parmesan cheese
pinch of nutmeg
2 tbsp chopped parsley
2 eggs, beaten
oil for frying

This recipe comes originally from the Apulia region. Sift the flour into a mound, make a well in the center and add the butter, cut into pieces, a pinch of salt and an egg yolk. Mix together, kneading and gradually adding sufficient water to obtain a smooth elastic dough. Shape into a ball, cover and leave to stand in a cool place for at least ½ hr. Roll out, folding the dough over on to itself a few times, as if making flaky pastry, then roll out into a thin sheet. Cut into circles about 3 in in diameter. Dice the Mozzarella, cut the ham into pieces and place in a bowl with the 2 whole eggs, grated Parmesan, pinch of nutmeg and chopped parsley. Mix well, then spoon a little into the center of each circle. Brush the edges with beaten egg, fold over and press gently.

Heat plenty of oil in a skillet. When hot, dip the crescents in beaten egg and then fry, a few at a time, until golden brown and puffed up. Drain well on kitchen paper and serve piping hot.

PITTA INCHIUSA
(Stuffed pizza)

basic bread dough (see p. 250), once risen
¼ cup + 2 tbsp lard
3 eggs
salt
freshly ground pepper
3 lb pig's skin with fat, to make 7 oz frittoli (pork cracklings)

This is a typical Calabrian dish, made with pizza dough which has already risen once. Place the already risen dough on a work surface, flatten it slightly and make a well in the middle. Add the softened lard, cut into pieces, two beaten eggs, a pinch of salt and a sprinkling of pepper; knead well until the dough is smooth and elastic and comes away from the work surface without sticking. Shape into a ball and place in a lightly floured bowl; cover and leave in a warm place for 1 hr. Cut the pig's skin into small squares and cook, fat side down, over gentle heat in a heavy saucepan with a little water for about 2 hr. Salt lightly. Roll out the dough into two circles, one larger than the other. Grease a 12-in pizza pan with lard and line with the larger circle of dough. Spread a layer of pork cracklings on top and cover with the smaller circle of dough. Press firmly round the edges, brush with the remaining beaten egg and bake in a preheated oven at 450°F for about 20–30 min until golden brown. This pizza can also be made with a filling of cooked green vegetables, fresh sardines in tomato sauce or cooked red peppers. Serve hot.

PANDORATO
(Golden bread)

1 loaf white bread, unsliced
12 oz Mozzarella
4 oz prosciutto, sliced
milk
all-purpose flour
2 eggs
salt
oil for frying

This dish is a specialty of the Latium region and may be eaten as an appetizer or snack. Cut the bread in the following way: Place the loaf on a chopping board and cut into ½-in slices. On alternate slices cut almost to the bottom, leaving each pair of slices joined. Cut the Mozzarella and prosciutto to the shape of the bread and fill each "sandwich" with a slice of each. Press the two slices firmly together, dip very briefly in milk and then in flour. Place in a deep dish. Beat the eggs well, add salt and pour over the filled sandwiches. Leave to stand for 2 hr. About ½ hr before serving, heat plenty of oil in a skillet. When very hot, deep fry the sandwiches a few at a time until golden brown on both sides. Drain well on kitchen paper, set aside on a warm serving dish and keep hot. When all the sandwiches are cooked, serve at once, piping hot.

PIZZA DI PASQUA
(Easter pizza)

basic bread dough (see p. 250)
3 eggs
salt
⅓ cup grated Parmesan cheese
⅓ cup grated Pecorino cheese
1¼ cups all-purpose flour
½ cup olive oil
lard
1 small black truffle, sliced

This dish is typical of the region known as the Marches. Beat together in a bowl the eggs, salt and grated Parmesan and Pecorino cheese. Leave to stand while preparing the dough. Work the flour and oil into the basic pizza dough, kneading well. Make a well in the middle, pour in the egg and cheese mixture and knead again until the dough is smooth and soft and comes away easily from the work surface without sticking. Place in a bowl, cover with a cloth and leave to rise in a warm place for about 2 hr. Roll out the dough and place in a deep pizza pan greased with lard. Cover and leave to rise in a warm place for 1 hr. Bake in a preheated oven at 450°F for about 20–30 min until golden brown. Serve hot with slices of black truffle. If desired, garnish with salami and hard-boiled eggs.

PANE AL RAMERINO
(Rosemary bread)

12 oz basic bread dough (see p. 250), once risen
3 tbsp seedless white raisins
5 tbsp olive oil
1 sprig rosemary

This is a Tuscan recipe. Soak the seedless white raisins in warm water. Pour the oil into a saucepan, add the rosemary and heat gently for a few minutes. Strain the oil before the rosemary turns black. Place the dough on a work surface, make a well in the middle and pour in the flavored oil. Knead well until the oil is incorporated, then work in the drained and dried seedless white raisins. Knead well again and shape into small round or oval loaves. Make a cross on the top of each with a sharp knife; place on a floured cookie sheet, cover with a cloth and leave to rise in a warm place for about ½ hr. Bake in a preheated oven at 400°F for 15–20 min. This delicious bread can be served at breakfast or with any meal.

CALZONI PUGLIESI
(Mini calzoni with anchovies and olives)

basic bread dough (see
  p. 250)
7 tbsp olive oil
1½ cups sliced onions
½ cup pitted olives
1½ oz anchovy fillets
2 tbsp capers
or
¾ cup tomatoes, peeled, seeded
  and cut into strips
3 oz Pecorino cheese
1 cup sliced onions
1 oz anchovy fillets

Place the dough on a work surface and knead lightly, incorporating 2 tbsp oil. When the dough is smooth roll out into a sheet ⅛ in thick and cut into 3-in squares.

Slice the onions and sauté in 5 tbsp oil without letting them brown; cut the olives in half. Place a spoonful of onions, a piece of anchovy and a few capers and olives in the middle of each square. Add a few drops of oil, then fold the dough over into a rectangle. Press around the edges with the prongs of a fork to seal. Place the calzoni on a greased cookie sheet and brush with oil. Cook in a preheated oven at 450°F for ¼ hr until lightly browned. Serve very hot. For a variation in the filling use strips of tomato, grated cheese, fried onions and pieces of anchovy.

PAN MOLLE DEL GHIOTTONE
(Soaked savory bread)

2¼ cups dry white wine
1 sprig rosemary
1 bay leaf
2 cloves
black peppercorns
salt
12 slices dry wholemeal bread
3 cloves garlic
4 gherkins
8 oz mushrooms (bottled in oil)
1 sprig parsley
1 basil leaf
1 onion
20 black olives
6 salted anchovies
freshly ground pepper
⅓ cup olive oil
3 tbsp vinegar
6 hard-boiled eggs
1 cucumber

Prepare a marinade: Pour the wine and a little water into a bowl and add the rosemary, chopped bay leaf, the cloves, a few whole black peppercorns and a pinch of salt. Leave to stand for 24 hr. Rub the slices of bread with the cut cloves of garlic, then dip them in the strained marinade. Coarsely chop the gherkins, mushrooms, parsley, basil, onion, 8 pitted olives and the rinsed and boned anchovies. Place the soaked slices of bread on a serving dish and cover with the chopped ingredients. Season with salt and freshly ground black pepper and pour over a dressing of olive oil beaten with vinegar. Place half a boiled egg and a black olive on each slice and garnish with cucumber slices.

CALZONE ALLA RICOTTA
(Calzone with ricotta cheese)

basic bread dough (see
  p. 250)
⅔ cup ricotta cheese
1 oz mortadella or ham
1 hard-boiled egg
2 basil leaves

This recipe originates from the countryside round Rome. Roll out the dough into one large or several small circles. Mix the filling ingredients together and spoon into the center. Fold over to make a crescent and press the edges firmly together to seal. Bake at 450°F for 20–30 min until lightly browned. Serve hot or cold.

FITASCETTA
(Onion bread ring)

12 oz basic bread dough (see
  p. 250)
3 tbsp olive oil
1 lb mild red onions
¼ cup butter
salt
pinch of sugar
oil or butter for greasing
1 Mozzarella cheese (optional)

This bread is a specialty of Lombardy. Knead the dough, incorporating the olive oil. Leave to rise in a warm place. Meanwhile prepare the onions. Peel and finely slice the onions, then sauté in the butter until soft. Sprinkle with salt and a pinch of sugar. Knead the dough lightly and shape into a long sausage. Coil into a ring, place on an oiled cookie sheet and leave to rise in a warm place. When doubled in size, spread the onions around the top and bake in a preheated oven at 350°F for about ½ hr. Serve hot or cold, sliced and spread with butter.

Onion bread ring is delicious as it is but can be made even richer by covering the onions with thinly sliced Mozzarella before baking.

SFINCIONE DI SAN VITO
(Sardine and cheese pizza)

14 oz basic bread dough (see
  p. 250)
olive oil
1 lb ripe tomatoes
1 onion or clove garlic, chopped
salt
freshly ground pepper
10 oz salted sardines
4 oz Caciocavallo cheese

Sfincione di San Vito is a specialty of the area around Palermo. Knead the dough incorporating 4 tbsp olive oil. Leave to rise. Leave the tomatoes in boiling water for 1 min, then peel and chop them, discarding the seeds. Heat ½ cup oil in a saucepan and fry the onion (or garlic). As soon as they begin to brown add the tomatoes; season with salt and pepper and simmer for ½ hr. Rinse the sardines and remove the head and tail. Open up and discard the backbone. Add half to the tomato sauce and cook for 10 min. Lightly oil a 10-in pizza pan and roll out the dough to fit. Spread half the tomato sauce and the diced cheese on top and bake at 350°F for 20 min. Pour over the remaining sauce and sardines, sprinkle with a little olive oil and bake for a further 10 min.

TORTA PASQUALINA *
(Easter pie)

5¼ cups all-purpose flour
⅓ cup olive oil
salt
1 lb spinach or spring greens or 5
    young artichokes
½ onion
1¾ cups ricotta cheese
1½ cups milk
2 tbsp butter
4 eggs
freshly ground pepper
marjoram
¼ cup grated Parmesan cheese

Sift the flour into a mound and make a well in the center. Add 3 tbsp oil, a generous pinch of salt and work in sufficient water to make a firm dough. Knead well until smooth and elastic. Divide into 6 or 7 balls and place them on a damp teacloth. Cover with another damp cloth and leave to stand for about ¼ hr. Trim and rinse the spinach or greens and cook in a little salted water for 5–10 min or until tender. If young artichokes are used, cut off any hard outer leaves and place in water acidulated with lemon juice to prevent discoloration. Chop the onion finely and fry in the remaining oil. Add the drained and chopped spinach (or sliced artichokes). Season with salt and cook for a few minutes, stirring constantly. Mix the ricotta and milk together in a bowl. Add a pinch of salt and mix well with a wooden spoon. Roll out each ball of dough into a very thin circle. Butter and lightly flour a pie pan and line with the first circle of pastry which should overlap the edges. Brush lightly with oil and place a second circle of pastry on top. Spread a few flakes of butter around the sides then repeat the operation with the third and fourth circles. Spread the fourth layer with the onion and vegetable mixture, then with the ricotta. Make four holes in the filling and place a little butter in each. Break an egg into each hole and sprinkle with salt, pepper, marjoram and ½ tbsp grated Parmesan. Cover with the remaining circles of pastry, brushing each one lightly with oil. Fold the overlapping edge of pastry on to the top and press well to seal. Brush the top and edges with oil, prick with a fork and bake in a preheated oven at 400°F for ¾ hr until golden brown. Serve the pie hot or cold.

Desserts

*I*talian desserts are sometimes unfairly dismissed as dull and unimaginative, but a look at some of the best known ones will persuade the most exigent of gourmets that this is not so. Just consider a traditional Sicilian cassata prepared with fresh ricotta and soft fondant frosting; creamy Lat brûlé from Emilia-Romagna; apple flan served with date ice cream and wine caramel sauce; and soft fondant frosting; creamy Lat brûlé from Emilia-Romagna; apple flan served delicious little almond macaroons and cookies, and a variety of airy little cakes and pastries such as castagnole fritte and chiacchiere, which are prepared around Carnival time.

Of all the courses the dessert is the most frivolous, intended exclusively for pleasure rather than nourishment. There can surely be no better way to end a celebratory repast than by producing a triumphant zuccotto made with chocolate, cream and nuts and flavored with a dash of brandy, or such mouthwatering classic cakes as a feather-light pandoro or a wickedly rich, dark and moist Tuscan chestnut cake.

ALBICOCCHE ALLA PANNA
(Apricots with cream)

8 large ripe apricots
½ cup + 3 tbsp sugar
1 cup water
1 cup heavy cream
few drops vanilla extract
¾ cup confectioners' sugar
3 tbsp maraschino liqueur
16 macaroons (amaretti)

Rinse and dry the apricots, cut in half and remove the pits. Put the sugar and water in a saucepan. Stir to dissolve and bring to a boil over low heat. Dip the apricots into this syrup a few at a time. Whip the cream, flavor it with vanilla extract and sweeten with the confectioners' sugar. Pour the maraschino into a large shallow dish and soak the macaroons. Use some of the whipped cream to pipe a rosette on each apricot half. Pile the remainder of the cream into a round serving dish and surround it with half the macaroons. Press the apricot halves into the cream and place a macaroon on each cream rosette. Drizzle any remaining liqueur over the top.

AMARETTI DI SARONNO
(Almond macaroons)

¾ cup sweet almonds
¾ cup bitter almonds
1 cup sugar
2 egg whites
confectioners' sugar

Blanch the almonds and peel off the skins. Lay them on a cookie sheet and dry them out in the oven without allowing them to brown. Grind to a powder in a mortar or food processor, together with ½ cup sugar. Whip the egg whites until stiff and fold in the remaining sugar with a spoon. Then fold in the almond powder. Place the mixture in a pastry bag fitted with a plain tube and pipe small, walnut-sized mounds of the mixture on to a greased and floured cookie sheet, spacing them well apart to allow for spreading. Flatten the mounds gently and dust with confectioners' sugar. Leave to stand for a few hours. Bake at 350°F for about ¼ hr.

BRIGIDINI
(Aniseed cookies)

1 cup all-purpose flour
pinch of salt
1 tsp double acting baking powder
7 tbsp butter, softened
3 tbsp sugar
1 egg
1 tsp anise seeds
milk

These are a Tuscan specialty. Sift the flour, salt and baking powder into a bowl and rub in the butter. Add the sugar, egg, anise seeds and enough milk to bind the mixture to a smooth, firm dough. Knead well on a floured surface, then shape into nut-sized balls. Flatten these gently and cook, a few at a time, on a greased hot griddle or in a heavy skillet. Serve at once while still hot.

BUDINO DI RICOTTA *
(Ricotta cheese pudding)

1 tbsp seedless white raisins
2 tbsp rum
1 cup water
¼ cup fine semolina
4 eggs
1¾ cups ricotta cheese
6 tbsp confectioners' sugar
½ cup mixed candied peel
pinch of cinnamon
grated peel of ½ lemon
butter and flour for mold
vanilla sugar

Soak the seedless white raisins in the rum. Bring the water to a boil and drizzle in the semolina. Mix well, and remove from the heat after a couple of minutes. Spoon the mixture into a bowl and leave to cool. Separate three eggs. In another bowl mix together the ricotta, confectioners' sugar, one whole egg and three yolks, the candied peel, seedless white raisins, cinnamon and lemon peel. Whip the remaining egg whites until stiff. Add the semolina mixture to the Ricotta mixture and mix well. Fold in the egg whites. Butter and flour a large 2½-pint mold and pour in the mixture. Cook at 350°F for about 1 hr. Leave to cool, then turn out. Dust with vanilla sugar before serving.

BUDINO ARIANNA
(Arianna pudding)

½ cup seedless white raisins
3 tbsp rum
2 eggs (room temperature)
6 tbsp sugar
1 cup milk
1 vanilla bean
butter for greasing
confectioners' sugar
4 oz sponge cake, cut in slices
1¾ cups candied peel
zabaglione (see p.280) made with 2
    eggs and ¼ cup heavy cream,
    whipped
candied fruit to decorate

Soak the seedless white raisins in the rum. Beat the eggs and sugar in a bowl until light and frothy. Pour the milk into a saucepan with the vanilla bean and bring to a boil. Remove the vanilla bean and pour the hot milk over the egg and sugar mixture. Butter a mold, dust it with confectioners' sugar and line it with a layer of sponge cake slices, trimming them to fit as necessary. Arrange a layer of candied peel and soaked seedless white raisins on top, followed by a further layer of sponge cake slices. Continue layering until the mold is nearly full. Pour the egg and milk mixture slowly into the mold. Place in a roasting pan half-filled with water and cook gently in the oven until the custard has set. Remove from the oven and leave to cool, then turn out on to a serving dish. Prepare the zabaglione (see recipe on p.280) and once this has cooled, gently fold in the whipped cream. Pour this sauce over the pudding and decorate with candied fruit.

CANDELAUS
(Sardinian almond cookies)

3 cups sweet almonds
1½ cups + 3 tbsp sugar
1¼ cups confectioners' sugar
grated peel of 1 lemon
3 tbsp orange flower water

These cookies are a Sardinian specialty. Blanch the almonds in boiling water, then peel off the skins. Spread on a cookie sheet and dry out in a cool oven (250°F). Do not allow them to brown. Chop them finely, or grind in a food processor. Put the granulated sugar in a saucepan, preferably copper-based, with ¼ cup water and heat until the sugar has dissolved. Add the confectioners' sugar, almonds, lemon peel and orange flower water. Cook for 5 min until the mixture leaves the sides of the saucepan. Remove from the heat and leave to cool. When cool enough to handle, wet your hands and shape the mixture into little animals, flowers, figures and so on. Place these on a cookie sheet and bake at 350°F for about 5 min. Dissolve a little more sugar in a very small amount of water and brush the glaze on to the cookies.

CANESTRELLI
(Ligurian almond cookies)

1¾ cups almonds
¾ cup sugar
orange flower water
1 tsp butter
3 tbsp fruit syrup
nonpareils to decorate

These sweets are typical of Liguria. Blanch the almonds for 2-3 min in boiling water. Rub off the skins and pound the nuts in a mortar or food processor. In a bowl stir together the sugar and ground almonds and moisten with enough orange flower water to bind the mixture. Butter a cookie sheet. Shape the mixture into flat rounds and bake for ¼ hr at 325°F near the top of the oven. When the cookies are golden, remove them from the oven, glaze with fruit syrup and sprinkle with nonpareils.

CANNOLI ALLA SICILIANA
(Sicilian cream horns)

for the dough:
1¼ cups all-purpose flour
1 tsp cocoa powder
½ tsp instant coffee powder
pinch of salt
1 tbsp sugar
2 tbsp lard or butter
⅔ cup red or white wine or Marsala
oil for frying

261

for the filling:
¾ cup + 2 tbsp ricotta cheese
1¼ cups confectioners' sugar
1 tbsp orange flower water
½ cup chopped candied orange,
   lemon and pumpkin, or ground
   pistachios
1 oz semisweet chocolate, grated
1 tbsp cocoa powder (optional)
8 glacé cherries
vanilla sugar

Cannoli are similar in shape to cream horns, and special metal cannoli molds are needed to make them. The cannoli are made of a pastry known as *scorza*, with a ricotta cheese filling. Sift the flour, cocoa, coffee, salt and sugar into a bowl. Rub in the lard or butter with your fingers. Add as much wine or Marsala as necessary to bind the mixture to a firm dough. Knead until the dough is smooth and elastic. Cover with a teacloth and let it rest for about 1 hr. Roll out very thinly and cut out eight squares, with 3-in sides. Lay a cannoli mold diagonally across each square and wrap the two corners around it. Press to seal. Deep fry two at a time until crisp and golden. Drain on kitchen paper. When the molds are cool enough to handle, gently slide off the pastry horns. Leave to cool. In a bowl mix together the ricotta, sugar, orange flower water, candied fruit (or pistachios) and the grated chocolate. If using cocoa powder spoon half the mixture into a second bowl and mix in the cocoa. With a teaspoon or pastry bag fill the cannoli with the ricotta cream; if using cocoa, fill one end of each horn with the white cream and the other with the dark cream. Smooth out the cream and press half a glacé cherry on to each end. Lay the cannoli in a row on a serving plate and dust with vanilla sugar.

CASSATA ALLA SICILIANA *
(Sicilian cheesecake)

1½ lb ricotta cheese
1¼ cups + 3 tbsp sugar
pinch of cinnamon
4 oz semisweet chocolate, grated
3 cups candied peel, finely chopped
½ cup peeled pistachio or pine nuts

4-5 tbsp maraschino liqueur
12 oz sponge cake

for the fondant frosting:
½ cup + 3 tbsp sugar
1 cup water
juice of ½ small lemon
pinch of cream of tartar

How to make puff pastry

(makes 2 9-in pie crusts)
3½ cups all-purpose flour
1¾ cups butter
cold water
pinch of salt

Sift two-thirds of the flour and the salt into a bowl and add enough cold water to mix to a smooth, firm dough. Leave to chill in the refrigerator for ½ hr.

In a second bowl, work the remaining flour into the butter. Shape into balls and chill this mixture also.

Roll out the dough into a thick rectangle. Take the butter and flour balls out of the refrigerator, place at intervals over one half of the dough and fold the other half to cover them.

Now the most delicate part of the operation begins: Gently roll out the dough, taking care not to break the outer layer, until it is double in size. Fold again, as before, then roll out once more. Repeat the folding and rolling out at least five times, leaving it to rest for ¼ hr each time.

This is the traditional recipe for cassata, although a popular frozen version also exists (illustrated).

Beat the ricotta until smooth. Dissolve the sugar in a saucepan with a little water; before it begins to color add it to the ricotta, mix cinnamon. Add the chocolate, 1 cup candied peel (reserve the best pieces to decorate), the chopped nuts and half the maraschino. Cut the sponge cake into slices and dip into the remaining maraschino. Line the base and sides of a deep-sided 10-in mold or soufflé dish with a few of the slices. Spoon the ricotta mixture into the center and smooth the surface with a spatula. Place the rest of the sponge cake slices on top. Chill for at least 3 hr. Carefully turn out the cassata on to a serving plate. To prepare the fondant frosting: Gently heat the sugar, water and lemon juice in a heavy copper-based saucepan, stirring constantly until the sugar has dissolved. Bring the syrup to a boil, add the cream of tartar and boil steadily without stirring until it reaches 240°F. The syrup is the correct consistency when a tea-spoonful forms a soft ball when dropped into cold water. The ball should flatten when removed from the water. Sprinkle a little water over the inside of a large bowl, pour the syrup into it and leave to cool for ¼ hr. Work the mixture well with a spatula, constantly turning it until it becomes opaque and thickens. Turn the fondant on to a work surface sprinkled with cold water and knead it until white and smooth. The fondant can be stored almost indefinitely in an air-tight jar in the refrigerator. When the fondant is required warm it in a saucepan with a little water and a few drops of food coloring if desired. Spread it evenly over the top and sides of the cassata using a spatula dipped in cold water. The fondant icing can then be decorated with candied fruit or small marzipan candies. The fondant frosting may be omitted, in which case dust the cassata with confectioners' sugar before decorating. Serve immediately.

CASTAGNACCIO ALLA TOSCANA
(Tuscan chestnut cake)

1 small sprig rosemary
3 tbsp seedless white raisins
3½ cups chestnut flour
6 tbsp olive oil
4 tbsp sugar
pinch of salt

2¼ cups milk
2¼ cups water
fine fresh breadcrumbs
chopped mixed nuts (optional)
3 tbsp pine nuts

Chop the rosemary very finely. Soak the seedless white raisins in lukewarm water for about 20 min. Drain and squeeze out excess moisture. In a bowl combine the chestnut flour, olive oil, sugar and salt. Beat well, then, stirring constantly, pour in the milk and water (and the mixed nuts, if desired), and mix until smooth and liquid. Grease a mold or cake pan (7 or 8 in in diameter) and sprinkle a few breadcrumbs over the base. Pour in the mixture and cover the top evenly with the seedless white raisins, pine nuts and rosemary. Sprinkle with olive oil and bake in a moderate oven (350°F) for about 1 hr. When the cake is ready it should be soft in the middle and crisp on the outside. Serve warm or cold.

CHIACCHIERE
(Carnival sweetmeats)

3 cups all-purpose flour
2 eggs
¼ cup butter
½ cup sugar
pinch of salt
grated peel of 1 orange and ½ lemon
4-5 tbsp white wine
vanilla sugar

Chiacchiere or *nastri* ("ribbons") are traditionally eaten at Carnival time. Pour the flour on to a working surface, make a well and add the eggs, the softened butter, sugar, salt, orange and lemon peel and the white wine. Mix and work into a dough. Shape the dough into a ball and let rest for 1 hr. Roll out thinly and, using a pastry cutter, cut strips which can then be tied like ribbons, or rectangles with two or more slits in the middle (see illustration on pp. 258–9). Shallow fry the chiacchiere a few at a time in hot oil. When golden, remove with a slotted spoon, drain and leave to cool on kitchen paper. When cold, dust with vanilla sugar.

CASTAGNOLE FRITTE *
(Lemon fritters)

2 eggs
3 tbsp sugar
1¾ cups all-purpose flour
4 tbsp olive oil
3 tsp brandy
pinch of salt
½ tsp vanilla extract
grated peel of 2 lemons
oil for deep frying
confectioners' sugar

Beat the eggs with the sugar until light and fluffy. Add the flour, oil, brandy, salt, vanilla extract and lemon peel. Mix with a wooden spoon until well blended. Heat a large saucepan of oil for deep frying, and drop teaspoonfuls of the mixture into the hot oil. Use two teaspoons to achieve the characteristic rounded shape of the *castagnole*, illustrated below. The fritters will puff up, so deep fry only a few at a time. Drain on kitchen paper and dust generously with confectioners' sugar. Serve immediately.

CREMA AL MASCARPONE
(Mascarpone cream)

2 whole eggs + 1 egg yolk
¾ cup mascarpone (cream cheese)
½ cup + 3 tbsp sugar
3 tbsp rum

Separate the two whole eggs and beat the whites until stiff. Beat all three yolks with the sugar; then add the mascarpone and mix well. Pour over the rum and fold in the two egg whites. When the mixture is evenly blended, pour into four small coffee cups and chill in the refrigerator for a few hours. Serve with plain cookies.

DOLCE DI CASTAGNE E RISO
(Chestnut rice pudding)

¾ cup dried chestnuts
2 cups milk or water
pinch of salt
¾ cup short-grain rice
6 tbsp sugar
½ cup seedless white raisins
¼ cup + 2 tbsp butter

Place the chestnuts in a bowl, pour over lukewarm water and soak overnight. Peel off any filmy outer layer from the chestnuts, pat dry and place in a saucepan. Cover with milk or water, add a pinch of salt and simmer gently for ½ hr. Then add the rice, the softened seedless white raisins and the sugar. Cook, stirring constantly for a further 20–25 min, until the rice is tender and a risotto-like mixture is obtained. Add more milk if necessary. Add the butter, and allow it to melt over the pudding mixture. Stir well, pour into a serving bowl and leave to cool. Serve cold.

CROSTATA DI VISCIOLE
(Cherry tart)

2½ cups all-purpose flour
1¼ cups confectioners' sugar
pinch of salt
¼ cup + 2 tbsp butter
¼ cup lard
2 whole eggs + 1 egg yolk
juice of 1 lemon
1 14-oz jar sour or black cherry jam

This recipe is typical of the countryside around Rome. Sift the flour, confectioners' sugar and a pinch of salt into a bowl, rub in the softened butter and lard, then add the two whole eggs and the lemon juice. Mix together lightly, working the mixture as little as possible. Add a little milk if necessary to make the dough more elastic and malleable. Form into a ball. Put the dough in a bowl, cover with a tea-cloth and let it rest in the refrigerator for 1 hr. Grease and flour a 10-in tart pan with a removable base. Roll out half the dough and line the base of the tart pan. Spread the cherry jam over the dough and smooth it out with a spatula. Roll out the remaining dough and, using a pastry cutter, cut it into long strips. Lay these in a crisscross pattern over the jam filling. Beat the egg yolk and glaze the strips of pastry. Bake at 350°F for about ¾ hr until golden. Leave to cool. Transfer to a serving plate. This pie is best served the day after it is made.

CROSTATA DI PRUGNE E ALBICOCCHE'
(Prune and apricot flan)

2¼ cups all-purpose flour
½ cup + 2 tbsp butter, melted
6 tbsp sugar
1 egg
grated peel of 1 lemon
pinch of salt
sponge fingers
raspberry jam
1 small can prunes
1 small can apricots.

Sift the flour into a bowl. Add the melted butter, sugar, egg, lemon peel and a pinch of salt. Blend together with a fork and, without overworking the dough, form into a ball. Cover the dough and leave to rest for 1 hr. Roll out to a thickness of ¼ in and line the base and sides of a buttered springform pan. Prick the pastry all over with a fork and bake blind at 350°F for 20 min. Cool on a wire rack. When the pastry is cold, spread a layer of warmed jam on the bottom. Top this with a layer of sponge fingers and then another layer of warmed jam. Decorate with the halved

prunes and apricots and place on a serving dish.

DOLCETTI DELLA NONNA
(Grandmother's petits fours)

Arranged on a three-tiered cake stand, this selection of petits fours is both attractive and appetizing.

Almond rocks

2 egg whites
1¼ cups confectioners' sugar
1 cup blanched almonds, toasted and chopped

Beat the egg whites with half the sugar (preferably in a copper bowl to achieve more volume), adding the remaining sugar gradually while beating. Fold in the toasted and chopped almonds. Spoon the mixture into baking cases and cook in a cool oven (250°F) for about ¾ hr. Leave to cool.

Chestnut truffles

1 cup marrons glacés, chopped
1 tbsp butter, softened
3 tbsp rum
1 cup cashew nuts
grated chocolate
chopped filberts or almonds

Sieve the marrons glacés into a bowl and add the butter, rum and cashew nuts. Shape this mixture into little balls, roll some of them in grated chocolate and some in the chopped nuts.

Chocolate sponge slices

1 cup mascarpone (cream cheese)
¼ cup sugar
3 tbsp brandy
sponge cake slices
11 oz chocolate
4-5 tbsp water
filberts, toasted and chopped

Beat the mascarpone, sugar and brandy with a wooden spoon. Cut the sponge cake into little rectangles, spread each with the mascarpone mixture and press together to make sandwiches. Melt the chocolate with 4–5 tbsp water in a double boiler. Remove from the heat and, before it cools, dip the

mascarpone-filled rectangles into it with the help of two spoons, coating them evenly. Sprinkle the chopped nuts on top.

FICHI AL CIOCCOLATO
(Chocolate figs)

14 oz large, dried figs
scant 1 cup toasted almonds
scant 1 cup chopped candied peel
1 clove, minced
3 oz chocolate powder (or grated chocolate)
scant 1 cup confectioners' sugar

Make a slit in each fig and fill with an almond, a few pieces of candied peel and a pinch of minced clove. Pinch them together again, place on a cookie sheet and place in a preheated oven (325°F) for about ¼ hr until they begin to turn golden. Remove from the oven and roll them in a mixture of sugar and chocolate powder. Alternatively dip them into melted chocolate and sugar with a little water added.

DOPOSCUOLA PER BAMBINI
(Children's after-school treat)

for the pâte sucrée:
1¾ cups all-purpose flour
½ cup sugar
pinch of salt
2 eggs
grated peel of ½ lemon
scant ½ cup butter

2¼ cups milk
grated peel of 1 lemon
4 egg yolks
½ cup sugar
½ cup all-purpose flour
16 sponge fingers
2 tbsp Marsala
16 cherries, pitted
1 egg yolk for glazing

Make the pâte sucrée following the method given on page 267 and roll it out on a floured board. Grease a springform cake pan and line it with the pastry, pressing the edges closely to the sides. Trim to fit and reserve the pastry trimmings. Heat the milk to boiling point and add the lemon peel. Beat the egg yolks with the sugar until light and

fluffy. Add the flour and the hot milk. Heat gently until the custard thickens, stirring constantly. Remove from the heat and leave to cool. Sprinkle the sponge fingers with the Marsala. When the custard is cold, spoon a layer of it over the pastry base. Lay the sponge fingers on top and cover them with the remaining custard. Cut long, narrow strips out of the remaining pastry with a pastry cutter and lay them crisscross on the top in a diamond pattern. Decorate with the cherries. Cook at 425°F for 10 min, then reduce the heat (350°F) and cook for a further 20 min. Halfway through the cooking (after about 10 min) glaze the pastry strips with the beaten egg yolk. When the top is golden, remove from the oven and leave to cool.

COPPA DI MARRONS GLACÉS
(Marrons glacés dessert cup)

2 cups heavy cream
¾ cup confectioners' sugar
1 cup marrons glacés
2 tbsp grated chocolate
1 tbsp chopped pistachio nuts

Whip the cream. When it starts to thicken, carefully add the confectioners' sugar a little at a time, beating constantly until stiff. Reserve four whole marrons glacés and roughly chop the rest. Divide the chopped pieces between four cocktail glasses, cover with some of the whipped cream and top each serving with a whole marron glacé. Sprinkle with the grated chocolate and nuts. Serve the remaining cream in a separate dish.

FOCACCIA RUSTICA
(Country ring cake)

1 cup butter
1 cup sugar
3 eggs, beaten
1 tbsp double acting baking powder
1 cup milk
1 tbsp salt
grated peel of 1 lemon
few drops vanilla extract
7 cups all-purpose flour

Using a wooden spoon or electric mixer, cream together the butter and the sugar in a bowl and beat in the eggs one at a time. Dissolve the baking powder in the milk and add to the mixture together with the salt, grated lemon peel and vanilla extract. Mix well. Sift the flour into another bowl and make a well in the center. Gradually stir in the egg mixture to make a stiff dough. Roll into a ball, cover and leave to stand for ½ hr. Knead the dough and shape into a thick sausage. Join the ends firmly to make a large ring. Place on a greased cookie sheet and bake in a moderate oven (350°F) for about 40 min. Leave to cool. Serve cold, in slices.

LAT BRÛLÉ
(Cream caramel)

4 cups milk
2 eggs
4 egg yolks
few drops vanilla extract
9 tbsp sugar

This sweet comes originally from Emilia-Romagna. Simmer the milk very slowly in a non-stick saucepan to allow it to reduce to less than half the volume (about 1¾ cups). Pour into a bowl and allow to cool. In another bowl beat together the eggs, egg yolks, vanilla extract and 6 tbsp sugar until thick and creamy. Gradually pour in the cooled milk, stirring constantly. Over a gentle heat melt the remaining sugar in the bottom of a deep metal pudding mold and allow it to caramelize. The caramel is ready when it has turned golden brown. Take care not to let it burn, by continuously turning the mold so the melted sugar runs over the edges and changes color evenly. Carefully pour the milk and egg mixture on to the caramel in the mold. Do not stir. Put the mold into a large saucepan half filled with boiling water so that it floats slightly above the bottom of the saucepan. Cover and simmer for about 3 hr, topping up the saucepan with boiling water as necessary. Remove from the saucepan and loosen the cream caramel by inserting a knife round the edge of the mold. While it is still warm turn it out on to a serving plate, letting the caramel syrup run down the sides. Leave to cool and serve cold with cream if desired.

MARZAPANE
(Almond tart)

for the pastry:
1¾ cups all-purpose flour
½ cup sugar
pinch of salt
⅓ cup butter
2 egg yolks
grated peel of 1 lemon

for the filling:
1¾ cups confectioners' sugar
1¾ cups ground almonds
⅔ cup light cream
3 eggs
2 tbsp orange flower water

Sift together the flour, sugar and salt and add in the butter, egg yolks and grated lemon peel. Mix together to form a dough. Roll into a ball, cover with a cloth and leave in a cool place for at least ½ hr. In a bowl add the confectioners' sugar to the ground almonds and stir in the cream. Separate the eggs and add the yolks to the mixture one at a time. Flavor with the orange flower water. Finally, using a metal spoon, fold in the three stiffly beaten egg whites. On a floured board roll out the pastry dough. Grease a deep tart pan, about 10 in in diameter, and line it with the pastry. Pour in the almond mixture and spread it out evenly with a knife. Bake in a moderate oven (350°F) for about 1 hr. Serve cold, cut into slices.

MONTE BIANCO
(Mont Blanc)

2 lb chestnuts
6¼ cups milk
2½ cups confectioners' sugar
2 tbsp rum
few drops vanilla extract
4½ cups heavy cream

Shell the chestnuts and carefully remove the inner skins. Simmer them in the milk for about 1 hr.

When soft, drain the chestnuts and pass them through a food mill into a bowl while they are still hot. Mix the confectioners' sugar, rum and vanilla extract together with the chestnut purée. Pass through the food mill again, this time letting the purée fall lightly on to a circular serving plate in a cone-shaped mound. Do not flatten. Whip the cream until stiff and sweeten with confectioners' sugar. Gently cover the mound of chestnut purée with the cream to give the effect of a mountain covered in snow.

PANDOLCE
(Sweet bread)

1 cake compressed yeast
4 cups cake flour
⅓ cup butter
½ cup sugar
1 cup pine nuts
⅔ cup candied citron peel
½ cup seedless white raisins
pinch of salt

This is a typical Ligurian cake. Dissolve the yeast in about 4 tbsp tepid water and then mix to a paste with 1 cup flour. Shape into a bun, cover and leave to rise in a warm place for at least 12 hr. Soak the seedless white raisins in tepid water for about 20 min until soft; drain and dry well. Mix the risen dough together with the remaining flour and add in the butter, sugar, pine nuts, coarsely chopped citron peel, seedless white raisins and salt. Knead well to obtain a smooth, even dough. Cover and leave to rise again for about 4 hr. Shape into a large round loaf then place on a buttered and floured

How to make pâte sucrée

This type of pastry is mostly used for sweet tarts and pies, although it naturally has many other uses and always gives good results. The basic ingredients are as shown in the recipe for "Italian shortcrust cookies" on p.269 although the quantities will often vary. The pastry is made as follows:

Sift the flour into a bowl and make a well in the center. Mix in the eggs, salt, grated lemon peel and sugar.

Lastly add the butter, slightly softened so that it is easy to work. Mix together well using a wooden spoon.

When the ingredients are thoroughly blended, knead the dough until it is smooth and pliable, adding a little water or milk if necessary.

Shape the dough into a ball, cover and refrigerate for about 1 hr before using.

cookie sheet. Cut a deep cross on the surface and bake for about 1 hr in a moderate oven (350°F) or until a toothpick inserted into the center comes out clean. Leave to cool before serving.

MOSTACCIOLI
(Honey cookies)

1¼ cups cake flour
¾ cup clear honey
1 tbsp aniseed liqueur
butter

These attractive little cookies come originally from Calabria. Sift the flour into a bowl and make a well in the center. Pour in the honey and liqueur and work the ingredients together until the mixture is smooth and even textured

267

like bread dough. Roll the dough out on a floured surface to a thickness of about ½ in and, using a pastry wheel, cut out small fancy shapes. Butter a cookie sheet and arrange the pastry shapes on it, evenly spaced apart. Bake in a cool oven (300°F) until golden. Leave to cool. These cookies are usually kept for a few days before they are eaten, to allow them to become soft. Stored in an airtight tin they will keep well.

PANDORO DI VERONA *

½ cake compressed yeast
2½ cups all-purpose flour
1 tbsp tepid water
6 tbsp sugar
2 eggs
3 egg yolks
¾ cup butter
few drops vanilla extract
pinch of salt
confectoners' sugar

In a cup work together the yeast, 1 tbsp flour and the tepid water to obtain a ball of soft dough. Cover and allow to rise in a warm place for about 20 min until the dough has more than doubled in size. In a bowl mix together two thirds cup flour, 1 generous tbsp sugar, 1 whole egg, 1 yolk and ½ tbsp softened butter. Add the leavened mixture from the cup and knead well for about 5 min until smooth and elastic. Cover and allow to rise in a warm place for about 1 hr until this second batch of dough has doubled in size. In another bowl mix together 1 cup flour, 2 tbsp sugar, 1 tbsp melted butter, 1 whole egg, 2 yolks, the vanilla extract and salt. Turn this on to a floured board together with the already leavened dough, and knead well for 10 min until smooth, soft and elastic. Gradually knead in another ½ cup flour until the dough acquires the consistency of very soft bread dough and is no longer sticky. Knead the dough for several minutes longer, repeatedly folding it, pushing it down with the heel of the hand and turning it around. Roll into a ball and place in a floured bowl in a warm place. Leave to rise for about 3 hr. Turn the risen dough on to a lightly floured sur-

face and kneed for 2–3 min to knock out the air bubbles. Roll out into a square and spread ½ cup + 2 tbsp butter in evenly spaced dots in the center. Fold the corners of the square to the middle to close in the butter then slightly flatten out the dough and fold it into three, as for flaky pastry. Roll out again and fold into three. Leave for about 20 min. Repeat the rolling and folding process twice more before folding the dough and leaving it to stand for a further 20 min. Lightly knead the dough, constantly turning it with one hand and folding it over with the over. Butter a traditional *pandoro* mold. Place the dough in the mold and leave to prove in a warm place until it rises to the top. Bake in a moderate oven (350°F), remembering to reduce the heat slightly after ¼ hr so that the pandoro cooks through to the middle without burning. After ½ hr check that the pandoro is ready by inserting a toothpick into the center. When this comes out perfectly clean remove the pandoro from the oven and turn it out onto a wire rack. Leave to cool. Sprinkle generously with confectioners' sugar before serving.

PANE BOLOGNESE
(Bolognese fruit bread)

1 tbsp pine nuts
1 tbsp candied citron peel
2 tbsp seedless white raisins
2¼ cups all-purpose flour
1 tbsp double acting baking powder
scant 1 cup confectioners' sugar
pinch of salt
½ cup milk
¼ cup + 2 tbsp butter
1 egg, beaten
few drops vanilla extract
1 egg yolk

Coarsely chop the pine nuts and finely slice the candied citron peel. Soak the seedless white raisins for 20 min in lukewarm water, then drain and dry. Sift the flour, baking powder, sugar and salt into a large bowl. Gently heat the milk until tepid, melt the butter into it and add the beaten egg and vanilla extract. Mix to a fairly stiff dough. Add the pine nuts, candied citron peel and seedless white raisins and knead until evenly distributed. Divide the dough into two and shape into ovals 1 in thick. Brush with the egg yolk and bake in a hot oven (400°F) for 20–30 min or until golden. Take care not to open the oven during cooking or the dough will not rise properly. Turn out on to a wire rack and leave to cool. Serve in slices.

PASTA FROLLA
(Italian shortcrust cookies)

3½ cups all-purpose flour
1 cup sugar
pinch of salt
4 eggs
grated peel of 1 lemon
¾ cup + 2 tbsp butter
confectioners' sugar

Sift the flour into a bowl and make a well in the center. Mix in the sugar, salt, eggs, grated lemon peel and softened butter. Mix together well with a wooden spoon until the ingredients are evenly blended. Knead the mixture thoroughly until smooth and pliable and shape into a ball. Cover and refrigerate for about 1 hr. On a floured board roll out the pastry a third at a time to about ¼ in thick and cut out a variety of shapes using cookie cutters. Place the cookies ½ in apart on greased cookie sheets. Bake in a moderate oven (375°F) for about ¼ hr or until light brown. Cool and dust with confectioners' sugar.

PESCHE AL FORNO
(Baked stuffed peaches)

4 large yellow peaches
1½ cups crushed macaroons
  (amaretti)
2–3 tbsp almond liqueur (amaretto)
6 tbsp sugar
1 egg yolk
8 blanched almonds
2 tbsp butter
1 cup white wine

Rinse and dry the peaches, cut them in half and remove the stones. Using a pointed teaspoon scoop out a little of the flesh from each and mix well together with the crushed macaroons, almond liqueur, sugar and egg yolk. Spoon the filling into the peach halves and decorate with an almond. Place the peaches in a buttered ovenproof dish and pour over the white wine. Bake in a moderate oven (350°F) for about ½ hr. Serve the peaches warm, decorated with macaroons and almonds.

PINOCCHIATE
(Pine nut candies)

generous 1 cup pine nuts
⅔ cup water
1⅓ cups sugar
grated peel of 1 lemon

These candies from Umbria are traditionally eaten at Christmas and date back to the fifteenth century. Toast the pine nuts in the oven for a few minutes until dry and crunchy, but do not allow them to change color. Put the sugar and water in a heavy saucepan and bring slowly to a boil, stirring constantly until the sugar dissolves. Continue to boil steadily without stirring until a small amount of the syrup dropped into cold water forms a ball which holds its shape when it is removed. Take the saucepan off the heat and add the pine nuts and the lemon peel, stirring constantly. Turn the mixture out immediately on to a work surface sprinkled with cold water, and level it out using a wet spatula. Working quickly before the mixture cools and sets hard, cut into rough shapes and leave to cool.

When cold, place candies in colorful wrappers.

A chocolate flavor can be substituted for the lemon flavor by replacing the grated lemon peel with 1 tbsp grated semisweet chocolate.

PINZA DI PANE
(Bread and butter pudding)

6 medium slices white bread
1¾ cups milk
2 tbsp sugar
⅓ cup seedless white raisins
2 eggs, beaten
grated peel of 1 lemon
1 tbsp all-purpose flour
¼ cup pine nuts
2 tbsp butter

Break up the bread in a basin and cover with the tepid milk. Add the sugar and mix until the bread is completely soft. Leave it to stand for ½ hr. Soak the seedless white raisins in warm water. Mix the bread and milk mixture to a soft paste, add the eggs, grated lemon peel, flour, seedless white raisins and pine nuts. Spread the mixture evenly in a buttered cake pan (the pudding should be 1-1½ in deep) and sprinkle with a few flakes of butter. Bake in a preheated oven at 350°F for about ½ hr or until brown. Eat hot or cold.

RICCIARELLI DI SIENA
(Sienese macaroons)

1¾ cups blanched almonds,
  toasted
1 cup sugar
1¾ cups confectioners' sugar
few drops vanilla extract
2 egg whites, stiffly beaten
rice paper

Grind the almonds to a fine powder using a pestle and mortar or an electric blender. Mix together the almonds, sugar and half the confectioners' sugar. Add the vanilla and gradually fold in the egg whites until the mixture is smooth, but not too runny. Put a little of the mixture, evenly spaced, on to the rice paper. Shape into diamonds and sprinkle with the remaining confectioners' sugar. Leave overnight.

Bake in a low oven (325°F) for 20 min until they are dry, but not brown. Leave to cool and dust with confectioners' sugar.

SFOGLIATELLE FROLLE
(Sweet ricotta turnovers)

for the pastry:
1¾ cups all-purpose flour
6 tbsp sugar
pinch of salt
3–4 tbsp cold water
¼ cup lard
1 egg yolk to brush the pastry

for the filling:
2 cups water
scant 1 cup semolina
pinch of salt
scant 1 cup ricotta cheese
¾ cup sugar
1 egg, beaten
1 cup mixed candied peel
few drops vanilla extract
pinch of ground cinnamon
confectioners' sugar

Sift together the flour, sugar and salt and make a well in the center. Gradually mix in enough water to make a stiff dough. Cut the lard into small pieces and work into the dough. Knead the dough quickly until smooth and pliable. Leave to rest in a cool place for ½ hr. To make the filling bring the water to a boil in a small saucepan and sprinkle in the semolina, stirring constantly. Add the salt and cook briskly for 5 min, stirring vigorously with a wooden spoon. Turn the mixture into a large bowl and leave to cool. Mix together the ricotta cheese, sugar, egg, finely chopped candied peel, vanilla extract and cinnamon. Add the mixture to the semolina and mix to an even consistency.

Divide the pastry dough into twelve pieces and roll them into ovals ¼ in thick. Put a little filling on one half of each oval of pastry, fold over the other half and press the edges well to seal. Place on a greased cookie sheet and brush with beaten egg yolk. Place in the hottest part of a preheated oven at 375°F and bake for about ¼ hr or until golden brown. Dust with confectioners' sugar and serve warm or cold.

STRUDEL *

for the pastry:
1¼ cups all-purpose flour
pinch of salt
1½ tbsp sugar
1 egg
2 tbsp butter
2 tbsp warm water

for the filling:
¼ cup seedless white raisins
¼ cup shelled nuts (walnuts, pine
   nuts, almonds)
1 lb apples
2 tbsp fresh breadcrumbs
2 tbsp butter
¼ cup sugar
1 level tsp ground cinnamon
grated peel of 1 lemon
1 tbsp fruit jelly (optional)
4 tbsp butter to grease the cookie
   sheet

This sweet comes originally from the Alto Adigé. Sift together the flour, salt and sugar. Make a well in the center and stir in the lightly beaten egg and melted butter, gradually add the warm water as necessary, mixing until the dough becomes soft. Knead the dough thoroughly for 10–15 min until elastic. Place the dough under an inverted bowl, to prevent it from drying out, and leave it to rest in a warm place for at least ½ hr. Soak the seedless white raisins for a few minutes in warm water and roughly chop the nuts. Peel and core the apples and slice thinly. Gently fry the breadcrumbs in the butter until golden, taking care not to let them burn as this will give them an unpleasant bitter flavor. Place the dough on a floured teacloth and roll out as thinly as possible into a rectangle, using a well floured rolling pin to prevent it sticking. Lift and stretch the dough using the backs of the hands until it is paper thin. Trim the edges with a knife. Spread fried breadcrumbs and melted butter over the dough. Mix together the sugar, cinnamon, grated lemon peel, nuts, seedless white raisins and apple and spoon the mixture on to the dough, leaving a border of 2 in on all sides. Spread the jelly on top of the filling. Using the floured cloth carefully roll up the strudel lengthways, like a jelly roll. Seal the join with water. Slightly dampen the dough at each

272

end of the rolled up strudel with water and press it together to prevent the filling leaking out during cooking. Lightly grease the cookie sheet with half the melted butter, and still using the cloth, roll the strudel on to it with the join underneath. Brush the surface with the rest of the melted butter. Place in a preheated oven at 325–350°F for about 1 hr until golden. Dust the strudel with confectioners' sugar and serve hot or cold with cream.

TARALLUCCI
(Little ring cookies)

2 eggs
1 tbsp sugar
2 tsp liqueur (Chartreuse, Grand
    Marnier, etc.)
1 tsp vanilla extract
pinch of ground cinnamon
2 cups all-purpose flour
oil for deep frying

These cookies are a specialty of the Campania, Apulia and Lucania regions. In a bowl mix together the eggs, sugar, liqueur, vanilla extract and ground cinnamon. Gradually add the flour until the mixture binds together to form a smooth and pliable dough. Knead the dough well on a floured board and roll into a ball. Cover and leave to rest for ½ hr. Divide the dough into thirty small pieces of equal size and roll into sausages about 3 in long. Join the ends to make small rings. Heat plenty of oil in a deep skillet and immerse several dough rings, taking care not to overfill the skillet as they will puff up. When the rings are light golden remove them from the skillet, keeping the oil over the heat, and score them with a sharp knife. Return to the skillet for a few minutes until deep golden brown. Drain on kitchen paper. Repeat until all the rings are cooked. These cookies are delicious eaten hot or cold.

STRUFFOLI ALLA NAPOLETANA
(Neapolitan honey sweets)

for the dough:
4 generous cups all-purpose flour
8 eggs
2 egg yolks
pinch of salt
¼ cup butter or lard
grated peel of ½ lemon
grated peel of ½ orange
olive oil for frying

for the coating:
⅔ cup clear honey
¼ cup sugar
¾ cup diced candied orange peel
¾ cup diced candied citron
¼ cup diced candied pumpkin
    (optional)
¼ cup nonpareils

How to prepare crêpes

(makes 12)
3 eggs
1 cup all-purpose flour
¼ cup sugar
pinch of salt
1¼ cups milk
butter for frying

In a bowl beat the eggs, then add the flour. Beat quickly with a whisk to avoid lumps. Stir in the sugar and salt.

Add the milk and whisk. The mixture should be smooth with no lumps.

In a skillet gently heat a small piece of butter. When it has melted spread 4–5 tbsp of the crêpe mixture over the bottom of the skillet.

As soon as the underside of the crêpe turns golden brown, using a spatula, carefully flip it over to cook the other side.

Continue until all the mixture is used, keeping the crêpes hot until ready to serve.

This is a typical Christmas sweet. In a bowl mix together all the ingredients for the dough. Work until smooth and knead well. Leave in the bowl for 1 hr covered with a damp cloth. Break off pieces of the dough and roll into sausages ½ in thick. Cut into ½-in pieces. Heat the oil in a deep skillet and, adding a few pieces of dough at a time, fry until golden brown. Drain well on kitchen paper. Put the honey, sugar and a few tablespoons of water in a small saucepan. Bring to a boil and simmer until the foam disappears and the mixture is yellow and clear. Lower the heat, add the fried struffoli with half of the diced candied fruit and stir well. Pour on to a serving plate. Wet your hands with cold water and quickly arrange the struffoli in a ring or a mound. Sprinkle with the nonpareils and decorate with the remaining candied peel. Leave a few hours before serving.

TORRONE DI CIOCCOLATO
(Chocolate nougat)

⅔ cup clear honey
3 cups shelled filberts
generous 1 cup sugar
8 squares semisweet chocolate
2 egg whites
wafers

There are many types of hard and soft nougat, but the soft varieties require much less preparation and cooking time. This soft chocolate nougat is quick and easy to make. Pour the honey into the top of a double boiler. Heat over boiling water, stirring constantly with a wooden spoon until the honey liquefies. Allow to cook over simmering water for a further 1 hr, stirring frequently, or until a small amount of the honey dropped in cold water forms a hard ball. While the honey is cooking, prepare the remaining ingredients: Toast the filberts in a moderate oven (375°F), then remove the outer skins. Dissolve ¼ cup of the sugar in an equal quantity of water and cook slowly until the mixture thickens. Add the chocolate, broken into pieces and, stirring constantly, continue cooking until the chocolate has melted and blended with

273

the sugar. Put to one side but keep the mixture warm. Dissolve the remaining sugar in 1–2 tbsp water and cook gently without stirring until it caramelizes. Beat the egg whites until very stiff. At this point the honey should be ready. Keeping the saucepan over heat, add the stiff egg whites to the honey, beat constantly until mixture is white and fluffy. Stir the caramelized sugar into the mixture, and when thoroughly blended add the warm chocolate. With the saucepan still over the heat, mix well and stir in the toasted filberts. Remove from the heat and spread the mixture over a layer of wafers. Quickly smooth out the nougat with a wet spatula into a layer 1½–2 in thick. If desired, the nougat can be covered with another layer of wafers. Leave to cool for 20 min. Then using a sharp, wet knife cut the torrone into two long strips and then into equal-sized pieces. To store, wrap each piece in foil and keep in a cool, dry place.

TORTA PARADISO
(Paradise cake)

1¼ cups butter
1¼ cups sugar
3 eggs
5 egg yolks
1¼ cups all-purpose flour
1 tsp baking powder
1¼ cups cornstarch
grated peel of 1 lemon
butter and fine breadcrumbs for the
    baking pan
confectioners' sugar

Cream the butter with a wooden spoon until light and fluffy, then add the sugar. In a separate bowl beat the eggs with a whisk and then add slowly to the butter and sugar mixture. Stir well. Sift together the flour, baking powder, cornstarch and the grated lemon peel and gradually stir into the mixture. Mix well. Pour into a deep 10-in round cake pan, buttered and coated with breadcrumbs. Bake in a moderate oven (375°F) for 40 min. Do not open the oven door for the first ½ hr of cooking or the cake will sink in the middle. The cake is ready when a toothpick inserted into the center comes out clean.

Turn the cake on to a wire rack and leave to cool. Before serving dust with confectioners' sugar.

TORTA DI ALBICOCCHE
(Apricot sponge cake)

scant 1 cup all-purpose flour
1 tsp double acting baking powder
1 cup cornstarch
6 eggs, separated
1¾ cups confectioners' sugar
few drops vanilla extract
small jar apricot jam
8-10 canned apricot halves
small jar apricot jelly
chopped almonds

Sift the flour, baking powder and the cornstarch into a bowl. In another bowl beat the egg yolks, sugar and vanilla extract until light and fluffy. Whisk the egg whites until stiff and fold into the yolk mixture. Gradually add to the dry ingredients and mix together well until the mixture is thick and creamy. Butter and flour a deep 9-in round cake pan and pour in the mixture. Bake in a preheated oven (400°F) for about ½ hr. The cake is ready when a toothpick inserted into the center comes out clean. Remove from the oven and leave to cool. Using a long sharp knife, slice the cake horizontally into two or three layers of equal thickness. Sandwich the layers of sponge together with apricot jam. Spread jam over the cake and arrange the drained apricot halves on top. Using a pastry brush carefully glaze the top and sides of the cake with the warmed apricot jelly. Press the chopped almonds around the sides.

TORTA ALLA PANNA
(Cream gateau)

scant ¼ cup butter
2 eggs
1 cup sugar
1 cup all-purpose flour
scant ¼ cup cornstarch
1 tsp double acting baking powder,
fine breadcrumbs
2¼ cups whipping cream
candied pineapple and cherries
confectioners' sugar
cocoa powder

Melt the butter in a saucepan over gentle heat. In a bowl beat the eggs and sugar, using a wooden spoon, until light and fluffy. Sift together the flour, cornstarch and baking powder and gradually stir into the egg mixture, together with the melted butter. Butter an 8-in round cake pan and coat with fine breadcrumbs. Pour in the cake mixture and bake in a preheated oven (400°F) for about ½ hr or until a toothpick inserted into the middle comes out clean. Remove the cake from the oven and turn out on to a wire rack to cool. When it is quite cold, slice the cake horizontally into two equal pieces using a long sharp knife. Whip the cream with a whisk until it stands in peaks, sweeten with confectioners' sugar to taste and spread over the bottom layer of the cake. Sandwich the two layers together. Fill a pastry bag fitted with a metal tube with any remaining cream and decorate the top of the cake. Sprinkle with the diced candied fruit and dust the center with cocoa powder.

TORTA SAN REMIGIO
(Mascarpone sponge cake)

6 eggs, separated
1½ cups sugar
¼ cup + 2 tbsp butter
3 cups all-purpose flour
1 tsp double acting baking powder
fine breadcrumbs
¾ cup + 2 tbsp mascarpone (cream cheese)
¾ cup confectioners' sugar
few drops vanilla extract

Beat the egg yolks with the sugar in a large bowl until light and fluffy. Melt the butter in a double boiler. Sift together the flour and baking powder and gradually add to the beaten eggs and sugar, together with the melted butter. Whisk the egg whites until stiff and carefully fold them into the mixture using a metal spoon. Butter one round and one rectangular baking pan and coat with fine breadcrumbs. Divide the mixture between the two pans and bake in a preheated oven (400°F) for 35–40 min. Turn out on to a wire rack and leave to cool. Cut the rectangular layer into cubes of about ¾ in square. Pre-pare the cream filling: Beat the mascarpone with a wooden spoon and gradually add the confectioners' sugar and a few drops of vanilla extract. Using a sharp knife, slice the round cake into two layers and place one on a large round serving plate. Spread half the cream filling over the bottom layer of sponge and sandwich the two layers together. Spread the remaining cream filling over the top of the cake. Pile the cubed sponge over the cake, dust with confectioners' sugar and serve.

TORTA DI NOCI
(Walnut cake)

1½ cups shelled walnuts
butter and flour for the cake pan
4 eggs, separated
1¼ cups sugar
grated peel of 1 lemon
confectioners' sugar

Finely chop or grind the walnuts. Grease a deep, 12-in round cake pan and dust lightly with flour. Beat the egg yolks, add the sugar and continue beating until light and fluffy. Stir in the grated lemon peel. Whisk the egg whites until stiff and fold a few tablespoons into the egg yolk mixture to make it lighter. Add the ground walnuts, stir well and when thoroughly blended fold in the remaining egg whites. Pour the mixture into the prepared baking pan and bake in a moderate oven (375°F) for approximately 1 hr until the cake is golden brown. Leave to cool on a wire rack and, before serving, dust with confectioners' sugar.

This cake is also delicious if split and filled with a lemon butter icing. If stored in an airtight tin it will stay moist for several days.

TORTA DI CASTAGNE
(Chestnut cake)

2 cups chestnuts
1 cup sugar
scant ½ cup butter
generous ½ cup blanched almonds
4 eggs, separated
grated peel of 1 lemon
½ cup all-purpose flour
confectioners' sugar

Cook the chestnuts in boiling water for 5 min. Remove the shells and inner skins at once. While they are still hot, sieve the chestnuts into a bowl. Chop the almonds. Put the egg yolks in a bowl with the sugar and beat until light and frothy. Reserve 1 tbsp of the butter and soften the rest. Stir in to the eggs and sugar, together with the grated lemon peel, chopped almonds and sieved chestnuts. Beat the mixture vigorously with a wooden spoon, making sure all the ingredients are well blended. Whisk the egg whites until stiff and gradually fold into the mixture. Use the reserved tbsp of butter to grease a 10-in cake pan and dust with flour. Pour in the mixture and bake in a preheated oven at 350°F for about 40 min. Turn out on to a wire rack. Leave to cool, then dust liberally with confectioners' sugar before serving.

TORTA DI MACEDONIA DI FRUTTA ✳
(Fresh fruit tart)

for the pâte sucrée:
2¼ cups all-purpose flour
1 egg
pinch of salt
grated peel of 1 lemon
6 tbsp sugar
½ cup + 2 tbsp butter

slices of sponge cake
fresh fruit of your choice (grapes, oranges, pineapple, bananas, glacé cherries, kiwis)
apricot jam

Prepare the pâte sucrée following the method given on p. 267. Roll out on a floured board to a thickness of ½ in. Butter and flour a large round tart pan with a removable bottom and line with the rolled out pastry. Prick all over with a fork to prevent puffing during baking. Bake blind in a hot oven (400°F) for about ¼ hr or until golden. Leave to cool, then cover the pastry base with a layer of sponge cake. Decorate the top with the fresh fruit of your choice, peeled, sliced, and arranged as illustrated opposite. Gently warm the apricot jam in a small saucepan, then spoon over the fruit to form a glaze.

TORTA ALLE MANDORLE
(Almond cake)

4 eggs, separated
½ cup + 3 tbsp sugar
½ cup almonds, blanched and finely chopped
½ cup all-purpose flour
½ tsp double acting baking powder
grated peel of 1 lemon
1 tbsp butter
confectioners' sugar

A typical Sardinian cake. Beat the egg yolks with the sugar until light and frothy. Finely chop the almonds and add to the flour, baking powder and grated lemon peel. Whisk the egg whites until stiff and carefully fold into the cake mixture using a metal spoon. Butter and flour a 10-in round cake pan and pour in the mixture. Bake in a preheated oven at 350°F for about 35 min. The cake is ready when a toothpick inserted into the center comes out clean. Remove from the oven, turn out on to a wire rack and leave to cool. Place the cake on a serving plate and dust generously with confectioners' sugar.

TORTA CASALINGA
(Plain sponge cake)

5 eggs, separated
½ cup + 3 tbsp sugar
juice of 1 lemon
few drops vanilla extract
¾ cup cornstarch
½ tsp double acting baking powder
butter and flour for cake pan

Put the egg yolks and sugar in a bowl over a saucepan of warm water. Beat with a whisk until the mixture is light and fluffy. Add the lemon juice and vanilla extract. Sift together the cornstarch and baking powder and add to the mixture. Whisk the egg whites until stiff and carefully fold into the mixture. Pour into a greased and floured cake pan 8 in in diameter and bake in a preheated oven at 375°F for about ½ hr. The cake is ready when a toothpick inserted into the center comes out clean. Turn out on to a wire rack and leave to cool before serving.

TORTA GLASSATA
(Sponge cake with fondant frosting)

generous ¾ cup all-purpose flour
¾ cup cornstarch
1 tsp double acting baking powder
6 eggs, separated
1¾ cups sugar
few drops vanilla extract
1 tbsp butter

for the fondant frosting:
⅔ cup cold water
1 cup sugar
pinch of cream of tartar
2-3 tbsp orange liqueur, or similar

Sift the flour, cornstarch and baking powder into a bowl. In a separate bowl beat the egg yolks and gradually add in the sugar and vanilla extract. Whisk the egg whites until stiff and fold into the egg yolks and sugar. Gradually pour the mixture into the bowl of sifted dry ingredients and stir well with a wooden spoon until the mixture is light and creamy. Grease a 10-in round cake pan with the butter and pour in the mixture. Bake in a preheated oven at 400°F. The cake is ready when a toothpick inserted into the center comes out clean. Turn out on to a wire rack and leave to cool.
   Prepare the fondant frosting: Gently heat the water and sugar in a heavy copper-based saucepan, stirring constantly until the sugar has dissolved. Bring the syrup to a boil, add the cream of tartar and boil steadily without stirring until it reaches 240°F. The syrup is the correct consistency when a teaspoonful dropped into cold water forms a soft ball that flattens when it is removed. Sprinkle a little water over the inside of a large bowl. Pour the syrup into it and leave to cool for ¼ hr. Work the mixture well until it becomes opaque and thickens. Turn the fondant out and knead it until white and smooth. This part of the preparation can be carried out in advance and the fondant stored in a screw top jar in the refrigerator. When the fondant is required, warm it in a saucepan over gentle heat. Add the liqueur and pour the fondant over the top and sides of the cake. Decorate with candied fruit or small marzipan candies.

TORTINO DI CIOCCOLATO E AMARETTI
(Chocolate and almond cake)

for the caramel:
6 tbsp sugar
6 tbsp water

8 eggs
½ cup cocoa powder
1 cup sugar
1 cup rum
4½ cups milk
4 cups crushed macaroons
   (amaretti)

Dissolve the sugar in the water in a small saucepan and bring to a boil, stirring constantly. Boil briskly, without stirring, until the liquid turns golden brown and caramelizes. Pour the caramel into the base of a cake pan. In a large bowl with a mixer at low speed, beat the eggs, cocoa and sugar. Gradually add the rum, milk and macaroons and beat until the ingredients are well blended. Pour on to the caramel and cook in the oven in a bain-marie at 250°F for 1½ hr. Allow to cool then refrigerate for 4hr before serving.

TORTA SOVRANA
(Sovereign cake)

scant ½ cup sugar
¾ cup blanched almonds
1 cup all-purpose flour
2 egg yolks
pinch of salt
½ cup heavy cream
½ cup softened butter
½ cake compressed yeast
confectioners' sugar
1 whole egg

Grind half the sugar and the almonds to a fine powder using a pestle and mortar or electric blender. Dissolve the yeast in a few tablespoons of warm water. Sift the flour into a bowl, make a well in the center and pour in the egg yolks, salt, cream, softened butter and yeast solution. Mix the ingredients together well, until they bind together to form a smooth, soft and elastic dough. Add in the remaining sugar, then turn the dough on to a floured surface and knead for a few minutes. Cover and leave to rise in a warm place

for about 1 hr until it has doubled in size. Roll out the dough to a thickness of ½ in. Grease an 8-in round, shallow cake pan and dust with confectioners' sugar. Line with a layer of the dough and sprinkle with the ground almonds and sugar. Cut the remaining dough into narrow strips and make a crisscross design over the top. Brush with the beaten egg and bake in a moderate oven (375°F) for 35 minutes, or until golden brown.

TORTA DI RISO
(Rice cake)

¼ cup blanched almonds
¼ cup candied fruit (orange and
   citron)
4 cups milk
¾ cup short-grain rice
½ cup + 3 tbsp sugar
pinch of salt
2 eggs, separated
grated peel of 1 lemon
¼ cup pine nuts
vanilla extract

Finely chop the almonds and dice the candied fruit. Bring the milk to a boil then add the rice, ¼ cup sugar, and the salt. Cook gently until the rice is soft and tender, then leave to cool. Beat the egg yolks in a bowl with the remaining sugar until light and fluffy. Add the cooked rice, grated lemon peel, almonds, diced candied peel, pine nuts, and vanilla extract and mix well. Whisk the egg whites until stiff and gradually fold into the mixture. Butter a 10-in tube pan and coat with fine breadcrumbs. Pour in the mixture and bake in a preheated oven at 325°F for about 1 hr. This cake is best eaten the following day.

TORTA ALLE NOCCIOLE
(Filbert cake)

1 cup whole, shelled filberts
1½ cups all-purpose flour
⅓ cup cornstarch
1 cup sugar
½ cup powdered milk chocolate
¼ cup butter
4 eggs
⅓ cup seedless white raisins
grated peel of 1 lemon
1 tbsp double acting baking powder
1 cup + 2 tbsp warm milk
2 tbsp apricot jam
1 cup finely chopped almonds

Toast the filberts in the oven and chop them finely. Sift the flour and cornstarch into a bowl and mix in the sugar, chocolate powder, chopped filberts and butter. Add the eggs separately, stirring constantly, followed by the seedless white raisins, lemon peel and baking powder dissolved in the warm milk. Mix all the ingredients together well. Butter and flour a 9-in cake pan and pour in the mixture. Bake in a hot oven (400°F) for about ½ hr. When the cake is ready, remove it from the pan and leave to cool on a wire rack. Spread the top and sides of the cake with apricot jam and cover it with a layer of very finely chopped almonds.

TORTA DI FRUTTA
(Cherry sandwich cake)

1 tbsp butter
4 eggs
¾ cup sugar
2 cups all-purpose flour
1 tbsp double acting baking powder
few drops vanilla extract
liqueur to taste
2 cups pitted cherries

for the cream filling:
2 cups milk
grated peel of 1 lemon
4 egg yolks

½ cup sugar
¼ cup all-purpose flour

Melt the butter. Beat together the eggs and sugar until light and fluffy. Sift the flour with the baking powder and gradually add to the egg mixture together with the melted butter and vanilla extract. Butter and flour a 9-in round cake pan. Pour in the mixture and bake in a hot oven (400°F) for ½ hr or until golden brown. Remove the cake from the oven and cool on a wire rack. Slice the cake horizontally into two layers. Carefully reduce the diameter of one layer of sponge by cutting away ½ in around the edge. Prepare the filling: Bring the milk to a boil and add the grated lemon peel. With a wooden spoon beat the egg yolks together with the sugar in a heavy saucepan. Stir in the flour and beat well then gradually pour in the milk. Thicken the cream by stirring over moderate heat. Boil for a few minutes and allow to cool. Place the larger of the two layers of sponge on a serving plate and soak with liqueur. Cover with a thick layer of the filling and arrange three quarters of the cherries around the outer edge. Soak the top layer with liqueur, cover with the cream filling and place over the bottom layer. Decorate the top with the remaining cherries and serve.

TORTA DI TAGLIATELLE
(Tagliatelle cake)

3 cups all-purpose flour
4 eggs
small glass cherry liqueur
1 cup blanched almonds, chopped
1 generous cup crushed macaroons (amaretti)
1 cup sugar
few drops vanilla extract
½ cup butter

Sift the flour into a bowl. Make a well in the center and pour in the eggs, cherry liqueur and enough warm water to form a smooth dough. Knead well. Turn out on to a floured board and roll out thinly. Leave for a few minutes to dry, then roll up like a jelly roll. Slice the roll of dough into narrow strips and

carefully open out into strips resembling *tagliatelle*. Toast the almonds in the oven and mix with the crushed macaroons, sugar and vanilla extract. Butter and flour an 8-in round cake pan. Arrange a layer of the strips of dough over the bottom of the pan and cover with a few tablespoons of the mixture. Continue alternating layers of dough strips and almond mixture, finishing with a layer of dough strips. Dot with flakes of the butter and bake in a preheated oven at 350°F for about ½ hr. Serve while still warm.

TORTA DI MELE
(Apple cake)

½ cup butter
1¼ cups sugar
pinch of salt
3 eggs
grated peel of 1 lemon
few drops of vanilla extract
1 cup milk
3½ cups all-purpose flour
1 tbsp double action baking powder
4 apples, peeled and sliced

Soften the butter then beat it together with the sugar and salt. When it is soft and creamy add in the eggs one at a time, the lemon peel and the vanilla extract and the milk, a spoonful at a time. Sift the flour and the baking powder and add to the mixture. Mix well and let the mixture stand in a covered bowl. Butter and flour an 11-in round springform pan and pour in half the mixture. Cover with a layer of sliced apples and then put in the rest of the mixture. Arrange the remaining apple slices on the top of the cake and bake in a moderate oven (350°F) for 30–40 min or until golden brown. Cool on a wire rack and serve.

TORTELLINI DI MARMELLATA *
(Jam turnovers)

1¾ cups all-purpose flour
6 tbsp sugar
pinch of salt
½ cup + 2 tbsp butter
2 eggs

grated peel of 1 lemon
jam for filling
1 beaten egg for brushing the pastry
confectioners' sugar

Sift together the flour, sugar and salt. Make a well in the center and stir in the softened butter, eggs and grated lemon peel. Knead the mixture thoroughly until smooth and pliable and shape into a ball. Cover with a cloth and leave to stand for about 1 hr. On a floured board roll out the pastry to about ⅛ in thick and cut out as many circles of 3 in diameter as possible. Put ½ tsp of jam in the center of each circle, brush the edges with the beaten egg and fold them in half, firmly sealing them. Place on a greased cookie sheet and brush with the rest of the beaten egg. Bake in a medium oven (350°F) for about 20 min until golden brown. Serve hot or cold, sprinkled with confectioners' sugar.

ZALETI
(Polenta cake and cookies)

scant 1 cup seedless white raisins
2¼ cups milk
1 cup sugar
2 tsp salt
2½ cups polenta (corn meal)
scant 1 cup all-purpose flour
scant ½ cup butter
5 eggs
1¼ cups pine nuts
grated peel of 1 lemon
few drops vanilla extract
2 level tsp baking powder
confectioners' sugar

These little cakes are typical of the Veneto region. Soak the seedless white raisins in warm water to soften them. Heat the milk in a large saucepan and as soon as it comes to a boil add the sugar and salt. Gradually add in the polenta and flour, stirring constantly. Lower the heat and cook gently for ½ hr or until the mixture is thick and smooth. Pour into a bowl and add the butter, eggs, seedless white raisins, pine nuts, grated lemon peel, vanilla extract and baking powder. Butter and flour an ovenproof pudding mold and three-quarters fill it with the mixture. Place level tablespoons of the remaining mixture on to a greased cookie sheet to make small cookies. Bake the cake and cookies in a hot oven (400°F) for 20–30 min or until golden brown. Serve hot or cold sprinkled with confectioners' sugar.

ZABAIONE FREDDO
(Cold zabaglione)

½ cup sugar
4 egg yolks
1 cup Marsala
grated peel of 1 lemon
pinch of ground cinnamon
few drops of vanilla extract
1 cup heavy cream

Put the sugar and egg yolks in a deep, preferably copper, basin and beat vigorously until light and frothy. Add the Marsala, grated lemon peel, cinnamon and vanilla. Place the bowl over a saucepan of hot, but not boiling, water over very low heat. Continue to beat until the zabaglione is light and fluffy. Remove from the heat and stir until cool. Whip the cream until stiff peaks form and carefully fold in to the egg mixture using a metal spoon. Serve the zabaglione cold in cocktail glasses. Decorate with piped cream rosettes and candied fruit.

ZEPPOLE
(Neapolitan sweet pastry rings)

1¼ cups all-purpose flour
4 tbsp semolina
2¼ cups water
pinch of salt
½ cup sugar
1 bay leaf
½ cup Marsala
3 egg yolks
oil for deep frying
confectioners' sugar

This dessert comes originally from Campania. Sift together the flour and semolina. Heat together in a saucepan the water, salt, sugar and bay leaf. As soon as the liquid begins to boil remove from the heat and add the flour mixture all at once, stirring vigorously with a wooden spoon. As soon as the flour is well mixed in, return the saucepan to the heat for another 10 min, stirring constantly. Remove from the heat again, take out the bay leaf and allow the mixture to cool slightly before adding the Marsala and the egg yolks. Beat until very smooth and then turn out on to an oiled marble slab or pastry board. When the dough is cold break off small pieces and shape them into little rings. Heat plenty of oil for deep frying. Add the rings a few at a time and fry until crisp and golden, constantly moving them about during cooking so the dough forms little nodules over the surface, typical of this Neapolitan specialty. Remove from the saucepan with a perforated spoon and drain on kitchen paper. Serve sprinkled with confectioners' sugar.

ZUCCOTTO *

for the sponge cake:
4 eggs, separated
1 tsp vanillia extract
1 cup confectioners' sugar
⅓ cup all-purpose flour
⅓ cup cornstarch

for the filling:
½ cup blanched almonds
½ cup shelled filberts
scant 4½ cups heavy cream
¾ cup confectioners' sugar
1¼ cup grated semisweet chocolate
2 tbsp cognac
2 tbsp sweet liqueur
cocoa powder

This is a traditional dessert from Tuscany. To make the sponge, beat the egg yolks, vanilla extract and sugar in a bowl until light and frothy. Whisk the egg whites stiffly and fold carefully into the egg mixture. Gradually add the flour and cornstarch, mixing continuously. Butter and flour a moderately deep cake pan, about 10 in diameter. Spoon in the sponge mixture and bake in a moderate oven (350°F) for about 40 min until light golden brown. Cool on a wire rack. To make the filling, toast the almonds and filberts and roughly chop them. Whip the cream in a bowl with the confectioners' sugar and mix in the chopped nuts and grated chocolate. Cut the sponge horizontally into slices ½ in thick and sprinkle them with the cognac and sweet liqueur, mixed together. Line a semispherical mold or basin with well-buttered wax paper and then with some of the sponge slices. Fill up to the brim with the whipped cream, level the top with a spatula and cover the dessert with the remaining sponge slices. Refrigerate for at least 2 hr. Turn out on to a round serving plate and sprinkle with cocoa and confectioners' sugar mixed, or with first one and then the other to give alternate brown and white segments.

CROSTATA DI MELE CON * GELATO DI DATTERI E CARAMELLO DI VINO
(Apple tart with date ice cream and caramel wine sauce)

for the pastry:
scant 1 cup all-purpose flour
¼ cup sugar
1 whole egg
1 egg yolk
1 tsp vanilla extract
¼ cup butter

for the filling:
*1½ lb rennet apples, peeled and
  sliced*

for the caramel:
½ cup sugar
½ cup sweet red wine
juice of ½ lemon

for the ice cream:
½ cup pitted dates
½ cup milk
2 eggs, separated

To make the pastry, sift together the flour and the sugar and mix in the egg and the vanilla extract. Add the butter and mix to a soft dough then cover and refrigerate for ½ hr. Butter and flour a 7-in pie dish. On a floured board roll out the pastry into two circles, the same diameter as the dish and about ⅛ in thick. Place one circle in the bottom of the dish and cover it with the sliced apple. Place the second pastry circle on top of the apples and bake in the oven for 1 hr at 250°F. To make the caramel dissolve the sugar in the wine and lemon juice and boil briskly in a saucepan for about 10 min until it caramelizes to dark brown. To make the ice cream, gently simmer the dates in the milk for ½ hr. Mix together in a blender. Add the separately beaten egg yolks and whites. Blend the ingredients together, cover and place in the freezer. During the first hour of freezing, whisk the mixture at regular intervals until slushy then leave undisturbed for 2–3 hr until set.

Sprinkle the pie with confectioners' sugar and cut into small slices. Serve with a ball of ice cream and a little caramel sauce.

PANNA COTTA CON SALSA DI FRAGOLE *
(Crème brûlée with strawberry sauce)

for the sauce:
3 cups strawberries, washed and
   hulled
¼ cup sugar

2¼ cups light cream
¼ cup sugar
1 tsp vanilla extract
2 level tsp powdered gelatin
   (unflavored)

First make the sauce: purée the strawberries and sugar in a blender and pass through a fine metal strainer. To make the custard, heat the cream with the sugar and the vanilla for ¼ hr. Sprinkle the gelatin on to a small amount of cold water to soften it then add to the mixture in the saucepan and stir well. Pour the mixture into four cups and refrigerate for 10 hr. Turn the custards out into individual dishes and serve with the strawberry sauce.

Cheeses

Nutritious and versatile, cheese has for centuries formed an integral part of the Italian diet. Nearly 2,000 years ago in the markets of Imperial Rome it was possible to buy more than a dozen types of cheese from many different parts of the Empire. The great range of cheeses produced in Italy today is largely due to the varied geography of the country. From the lush green pastures of the north come the richer and fattier cow's milk cheeses such as the world-famous Gorgonzola and Pannerone from Lombardy, the harder Asiago from the Veneto and the noble Parmigiano-reggiano from Emilia-Romagna. The more hilly central regions of the Abruzzi, Latium and Campania are the home of spun-curd cheeses such as Scamorza as well as a number of sheep's and goat's cheeses. The mountainous south and the islands of Sicily and Sardinia are recognized for their sheep's milk cheeses such as Pecorino and the traditional Ricotta. This wealth of choice is reflected in Italian cooking and cheese provides an indispensable ingredient for many popular recipes from pasta dishes, soups and pizzas to desserts such as the traditional Sicilian cassata made with Ricotta. Cheese, soft or hard, fresh or matured, used in cooking or eaten simply on its own with freshly baked bread, is as much a part of the Italian table as pasta, olive oil and good local wine.

Asiago

A semi-hard cheese, low in fat content, made with whole cow's milk; either dry-salted or immersed in a weak brine. Usually eaten unmatured, when it is only 4–5 months old. When matured for over a year, Asiago can be grated and used for cooking. The cheeses are wheel-shaped, 12–16 in in diameter, with almost straight sides about 4 in thick. Weight varies between 22–31 lb. The paste (inside) is a very pale straw color with fairly evenly distributed small-to-medium holes. The unmatured cheeses have a very delicate taste which becomes more pronounced when aged.

A much stronger-flavored variety of Asiago is produced from the high pastures of the Altopiano di Vezzena, and is usually matured for a year or even longer. This cheese is deep yellow in color with small, evenly distributed holes occurring throughout the paste. In the region of its production, "vezzena" – as the cheese is known – is almost always eaten with polenta.

Bitto

Named after the Bitto valley in the Valtellina region of northern Italy, this cheese is widely known through two local specialties: *pizzoccheri* ("ribbon noodles") and *taragna* polenta. Once mixed with goat's or sheep's milk, these scalded-curd cheeses are now made with whole cow's milk.

The shape of the cheese varies, usually weighing 17½–22 lb, although they can sometimes be heavier than a Parmesan cheese. Bitto ages slowly and is rarely eaten before it is 6 months old. It is a hard cheese, varying in color, with tiny holes and a fairly high fat content. When cured for a year or longer, Bitto gains in strength and aroma, the paste gradually hardening until it acquires a dense, almost crumbly consistency not unlike Parmesan.

Burrata

Apulia, in southern Italy, is the home of this cheese which at first sight looks just like a large Mozzarella, weighing about 1 lb. Like Mozzarella, Burrata would traditionally have been made from buffalo milk, but today cow's milk is used. As its name ("buttery") suggests, it has a higher fat content than Mozzarella. The outer (edible) layer of Burrata has the appearance of a protective coating, enclosing the softer, creamy part of the cheese.

Burrata is considered by many the best fresh cheese in the world.

Caciocavallo

A large number of hard, plastic-curd (or spun-curd) cheeses come under this heading. The cow's milk cheeses are salted in brine and shaped like flasks with their necks constricted where they have been tied tightly with twine for curing. Their name "cheese on horseback" derives from the custom of hanging string-linked pairs of cheese astride a horizontally placed pole where they are left to mature.

Weight varies between 2–4½ lb. The paste is white, sometimes with a faint straw-colored tinge, very dense and even-textured when young. Some cheeses are smoked during aging. Caciocavallo is most often eaten as a table cheese when matured for up to 6 months; longer aging (up to a year) produces a grating cheese. The sweet, delicate taste of the unmatured cheese changes in the older, aged cheeses to a stronger, more pronounced flavor. This cheese is produced in almost every region of southern Italy.

Caciofiore umbro

In the past, large quantities of consistently high quality Caciofiore were made throughout Latium; today production is confined to the Pian di Chiavano area near Cascia. Skimmed cow's milk is used to produce this soft cheese, which is eaten fresh or briefly matured. It has a mild taste, with a slight aromatic overtone, which is probably a result of the type of pasturage on which the cows graze. Disk-shaped, a Caciofiore cheese weighs just over 2 lb.

Caciotta romana

Made by cottage-industry producers in the hills around Rome and in the Nepi and Riano districts. Usually a mixture of sheep's and cow's milk, although occasionally just one type of milk is used. Consumed in large quantities in Rome during the nineteenth century, Caciotta still accounts for a sizeable proportion of the region's cheese production. Cylindrical in shape, they weigh a little over 2 lb. This cheese is most often eaten fresh as a table cheese but is also widely used in cooking; in Rome, Caciotta and Scamorza are eaten broiled or lightly fried in a little olive oil.

Caciotta toscana

The group of cheeses classified under the general heading Caciotta includes an endless variety of cow's, goat's and sheep's milk products from the upland areas of Tuscany, Latium, the Marches and Umbria. The most noteworthy is probably Tuscan Caciotta, made with all cow's milk, which can be eaten fresh or matured. The cheeses are usually disk-shaped, small with straight or slightly convex sides. The best come from San Gimignano, Monte Amiata, the Maremma and Casentino; in the latter two, sheep's milk is sometimes used.

Crescenza

A traditional, cheese from Lombardy, with at least 50 percent fat content made with whole cow's milk. Eaten as fresh as possible as it spoils quickly; mainly produced in 6-in square molds, 2 in deep. Large-scale producers make smaller cheeses as well, also square, weighing ½–1 lb. The paste is white, without rind or holes; if left in a warm place, however, the cheese expands and rises while holes form inside (this process probably gave the cheese its name, *crescere* meaning "to grow" in Italian). The fat content varies according to the time of year, being predictably lower in winter and higher in summer. Other similar but smaller cheeses, known as Crescenzine, fall within this group.

Crescenza used to be known under the alternative name of Stracchino, indicating that it belonged to the family of fresh, uncooked and rindless curd cheeses produced throughout the Lombardy plain.

The name Stracchino (dialect for "tired") is thought to derive from the fact that the cheese was traditionally made with the evening's milk, mixed with cream, when the cows were weary after a long day's grazing in the pastures.

Although traditional methods of making the cheese have given way to special modern techniques, the cheese has retained its original consistency and character.

Fior di latte abruzzese

Originally made only in certain parts of Campania, this cheese is now made throughout the region with production centered in Abruzzo. Made with cow's milk, Fior di latte is described as the poor relation of buffalo milk Mozzarella; it is similar in appearance, produced in oval shapes and braids. Unlike Mozzarella, however, this is not a spun-curd cheese and its color is milky white as opposed to chalk white. It is used as a table cheese and a cooking cheese, especially in regional dishes, in much the same way as Mozzarella.

Fontal

This cheese belongs to the same family as Fontina and Montasio, which are made with whole cow's milk and come from the Alpine region.

Pale straw yellow in color, the paste is dense yet tender and easy to cut with sparse, evenly distributed tiny holes. Wheel-shaped, about 16 in in diameter with slightly convex sides approximately 4 in high. Like Fontina this is a very palatable table cheese and a main ingredient in many regional dishes. Similar in taste to Emmental it is particularly well suited to cold meals, such as mixed rice salads.

Fontina

This cheese almost certainly takes its name from Fontin in the Italian Alps, but other places also lay

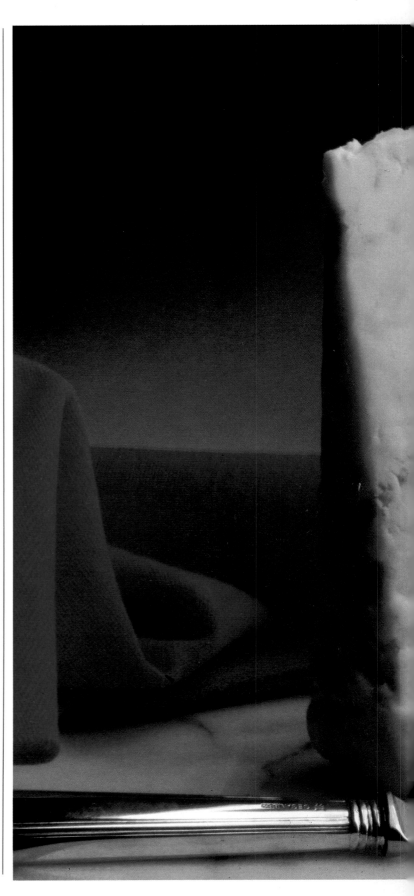

claim to its origin; it is a typical cheese of the Val d'Aosta and its production dates back to ancient times. Protected by the denomination system as a fine, classic cheese.

Fontina is made with whole cow's milk and there are two types, one made with summer milk when the cows are feeding on the high mountain pastures; the other with winter milk when the cows are forage-fed in their cowsheds. The wheel-shaped cheeses, 18–22 in wide, have almost completely straight sides and are usually 3–4 in high. Weight varies from 17–40 lb; the thin rind, varying from russet to dark brown, encloses a fairly soft, pale to deep straw-colored paste with few holes. The aromatic bouquet is more pronounced in the cheeses produced in summer.

Fontina is a full-fat, dry-salted cheese which is matured for 90–100 days; it makes a good table cheese and is also used in cooking.

Formaggetta

A vast range of cheeses produced in the Ligurian Apennine region falls under this heading. Varying in size but always fairly small, these molded cheeses are made with a mixture of goat's and cow's milk; traditional artisan's cheeses are, however, often made with all cow's milk or all goat's milk. Invariably eaten fresh; it is extremely rare to see this cheese matured, but it can be preserved in oil, which produces a stronger and sharper flavor. When the goat's milk cheeses are aged, they are used for grating; particularly recommended in Genoese pesto sauce for a more pronounced flavor. Cheeses made in the border region between the Ligurian and the Tuscan Apennines are slightly different, having a more robust taste and a brownish rind.

Gorgonzola

This classic cheese is heir to a long tradition and has a distinctive appearance due to the presence of molds which are introduced by piercing the cheese in several places. These molds are encouraged to grow during the maturing process. The *penicillium glaucum* which produces these molds gives the cheese a greenish-veined appearance and a sharp flavor.

It is claimed that the first Gorgonzola cheeses were made as early as 879 A.D., and that Gorgonzola was preceded by Roquefort, another veined or blue cheese. Legend has it that Charlemagne tasted one of these ancient French cheeses eighty years earlier when offered shelter by a hermit during a long journey through France.

Gorgonzola is produced with whole cow's milk in squat drum-shaped forms with straight sides 6–8 in high and 10–12 in in diameter, weighing 15½–28½ lb. The fat content is very high (about 50 percent) and the cheeses are dry-salted and then aged for several months. Recent trends have led to the marketing of several different kinds of Gorgonzola, varying in pungency, produced by adjusting the maturing period and the fat content. If the cheeses are not pierced while they are maturing, no mold develops, and the cheese is known as Pannerone.

Grana padano

The name "Grana padano" embraces the entire production of this type of cheese north of the River Po. It is a hard cheese, low in fat content, that ages slowly and is made with milk from cows fed on fresh pasture or forage. The milk is allowed to stand and the cream that rises to the surface is skimmed off. Production goes on throughout the year. Grana padano cheeses weigh 53–88 lb and are wheel-shaped with slightly convex sides 7–10 in high, 14–18 in in diameter; inside the ⅛–¼ in-thick rind the paste is pale, straw-tinged white with a fragrant and delicate taste and aroma. The natural aging process lasts for up to 2 years at a temperature of 60–70° F.

Grana padano is produced in the provinces of Alessandria, Asti, Cuneo, Novara, Turin, Vercelli, Bergamo, Brescia, Como, Cremona, Mantua (the left bank of the River Po), Milan, Pavia, Sondrio, Varese, Trento, Padua, Rovigo, Treviso, Venice, Verona, Vicenza, Bologna (the right bank of the River Reno), Ferrara, Forli, Piacenza and Ravenna. The cheeses are categorized into three types, depending on when pro-

289

duction takes place: *Vernengo* or *invernengo*, made from December through March; *di testa*, from April through June, and *tardivo* or *terzolo*, produced during October and November. Predictably, *di testa* is the best Grana padano, when the cows are feeding on fresh grass.

Marzolino
Production of this, the original Pecorino which comes from the Val di Chiano, used to begin in March. The cheese was well known throughout Tuscany and several mentions are made of it in Italian literature.

Marzolino is oval in shape with a diameter of about 5 in at its widest point; the rind is thin and whitish on the fresh cheeses. Tomato paste is rubbed over the surface of cheeses which are to be matured (replacing the traditional sheep's blood), giving it a reddish hue. The fairly dense paste (white, becoming pale orange when aged) has some holes; a cheese for the table and for grating.

Mascarpone
Tradition has it that when Spain ruled parts of Italy in the seventeenth century, one of her governors tasted this cheese and exclaimed:—¡*Mas que bueno!*—("Better than good!"), from which came *mascarpone*. True or not, the name can certainly be linked to *mascherpa* or *mascherpin*, the old Lombard words for Ricotta. This cheese originally came from the flood plain of the River Lodi; it has become so popular that nowadays it is produced in most regions of Italy.

Citric acid is used to curdle cream and the end product, Mascarpone, looks like extremely thick cream. It is a spreading cheese with a very high fat content and the color and flavor of milk. Highly perishable, it is best made during the winter months. Besides being served as a table cheese, it is also used for desserts (mixed with grated or melted chocolate, ground coffee, or a variety of liqueurs), as a filling for cakes or in the preparation of delicately flavored pasta dishes (instead of butter or cream).

Montasio
Typical of the eastern Alps but nowadays widely produced elsewhere. Whole cow's milk is used during the summer Alpine pasturing season. A winter version, also called Montasio, has a slightly lower fat content as partially skimmed cow's milk is used, but, unlike summer Montasio, it is eaten fresh. Classic Montasio is disk-shaped with straight sides about 4 in high, 14–16 in in diameter and usually weighing under 22 lb. Low in fat content, this cheese is fairly even textured with sparse holes; it is salted in a weak brine solution or may be dry-salted. Mild when briefly ripened, the taste intensifies when the cheese is aged for around a year. The taste of mature Montasio has led to its being called "Pecorino" (*i.e.* sheep's milk cheese), belying its content of all cow's milk. Strict quality control during aging means that any slightly sub-standard forms (too many holes, faulty rind) are sold for immediate consumption, leaving only perfect examples to complete the maturing process.

This type of cheese dates back to late medieval times, when the monks of the Abbey of Moggio began making cheese.

Morlacco
A cheese that comes from the northern part of the province of Vicenza, probably taking its name from the Morlacchia region of Zara where production originated. In Vicenza it used to be known as "the poor man's cheese" because its relatively high nutritional value and inexpensive price made it a staple food.

Partially skimmed cow's milk is used to make this slightly salty white cheese with the occasional tiny hole; the taste becomes sharper with age. Morlacco is noted for its tendency to develop a greenish-blue surface mold from which it acquires a distinctive taste. The disk-shaped cheeses vary in size from 10–12 in in diameter and have slightly convex sides 4–6 in high.

Mozzarella
Always eaten fresh, this world-famous cheese takes its name from a stage in its manufacture: As the spun curd is produced it is cut into small pieces, the Italian word for this being *mozzare* ("to cut").

Mozzarella has been made for centuries. Traditionally only buffalo's milk was used but nowadays this type is less readily available and costs more; the Battipaglia plain in the province of Salerno, and the Volturno plain still produce the original (and superior) type. The soft spun curd cheese is very dense with a bland, milky taste. The shape varies from round (*bocconcini* – "mouthfuls") to egg-shaped (*ovolini*). Such is the demand for Mozzarella (which must be eaten very fresh) that a very good cow's milk version is manufactured; however, this cannot be compared with the buffalo milk cheeses. Mozzarella is a very digestible fresh cheese and when made with cow's milk has a fairly low fat content. It is used in a great many southern Italian dishes as well as for pizzas.

Pannerone
The region around Lodi in the Lombardy plain is the home of this whole cow's milk cheese. Drum-shaped, with straight sides about 8 in high and varying in diameter from 10–12 in, these high fat content cheeses have minute holes evenly distributed through the milky white, sometimes straw-colored, paste. Pannerone is in fact moldless Gorgonzola; it is not salted and after a period of aging (never longer than 2 months) it acquires quite a distinctive, slightly sour flavor. It is eaten only as a table or dessert cheese.

Parmigiano reggiano
Parmesan reigns supreme among Italian cheeses and is used, freshly grated, on most pasta dishes. The region which has been granted the right to call its product Parmigiano reggiano extends from the province of Parma to that of Mantua (on the right bank of the River Po) and to the province of Bologna (left bank of the River Reno).

This hard cheese, low in fat content, is made with milk from cows fed mainly on fresh field or meadow pasturage. The morning's milk is left to stand and is then partially skimmed. Production must fall between the dates of April 1 and November 11. Salting is carried out when the cheeses are a few days old and lasts 20–30 days. The shortest period of aging, involving no artificial processes, lasts until the end of the summer of the year after production, and the cheeses are often aged for far longer. The forms are drum-shaped with slightly convex sides 7–9½ in high, 14–18 in in diameter and weigh at least 53 lb. The pale straw-colored paste has a pronounced but subtle flavor and aroma with no hint of bitterness. It is granular in texture, breaking along natural lines of separation into large, thick "flakes"; the holes are so small as to be almost invisible and the rind is about ¼ in thick. An association of producers of genuine Parmesan cheese from the authorized provinces governs the use of a special Parmigiano reggiano stamp on the surface of the rind and also controls manufacture and marketing.

Pecorino romano
One of the best known Pecorino or sheep's milk cheeses, both in Italy and abroad. About half the total production is exported, much of it to the United States. These hard cheeses are made exclusively with sheep's milk, from March through June. An operation known as *frugatura* peculiar to this cheese entails pressing the curd to expel all the whey as soon as it has been placed in the mold. Dry-salting lasts about 90 days, during which time the cheese undergoes frequent washings and is pierced in several places to allow the salt to penetrate more readily; it then takes about 8 months to mature. These drum-shaped cheeses, low in fat content, measure 5½–8½ in in height, and weight varies from 17–44 lb; the paste is white and dense with a distinctive, sharp taste. Production is concentrated in the provinces of Cagliari, Frosinone, Grosseto, Latina, Rome, Sassari, Nuoro and Viterbo.

Pecorino sardo *or* Fiore sardo
As its names imply, this version of Pecorino is made in Sardinia from sheep's milk. The curd is shaped in special cone-shaped molds, pairs of which are stuck base to base to form an unusual, instantly recognizable form. The cheeses are soaked in brine, then dry-salted;

up to 3 months afterward they can be eaten as table cheeses for slicing. When aged for 6 months or more they are used for grating. Weight varies from 3¼–8¾ lb. The rind is yellow, turning brownish-gray when aged; the color of the paste inside is white to pale straw and the taste changes and becomes stronger as the cheese matures.

Pecorino senese

A Sienese sheep's milk cheese that really belongs to the large family of Caciottas; when aged, however, its taste sets it apart from other sheep's milk cheeses of this type. Even when mature it does not develop much "bite" but has a slightly bitter aroma derived from certain plants that grow where the sheep graze. The best cheeses are made in springtime when these plants are young and tender, and less bitter. The drum-shaped cheeses have convex sides and weigh 2¼–4½ lb. Their name denotes the centuries-old tradition in the province of Siena of making fine, aged cheeses and this region still accounts for the greatest production in both volume and quality.

Pecorino siciliano

Most of this cheese, predictably, comes from Sicily and during the first few days of the manufacturing process it is shaped in wicker molds, hence its other name Canestrato (*canestro* – "basket").

It is a hard cheese, made with whole sheep's milk during the months October through June, and takes at least 4 months to mature. The cylindrical forms are dry-salted and weigh from 8¾–26½ lb. The rind is yellowish-white and shows the imprint of its wicker mold, enclosing a dense paste with few holes. Sometimes a few peppercorns are incorporated into the cheese curd and it then becomes Pecorino peppato or Maiorchino.

Provola

Central and southern Italy produce these small spun-curd cheeses, which were once made with buffalo milk but now may also be made with cow's milk. Roughly spherical and weighing 1½–1¾ lb, Provola is marketed as fresh, mature, smoked fresh or smoked mature.

When very fresh the taste is mild and not unlike Mozzarella; when mature it is reminiscent of Caciocavallo. Mass-produced Provolas are wax-coated to prevent them becoming dry.

Provolone

Production of this cheese is governed by the regulations of a decree that conferred the status of a "typical" cheese on Provolone. Provolone has been likened to Caciocavallo (see page 287) and both these cheeses are made with whole cow's milk. Provolone varies in shape, being produced as cone, pear, melon or long sausage-shaped cheeses. This last form is most common, with rounded ends, 14–17½ in long and weighing 2¼–13¼ lb; huge versions of these cheeses are also made, their impressive weight and size earning them the name Provolone gigante. The cheeses are netted and tied up in pairs to mature like Caciocavallo. The paste is white or tinged a pale straw yellow and as it matures may develop a few holes. Three varieties are marketed: mild, strong (when aging has produced a more pronounced flavour), and smoked.

Ragusano

A classic product of the Ragusa region, Ragusano is a hard, spun-curd cheese. These Sicilian cheeses are made with whole cow's milk, salted in brine and are occasionally smoked. They are strung up together in pairs and hung over poles to mature. They are ready for consumption as table cheese after 6 months; older cheeses are used for grating. The straight-sided, oblong cheeses with slightly rounded corners show the marks of having been tied up to mature; they usually weigh 13¼–26½ lb. The rind is thin and pale straw colored when fresh, turning light to dark brown when aged and encloses a paste which is white, acquiring a pale straw tinge as it matures, with the occasional hole. The fresh cheese is mild and delicate but the flavor becomes sharper with age.

Ricotta stagionata

Mature and "dry" Ricottas are a Sicilian specialty. Small molded Ricotta cheeses are drained and

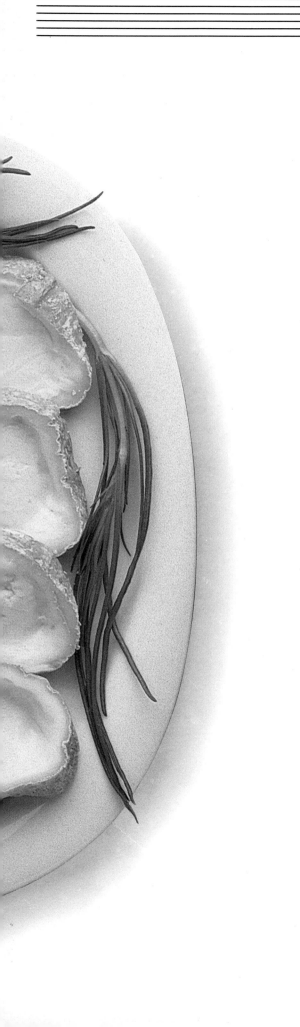

then left to dry in the sun until they become hard and compact enough for grating. Ricotta from the Norcia region has a far higher fat content than most and is used to enhance plain pasta dishes as an alternative to Parmesan, giving a delightfully mild milky flavor. A similar type of Ricotta, from the Apulia region of southern Italy, takes longer to make and this aged Ricotta is also sprinkled on pasta dishes. Some varieties of Ricotta are also smoked.

Robiola
Robiola is most probably named after Robbio in Lomellina, but an alternative etymology traces it back to the Latin *rubeola* ("little reddish one") because these small cheeses once had a reddish rind.

More often than not made with cow's milk and high in fat content, these diminutive square cheeses are usually eaten fresh; sometimes cow's milk is mixed with sheep's or goat's milk. Robiola ripens in 8–15 days, when it can be classified as a Crescenza or Stracchino, but if matured it acquires a sharper taste with its own distinctive aroma: Robiolas produced in Valsassina, Ballabio, Introbio and Pasturo belong to this latter type. Robiola bears a close resemblance to Taleggio but is somewhat smaller. Bec is a noteworthy variety of Robiola, from the Langhe region of Piedmont, and is made with cow's milk mixed with goat's milk during the goats' mating season (*becco* or *bec* in Piedmontese dialect means "billy goat"). Other good Robiolas come from Roccaverano, Ceva, Bossolasco and Monferrato. Some of these are preserved with oil and herbs in glass jars.

Scamorza
Throughout central and southern Italy, in those parts of the country traditionally associated with the rearing of buffalos, a cheese is made which is almost as widely used in cooking as Caciocavallo and Mozzarella. Smaller than Caciocavallo, the best Scamorza comes from Calabria (where they are slighty elongated in shape) and Apulia (where they are stubbier and sometimes shaped to look like pigs). Slices of Scamorza are dressed with oil and pepper and broiled or baked in the oven on a slice of toast; the cheese can also be used instead of Mozzarella for a deep-fried cheese sandwich (*Mozzarella in carrozza* – "Mozzarella in a carriage").

Taleggio
The fame of this cheese has spread beyond the confines of its native Lombardy where it originated in the foothills of the Alps near Bergamo. Taleggio is made only with whole cow's milk and is dry-salted; the soft, fat cheese is fully ripe after 40–50 days. The oblong, straight-sided cheeses weigh approximately 4½ lb. Few or no holes occur in the paste, which is white or occasionally palest straw yellow, and its subtly aromatic taste strengthens with age. The rind is soft and thin.

Toma
Toma is a general heading under which can be grouped a variety of hard cheeses from the Piedmontese Alpine region and lower slopes of the Alps. Besides these parts of Lombardy, Toma is also found in the Apennines and even in Sicily where the name is Tuma, but although these products share the same name they may differ widely.

A much smaller version, called Tometta, with the same drum shape, never exceeds 4½ lb in weight, whereas a classic Toma cheese can weigh as much as 17½–20 lb. There is also Tomino, around ½ lb in weight, a disk-shaped, spreadable cheese with an acidulated taste, which is eaten fresh. All these cheeses are usually made with cow's milk, occasionally mixed with goat's or sheep's milk. White when fresh, the color of the cheese turns yellow as it matures and its mild taste gradually sharpens. When aged, Toma is hard enough to grate and is used to flavor polenta. Tometta can also be matured, when the paste's delicate, creamy texture turns into a stronger cheese with small holes. Tomino cheeses, however, must be eaten fresh and can be served with a variety of sauces, tomatoes and red chili peppers. Alternatively they can be preserved in oil with herbs and seasonings.

Preserves, Pickles and Liqueurs

*I*t can be very rewarding to make your
own preserves, taking advantage of a
glut of seasonal fruits or vegetables in order
to enjoy them throughout the year. Fruit
preserved in alcohol, candied fruit, vegetables
in oil or vinegar, homemade relishes, fruit
jellies and preserves are all very satisfying to
make and well worth the time and effort
involved.

Take care, when canning or bottling any
fruit, preserves or liqueur, to observe certain
hygiene guidelines. For all preserving in jars
it is important that you follow the
manufacturer's sterilization instructions
carefully. The jars should be free of chips or
cracks (rinse and then warm in the oven
before use to lessen the risk of cracking) and
seals must be hermetic. Rubber rings are
useful for this purpose, and may be
purchased with the preserving jars.

To see if the mixture has set when making
preserves, spoon a small amount on to a cold
plate and allow it to cool; push your finger
across the surface and if it wrinkles, the
preserves have set. If not, return the mixture
to the saucepan and continue boiling until
setting point is reached (this takes place at
221°F). A special thermometer is useful.

Homemade liqueurs and fruit cordials are
delicious and easy to make. In Italy, 80°
alcohol is used, which is readily available for
this purpose, but any clear, flavorless spirit
may be substituted, such as vodka, schnapps
or aquavit.

RATAFIÀ DI ALBICOCCHE
(Apricot ratafia)

2¼ lb apricots
20 apricot kernels
1 cup + 3 tbsp sugar
2 quarts 80° clear, flavorless spirit
  (e.g. vodka, schnapps, aquavit)
4 vanilla beans
6–8 cloves

Wash the apricots well and chop. Pound the skinned kernels in a mortar then mix with the other ingredients and leave to stand for at least 20 days, preferably in a cool dark place. Strain through muslin before bottling and wait at least 3 months before sampling.

LIQUORE DI CILIEGIE
(Cherry cordial)

2¼ lb cherries
2 cups sugar
1 quart 80° clear, flavorless spirit
  (e.g. vodka, schnapps, aquavit)
about 40 young cherry leaves
2 pieces cinnamon

Rinse the cherries thoroughly and place them in a large glass jar with the sugar. Seal with an airtight lid and leave to stand in full sun for 7–8 days. Open the jar and transfer the contents to another jar large enough to take the liquid as well; add the cherry leaves and cinnamon. Leave for a month, then pour slowly through a paper coffee filter. Bottle and leave for 2 months before drinking.

NOCINO
(Walnut liqueur)

20 green (fresh) walnuts
1 quart 80° clear, flavorless spirit
  (e.g. vodka, schnapps, aquavit)
6–7 cloves
1 piece cinnamon
2½ cups sugar
scant ½ cup water

Pound the tender, freshly shelled walnuts to a paste with a pestle. Pour the liquor into a large glass jar, add the walnut paste, cloves, and cinnamon and leave to stand for 40 days. Afterward, filter through muslin. Boil the sugar and water for 2–3 min; strain this syrup into the bowl containing the flavored liquor. Mix well. Bottle and leave for 2 months.

MARASCHINO

4 cups Morello cherry pits
2 cups 80° clear, flavorless spirit
  (e.g. vodka, schnapps, acquavit)
2 cups sugar
1¾ cups water

Place the cherry pits in a jar, pour in the liquor and leave for at least 2½ months. Strain through muslin. Make a sugar syrup by boiling the sugar and water together for about 10 min; strain into the bowl containing the flavored liquor. Pour into bottles and leave to stand for 24 hr; strain, bottle and seal. If the liquid is not completely clear strain again, through a paper coffee filter.

ROSOLIO
(Citron cordial)

grated peel of 5 citrons (no pith)
2 cups 80° clear, flavorless spirit
  (e.g. vodka, schnapps, aquavit)
2 cups water
2½ cups sugar

Grate only the outer layer of the citrons, leaving all the bitter pith behind. Pour the liquor into a bowl and stir in the peel. Leave to stand for 10 days, then strain. Boil the sugar and water together for 10 min; leave to cool slightly before straining and mixing with the alcohol. Bottle. Wait 2 months before opening to drink.

GINEPRO
(Juniper liqueur)

generous ½ cup juniper berries
2½ cups sugar
1 quart clear, flavorless spirit (e.g. vodka, schnapps, aquavit)
1 tsp anise seeds
1 tsp whole coriander seeds

Mix all the ingredients except the alcohol and leave to stand in a glass jar for 8–9 days, preferably in a sunny position. Add the alcohol and leave for a further 40 days. Strain before bottling.

CONFETTURA DI ALBICOCCHE
(Apricot preserves)

2¼ lb apricots
4 cups sugar

Wash the fruit, pit, and chop finely. Mix with the sugar in a bowl and leave to stand overnight. The next day, transfer to a saucepan and boil rapidly until setting point is reached. Place in jars while still warm; wait until cold before sealing the jars.

ALBICOCCHE SCIROPPATE
(Apricots in syrup)

2¼ lb apricots
scant 1 pint water
3 cups sugar
peel of 1 lemon (no pith)
1 piece cinnamon

Wash the apricots well. Make a flavored sugar syrup by boiling the water, sugar, lemon peel and cinnamon together for about 10 min. Add the whole apricots and boil for a further 3 min; remove the fruit with a slotted spoon and pack in glass jars. Reduce the sugar syrup by boiling for 7–8 min more, and leave to cool before pouring sufficient into the jars to come to just below the rim. Seal. Wait 2 months before opening; turn the jar upside down at intervals to distribute the syrup evenly.

SCIROPPO DI AMARENE
(Morello cherry cordial)

4½ lb very ripe Morello cherries
sugar
cinnamon

Wash the cherries, pit them and detach the stalks. Place cherries and stalks in a bowl. Crush the cherries with a wooden spoon to release the maximum amount of juice. Add a crumbled piece of cinnamon. Leave to stand at room temperature for 48 hr, stirring and turning at intervals. Strain through muslin, measure out the juice and then boil with the equivalent weight of sugar for 5 min. Allow to cool before bottling, and seal when cold.

GELATINA DI ALBICOCCHE
(Apricot jelly)

2¼ lb ripe apricots
2½ cups sugar

Purée the apricots in a blender and measure out 2¼ cups liquid; mix with the sugar and boil rapidly until setting point is reached.

BUCCE DI ARANCE CANDITE
(Candied orange peel)

fresh orange peel
sugar
water

Scrape every trace of pith off the peel; wash the peel well, cut into very thin strips and boil in water for about ½ hr. Drain the peel; weigh it and measure the same weight of sugar into a small saucepan. Stir in the peel and cook over low heat until the peel has absorbed all the sugar. Spread the peel out on a wooden board and leave to dry. This candied peel will keep almost indefinitely.

GELATINA DI ARANCE
(Orange jelly)

juice of 2¼ lb oranges
juice of 1 lemon
2 cups sugar
liquid pectin

Boil the orange and lemon juice with the sugar. Once the sugar has completely dissolved add 3 tbsp pectin for each (approximate) quart of liquid. Bring to a boil and continue boiling until the jelly sets when tested.

AMARENE SOTTO SPIRITO
(Tipsy cherries)

2¼ lb Morello cherries
generous 1 lb sugar
scant 1 cup brandy or other spirit
1 piece cinnamon

Rinse the cherries, drain and pack into glass jars with the sugar and crumbled cinnamon bark. Seal the jars and leave in a sunny position for at least 8 days. Open the jars and add the alcohol. Reseal and wait at least 2 weeks and preferably longer before serving.

MARMELLATA DI ARANCE
(Marmalade)

12 ripe oranges
2 lemons
sugar
water

Choose oranges and lemons that are in good condition. Rinse well, and peel. Slice horizontally into rounds, reserving all the juice. Cut the pith away from the peel and slice the latter into very thin strips. Place the peel in a bowl, add enough water to cover and leave to stand for 24 hr. Drain and cook in fresh water until tender; discard cooking liquid. Add the orange and lemon slices and juice; cook for 10 min. Measure this mixture and add an equal amount of sugar; return to the saucepan and boil until the jelling point is reached.

MARMELLATA DI CACHI
(Persimmon preserves)

2¼ lb very ripe persimmons
3½ cups sugar
juice of 2 lemons
scant ½ cup water

Rinse the persimmons before pulling the stalk and skin away from the contents. Sieve the fruit; Boil the sugar and water hard for 2 min. Add the sieved fruit to this syrup. Continue boiling until the mixture sets when tested. Gently stir in the lemon juice 5 min before the jam has finished cooking.

MARMELLATA DI CASTAGNE
(Chestnut preserves)

2¼ lb sweet (Spanish) chestnuts
2½ cups sugar
2 cups water
¼ cup rum

Wash the chestnuts, prick their hard casings and boil until very tender. Peel while warm and sieve. Boil the water and sugar together for 10 min, add the chestnut purée to this syrup, and boil until setting point is reached, stirring in the rum before transferring to jars.

CASTAGNE CANDITE *
(Marrons glacés)

To make your efforts worthwhile when you undertake the fairly difficult and fiddly process of candying chestnuts you must use only the largest, soundest sweet chestnuts. A lot of wastage is inevitable, so allow plenty to spare. Remove the hard, brown outer casing and add to the chestnuts in a large saucepan of hot water; cook to *just below* boiling point (this is important) until a small skewer or needle penetrates easily. Remove from the heat and remove only one chestnut at a time to peel off the thin inner skin very carefully. This operation becomes much more difficult when the chestnuts cool. Do not get discouraged when quite a few of the chestnuts break up as you peel them. Place in a shallow flameproof dish in a single layer when peeled. Boil equal quantities of water and sugar, skimming off any foam to keep the syrup clear, for about 10 min, taking care that the syrup does not reach 230°F; check this with a candy thermometer if you have one. Remove from the heat immediately so that it does not reach thread stage.

Pour the boiling syrup evenly all over the chestnuts and leave to stand. The following day tip up the dish containing the chestnuts to drain off all the syrup into a saucepan and cook until it reaches thread stage (230–234°F); pour the hot syrup all over the chestnuts once more and leave to stand for another 24 hr. On the third day drain the syrup into the saucepan once more and add a little vanilla extract as well as a few drops of liquid glucose or honey (both prevent crystallization). Cook until the syrup reaches soft ball stage (234–240°F). Repeat the pouring process, coating all the chestnuts and leave to stand until the next day. Transfer very carefully to a wide-necked jar together with the remaining syrup. Seal the jar. This is the best way to preserve chestnuts for a considerable length of time.

The alternative "dry" method is for short-term preserving; confectioners use special pans with racks on which the chestnuts are placed and which can be raised (for draining) and lowered for another immersion in the syrup. Once the chestnuts have drained completely the syrup is thickened one stage further and the rack with the chestnuts lowered once more to complete another stage of the "glazing" process. Although many cookery books favor this method (using a fork to remove the chestnuts for each draining), more chestnuts will be broken this way, making a tricky operation even more hazardous. As a compromise, drain off the syrup after completing the whole of the first process given above and cook it until it reaches soft ball stage (234–240°F), then add the chestnuts and heat through (do not allow to boil). A skin will form on top, which should be removed; as you run your spatula round the sides of the pan the sugar will start to whiten. Remove the chestnuts very gently with a slotted spoon and leave them to drain, well spaced out, on a rack. Do not touch until they have completely drained and are cold. Place in an airtight tin lined with wax paper, separating the layers with more wax paper.

CHINOTTI CANDITI
(Candied sour oranges)

Wash the sour (or myrtle-leaved) oranges well and pierce them in three or four places with a large needle; place in a bowl and cover completely with cold water; leave to soak for 2 days, changing the water at least 2 or 3 times a day. Transfer the oranges to a saucepan full of fresh water, bring to a boil and simmer over low heat for ¼ hr. While they are cooking, bring 6¼ cups water to a boil in another saucepan. Use a slotted spoon to transfer the oranges from the first saucepan of boiling water straight into the fresh saucepanful; simmer for a further 10 min. Remove the oranges once more, retaining the water this time, and adding generous 5 cups sugar to it; cook these until the resulting syrup nears thread stage. Return the oranges to the saucepan and cook in the syrup for 2 or 3 min before pouring the contents of the pan into a bowl. Leave to stand for 24 hr, then drain off the syrup into a saucepan, bring to a boil and add the oranges. Repeat this last operation 5 more times, ensuring that the syrup ends up at the hard ball stage (250–266°F). If wished, add ¼–½ cup grappa while still warm and leave to stand overnight before transferring to a large, wide-necked jar, with an airtight seal.

CILIEGIE IN AGRODOLCE
(Sweet and sour cherries)

2¼ lb cherries
1¼ cups sugar
ground cinnamon
4–6 cloves
generous 1 cup red wine vinegar
grated peel of ½ lemon

For this recipe use Bigarreau or an equivalent type of cherries: firm even when ripe and less soft than black cherries. Wash, dry and pit, before arranging in neatly packed layers alternating with layers of the sugar, cinnamon and cloves. Boil the vinegar with the lemon peel for 2–3 min; leave to cool completely before pouring into the jar containing the layered cherries. If there is not quite enough vinegar to cover the contents of the jar completely, boil up some more, cool and top up. Use a patent canning jar with a fresh rubber seal. Make sure it is airtight and store in a cool, dark place. Serve as an accompaniment to game or boiled meats.

CILIEGIE SCIROPPATE
(Cherries in syrup)

2¼ lb cherries
3 cups sugar
1¾ cups water
1 small piece cinnamon

Wash the cherries well and remove their stalks. Boil the sugar, cinnamon and water together for 10 min; add the cherries to this syrup, bring back to a boil and then, using a slotted spoon, transfer the cherries to preserving jars. Reduce and thicken the syrup by cooking for a further 10 min. When cold pour into the jar(s) to come just below the rim. Seal and sterilize for 20 min.

GELATINA DI CILIEGIE
(Cherry jelly)

2¼ lb cherries
water
sugar
peel of 1 lemon
1 piece cinnamon

Wash the cherries thoroughly, then remove the pits and tear off the stalks. Wrap half the pits in a piece of muslin and place with the cherries in a saucepan. Add a handful of the cherry stalks. Add sufficient water to cover and boil gently for 10 min. Strain the juice and leave to stand overnight. Measure the juice, add an equal weight of sugar and boil in a saucepan with the lemon peel and cinnamon until setting point is reached.

CILIEGIE CANDITE
(Candied cherries)

Choose red, ripe but firm cherries; black cherries look less attractive and are less easy to handle when pitted and candied. Wash the fruit, pit and weigh. Place in a bowl, alternating layers of cherries with layers of sugar (use an equal amount of sugar and cherries); leave to stand overnight. Strain off the juice into a saucepan (if the cherries you use are not very juicy, add a very little water to the cherry juice) and bring to a boil while stirring and removing any scum. When the boiling syrup has thickened to thread consistency pour it over the cherries and leave to stand for 24 hr. Drain off the syrup into the saucepan, add scant 1 cup apple juice and bring to a boil; add the cherries and cook for 5 min to thicken the syrup further. Leave to stand for 2 days, then repeat the process of draining off the syrup, boiling it and adding the cherries twice more (do not add any more apple juice). Allow the cherries to stand in the syrup for 2 days each time. By now the syrup should be at hard ball stage. Leave to stand for a final 24 hr, then transfer to jars with an airtight seal.

MARMELLATA DI FRAGOLE
(Strawberry preserves)

2¼ lb strawberries
4 cups sugar

Choose slightly underripe strawberries to obtain a better set. Rinse and hull, handling as little as possible. Simmer the strawberries with the sugar in a flameproof casserole until the sugar has completely dissolved; transfer all the fruit and liquid to a saucepan and boil until setting point is reached.

MARMELLATA DI FICHI
(Fig preserves)

2¼ lb figs
3½ cups sugar
juice of 1 lemon

Choose ripe, thin-skinned figs with no splits or blemishes. Rinse, chop finely and place in an earthenware receptacle with the sugar. Leave to stand for at least 12 hr. Boil the figs and sugar and juice in a heavy saucepan until set. Stir in the lemon juice gently a few minutes before removing from the heat.

GELATINA DI LAMPONI
(Raspberry jelly)

2½ cups fresh raspberry juice
generous 2½ cups sugar
scant ½ cup water

Wash the raspberries well and cook until very soft. Spoon the mixture into a jelly bag or fine hair sieve with a bowl placed underneath and leave overnight to allow all the juice to drain off. (If you find you have less than the required amount of juice, measure it and put the same weight of sugar in a saucepan with a little less water, otherwise stick to the quantities given above.) Simmer the sugar and water to make a syrup, then stir in the raspberry juice and boil rapidly until it jells when tested.

MARMELLATA DI LAMPONI
(Raspberry preserves)

2¼ lb raspberries
3½ cups sugar

Handle the ripe raspberries carefully when rinsing and picking them over. Cook gently for about 10 min then add the sugar and boil rapidly until the jam sets when tested.

BUCCE DI LIMONI CANDITE
(Candied lemon peel)

lemon peel
water
sugar

Boil the fresh lemon peel (all pith removed) in water for 20 min; drain well and cut into thin strips. Weigh the peel and cook with the same weight of sugar in a saucepan until all the sugar has been absorbed. Spread the peel out on a wooden chopping board to dry off.

MARMELLATA DI MELE
(Apple preserves)

2¼ lb apples
4 cups sugar
2 small pieces vanilla bean

Use early varieties of apple for this recipe. Do not peel or core. Chop the apples and cook for 15 min in a saucepan with very little water. Purée by pushing through a fine sieve into another saucepan, add

Wash and peel the fruit but do not core. Chop and cook in the white wine until very soft. Push through a fine sieve into another saucepan; add the sugar and the coarsely chopped peel. Simmer to reduce and thicken, adding the mustard powder just before removing from the heat.

SCIROPPO DI MIRTILLI
(Blueberry syrup)

2¼ lb blueberries
sugar

Rinse the fruit, handling as little as possible, and place in a large bowl. Crush to release all the juice. Leave to stand for at least 48 hr before straining through a canvas jelly bag or piece of muslin by hanging up to drip into a bowl overnight. Measure out the juice and boil with the same weight of sugar in a saucepan for 5 min exactly. Pour into preheated bottles while still hot.

GELATINA DI MORE
(Blackberry jelly)

2¼ lb blackberries
generous 1 cup water
2½ cups sugar

Wash the fruit and cook with a little water for just 5 min. Push through a sieve, then drain the resulting purée in a canvas jelly bag suspended over a bowl overnight. Pour the juice into a saucepan and boil with the sugar until the correct setting consistency is reached.

MARMELLATA DI PESCHE
(Peach preserves)

2¼ lb peaches
3¾ cups sugar

Place the peaches in a large bowl and pour boiling water over them; after a minute or so they will be much easier to peel. Coarsely chop the peeled, pitted peaches and cook for 10 min. Add the sugar and boil rapidly, stirring gently from time to time, until set.

the sugar and vanilla and boil rapidly until set.

SCIROPPO DI MORE
(Blackberry cordial)

Choose large, fleshy berries. Wash them by holding under cold running water in a sieve, drain well and spread out to dry on kitchen paper. Push through a sieve, crushing them with the base of a cup (blackberries stain, so take care), allowing the purée to collect in a large bowl underneath. Leave to ferment in a warm, dark place for 2 days. Skim off the thicker top layer and discard, pouring the liquid underneath through a coffee filter paper or a colander lined with muslin; the strained liquid must be very clear. For every 2¼ lb net weight of liquid allow 7⅔ cups sugar. Mix this with the strained juice of 2 lemons in a stainless steel

pan and stir in the blackberry juice. Bring slowly to a boil, removing any scum (but no liquid); simmer for 3 min. When it has cooled a little pour the syrup into bottles and, when completely cold, seal with sterilized patent bottle tops.

GELATINA DI MELE
(Apple jelly)

2¼ lb underripe apples
sugar

Do not peel, core or remove the seeds. Slice the apples thinly into a saucepan and cook until mushy. Spoon into a muslin bag and hang up to drain into a large bowl overnight. Measure out the juice and cook with the same weight of sugar over low heat, spooning off any scum. When the sugar has dissolved, bring to a boil and boil rapidly, until the jelly sets when tested.

CONFETTURA DI PERE
(Pear preserves)

2¼ lb pears
4 cups sugar
juice of 1 lemon

Wash and chop the pears. Place in a large bowl with the sugar and leave to stand for a few hours. Transfer the contents of the bowl to a saucepan and boil rapidly until set. Shortly before taking the saucepan off the heat, gently stir in the lemon juice.

MOSTARDA DI MELE
(Quince and mustard relish)

2¼ lb quinces
1½ lb apples
1 quart white wine
5 cups sugar
generous 1 cup mixed orange and
    citron peel
3 tbsp mustard powder

UVA SOTTO GRAPPA
(Grapes in grappa)

2¼ lb white grapes
2½ cups sugar
1 piece cinnamon
2–3 cloves
grappa

Wash the grapes and remove their stalks as neatly as possible. Fill glass preserving jars with the grapes, sugar, crumbled cinnamon bark and cloves. Pour in enough grappa to cover. Seal tightly and wait at least 2 months before sampling.

SCIROPPO D'UVA
(Grape syrup)

To make 1 quart syrup you will need 4½ lb grapes. Wash the grapes, remove stalks and pat dry with kitchen paper. Place them in a large bowl. Squeeze and crush the grapes by hand as thoroughly as possible. Cover this grape must with a clean cloth and leave to ferment for 1 week, after which sieve to eliminate the skins. Pour the remaining juice and pulp into a colander lined with fine muslin and place over a bowl; leave to drip into the bowl. The resulting liquid should be clear; if it is not, strain through a large paper coffee filter placed in the appropriate conical holder. Measure the liquid and pour into a stainless steel pan, adding 6¼ cups sugar for every quart of juice. Stir the sugar in slowly. Heat to a gentle boil, skimming any scum off the surface; simmer for

CONFETTURA DI PRUGNE
(Plum preserves)

2¼ lb plums
3⅔ cups sugar
peel of 1 lemon (no pith)
1 piece cinnamon

Wash and pit the plums. Put the fruit in a bowl with the sugar and leave to stand for at least 12 hr, then transfer to a saucepan. Boil rapidly with the lemon peel and the cinnamon, stirring continuously until the correct consistency is reached.

MARMELLATA DI RIBES
(Redcurrant preserves)

2¼ lb redcurrants
4 cups sugar

Wash the redcurrants, drain and remove their stalks. Cook the fruit for 10 min or until very soft, then add the sugar. Once this has dissolved, boil rapidly until set.

GELATINA DI UVA BIANCA
(White grape jelly)

2¼ lb white grapes
3½ cups sugar

Wash the grapes, remove their stalks and press through a sieve. Weigh the pulp; measure out the same weight of sugar and cook these together over a moderate heat until the sugar dissolves. Bring to a boil, and boil rapidly until the grape jelly reaches setting point.

PESCHE INTERE AL BRANDY
(Whole peaches in brandy)

2¼ lb peaches
1⅔ cups sugar
1 pint brandy

Wash and dry the peaches; pierce in several well-spaced places with a fork and arrange neatly inside several canning jars (or 1 large jar). Pour in the sugar and sufficient brandy to cover. Seal hermetically. Leave to mature for 3 months.

10 min. Turn off the heat, leave to cool a little and pour into bottles. When completely cold, seal with patent bottle tops.

MACEDONIA SCIROPPATA
(Fruit salad preserved in syrup)

2¼ lb mixed fruit (e.g. apples, pears, peaches, cherries)
2 lemons
2¼ cups water
2½ cups sugar

Wash and peel the fruit. Core, pit, chop and place in a bowl of iced water acidulated with the juice of 1 lemon. Boil the water and sugar with the juice of the remaining lemon for 10 min to make a syrup. Drain off the acidulated water from the fruit and cook in the syrup for 3 min. Using a slotted spoon, transfer the fruit to preserving jars. Boil the syrup for 10 min more to thicken it; when it is just warm pour into the jars to come just below the rim; seal and sterilize for 20 min.

SUCCO DI POMODORO
(Tomato juice)

Although homemade tomato juice will keep only for a few months, it is a good way of profiting from a tomato glut. Choose very ripe, juicy tomatoes. Wash them well, dry and sieve (or purée in a blender), collecting all the liquid in a large bowl. Add a little salt to a cupful of this thick juice and stir thoroughly, making sure the salt dissolves. Add to the bowlful of juice and mix well. Bottle and seal as usual, then sterilize for 1 hr. If you prefer, bottle small quantities in little beer bottles; sterilize for ½ hr (or for 20 min if you add salt to the sterilizing water, after which the water will boil at a higher temperature).

MOSTARDA CASALINGA
(Fruit relish)

10 apricots
10 figs

14 oz watermelon peel
2¼ cups water
2½ cups sugar
1 chili pepper
peppercorns

Wash the fruit but do not peel. Simmer the watermelon peel in two changes of water for 10 min each time, then cut into thin strips. Make a syrup by boiling the water and sugar for 10 min. Add the fruit and strips of watermelon peel and boil gently until tender. Remove both fruit and peel with a slotted spoon and place in the jars with the crumbled chili pepper and a few peppercorns. Boil the syrup for about 10 min to reduce and then pour over the fruit. Seal immediately while hot to set up a vacuum inside the jars.

CIPOLLINE SOTT'ACETO
(Pickled onions)

The best onions for pickling, or preserving in oil, have a small, rather flattened bulb and are sown in February–March to be ready in late summer–early autumn or later, depending on the variety.

Peel off the outer skin of 2¼ lb pickling onions, working with the onion under cold running water to prevent your eyes from watering. Take great care not to cut into the lower layers of the onion. Blanch the onions for 1 min in boiling, lightly salted water, then remove with a slotted spoon and drain well. You can choose either to hot-pickle or cold-pickle them i.e. to boil the onions for 10 min in spiced vinegar or simply to pour cold vinegar and spices over them in their jars and seal. With the second method they will not be ready to eat quite so soon but are more likely to remain firm and crisp.

Cold pickling method: Place the onions in a non metallic bowl, boil sufficient white vinegar to completely cover them for 2 min; pour straight over the onions, leave to stand for 24 hr. Use a slotted spoon to transfer the onions to jars, discard the used vinegar and boil up a fresh saucepanful. Add a few peppercorns and 3–4 cloves to each jar, then pour in sufficient boiling vinegar to cover the con-

tents. When cold, dribble 2 or 3 tbsp olive oil on to the surface of the vinegar which will act as a seal. Close the jars tightly and store in a cool place.

Hot pickling method: Blanch the onions, and add to boiling vinegar with a few peppercorns, 1 small piece cinnamon, 1 bay leaf and, if wished, 1 clove garlic. Simmer for 10 min; drain, pack into jars and cover with fresh boiled and cooled vinegar. Add a layer of olive oil and seal. Leave to mature for 2 months.

FUNGHI SOTT'ACETO
(Pickled mushrooms)

When pickling mushrooms, or preserving them in oil, choose small, firm compact varieties. Porcini (cèpes) are probably the best. The freshest, whitest cultivated button mushrooms will also keep well. Discard any mushrooms which are damp, floppy or blemished. Trim off the stalks, wash in a large bowl of water acidulated with the juice of 1 lemon; when clean, drain, pat dry with kitchen paper and place in a

303

non metallic pan (earthenware is best). Cover with wine or cider vinegar and add a few bay leaves. Good red wine vinegar enhances the chestnut brown color of small porcini mushrooms. Bring to a boil, then simmer for up to ¼ hr, depending on the size and type of mushrooms. Drain thoroughly; spread out on several layers of kitchen paper to dry in a well ventilated spot. Change the paper to complete drying. Pack closely into glass preserving jars, taking care not to break off the stems. Cover with fresh white vinegar, adding a few peppercorns if wished. Seal tightly and leave for at least 1 month before using.

FUNGHI SOTT'OLIO
(Mushrooms preserved in oil)

Use porcini (cèpes) or cultivated button mushrooms for this recipe. Pick out only the freshest, firmest and smallest mushrooms. Wipe free of any grit and earth and leave whole; do not wash. Place in a flameproof casserole with just enough water and vinegar to moisten, salt, pepper and a bay leaf. Simmer for 5 min. Lift out with a slotted spoon and spread out on clean cloths to dry for a few hours. Pack carefully into glass jars with peppercorns, bay leaves, a little salt and enough good quality olive oil to cover. Seal in airtight jars and store in a cool place for several weeks before serving.

PEPERONI SOTT'ACETO
(Pickled sweet peppers)

While ordinary sweet peppers (capsicums) can be pickled if they are first broiled briefly to make the skins come off more easily before bottling, more successful results are obtained with special dwarf fruiting varieties, be they small, thin sweet varieties (e.g. Golden Greek); mild "Peperoncini;" "Sweet Cherry" (small and round) or the "Anaheim" variety when young, before it becomes hot.

Use these small peppers whole, after trimming the stem to within about ⅛ in of the fruit, then wash,

dry and place on racks in a well ventilated, sunny place for 2 days (bring them inside before dusk). After they have lost some of their moisture by this process, put them in a non metallic bowl and completely cover with boiling, lightly salted vinegar. Cover with a cloth and leave to stand for ¼ hr. This will draw out any residual moisture. Drain off all the vinegar; pack the peppers into jars and cover with fresh, unboiled white vinegar. Seal and store for at least 2 months before opening.

If you choose to use the larger sweet (bell) peppers or capsicums, select red or yellow, juicy, square-ish-shaped fruit with very smooth skins. Push the prongs of a fork into the stalk end and hold the pepper over the gas flame (or broil), turning frequently so that the skin is loosened without cooking the underlying flesh. Peel off the scorched skin, and cut the peppers lengthwise in quarters; remove seeds and whitish pith. Place the pieces on a tilted plate, sprinkle with fairly coarse salt and leave for the moisture to drain off. Rinse off the salt, drain and add to a panful of boiling vinegar. Remove with a slotted spoon after 10 min and leave to dry. Cut into strips or leave whole, if you prefer, and pack into jars in layers, alternating with blanched onion rings, peppercorns and (optional) chili peppers. Bring the vinegar used for cooking back to the boil for a few minutes; when cold pour into the jars to completely cover the peppers. Dribble a film of olive oil on the surface. Seal and wait for 1 month before eating.

MELANZANE SOTT'OLIO
(Eggplant in oil)

Choose round eggplant as they are very easy to pack neatly into jars when sliced lengthwise into rounds. Use white or purple varieties. Peel and slice lengthwise; sprinkle the slices with salt and place in a colander with a weight on top if necessary. Leave to stand for 2 hr to draw out the bitter juices, then rinse well in cold water and pat dry with kitchen paper. Fill a large pan with vinegar and bring to

a boil, add the eggplant slices and simmer gently for 5 min. Drain well and spread out on kitchen paper in a well ventilated spot for a few hours, turning them and replacing the paper several times. When they are dry, pack into jars with a little salt and a few peppercorns; coarsely chopped garlic and chili pepper (both optional) add an interesting extra flavor. Fill the jars with good olive oil; cover with cloths and then top up the oil level as the vegetables absorb it. When the oil is no longer being soaked up, seal the jars.

PEPERONI SOTT'OLIO
(Sweet peppers in oil)

See the recipe for pickled sweet peppers (p. 304) for the varieties to choose. When preserving in oil you should again use the small, mild peppers but the larger sweet (bell) peppers or capsicums (red or yellow) will do just as well. Follow the method given for pickled sweet peppers, topping the jars with best olive oil instead of vinegar; some of the oil will be absorbed, so unseal and top up the oil level after a few days. Reseal and leave for about 1 month before opening.

ZUCCHINE SOTT'OLIO
(Zucchini in oil)

Follow the method given for pickled sweet peppers (p. 304), discarding the vinegar in which the vegetables have been cooked. Make sure the zucchini have dried off as much as possible before packing them neatly into jars with peppercorns and, if you like, garlic. Avoid adding parsley as it does not keep well in oil, but if you wish to give the vegetables a herbal flavor when you serve them, marinate them for an hour or two in a shallow dish in their oil, with chopped parsley and mint. Fill up the jars with good olive oil, cover with cloths and keep topping up the level as the vegetables absorb the oil. Once the level remains constant, seal and wait at least 1 month before sampling.

D.O.C. Wines

*N*o Italian meal would be complete
without a good local wine to excite
the palate and enhance the flavor of the food.
An abundance of wine is produced in Italy to
match every occasion and accompany most
foods: Try a slightly chilled fragrant white
such as a Tocai Friulano or Soave to
accompany white meats and fish or a full-
bodied, earthy red such as a Barolo or
Barbaresco with red meats and game.
Dessert wines with which to end a meal
include the famous Vinsanto and Sangue di
Giuda, and there are many impressive
sparkling wines to choose from including
Prosecco and Asti Spumante. Wine can also
be used in cooking to add extra interest to
soups, sauces and casseroles or, mixed with
other ingredients it can form the basis of a
marinade with which to tenderize and flavor
meat.
  Wine production in Italy is strictly
controlled and in order to qualify for D.O.C.
status (Denominazione di Origine
Controllata), Italy's equivalent to France's
Appellation Contrôlée, wines must comply
with set regulations concerning geographic
origin, grape variety, yields per acre, methods
of vinification, alcoholic strength and aging
requirements.

Val d'Aosta

Donnaz

Color bright transparent red tending to light garnet. Delicate bouquet with a faint almond fragrance. Soft flavor with not too much body and a slightly bitter almond aftertaste. Minimum alcoholic strength 11.5%. Donnaz provides a good accompaniment to traditional dishes from the Val d'Aosta region made with Fontina cheese, game and other meats. Serve at 68°F.

This wine is produced in the *comuni* of Donnaz, Perloz, Bard and Pont S. Martin, which lie along the Dora Baltea river.

Enfer d'Arvier

Color moderately light garnet. Distinctive bouquet. Soft flavor with very little body and pleasantly bitter. Minimum alcoholic strength 11.5%. It goes well with antipasti of cured meats, local soups, fried foods and the typical regional dishes of *saucisse* and *moccetta*. Serve at 65°F.

This wine is produced exclusively in the *comune* of Arvier.

Piedmont

Barbaresco

Color garnet with shades of orange. Scent characteristic, ethereal, pleasant, intense. Flavor dry, full, robust, austere, yet velvety and harmonious. Minimum alcoholic strength 12.5%. Barbaresco is a superior partner to roasts (particularly feathered game), braised and broiled meats, steak, and cheese. It should be served at a minimum temperature of 68°F, and uncorked a few hours in advance. Produced in four *comuni* in the province of Cuneo: Barbaresco, Neive, Treisco and part of S. Rocco Senodelvio near Alba.

Barbera d'Alba

Color deep ruby red when young, tending to garnet as it ages. Odor vinous, intense, yet delicate. Flavor dry, with body, faintly bitter, with a fairly marked acidity, slightly tannic and, after adequate

aging, full and harmonious. Minimum alcoholic strength 12%. Barbera d'Alba goes well with roasts, strong cheeses and strongly flavored dishes of red meat, such as stews and game. Serve at 65°F (*superiore* type at 68°F).

Barbera d'Asti

Color deep ruby red when young, tending to garnet after aging. Vinous odor with characteristic fragrance. Flavor dry or even faintly sweet, full bodied. After aging it becomes more harmonious, pleasant and full-tasting. Minimum alcoholic strength 12.5%. Barbera d'Asti is typically drunk with antipasti, red meats, stews and cured meats. The *superiore* type, produced by a special aging process, is a perfect foil for roasts. Serve at 65–68°F.

This wine is produced in a number of *comuni* in the provinces of Asti and Alessandria.

Barbera del Monferrato

Color lively red, varying in intensity. Vinous odor. Flavor dry, occasionally slightly sweet, acidulous, of medium body, sometimes sparkling. Minimum alcoholic strength 12%. Barbera del Monferrato is well suited to main course dishes. Serve at room temperature (65°F) or very slightly chilled (59–60°F).

The zone of production includes the Monferrato area in the province of Alessandria and some *comuni* in the province of Asti.

Barolo

Color garnet with orange tints. Bouquet characteristic, ethereal, pleasant, intense. Flavor dry, full, robust, austere yet velvety, harmonious. Minimum alcoholic strength 13%. Because of its full flavor and aristocratic qualities Barolo is a classic wine for accompanying special meals of roast and braised meats, game and cheese. Serve at about 68°F, uncorking several hours in advance.

This wine is produced in 13 *comuni* in the hills of the province of Cuneo.

Boca

Color bright ruby red with subtle shades of garnet. Characteristic bouquet, with a pleasant scent of

Barbera del Monferrato

Barolo

Carema

Grignolino del Monferrato Casalese

Moscato d'Asti

Freisa d'Asti

violets. Flavor lively, dry, harmonious with an aftertaste of pomegranate. Minimum alcoholic strength 12%. Boca provides an ideal accompaniment to red meat, game and most regional dishes. It should not be served below 65–66°F.

It is produced in the *comune* of the same name in another four *comuni* in the province of Novara.

Bracchetto d'Acqui

Color ruby red of moderate intensity, tending to light garnet or rosé. Musty, very delicate bouquet. Flavor sweet, soft, lightly sparkling, persistently frothy. Minimum alcoholic strength 11.5%, at least 6% of which is actual alcohol. It is a pleasant wine with dried fruit and desserts (particularly those served hot). Serve at 50–54°F.

Bracchetto d'Acqui is produced in the province of Asti in 18 *comuni*, and in the province of Alessandria in eight *comuni*. Vinification can take place in the provinces of Asti, Alessandria and Cuneo.

Bramaterra

Color garnet with orange tints, fading with time. Fragrance characteristic, intense, slightly ethereal, improving with age. Flavor full and dry, velvety with pleasantly bitter undertones, lively and harmonious. Minimum alcoholic strength 12%. Bramaterra goes very well with roasts and game. Serve at 68°F.

The production zone includes the *comuni* of Massarano, Brusnengo, Curino, Roasio, Villa del Bosco, Sostegno and Lozzolo in the province of Vercelli.

Carema

Color pale garnet. Subtle fragrance, reminiscent of roses. Flavor soft, velvety, full-bodied. Minimum alcoholic strength 12%. Carema is a particularly good accompaniment to roasts, braised and broiled meats, kid and lamb. Serve at a minimum temperature of 68–71°F.

This wine is produced solely in the *comune* of the same name, which is in the province of Turin.

Colli Tortonesi Barbera

Color fairly deep ruby which will

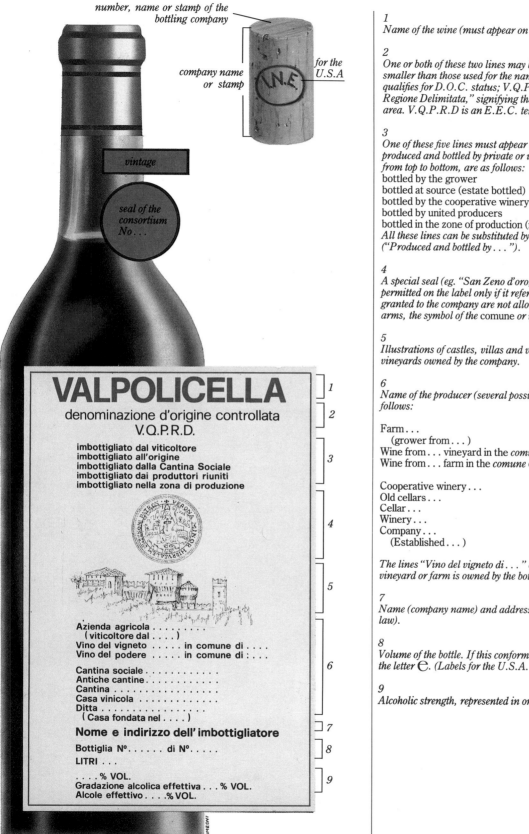

number, name or stamp of the
bottling company

company name
or stamp

for the
U.S.A

I.N.E.

vintage

seal of the
consortium
No...

VALPOLICELLA

denominazione d'origine controllata
V.Q.P.R.D.

imbottigliato dal viticoltore
imbottigliato all'origine
imbottigliato dalla Cantina Sociale
imbottigliato dai produttori riuniti
imbottigliato nella zona di produzione

Azienda agricola . . . .
   (viticoltore dal . . . .)
Vino del vigneto . . . . . in comune di . . . .
Vino del podere . . . . . in comune di : . . .

Cantina sociale . . . .
Antiche cantine . . . .
Cantina . . . .
Casa vinicola . . . .
Ditta . . . .
   (Casa fondata nel . . . .)

Nome e indirizzo dell' imbottigliatore

Bottiglia Nº . . . . . . di Nº . . . . .
LITRI . . .

. . . . % VOL.
Gradazione alcolica effettiva . . . . % VOL.
Alcole effettivo . . . . % VOL.

1
2
3
4
5
6
7
8
9

1
Name of the wine (must appear on the label by law).

2
One or both of these two lines may be used but the size of the characters must be smaller than those used for the name of the wine. The first line proves that the wine qualifies for D.O.C. status; V.Q.P.R.D. stands for "Vino di Qualità Prodotto in una Regione Delimitata," signifying that it is a quality wine, produced within a stated area. V.Q.P.R.D is an E.E.C. term that qualifies all D.O.C. wines.

3
One of these five lines must appear on the bottle to indicate whether the wine was produced and bottled by private or united producers. The translations in English, from top to bottom, are as follows:
bottled by the grower
bottled at source (estate bottled)
bottled by the cooperative winery
bottled by united producers
bottled in the zone of production (not estate bottled)
All these lines can be substituted by the words "Vinificato e imbottigliato da . . ." ("Produced and bottled by . . .").

4
A special seal (eg. "San Zeno d'oro," "Duja d'or," or "Pramaggiore," etc.) is permitted on the label only if it refers to the wine in the bottle. Any special awards granted to the company are not allowed to appear. Seals based on family coats of arms, the symbol of the comune or imaginary symbols are permitted.

5
Illustrations of castles, villas and vineyards are permitted only if the wine comes from vineyards owned by the company.

6
Name of the producer (several possibilities). The translation from top to bottom is as follows:

Farm . . .
   (grower from . . .)
Wine from . . . vineyard in the comune of . . .
Wine from . . . farm in the comune of . . .

Cooperative winery . . .
Old cellars . . .
Cellar . . .
Winery . . .
Company . . .
   (Established . . .)

The lines "Vino del vigneto di . . ." or "Vino del podere di . . ." are only included if the vineyard or farm is owned by the bottler.

7
Name (company name) and address of the bottler (this information must appear by law).

8
Volume of the bottle. If this conforms with E.E.C. regulations; it will be followed by the letter ℮. (Labels for the U.S.A. will show volume in fluid ounces.)

9
Alcoholic strength, represented in one of the three ways illustrated.

become lighter with age and take on garnet tints. It has an agreeably vinous nose with a persistent, characteristic scent. Flavor dry, fresh, lively, vigorous, robust, mellowing with age to become full, round, harmonious. Minimum alcoholic strength 12%. Although an excellent accompaniment to all foods it is particularly good with cured meats, pasta dishes, risottos, strong mature cheeses. Serve at room temperature (65°F).

This wine is produced in the hills surrounding the *comune* of Tortona and in another 31 *comuni* in the province of Alessandria.

Colli Tortonesi Cortese

Color pale straw yellow with greenish tints. Bouquet delicate, agreeable and persistent, characteristic fragrance. Flavor fresh, light, with a slight hint of bitter almonds. Minimum alcoholic strength 10.5% unless sparkling in which case it is 11.5%. An excellent wine both as an apéritif and as an accompaniment to antipasti, and delicately flavored dishes of white meat and fish. It should be served slightly chilled (47–50°F).

For the zone of production see Colli Tortonesi Barbera.

Cortese dell'Alto Monferrato

Color very pale straw yellow, sometimes greenish. Bouquet characteristic, delicate, gentle yet persistent. Flavor dry, harmonious, lively, pleasantly bitter. Minimum alcoholic strength 10%. This type of Cortese is suitable for drinking with antipasti, risottos, fish and egg dishes. Serve at 50°F.

The zone of production includes 33 *comuni* in the province of Asti and 51 *comuni* in the province of Alessandria.

Dolcetto d'Acqui

Color deep ruby red, tending to brick red with age. Odor vinous, subdued, characteristic. Flavor soft, harmonious, with a slightly bitter or almond aftertaste. Minimum alcoholic strength 11.5%. Dolcetto d'Acqui goes well with meat dishes and local Piedmontese specialties. The minimum recommended serving temperature is 65°F.

This wine is produced in the province of Alessandria in 24 *comuni*, one of which is Acqui Terme, from which it takes its name. An ancient and well known tradition permits vinification in six provinces: Asti, Alessandria, Cuneo, Turin, Genoa and Savona.

Dolcetto d'Alba

Color ruby red, tending occasionally to appear violet at the edges. Characteristic, vinous odor. Flavor dry, pleasantly bitter, of medium acidity, full-bodied, harmonious. Minimum alcoholic strength 11.5%. Dolcetto d'Alba is an excellent accompaniment to most local dishes from the Langhe area. Serve at 65–68°F.

This wine is produced in and around the town of Alba, in the province of Cuneo.

Dolcetto d'Asti

Color lively ruby red. Odor vinous, pleasant, characteristic. Flavor dry, slightly bitter, of medium acidity and body. Minimum alcoholic strength 11.5%. It goes very well with antipasti, appetizers and main courses and is an excellent accompaniment to agnolotti, escalopes, risottos, and tagliatelle with mushrooms. Serve at 65°F.

Dolcetto d'Asti is produced in 24 *comuni* of the province of Asti (from Mombaruzzo in the north down to Bobbio and Serole). Ancient tradition permits vinification in seven provinces: Asti, Genoa, Savona, Imperia, Alessandria, Cuneo, Turin.

Dolcetto delle Langhe Monregalesi

Color lively ruby red. Characteristic, vinous odor. Flavor dry, pleasing, slightly bitter, of medium acidity and body. Minimum alcoholic strength 11%. This wine goes well with main courses and meats. Serve at a minimum temperature of 62–65°F.

Dolcetto delle Langhe is produced in 12 *comuni* around the town of Mondovì.

Dolcetto di Diano d'Alba

Color ruby red. Characteristic, vinous odor. Flavor dry, with a pleasant hint of almond, moderately acidic, full-bodied, harmonious. Minimum alcoholic strength 12%. This wine is an excellent complement to the local cuisine of Alba.

Serve at 62–68°F.

This type of Dolcetto is produced solely in the *comune* of Diano d'Alba.

Dolcetto di Dogliani

Color ruby red, tending toward violet. Characteristic, vinous odor. Flavor dry, of medium acidity, faintly bitter, delicate, agreeable, not much body, harmonious. Minimum alcoholic strength 11.5%. This wine is particularly good with specialties from the Langhe, but generally goes well with most food, with the exception of fish. Serve at 62°F when young and 67–68°F when more mature.

This type of Dolcetto is produced in the *comune* of Dogliani as well as in another ten *comuni* in the surrounding area.

Dolcetto di Ovada

Color deep ruby red, tending toward garnet as it ages. Odor vinous. Flavor dry, soft, harmonious, pleasantly bitter or with a slight almond taste. Minimum alcoholic strength 11.5%. Dolcetto di Ovada is a good choice for serving with all traditional Piedmontese dishes and should be served at 60–68°F.

This wine is produced in the province of Alessandria in the

comune of Ovada and in another 21 surrounding *comuni*. Vinification takes place in six provinces: Asti, Alessandria, Cuneo, Turin, Genoa and Savona.

Erbaluce di Caluso and Caluso passito

Color straw yellow. Bouquet vinous, refined, characteristic. Flavor dry, fresh. Minimum alcoholic strength 11%. It is a good accompaniment to fish and should be served at 50°F.

Caluso passito varies in color from golden yellow to dark amber; bouquet delicate, characteristic; flavor sweet, harmonious, full and velvety. Minimum alcoholic strength 13.5% (natural residual sugars not less than 8%). This is principally a dessert wine but can also be enjoyed with strong cheeses. Serve at 59–60°F or at room temperature (65°F). There is also a fortified version of this wine, known as Caluso passito liquoroso.

Both these wines are produced in 32 *comuni* in the province of Turin and in four *comuni* in the province of Vercelli.

Fara

Color ruby red. Delicately violet-scented. Flavor dry, vigorous, harmonious. Minimum alcoholic strength 12%. Fara goes well with red meats, roasts and game. It should be served at 65–68°F; it is advisable to uncork the bottle several hours before drinking.

Fara is produced in the *comuni* of Fara and Briona in the province of Novara.

Freisa d'Asti

Color bright garnet or light cherry red, becoming deep orange with age. Characteristic bouquet reminiscent of raspberries and roses. The flavor of the *amabile* (semisweet) version has pleasant raspberry undertones; in the *secco* (dry) version it is lively, tart, becoming softer after a short period of aging. Minimum alcoholic strength 11%. The *amabile* is served typically with fruit; the *secco* goes perfectly with bagna cauda (see p. 130) but is equally good with white meats, stews and fried dishes. Both versions are served at room temperature (65°F).

The zone of production is the hilly district in the province of Asti.

Freisa di Chieri

Color not very deep ruby red. Delicate scent reminiscent of raspberries and violets. Flavor dry, acidulous; with aging the *secco-amabile* (semisweet) type becomes more delicate, and the *amabile* (sweet) type more aromatic. Minimum alcoholic strength 11% (Freisa *amabile* must be at least 7% actual alcohol). *Frizzante* (slightly sparkling) and *spumante* (sparkling) versions of Freisa di Chieri are also produced by refermenting the natural residual sugars. The *secco* (dry) type, served at room temperature, goes particularly well with white meats, lamb, kid and with antipasti. The *amabile*, *frizzante* and *spumante* types are classic dessert wines and should be served slightly chilled (47–50°F).

The zone of production is in the province of Turin in 12 *comuni*, one of which is Chieri.

Gattinara

Color garnet red, aging toward orange. Delicate fragrance reminiscent of violets, particularly when aged. Flavor dry, mellow with a characteristic slightly bitter undertone. Minimum alcoholic strength 12%. Gattinara goes well with roasted meats, game and hard cheeses. Serve at 68°F; uncork bottle several hours before drinking.

Produced in the *comune* of Gattinara, from which it takes its name.

Gavi or Cortese di Gavi

Color brilliant straw yellow. Light distinctive fragrance. Flavor dry, pleasant, fresh. Minimum alcoholic strength 10.5%. Gavi, which is also produced in sparkling and lightly sparkling form, is a very good apéritif wine and is often served with meatless antipasti, oysters, seafood, cold fish salads, trout and other freshwater fish. Serve at 50°F.

This wine is produced in 12 *comuni* in the province of Alessandria, one of which is Gavi.

Ghemme

Color garnet red. Delicate scent of violets. Flavor dry, vigorous. Minimum alcoholic strength 12%. Ghemme is an excellent choice for accompanying roasts, game and mature cheeses. Serve at 67–68°F. Produced in the province of Novara in the *comuni* of Ghemme and Romagnano Sesia.

Grignolino d'Asti

Color ruby red, varying in brilliance, turning orange with age. Characteristic, delicate aroma. Flavor dry, slightly tannic, pleasantly bitter with a persistent aftertaste. Minimum alcoholic strength 11%. A delicate table wine, Grignolino d'Asti goes well with antipasti of cured meats, and soups. Serve at 60–65°F.

Produced in the province of Asti in 37 *comuni*.

Grignolino del Monferrato Casalese

Color light ruby red turning orange with age. Distinctive, delicate aroma. Flavor dry, slightly tannic, pleasantly bitter with a distinctive aftertaste. Minimum alcoholic strength 11%. A good accompaniment to pasta dishes, stews, bagna cauda (see p. 130), and roast poultry. Serve at about 59°F.

This type of Grignolino is produced in 36 *comuni* in the hilly district around Casale Monferrato in the province of Alessandria.

Lessona

Color garnet red, acquiring orange tints with age. Characteristic fragrance reminiscent of violets, subtle and intense. Flavor dry, pleasantly tannic with characteristic liveliness and agreeable, lingering aftertaste. Minimum alcoholic strength 12%. Lessona is an excellent wine for serving with roasts, game, broiled and barbecued meats. Serve at 68°F.

This wine is produced in the *comune* of Lessona in the province of Vercelli.

Malvasia di Casorzo d'Asti

Color ruby red to cherry pink. Characteristic, fragrant aroma. Sweet, slightly aromatic flavor. Minimum alcoholic strength 10.5% (of which not less than ⅓ is made up of residual sugars for conversion). Both this wine and the sparkling type are recommended for desserts and ices. Serve chilled.

Produced around Asti and Alessandria in a total of six *comuni*.

Malvasia di Castelnuovo Don Bosco

Color cherry red. The bouquet is characterized by the fragrant aroma of the grapes from which it is made. Sweet, slightly aromatic flavor. Minimum alcoholic strength 10.5%, of which not less than 2/5 of the total residual sugars are still to be converted. It is possible to find *spumante* (sparkling) and *frizzante* (slightly sparkling) versions of Malvasia di Castelnuovo Don Bosco. This is a wine to be drunk young, preferably with desserts and fruit. Serve chilled at 50–54°F.

Produced in the province of Asti in six *comuni*, one of which is Castelnuovo Don Bosco, from which it takes its name.

Moscato d'Asti

Color straw yellow or fairly deep yellow. Fragrant aroma of the muscat grape. Sweet aromatic flavor, characteristic of the muscat grape. Minimum alcoholic strength 10.5%. This wine goes particularly well with cakes, pastries and desserts in general. Serve at 59°F. Produced principally in the province of Asti in 28 *comuni*, in the province of Cuneo in 15 *comuni* and in the province of Alessandria in nine *comuni*.

Moscato d'Asti spumante or Asti

Color straw yellow or soft golden yellow with occasional greenish tints. Fragrance characteristic of the muscat grape, quite marked yet delicate. Delicately sweet, aromatic flavor. Minimum alcoholic strength 12%. This is a wine for serving at the end of a meal to accompany the dessert; it is also excellent as an apéritif. It should be served chilled and the bottle uncorked just before drinking.

For the zone of production see Moscato d'Asti.

Nebbiolo d'Alba

Color fairly deep ruby red, with garnet tints in older wines. The bouquet is characterized by a soft, delicate scent reminiscent of raspberries and violets, which becomes fuller and improves with age. Flavor varying from dry to pleasantly sweet, full-bodied, moderately tannic when young, velvety,

harmonious. Minimum alcoholic strength 12%. The *secco* (dry) type goes well with risottos, lightly fried food, and white meats; when matured it is good with roasts and game. Serve at 65–68°F. The *dolce* (sweet) type should be served slightly cooler at about 59°F at the end of a meal with cakes and pastries.

There is also a *spumante* (sparkling) version of this wine. The production zone lies within the province of Cuneo in 25 *comuni*.

Rubino di Cantavenna

Color light ruby red with garnet tints. Vinous odor with a light, delicate bouquet. Flavor dry, harmonious and full. Minimum alcoholic strength 11.5%. Cantavenna is a fine wine and can be drunk throughout a meal. Serve at 60–65°F.

The zone of production includes four *comuni* in the province of Alessandria.

Sizzano

Color ruby red with garnet tints. Vinous odor with characteristic violet perfume, fine and agreeable. Flavor dry, lively and harmonious. Minimum alcoholic strength 12%. This wine goes particularly well with roasts, game and stews, but can be enjoyed with all dishes typical of the Piedmont region, except fish. Serve at 68°F.

Produced exclusively in the *comune* of the same name in the province of Novara.

Lombardy

Botticino

Color deep ruby with garnet tints. Odor vinous, intense, slightly ethereal. Warm, full flavor, moderately tannic. Minimum alcoholic strength 12%. Although this is considered a wine suitable for all courses of a meal, it goes particularly well with roasts, game and cured meats typical of the area around Brescia. Serve at 68°F, if possible uncorking and decanting several hours beforehand.

Botticino is produced in the *comuni* of Brescia, Botticino and Rezzato.

Capriano del Colle

Color lively and brilliant ruby red. Characteristic, vinous odor. Flavor vigorous, dry, firm, harmonious. Minimum alcoholic strength 11%. It is recommended as an accompaniment to meat dishes, especially roasts. Serve at room temperature (65°F).

Produced in the province of Brescia in the *comuni* of Capriano del Colle and Poncarale.

Capriano del Colle Trebbiano

Color oscillating between greenish and straw yellow. Pleasant, delicate bouquet. Flavor dry and slightly tart when young. Minimum alcoholic strength 11%. Goes well with antipasti and fish. Serve at 50°F. For the zone of production see Capriano del Colle.

Cellatica

Color ruby red. Typical, vinous bouquet. Flavor vigorous and dry. Minimum alcoholic strength 11.5%. Cellatica is a fine table wine, well suited to most main course dishes, with the exception of fish. Serve at room temperature (65°F).

Produced in the hills that extend westward from Brescia, toward the *comuni* of Cellatica and Gussago.

Colli Morenici Mantovani del Garda bianco

Color straw yellow. Bouquet characterized by a soft, delicate, lingering fragrance. Flavor dry, vigorous, harmonious. Minimum alcoholic strength 11%. This wine is a suitable accompaniment to fish and rice salad. Serve at 50°F.

Produced in six *comuni* within the province of Mantua: Castiglione delle Stiviere, Cavriana, Monzambano, Ponti sul Mincio, Solferino, Volta Mantovana.

Colli Morenici Mantovani del Garda rosso and rosato

Color pink or light ruby red, tending toward cherry red when aged. Aroma vinous, delicate, pleasant. Flavor dry, harmonious, slightly bitter. Minimum alcoholic strength 11%. Goes well when young with white meats and pasta dishes. Serve at 65–68°F.

For the zone of production see previous wine.

Franciacorta Pinot

Color straw with greenish tints. Characteristic, delicate fragrance. Smooth, vigorous flavor. Minimum alcoholic strength 11.5%. This is an excellent table wine that goes well with meatless antipasti, soufflés and freshwater fish. Serve at 50°F.

Franciacorta is produced in 21 *comuni* situated in the hilly area of the same name in the province of Brescia.

Franciacorta rosso

Color bright red with violet tints when young, red with garnet tints when aged. Noted for its characteristic fragrance which alters as it matures. Flavor dry, of medium body, vinous, harmonious. Minimum alcoholic strength 11%. Particularly suitable to serve with ravioli in broth, risottos, meat dishes, poultry and stews. Excellent with the traditional *polenta e uccelli*. Serve at room temperature (65°F).

For the zone of production see Franciacorta Pinot.

Lugana

Color straw white or greenish, tending to become a slightly golden yellow as it ages. Bouquet delicate, pleasing and characteristic. Flavor cool, soft, smooth, particularly delicate. Minimum alcoholic strength 11.5%. Lugana is an excellent accompaniment to all fish dishes and also meatless antipasti. Serve at 50°F.

The zone of production is situated on the southern tip of Lake Garda, around Peschiera and Desenzano in the provinces of Verona and Brescia.

Oltrepò Pavese Barbacarlo

Color deep ruby red. Marked vinous odor with a characteristic fragrance of violets and raspberries. Flavor full, slightly tannic, moderately sweet. Minimum alcoholic strength 12%. The *secco* (dry) type goes well with savory dishes and strongly flavored sauces; the *amabile* (semisweet) and *frizzante* (lightly sparkling) types are best served at the end of the meal. Serve at 65–68°F.

Produced around Broni in a small area south of the River Po (Oltrepò) bounded by two tributaries, the Versa in the east and the Scuropasso in the west.

Oltrepò Pavese Barbera

Color deep, ruby red. Vinous odor and after aging a characteristic fragrance. Flavor dry, vigorous, full-bodied, slightly tannic and acidulous. Minimum alcoholic strength 11.5%. A classic wine for accompanying strongly flavored, savory dishes; excellent with braised and barbecued meats and game. Serve at 68°F.

The production zone covers a hilly area south of the River Po and includes 42 *comuni* within the province of Pavia.

Oltrepò Pavese Bonarda

Color deep ruby red. Strong, agreeable bouquet. Flavor soft, full, slightly tannic, fresh. Minimum alcoholic strength 11%. It is typically drunk with soup, rabbit and poultry; when matured it goes well with roast pork and beef, and braised meats, especially hare. Serve at room temperature (65°F).

For the zone of production see Oltrepò Pavese Barbera.

Oltrepò Pavese Buttafuoco

Color ruby red. Intense, vinous odor. Flavor full, slightly tannic, full-bodied. Minimum alcoholic strength 12%. Excellent with strongly flavored dishes, ravioli with Parmesan cheese and butter, roasts and game. Serve at 54–57°F.

Produced in a very small area around Broni and Stradella.

Oltrepò Pavese Cortese

Color light straw yellow. Characteristic, vinous odor. Flavor dry, soft, fresh, pleasant. Minimum alcoholic strength 11%. Well suited as an accompaniment to fish soups, meat stews, and frogs' legs. Serve chilled 44–47°F.

For the zone of production see Oltrepò Pavese Barbera.

Oltrepò Pavese Moscato

Color straw yellow. Characteristic, aromatic fragrance, deep, delicate bouquet. Flavor sweet, agreeable. Minimum alcoholic strength 10.5%. Classic dessert wine, for fruit salads and almond tart. Ideal for drinking on its own. The *spumante* (sparkling) type is drunk

Lugana

Oltrepò Pavese Pinot

Franciacorta Pinot

Oltrepò Pavese Bonarda

Riviera del Garda Bresciano

Valcalepio

Valtellina

with desserts. Serve at 41–44°F.

For the zone of production see Oltrepò Pavese Barbera.

Oltrepò Pavese Pinot

Color greenish straw yellow, very pale, or rosé or red according to the type of grape and system of vinification used. Characteristic bouquet. Flavor dry, fresh, lively, fine and very pleasant. Minimum alcoholic strength 11%. The white type is excellent as an apéritif, with fish, shellfish and light antipasti. Serve slightly chilled 48–50°F. The *spumante* (sparkling) type (generally white but also produced as a rosé) can accompany an entire meal through to the dessert besides making a superb apéritif. It should be drunk chilled at 42–47°F and uncorked immediately before serving.

For the zone of production see Oltrepò Pavese Barbera.

Oltrepò Pavese Riesling

Color pale straw yellow, greenish. Characteristic, agreeable aroma. Flavor dry, full and fresh. Minimum alcoholic strength 11%. A wine to accompany fish, especially if fried, and savory antipasti; it is also excellent with frogs' legs and potato gnocchi. The sparkling *brut* types goes very well with fish and cheese. This wine should be served chilled 44–48°F, and the sparkling type at 41°F.

For the zone of production see Oltrepò Pavese Barbera.

Oltrepò Pavese rosso

Color ruby red. Intense, vinous odor. Full-bodied, slightly tannic flavor. Minimum alcoholic strength 11.5%. A wine for drinking with most food: it goes well with flavorsome rustic dishes, mushrooms and game. Serve at 65°F.

For the zone of production see Oltrepò Pavese Barbera.

Oltrepò Pavese Sangue di Giuda

Color ruby red. Intense, vinous odor. Flavor moderately sweet, original, superb, decisive and lightly sparkling. Minimum alcoholic strength 12%. A typical dessert wine, it should be served at 60–65°F.

Produced in a small area around the *comune* of Broni.

Riviera del Garda Bresciano chiaretto

Color pale cherry pink tinged with ruby. Delicate, agreeable bouquet. Flavor soft with neutral and slightly bitter undercurrents reminiscent of bitter almonds. Minimum alcoholic strength 11.5%. A wine that goes well with light dishes, fish, roasted white meats. Serve at 60–62°F.

Produced in 30 *comuni* in the hills on the western shore of Lake Garda, within the province of Brescia.

Riviera del Garda Bresciano rosso

Color brilliant ruby red. Characteristic, vinous odor. Lively flavor with a slightly bitter undertone.

tent, characteristic perfume. Flavor dry, slightly fruity, tannic. Minimum alcoholic strength 11%. A perfect accompaniment for red meat, and game (particularly roast pigeon) and pizzoccheri della Valtellina (see p. 77). Serve at 68–71°F and uncork the bottle a few hours before drinking. The *sfurzat* type is particularly good with matured, full-fat and strongly flavored cheeses.

Produced in the valley of the River Adda in the province of Sondrio.

Valtellina Superiore
Color ruby red, turning to garnet. Characteristic, persistent bouquet mellowing with age. Flavor dry, slightly tannic, austere, velvety, harmonious and characteristic. Minimum alcoholic strength 12%. All four Valtellina Superiore wines – Sassella, Grumello, Inferno, Valgella – are fine wines for drinking throughout a meal. They go perfectly with meat dishes, Speck, bresaola, cheese, cured and broiled meats, game, steak and, especially, traditional Lombard dishes. They should be drunk mature. Serve at around 68–71°F, uncorking the bottle several hours beforehand.

Valtellina Superiore is produced exclusively in the four geographic subzones of Sassella, Grumello, Inferno and Valgella.

Veneto

Minimum alcoholic strength 11%. This wine should preferably accompany stews and well flavored dishes in general, strong and matured cheeses. Serve at 60–62°F when young and 65–68°F when aged.

For the zone of production see the previous chiaretto type.

Tocai di San Martino della Battaglia
Color lemon yellow, tending toward golden with age. Bouquet moderately intense, characteristic and pleasant. Flavor dry with typical bitterish aftertaste. Minimum alcoholic strength 12%. This wine is especially recommended for drinking with antipasti, fried fish,

light dishes and clear soups. Serve at 50–54°F.

Produced in an area encompassing the *comuni* of Sirmione, Desenzano, Lonato, Pozzolengo and Peschiera in the provinces of Brescia and Verona.

Valcalepio bianco
Color straw yellow varying in depth. Characteristic, delicate bouquet. Flavor dry, harmonious, characteristic. Minimum alcoholic strength 11.5%. Particularly suitable for accompanying fish and boiled meats, this is also an excellent apéritif. Served chilled 47–50°F.

Valcalepio bianco is produced in 15 *comuni* within the province of

Bergamo, in the Calepio valley.

Valcalepio rosso
Color ruby red, varying in depth, with garnet tints. Strong, ethereal bouquet, agreeable and distinctive. Flavor dry, full, harmonious, persistent. Minimum alcoholic strength 12%. An excellent wine with roasts, much in keeping with the traditional Bergamo cuisine. Serve at 60°F when young and at 65–68°F when aged; it is advisable to open the bottle some time before drinking.

For the zone of production see Valcalepio bianco.

Valtellina
Color bright red. Subtle, persis-

Bardolino
Color light ruby red, occasionally tending toward cherry, which turns to garnet with age; when young it may be rosé, in which case it is also called Chiaretto. Vinous aroma, with a light, delicate bouquet. Flavor dry, fresh, slightly bitter, harmonious, subtle, occasionally *frizzante* (lightly sparkling). Minimum alcoholic strength 10.5%. Bardolino is an excellent accompaniment to soups, white meats (both casseroled and roasted) and light game. Serve at 59–65°F. Uncorking the bottle one hour before drinking will improve the characteristic aroma.

315

Bardolino, produced at the center of the production zone in the *comuni* of Bardolino, Garda, Costermano, Cavaion Veronese, Lazise and Affi, is qualified as *classico*. The D.O.C. zone, however, also includes the part of the moraine hills in the *comuni* of Pastrengo, Rivoli Veronese, Bussolengo, Sona, Sommacampagna, Castelnuovo, Peschiera, Valeggio sul Mincio, all in the province of Verona.

Bianco di Custoza

Color straw yellow. Vinous odor, very fragrant and slightly aromatic. Flavor soft, full, delicate. Minimum alcoholic strength 11%. Ideal for accompanying shellfish and fish soups. Serve at 50°F.

Bianco di Custoza is produced in the province of Verona in nine *comuni* centered around Custoza in the *comune* of Sommacampagna.

Breganze bianco

Color straw yellow. Vinous, delicately intense bouquet. Flavor dry, rounded, fresh. Minimum alcoholic strength 11%. A wine for fish and egg dishes. Serve at around 50°F.

Breganze is produced north of Vicenza on the fertile slopes around the small town of Breganze and in 12 further surrounding *comuni*.

Breganze Cabernet

Color ruby red with garnet tints. Deep, pleasing bouquet. Flavor dry, robust, moderately tannic. Minimum alcoholic strength 11.5%. A good wine for serving with white and red meats and with mature cheeses. Serve at a minimum temperature of 68°F.

For the zone of production see Breganze bianco.

Breganze Pinot bianco

Color pale straw yellow. Delicate, pleasing, characteristic bouquet. Flavor harmonious, rounded, velvety. Minimum alcoholic strength 11.5%. Goes well with artichokes, seafood antipasti, lobster, and fish in general. Serve at 47–50°F.

For the zone of production see Breganze bianco.

Breganze Pinot nero

Color ruby red with tints of brick red. Delicate bouquet. Flavor dry, vigorous, with a slightly bitter aftertaste. Minimum alcoholic strength 11.5%. An excellent accompaniment to lamb and pork. Serve at a minimum temperature of 65°F.

For the zone of production see Breganze bianco.

Breganze rosso

Color lively ruby red. Characteristic vinous odor. Flavor harmonious, dry, robust, slightly tannic. Minimum alcoholic strength 11%. A wine to drink throughout a meal. Serve at 60–65°F.

For the zone of production see Breganze bianco.

Breganze Vespaiolo

Color straw yellow or moderately dark pink. Strong, fruity bouquet. Flavor full and fresh. Minimum alcoholic strength 11.5%. This wine goes well with Parma ham, cured meats and certain cheeses such as Asiago and Robiola. Serve at 54–55°F.

For the zone of production see Breganze bianco.

Cabernet del Piave

Color ruby red, almost garnet after aging. Intense, pleasing, characteristic bouquet. Flavor dry, lively, full-bodied, slightly grassy, harmonious. Minimum alcoholic strength 11.5%. A good wine for roasts, cutlets, game and strong cheeses. Serve at 60–62°F when young and at 68°F when aged (after three years' aging it becomes known as *riserva*).

As the name suggests this wine is produced in the basin of the River Piave in the provinces of Treviso (51 *comuni*) and Venice (12 *comuni*).

Cabernet di Pramaggiore

Color deep ruby red, tending toward brick red with age. Characteristic, strong, grassy aroma becoming more marked as it ages. Flavor dry, full, with a certain amount of tannin, full-bodied, austere and velvety with age. Minimum alcoholic strength 11.5%. Excellent with red meat and game but more suited to cold meats and poultry when young. Serve at 65°F; the *riserva* at 67–69°F.

Produced in the vineyards of the

comune of Pramaggiore, ten *comuni* in the province of Venice, two in the province of Treviso and six in the province of Pordenone.

Colli Berici Cabernet

Color deep ruby red, tending toward orange with age. Strong, pleasant aroma characteristic of the variety. Flavor dry, robust, tannic. Minimum alcoholic strength 11%. Excellent with game. The young wine is generally served at room temperature 60–65°F, the *riserva* at 68–69°F.

The D.O.C. Colli Berici covers seven wines (Cabernet, Garganega, Merlot, Pinot bianco, Sauvignon, Tocai italico and Tocai rosso) produced in 27 *comuni* in the hilly region of the same name, south of Vicenza.

Colli Berici Garganega

Color straw yellow tending toward pale gold. Slightly vinous odor with a delicate, characteristic fragrance. Flavor dry, delicately bitter, of medium body, harmonious. Minimum alcoholic strength 10.5%. A wine to drink with most food; recommended with fish, especially pike. Serve at 50–54°F.

For the zone of production see Colli Berici Cabernet.

Colli Berici Merlot

Color ruby red. Vinous odor, pleasantly intense, characteristic. Flavor soft, harmonious, full-bodied. Minimum alcoholic strength 11%. Although a wine suitable for drinking throughout a meal it goes particularly well with roasts, stews, kabobs, and cheeses. Serve at 59–62°F.

For the zone of production see Colli Berici Cabernet.

Colli Berici Pinot bianco

Color pale straw yellow. Delicately intense bouquet, characteristic of the variety. Flavor harmonious, full, velvety. Minimum alcoholic strength 11%. A good accompaniment to antipasti, risottos, fish, and shellfish. Serve at 47–50°F.

For the zone of production see Colli Berici Cabernet.

Colli Berici Sauvignon

Color straw yellow. Delicate bouquet, characteristic of the variety. Flavor dry, harmonious, fresh, with body. Minimum alcoholic strength 11%. Goes well with antipasti, fish and polenta. Serve slightly chilled at 50–54°F.

For the zone of production see Colli Berici Cabernet.

Colli Berici Tocai italico

Color straw yellow. Slightly vinous odor. Flavor dry, harmonious, fresh, with body. Minimum alcoholic strength 11%. A good accompaniment to soups, frogs' legs, snails, egg and fish dishes. It is best served chilled at 47–50°F.

For the zone of production see Colli Berici Cabernet.

Colli Berici Tocai rosso

Color not very deep, but lively ruby red. Strong, vinous odor, characteristic of the variety. Flavor pleasant, a little bitter, harmonious, moderately tannic. Minimum alcoholic strength 11%. This wine goes perfectly with *baccalà* (dried salt cod), light roasts and cured meats. Serve at room temperature (65°F), or very slightly below (60–62°F). For zone of production see Colli Berici Cabernet.

Colli Euganei bianco

Color straw yellow varying in depth. Vinous odor with an agreeable, characteristic bouquet. Flavor dry or slightly sweet, lively, soft, fine and velvety. Minimum alcoholic strength 10.5%. A good accompaniment to pasta dishes, fish and fried food. Serve chilled at 50°F.

Produced on the slopes of the Euganei hills in 17 *comuni* in the province of Padua.

Colli Euganei moscato

Color golden yellow. Strong nose, characteristic of the muscat grape. Flavor sweet, intense, still or slightly sparkling. Minimum alcoholic strength 10.5%. Typically served with desserts and ice cream. Serve cold at 42–44°F.

For the zone of production see Colli Euganei bianco.

Colli Euganei rosso

Color ruby red, varying in intensity. Vinous odor with characteristic bouquet. Flavor dry or slightly sweet, lively, soft, full-bodied, fine and velvety. Minimum alcoholic strength 11%. Strongly recommended with cured meats, local meat dishes, chicken cooked on a spit. Serve at 62–65°F. The sweet *spumante* type goes well with desserts and the *brut* with a variety of local specialties.

For the zone of production see Colli Euganei bianco.

Gambellara

Color yellow, from straw to pale gold. Slightly vinous odor with a strong, characteristic bouquet. Flavor dry, velvety. Minimum alcoholic strength 11%. It is a wine that goes well with meatless antipasti, soups and fish. Serve at a maximum temperature of 50°F.

Gambellara is produced from vines grown in the *comuni* of Gambellara, Montebello, Vicentino, Montorso and Zermeghedo, in the province of Vicenza.

Gambellara Recioto

Color golden yellow. Strong, fruity bouquet. Flavor characteristic, harmonious, with a slight taste of raisins, semi sweet, still or sparkling to a greater or lesser degree, with a slightly bitter aftertaste. Minimum alcoholic strength 12%. Best with desserts and shellfish. Serve slightly chilled at 55–57°F.

For the zone of production see Gambellara (above).

Gambellara Vinsanto

Color deep amber yellow. Strong, characteristic bouquet of raisins. Flavor sweet, harmonious, velvety. Minimum alcoholic strength 14%. This is a dessert wine; especially good with dry pastries. Serve at 59–60°F.

For the zone of production see Gambellara.

Merlot del Piave

Color red, aging to garnet. Strong bouquet, becoming more delicate and pleasing. Flavor dry, lively, full-bodied, tannic, harmonious. Minimum alcoholic strength 11%. It is a wine for the whole meal, but goes particularly well with cured meats, roasts, pork. Serve at room temperature (65°F).

Produced in the basin of the River Piave in the provinces of Treviso (51 *comuni*) and Venice (12 *comuni*).

Merlot di Pramaggiore

Color ruby red when young, tending toward garnet as it ages. Vinous, rather intense odor, slightly grassy, characteristic, with a pleasant bouquet. Flavor dry, quite tannic, full bodied, agreeable, characteristic. Minimum alcoholic strength 11.5%. The young wine goes well with risottos and pasta dishes made with meat, roast poultry and the traditional fritto misto. The *riserva* type is good with broiled meats and strongly flavored cheeses. The ideal temperature for drinking depends on the age of the wine, but 65–69°F should be suitable.

Produced from vines grown in the *comune* of Pramaggiore, in ten *comuni* in the province of Venice, two in the province of Treviso and six in the province of Pordenone (partly in the Veneto and partly in Friuli).

Prosecco di Conegliano e Valdobbiadene Superiore di Cartizze

Tocai di Lison

Colli Berici

Prosecco di Conegliano e Valdobbiadene

Bardolino

Vini del Piave or Piave Merlot

Bianco di Custoza

Gambellara

Valpolicella

Colli Euganei rosso

Soave

Montello and Colli Asolani Cabernet

Color ruby red, becoming almost garnet with age. Odor vinous, intense, characteristic, agreeable. Flavor dry, lively, full-bodied, very slightly grassy, quite tannic, harmonious and characteristic. Minimum alcoholic strength 11.5%. An excellent accompaniment to special roasts, game and fermented cheeses. Serve at 65–68°F.

Produced from vines grown in the whole of the *comune* of Monfumo and in part of the *comuni* of Asolo, Caerano S. Marco, Castelcucco, Cavaso del Tomba, Cornuda, Crocetta del Montello and of other *comuni* in the Montello zone as far as Nervesa.

Montello and Colli Asolani Merlot

Color ruby red, tending to garnet with age. The young wine has a strong, characteristic, vinous odor, which becomes more delicate, ethereal and pleasing with age. Flavor dry, lively, robust, full-bodied, moderately tannic, harmonious. Minimum alcoholic strength 11%. This wine goes very well with roasts and game but is also pleasant with stews and casseroles. Serve at 65–68°F.

For the zone of production see Montello and Colli Asolani Cabernet.

Montello and Colli Asolani Prosecco

Color straw yellow, occasionally becoming a deep golden, varying in intensity. Bouquet characteristic, vinous, fruity. Flavor dry, rounded, with a slight hint of almonds, semisweet in the *frizzante* (lightly sparkling) type. Minimum alcoholic strength 10.5%. It is a suitable accompaniment to antipasti and fish. Serve at 50°F. The *spumante* (sparkling) type, which is served even cooler (44–47°F) goes well with local dessert specialties and panettone.

For the zone of production see Montello and Colli Asolani Cabernet.

Prosecco di Conegliano e Valdobbiadene

Color straw yellow, varying in intensity. Characteristic, vinous odor with a slightly fruity fragrance, particularly evident in the *dolce* (sweet) and *amabile* (semisweet) types. Flavor pleasantly bitter, not much body in the *secco* (dry) type; sweet or semisweet and fruity in the *dolce* and *amabile* types. Minimum alcoholic strength 10.5%; 11% for the Superiore di Cartizze. This wine can be drunk throughout a meal, with antipasti, savory snacks, fish, shellfish; it is also excellent with barbecued fish. Serve chilled at 35–50°F.

Produced in the province of Treviso in 13 *comuni* situated in the hilly area that lies between Conegliano and Valdobbiadene, from which two *comuni* it takes its name. Cartizze is produced in the area of the same name in the *comune* of Valdobbiadene.

Prosecco di Conegliano e Valdobbiadene frizzante

Color brilliant straw yellow with plenty of bubbles. Pleasant, characteristically fruity bouquet. Flavor dry, semisweet, lightly sparkling, fruity. Minimum alcoholic strength 10.5% (11% for the Superiore di Cartizze). This wine is good as an apéritif drunk on its own, but is also pleasant with antipasti and fish dishes, while the *amabile* type can be served with desserts. Serve at 42–47°F.

For the zone of production see Prosecco di Conegliano e Valdobbiadene.

Prosecco di Conegliano e Valdobbiadene spumante

Color brilliant straw yellow, with persistent bubbles. Characteristic, pleasant, fruity bouquet. Flavor dry, semisweet or sweet, pleasantly fruity, characteristic. Minimum alcoholic strength 11%. The *brut* is good as an apéritif and with all courses, especially those with fish; the *demi-sec* or *amabile* goes well with desserts, panettone and pandoro. Serve chilled at 42–47°F.

For the zone of production see Prosecco di Conegliano e Valdobbiadene.

Soave

Color straw yellow, occasionally with a greenish tint. Vinous odor, with a deep, delicate bouquet. Flavor dry, of medium body, harmonious, slightly bitter. Minimum alcoholic strength 10.5%. This

wine goes well with antipasti, rice, fish and egg dishes and is excellent with poached trout and mayonnaise. Serve at 50°F.

Soave *classico* is produced in the hilly part of the *comuni* of Soave and Monteforte d'Alpone; D.O.C. Soave is produced in the adjoining *comuni* of Montecchia di Crosara, Cazzano di Tramigna, Illasi, Caldiero, San Martino Buon Albergo, Colognola ai Colli, Roncà and San Giovanni Ilarione.

Soave Recioto

Color pale golden yellow. Bouquet intense, vinous, fruity. Flavor semisweet, velvety, harmonious, full-bodied. Minimum alcoholic strength 14% (of which at least 11.5% is converted alcohol). An ideal accompaniment to desserts, particularly Veronese specialties and Milanese panettone.

For the zone of production see Soave.

Tocai del Piave

Color pale straw yellow, tending to greenish. Delicate, pleasing bouquet. Flavor dry, harmonious, fresh, aromatic. Minimum alcoholic strength 11%. A wine for accompanying seafood risottos, fish and antipasti.

This wine is produced from vines grown in the basin of the River Piave in the provinces of Treviso (in 51 *comuni*) and Venice (in 12 *comuni*).

Tocai di Lison

Color straw yellow. Light, fruity bouquet. Flavor dry, characteristic, lively, harmonious, with a slight hint of almonds. Minimum alcoholic strength 11.5%. This wine goes well with antipasti, white meats and cheeses and should be served slightly chilled at 50–54°F.

This type of Tocai is produced in several *comuni* belonging to the provinces of Venice, Treviso and Pordenone. The *classico* zone includes Lison, Sumaga and Pradipozzo in the *comune* of Annone Veneto, and Belfiore, Bessaglia and Salvarolo in the *comune* of Pramaggiore.

Valpolicella

Color medium ruby red, aging to garnet. Intense vinous odor with a delicate, characteristic perfume, occasionally reminiscent of bitter almonds. Flavor dry or velvety, full-bodied, bitterish, lively and harmonious. Minimum alcoholic strength 11% (with a maximum of 0.3% unconverted alcohol). Valpolicella is an excellent wine with the main course, roasts in particular, and is also good with mature cheeses. It is important to serve it at 65–68°F.

The *classico* type is produced in the geographical region of Valpolicella, in the *comuni* of Sant'Ambrogio, Fumane, San Pietro Incariano, Negrar, Marano; the D.O.C. region extends into the eastern part of the Verona hills as far as Illasi and Cazzano di Tramigna. The production zone also includes the region of Valpolicella-Valpantena, since grapes are also used from vines in Valpantena, principally from the *comuni* of Grezzana and Verona.

Valpolicella Recioto

Color fairly deep ruby red. Marked characteristic odor. Flavor delicate, full, warm, velvety, semisweet, with a lot of character. The *amarone* type is excellent with roasts and strongly flavored

cheeses and should be served at 68–71°F, uncorking the bottle several hours beforehand. Good with desserts; the *spumante* goes well with pandoro and panettone. Serve at 59°F.

For the zone of production see Valpolicella.

Verduzzo del Piave

Color pale golden yellow, tending toward greenish. Delicate, pleasant, characteristic bouquet. Flavor dry, lively, harmonious, pleasing. Minimum alcoholic strength 11%. Particularly good with pasta served in broth, antipasti, and fish in general. Serve chilled at 44–50°F.

This wine is produced from vines grown in the basin of the River Piave, in the provinces of Treviso (in 51 *comuni*) and Venice (in 12 *comuni*).

Trentino Alto Adige

Alto Adige Cabernet

Color deep ruby red with orange tints when aged. Bouquet characteristic, slightly grassy, ethereal, pleasant. Flavor dry, full, slightly tannic, full-bodied. Minimum alcoholic strength 11.5%. This is a wine for drinking with traditional game dishes, broiled meats, strongly flavored cheeses. Serve at room temperature (65°F).

Alto Adige wines are produced in a region that includes 32 *comuni* in the province of Bolzano.

Alto Adige Lagrein rosato (Lagrein Kretzer)

Color light ruby, rosé. Bouquet delicate, pleasant, not very intense. Flavor harmonious, pleasing, not much body. Minimum alcoholic strength 11.5%. A suitable wine for accompanying light meals and the traditional *knödel*. Serve slightly chilled at 55–59°F.

For the zone of production see Alto Adige Cabernet.

Alto Adige Lagrein scuro (Lagrein Dunkel)

Color deep ruby. Bouquet marked, pleasant, characteristic. Flavor mellow, velvety, full. Minimum al-

coholic strength 11.5%. A wine to drink throughout the meal espcially main-course meat dishes. Serve at 65°F.

For the zone of production see Alto Adige Cabernet.

Alto Adige Malvasia (Malvesier)

Color ruby red with orange tints. Pleasing bouquet. Flavor full and harmonious. Minimum alcoholic strength 11.5%. It goes well with Parma ham and melon and well flavored antipasti. Serve chilled at 50–54°F.

For the zone of production see Alto Adige Cabernet.

Alto Adige Merlot

Color ruby red. Characteristic, pleasing bouquet. Flavor full, lively, dry, slightly grassy. Minimum alcoholic strength 11%. This wine goes well with succulent first courses, roasted and barbecued red meats. Serve at around 65°F.

For the zone of production see Alto Adige Cabernet.

Alto Adige Moscato Giallo (Goldenmuskateller)

Color straw yellow. Characteristic, strong, delicate aroma. Flavor dry, aromatic, agreeable. Minimum alcoholic strength 11%. A classic wine for serving with desserts and sweets. Serve at 60–62°F.

For the zone of production see Alto Adige Cabernet.

Alto Adige Moscato rosa (Rosenmuskateller)

Color rosé. Bouquet delicate, pleasant, aromatic. Flavor sweet, agreeable, characteristic. Minimum alcoholic strength 12.5%. It is a wine that goes well with desserts, ice cream, sweets. Serve slightly chilled (55–59°F).

For the zone of production see Alto Adige Cabernet.

Alto Adige Pinot bianco (Weissburgunder)

Color straw yellow. Characteristic, agreeable odor. Flavor dry, lively. Minimum alcoholic strength 11%. It is an excellent wine for accompanying all antipasti. Serve chilled, at around 50–54°F.

For the zone of production see Alto Adige Cabernet.

Alto Adige Pinot grigio (Ruländer)

Color straw yellow. Bouquet not marked, pleasant. Flavor dry, full, harmonious. Minimum alcoholic strength 11.5%. An excellent apéritif wine; a perfect accompaniment to delicately flavored dishes. Serve chilled, at 50–54°F.

For the zone of production see Alto Adige Cabernet .

Alto Adige Pinot nero (Blauburgunder)

Color bright ruby, with orange tints when aged. Bouquet ethereal, pleasing, elegant, characteristic, intense. Flavor dry, soft and full, with an agreeable, slightly bitter aftertaste, harmonious. Minimum alcoholic strength 11.5%. This wine goes particularly well with traditional game dishes, broiled meats, roasts and stews. Serve at room temperature (65°F), taking care to uncork the bottle at least two hours before drinking.

For the zone of production see Alto Adige Cabernet.

Alto Adige Riesling italico (Welschriesling)

Color pale straw yellow, greenish. Characteristic, agreeable bouquet. Flavor dry, full, fresh, pleasant. Minimum alcoholic strength 11%. It is an agreeable wine to drink with all kinds of food. Serve slightly chilled at about 50–54°F.

For the zone of production see Alto Adige Cabernet.

Alto Adige Riesling renano (Rheinriesling)

Color straw yellow, tending to greenish. Bouquet delicate, pleasantly acidulous, fruity. Minimum alcoholic strength 11%. An excellent wine with fish cooked *en papillote* and antipasti. Serve slightly chilled at about 50–54°F.

For the zone of production see Alto Adige Cabernet.

Alto Adige Riesling Sylvaner (Müller-Thurgau)

Color straw yellow, tending to greenish. Bouquet delicate, characteristic. Flavor dry, acidulous, fruity. Minimum alcoholic strength 11%. Excellent with antipasti, especially fish. Serve chilled (50–54°F). For zone of production see Alto Adige Cabernet.

Alto Adige Sauvignon

Color yellow, tending to greenish. Characteristic, agreeable bouquet. Flavor characteristic, dry, fruity. Minimum alcoholic strength 11.5%. Goes well with most food, but particularly good with oily sea- or freshwater fish. Serve slightly chilled (50–54°F).

For the zone of production see Alto Adige Cabernet.

Alto Adige Schiave (Vernatsch)

Color from garnet to ruby. Bouquet not very strong, pleasant, characteristic. Flavor soft, with a slight hint of almonds. Minimum alcoholic strength 10.5%. This wine is recommended with white meats and chicken; particularly good with local cuisine. Serve at room temperature (65°F).

For the zone of production see Alto Adige Cabernet.

Alto Adige Sylvaner

Color straw yellow. Characteristic, pleasant bouquet. Flavor delicate, fresh, harmonious. Minimum alcoholic strength 11%. A particularly good accompaniment to sauces and broiled meats. Serve slightly chilled at around 50–54°F.

For the zone of production see Alto Adige Cabernet.

Alto Adige Traminer Aromatico (Gewürztraminer)

Color golden yellow. Intense, characteristic odor. Flavor full, slightly bitter, pleasantly aromatic. Minimum alcoholic strength 11.5%. This is a wine for drinking with spicy dishes; excellent also with broiled shellfish. Serve slightly chilled (50–54°F).

For the zone of production see Alto Adige Cabernet.

Caldaro or Lago di Caldaro (Kalterer or Kalterersee)

Color ruby red to garnet. Bouquet pleasant, perfumed, fruity. Flavor soft, harmonious with a hint of almonds. Minimum alcoholic strength 10.5%. This wine is particularly recommended with white meats, chicken and traditional, regional cuisine. Serve at room temperature (65°F).

The zone of production covers the hills around Lake Caldaro in the province of Bolzano, and includes several nearby *comuni* in the province of Trento.

Casteller

Color pink to ruby. Bouquet vinous, with a delicate, agreeable perfume. Flavor dry and very slightly sweet, harmonious, velvety. Minimum alcoholic strength 11%. An excellent wine with most food, it goes well with all kinds of soups, meat, game, poultry, stews and cheese. Serve at room temperature (65°F).

Casteller is produced in the province of Trento in 28 *comuni*.

Colli di Bolzano (Bozner Leiten)

Color ruby red to garnet. Bouquet characteristic. Flavor full, soft, harmonious. Minimum alcoholic strength 11%. A typical wine for accompanying all courses; excellent with stews and meat. Serve at 60–62°F.

Colli di Bolzano is produced in the Bolzano hills, in seven *comuni*, one of which is Bolzano itself.

Meranese or Meranese di Collina (Meraner Hügel)

Color ruby red. Characteristic bouquet, delicately scented. Flavor harmonious, lively. Minimum alcoholic strength 10.5%. Goes with most food, soups, vegetables, poultry, roasts, cheeses. Serve at room temperature (65°F).

The zone of production includes the *comune* of Merano and 12 other *comuni* in the province of Bolzano.

Santa Maddalena (St. Magdalener)

Color ruby red to garnet, aging to brick red. Bouquet intense, with a fragrance reminiscent of violets and almonds, becoming more accentuated with age. Flavor velvety, lively. Minimum alcoholic strength 11.5%. An excellent wine with red and white meats, game and dry meats. Serve at room temperature (65°F).

Produced in the *comune* of Bolzano in S. Maddalena and also, to a lesser degree, in the *comuni* of Terlano, S. Genesio and Renon.

Sorni bianco

Color straw yellow. Bouquet characteristic, agreeable, delicate. Flavor fresh, harmonious, occasionally soft. Minimum alcoholic strength 10%. This wine goes excellently with antipasti of vegetables, asparagus, soups, trout and other fish from the Adige region. Serve slightly chilled, preferably around 50–54°F.

Sorni is produced in the *comuni* of Lavis, Giovo and S. Michele all'Adige in the province of Trento; the center of production is Sorni in the *comune* of Lavis.

Sorni rosso

Color ruby red, varying in depth. Delicately scented. Flavor harmonious, soft, characteristic. Minimum alcoholic strength 10.5%. An excellent wine for all courses, which goes well with the traditional dishes of the Trentino region, Parma ham, feathered game, mature cheeses. Serve at room temperature (65°F).

For the zone of production see Sorni Bianco.

Terlano (Terlaner)

Color pale straw yellow. Bouquet characteristic, delicate, fruity. Flavor dry, well balanced. Minimum alcoholic strength 11.5%. Goes well with most dishes; particularly good with fish and light meats. Drink slightly chilled at around 50–54°F.

The zone of production is situated in and around the *comune* of Terlano in the province of Bolzano.

Terlano Müller-Thurgau

Color straw yellow, tending to greenish. Characteristic, delicate bouquet. Flavor dry, pleasantly acidulous, fruity. Minimum alcoholic strength 11%. Goes well with antipasti and fish. Serve at 50°F.

For the zone of production see Terlano (Terlaner).

Terlano Pinot bianco

Color greenish yellow to golden yellow. Characteristic aroma. Flavor dry. Minimum alcoholic strength 11%. Recommended as an accompaniment to fatty, cured meats, seafood antipasti, preserved fish. Serve at 50°F.

For the zone of production see Terlano (Terlaner).

Terlano Riesling italico

Color greenish yellow. Charac-teristic scent of the vine. Flavor dry, lively, and harmonious. Minimum alcoholic strength 10.5%. An easy wine to drink, it goes well with all courses. Serve at 50°F.

For the zone of production see Terlano (Terlaner).

Terlano Riesling renano

Color greenish yellow, tending to yellow. Characteristic smell of the vine. Flavor dry, full-bodied, harmonious. Minimum alcoholic strength 11.5%. An excellent wine to serve with fish. Serve slightly chilled at 50°F.

For the zone of production see Terlano (Terlaner).

Terlano Sauvignon

Color greenish yellow. Delicate, slightly aromatic bouquet. Flavor full, characteristic. Minimum alcoholic strength 12%. Its strong fragrance makes it a perfect foil for oily fish, octopus, squid, mackerel, and trout. Serve slightly chilled at 50–54°F.

For the zone of production see Terlano (Terlaner).

Terlano Sylvaner

Color greenish yellow. Delicate bouquet. Flavor full-bodied, harmonious. Minimum alcoholic strength 11.5%. Goes well with fish in mayonnaise and other sauces, liver croûtons, mussels. Serve at 50°F.

For the zone of production see Terlano (Terlaner).

Teroldego Rotaliano

Color red, tending to garnet (the rosé type) of a deep ruby red, often bordered with violet (the red type). Characteristic, pleasantly fruity bouquet, particularly marked in the red. Flavor dry, lively, slightly bitter with a delicate hint of almonds; the red has a little more body and is slightly tannic. Minimum alcoholic strength 11.5%. A fine wine to serve with all courses; the rosé is excellent with antipasti, cheese fritters and soufflés; the red goes well with boiled, broiled meats and white meats. Serve at 62–65°F. The *superiore* is a good accompaniment to roast game.

The zone of production lies within the province of Trento, between Mezzolombardo, Mezzocorona and S. Michele all'Adige.

Trentino Cabernet

Color deep ruby red with orange tints. Bouquet characteristic, grassy, ethereal, pleasing. Flavor dry, full, slightly tannic. Minimum alcoholic strength 11%. This wine goes well with roast meats and stews. Serve at 65–68°F.

The wines that are classed as Trentino and further defined by the name of the particular grape variety are produced in 38 *comuni* in virtually the whole wine-producing region in the province of Trento.

Trentino Lagrein

Color rosé, light garnet or ruby. Characteristic, fruity bouquet. Flavor agreeable, dry. Minimum alcoholic strength 11%. Goes well with pasta served with butter and cheese and roasts. Serve at room temperature (65°F).

For the zone of production see Trentino Cabernet.

Trentino Marzemino

Color ruby red with orange tints. Deep, delicate, characteristic bouquet. Flavor dry, lively, full, harmonious. Minimum alcoholic strength 11%. A good choice of wine with ravioli and roast meats. Serve at 65–68°F.

For the zone of production see Trentino Cabernet.

Trentino Merlot

Color ruby red. Marked characteristic bouquet. Flavor dry, full, pleasing, grassy. Minimum alcoholic strength 11%. Goes well with all foods. Serve at room temperature (65°F).

For the zone of production see Trentino Cabernet.

Trentino Moscato

Color deep straw yellow. Bouquet ethereal, aromatic, characteristic. Delicate, sweet flavor typical of the muscat grape. Minimum alcoholic strength 13%. A classic wine to serve with the dessert. Serve at 55–59°F.

For the zone of production see Trentino Cabernet.

Trentino Pinot bianco

Color straw yellow. Bouquet delicate, ethereal, characteristic. Flavor dry, slightly bitter, harmonious, smooth. Minimum alcoholic strength 11%. An excellent accompaniment to seafood antipasti and vegetable soups. Serve at 47–50°F.

For the zone of production see Trentino Cabernet.

Trentino Pinot nero

Color ruby red or occasionally rosé. Bouquet delicate, agreeable, characteristic. Flavor dry, pleasantly bitter. Minimum alcoholic strength 11.5%. A good accompaniment to antipasti and meat dishes. Serve at 67–68°F.

For the zone of production see Trentino Cabernet.

Trentino Riesling

Color straw yellow. Delicate, characteristic bouquet. Flavor dry, pleasantly acidulous, fruity. Minimum alcoholic strength 11%. This wine goes well with Parma ham and melon, fish risottos, shellfish and fish soup. Serve at 47–50°F.

For the zone of production see Trentino Cabernet.

Trentino Traminer aromatico

Color straw yellow, tending to golden. Bouquet harmonious and strong. Flavor aromatic, fine, delicate, characteristic. Minimum alcoholic strength 12%. This wine goes well with antipasti, pasta served with butter and cheese, and strong cheeses. Serve slightly chilled at 50°F.

For the zone of production see Trentino Cabernet.

Trentino Vinsanto

Color amber yellow. Bouquet pleasing, aromatic, elegant, delicate. Flavor pleasantly sweet, of raisins, full-bodied, harmonious. Minimum alcoholic strength 16% (of which at least 7% converted). A dessert wine. Serve at 55–59°F. It is advisable to open the bottle ½hr before drinking.

For the zone of production see Trentino Cabernet.

Valdadige bianco

Color straw yellow. Pleasant, vinous odor. Flavor harmonious, moderately acidic, occasionally slightly sweet. Minimum alcoholic strength 10.5%. This wine goes well with all foods but is a particularly good complement to meatless antipasti, clear soups, and fish. Serve slightly chilled at 50–54°F.

The zone of production comprises 38 *comuni* in the province of Trento, 33 in the province of Bolzano and four in the province of Verona.

Valdadige rosso

Color fairly deep rosé to ruby. Pleasant vinous odor. Flavor harmonious, moderately acidic, occasionally slightly sweet. Minimum alcoholic strength 11%. A good wine with most foods; excellent with pasta, cured meats, vegetable and cheese dishes, and white meats. Serve at room temperature (65°F).

For the zone of production see Valdadige bianco.

Valle Isarco Müller-Thurgau

Color straw yellow with greenish tints. Light, vinous odor with a characteristic bouquet. Flavor dry, fresh, not much body, vigorous. Minimum alcoholic strength 10.5%. An easy wine for drinking with most plain foods. Serve slightly chilled at 50°F.

The zone of production lies in 11 wine-producing *comuni* in the Isarco valley in the province of Bolzano.

Valle Isarco Pinot grigio

Color straw yellow. Odor vinous with a light, characteristic bouquet. Flavor dry, full-bodied, fresh, vigorous, pleasant, characteristic. Minimum alcoholic strength 11%. A good accompaniment to antipasti, white meats, and fish. Serve slightly chilled at 50°F.

For the zone of production see Valle Isarco Müller-Thurgau.

Valle Isarco Sylvaner

Color greenish yellow. Vinous odor with a light, delicate bouquet. Flavor dry, delicate, fresh, of medium body. Minimum alcoholic strength 10.5%. An easy wine for drinking with most plain foods. Serve slightly chilled at around 50°F.

For the zone of production see Valle Isarco Müller-Thurgau.

Valle Isarco Traminer aromatico

Color very pale yellow with greenish tints. Delicate, intense bouquet with a characteristic aroma. Flavor dry, fresh, velvety, pleasantly aromatic. Minimum alcoholic strength 11%. Because of its marked aroma this wine goes very well with hot spicy dishes and strongly flavored seafood. Serve at 54–55°F.

For zone of production see Valle Isarco Müller-Thurgau.

Valle Isarco Veltliner

Color pale yellow tending toward greenish. Vinous odor, with a light perfume, characteristic of the grape. Flavor dry, fresh, fruity, vigorous. Minimum alcoholic strength 10%. A wine that goes well with light meals. Serve at 50°F.

For the zone of production see Valle Isarco Müller-Thurgau.

Friuli Venezia Giulia

Aquileia Cabernet

Color deep ruby red. Bouquet grassy, pleasant, intense. Flavor characteristic, agreeable, slightly grassy, soft. Minimum alcoholic strength 11.5%. This wine goes well with most foods, roasts (particularly roast pork), succulent meats, and cured meats in general. Serve at 65–68°F.

Produced in the province of Udine in a total of 18 *comuni*, one of which is Aquileia.

Aquileia Merlot

Color ruby red. Characteristic, vinous odor. Flavor dry, soft, aromatic. Minimum alcoholic strength 11%. This wine goes well with most foods, roasts (particularly roast pork), succulent meats, and cured meats in general. Serve at around 65°F.

For the zone of production see Aquileia Cabernet.

Aquileia Pinot bianco

Color varying from straw to golden yellow. Light, characteristic fragrance. Flavor velvety, soft. Minimum alcoholic strength 11.5%. A good apéritif wine; excellent with antipasti, fish and white meats. Serve chilled (47–50°F).

For the zone of production see Aquileia Cabernet.

Aquileia Pinot grigio

Color golden yellow. Characteristic bouquet. Flavor dry, full, harmonious. Minimum alcoholic strength 11%. A pleasant apéritif wine; excellent with antipasti, fish and white meats. Serve chilled (47–50°F.)

For the zone of production see Aquileia Cabernet.

Aquileia Refosco

Color deep violet-ruby red. Vinous odor. Flavor dry, full, slightly bitter. Minimum alcoholic strength 11%. Goes with most food, except fish. Serve at room temperature (65°F).

For the zone of production see Aquileia Cabernet.

Aquileia Riesling renano

Color pale golden yellow. Characteristic odor. Flavor dry, full-bodied, harmonious. Minimum alcoholic strength 11%. A particularly good accompaniment to antipasti, white meats, fish, mild cheeses. Serve chilled at 50–52°F.

For the zone of production see Aquileia Cabernet.

Aquileia Tocai italico

Color straw to pale gold. Bouquet delicate, agreeable, characteristic. Flavor dry, harmonious, with an aromatic aftertaste. Minimum alcoholic strength 11%. A wine to serve with fish, shellfish and mild cheeses. Serve slightly chilled at around 50–54°F.

For the zone of production see Aquileia Cabernet.

Colli Orientali del Friuli Cabernet

Color deep ruby red. Bouquet vinous, intense, agreeable. Flavor full-bodied, soft, fine, grassy. Minimum alcoholic strength 12%. It is a wine that goes well with cold roast meats, especially lamb and kid; the *riserva* makes a good accompaniment for all roasts. Serve at 65–68°F.

This wine is produced in the hilly part of the province of Udine, which can be considered a continuation of the hilly Collio Goriziano.

Colli Orientali del Friuli Pinot bianco

Collio Goriziano or Collio Tocai italico

Latisana

Isonzo

Grave del Friuli Merlot

Colli Orientali del Friuli Merlot

Color deep ruby red. Bouquet vinous, intense, pleasant, and perfumed. Flavor fine, soft, grassy. Minimum alcoholic strength 12%. This wine is a good accompaniment to roast and broiled meats. Serve at room temperature (65°F).

For the zone of production see Colli Orientali del Friuli Cabernet.

Colli Orientali del Friuli Picolit

Color deep straw yellow. Delicately semisweet or sweet, warm, well balanced, pleasant, delicate. Minimum alcoholic strength 15%. This is an extremely delicate wine to accompany light desserts, but it is also very palatable served with shellfish and strong cheeses. Serve chilled (43–47°F).

For the zone of production see Colli Orientali del Friuli Cabernet.

Colli Orientali del Friuli Pinot bianco

Color pale straw yellow or golden. Delicate bouquet. Flavor velvety, soft, harmonious. Minimum alcoholic strength 12%. Goes well with antipasti and fish dishes. Serve chilled (47–50°F.)

For the zone of production see Colli Orientali del Friuli Cabernet.

Colli Orientali del Friuli Pinot nero

Color not very bright ruby red, or slightly garnet after aging. Bouquet marked, characteristic and delicate. Flavor slightly aromatic, pleasantly bitter, velvety. Minimum alcoholic strength 12%. This wine should be served with cured meats, white meats and stews. Drink at room temperature (65°F).

For the zone of production see Colli Orientali del Friuli Cabernet.

Colli Orientali del Friuli Refosco

Color deep violet-red or garnet red after aging. Bouquet vinous and slightly special, characteristic. Flavor dry, warm, slightly bitter, full. Minimum alcoholic strength 12%. When aged it goes very well with roasts, hare and various kinds of game. Serve at 68°F.

For the zone of production see Colli Orientali del Friuli Cabernet.

Colli Orientali del Friuli Ribolla

Color straw yellow, tending to greenish. Bouquet fragrant, characteristic. Flavor dry, vinous, fresh, harmonious. Minimum alcoholic strength 12%. A good accompaniment to antipasti, cured meats, freshwater fish. Serve chilled (44–47°F).

For the zone of production see Colli Orientali del Friuli Cabernet.

Colli Orientali del Friuli Riesling renano

Color pale golden yellow. Characteristic bouquet. Flavor dry, well balanced. Minimum alcoholic strength 12%. Goes well with antipasti, rice, fish. Serve chilled (44–47°F).

For the zone of production see Colli Orientali del Friuli Cabernet.

Colli Orientali del Friuli Sauvignon

Color pale golden yellow. Delicate, almost aromatic bouquet. Flavor dry, full-bodied, warm, velvety. Minimum alcoholic strength 12%. A good accompaniment to antipasti, fish and eggs. Serve at 44–47°F.

For the zone of production see Colli Orientali del Friuli Cabernet.

Colli Orientali del Friuli Tocai italico

Color pale golden straw, tending to lemon. Bouquet pleasant, delicate, with a characteristic fragrance. Flavor dry, warm, with a slight aromatic aftertaste. Minimum alcoholic strength 12%. Goes well with antipasti and fish. Serve chilled (47–50°F).

For the zone of production see Colli Orientali del Friuli Cabernet.

Colli Orientali del Friuli Verduzzo

Color golden yellow. Characteristic, fruity bouquet, particularly in the sweet Ramandolo type. Flavor dry or semisweet, fruity, full-bodied, slightly tannic. Minimum alcoholic strength 12%. Suitable as an accompaniment to egg dishes and steamed fish. Serve chilled (47–50°F).

For the zone of production see Colli Orientali del Friuli Cabernet.

Collio or Collio Goriziano

Color straw yellow, varying in intensity. Neutral odor. Flavor dry, slightly sparkling, with body. Minimum alcoholic strength 11%. This wine goes well with most foods, but especially fish, vegetables and soup. Serve chilled (47–50°F).

Produced in the hilly area of the same name on the border with Yugoslavia.

Collio Cabernet franc

Color not very bright but lively ruby red. Bouquet grassy, distinctive, characteristic, pleasant. Flavor dry, rounded, well balanced. Minimum alcoholic strength 12%. An excellent wine with broiled foods, and when aged, with roasts and Parmesan cheese. Serve at room temperature (65°F).

For the zone of production see Collio (above).

Collio Malvasia

Color straw. Bouquet distinctive, pleasant, characteristic. Flavor dry, rounded, well balanced, distinctive. Minimum alcoholic strength 11.5%. This wine goes well with spicy fish dishes as well as antipasti and thin soups. Best served chilled at about 47–50°F.

For the zone of production see Collio.

Collio Merlot

Color not very bright but lively ruby red, with red bubbles. Bouquet distinctive, grassy. Flavor slightly bitter, grassy, lively, full-bodied, well balanced. Minimum alcoholic strength 12%. This wine goes well with most foods, especially white and red meats. Serve at room temperature (65°F).

For the zone of production see Collio.

Collio Pinot bianco

Color golden straw. Distinctive, characteristic bouquet. Flavor dry, full, harmonious. Minimum alcoholic strength 12%. Goes excellently with cured meats, Parma ham and freshwater fish. Serve at 47–50°F.

For the zone of production see Collio.

Collio Pinot grigio

Color golden yellow. Bouquet dis-tinctive, characteristic. Flavor dry, full, harmonious, characteristic. Minimum alcoholic strength 12.5%. It is a wine for accompanying antipasti, soups and shellfish. Serve chilled at around 47–50°F.

For the zone of production see Collio.

Collio Pinot nero

Color not very bright but lively ruby red. Bouquet marked and characteristic, delicate. Flavor slightly aromatic, pleasant, slightly bitter, velvety. Minimum alcoholic strength 12.5%. This wine provides a very good accompaniment to lamb, pork, kidneys, rabbit *alla cacciatora* (see p. 153) and stews. Serve at room temperature (65°F).

For the zone of production see Collio.

Collio Riesling italico

Color pale golden yellow. Bouquet distinctive, characteristic. Flavor dry, with body, harmonious. Minimum alcoholic strength 12%. Goes well with seafood antipasti and fish served in a sauce. Serve chilled (47–50°F).

For the zone of production see Collio.

Collio Sauvignon

Color deep straw yellow. Bouquet delicate, slightly aromatic. Flavor dry, with body, fresh, well balanced, distinctive. Minimum alcoholic strength 12.5%. Goes with oily fish, octopus, and squid. Serve chilled, at around 47–50°F.

For the zone of production see Collio.

Collio Tocai italico

Color ranging from lemon yellow to straw yellow. Bouquet vinous, delicate and pleasant with a characteristic fragrance. Flavor dry, warm, full, with an almond-like bitterness. Minimum alcoholic strength 12%. An excellent accompaniment to shellfish and fish soups. Serve chilled at 47–50°F.

For the zone of production see Collio.

Collio Traminer

Color deep straw yellow. Bouquet distinctive, with a characteristic aroma. Flavor aromatic, intense, full, robust, with body. Minimum alcoholic strength 12%. Besides complementing shellfish this wine goes well with strong cheeses such as Gorgonzola, Provolone and Pecorino. Serve chilled at 47–50°F.

For the zone of production see Collio.

Grave del Friuli Cabernet

Color bright ruby. Pleasant, grassy bouquet. Flavor dry, soft and aromatic. Minimum alcoholic strength 11.5%. Goes well with main courses, meats and game. Drink at room temperature (65°F) or 68°F if aged.

The zone of production is extensive and lies in the provinces of Udine and Pordenone.

Grave del Friuli Merlot

Color ruby red. Characteristic, vinous odor. Flavor dry, soft and aromatic. Minimum alcoholic strength 11%. Serve with main courses in general and roasts. Drink at room temperature (65°F).

For the zone of production see Grave del Friuli Cabernet.

Grave del Friuli Pinot bianco

Color from straw yellow to golden yellow. Bouquet light, perfumed, characteristic. Flavor velvety, well balanced, soft. Minimum alcoholic strength 11.5%. Well suited to antipasti, risottos and fish dishes. Served chilled (47–50°F).

For the zone of production see Grave del Friuli Cabernet.

Grave del Friuli Pinot grigio

Color golden yellow. Distinctive, characteristic bouquet. Flavor dry, full and well balanced. Minimum alcoholic strength 11%. A good choice to accompany cured meats, antipasti and fish. Serve chilled (47–50°F).

For the zone of production see Grave del Friuli Cabernet.

Grave del Friuli Refosco

Color bright violet red. Vinous odor. Flavor dry, full, bitterish. Minimum alcoholic strength 11%. Goes very well with fermented cheeses and meats. Serve at room temperature (65°F).

For the zone of production see Grave del Friuli Cabernet.

Grave del Friuli Tocai italico

Color pale golden straw tending to lemon. Bouquet delicate, pleasant, characteristic. Flavor dry, harmonious, with an aromatic aftertaste. Minimum alcoholic strength 11%. Goes well with broiled or boiled fish. Serve chilled (47–50°F).

For the zone of production see Grave del Friuli Cabernet.

Grave del Friuli Verduzzo

Color golden yellow. Typical bouquet. Flavor slightly tannic, full, with body, dry. Minimum alcoholic strength 11%. A good accompaniment to egg dishes and fish. Serve chilled (47–50°F).

For the zone of production see Grave del Friuli Cabernet.

Isonzo Cabernet

Color deep ruby red. Bouquet vinous, deep, agreeable, with a characteristic perfume. Flavor dry, full-bodied, soft, grassy, characteristic, pleasant. Minimum alcoholic strength 11%. Goes well with all main courses, especially roasts. Serve at room temperature (65°F).

Produced in the Isonzo valley north of Monfalcone and to the south of Gorizia.

Isonzo Malvasia istriana

Color straw. Pleasant bouquet. Flavor dry, delicate, not much body, pleasant. Minimum alcoholic strength 10.5%. Goes well with risottos, antipasti and most types of fish. Serve at around 50°F.

For the zone of production see Isonzo Cabernet.

Isonzo Merlot

Color ruby red. Pleasant, characteristic bouquet. Flavor full, vigorous, dry, slightly grassy. Minimum alcoholic strength 10.5%. A good accompaniment to main courses and roast meats; excellent with all kinds of game. Serve at room temperature (65°F).

For the zone of production see Isonzo Cabernet.

Isonzo Pinot bianco

Color light straw yellow or slightly golden. Bouquet delicate, characteristic, pleasant. Flavor velvety, soft, well balanced. Minimum alcoholic strength 11.5%. This wine can be served as an apéritif but is also excellent with antipasti and fish. Serve chilled at around 50°F.

For the zone of production see Isonzo Cabernet.

Isonzo Pinot grigio

Color yellow with pink hues. Bouquet distinctive, characteristic, pleasant. Flavor well balanced, characteristic. Minimum alcoholic strength 11%. This wine goes well with egg dishes, risottos and fish. Serve chilled at 48–50°F.

For the zone of production see Isonzo Cabernet.

Isonzo Riesling renano

Color straw yellow. Bouquet quite strong and characteristic, delicate, agreeable. Flavor dry, with medium body, well balanced, characteristic. Minimum alcoholic strength 11%. Drink with antipasti, risottos, fish and soft cheeses. Serve chilled at 47–50°F.

For the zone of production see Isonzo Cabernet.

Isonzo Sauvignon

Color light straw yellow. Bouquet delicate, almost aromatic. Flavor dry, full-bodied, velvety, pleasing. Minimum alcoholic strength 11%. Excellent with broiled fish. Serve chilled at 50°F.

For the zone of production see Isonzo Cabernet.

Isonzo Tocai

Color straw or light golden, tending to lemon. Bouquet delicate, pleasant, with characteristic fragrance. Flavor dry, warm, full, with a slight, aromatic aftertaste. Minimum alcoholic strength 10.5%. A good accompaniment to antipasti, particularly Parma ham and melon; also goes well with fish. Serve chilled at 50°F.

For the zone of production see Isonzo Cabernet.

Isonzo Traminer aromatico
Color deep straw yellow. Pleasant bouquet with a marked, characteristic aroma. Flavor slightly aromatic, intense, characteristic, full-bodied, pleasant. Minimum alcoholic strength 11%. A wine to accompany spicy antipasti; also goes well with Parma ham and melon, white meats and fish. Serve at 47–50°F.

For the zone of production see Isonzo Cabernet.

Isonzo Verduzzo friulano
Color varying depths of golden yellow. Bouquet vinous, characteristic, fruity. Flavor dry, fruity, full-bodied, slightly tannic. Minimum alcoholic strength 10.5%. Goes well with most food but particularly good with fish. Serve at around 50°F.

For the zone of production see Isonzo Cabernet.

Latisana Cabernet
Color bright ruby red. Bouquet grassy, pleasant, intense. Flavor slightly grassy, fine, soft. Minimum alcoholic strength 11.5%. Excellent with cold meat and poultry; when aging it is particularly suited to game. Serve at room temperature (65°F).

The zone of production includes the *comune* of Latisana and another 11 *comuni* in the province of Udine.

Latisana Merlot
Color ruby red. Bouquet vinous, characteristic, flavor dry, soft, harmonious. Minimum alcoholic strength 11%. This is a superior red wine which may be drunk throughout a meal; particularly pleasant with roasts and stews. Serve at room temperature (65°F).

For the zone of production see Latisana Cabernet.

Latisana Pinot bianco
Color light straw yellow to golden yellow. Light, characteristic bouquet. Flavor velvety, soft, charac-

teristic. Minimum alcoholic strength 11.5%. It is a good wine to accompany all courses; particularly recommended with antipasti, fish and white meat. Serve chilled at 47–50°F.

For the zone of production see Latisana Cabernet.

Latisana Pinot grigio
Color golden yellow. Characteristic bouquet. Flavor dry, full, well balanced. Minimum alcoholic strength 11%. This wine is particularly good with fish dishes and antipasti. Serve chilled at 47–50°F.

For the zone of production see Latisana Cabernet.

Latisana Refosco
Color bright violet-ruby red. Characteristic, vinous bouquet. Flavor dry, full, bitterish. Minimum alcoholic strength 11%. A good accompaniment to all courses of a meal. Serve at room temperature (65°F).

For the zone of production see Latisana Cabernet.

Latisana Tocai italico
Color straw or light golden, tending to lemon. Bouquet delicate, pleasant, characteristic. Flavor well balanced, characteristic. Minimum alcoholic strength 11%. It is a wine for all courses, particularly good with cooked fish dishes and cheese. Serve chilled at 50–54°F.

For the zone of production see Latisana Cabernet.

Latisana Verduzzo
Color golden yellow. Characteristic, vinous bouquet. Flavor slightly tannic, full-bodied. Minimum alcoholic strength 11%. Goes well with most food, particularly antipasti of cured meats, rich pasta dishes and white meats. Serve chilled at 47–50°F.

For the zone of production see Latisana Cabernet.

Liguria

Cinque Terre
Color varying depths of straw yellow. Typical, fresh, delicate bouquet. Flavor dry, slightly

aromatic, characteristic, agreeable. Minimum alcoholic strength 11%. Particularly good with fish soups, fish cooked *en papillote* and shellfish; it also goes well with stuffed vegetables. Serve at 48–52°F.

This wine is produced in the *comuni* of Riomaggiore, Vernazza and Monterosso in the province of La Spezia, as well as in part of the *comune* of La Spezia.

Cinque Terre Sciacchetrà
Color golden yellow to amber yellow. Pleasant bouquet. Flavor sweet to almost dry. Minimum alcoholic strength 17% (of which at least 13.5% converted). When almost dry this wine is an excellent apéritif, otherwise it goes well with fruit salads, cookies and ice cream. As an apéritif, serve very chilled, at (43–47°F), otherwise at 50–57°F.

For the zone of production see Cinque Terre.

Rossese di Dolceacqua or Dolceacqua
Color ruby red, garnet after aging. Bouquet vinous, intense but delicate, characteristic. Flavor soft, aromatic, warm. Minimum alcoholic strength 12%. Excellent with local ravioli specialties, casseroled hare, and roasts. Serve at room temperature (65°F); the *superiore* type slightly warmer, at 68°F.

The zone of production lies on the border with France and includes the *comune* of Dolceacqua and another ten neighboring *comuni*; it also includes part of two further *comuni*, one of which is Ventimiglia.

Emilia Romagna

Albana di Romagna secco
Color straw or golden yellow. Bouquet light, characteristic of the Albana grape. Flavor dry, slightly tannic, warm. Minimum alcoholic strength 11%. It is a good accompaniment to antipasti, which goes well with lasagne bolognesi (see p. 74), a variety of cured meats,

sea- and freshwater fish and eel. Serve chilled (50–54°F).

The zone of production includes a number of *comuni* in the provinces of Forlì, Ravenna and Bologna.

Albana di Romagna amabile
Color golden yellow. Characteristic, delicate bouquet. Flavor fruity, varying in sweetness, pleasant, characteristic. Minimum alcoholic strength 12.5%. Goes well with savory dishes but is also suitable served at the end of a meal. Serve chilled (50–54°F), also the *spumante* (sparkling) type.

For the zone of production see Albana di Romagna secco.

Bianco di Scandiano secco
Color straw of varying depth. Bouquet characteristic, aromatic. Flavor characteristic, sweet or semisweet, vigorous, fresh, well balanced, with medium body. Minimum alcoholic strength 10.5%. An excellent accompaniment to the local Emilian cuisine. Serve chilled (50°F).

The zone of production includes the *comune* of Scandiano and another five *comuni* in Reggio Emilia.

Bianco di Scandiano semi-secco
Color straw of varying depth. Bouquet characteristic, pleasantly aromatic. Flavor characteristic, sweet, vigorous, fresh, well balanced, with medium body. Minimum alcoholic strength 10.5%. A good wine with sweets, ice cream and desserts. Served chilled (50°F).

For the zone of production see Bianco di Scandiano secco.

Colli Bolognesi (Monte San Pietro or Castelli Medievali) Barbera
Color deep ruby red, tending to violet. Characteristic, vinous odor. Flavor harmonious, moderately tannic. Minimum alcoholic strength 11.5%. The young wine is excellent with antipasti, cured meats, lasagne and tortellini; the *riserva* is also good with game, barbecued meat and kid. Serve the young wine at room temperature (60–65°F); the *riserva* at 68°F.

The zone of production lies in

ten traditionally wine-producing *comuni* in the Bolognese hills. The denominations of Colli Bolognesi Monte San Pietro and Colli Bolognesi Castelli Medievali originate from two places which have given their geographical names to the wines they produce: Monte San Pietro is a *comune*; Castelli Medievali is the state highway 569, so called because of the medieval castles found along it.

Colli Bolognesi (Monte San Pietro or Castelli Medievali) bianco

Color light golden yellow. Vinous odor with fragrance of the Albana grape. Flavor dry or semisweet, vigorous, slightly tannic. Minimum alcoholic strength 11% (of which not more than 0.5% unconverted). This wine may be drunk throughout the meal and is particularly good with soups, pasta dishes served with meat sauce, white meats, antipasti. Serve chilled at 50°F.

For the zone of production see Colli Bolognesi Barbera.

Colli Bolognesi (Monte San Pietro or Castelli Medievali) Merlot

Color ruby red with violet hues. Characteristic bouquet. Flavor dry or slightly sweet, vigorous, well balanced. Minimum alcoholic strength 11.5% (of which not more than 0.5% unconverted). This is a wine to accompany traditional Emilian specialties, braised meats, rotisseried poultry, and cured meats. Serve at room temperature (65°F).

For the zone of production see Colli Bolognesi Barbera.

Colli Bolognesi (Monte San Pietro or Castelli Medievali) Pinot bianco

Color straw yellow with occasional greenish tints. Delicate, ethereal bouquet. Flavor dry or semisweet, well balanced. Minimum alcoholic strength 12% (of which not more than 0.5% unconverted). An excellent wine with antipasti, cured meats, pasta served in clear broth, omelets, white meats. Colli Bolognesi should be served chilled at around 50°F.

For the zone of production see Colli Bolognesi Barbera.

Colli Bolognesi (Monte San Pietro or Castelli Medievali) Riesling italico

Color varying depths of straw yellow. Delicate, characteristic bouquet. Flavor dry or slightly sweet, characteristic, well balanced. Minimum alcoholic strength 12%. Goes well with antipasti, omelets, salads, fish, white meats, cheeses. Serve at 47–50°F.

For the zone of production see Colli Bolognesi Barbera.

Colli Bolognesi (Monte San Pietro or Castelli Medievali) Sauvignon

Color straw yellow. Bouquet delicate, slightly aromatic, characteristic. Flavor dry or semisweet, with body, fresh, well balanced. Minimum alcoholic strength 12% (of which not more than 0.5% unconverted). An excellent accompaniment to pasta in broth, white meats, fish. Serve chilled (47–50°F).

For the zone of production see Colli Bolognesi Barbera.

Gutturnio dei Colli Piacentini

Color bright red. Vinous odor. Flavor dry and slightly sweet. Minimum alcoholic strength 12%. Goes well with risottos, pasta served with butter and cheese, roasts, poultry and rabbit; the *amabile* (sweet) type is good with fruit salads and desserts. Serve at room temperature (65°F).

Gutturnio is produced in three hilly areas in the province of Piacenza.

Lambrusco di Sorbara

Color ruby red or varying depths of garnet. Agreeable bouquet, reminiscent of violets. Flavor dry or semisweet, full-bodied, fresh, vigorous and well balanced. Minimum alcoholic strength 11%. This wine is particularly recommended with traditional Emilian dishes. Serve at 59°F, or cooler in summer.

This type of Lambrusco is produced in Sorbara in the *comune* of Bomporto as well as in nine other *comuni* in the province of Modena.

Lambrusco Grasparossa di Castelvetro

Color ruby red, violet at the edges. Bouquet markedly vinous with a strong perfume. Flavor dry or slightly sweet, vigorous, well balanced. Minimum alcoholic strength 10.5%. This is a lively wine that goes well with all courses but it is particularly pleasant with traditional Emilian specialties such as risottos, *zampone, cotechino,* and tortellini with meat sauce; the *amabile* is more suited to the end of the meal. Serve slightly chilled at 55°F.

Produced in the province of Modena in 14 *comuni*, including Castelvetro.

Lambrusco Reggiano

Color rosé to lively ruby. Pleasant, characteristic bouquet. Flavor dry or semisweet, slightly sparkling, not too much body, harmonious, fresh and pleasing. Minimum alcoholic strength 10.5%. This wine goes well with local specialties, hot cured meats and stews. Serve at 57–59°F.

Produced in the province of Reggio Emilia in around 20 *comuni* between Secchia and Enza.

Lambrusco Salamino di S. Croce

Color varying depths of ruby red. Intense, vinous odor with characteristic, fruity bouquet. Flavor dry or semisweet, noticeably vinous, pleasant, full-bodied, vigorous, fresh and slightly sparkling. Minimum alcoholic strength 11%. It is a particularly good foil to the oiliness of traditional Emilian cuisine. Serve at 59°F (even cooler in summer).

Production of this type of Lambrusco in the province of Modena is centered around the village of S. Croce in the *comune* of Carpi; it also extends to ten further *comuni* in the province.

Monterosso Val d'Arda

Color straw yellow or slightly golden yellow. Delicate, characteristic bouquet. Flavor dry or slightly sweet, occasionally slightly sparkling, fine and with subtle body. Minimum alcoholic strength 11% The *secco* (dry) is excellent with fettucine, panzerotti, and rice with mushrooms; the *amabile* (semisweet) or *frizzante* (slightly sparkling) types are recommended with fruit salads and desserts; the *spumante* (sparkling) type is best served at the end of a meal with sweets or ice cream. Always serve chilled at 47–50°F.

Monterosso is produced in the province of Piacenza in the *comuni* of Vernasca, Alseno, Lugagnano, Castell'Arquato, Gropparello and Carpaneto situated in the hills of the Arda valley.

Sangiovese di Romagna

Color ruby red occasionally with hints of violet. Vinous bouquet with a delicate fragrance reminiscent of violets. Flavor dry, well balanced, occasionally slightly tannic, with a pleasant, bitterish aftertaste. Minimum alcoholic strength 11.5%. An excellent table wine to accompany most foods. Drink at room temperature (65°F) or slightly chilled (59–60°F).

Produced in 44 *comuni* in the province of Forlì, in six *comuni* in the province of Ravenna and in seven *comuni* in the province of Bologna.

Trebbianino Val Trebbia

Color straw yellow or light golden yellow. Vinous, slightly aromatic bouquet. Flavor dry or very slightly sweet, delicate, at times with a sparkle, subtle, not too much body. Minimum alcoholic strength 11%. Goes well with light antipasti, shellfish, omelets. Serve at 47–50°F.

This type of Trebbiano is produced in five *comuni* in the valley of the River Trebbia (Bobbio, Coli, Travo, Rivergaro, Gazzola) in the province of Piacenza.

Trebbiano di Romagna

Color straw, varying in brightness. Pleasant, vinous odor. Flavor dry, vigorous, well balanced. Minimum alcoholic strength 11.5%. A good accompaniment to fish dishes, eggs and antipasti; the *spumante* (sparkling) type should be served with the dessert. Drink the table wine at 50°F, the *spumante* at 41–44°F.

This Trebbiano is produced in ten *comuni* in the province of Bologna, in 30 *comuni* in the province of Forlì and in 14 *comuni* in the province of Ravenna.

Tuscany

Bianco della Valdinievole

Color light golden yellow, tending to straw. Pleasant, slightly vinous

Barbera

Cabernet franc

Carignano

Müller-Thurgau

Trebbiano toscano

Riesling-Sylvaner

nose. Flavor dry, lively, well balanced, at times slightly sparkling. Minimum alcoholic strength 11%. Excellent with antipasti, fish, white meats. Serve at room temperature (65°F) or slightly chilled (59°F).

The zone of production includes the *comuni* of Buggiano, Montecatini Terme, Uzzano and part of six further *comuni* in the province of Pistoia.

Bianco della Valdinievole Vinsanto

Color straw to more or less tawny amber. Bouquet intense, ethereal, typical. Flavor harmonious, soft, with a characteristic, bitterish aftertaste. Minimum alcoholic strength 17% (of which one part unconverted). Recommended with desserts, particularly with traditional Tuscan cakes. Serve at room temperature (65°F) or slightly chilled (59°F).

For the zone of production see Bianco della Valdinievole.

Bianco di Pitigliano

Color straw yellow, with greenish hues. Delicate bouquet. Flavor dry, neutral, with a slightly bitter background, of medium body, soft. Minimum alcoholic strength 11.5%. A suitable wine for most courses, particularly antipasti, beef dishes and fish. Serve chilled at 47–50°F.

Produced in the *comuni* of Pitigliano and Sorano and also in Scansano and Manciano in the province of Grosseto.

Bianco Pisano di S. Torpé

Color straw yellow, occasionally with noticeable greenish tints. Bouquet clean, fragrant, delicate, intense, lasting, with an aromatic background. Flavor dry, balanced, with a slightly bitter aftertaste, characteristic. Minimum alcoholic strength not yet established. Goes well served with fish or at the end of the meal; occasionally also served with the first course. Drink chilled at 47–50°F.

Produced in the Chianti zone, in the province of Pisa.

Bianco Vergine Val di Chiana

Color straw with greenish tints. Bouquet neutral, characteristic, with a pleasant, delicate perfume. Flavor dry, and slightly sweet, with a faint aftertaste of bitter almonds. Minimum alcoholic strength 11%. A good accompaniment to antipasti, fish, soups and white meats. Serve chilled at 50–54°F.

Produced in part of the following *comuni*: Arezzo, Castiglion Fiorentino, Cortona, Foiano, Marciano, Monte S. Savino, Civitella in Valdichiana, Sinalunga, Torrita di Siena, Chiusi and Montepulciano, in the provinces of Arezzo and Siena.

Brunello di Montalcino

Color bright ruby red, tending to garnet with age. Intense, characteristic bouquet. Flavor dry, warm, slightly tannic, robust and lively but soft. Minimum alcoholic strength 12.5%. Goes well with large roasts and game. Serve at 68–71°F; uncork the bottle at least 2 hr before drinking.

Produced in the *comune* of Montalcino in the province of Siena.

Candia dei Colli Apuani

Color straw yellow, varying in brightness. Bouquet delicate, intense, slightly aromatic, characteristic. Flavor dry, occasionally slightly sweet, full, harmonious, with a bitterish aftertaste. Minimum alcoholic strength 11.5%. Recommended with fish. Serve chilled at 47°F.

The zone of production is in the *comuni* of Carrara, Massa and Montignoso, in the province of Massa-Carrara.

Carmignano

Color lively ruby tending to garnet with age. Bouquet vinous with a strong scent of violets, becoming more refined with age. Flavor dry, vigorous, harmonious, mellow. Minimum alcoholic strength 12.5%. A good-quality wine to accompany roasts and matured cheeses. Serve at 65–68°F. The *riserva* should be served at 68–71°F, remembering to uncork the bottle a few hours beforehand.

Produced in the *comuni* of Carmignano and Poggio a Caiano in the province of Florence.

Chianti

Color bright ruby. Strongly vinous bouquet. Flavor well balanced, dry, vigorous, slightly tannic. Minimum alcoholic strength 11.5%. Goes well with all courses. Serve at room temperature (65°F).

Produced in the provinces of Florence, Siena, Arezzo, Pisa and Pistoia; the D.O.C. covers several geographical areas: Montalbano, Rufina, Colli Fiorentini, Colli Senesi, Colli Aretini, Colline Pisane. The *classico* zone includes the *comuni* of Radda, Gajole, Castellina in Chianti, Greve and S. Casciano Val di Pesa.

Chianti Classico
Color bright ruby tending to garnet with aging. Vinous bouquet, with a typical lasting aroma of sweet violets, fine. Flavor well balanced, dry, vigorous, slightly tannic, becoming more refined, mellow and velvety with age. Minimum alcoholic strength 12%. A distinctive wine to accompany all courses. Serve at 68–71°F, uncorking the bottle several hours before drinking.

For the zone of production see Chianti.

Elba bianco
Color light straw yellow. Bouquet vinous, delicately perfumed. Flavor dry and harmonious. Minimum alcoholic strength 11%. Goes well with boiled and baked fish and egg dishes. Serve at around 50°F; the *spumante* (sparkling) type is generally served chilled with the dessert (41–44°F).

The zone of production covers the entire island of Elba.

Elba rosso
Color bright ruby red. Vinous odor. Flavor dry, slightly aromatic, harmonious. Minimum alcoholic strength 12%. A wine to accompany the entire meal. Serve at 65°F.

For the zone of production see Elba bianco.

Montecarlo
Color bright straw. Delicate bouquet. Flavor dry, velvety, harmonious. Minimum alcoholic strength 11.5%. A perfect accompaniment to fish and antipasti. Serve chilled at 48–50°F.

The zone of production lies in the province of Lucca, extending toward the province of Pistoia

Lambrusco di Sorbara

Sangiovese di Romagna

Colli Bolognesi Barbera

Trebbiano di Romagna

Gutturnio dei Colli Piacentini

Chianti

Chianti Classico

Bianco Vergine Val di Chiana

Montecarlo

Vernaccia di S. Gimignano

Brunello di Montalcino

and includes the *comuni* of Montecarlo, Altopascio, Capannori and Porcari.

Montescudaio bianco
Color straw yellow. Delicate, vinous bouquet. Flavor dry, harmonious, pleasant. Minimum alcoholic strength 11.5%. A pleasant accompaniment to cured meats, antipasti and fish. Serve chilled at around 50°F.

Produced in the *comune* of the same name and six other *comuni* in the province of Pisa.

Montescudaio rosso
Color deep ruby red. Bouquet vinous, soft, fruity. Flavor dry, good body, moderately tannic, harmonious. Minimum alcoholic strength 11.5%. This wine is particularly good served with the main course, especially with red meats. Serve at room temperature (65°F).

For the zone of production see Montescudaio bianco.

Montescudaio Vinsanto
Color straw to tawny amber. Bouquet intense, ethereal, typical. Flavor well balanced, soft, with bitterish aftertaste, characteristic. Minimum alcoholic strength 17% (of which 14% converted). A prized dessert wine that can also be served at the end of the meal with traditional dry pastries that are dipped into it. Serve at room temperature (65°F) or slightly chilled.

For the zone of production see Montescudaio bianco.

Morellino di Scansano
Color ruby red, tending to garnet with aging. Bouquet vinous, becoming intense, ethereal, pleasing, elegant, with a fragrance reminiscent of sweet violets as it ages. Flavor dry, austere, warm, slightly tannic. Minimum alcoholic strength 11.5%. When young it will go well with the entire meal; as it ages it is a good accompaniment to rotisseried meats, steaks and roasts. Serve at room temperature (65°F).

Produced in the *comune* of Scansano in the province of Grosseto and in another six *comuni* situated in the hilly area between the rivers Ombrone and Albegna.

Rosso delle Colline Lucchesi

Vino Nobile di Montepulciano

Parrina bianco
Color slightly golden straw yellow. Bouquet vinous, fine. Flavor dry but velvety with a slightly bitter aftertaste. Minimum alcoholic strength 11.5%. An excellent accompaniment to meatless antipasti, fish, and white meats. Serve chilled at 50°F.

Produced in Parrina, in the *comune* of Orbetello in the province of Grosseto.

Parrina rosso
Color ruby red. Bouquet vinous, delicate, pleasant. Flavor harmonious, velvety, dry. Minimum alcoholic strength 11.5%. A pleasant accompaniment to cured meats and first courses. Serve at 65°F.

For the zone of production see Parrina bianco.

Rosso delle Colline Lucchesi
Color brilliant ruby red. Bouquet pleasant and characteristic. Flavor dry, harmonious, soft; lively if drunk the same year it is made.

Minimum alcoholic strength 11.5%. A wine for immediate drinking, to accompany the entire meal, also particularly recommended with red meats and roasts. Serve at 65–68°F.

Produced in the *comuni* of Lucca, Capannori and Porcari.

Vernaccia di San Gimignano
Color light, golden yellow. Fine and penetrating bouquet. Flavor dry, fresh, harmonious. Minimum alcoholic strength 12%. Although mainly a wine to accompany fish it also goes well with antipasti, rice salad and cappelletti in clear broth. Serve chilled (47–50°F).

Produced in the *comune* of San Gimignano in the province of Siena.

Vino Nobile di Montepulciano
Color garnet varying in brightness, tending to reddish brown with age. Bouquet delicate and intense, of sweet violets. Flavor dry, slightly tannic. Minimum alcoholic strength 12%. A good wine of superb quality for accompanying roasts. Serve at around 68°F, uncorking the bottle some time in advance of serving.

Produced in the *comune* of Montepulciano in the province of Siena.

Umbria

Colli Altotiberini bianco
Color varying depths of straw yellow. Pleasant, characteristic bouquet. Flavor dry, well balanced. Minimum alcoholic strength 10.5%. Particularly suited to seafood specialties and antipasti. Serve chilled at 50°F.

The zone of production includes parts of the *comuni* of S. Giustino, Cisterna, Città di Castello, Monte S. Maria Tiberina, Montone, Umbertide, Gubbio, Perugia.

Colli Altotiberini rosato
Color pale rosé. Bouquet faintly fruity. Flavor fresh, lively. Minimum alcoholic strength 11.5%. A wine to accompany all courses, generally drunk young. Serve at around 54–57°F.

For the zone of production see Colli Altotiberini bianco.

Colli Altotiberini rosso
Color ruby red. Pleasant bouquet.

Flavor dry, rounded. Minimum alcoholic strength 11.5%. An excellent accompaniment to more sophisticated main courses. Serve at room temperature (65°F).

For the zone of production see Colli Altotiberini bianco.

Colli del Trasimeno bianco
Color straw yellow. Pleasant bouquet. Flavor well balanced. Minimum alcoholic strength 11%. Goes well with antipasti, fish, risottos. Serve at 50–54°F.

The zone of production includes parts of the *comuni* of Castiglione del Lago, Città della Pieve, Paciano, Piegaro, Panicale, Perugia, Corciano, Magione, Passignano sul Trasimeno, Tuoro sul Trasimeno.

Colli del Trasimeno rosso
Color varying depths of garnet, tending to brick red with age. Bouquet delicate, of violets, becoming more refined with age. Flavor dry, harmonious, slightly tannic. Minimum alcoholic strength 11.5%. A pleasant accompaniment to meats, game and main courses. Serve at room temperature (65°F).

For the zone of production see Colli del Trasimeno bianco.

Montefalco
Color ruby, tending to garnet. Characteristic, vinous bouquet. Flavor harmonious, dry, velvety. Minimum alcoholic strength 11.5%. Goes well with main courses, especially meats. Serve at room temperature (65°F).

Produced in the province of Perugia in the registered zone, which includes the entire *comune* of Montefalco and part of the *comuni* of Bevagna, Gualdo, Cattaneo, Castel Ritaldi, Giano dell'Umbria.

Montefalco Sagrantino
or Sagrantino di Montefalco
Color ruby red, tending to garnet with age. Bouquet delicate, similar to that of blackberries, characteristic. Flavor dry, harmonious. Minimum alcoholic strength 12.5%. Goes well with main courses; the *passito* type is an excellent accompaniment to desserts and pastries. Serve at room temperature (65°F); the *passito* at 59–62°F.

For the zone of production see Montefalco.

Orvieto
Color varying depths of straw. Pleasant, delicate bouquet. Flavor dry with a faintly bitter aftertaste, or slightly sweet, elegant and delicate. Minimum alcoholic strength 12%. It is particularly recommended with fish and antipasti; the *abboccato* (slightly sweet) type goes well with the entire meal, and is especially good with Parma ham and melon. Serve chilled at 50°F.

Produced throughout or in parts of the *comuni* of Orvieto, Allerona, Baschi, Castel Giorgio, Castel Viscardo, Ficulle, Montecchio, Fabro, Montegabbione, Monteleone d'Orvieto, Castiglione in Teverina, Civitella d'Agliano, Graffignano, Lubriano, Bagnoregio, Porano. The *classico* zone, which is older and more traditional, covers the right and left banks of the Paglia.

Torgiano bianco
Color straw yellow. Bouquet vinous, quite pleasant, with the delicate fragrance of wild flowers. Flavor very slightly fruity, acidic. Minimum alcoholic strength 11.5%. It is an excellent apéritif wine but also goes well with antipasti, fish and pasta dishes. Serve chilled at 47–50°F.

The zone of production lies in the hilly area to the north of the *comune* of Torgiano, toward Ponte S. Giovanni-Collestrada, in the province of Perugia.

Torgiano rosso
Color bright ruby red. Bouquet delicate and delicately fruity. Flavor dry, well balanced, of medium body. Minimum alcoholic strength 12%. Goes well with roasts and game. Serve at 65–68°F; the *riserva* type at 68–71°F, uncorking the bottle several hours before drinking.

For the zone of production see Torgiano bianco.

The Marches

Bianchello del Metauro
Color straw yellow. Bouquet delicate, characteristic, fruity with a vague aroma of ripe peaches.

Flavor dry, fresh, harmonious, pleasant. Minimum alcoholic strength 11.5%. An excellent accompaniment to fish, antipasti and white meats. Serve chilled at around 50–54°F.

Produced in 18 *comuni* in the lower part of the valley of the River Metauro.

Bianco dei Colli Maceratesi

Color pale straw yellow. Pleasant, characteristic bouquet. Flavor dry, well balanced. Minimum alcoholic strength 11%. It is a wine that goes particularly well with fish delicacies from the Adriatic coast; excellent also with antipasti, soups, light meats. Serve chilled (47–50°F).

The zone of production includes the entire province of Macerata and the *comune* of Loreto in the province of Ancona.

Falerio dei Colli Ascolani

Color pale straw yellow. Bouquet faintly perfumed. Flavor dry, vigorous, harmonious, slightly acidulous, pleasant. Minimum alcoholic strength 11.5%. A wine suited to meatless antipasti, baked fish and subtle dishes. Serve at 47–50°F.

Produced in the hills in the province of Ascoli Piceno.

Rosso Conero

Color bright ruby red. Pleasant, vinous bouquet. Flavor vigorous, well balanced, dry, clean, full-bodied. Minimum alcoholic strength 11.5%. This wine goes well with red meats and broiled food. Serve at 65°F.

Rosso Conero is produced in the entire *comuni* of Ancona, Offagna, Camerano, Sirolo, Numana and in parts of the *comuni* of Castelfidardo and Osimo.

Rosso Piceno

Color moderately dark ruby red, tending to garnet with age. Bouquet pleasant, vinous, slightly ethereal. Flavor vigorous, well balanced, dry. Minimum alcoholic strength 11.5%. This wine goes well with thick soups and meats; the *superiore* type is best served with roasts, grills and game. Serve at room temperature (65°F).

Rosso Piceno is produced along the Adriatic coast in the province of Ascoli Piceno.

Sangiovese dei Colli Pesaresi

Color not very deep garnet red. Bouquet delicate, vinous, characteristic. Flavor dry. Minimum alcoholic strength 11.5%. May be drunk throughout a meal but is particularly good with poultry or the typical local dish of rabbit with fennel. Serve at room temperature (65°F).

Produced in 37 *comuni* in the hills in the province of Pesaro.

Verdicchio dei Castelli di Jesi

Color pale straw. Delicate, characteristic bouquet. Flavor dry, harmonious. Minimum alcoholic strength 12%. Goes well with antipasti, fish and egg dishes; the *spumante* (sparkling) type is good with desserts. Serve chilled (50°F); the *amabile* (semisweet) type colder (43–44°F).

This Verdicchio comes from a *classico* zone which includes the older, original area and excludes the area on the left bank of the River Misa and the *comuni* of Ostra and Senigallia; the entire zone includes all or part of 27 *comuni* in the province of Ancona.

Verdicchio di Matelica

Color pale straw. Characteristic, delicate bouquet. Flavor dry, harmonious, with a pleasantly bitter aftertaste. Minimum alcoholic strength 12%. This wine goes well with cold antipasti, egg dishes and fish. Serve at 50–54°F.

This type of Verdicchio is produced in six *comuni* in the province of Macerata, one of which is Matelica, and in two *comuni* in the province of Ancona.

Vernaccia di Serrapetrona

Color garnet to ruby. Bouquet characteristic, aromatic, vinous. Flavor semisweet or sweet, with a pleasant, bitterish aftertaste. Minimum alcoholic strength 11.5%. This is a sparkling red wine to serve at the end of the meal or with the dessert. Serve slightly chilled at 57–59°F.

Produced in the entire *comune* of Serrapetrona and partly in Belforte del Chienti; and Sanseverino Marche in the province of Macerata.

Abruzzo

Montepulciano d'Abruzzo

Color bright ruby red with slight violet tints; as it ages it tends to turn orange. Bouquet vinous, light, agreeable. Flavor dry mellow, lively, tannic. Minimum alcoholic strength 12%. A good wine for accompanying traditional local specialties such as tagliatelle with meat sauce, partridge, game, lamb, and sausages; the *cerasuolo* type goes well with pasta dishes, feathered game, tripe and omelets. Serve at 62–68°F (the *cerasuolo* type at 59°F).

Montepulciano d'Abruzzo is produced in the wine-growing areas in the provinces of Chieti, L'Aquila, Pescara and Teramo.

Trebbiano d'Abruzzo

Color straw. Bouquet vinous, pleasant, delicately scented. Flavor dry, lively, harmonious. Minimum alcoholic strength 11.5%. A wine to drink throughout the meal; excellent with antipasti of fish, shellfish, artichokes and omelets. Serve at a maximum temperature of 47–50°F.

This type of Trebbiano is produced throughout the region's wine-growing area, in the provinces of Chieti, Pescara, Teramo and part of L'Aquila.

Molise

Biferno

Color ruby red, varying in intensity, acquiring orange tints when aged. Vinous bouquet with an ethereal fragrance when aged. Flavor dry, harmonious, velvety. Minimum alcoholic strength 11.5%. Goes well with roast meats and game. Serve at 62°F.

Produced in 43 *comuni* in the province of Campobasso. There are also a rosé and a white version of this wine.

Pentro di Isernia

Color ruby red, varying in intensity. Pleasant, characteristic bouquet. Flavor dry, harmonious, velvety and slightly tannic. Minimum

alcoholic strength 11%. Goes well with stews and roast meats. Serve at 65°F. There are also a rosé and a white version of this wine.

Latium

Aleatico di Gradoli
Color garnet red with violet tints. Bouquet delicately aromatic, characteristic. Flavor of fresh fruit, soft, velvety, sweet. Minimum alcoholic strength 12% (of which at least 9.5% unconverted). It is a good accompaniment to cake and desserts. The *liquoroso* (fortified dessert wine) type is a good conclusion to any meal. Serve at 50–54°F.

Produced in the *comuni* of Gradoli, Grotte dei Casto, S. Lorenzo Nuovo and Lattera, all in the province of Viterbo.

Bianco Capena
Color straw yellow, tending to golden, with greenish tints. Bouquet slightly aromatic, characteristic, agreeable. Flavor dry or slightly sweet, soft, scented. Minimum alcoholic strength 11.5%. A wine for drinking with all courses, it is particularly good with Roman specialties and also with vegetables, soups and pizza. It must be drunk chilled at 50–54°F.

Produced in the *comune* of Capena and in another 13 *comuni* in the province of Rome.

Cerveteri bianco
Color straw yellow, varying in intensity. Bouquet vinous, pleasant, delicate. Flavor dry, slightly sweet, with a slightly bitter undertaste, lively, full, harmonious. Minimum alcoholic strength 11.5%. A wine to accompany the entire meal, it goes well with local specialties. Drink at 50–54°F.

Produced in the *comune* of Cerveteri and in another seven *comuni* in the province of Rome.

Cerveteri rosso
Color ruby red, varying in intensity. Bouquet vinous. Flavor dry

with a slightly bitter undertaste, lively, full-bodied, harmonious. Minimum alcoholic strength 12%. Goes well with roasted and broiled meats. Serve at 65–68°F.

For the zone of production see Cerveteri bianco.

Cesanese del Piglio

Color ruby red, tending to garnet with age. Delicate, characteristic bouquet. Flavor soft, slightly bitter, dry and clean or slightly sweet. Minimum alcoholic strength 10%. The dry type goes excellently with first courses, roasts, meats, baked mushrooms, kidneys, mature cheeses; the *amabile* (semisweet) and especially the *dolce* (sweet) types are good served at the end of the meal with sweets and dessert. Serve at 68°F; the *spumante* type should be drunk a little cooler at 59–60°F.

Produced in the *comune* of Piglio and another four *comuni* in the province of Frosinone.

Cesanese di Affile or Affile

Color ruby red, tending to garnet with age. Delicate bouquet, characteristic of the vine. Flavor soft, slightly bitter, clean, dry, slightly sweet or sweet according to the type. Minimum alcoholic strength 12%. When aged the *secco* (dry) type is particularly good with roasts. Serve at 68°F. *Spumante* (sparkling) and *frizzante* (semisparkling) versions are also made.

This wine is produced in the province of Rome in the *comuni* of Affile, Roiate and part of Arcinazzo.

Cesanese di Olevano Romano

Color ruby red, tending to garnet with age. Delicate, characteristic bouquet. Flavor soft, slightly bitter. Minimum alcoholic strength 12%. The *secco* (dry) type goes well with main courses and meats; the *amabile* (semisweet) and *dolce* (sweet) types can be drunk on their own or with desserts and pastries. Serve the *secco* at room temperature (65°F), the *amabile* and *dolce* a little cooler (59°F).

Produced in the *comuni* of Olevano and Gennazzano (Rome).

Colli Albani

Color straw yellow to deep yellow. Bouquet vinous, delicate, aromatic. Flavor dry or semisweet, fruity. Minimum alcoholic strength 11.5%. This wine goes excellently with traditional Roman specialties, mixed antipasti, and bruschetta (see p. 12). Serve at 50–54°F.

Produced in the *comuni* of Rome, Pomezia, Castelgandolfo and Lanuvio.

Colli Lanuvini

Color varying shades of straw yellow. Bouquet vinous, delicate and pleasant. Flavor dry or semisweet, lively, medium-bodied, harmonious, velvety. Minimum alcoholic strength 11.5%. This wine goes well with antipasti, cured meats and fish. Serve chilled at 50°F.

The area of production includes the entire *comune* of Genzano and part of the *comune* of Lanuvio, south of Lake Nemi.

Cori bianco

Color straw yellow. Bouquet vinous, agreeable, characteristic. Flavor delicate, soft, harmonious; dry, semisweet or sweet. Minimum alcoholic strength 11%. Goes well with a variety of dishes; the *secco* (dry) is excellent with fish. Serve chilled at 50°F.

Produced in the province of Latina in the entire *comune* of Cori and part of the *comune* of Cisterna.

Cori rosso

Color ruby red. Bouquet vinous, pleasant, characteristic. Flavor dry, soft, velvety, fresh. Minimum alcoholic strength 11.5%. It is a wine to drink with any meal in which meat predominates. Serve at room temperature (65°F).

For the zone of production see Cori bianco.

Est! Est!! Est!!! di Montefiascone

Color straw yellow, clear, brilliant. Bouquet vinous. Flavor lively, full-bodied, harmonious, dry. Minimum alcoholic strength 10.5%. A wine for the entire meal; goes well with traditional cooking from around the town of Viterbo. Serve chilled at 50–54°F.

Produced north of Rome in the *comuni* of Montefiascone, Bolsena, S. Lorenzo Nuovo, Grotte di Castro, Gradoli, Capodimonte and Marte.

Frascati

Color clear, brilliant, straw yellow. Bouquet vinous, delicately scented, characteristic. Flavor lively, soft, fine, velvety, dry and clean. Minimum alcoholic strength 11.5%. It is a wine to accompany the entire meal and goes excellently with Roman specialties. Serve chilled at 47–50°F. There are also semisweet, sweet (*canellino*) and *superiore* versions of this wine.

The zone of production includes the *comune* of Frascati and the neighboring *comuni* of Rome, Monteporzio Catone, Montecompatri, Grottaferrata.

Marino

Color straw yellow. Delicate, vinous bouquet. Flavor dry or semisweet, soft, characteristic, fruity, harmonious. Minimum alcoholic strength 11.5%. Recommended with fish and egg dishes. Serve chilled at 50°F.

Produced in the *comune* of Marino and part of the *comuni* of Rome and Castelgandolfo.

Merlot di Aprilia

Color garnet red, occasionally tending to brick red with age. Pleasant, vinous bouquet. Flavor full, soft, harmonious, of medium body. Minimum alcoholic strength 12%. A wine for the entire meal, it is particularly suited to roasted meats, pork, chicken, wild boar and strong-flavored dishes. Serve at room temperature (65°F)

Produced in the province of Latina in the *comuni* of Aprilia, Cisterna and Latina and in the province of Rome in the *comune* of Nettuno.

Montecompatri Colonna

Color varying depths of straw yellow. Bouquet vinous, delicate, pleasing. Flavor dry, soft, characteristic. Minimum alcoholic strength 11.5%. May be drunk throughout the meal; particularly good with boiled and meatless dishes. Serve chilled at 47–50°F.

Produced in the *comune* of Colonna and part of the *comuni* of Montecompatri, Zagarolo and Roccapriora.

Verdicchio dei Castelli di Jesi

Falerio dei Colli Ascolani

Frascati

Rosso Conero

Rosso Piceno

Colli Altotiberini bianco

Orvieto

Sangiovese dei Colli Pesaresi

Verdicchio di Matelica

Sangiovese di Aprilia

Color varying depths of rosé. Bouquet vinous with a characteristic fragrance. Flavor dry, balanced. Minimum alcoholic strength 11.5%. A good accompaniment to risottos, pasta dishes, broiled poultry and spring lamb. Drink chilled at 47–50°F.

Produced in the province of Latina in the *comuni* of Aprilia, Cisterna and Latina and in the province of Rome in the *comune* of Nettuno.

Trebbiano di Aprilia

Color varying depths of straw yellow. Bouquet vinous with a characteristic scent. Flavor delicate, harmonious, characteristic. Minimum alcoholic strength 11%. A good accompaniment to cold antipasti, shellfish, fish, fish soups and mussels. Serve chilled at 47–50°F.

For the zone of production see Sangiovese di Aprilia.

Velletri bianco

Color varying depths of straw yellow. Bouquet vinous, agreeable, delicate. Flavor dry or semi-sweet. Minimum alcoholic strength 11.5%. A wine suitable for the entire meal, it goes very well with fish, antipasti and soups. It should be served chilled at 47–50°F.

Produced in the *comuni* of Velletri and Sariano and part of the *comune* of Cisterna.

Velletri rosso

Color varying depths of ruby red. Intense, vinous odor. Flavor dry, velvety, harmonious, moderately tannic. Minimum alcoholic strength 12%. Goes well with antipasti, cured meats, spaghetti alla carbonara, artichokes; when aged it is excellent with roasted and braised meats. Serve at 65°F.

For the zone of production see Velletri bianco.

Zagarolo

Color varying depths of straw yellow. Bouquet vinous, delicate, agreeable. Flavor dry or semi-sweet, soft, characteristic, harmonious. Minimum alcoholic strength 11.5%. This wine goes well with cured meats, antipasti and white meats. Serve chilled at about 50°F.

Produced in the province of Rome in the *comuni* of Zagarolo and Gallicano.

Campania

Capri bianco

Color varying depths of straw yellow. Bouquet agreeable with a characteristic fragrance. Flavor dry, fresh. Minimum alcoholic strength 11%. Goes well with fish, particularly saltwater fish, fish soup, oysters, and seafood risotto. Serve at 47–50°F.

Produced throughout the island of Capri.

Capri rosso

Color varying depths of ruby red. Bouquet pleasantly vinous. Flavor dry, lively. Minimum alcoholic strength 11.5%. This wine goes nicely with thick soups, and tripe. Drink slightly chilled at 59–60°F.

For the zone of production see Capri bianco.

Fiano di Avellino

Color varying depths of straw yellow. Bouquet agreeable, intense, characteristic. Flavor dry, harmonious. Minimum alcoholic strength 11.5%. This wine can be drunk with the entire meal and is especially good with antipasti, white meats, mussels, fish soup, and broiled fish. Serve chilled at 47–50°F.

The zone of production includes the *comune* of Avellino and several other *comuni* in the province.

Greco di Tufo

Color straw yellow or golden yellow. Bouquet clean, agreeable, characteristic. Flavor thin, dry, harmonious. Minimum alcoholic strength 11.5%. This wine (especially the *spumante* type) goes well with cold antipasti; the normal type is excellent with specialties prepared with tuna fish, *baccalà* (dried salt cod), herrings, and with baked mussels and lobster. Serve at 50–54°F.

The zone of production, in the province of Avellino, includes the *comune* of Tufo and seven other *comuni*.

Ischia bianco

Color straw tending to golden. Bouquet vinous, delicate and agreeable. Flavor dry, of medium body, harmonious. Minimum alcoholic strength 11%. Goes well with risottos, antipasti and fish dishes. Serve at 50°F.

Produced throughout the island of Ischia.

Ischia bianco superiore

Color straw yellow or tending to golden. Fragrance agreeable, aromatic. Flavor characteristic, harmonious, dry. Minimum alcoholic strength 12%. Excellent with fish but goes well with most dishes and can be served throughout the meal. Serve chilled at 50°F.

For the zone of production see Ischia bianco.

Ischia rosso

Color varying depths of ruby red. Bouquet vinous. Flavor dry, of medium body, tannic. Minimum alcoholic strength 11.5%. It is a wine that can accompany the entire meal but it goes particularly well with main courses and meat. Serve at room temperature (65°F).

For the zone of production see Ischia bianco.

Solopaca bianco

Color varying depths of straw yellow. Pleasant, vinous bouquet. Flavor dry, velvety. Minimum alcoholic strength 12%. Goes very well with risottos. Serve at 44–47°F.

The zone of production lies in the province of Benevento in 11 *comuni*, one of which is Solopaca.

Solopaca rosso

Color ruby red, becoming paler with age. Bouquet intense, characteristic. Flavor dry, harmonious and velvety. Minimum alcoholic strength 12%. When young this wine is a good partner for pasta with meat sauce; after a short period of aging it is particularly good with roast chicken, lamb, stuffed pigeon. Serve at room temperature (65°F).

For the zone of production see Solopaca bianco.

Taurasi

Color deep ruby red with orange tints after aging. Bouquet characteristic, agreeable, intense. Flavor dry, full, robust, aromatic. Minimum alcoholic strength 12%. Goes well with roasts, wild boar in a sweet and sour sauce, kid, cold roast beef and lamb. Serve at 68°F.

Produced in the province of Avellino in 16 *comuni*, one of which is Taurasi.

Vesuvio bianco

Color light, brilliant straw yellow. Fragrance clean, intense, fruity. Flavor dry, full, very well balanced. Minimum alcoholic strength not yet established. It is a wine suited to seafood antipasti. Serve chilled at 47–50°F.

The zone of production lies at the base of Mount Vesuvius in the province of Naples (Torre del Greco, Boscoreale, etc.).

Vesuvio rosato

Color light cherry red. Fragrance clean, delicate, fruity. Flavor full with undertones of almond. Minimum alcoholic strength not yet established. Recommended for drinking throughout the meal. Serve at 57°F.

For the zone of production see Vesuvio bianco.

Vesuvio rosso

Color deep ruby red when young, garnet after aging. Fragrance clean, with a scent of sweet violets, ethereal, elegant. Flavor dry, full, often generous. Minimum alcoholic strength not yet established. Goes well with roasts or stewed meats. Serve at 65°F.

For the zone of production see Vesuvio bianco.

Basilicata

Aglianico del Vulture

Color varying depths of ruby red or lively garnet; after aging it acquires orange tints. Bouquet vinous, delicately scented, characteristic. Flavor dry, lively, fresh, harmonious, moderately tannic. Minimum alcoholic strength 11.5%. When young this wine goes well with stews, chicken, spring lamb, rabbit *alla cacciatora* and broiled meats; when aged it goes well with roasted game and dishes containing

truffles. Serve at 65–68°F depending on age.

Produced in the province of Potenza in 15 *comuni* situated to the south of the Vulture massif.

Calabria

Cirò bianco

Color varying depths of straw yellow. Characteristic, aromatic bouquet. Flavor delicate, harmonious, characteristic. Minimum alcoholic strength 12%. This wine can be drunk as an apéritif or served with broiled fish steaks such as tuna and swordfish. Serve chilled at 50–54°F.

The zone of production includes the entire *comuni* of Cirò and Cirò Marina and part of the *comuni* of Melissa and Crucoli.

Cirò rosso or rosato

Color ruby red to rosé. Bouquet agreeable and delicate, even if strongly vinous. Flavor full-bodied, warm, harmonious, velvety when aged. Minimum alcoholic strength 13.5%. An excellent accompaniment to roasts. Serve at room temperature (68–71°F).

For the zone of production see Cirò bianco.

Donnici

Color ruby red to varying depths of cherry red. Bouquet pleasantly vinous. Flavor dry, harmonious. Minimum alcoholic strength 12%. A wine for the entire meal; excellent with meats. Serve at room temperature (65°F).

The zone of production extends to the outskirts of Cosenza in the hilly area south of the populated center. It includes Consenza and about ten other surrounding *comuni*.

Greco di Bianco

Color golden yellow, often very deep, tending to amber. Fragrance clean, pronounced, persistent, agreeable, with an undertone reminiscent of orange blossom. Flavor sweet but not sickly, fresh, generous, harmonious. Minimum alcoholic strength not yet established. An excellent dessert wine. Serve chilled at 47–50°F.

The zone of production lies partly in the flat area and partly in the hills in the *comune* of Bianco, in the province of Calabria.

Lamezia

Color varying depths of cherry red. Bouquet pleasant, delicately vinous. Flavor dry, of medium body, harmonious. Minimum alcoholic strength 12%. This wine can accompany the entire meal and goes well with most meats. Serve at about 65°F.

Produced in ten *comuni* in the province of Catanzaro, one of which is Lamezia Terme.

Melissa bianco

Color pale straw yellow. Characteristic, vinous bouquet. Flavor dry, delicate, harmonious. Minimum alcoholic strength 11.5%. An excellent accompaniment to fish, it also goes well with traditional local cuisine. Serve chilled at 48–50°F.

Produced in the province of Catanzaro in a number of *comuni*, one of which is Melissa.

Melissa rosso

Color deep rosé to ruby red, with orange tints when aged. Characteristic, vinous bouquet. Flavor dry, full-bodied, lively, characteristic. Minimum alcoholic strength 12.5%. Particularly when aged this wine goes with roasts, mushrooms, game and most meats. Serve at room temperature (65°F).

For the zone of production see Melissa bianco.

Pollino

Color ruby red or cherry red. Characteristic fragrance. Flavor full and dry. Minimum alcoholic strength 12%. This wine can be drunk with the entire meal; when aged it is suited to game and poultry. Serve at room temperature (65°F).

The zone of production is situated in the hills north of Cosenza, spurs of the Pollino massif, and includes the *comuni* of Castrovillari, S. Basile, Saracena, Cassano Ionio, Covita and Frascineto.

Sant'Anna di Isola Capo Rizzuto

Color varying depths of pinkish red. Characteristic, vinous bou-

quet. Flavor dry, harmonious, round. Minimum alcoholic strength 12%. This is a wine for the entire meal; particularly good with meats. Serve chilled at 59–60°F.

Produced on the island of Capo Rizzuto and in part of the *comuni* of Crotone and Cutro in the province of Catanzaro.

Savuto

Color varying depths of ruby red, or rosé. Characteristic bouquet. Flavor full, dry. Minimum alcoholic strength 12%. It is an excellent table wine; when aged it goes particularly well with meat dishes; the rosé type goes nicely with lean meat antipasti, white meats, asparagus, artichokes and cheeses. Serve at 54–68°F, depending on the age of the wine.

The zone of production is situated on the arid hill slopes that form the valley along which the River Savuto runs. It includes 14 *comuni* in the province of Cosenza and six in the province of Catanzaro.

Apulia

Aleatico di Puglia

Color varying depths of garnet red, with violet tints; tending to orange as it ages. Characteristic, delicately aromatic bouquet. Flavor full, sweet, velvety. Minimum alcoholic strength 15% (of which at least 13% converted). Drink with fresh fruit, fruit salad and ice cream. Serve at 54–57°F.

Aleatico di Puglia is produced throughout the provinces of Foggia, Bari, Brindisi, Lecce and Taranto.

Aleatico di Puglia liquoroso

Color varying depths of garnet red, with hints of violet; as it ages it tends to orange. Characteristic, delicately aromatic bouquet. Flavor full, warm, sweet, harmonious, pleasing. Minimum alcoholic strength 18.5% (of which at least 16% converted). It is a dessert wine and is best served at 54–57°F.

For the zone of production see Aleatico di Puglia.

Brindisi

Color varying depths of ruby red, with light orange hues when aged. Bouquet vinous with an intense fragrance. Flavor dry, harmonious, with a bitter aftertaste, velvety and moderately tannic. Minimum alcoholic strength 12%. This wine provides a perfect accompaniment to sophisticated meat dishes. Serve at 65–68°F.

Produced in the *comuni* of Brindisi and Mesagne.

Brindisi rosato

Color coral red, tending to light cherry. Bouquet lightly fruity, delicate and characteristic when young. Flavor dry, well balanced, pleasantly bitter. Minimum alcoholic strength 12%. Goes well with cured meats, broiled or rotisseried fish and white meats. Serve moderately chilled at 54–57°F.

For the zone of production see Brindisi.

Cacc'e mmitte di Lucera

Color varying depths of ruby red. Bouquet characteristic, intense. Flavor full, harmonious, with a characteristic aftertaste. Minimum alcoholic strength 11.5%. It is a wine to drink throughout the meal. Serve at room temperature (65°F).

Produced in the *comuni* of Lucera, Troia and Biccari in the province of Foggia.

Castel del Monte bianco

Color straw yellow, Bouquet pleasant, slightly vinous, delicate. Flavor dry, fresh, harmonious. Minimum alcoholic strength 11.5%. Goes well with fish, broiled eggplant, peppers and antipasti. Serve at about 50°F.

Produced in the whole *comune* of Minervino Murge and, to a lesser extent, in the *comuni* of Andria, Corato, Trani, Ruvo, Terlizzo, Bitonto, Palo del Colle, Toritto, Binetto, in the province of Bari.

Castel del Monte rosato

Color varying depths of ruby pink. Bouquet vinous, pleasant, with a characteristic scent. Flavor dry, harmonious, moderately tannic. Minimum alcoholic strength 11.5%. It is a popular wine with antipasti, but is also excellent with fish or as an apéritif. Generally served at 50–54°F, cooler if served as an apéritif (44–47°F).

For the zone of production see Castel del Monte bianco.

Castel del Monte rosso

Color from ruby red to garnet, tending to orange. Bouquet vinous, pleasant, with a characteristic fragrance. Flavor dry, harmonious, moderately tannic. Minimum alcoholic strength 12%. It is a wine to drink with the whole meal, particularly good with thick soups, roasts and broiled poultry and rabbit; the *riserva* type goes well with roasts and mature local sheeps' milk cheeses. Serve at 62–68°F, depending on age.

For the zone of production see Castel del Monte bianco.

Copertino rosato

Color salmon pink, occasionally tending to light cherry. Bouquet slightly vinous, distinctive. Flavor dry, without sharpness, with a grassy undertone and bitterish aftertaste. Minimum alcoholic strength 12%. Goes well with antipasti, fried food and cheese. Serve at 50–54°F.

Produced in the *comune* of Copertino and another five *comuni* in the province of Lecce.

Copertino rosso

Color varying shades of ruby red, with light orange hues when aged. Lingering, vinous bouquet. Flavor dry, with a bitterish aftertaste, velvety, vigorous, generous. Minimum alcoholic strength 12%. It is a wine to drink with the entire meal. Serve the young wine slightly chilled at about 60°F; the *riserva* at about room temperature (65°F), uncorking the bottle several hours beforehand.

For the zone of production see Copertino rosato.

Leverano bianco

Color varying depths of straw yellow. Bouquet pleasant, slightly vinous, delicate. Flavor dry, soft, harmonious, characteristic. Minimum alcoholic strength 11%. It provides a good accompaniment to pasta served with cream, seafood risottos, vegetables, mussels, fish, white meats. Serve chilled at 47–50°F. Produced in the *comune* of Leverano, Lecce province.

Leverano rosato

Color rosé tending to light cherry, occasionally with orange tints. Bouquet slightly vinous, with a fruity fragrance when young. Flavor dry, fresh, harmonious. Minimum alcoholic strength 11.5%. It is well suited to antipasti, fried foods, *baccalà* (dried salt cod), soups. Serve chilled at about 54°F.

For the zone of production see Leverano bianco.

Leverano rosso

Color ruby red to garnet, acquiring orange tints as it ages. Bouquet vinous, pleasant, with a characteristic fragrance. Flavor dry, harmonious, with a delicate bitter undertaste. Minimum alcoholic strength 12%. This wine goes very well with pasta dishes, most meats, and cheeses. Serve at room temperature (65°F).

For the zone of production see Leverano bianco.

Locorotondo

Color pale straw or greenish. Bouquet delicate, characteristic, pleasing. Flavor dry, delicate. Minimum alcoholic strength 11%. This wine goes excellently with specialties of fish and shellfish, vegetables, subtly flavored risottos, eggs and cheeses, especially Pecorino. Serve at 48–50°F.

Produced in the *comuni* of Locorotondo, Cisternino and part of Fasano, in the provinces of Bari and Brindisi.

Martina or Martina Franca

Color greenish or pale straw. Bouquet vinous, delicate, characteristic, pleasant. Flavor dry, delicate, harmonious. Minimum alcoholic strength 11%. This is an excellent wine to serve with risottos, fish, shellfish, vegetables. Serve chilled at 47–50°F.

The zone of production includes the *comuni* of Martina Franca and Alberobello and part of Cegio Messapico and Ostuni, in the provinces of Bari, Taranto and Brindisi.

Matino rosato

Color deep rosé with light golden yellow tints after the first year. Slightly vinous bouquet. Flavor dry, characteristic, harmonious. Minimum alcoholic strength 11.5%. This wine goes well with cured meats, Parma ham, pasta with tomato sauce, vegetables, white meats, tripe and fried food. Serve at 50–54°F.

The zone of production includes the whole *comune* of Matino and part of six other *comuni* in the province of Lecce.

Matino rosso

Color ruby red with orange tints after aging. Vinous bouquet. Flavor dry, harmonious. Minimum alcoholic strength 11.5%. It can be served throughout the meal and goes excellently with meats and cheeses. Serve at room temperature (65°F).

For the zone of production see Matino rosato.

Moscato di Trani

Color golden yellow. Intense, characteristic bouquet. Flavor sweet, velvety. Minimum alcoholic strength 15% (of which at least 13% converted). This is a classic wine for drinking at the end of a meal with sweets, pastries or dessert; it is also excellent drunk on its own. Serve chilled at 47–50°F.

Produced in the *comune* of Trani and in another 11 *comuni* in the province of Bari.

Moscato di Trani liquoroso

Color golden yellow. Intense, characteristic bouquet. Flavor sweet, velvety. Minimum alcoholic strength 18% (of which at least 16% converted). It is a wine to be drunk at the end of the meal with desserts and pastries; it can also be drunk on its own. Serve very chilled at 41–43°F.

For the zone of production see Moscato di Trani.

Ostuni bianco

Color straw yellow. Delicate, vinous bouquet. Flavor dry, of medium body, harmonious. Minimum alcoholic strength 11%. This wine goes excellently with fish. Serve at a maximum of 54°F.

Produced in the *comune* of Ostuni and in another six *comuni* in the province of Brindisi.

Ottavianello di Ostuni

Color light ruby red. Bouquet delicate. Flavor dry, harmonious. Minimum alcoholic strength

337

11.5%. This wine goes well with stews, fried meats, pork, broiled steaks, lamb. Serve at 59°F.

For the zone of production see Ostuni bianco.

Primitivo di Manduria
Color red, tending to violet, acquiring orange tints with age. Bouquet light, characteristic. Flavor pleasing, full, harmonious, becoming velvety with aging. Minimum alcoholic strength 14%. The normal type is excellent with soups, pork and cured meats; the *liquoroso* versions, both *dolce* (sweet) and especially the *secco* (dry), are generally drunk on their own as an apéritif. Serve at about 65°F; the *liquoroso* type slightly cooler but not below 59°F.

Produced in the province of Taranto in the 16 *comuni*, one of which is Manduria.

Rosso Barletta
Color ruby to garnet, tending to acquire deep orange tints with aging. Characteristic, vinous odor. Flavor dry, harmonious, full-bodied. Minimum alcoholic strength 12%. It is a wine for the entire meal, excellent with meats. Serve slightly chilled at 59–60°F when young and at about 68°F when aged.

The zone of production lies in the province of Bari and Foggia and includes the *comune* of Barletta and four other *comuni*.

Rosso Canosa
Color varying depths of ruby red, tending to acquire deep orange tints after aging. Bouquet vinous, agreeable, with a characteristic fragrance. Flavor dry, vigorous, full-bodied, moderately tannic, with a pleasant, slightly bitter aftertaste. Minimum alcoholic strength 12%. When young it can be drunk throughout the meal; when aged it goes well with roasts, game, lamb, kid and broiled foods. Serve, depending on age, at 60–68°F.

Produced solely in the *comune* of Canosa di Puglia in the province of Bari.

Rosso di Cerignola
Color varying shades of ruby red to brick red after aging. Bouquet vinous, alcoholic, agreeable. Flavor dry, vigorous, full-bodied, moderately tannic, harmonious, with a pleasant, slightly bitter aftertaste. Minimum alcoholic strength 12%. It is an excellent wine to accompany the entire meal and goes particularly well with roast white meats, chicken and game. Drink at 65–68°F.

The zone of production includes the *comuni* of Cerignola, Stornara and Stornarella in the province of Foggia.

Salice Salentino rosato
Color light cherry red tending to deeper pink with age. Bouquet slightly vinous, moderately persistent. Flavor dry, velvety, warm. Minimum alcoholic strength 12%. This wine is suited to antipasti, lightly fried food, soups and cheeses. Serve chilled at 50–57°F.

The zone of production includes the *comune* of Salice Salentino and another five *comuni* in the provinces of Brindisi and Lecce.

Salice Salentino rosso
Color varying shades of ruby red, with deep orange tints after aging. Bouquet vinous, ethereal, characteristic, pleasant, intense. Flavor full, dry, robust but velvety, warm, harmonious. Minimum alcoholic strength 12.5%. It is an excellent accompaniment to roasts, especially when aged. Serve at 65–68°F.

For the zone of production see Salice Salentino rosato.

San Severo bianco
Color light straw yellow. Bouquet slightly vinous, pleasant. Flavor dry, fresh and harmonious. Minimum alcoholic strength 11%. This versatile wine goes excellently with fish soups, various pasta dishes, veal in tuna sauce, and fish. Serve at 50–52°F.

Produced in eight *comuni* in the province of Foggia.

San Severo rosso, or rosato
Color red tending to ruby or ruby red tending to brick with age. Bouquet vinous with a pleasant, characteristic fragrance. Flavor dry, full-bodied, vigorous, harmonious. Minimum alcoholic strength 11.5%. The red may be drunk throughout the meal; the rosé goes well with antipasti, fried

Cirò rosso or rosato

San Severo Bianco

Marsala

foods, cheeses, soups, and roasts. Serve chilled at about 50°F, especially the rosé.

For the zone of production see San Severo bianco.

Squinzano rosato

Color pale ruby red to light cherry. Bouquet vinous and perfumed. Flavor lively, fine, velvety. Minimum alcoholic strength 12.5%. This wine is well suited to antipasti, fried foods, cheeses, soups, baked mussels. Serve chilled at 50–52°F.

Produced in the *comune* of Squinzano and in another six *comuni* in the province of Lecce.

Squinzano rosso

Color varying shades of ruby red, acquiring deep orange tints when aged. Bouquet vinous, ethereal, characteristic, intense. Flavor full, dry, robust but velvety. Minimum alcoholic strength 12.5%. When sufficiently aged this wine goes excellently with roasts and can be enjoyed throughout the meal; it is very good with most pasta dishes, antipasti of cured meats, lamb, kid,

broiled cutlets and roast pork. Serve at 65–68°F.

For the zone of production see Squinzano rosato.

Sicily

Alcamo, or Bianco di Alcamo

Color straw yellow with greenish tints. Bouquet neutral with a slight scent of the grape. Flavor dry, lively, fresh, fruity. Minimum alcoholic strength 11.5%. It can be drunk throughout the meal. Serve at 47–50°F.

Produced in the province of Trapani in the area that slopes down to Alcamo.

Cerasuolo di Vittoria

Color bright cherry red. Bouquet vinous, delicately perfumed. Flavor warm, dry, full, harmonious and full-bodied. Minimum alcoholic strength 13%. This wine goes well with roasted red meats, rotisseried rabbit, pork and lamb. Serve at 59–62°F.

Produced in the province of Ragusa in five *comuni*, one of which is Vittoria, in the province of Caltanissetta in two *comuni*, and in the province of Catania in another two *comuni*.

Etna bianco

Color straw yellow, occasionally with light golden tints. Typical, delicate fragrance. Flavor dry, fresh, harmonious, with light, bitterish undertones. Minimum alcoholic strength 11.5%. This wine is a good accompaniment to fried fish. Served chilled at about 50°F.

Produced in the province of Catania in 20 *comuni* situated on the lower slopes of Mount Etna. These include Paternò, Giarre, Acireale and Linguaglossa.

Etna bianco superiore

Color very light straw yellow. Bouquet delicately fruity. Flavor dry, light, fresh, harmonious. Minimum alcoholic strength 12%. Goes very well with broiled fish, fish cooked *en papillote* and traditional Sicilian pasta dishes made with sardines and cuttlefish. Serve at 50°F.

For the zone of production see Etna bianco.

Etna rosso, or rosato

Color ruby red with light garnet tints when aged, or rosé tending to ruby. Bouquet vinous, strongly perfumed. Flavor dry, warm, robust, full, harmonious. Minimum alcoholic strength 12.5%. The red provides a good accompaniment to the entire meal; the rosé goes well with cold dishes, vegetables, couscous, tuna with onions. Serve the red at 65–68°F and the rosé at 60°F.

For the zone of production see Etna bianco.

Faro

Color varying shades of ruby red, tending to brick red with aging. Bouquet delicate, ethereal, persistent. Flavor dry, harmonious, of medium body, characteristic. Minimum alcoholic strength 12%. A wine to be drunk with the entire meal. Serve at 68°F.

Produced in the *comuni* of Messina and Ganzirri.

Malvasia delle Lipari

Color golden yellow or amber. Characteristic, aromatic bouquet. Flavor sweet, aromatic. Minimum alcoholic strength 11.5% (of which at least 8% converted). It is a dessert wine that can also be drunk on its own and goes well with pastries and ice cream. Serve chilled at about 47°F.

This type of Malvasia is produced on the Aeolian islands in a number of *comuni* including Salina in the province of Messina.

Marsala

Color brilliant amber yellow, tending to brown. Bouquet characteristic, agreeable, persistent. Flavor dry or sweet, warm, aromatic, with good body. Minimum alcoholic strength 17–18%. The *secco* (dry) type can be drunk as an apéritif; the semisweet type is very good drunk on it own or with cookies; the *dolce* (sweet) type is an excellent dessert wine. Dry Marsala is served chilled at 50°F; the sweet type at room temperature (65°F).

This traditional Sicilian wine is produced in several *comuni* in the provinces of Trapani, Agrigento and Palermo.

Moscato di Noto

Color varying shades of golden yellow to amber. Bouquet characterized by the fragrant aroma of the muscat grape. Flavor slightly aromatic, characteristic. Minimum alcoholic strength 11.5% (of which at least 8% converted). It goes particularly well served at the end of the meal with dessert and fruit in syrup. Serve chilled at 50°F.

Produced in the *comuni* of Noto, Rosolini, Pachino and Avola in the province of Siracusa.

Moscato di Noto liquoroso

Color varying shades of golden yellow. Delicate, aromatic bouquet. Flavor sweet, pleasant, warm, velvety. Minimum alcoholic strength 22% (of which at least 16% converted). A wine to end the meal. Serve at 50°F.

For the zone of production see Moscato di Noto.

Moscato di Noto spumante

Color straw yellow or light golden yellow. Characteristic aroma. Flavor delicate, sweet, aromatic. Minimum alcoholic strength 13% (of which at least 8% converted). A classic wine for the end of the meal. Serve chilled at about 50°F.

For the zone of production see Moscato di Noto.

Moscato di Pantelleria

Color golden yellow to amber. Bouquet delicate, with characteristic fragrance of the muscat grape. Flavor sweet, aromatic, characteristic. Minimum alcoholic strength 12.5% (of which at least 8% converted). It is an excellent dessert wine and can also be drunk on its own or with cookies. Serve at 50–54°F.

Produced on the island of Pantelleria (Trapani).

Passito di Pantelleria

Color amber. Delicate aroma of the muscat grape. Minimum alcoholic strength 14%. It is a classic wine for drinking on its own. Serve at about 50–54°F, preferably in chilled glasses.

For the zone of production see Moscato di Pantelleria.

Moscato di Siracusa

Color deep golden yellow, acquiring amber tints. Delicate, characteristic bouquet. Flavor sweet, velvety, agreeable. Minimum alcoholic strength 16.5% (of which at least 14% converted). This is a rather rare wine that goes well with cakes, pastries and desserts. Serve at 47–54°F.

The zone of production covers the entire *comune* of Siracusa.

Sardinia

Campidano di Terralba or Terralba

Color varying shades of pale ruby red. Intense, vinous bouquet. Flavor dry, vigorous, full, characteristic. Minimum alcoholic strength 11.5%. It is a wine to drink young and goes well with soups, pasta dishes, meats, olives and cured meats. Serve at 60–65°F.

The zone of production includes a number of *comuni*, one of which is Terralba, in the provinces of Cagliari and Oristano in the luxuriant Campidano region.

Cannonau di Sardegna

Color varying depths of ruby red, tending to deep orange with age. Bouquet very characteristic, perfumed, agreeable. Flavor varying from dry to semisweet, lively, characteristic. Minimum alcoholic strength 13.5%. This a is particularly versatile wine, owing to the many different types available. The normal *secco* (dry) type may be drunk throughout the meal; the *secco superiore* or *liquoroso* is a good accompaniment to roasts, wild boar and red meat; the *dolce* (sweet) type is a dessert wine and goes excellently with cookies. Serve the normal type at 60–65°F; and the *superiore* at 65–68°F.

Produced throughout the whole of Sardinia.

Carignano del Sulcis rosato

Color varying depths of rosé. Pleasantly vinous bouquet. Flavor dry, harmonious, velvety, characteristic. Minimum alcoholic strength 11.5%. Goes well with all courses: Pasta, cured meats, traditional main course dishes, stews. Serve at 60–65°F.

Produced in the Sulcis region in the province of Cagliari.

Carignano del Sulcis rosso

Color varying shades of ruby red. Bouquet vinous, pleasantly intense. Flavor dry, lively, harmonious. Minimum alcoholic strength 11.5%. This wine is recommended with roasted red meats, lamb, game, etc. Serve at 65–68°F.

For the zone of production see Carignano del Sulcis rosato.

Girò di Cagliari

Color light, brilliant ruby red. Bouquet delicate, with the aroma of the grape. Flavor pleasant, warm, velvety. Both sweet and dry types of this wine are produced. The minimum alcoholic strength of the sweet type is 14.5% (of which at least 12% converted) and of the dry type is 14% (of which at least 13.5% converted). The sweet type is a dessert wine; the dry makes a good accompaniment for roasts. Both should be served at 59–62°F.

Produced in the province of Cagliari and to a lesser extent in the province of Oristano.

Girò di Cagliari liquoroso

Color light, brilliant ruby red. Bouquet fine and markedly aromatic. Flavor sweet or dry, according to the type. Minimum alcoholic strength 17.5% (of which at least 15% converted). This wine is drunk much in the same way as port. Serve at 59–62°F.

For the zone of production see Girò di Cagliari.

Malvasia di Bosa

Color straw yellow to golden. Very delicate, intense bouquet. Flavor from sweet to dry, according to the type, with a slightly bitter aftertaste. Minimum alcoholic strength 15% (of which at least 13% converted in the sweet type, and 14.5% in the dry type). The sweet Malvasia di Bosa goes very well with desserts and cookies; the dry type is good with antipasti of shellfish, molluscs, oily fish and also Sardinian Pecorino cheese. These wines should be served chilled at 47–50°F.

Produced in the *comune* of Bosa and in another six *comuni* in the province of Nuoro.

Malvasia di Bosa liquoroso

Color straw yellow to golden. Bouquet very fine, markedly aromatic.

Flavor sweet or dry, according to type, very refined. Minimum alcoholic strength 17.5% (of which at least 15% converted in the sweet type, and 16.5% in the dry type). The sweet version goes very well with cookies or desserts; the dry type is excellent as an apéritif or mixed in cocktails. Both types are served at 47–50°F.

For the zone of production see Malvasia di Bosa.

Malvasia di Cagliari

Color straw yellow tending to golden. Bouquet intense, delicate, characteristic. Flavor sweet or dry, according to type, with slightly bitter undertones reminiscent of toasted almonds. Minimum alcoholic strength 14% (of which at least 12% converted in the sweet type, and 13.5% in the dry type). The sweet Malvasia di Cagliari is suitable to drink with dessert and with cookies; the dry version goes well with antipasti of shellfish, molluscs, oily fish and also with Sardinian Pecorino cheese. Both types are served chilled at 47–50°F.

Produced in the whole of the provinces of Cagliari and Oristano.

Malvasia di Cagliari liquoroso

Color straw yellow tending to golden. Bouquet very fine with a marked aroma. Flavor sweet or dry according to type. Minimum alcoholic strength 17.5% (of which at least 15% converted in the sweet type, and 16.5% in the dry type). The sweet type goes well with cookies and desserts, whereas the dry type makes a good apéritif or can be used in cocktails. Serve both types at 47–50°F.

For the zone of production see Malvasia di Cagliari.

Monica di Cagliari

Color light ruby red. Bouquet ethereal, intense but delicate. Flavor agreeable, soft, velvety. This wine is produced in a sweet and dry type. The minimum alcoholic strength for the sweet type is 14.5% (of which at least 13% are

converted); for the dry type it is 14% (of which at least 13.5% are converted). The sweet type goes well with pastries and fruit, while the dry is a good accompaniment to roasts, typical local dishes and game. Both are served at about 60°F.

The zone of production covers the whole province of Cagliari and part of the province of Oristano.

Monica di Cagliari liquoroso

Color light ruby red, tending to orange with aging. Bouquet very fine, with marked aroma. Flavor sweet or dry according to the type. Minimum alcoholic strength 17.5% (of which at least 15% converted in the sweet type, and 16.5% converted in the dry type). The sweet goes very well with pastries and fruit while the dry is a good accompaniment to roasts, traditional local dishes and game. Both are served at about 60°F.

For the zone of production see Monica di Cagliari.

Monica di Sardegna

Color pale, brilliant ruby red, tending to purplish red with age. Bouquet intense, vinous, pleasant. Flavor dry, vigorous. Minimum alcoholic strength 12%. A wine to accompany soups, roasts and game. Serve at room temperature (65°F).

Produced throughout Sardinia.

Moscato di Cagliari

Color brilliant, golden yellow. Intense, characteristic bouquet. Exquisitely sweet, velvety flavor. Minimum alcoholic strength 15% (of which at least 12% converted). An excellent dessert wine. Serve at 50–54°F.

Produced throughout the province of Cagliari and in several comuni in the province of Oristano.

Moscato di Cagliari liquoroso

Color brilliant, golden yellow. Bouquet very fine with an intense aroma of the muscat grape. Flavor very subtle, exquisitely sweet, re-

miniscent of fresh grapes. Minimum alcoholic strength 17.5% (of which at least 15% converted). A dessert wine. Serve at 57°F.

For the zone of production see Moscato di Cagliari.

Moscato di Sardegna

Color brilliant straw yellow. Bouquet aromatic, delicate, fruity, characteristic. Minimum alcoholic strength 11.5% (of which at least 8% converted). It is a dessert wine and is excellent with ice cream; it can also be drunk on it own. Serve chilled at 41–43°F, and uncork the bottle some time in advance of drinking.

Produced throughout Sardinia.

Moscato di Sorso-Sennori

Color deep golden yellow. Intense, characteristic aroma. Flavor sweet, full, fine. Minimum alcoholic strength 15% (of which at least 13% converted). This wine goes well with desserts and can also be drunk on its own or with cookies. Serve at 47–50°F.

Produced in the comuni of Sorso and Sennori in the province of Sassari.

Nasco di Cagliari

Color straw yellow to golden yellow. Bouquet delicate, slightly aromatic. Flavor agreeable with a bitter tang. There is both a sweet and a dry type. The minimum alcoholic strength for the sweet type is 14.5% (of which at least 12% converted); for the dry type it is 14% (of which at least 13.5% converted). Sweet Nasco goes well with fruit and desserts; the dry accompanies typical Sardinian dishes especially those based on shellfish, seafood, squid and lobster. Serve at 50–54°F.

Produced throughout the province of Cagliari and in a number of comuni in the province of Oristano.

Nasco di Cagliari liquoroso

Color straw yellow to golden yellow. Bouquet fine, with marked aroma. Flavor sweet or dry, ac-

cording to the type. Minimum alcoholic strength 17.5% (of which at least 15% converted in the sweet type, and 16.5% converted in the dry). Sweet Nasco liquoroso is best with pastries or drunk on its own; the dry makes an excellent apéritif. Serve both at about 47–50°F.

For the zone of production see Nasco di Cagliari.

Nuragus di Cagliari

Color pale straw yellow, occasionally with light greenish tints. Bouquet pleasant and agreeable. Flavor dry, lively, harmonious, slightly acidulous, pleasant, palatable. Minimum alcoholic strength 11%. This wine is suitable to serve with all courses. Serve chilled at 50°F.

Produced in the whole of the province of Cagliari, in part of the province of Oristano and in several comuni in the province of Nuoro.

Vermentino di Gallura

Color straw yellow with light tints of brilliant green. Bouquet subtle, intense, delicate. Flavor dry, soft, bitterish. Minimum alcoholic strength 12%. An excellent apéritif wine. Serve chilled at 47–50°F.

The zone of production comprises several comuni in Gallura, in the province of Sassari (Calangius, Tempio Pausania, S. Teresa di Gallura), and two comuni in the province of Nuoro.

Vernaccia di Oristano

Color golden yellow, tending to amber with age. Bouquet delicate with hints of almond blossom. Flavor fine, subtle, warm with a slight pleasant aftertaste of bitter almonds. Minimum alcoholic strength 15%. It is an excellent apéritif wine; recommended with shellfish and oysters. Serve at 47–50°F; as an apéritif it should be served chilled.

Produced in the comune of Oristano and another 15 comuni in the provinces of Cagliari and Oristano in the Tirso valley.

Glossary

Abbacchio (spring lamb)
In Latium and other parts of Italy, this name indicates a lamb not yet weaned. The term, for some etymologists, is derived from the fact that the lamb will be slaughtered by a blow to the head (thus, by *abbacchiare*, "knocking down"). For others, it derives from the Latin *ad baculum*, which means "tied to a staff."

Acciughe (anchovies)
Much used in Italian cooking, anchovies feature in many classic dishes, such as bagna cauda (see p. 130). They form a principal ingredient of pizza toppings, and add a distinctive flavor to pasta and meat sauces.

Affogare (to poach)
A method of gently stewing fish or seafood in barely simmering liquid. Especially in regional cooking, *affogato* ("poached") refers to octopus or squid cooked in a terracotta pot. The term also applies to chicken cooked in a tightly closed receptacle so that it steams in its own juices.

Affumicamento (smoking)
An ancient method of preserving meat or fish by placing it in a special brine and then exposing it for some time to the smoke created by burning fragrant wood (e.g. apple), or wood which has not been completely dried out.

Agnolotti
This is a kind of filled egg pasta, like ravioli, square or disk-shaped, typical of Italian cooking, especially in Piedmont, Lombardy and Tuscany. Generally, agnolotti are filled with meat stuffing, cheese, spinach or other vegetables.

Agresto
This name applies to the juice of unripened grapes. In cooking, it is used as a corrective or addition to sauces. It has a strongly astringent flavor.

Ajada
A sauce made with a pestle and mortar, using garlic, skinned walnuts, soft breadcrumbs and olive oil. It is used to accompany a lasagne dish of ancient origin, which is eaten on fast days.

Amatriciana
A type of sauce for pasta, especially the famous macaroni called bucatini. In Amatrice, where the sauce originated, the locals still honor this typical dish of Latium during the feast which takes place on the first Sunday after the August holiday of *ferragosto*.

Aranzada
A sweet typical of Sardinia. It is a type of nougat made from toasted almonds mixed with very finely sliced strips of orange peel, cooked in honey.

Arista (loin)
A cut of pork, specifically the loin, cooked on a rotisserie or in the oven. This is a roast long-established in tradition, since it appears in menus dating back to the Renaissance.

Baccalà (salt cod)
In the Veneto, this is cod, split, salted and dried, and exported in large quantities to Mediterranean countries.

Baci di dama (lady's kisses)
A specialty of Sanremo, Liguria and Tortona. These are little sweetmeats made with almonds, flour, butter, sugar, liqueur and vanilla, mixed with chocolate.

Bagna cauda (garlic and anchovy dip)
A specialty of Piedmontese cookery, this is a sauce made from anchovies, garlic, oil and a little butter or cream (see p.130). It is served hot but not boiling, and is eaten with raw vegetables which are dipped into it: fennel, celery, cardoons and artichokes. This sauce is served in special small pots, heated from underneath.

Bain-Marie
A method of cooking in which the receptacle containing solid or liquid ingredients is placed in an oven-proof dish (usually a deep roasting pan) half-filled with boiling water before being put into the oven. In this way, the maximum temperature will never exceed 100°C (112°F), since boiling water never rises above this. There are many theories about the name *bain-marie*, although no conclusion has

been reached. One is that it comes from Mary, the sister of Moses, who is supposed to have practised alchemy in Egypt.

Bagòss
This a cheese from the foothills of the Lombard Alps. It is produced in the Val Sabbia, more precisely in Bagolino (from whence it gets its name). Made from cow's milk, it is very piquant, and is served on slices of toasted bread. At one time this cheese was credited with being an aphrodisiac and was known as the "cheese of love" (*formaggio d'amore*).

Bandiera (flag)
This dish takes its name from the whiteness of the onion, the red of the tomato and the color of the green pepper, making up the three colors of the Italian flag. These ingredients are all lightly fried in olive oil, then cooked over low heat until they form a thick sauce. For a good *bandiera* the vegetables should not break down or be overdone. This is an Umbrian variation of peperonata (see p. 239).

Basilico (basil)
Highly aromatic and with a strong, distinctive flavor, basil is a herb very frequently used in Italian cooking. It is one of the main components of pesto sauce and a natural partner for any dish containing tomatoes.

Battuto (stuffing)
The cooking term for a seasoning obtained by finely chopping, in a chopping-bowl or on a board, using a *mezzaluna* (a crescent-shaped knife, q.v.) various ingredients such as parsley, celery, garlic, carrots, onions, bacon etc.

Bìgoli
In the Veneto, this name is given to noodles made from fine buckwheat flour and egg. A special instrument is necessary to make these noodles; outside Italy, most people buy the commericial variety. If the bìgoli are made from wholemeal flour they are called "false bìgoli."

Bomba di riso
A typical rice dish from Emilia, it is the equivalent of the Piedmontese "goffa" and the Neapolitan "sartù" (or "timballo"). A roast of meat with its juices is placed in an oiled mold lined with risotto rice and heated in the oven.

Bóndola (pork sausage)
Like the Lombard "bondiana" and the Emilian "bondéina" the Venetian Bóndola is the bondiola, or Italian pork sausage. All three terms apply to the prepared beef intestine into which the dressed pork, pork meat or pork mixed with beef, is packed.

Bottarga
This is the caviar of the Venetians, and is made from the roe of the gray mullet, dried in the sun, cut into thin slices and served as an hors d'oeuvre with olive oil, lemon juice and sometimes pepper.

Boudin (black pudding)
This a sausage made in the Val d'Aosta from boiled pig's blood, pork fat and pepper. It can be served sliced and fried, or boiled. The name *boudin* is used in France and Italy.

Brasato (braised)
This term applies to the lengthy cooking of meat in a tightly covered casserole or pot. The French equivalent is *daube*. This method of cooking by moist heat (instead of roasting) is especially effective for less expensive cuts of meat. In the country, farmworkers can prepare it before leaving the house in the morning, and return in the evening to find it perfectly cooked. The meat is browned before being placed on a bed of vegetables with a small amount of liquid, then placed in the oven for slow cooking.

Brodetto
A sauce made from broth containing beaten eggs and lemon juice. It is popular in many places around the Adriatic.

Brovada
In Friuli, this name applies to turnips put to mature in marc for about three months in special wooden vats. These turnips are cut into strips and used to prepare a "jota," a soup with a rather tart flavor. Stewed with bacon, brovada make a good accompaniment to pork.

Burrielli
This is the name for the *bocconcini* (morsels), that is, the little Mozzarella cheeses that, in Naples, are kept in earthenware pots called "lancelle." The name of these cheeses indicates that they are richer in butter (*burro*) content than ordinary Mozzarella.

Büsêca
From the Spanish *buseca*, this is the name for tripe in Milan. Some say that the Milanese are the greatest consumers of this type of variety meat, which is why they are given the name of "büsecón" (the equivalent to the name given to Venetians, "polentón" because of their consumption of polenta).

Bussolani *or* bussolai
In the Po valley this name is given to the ring-shaped cake called "ciambella." The ingredients vary from one locality to another, but the shape is nearly always the same.

Cacciucco (Leghorn fish stew)
The word *cacciucco*, originally Turkish, meaning very small fish, is used in Leghorn to denote a fish stew. For the people of Leghorn, cacciucco is a different dish from any other fish stew, both because of the choice of fishes used, and the special way in which it is prepared. A filling and substantial dish, it is served as a main course.

Caciuni
These are large ravioli made with bread dough. The filling is made of fresh Pecorino (ewe's milk cheese) and matured Pecorino, in proportions according to taste. The other ingredients include egg yolk, sugar and lemon juice to taste.

Calzone
The origin of the name of this Neapolitan dish is uncertain. Some believe it derives from a large-bellied musical instrument rather like a lute, called a *calizon*. It is made from bread dough, like pizza, but it can be folded over like an envelope after being filled with a mixture of ingredients, such as Mozzarella, ricotta, many other kinds of cheese, and ham. In other regions of central-southern Italy calzoni are made with local ingredients, sometimes only vegetables. At one time calzoni were not baked in the oven like pizza, but fried in a skillet with lard.

Candelaus (almond candies)
Sardinian candies made from peeled, chopped almonds and sugar. They are flavored with orange flower water (see p.261).

Cannellone
A kind of pasta, in tube shapes of ¾ in in diameter. The cannelloni are boiled before being rolled up. They are filled with chopped meat or vegetables, rolled up like little pancakes and baked in the oven, covered with tomato sauce. Cannellone is also the name for a kind of rolled pancake stuffed with meat and then baked.

Cannòlo
A typical Sardinian sweet, tubular

in shape, it is a fried, stuffed pastry filled with sweetened ricotta and chopped candied fruit, then sprinkled with vanilla-flavored confectioner's sugar (see p.268).

Caponata
This is a traditional dish from southern Italy, made with various vegetables, into which bread is dipped. Usually it consists of fresh tomatoes, onions, basil, garlic, green peppers and olives, seasoned with olive oil, wine vinegar, salt and pepper. In Tuscany it is called "panzanella." An important version from Sicily is known as "caponatina di melanzane" (eggplant caponata) in which eggplants are fried with celery, onion, capers, olives and tomatoes; its bittersweet taste comes from the inclusion of pears and sugar mixed with white wine vinegar.

Cappelletto (little hat)
This is a type of pork sausage (the same mixture as for zampone),

which is boiled and then eaten. Its tricorn shape is like a priest's biretta, and gives it its other name, "cappello da prete" (priest's hat).

Capperi (capers)
Capers, pickled and sharp-tasting, are used in many Italian dishes, from antipasti and sauces to meat, game and fish recipes.

Caramello (burnt sugar)
In cookery this is the transformation of saccharose or sugar when it is cooked to a temperature of 350–400°F. It is used as a coloring for fruit cakes, a sauce for desserts, or as gravy browning.

Carbonade
In Piedmont and in the Val d'Aosta this is a typical way to prepare beef which has been salted for preservation. Those who wish to reduce the taste of salt cook the meat with the same quantity by weight of onions. With the advent of refrigeration this method of preserving

meat was discontinued, but the traditional dish lives on in many restaurants, and can be compared to an ordinary stew with onions. The name probably derives from the typically dark color of the cooked meat, and also from the red wine used in the sauce.

Cartoccio
This is the Italian term for *"en papillote."* It indicates a way of cooking some foods, mainly meat or fish, wrapped in paper, which is greased on the inside with oil or butter. Nowadays, foil may be used instead. Cooking in this way helps to mix the flavors of the ingredients inside the paper or foil. Besides meat and fish, vegetables are now cooked like this and also dry food which needs to be made more flavorsome.

Casonsèi
In Brescia and Bergamo casonsèi are large ravioli filled with spiced pork sausage, spinach, seedless

white raisins, amaretti, soft breadcrumbs and cheese and seasoned with melted butter and sage. This is a very ancient dish, its name deriving – according to some etymologists – from the inclusion of cheese (in Latin, *caseus*) in the filling.

Cassata (Sicilian cheesecake)
A cake typical of Easter festivals in Sicily, which is now made all year round. It was prepared with sponge cake filled with sweetened ricotta, flavored with vanilla or chocolate. Other flavors may of course be added to these, according to taste. The name probably comes from the ricotta cheese, the Latin for cheese being *caseus*. For a long time these cakes were made only by the nuns in Sicilian convents. Later, similar cakes were made, using layers of different fruit-flavored ice creams, and from this came the commercially produced ice cream known as cassata.

Cassóla (fish soup)
In some Italian localities which experienced the Spanish presence "cassóla" indicates anything cooked in a casserole. In Sardinia it is a fish soup. (See also "cazzoeula," below.)

Cazzoeula (casserole of pork)
A dish typical of the Lombardy plain, eaten during the winter. Originally, it was made with pig's trotters and ears, some Luganega (or other) sausage, bacon rind, carrots, celery, tomatoes, cabbage. Variations of it exist in other localities, with different ingredients; thus we have a Milanese cassoeula, one from Como, another from Pavia and one from Novara. "Cazzoeula" derives from the dialect word from Lombardy meaning casserole.

Cenci (Tuscan fried pastries)
In Tuscany these are sweet pastries made with flour, egg, sweet wine and a raising agent, flavored with aniseed, vanilla, or orange peel. They are rolled out, cut and twisted to look like knots, then fried in very hot oil or lard. The Venetian *galani* are very like these pastries, as are the "sfrappole" from Bologna, "donzelline," "nastrini di monaca" and "chiacchere."

Certosina

"Alla certosina" (literally, "charter-house style") is a method of preparing risotto. It seems to have originated in the kitchens of the Carthusian charterhouse in Pavia. The risotto was made with peas, shrimp, mushrooms, garlic and olive oil. The original methods of preparation are found quite frequently wherever rice-growing was widespread in the past.

Chitarra

A special instrument used for cutting macaroni "alla chitarra" (see p.51). In the Abruzzo this means a rectangular frame with numerous steel wires as in a guitar. The rolled egg pasta is laid on the wires, and pressed through them with a rolling pin and thus cut into fine strips. Passing a finger across the wires as though strumming a guitar frees the macaroni, which fall into the lower part of the apparatus.

Cicenielli

This Neapolitan word refers to the very small anchovy fish which resemble tiny beans, hence their name, "cicenielli" from *ceci*, beans. They are served as a garnish on pizzas, and can also be eaten in a special type of omelet.

Cicerchiata (honey cake)

This is a cake made in the Abruzzo at carnival time. Essentially, it consists of small pea-sized balls of sweet pastry, fried in oil. These are then stirred together in a saucepan of heated honey. When cooled, the cake may be formed into rings or heart shapes.

Cieche (baby eels)

These are newly-hatched baby eels, for which there is a recipe in every Mediterranean cuisine. In Pisa, they are fried with sage and garlic; elsewhere they are fried with scrambled eggs, cheese and breadcrumbs, almost always flavored with sage leaves, pepper and lemon juice.

Cima (stuffed veal)

Stuffed veal ("cima ripiena") is a typical dish of the Ligurian coast, although it is found in many other regions, under different names, the most usual being "tasca ripie-

na" (which may be translated as stuffed pouch or pocket). It is made from shoulder of veal which is cut in a particular way so as to form a bag or pouch to be stuffed and rolled up. The filling is made from lightly beaten eggs, calf's brains, finely chopped lean veal, cooked peas, parsley and a lot of grated Parmesan. Many variations have been developed from this basic recipe. All may be served hot or cold.

Ciriole

These small eels take their name from the Latin *cereus*, because they are like candles. They are prepared with oil, capers, anchovies, chili pepper and white wine. In Umbria this name refers to the large spaghetti made at home, usually seasoned with garlic, oil and chili pepper.

Civét

In the Val d'Aosta this is the tech-

nique for cooking hare, venison and kid. The meat, left to marinate in red wine with herbs, is then lightly fried and sprinkled with grappa.

Connita

In the Abruzzo, this stands for "seasoned." In thick soups in which pieces of pancetta are cooked, eggs beaten with cheese and parsley are added. This soup looks like "stracciatella alla romana," but is more savory.

347

Coppiette (courting couples)
These are a specialty of the Maremma, and are very popular with the shepherds of that region. The lean meat of wild boar, or even pork and beef, is cut into thin strips, salted and seasoned with ginger. After this first stage, the meat strips are dried and smoked, then folded and tied together. It is this final operation which gives them their name.

Crauti (Sauerkraut)
This is made in the Alto Adige and serves as an accompaniment to numerous dishes, usually based on pork. In Germany it is called "Sauerkraut" (sour cabbage), and is made with cabbage, shredded very thinly and fermented in brine for four to six weeks. After washing, it is cooked with bacon. Another type of Sauerkraut is made in the Veneto, without fermentation, but with the addition of white wine.

Cren (horseradish)
A piquant sauce which is made from grated horseradish. In some parts of Italy, vinegar and breadcrumbs are added to the sauce to bring out its very sharp flavor.

Crostino (toast)
Crostini are one of the most typical Italian hors d'oeuvres, especially in Tuscan cookery. They are small slices of crusty bread, browned in butter and covered with a soft spread, such as one based on chicken livers stewed with onion, anchovies and capers. The spreads for these toasts vary from region to region: In Spoleto, for example, truffles pounded with butter and anchovies are most popular.

Crostone (large toast)
These are large slices of crusty bread fried in oil or butter or, simply, left in the oven to brown for a short time. In more modern regional cooking the bread is spread with cheese (Gorgonzola is typical), then put in the oven.

Crumiri
In Piedmont Crumiri are small sticks made with all-purpose flour, buckwheat flour, eggs and sugar. The homeland of these biscuits is Casale Monferrato.

Cubbàita
This specialty, a special kind of nougat made with honey, sesame seeds and almonds, probably belongs to the art of Arab sweetmaking which still survives in Sicily. Some people believe cubbàita to derive from the little cakes made for fertility rites in Magna Graecia.

Cuscùsu (Couscous)
This dish is found in many countries all around the Mediterranean, especially Libya, Tunisia, Algeria and Morocco ("cuscùsu" is the Sicilian adaptation of the Arab *kuskus*). It is composed of coarse semolina, made into a paste with water and steamed. It can be seasoned in many different ways: In Algeria it is usually meat and vegetable-based, with a piquant sauce. Sicilian couscous, typical of the area around Trapani, is made with fish.

Cuticùsu
An ancient dish from Macerata, made with beans dressed with oil, vinegar and anchovy fillets, and seasoned with marjoram and garlic minced in a mortar.

Dragoncello (tarragon)
An aromatic herb used for flavoring sauces, salads and chicken dishes. It is strong-tasting, and should be used sparingly.

Estratto (extract)
In cooking this is obtained by evaporating meat, fish or vegetable juices. This method was much in use before the advent of commercial meat extracts and glutamate; these are used to enrich the taste of various dishes.

Facciuni di Santa Chiara
Tradition has it that in the convent of Santa Chiara at Noto in Sicily, the nuns made little tartlets of almonds with a marmalade of lemon and orange and covered with chocolate. These tartlets were called "facciuni" because little angel faces (*faccie*) were modeled on the surface.

Farcia (stuffing)
A mixture of ingredients for flavoring poultry, meat and fish during cooking; also pasta (e.g. tortellini) and sweet dishes.

Farsumagro
This is a preparation of the "cima" variety (q.v.), Genoese-style. A piece of veal, usually the belly, is beaten flat with a meatbat; eggs, cheese, ground pork, and so on, are placed on it. It is then rolled up like a sausage and tied securely, then cooked in a heavy casserole. Like "cima," it can be served hot or cold, thinly sliced.

Favata
This bean stew is very renowned in Sardinia. There are, of course, many variations, but in every one the beans are soaked first, and cooked in a pork stew with a piece of salt pork fat.

Fave dei morti
Little crispy pastries, hardly longer than a bean, made of a mixture of sugar, almonds, pine nuts, egg white and flour. They are from Lombardy, but are made everywhere in the Po Valley.

Fiandoléin
This cream, made from milk, egg yolks, sugar and rum with a flavoring of orange peel is like a type of milk zabaglione. The ingredients must be beaten for a long time, and cooked in a double boiler while being continually whipped. This sweet, typical of the Val d'Aosta, may be served with toasted rye bread.

Finanziera
This Piedmontese dish has a long history, going back as far as the court of Charles Emmanuel I when he was Duke of Savoy. It is traditionally composed of veal sweetbreads, spinal cord and mushrooms, arranged in layers topped by slices of bread sautéed in butter.

Foiólo (honeycomb tripe)
This is the Milanese term for that part of tripe known in Italian as *centopello* (honeycomb), from the reticulum.

Fondüa (fondue)
This typical dish from the foothills of the Piedmontese Alps is a hot fondue of Fontina cheese melted with eggs and cream, some butter, salt and pepper, and garnished with chopped white truffle. It is accom-

panied by rice. Sometimes the name is Italianized to "fonduta."

Frégula
This is a Sardinian dish, based on semolina mixed with water like Sicilian "cuscùsu." These little grains, however, are cooked in a soup with plenty of cheese. As with couscous, the semolina base – made by rubbing the grains with dampened hands – is typical of the Mediterranean, but particularly of the Semitic peoples, and was probably imported into Sardinia very long ago.

Fritto misto (mixed fry)
The most famous *fritto misto* is from Bologna; it includes a wide variety of meat and vegetables, including artichokes, tomatoes, apple fritters, chicken croquettes, fried brains and zucchini, oranges, semolina fritters and bananas, all dipped in a batter of egg, milk and flour and deep fried in very hot oil. The Florentine fritto misto consists of fried croquettes of brains, sweetbreads, artichokes, zucchini and lamb cutlets. The mixture from Ascoli even contains large olives stuffed with beef and veal.

Frutti di pasta reale (Martorana fruits)
At one time these marzipan-like candies were made at the convent of Martorana in Palermo. They were imitations of real fruits, and closely resembled them, even in color. The mixture then used by the nuns is still used today by some of the city's confectioners; equal amounts of almonds and sugar are crushed with a pestle in a mortar, mixed with a sweet liqueur and flavored with cinnamon. The mixture, prepared in a special copper container, attains the right consistency while being stirred continuously over heat. A small piece of the paste is taken and molded into the shape of a fruit. It is then tinted with natural coloring and cooked in a cool oven.

Fumét (essence)
This is the precursor of all meat extracts and bouillon cubes. It is made by slowly boiling, in a small amount of water, bones and pieces of veal and beef with a little butter, pepper and herbs. After straining, the liquid is stored in jars and can be boiled again in a double boiler.

Fusilli
These noodles, or spaghetti, are wound round a stick when being made at home. When dry they remain coiled into spirals, as their name suggests. Commercially, they are shaped by machines. This type of pasta can be found in the Abruzzo, Latium, Campania, Apulia, Calabria and Basilicata.

Garmugia
This is a popular soup in Lucchesia. Thinly sliced veal is lightly browned in olive oil, with pork belly, some onion, peas, green beans, artichoke hearts and asparagus spears. Then plenty of boiling water is added and the mixture is allowed to boil until the vegetables are cooked. It is served with lightly toasted slices of bread.

Genepi liqueur
This typical liqueur is perhaps the oldest in the region around the western Alps. The original recipe is based on herbs found in the Alps, and a herbalist named Genepin, who lived in the second half of the fourteenth century, is said to have invented it. It is distilled in two colors, white or green.

Ghiotta
This word may come from the Arab *ghatta*, which means sauces and flavorings in general. When the name of an Italian dish is followed by "alla ghiotta" it means that a particular seasoning has been used in its preparation.

Giardiniera
This is a general term (literally, "gardener's style") for a vegetable soup without beans. The same word, however, can mean pickled vegetables such as carrots, celery and onion.

Giuliana
In French this word becomes *julienne* and indicates a way of presenting a garnish of vegetables cut into thin strips. By extension, the word also refers to a method of cutting meat used in mixed salads, especially chicken breasts, ham and tongue.

Goffa
See bomba di riso.

Guazzetto
This term is commonly used in regional cookery, especially in the Veneto, to mean stewing, that is, cooking in a rich broth.

Gubana
A sweet made in Friuli, gubana is rolled up like an apple strudel and twisted into scrolls. The wrapping which is rolled round the filling can be made with puff pastry, but some people prefer to use sweetened bread dough rolled out very thinly. The filling is made of skinned walnuts, seedless white raisins, pine nuts, prunes and dried figs, candied orange and lemon peel and powdered chocolate, all moistened with rum or sweet wine. The etymological derivation of the name appears to come from the Friulian *bubana*, which means plenty, abundance. At one time this sweet was eaten during Easter, almost as a propitiatory rite for a forthcoming good season.

Infarinata
A bean soup typical of the Garfagnana or of Versilia, where it is also called "intruglia." It can be mixed with a very liquid polenta and is made with maize cooked with beans, black cabbage, tomato sauce and rosemary, flavored with salt pork or sausage. It is eaten hot or cold. If left to get cold it can be sliced then lightly fried or broiled.

Jota
This recipe is typical both of Friuli and Venezia Giulia, though the two areas produce different kinds of jota. In Friuli, the main ingredients are beans, maize, brovada (a kind of turnip, q.v.) and milk; in the Venezia Giulia, they use beans, potatoes, cabbage and smoked bacon.

Lampascioni
In Apulia, this is the name for the grape hyacinth (*Muscari atlanticum*), the bulbs of which are eaten boiled, in salads, or hot, lightly fried. These have a strong diuretic action. They are especially appreciated for their rather bitter taste, which they retain even after cooking.

La Pigneti
This term indicates not so much a dish as a way of cooking lamb used in the Basilicata. The meat is cut into pieces and then placed in a terracotta dish with potatoes, onions, tomatoes, peppers, Pecorino cheese, a piece of sausage, and water to cover. The dish is covered and sealed with clay, then put in a hot oven.

Lattaiolo (sweet baked custard)
This is a very delicate dessert typical of the cookery of the Romagna. It is made with milk, sugar and egg yolks. When the ingredients have been beaten together, the custard is baked in the oven. Sometimes it is flavored with rum or alkermes.

Leccarda
A receptacle which is placed under meat when it is being roasted on a spit. The purpose is to catch the meat juices as they drip during the cooking; the meat can then be basted with its own juices, which keep it tender and give it a deep golden-brown color.

Legare (to thicken sauces)
In making a sauce or extract, binding thickens the liquid. For this operation butter, flour, cornstarch, eggs or cream can be used. The result will be more or less smooth and creamy according to the ingredients.

Lepudrida
The word comes from the Catalan *olla podrida*. Around Cagliari, it is a vegetable soup in which beef or pork is cooked.

Maccu
This is one of the oldest soup recipes from southern-central Italy. It is made with dried beans, soaked overnight, then cooked in water flavored with wild fennel and

seasoned with oil. The beans are then put through a sieve.

Mandolino (mandolin cutter)
In cooking, an implement for cutting vegetables into thin slices or matchsticks.

Mandorlato
A sweet made of almonds toasted in the oven and bound together with a honey-based paste.

Martinsec
In the Val d'Aosta and around the western Alps in general, this is the name for a very small pear with a tough skin and white, bittersweet flesh. Cooked slowly in red wine with sugar and a few cloves, it is usually eaten cold.

Mazzafegati
This word is used for a sausage of pork liver made throughout central Italy. If seedless white raisins, sugar and pine nuts are added the result is the sweet "mazzafegati." The savory "mazzafegati" are made with the addition of spicy sausage meat. They are broiled on skewers or cooked in the oven.

Mazzancolle
This is the Roman name for saltwater crayfish. They can be broiled whole, or shelled, floured, dipped in beaten egg and fried.

Messicani
This is one of the many made-up names of untraceable origin, which were given to certain regional dishes in the interwar years. "Messicani" (mexicans) are veal olives containing a filling of spiced sausage, chicken livers, grated cheese and nutmeg, and cooked in a skillet with butter.

Mestecanza *or* **mesticanza**
This word, which means "mixed things," refers generally to a salad of radicchio, watercress, chicory, lamb's lettuce and other salad vegetables, seasoned with oil and vinegar.

Mezzaluna
This implement, which is shaped like a crescent moon (hence its name) is widely used in Italian kitchens for finely chopping vegetables and herbs.

353

Morseddu

This Calabrian dish (the name of which derives from the fact that it is eaten in *morsi*, bites) is made from pork chitlings. Etymologically, the word recalls the Spanish *almuerzo* (luncheon), although for some Italians it is the first meal of the day. The chitlings are cooked with tomatoes and other variety meats (liver, heart, lights), generously flavored with hot chili pepper. In restaurants, morseddu is served in pita bread, split and filled with the morseddu and its sauce; it is eaten like a sandwich, without a knife and fork. Care must be taken by the uninitiated, because the sauce is very spicy, due to the quantity of chilis usually included.

Mortaio (mortar)

A heavy bowl of marble, stone or metal used for pounding certain ingredients, with the help of a pestle (with which the crushing is done). For certain preparations (such as pesto sauce), a beater is used today in the mortar to speed up the process.

Mósa

A more or less creamy mixture made in the Trentino – Alto Adige region and in some parts of the Veneto. It is prepared by cooking all-purpose flour and corn meal in milk. The addition of butter makes it smoother and creamier.

Mostaccióli (chocolate cookies)

As the name indicates, new wine or "must" is added to the flour used in making these sweet cookies. They are found more or less everywhere in southern Italy. Those of the Abruzzo are much more elaborate and include, besides the flour, almonds, honey, powdered cinnamon, and chocolate to coat the outside.

Mostarda di Cremona

A savory relish made of fruit preserved in a sweet syrup and flavored with mustard, which is served with boiled meats. The same name applies to a Sicilian sweet made from the must of grapes.

Muscoli

A regional name for mussels (*cozze*).

Mùstica

These are the fry of anchovies. After salting, these small white fish are preserved in oil in glass or terracotta containers. They are a true specialty of the Ionian coast, and their name derives from the type of terracotta container in which they are preserved.

Nocino

This liqueur is obtained by soaking walnuts in their shells while they are still green, in clear spirit, with a pinch of cinnamon and a few cloves. After one month, everything is passed through a filter and sugar is added. The most famous nocino comes from Emilia. Nowadays it is commercially mass produced.

Olio d'oliva (olive oil)

The oil most commonly used in Italian cookery, for dressing salads and seasoning antipasti, pasta and a variety of other dishes. For the most successful results and the best flavor it is advisable to buy the best quality "virgin" olive oil (*olio vergine*), which should be greenish-yellow in color.

Olla (pot)

An earthenware pot used either for cooking or for preserving foods.

Pabassinas

These cakes from Sardinia are made with a variety of raisin called "pabassa." They are mixed with flour, toasted almonds, skinned walnuts and sugar.

Paiolo (copper pot)

A semispherical copper pot with a curved iron handle that allows it to be hung from a hook and chain in the center of the fireplace. It is used for cooking polenta.

Pan de mej

"Pan de mej" or, as they say in Milan, "pane di miglio" is a maize-flour cake which would once have been served with cream: The contrast between the coarseness of the bread and the smoothness of the cream being very pleasing to the palate. Today pan de mej can be found in many places. Served as a sweet, it is made with corn meal and semolina, butter, sugar, eggs and yeast or other leavening.

Pandoro

This is a classic cake produced in Verona and made of flour, butter, eggs and yeast (see p.268) Although the name is said to come from *pan d'oro* (golden bread) it is actually derived from the Veronese "pandòlo," an old name for a local cake. From the end of the nineteenth century the Melegatti confectionery in Verona made this very soft cake covered with a layer of confectioner's sugar.

Panforte (fruit cake)

A cake in the ancient tradition from Siena, which is mentioned by Dante. Its preparation, however, links it to the bread, spiced and sweetened with honey, that was already being made in Tuscany at the beginning of the thirteenth century. At present, the panforte which is commercially produced in Siena is made with flour, sugar, crystallized fruit, almonds and various spices.

Paniscia *or* panissa

A soup, dating from medieval times, which is a thick mixture of rice and beans.

Pansòoti

In Liguria this is the name for ravioli filled with a mixture of herbs, cheese, egg and garlic. It is served with a sauce made of ground walnuts, oil, egg yolk and ricotta.

Panzanella

At one time this soup was very popular throughout Tuscany. Slices of homemade bread are soaked in water with anchovy fillets, onions, tomatoes, oil, vinegar, salt and pepper. The etymon of this soup's name is uncertain; in a sense it corresponds to the Venetian "pan moiéto" (damp bread). Soups of this kind, hot or cold, were eaten in peasants' kitchens throughout Italy in times past. It is a good way to use up old bread.

Pappardelle

Pappardelle in Tuscany are large pieces of lasagne or noodles, about 1 in wide, corresponding to the "paparèle" of the Veneto, which are usually flavored with various sauces. The most famous are served with a hare sauce, "pappardelle sulla lepre," (see p.33) prepared in the Aretino and other areas in Tuscany.

Passatelli
These homemade noodles are made by pressing a mixture of breadcrumbs, cheese and eggs through a special potato ricer with holes ¼ in in diameter (see p.97). It makes cylinders of 1–1½ in long, and the same width as the holes. The instrument used for making them is a passatello. Passatelli are a specialty of Romagna and are generally eaten with a generous amount of savory, thick meat soup.

Peòci
The name given to mussels (*cozze*) in the Veneto.

Pepatelle *or* pepatille
A peppery sweet made with fine bran or wholemeal flour, honey, sliced almonds and a lot of pepper.

Pepe di Caienna (cayenne pepper)
The powder from dried and ground red spicy chilies.

Peperoncino (chili pepper)
This is used throughout southern Italy to add a spicy flavor to many dishes. In the classic "spaghetti aglio e olio" (see p.44), spaghetti tossed in garlic- and chili-flavored olive oil, it imparts a distinctive spiciness.

Perciatelli
A spaghetti with holes; the term is synonymous with bucatini.

Pesto
This famous basil sauce is used for all kinds of pasta in Liguria, but "pasta al pesto" is also very popular outside Italy. It is made by using a pestle and mortar to pound basil leaves, oil, pine nuts and garlic, with grated Pecorino cheese.

Piatto elefante
In the Alto Adige this name refers to a wide variety of meats served together as a single dish, almost making a complete meal. (It is a specialty of a restaurant of the same name in Bressanone.)

Piccagge
The name given to the wide lasagne eaten mainly in Genoa.

Piccellati
In the Molise, these are candies made with a filling of breadcrumbs, walnuts and almonds, orange peel and spices, mixed with honey or concentrated must.

Pillotto
Pieces of fat threaded on a metal spike which serve to provide continuous basting of meat being cooked on a spit. The word is used in Umbrian cooking. At one time the fat was wrapped in paper which, on contact with the fire, burned, releasing the fat which would drop on to the meat. This method of cooking was widely practised in central Italy. A similar technique is still found in Sardinia, for cooking "porceddu" (see p.149).

Pinoli (pine nuts)
The seeds of the stone pine are used in a variety of savory and sweet preparations and are pounded with garlic and basil to make pesto.

Pinza
In the eastern Alps this word

means the same as "pizza," although its ingredients are very different. Pinza is sweet, made from stale bread softened in milk, sugar, eggs, a little butter to make it smoother and pine nuts. Other pinzas, always made with flour, sugar and eggs, are made for Easter celebrations in Friuli and Venezia Giulia.

Pizza al formaggio (cheese pizza)

In Umbria this is the hors d'oeuvres which is usually served at Easter meals. The ingredients are eggs, Pecorino cheese, Parmesan and olive oil, beaten together. This mixture can then be used with the same amount of once-risen bread dough, and the whole mixed well together until a smooth, soft dough is obtained. After being allowed to rise it is placed on a cookie sheet and put into a hot oven. If it rises well the dough almost doubles in thickness.

Pizzòccheri

This is a specialty of the Valtellina, consisting of wide ribbon noodles made with a mixture of buckwheat flour and all-purpose flour. They are cooked with potatoes, white cabbage and other vegetables. After draining, they are seasoned with melted butter, cheese (such as Taleggio) and a little garlic.

Polenta di patate

In parts of the Trentino, and particularly in the eastern Alps, a polenta is made in which corn meal is replaced by mashed potatoes. To bind it together, a small quantity of buckwheat flour is added. The mixture is served with a variety of sauces, with soft cheese, raw smoked meats (ham etc.).

Polenta taragna

This polenta is made with buckwheat flour, also called "furmentùn," and is made in the same way as polenta with corn meal. Toward the end of the cooking, butter is added and also cheese (Taleggio, Bel Paese, Mozzarella), which not only adds flavor, but also makes a smoother polenta. The term "taragna" almost certainly derives from "tarare," to mix or blend; "tarài" is the wooden knife used for cutting polenta.

Porcini (cèpes)

These mushrooms (*boletus edulis*) are renowned for their flavor. Before use, dried porcini should be soaked in water for 10–20 minutes, then any excess moisture squeezed out.

Potacchio *or* potaggio

This name originates from the French *potage*. It refers to the cooking of meat, usually chicken, rabbit or lamb, by stewing.

Potiza

In Friuli, *putiza* or *butiz* means the belly. The potiza is a rounded cake composed of an envelope of leavened dough made with flour, milk, eggs and sugar, and a filling of chocolate, milk, sugar, currants, walnuts, prunes, toasted breadcrumbs, dried figs, lemon peel and a little cinnamon or nutmeg. It is made in the area around Gorizia.

Prèsniz

Like the potiza, the prèsniz is a cake made of sweetened puff pastry, but with a richer filling: walnuts, almonds, breadcrumbs fried in butter, sugar, chocolate, seedless white raisins, crystallized lemon peel, rum flavored with vanilla and, lastly, lemon juice.

Probusti

Large garlic-flavored sausages in which the main ingredients are pork and veal. Lightly smoked with burning birch wood, they are boiled and served with Sauerkraut. It is an ancient specialty of Rovereto in the Trentino, and very hard to find.

Provatura

In some parts of Latium this is the name given to Mozzarella cheese. Indeed, the morsels of Mozzarella, in shape and size, are very like the portions of cheese which cheesemakers use as samples to taste (hence provatura, from *provae*, to taste).

Pùddica

This is a type of pizza made in Apulia. The dough is rolled out to a thickness of about ⅝ in and the ingredients which go on top are put into cavities or dents specially made here and there in the dough. They are filled up with slices of tomato, garlic and oil. Like pizza, pùddica is served very hot.

Puddighìnos

These are young fowl, stuffed with a mixture of egg, lightly browned giblets, breadcrumbs, cream and tomatoes, then roasted in the oven. Medium-sized birds bred in Sardinia are used.

Puìna

The name for ricotta in Friuli-Venezia Giulia and in the Veneto in general. It also refers to smoked ricotta.

Puntarella

This is a bitter-tasting chicory used for salads. A specialty of Latium, it curls up in cold water, and is served with a dressing of oil, vinegar and anchovy fillets.

Radicchio arrosto (grilled radicchio)

Around Treviso, but also in other parts of the Veneto, grilled radicchio (the long-leaved type) is served as a side dish. The tougher outer leaves and the stalk are removed, the heads split lengthways into four, or into two if they are small. They are sprinkled with oil and salt, put under the broiler and turned quickly so that the outer leaves do not burn. Toward the end of the cooking, when the radicchio has become slightly limp, it is sprinkled with lemon juice and served hot.

Ratafià

This liqueur is made by leaving wild black cherries, with added sugar, for two months in a jar which is exposed to the sun. After this time, alcohol is added until the alcoholic content reaches 25–30%.

Ricciarelli

Candies made in Siena, with chopped almonds and sugar. These sweets are now produced commercially, but they have been known for centuries.

Risotto alla pilota

The major rice-growing areas of Italy have generally produced characteristic ways of cooking their rice. In the Veronese and Mantovano lowlands a risotto with the addition of fresh salami (tastassal) is made; it came to be called "alla pilota" because of its first consumers, the "pilots," that is, the workers whose job was the husking (*pilatura*) of the rice. Others prefer to think that the name "pilota" comes from the method of cooking – *pilotato*, that is, guided, or controlled. Indeed, this risotto is prepared by pouring rice into a saucepan full of boiling water, so that it forms a cone, covering the bottom of the saucepan, and, in height, rising to the surface of the water. In geometry we know that a cone drawn in a cylinder has a volume that is one third of that of the cylinder itself, so we will have rice equal to one part and water equal to two parts. In these proportions, the water, toward the end of the cooking, will be completely absorbed into the rice. Risotto made in this way is "guided" (*pilotato*) cooking. So that the heat is well distributed and to avoid the rice sticking to the bottom of the saucepan, it should be cooked in the oven in a covered dish.

Rosada

This is a type of pudding which used to be made in the Trentino-Alto Adige for high prelates. It may be compared to a caramel custard made with ground almonds.

Rôstida

In the Po Valley "rôstida" and "rôtisciada" refer to the preparation of the hearts, lights and other parts of the pig, cut into small pieces and cooked in butter. This was a winter dish, traditionally made in Italy at the time of year when pigs were slaughtered.

Saltimbocca (veal cutlets)

Small skewers of lean veal and small slices of ham, threaded alternately with sage leaves.

Salvia (sage)

A herb which features in many Italian dishes, including saltimbocca alla romana (see p. 139). It is also used to flavor melted butter in the seasoning of pasta dishes.

Sambuca

Aniseed liqueur produced in Latium. At one time, in the Roman *campagna*, it was made by steeping the seeds of the anise plant in acquavit, and adding sugar afterward. The sambuca of Civitavecchia is highly renowned.

Sanguinaccio

When a pig is slaughtered the blood is allowed to drain so that the meat is left white. This blood, mixed with lard, breadcrumbs and pine nuts, and sometimes sweetened with sugar, is cooked and then made into sausages. These large sausages are broiled or cooked in the oven. Blood puddings or sausages used to be made in every region in Italy in the days when, in peasant households, nothing was thrown away: The pig was slaughtered and every part of the animal was used for food.

Saór

This typically Venetian sauce is made of vinegar and onions. Pilchards are marinated in it for two to three days; after draining, they are coated in flour and deep fried.

Sartù

An important, typically Neapolitan dish; in the country of spaghetti, rice produces excellent results in this preparation (see p. 109). Today sartù is not as rich as in times past.

Sbira

This was the favorite dish of the dockworkers of Genoa. Its name probably comes from the fact that it was eaten standing up in the trattorie, like the *sbirri*, or policemen, on watch duty. It is a very filling dish of tripe, with pieces of meat, served on slices of homemade bread.

Sbrisolona

A type of sweet made in the Veneto. It is filled with a considerable amount of butter, which gives it the characteristic flakiness from which it gets its name because it is easy to crumble (*sbricciolare*, or "*sbrisolare*" in Venetian dialect.)

Schizzòtti

A very thin, almost flat bun, hence its name. It is made with flour (with no raising agent), mixed with lard; these buns are cooked in special tins, placed on top of the embers of a fire. It is eaten folded over and filled like an ordinary bun. There are also sweet schizzòtti, made with flour, sugar, eggs and rum, flavored with rosemary, and cooked in the oven.

Sfogliatelle

These are little ring-shaped buns of flaky pastry or short pastry. The former are also called "sfogliatelle ricce"; some are ring-shaped, others have a filling of ricotta and candied fruit, and are eaten hot.

Sópa coada

This dish is typical of the Veneto, and has recently become very popular in restaurants. It is prepared with two layers of crusty bread between which are placed a layer of cheese and another of boned, roasted pigeon. The two layers, placed in a roasting pan, are covered with meat stock and left in the oven for 4–5 hours. This long cooking time is what gives the dish its name: *zuppa covata* (or "coadas," in dialect) from *covare*, to brood, or sit on eggs. The oven must not be too hot. Without burning, the bread absorbs all the flavors of the soup, meat and cheese. In some parts of the Veneto, such as Treviso, tripe is used instead of pigeon.

Stoccafisso

This name refers to dried salt cod. The flesh of the fish is dried until it is as hard and rigid as a wooden stick. In English, the name for dried fish is, appropriately, stockfish.

Stracciatella

A soup made in the Latium region. A beaten egg is poured into the hot soup and stirred thoroughly with a fork or wire whisk, until the egg is just breaking up into strands (*stracciatelle*).

Stracotto

See brasato.

Sugna piccante

This preparation is found all over southern Italy, especially in the region of Basilicata, where it consists of a large quantity of peppers cooked in fresh lard. Made in Italy at the time of pig slaughtering, it is spread on slices of hot fried or toasted bread, or used to flavor other vegetables.

Surecilli

In the Abruzzo, "surecilli" are little mice. This name is given to gnocchetti made with flour, water and beaten egg yolks, served with the juices of roast lamb and Pecorino cheese.

Taccozze

This is a type of puff pastry made in Umbria, the Marches, the Abruzzo, Molise and Campania. The pastry is rolled out into squares of 1¼–1½ in and is slightly thicker than that of ordinary tagliatelle; it is eaten like pasta, but can also be added to soup. In this latter case the squares are a little smaller. The name comes from *taccone* (patch), the patch sewn on to a coat, which the squares of pasta resemble.

Tajarìn

This is a type of very narrow tagliatelle made with flour and eggs. Tajarìn are prepared throughout Piedmont, but particularly in the area around Alba, where they are served with a sauce made with butter, onion and chicken livers.

Taralli (baked pastry rings)

These are little baked pastry rings made almost everywhere in southern Italy. They may be sweet or spicy; because they are very crumbly they should be precooked for a few moments in boiling water before being put into a moderate oven.

Tarallucci

This is the diminutive of taralli, and these are small ring-shaped, or disk-shaped pastries. Being very crumbly, they must be precooked in boiling water like taralli, before being placed in the oven. Tarallucci, which are made throughout southern Italy, have a festive theme because they are sold in large quantities on market stalls at country festivals.

Tartufi bianchi (Piedmontese white truffles)

Mushrooms of superior aroma and quality, truffles are greatly prized by gourmets. White truffles feature in many Piedmontese dishes, including fondüa (q.v.). Thinly sliced raw as a final garnish to pasta, risotto and other dishes, they impart a delicious flavor and a touch of luxury.

Tassa

In the Molise, "tassa" is a peasant soup of bread and scalded wine to which a good quantity of paprika is added. It is usually consumed during the coldest winter days. Its name comes from the fact that it is served in a *tazza* (cup) or bowl.

Testaroli

These are little pancakes made with flour and water, cooked in terracotta containers with shallow lids known as *testi*, from which they take their name. They are placed on the hearth and covered with

Timballo
This dish is a case of flaky pastry containing a filling of precooked food: meat, mushrooms, macaroni or other. Its name is probably derived from its resemblance to a tymbal, a hollow semispherical drum with a skin stretched over it. The same name is given to the mold in which this kind of dish is prepared.

Torrone (nougat)
A sweet made for winter festivals in many regions of Italy. It is prepared with lightly toasted almonds stirred into a mixture of honey, sugar and egg white. There are many variations in the ingredients (filberts, pistachios, walnuts etc), and chocolate or dried figs can be added to the egg white mixture.

Tortelli
The "tortello" is a little pie or omelet, sweet or savory. A liquid mixture of eggs, milk and flour, with various added herbs or flavorings, is cooked with oil or butter. "Tortelli" may be made either larger or smaller and, in this case, are comparable to tortellini, only larger.

Trofie
Very soft gnocchetti made with flour mixed with mashed potato, or only flour seasoned with pesto or meat sauce. This is a specialty of Ligurian cookery.

Uccelletti di mare
These are small cuttlefish, squid and seafood, threaded on skewers soaked in a fairly thick sauce of breadcrumbs, parsley and oil, and cooked over charcoal.

Vaccinara
In Rome, the *vaccinari* were the men who worked at the slaughtering of beef cattle. There are some dishes typical of Roman cooking, especially those using the less appreciated cuts of meat, which are labeled "alla vaccinara" because they were cooked in inns or trattorie near the abattoir, where the men took their meals.

Vincisgrassi
This historic gastronomic specialty is still prepared in the Marches; it is a kind of lasagne, arranged with meat sauce and white sauce between each layer of pasta, then baked in the oven. At one time the recipe was richer than now, mainly because it called for the inclusion of large quantities of truffles.

Zabaglione (Zabaione)
According to popular tradition, this name comes from a distortion of San Giovanni di Baylon, the patron saint of pastrycooks. Zabaglione is a specialty in Piedmont and the Veneto but is also made in other parts of the country and has become a worldwide favorite. A most notable recipe is that in which a heaped spoonful of sugar is beaten with the yolk of an egg. When the two are well mixed some Marsala is added, the amount being half as much again as the amount of egg. It is cooked in a double boiler, while being whipped continuously until it reaches the right consistency. One egg per serving is sufficient. Zabaglione is served with sweet cookies.

Zafferano (saffron)
A spice used to impart the characteristic flavor and yellow color to "risotto alla milanese" (see p.114). Obtained from the pistils of the crocus, it is a very expensive ingredient because a large quantity of pistils is needed to produce even the smallest amount of saffron.

Zelten
A classic sweet of the Alto Adige. A large quantity of dates, dried figs, seedless white raisins, pine nuts and walnuts sprinkled with brandy or rum are made into a paste with rye flour. It is cut into little squares ¾ in thick and coated with almonds and candied peel. After cooking in the oven, each square is spread with some honey mixed with water.

Zéppole
These are pastry rings of different kinds made throughout southern Italy. In most cases they are made of eggs and flour precooked in boiling water, then fried in oil and coated with honey.

embers and charcoal. These little pancakes are cut into squares or ribbons, boiled in water for a few minutes, drained and seasoned with oil, garlic, basil and generous amounts of Pecorino cheese or Parmesan.

Tiella
In Apulia a *tiella* is prepared by arranging layers of sliced potatoes, sliced onions and sliced mushrooms in a dish. Each layer is seasoned with salt, pepper, oil, garlic and a little parsley. On the top, a layer of breadcrumbs toasted in the oven is sprinkled. The Latian tiella or, more specifically, that from the town of Gaeta, is made, instead, from two rounds of leavened dough like that used for pizza. Between the two rounds is sandwiched a filling of either fresh cheese, eggs, smoked meat and tomato slices or of a mixture of seafood, tomatoes, pitted olives, capers and garlic. The tiella is then cooked with oil or lard.